Advanced Oracle Utilities
The Definitive Reference
Second Edition

Bert Scalzo
Andrew Kerber
Donald K. Burleson
Steve Callan

RAMPANT
TECHPRESS

To my loving Schnauzer Max, who makes every day wonderfully special - and enriches my life beyond words.

- Bert Scalzo

To my mother, who to this day, is the best proofreader I know.

- Andrew Kerber

To my wife, Janet.

- Donald Burleson

To my wife, who graciously lets me play with computers when we could be out doing other things.

- Steve Callan

Advanced Oracle Utilities
The Definitive Reference
Second Edition

By Bert Scalzo, Andrew Kerber, Donald K. Burleson, and Steve Callan

Copyright © 2014 by Rampant TechPress. All rights reserved.

Printed in the United States of America.

Published in Kittrell, North Carolina, USA.

Oracle In-focus Series: Book #31

Series Editor: Donald K. Burleson

Production Manager: Robin Rademacher

Editor: Valerre Aquitaine

Technical Editor: Jeff Smith

Production Editor: Teri Wade

Cover Design: Janet Burleson

Printing History: August 2009 for First Edition, March 2014 for Second Edition

Oracle, Oracle7, Oracle8, Oracle8i, Oracle9i, Oracle10g, Oracle 11g, and Oracle 12c are trademarks of Oracle Corporation.

Many of the designations used by computer vendors to distinguish their products are claimed as Trademarks. All names known by Rampant TechPress to be trademark names appear in this text as initial caps.

Flame Warriors illustrations are copyright © by Mike Reed Illustrations Inc.

The information provided by the authors of this work is believed to be accurate and reliable. However, because of the possibility of human error by our authors and staff, Rampant TechPress cannot guarantee the accuracy or completeness of any information included in this work and is not responsible for any errors, omissions, or inaccurate results obtained from the use of information or scripts in this work.

Special thanks to Dr. Tim Hall for allowing us to use excerpts from his book "Oracle Job Scheduling" in chapter 10 and Jon Emmons for his content on cron scheduling.

ISBN 13: 978-0-9916386-5-9

Library of Congress Control Number: 2014936286

Table of Contents

Using the Online Code Depot

Purchase of this book provides complete access to the online code depot that contains sample code scripts. Any code depot scripts in this book are located at the following URL in zip format and ready to load and use:

rampant.cc/adv_ora_util.htm

If technical assistance is needed with downloading or accessing the scripts, please contact Rampant TechPress at rtp@rampant.cc.

Conventions Used in this Book

It is critical for any technical publication to follow rigorous standards and employ consistent punctuation conventions to make the text easy to read. However, this is not an easy task. Within database terminology, there are many types of notation that can confuse a reader. For example, some Oracle utilities such as STATSPACK and TKPROF are always spelled in CAPITAL letters, while Oracle parameters and procedures have varying naming conventions in the database documentation. It is also important to remember that many database commands are case sensitive, and are always left in their original executable form, and never altered with italics or capitalization. Hence, all Rampant TechPress books follow these conventions:

Parameters – Database parameters will be *lowercase italics*. The exception is parameter arguments that are commonly capitalized (KEEP pool, TKPROF), which will be ALL CAPS.

Variables – Procedural language (e.g. PL/SQL) program variables and arguments will also remain in *lowercase italics* (i.e. *dbms_job*).

Tables & dictionary objects – Data dictionary objects are referenced in lowercase italics (*dba_indexes*, *v$sql*), ncluding *v$* and *x$* views (*x$kcbcbh*, *v$parameter*) and dictionary views (*dba_tables*, *user_indexes*).

SQL – All SQL is formatted for easy use in the code depot and displayed in lowercase. Main SQL terms (select, from, where, group by, order by, having) will appear on a separate line.

Programs & Products – All products and programs that are known to the author are capitalized according to the vendor specifications (CentOS, VMware, Oracle, etc). All names known by Rampant TechPress to be trademark names appear in this text as initial caps. References to UNIX are always made in uppercase.

Acknowledgements

This type of highly technical reference book requires the dedicated efforts of many people. Even though we are the authors, our work ends when we deliver the content. After each chapter is delivered, several Oracle DBAs carefully review and correct the technical content. After the technical review, experienced copy editors polish the grammar and syntax.

The finished work is then reviewed as page proofs and turned over to the production manager, who arranges the creation of the online code depot and manages the cover art, printing distribution, and warehousing.

In short, the authors play a small role in the development of this book, and we need to thank and acknowledge everyone who helped bring this book to fruition:

Robin Rademacher, for the production management, including the coordination of the cover art, page proofing, printing, and distribution.

Teri Wade, for help in the production of the page proofs.

Janet Burleson, for exceptional cover design and graphics.

John Lavender, for assistance with the web site, and for creating the code depot and the online shopping cart for this book.

With our sincerest thanks,

Bert Scalzo, Andrew Kerber, Donald K. Burleson, and Steve Callan

Introduction to Oracle Utilities

Introduction

This chapter provides the definition of a utility and introduces the reader to what an Oracle utility does. This chapter also provides a list of these utilities as well as a discovery mechanism that will aid in finding them in future releases of Oracle.

Due to the complexity of most utilities, and the number of programs that can accurately be termed utilities, they cannot all be explained in great detail. The rest of the book will explore the most useful utilities with as much detail as possible. This chapter will provide the complete lists for the different Oracle versions.

Definition of a Utility

Webster's Dictionary© defines a utility as the following:

The quality or condition of being useful; a useful article or device.

This is admittedly a broad definition, but as will be discovered in this book, there are many tools that can be considered utilities for the Oracle database that are not widely known. The average Oracle user would not consider many of these tools a utility, but said tools can actually be used extensively to make the life of an Oracle DBA or developer easier.

Tools are supplied with Oracle that can be very useful for DBAs, developers, and system administrators to maintain or enhance the Oracle products. For this reason, they will be known as "Oracle Utilities" in the chapters that follow.

An Oracle utility is an Oracle program, package, or PL/SQL script that is useful in a way that helps an Oracle DBA or developer do his or her job. It could be an operating system executable file, a Windows bat file, a UNIX shell script, an Oracle supplied package, a feature of an existing tool that is not widely known, or even user written.

What is a Hidden Utility?

A hidden utility is one that is not widely used, and its very existence may be unknown to most Oracle professionals. Hidden utilities are either undocumented or documentation is difficult to find.

Some executables are not supplied as part of the base Oracle installation. By default, some PL/SQL packages do not exist in the database, although the code to load them exists in the operating system. Other PL/SQL packages are only available through Oracle MetaLink, such as Trace Analyzer. Additionally, certain PL/SQL packages are only accessible to the SYS user by default (*dbms_system*) in some Oracle versions.

Although some utilities are included for reasons known only to Oracle Corporation, they are indeed present in the Oracle environment and can be used to solve specific problems.

Utility Locations

The main directories of interest regarding Oracle utilities are the following:

- $ORACLE_HOME/bin – This contains the binary executables used by the Oracle server. Most of the tools discussed in this book reside here.

- $ORACLE_HOME/rdbms/admin – This contains many SQL scripts used for creating PL/SQL packages and their required environments.

- $ORACLE_HOME/sqlplus/admin – This contains scripts used with autotrace and other utilities.

- $ORACLE_HOME/sysman (and subdirectories) – This is used by utilities such as oemctl and the Oracle Management Server (OMS).

Given the obscure location of many utilities, it is best to learn how to find the utilities, identify them, and figure out how to use them.

Methods of Discovery

Although many utilities are documented here, the ability to find them is important in order to know which ones exist. This ability can be transferred with each new release of the database, revealing the presence of new utilities that may or may not be useful for the task at hand.

It often takes months, or even years to become familiar with the key features of a new database version. It takes time for the features to become well known, and that timeline also applies to the utilities. The truly useful utilities often take much longer to find and become popular, though Oracle does not always document or publicize utilities well. In some cases, the utility has a use that Oracle did not envision when the utility was written, and it becomes the job of the Oracle user community to make use of and document the utility to its fullest.

The most popular technical sessions at Oracle Open World concern TKPROF even though the utility has existed for many years. There is no need to wait for complete documentation since these utilities can be found and applied by the individual. Once their existence is revealed, they can be investigated and their benefits and drawbacks can be identified.

Package Discovery

Fortunately, the PL/SQL packages that are installed in the database are the easiest utilities to find. To reveal the new packages, a database link must be created within the version of Oracle that contains the packages. The database link should point to a prior version of Oracle. This allows a query to be executed to determine the differences between the two databases.

The following query, through a database link, displays the packages that were added in Oracle version 10.2 as compared to 9.2.

```
select object_name
   from dba_objects
   where owner     = 'SYS'
    and object_type = 'PACKAGE BODY'
   minus
   select object_name
     from  dba_objects@Oracle92
        where owner    = 'SYS'
        and object_type = 'PACKAGE BODY';
```

This query simply displays all of the package bodies owned by SYS that exist in 10.2 but not in 9.2. The same query can be executed to compare packages in any two databases, provided that the database link object exists to connect the two instances.

Other Changes Worth Discovering

The same approach used to discover new PL/SQL packages can be applied to find other useful features in new versions of the database. The following new Oracle features can be easily revealed:

- Instance Parameters – New instance parameters can easily be identified with the following query:

```
  select name
    from v$parameter
minus
select name
    from v$parameter@PRIOR_VERSION;
```

- Obsolete Parameters – Oracle provides a list of obsolete parameters with each version of the database, beginning in 8.1.5.

```
select name
    from v$obsolete_parameter
minus
select name
    from v$obsolete_parameter@PRIOR_VERSION;
```

- *v$* Views - New *v$* and *gv$* views are usually an indicator of new functionality in the database. They are listed with the following query:

```
select view_name
    from v$fixed_view_definition
minus
select view_name
    from v$fixed_view_definition@PRIOR_VERSION;
```

- System Events – The new system events are also very interesting to DBAs. Some of them offer new tuning features. They can be obtained from the following query:

```
select name
    from v$event_name
minus
select name
    from v$event_name@PRIOR_VERSION;
```

The @PRIOR_VERSION contained in each query above represents a database link to another version of Oracle. This designation can be used to find any new characteristic of the database via an SQL statement.

The next section of this book will categorize the PL/SQL and binary utilities according to the version of the database.

Package Utilities

Oracle supplied 34 PL/SQL packages with version 7.3.4 of the database and this grew to an astonishing 287 packages in Oracle 9.2. This increase indicates that the number of new database features being supplied in PL/SQL packages has grown tremendously.

The table below lists the supplied Oracle packages, a brief description, and the version of Oracle that first made it available. Version 7.3.4 is the oldest included in this book, even though the package may have been available before 7.3.4.

Package	Description	First Available
dbms_alert	Asynchronous event notification	7.3.4
dbms_application_info	Application registration	7.3.4
dbms_ddl	DDL functions	7.3.4
dbms_debug	Server Side Debugger	7.3.4
dbms_defer	User interface to RPC facility	7.3.4
dbms_defer_query	Query deferred transactions queue	7.3.4
dbms_defer_sys	Manage default replication node lists	7.3.4
dbms_describe	Describes stored procedure arguments	7.3.4
dbms_job	Job Scheduler	7.3.4
dbms_lock	Interface to Lock Management Services	7.3.4
dbms_offline_og	Offline instantiation of master groups	7.3.4

Package	Description	First Available
dbms_output	PL/SQL Output Buffer	7.3.4
dbms_pipe	Inter-session message pipe	7.3.4
dbms_refresh	Refreshes materialized views (snapshots)	7.3.4
dbms_repcat	Replication Catalog and Environment Administration	7.3.4
dbms_reputil	Replication utilities	7.3.4
dbms_session	Session Utilities including ALTER Session	7.3.4
dbms_snapshot	Snapshots (see DBMS_MVIEW)	7.3.4
dbms_space	Segment space info	7.3.4
dbms_sql	Dynamic SQL	7.3.4
dbms_system	System utilities	7.3.4
dbms_transaction	Transaction control statements	7.3.4
dbms_utility	Miscellaneous utility routines	7.3.4
Standard	Built-in functions	7.3.4
utl_file	External File Access	7.3.4
utl_http	HTTP access from PL/SQL	7.3.4
utl_raw	SQL functions for RAW datatypes	7.3.4
dbms_aq	Advanced Queue Manipulation	8
dbms_distributed_trust_admin	Maintains Trusted Database List	8
dbms_lob	LOB Management	8
dbms_offline_snapshot	Offline instantiation of snapshots	8
dbms_random	Random number generator	8
dbms_rectifier_diff	Shows differences between two replicated sites	8
dbms_repcat_sna	Shows differences between two replicated sites	8
dbms_rowid	ROWID manipulation	8

Package	Description	First Available
utl_ref	Access to objects via references	8
dbms_support	Support (Tracing) Routines	8.0.6
dbms_logmnr	Log Miner	8.1.5
dbms_logmnr_d	Log Miner Dictionary Routines	8.1.5
dbms_mview	Materialized Views	8.1.5
dbms_outln	Stored Outline Administration	8.1.5
dbms_profiler	PL/SQL Performance Profiler	8.1.5
dbms_repair	Block Corruption	8.1.5
dbms_repcat_instantiate	Replication Instantiate Deployment Templates	8.1.5
dbms_repcat_rgt	Replication Refresh Group Templates	8.1.5
dbms_resource_manager	Plans, Consumer groups, plan directives	8.1.5
dbms_resource_manager_priv s	Consumer group privileges	8.1.5
dbms_rls	Row Level Security	8.1.5
dbms_rule	Rule evaluation	8.1.5
dbms_rule_adm	Rule administration	8.1.5
dbms_space_admin	Segment space administration	8.1.5
dbms_stats	Optimizer Statistics	8.1.5
dbms_summary	Summary Advisor	8.1.5
dbms_trace	PL/SQL Tracing	8.1.5
dbms_tts	Transportable Tablespaces	8.1.5
outln_pkg	Stored Outlines	8.1.5
utl_coll	Collection Locators	8.1.5
dbms_obfuscation_toolkit	Code Obfuscation	8.1.6
dbms_xmlquery	Database to XML routines (use DBMS_XMLGEN instead)	8.1.7

Package	Description	First Available
dbms_xmlsave	Save XML to Database routines	8.1.7
Htf	Web Agent Hypertext Functions	8.1.7
Htp	Web Agent Hypertext Print Routines	8.1.7
Owa	Oracle Web Agent Interface Procedures	8.1.7
owa_cache	Web Agent Content Caching Functions	8.1.7
owa_cookie	Web Agent Cookie Manipulation Functions	8.1.7
owa_custom	Web Agent Customization Functions	8.1.7
owa_image	Web Agent Image Handling Functions	8.1.7
owa_opt_lock	Web Agent Optimistic Locking Functions	8.1.7
owa_pattern	Web Agent String Manipulation Functions	8.1.7
owa_sec	WebServer Security Functions	8.1.7
owa_text	WebServer Text Handling Functions	8.1.7
owa_util	WebServer Utility Functions	8.1.7
utl_inaddr	Internet address API	8.1.7
utl_smtp	SMTP E-Mail Interface Library	8.1.7
utl_tcp	TCP/IP Interface Library	8.1.7
dbms_aqelm	Advanced Queueing Asynchronous Notification Administration	9.0.1
dbms_cdc_publish (renamed later in 10)	Change Data Capture Publishing Routines	9.0.1
dbms_cdc_subscribe (renamed later in 10)	Change Data Capture Subscription Routines	9.0.1
dbms_cdc_utility	Change Data Capture Utilities	9.0.1

Package	Description	First Available
dbms_drs	Hot Standby	9.0.1
dbms_fga	Fine Grained Auditing	9.0.1
dbms_flashback	Flashback Query	9.0.1
dbms_logstdby	Logical Standby routines	9.0.1
dbms_metadata	Metadata routines	9.0.1
dbms_odci	Extensible Optimizer	9.0.1
dbms_outln_edit	Stored Outline Editing	9.0.1
dbms_redefinition	Table Online Reorgs	9.0.1
dbms_repcat_admin	Replication User Administration	9.0.1
dbms_resumable	Resumable session management	9.0.1
dbms_transform	Advanced Queueing message format transformations	9.0.1
dbms_xmlgen	XML generation	9.0.1
outln_edit_pkg	Stored Outline Editing Routines	9.0.1
Urifactory	URI Manipulation Functions	9.0.1
utl_encode	Encodes raw data	9.0.1
utl_url	Escape mechanism for URL characters	9.0.1
utl_xml	XML/XSL Utility Library	9.0.1
dbms_apply_adm	Streams Apply Process Administration	9.2
dbms_capture_adm	Streams Capture Process Administration	9.2

Code Depot Username = reader, Password = advutil

Package	Description	First Available
dbms_propagation_adm	Streams Propagation Process Administration	9.2
dbms_storage_map	FMON Mapping operations	9.2
dbms_streams	Streams Utilities	9.2
dbms_streams_adm	Streams Administration	9.2
dbms_wm	Workspace Manager	9.2
dbms_xdb	XML Database Resource Management	9.2
dbms_xdbt	XDB ContextIndex routines	9.2
dbms_xdb_version	XDB Versioning routines	9.2
dbms_xmldom	XML DOM Parser	9.2
dbms_xmlparser	Access contents and structure of XML documents	9.2
dbms_xmlschema	XML Schema Manipulation	9.2
dbms_xplan	Explain Plan	9.2
dbms_xslprocessor	XSL Processor routines (Stylesheets)	9.2
utl_gdk	Globalization Development Kit	9.2
dbms_advanced_rewrite	Robust rewrite capability	10.1
dbms_advisor	Part of ADDM?	10.1
dbms_aq_bqview	Advanced Queuing?	10.1
dbms_cdc_dputil	Change Data Capture	10.1
dbms_cdc_expdp	Change Data Capture	10.1
dbms_cdc_expvd	Change Data Capture	10.1
dbms_cdc_impdp	Change Data Capture	10.1
dbms_cdc_ipublish	Change Data Capture	10.1
dbms_cdc_isubscribe	Change Data Capture	10.1
dbms_crypto	Cryptography	10.1
dbms_crypt_ffi	Supports DBMS_CRYPTO?	10.1
dbms_datapump	Data Pump	10.1
dbms_dbupgrade	Upgrade	10.1

Package	Description	First Available
dbms_dbverify	Verify datafiles at block level	10.1
dbms_dimension	Dimensions	10.1
dbms_fbt	Flashback Table	10.1
dbms_feature_usage	Usage Registration & Monitoring	10.1
dbms_feature_usage_internal	Usage Registration Internal	10.1
dbms_file_transfer	File Transfer	10.1
dbms_frequent_itemset	Frequent Itemset Counting	10.1
dbms_index_utl	Index Maintenance	10.1
dbms_internal_safe_scn	Logical Standby Administration	10.1
dbms_isched	Undocumented	10.1
dbms_i_index_utl	Index and Table Utilities	10.1
dbms_java_dump	Java Interface	10.1
dbms_jms_plsql	Streams	10.1
dbms_ldap	LDAP Server Access	10.1
dbms_ldap_utl	LDAP Server Access	10.1
dbms_jms_plsql	Streams	10.1
dbms_logrep_util_invok	Log File Replication	10.1
dbms_logstdby_public	Logical Standby routines	10.1
dbms_monitor	Tracing & Statistics	10.1
dbms_prvt_trace	Undocumented	10.1
dbms_registry_server	Registry	10.1
dbms_repcat_exp	Replication	10.1
dbms_repcat_migration	Replication	10.1
dbms_rule_utli		10.1
dbms_scheduler	Scheduler	10.1
dbms_sched_class_export	Scheduler	10.1
dbms_sched_export_callouts	Scheduler	10.1
dbms_sched_job_export	Scheduler	10.1
dbms_sched_main_export	Scheduler	10.1
dbms_sched_program_export	Scheduler	10.1
dbms_sched_schedule_export	Scheduler	10.1

Package	Description	First Available
dbms_sched_window_export	Scheduler	10.1
dbms_sched_wingrp_expor	Scheduler	10.1
dbms_schema_copy	Schema Pre-compilation and RAC	10.1
dbms_server_alert	Set and Retrieve Threshold Violation Alerts	10.1
dbms_server_alert_export	Export Threshold Violation Alerts	10.1
dbms_service	Tracing	10.1
dbms_shared_pool	Manage LRU Mechanism	10.1
dbms_sqltune	SQL Tuning Advice	10.1
dbms_sqltune_internal	Undocumented	10.1
dbms_stat_funcs	Statistical Functions	10.1
dbms_stat_funcs_aux	Statistical Functions	10.1
dbms_streams_adm_utl_invok	Streams	10.1
dbms_streams_auth	Streams Admin. Privileges	10.1
dbms_streams_cdc_adm	Streams Change Data Capture Admin	10.1
dbms_streams_datapump	Streams	10.1
dbms_streams_datapump_util	Streams Datapump Utility	10.1
dbms_streams_lcr_int	Streams Internal	10.1
dbms_streams_messaging	Enqueue & dequeue ANYDATA queue messages	10.1
dbms_streams_lcr_int	Streams Internal	10.1
dbms_streams_pub_rpc	Streams	10.1
dbms_streams_rpc	Streams	10.1
dbms_streams_rpc_internal	Streams	10.1
dbms_streams_tablespace_ adm	Copying tablespaces between databases	10.1
dbms_streams_tbs_int	Streams Internal	10.1
dbms_streams_tbs_int_invok	Streams Internal	10.1
dbms_sum_rweq_export	Undocumented	10.1
dbms_sum_rweq_export_ internal	Undocumented	10.1

Package	Description	First Available
dbms_swrf_internal	Automatic Workload Repository	10.1
dbms_swrf_report_internal	Automatic Workload Repository	10.1
dbms_transform_internal	Advanced Queuing Message Transformation	10.1
dbms_undo_adv	Undo Tablespace Management	10.1
dbms_upgrade_internal	Upgrade/Downgrade	10.1
dbms_warning	PL/SQL Compiler Warnings	10.1
dbms_warning_internal	PL/SQL Compiler Warnings Internal	10.1
dbms_workload_repository	Automatic Workload Repository	10.1
dbms_xmlstore	Store XML in relational tables	10.1
dbms_xsoq	Undocumented	10.1
dbms_xsoq_odbo	Undocumented	10.1
dbms_xsoq_util	Undocumented	10.1
dbms_amd	Move OLAP Catalog	10.2
dbms_apply_user_agent		10.2
dbms_aq_exp_cmt_time_ tables	Advanced Queuing	10.2
dbms_aq_inv	Advanced Queuing	10.2
dbms_ash_internal	Active Session History	10.2
dbms_assert	String Value Checking	10.2
dbms_aw_xml	OLAP	10.2
dbms_cdc_sys_ipublish	Streams Change Data Capture	10.2
dbms_change_notification	Notification of result set changes	10.2
dbms_datapump_utl	Data Pump Default Directory Create and Replace	10.2
dbms_dblink	Upgrade Database Links	10.2
dbms_epg	Invoke PL/SQL thru HTTP Listener	10.2

Package	Description	First Available
dbms_errlog	Creates Error Logging Table for DML	10.2
dbms_feature_usage_report	Usage Report	10.2

Table 1.1: *Complete List of Utilities for Oracle Packages*

Below are the new packages for Oracle 11g, as listed in the Oracle 11g PL/SQL reference manual:

Package	Description
APEX_CUSTOM_AUTH	The APEX_CUSTOM_AUTH package provides an interface for authentication and session management.
APEX_APPLICATION	The APEX_APPLICATION package enables users to take advantage of global variables
APEX_ITEM	The APEX_ITEM package enables users to create form elements dynamically based on a SQL query instead of creating individual items page by page.
APEX_UTIL	The APEX_UTIL package provides utilities for getting and setting session state, getting files, checking authorizations for users, resetting different states for users, and also getting and setting preferences for users.
DBMS_ADDM	The DBMS_ADDM package facilitates the use of Advisor functionality regarding the Automatic Database Diagnostic Monitor
DBMS_ASSERT	The DBMS_ASSERT package provides an interface to validate properties of the input value.
DBMS_AUTO_TASK_ADMIN	The DBMS_AUTO_TASK_ADMIN package provides an interface to AUTOTASK functionality. It is used by the DBA as well as Enterprise Manager to access the AUTOTASK controls. Enterprise Manager also uses the AUTOTASK Advisor.

Package	Description
DBMS_AW_STATS	DBMS_AW_STATS contains a subprogram that generates and stores optimizer statistics for cubes and dimensions. Generating the statistics does not have a significant performance cost.
DBMS_COMPARISON	The DBMS_COMPARISON package provides interfaces to compare and converge database objects at different databases.
DBMS_CONNECTION_POOL	The DBMS_CONNECTION_POOL package provides an interface to manage Database Resident Connection Pool.
DBMS_CSX_ADMIN	The DBMS_CSX_ADMIN package provides an interface to customize the setup when transporting a tablespace containing binary XML data.
DBMS_CUBE	DBMS_CUBE contains subprograms that create OLAP cubes and dimensions, and that load and process the data for querying.
DBMS_CUBE_ADVISE	DBMS_CUBE_ADVISE contains subprograms for evaluating cube materialized views to support log-based fast refresh and query rewrite.
DBMS_DG	The DBMS_DG package allows applications to notify the primary database in an Oracle Data Guard broker environment to initiate a fast-start failover when the application encounters a condition that warrants a failover.
DBMS_HM	This package contains constants and procedure declarations for health check management. Health Monitor provides facilities to run a check store and retrieve the reports through DBMS_HM package.
DBMS_HPROF	The DBMS_HPROF package provides an interface for profiling the execution of PL/SQL applications. It provides services for collecting the hierarchical profiler data, analyzing the raw profiler output and profiling information generation.

Package	Description
DBMS_HS_PARALLEL	The DBMS_HS_PARALLEL PL/SQL package enables parallel processing for heterogeneous targets access. This package is designed to improve performance when retrieving data from a large foreign table.
DBMS_MGD_ID_UTL	The DBMS_MGD_ID_UTL package contains various functions and procedures that make up several utility subprograms.
DBMS_NETWORK_ACL_ADMIN	The DBMS_NETWORK_ACL_ADMIN package provides the interface to administer the network Access Control List (ACL).
DBMS_NETWORK_ACL_UTILITY	The DBMS_NETWORK_ACL_UTILITY package provides utilities to the interface for administering the network Access Control List (ACL).
DBMS_RESCONFIG	The DBMS_RESCONFIG package provides an interface to operate on the resource configuration list and to retrieve listener information for a resource.
DBMS_RESULT_CACHE	The DBMS_RESULT_CACHE package provides an interface to allow the DBA to administer that part of the shared pool that is used by the SQL result cache and the PL/SQL function result cache. Both these caches use the same infrastructure. For example, DBMS_RESULT_CACHE.BYPASS determines whether both caches are bypassed or both caches are used, and DBMS_RESULT_CACHE.FLUSH flushes both all the cached results for SQL queries and all the cached results for PL/SQL functions.
DBMS_SPM	The DBMS_SPM package supports the SQL plan management feature by providing an interface for the DBA or other user to perform controlled manipulation of plan history and SQL plan baselines maintained for various SQL statements.

Package	Description
DBMS_SQLDIAG	The DBMS_SQLDIAG package provides an interface to the SQL Diagnosability functionality.
DBMS_STREAMS_ADVISOR_ADM	The DBMS_STREAMS_ADVISOR_ADM package, one of a set of Oracle Streams packages, provides an interface to gather information about an Oracle Streams environment and advise database administrators based on the information gathered. This package is part of the Oracle Streams Performance Advisor.
DBMS_WORKLOAD_CAPTURE	The DBMS_WORKLOAD_CAPTURE package configures the Workload Capture system and produces the workload capture data. Replay of this capture is implemented by way of the DBMS_WORKLOAD_REPLAY package.
DBMS_WORKLOAD_REPLAY	The DBMS_WORKLOAD_REPLAY package provides an interface to replay a workload capture that was originally created by way of the DBMS_WORKLOAD_CAPTURE package. Typically, the DBMS_WORKLOAD_CAPTURE package will be used in the production system to capture a production workload, and the DBMS_WORKLOAD_REPLAY package will be subsequently used in a test system to replay the captured production workload for testing purposes.
DBMS_XA	The DBMS_XA package contains the XA/Open interface for applications to call XA interface in PL/SQL. Using this package, application developers can switch or share transactions across SQL*Plus sessions or processes using PL/SQL.
DBMS_XDB_ADMIN	The DBMS_XDB_ADMIN package provides an interface to manage the XMLIndex on the XML DB repository.

Package	Description
DBMS_XDBRESOURCE	The DBMS_XDBRESOURCE package provides the interface to operate on the resource's metadata and contents.
DBMS_XEVENT	The DBMS_XEVENT package provides event-related types and supporting subprograms.
DBMS_XMLINDEX	The DBMS_XMLINDEX package provides an interface to implement asynchronous indexing.
DBMS_XMLTRANSLATIONS	The DBMS_XMLTRANSLATIONS package provides an interface to perform translations so that strings can be searched or displayed in various languages.
SDO_CSW_PROCESS	The SDO_CSW_PROCESS package contains subprograms for various processing operations related to support for Catalog Services for the Web (CSW).
SDO_GEOR_ADMIN	The SDO_GEOR_ADMIN package contains subprograms for administrative operations related to GeoRaster.
SDO_OLS	The SDO_OLS package contains subprograms for Spatial OpenLS support.
SDO_PC_PKG	The SDO_PC_PKG package contains subprograms to support the use of point clouds in Spatial.
SDO_TIN_PKG	The SDO_TIN_PKG package contains subprograms to support the use of triangulated irregular networks (TINs) in Spatial.
SDO_WFS_LOCK	The SDO_WFS_LOCK package contains subprograms for WFS support for registering and unregistering feature tables. Registering a feature table enables the table for WFS transaction locking; unregistering a feature table disables the table for WFS transaction locking.
SDO_WFS_PROCESS	The SDO_WFS_PROCESS package contains subprograms for various processing operations related to support for Web Feature Services.

Package	Description
SEM_APIS	The SEM_APIS package contains subprograms for working with the Resource Description Framework (RDF) and Web Ontology Language (OWL) in an Oracle database.
SEM_PERF	The SEM_PERF package contains subprograms for examining and enhancing the performance of the Resource Description Framework (RDF) and Web Ontology Language (OWL) support in an Oracle database.
UTL_SPADV	The UTL_SPADV package, one of a set of Oracle Streams packages, provides subprograms to collect and analyze statistics for the Oracle Streams components in a distributed database environment. This package uses the Oracle Streams Performance Advisor to gather statistics.

Table 1.2: *New Package List from 11g PL/SQL Reference Manual*

UNIX Utilities and Shell Scripts

The table below lists the UNIX binaries provided through Oracle 10gR2, a brief description, and the version of Oracle that first made it available.

Binary	Description	First Available
adapters	Installed Network Adapters	(7.3.4)
agentctl	Agent Control Utility	9.0.1
agtctl	Agent Control Utility	8.1.5
bulkmodify	Oracle Internet Directory bulk modify	8.1.6
cmadmin	Connection Manager Administrator	8.1.6
cmctl	Connection Manager Control Utility	8.1.6
cmgw	Connection Manager Gateway	8.1.6
coraenv	Oraenv command for Cshell	(7.3.4)
csscan	Character Set Scanner	8.1.7
ctxkbtc	InterMedia	8.1.5
ctxload	InterMedia	(7.3.4)
ctxsrv	InterMedia	(7.3.4)

Binary	Description	First Available
cursize	Cursor Size Tool	8.0
dbca	Database Creation Assistant	9.0.1
dbfmig	Datafile Migrator	8.1.5
dbfsize	Datafile Size	(7.3.4)
dbhome	displays Oracle$HOME	(7.3.4)
dbshut	shuts down Oracle	(7.3.4)
dbsnmp	Intelligent Agent	8.0
dbsnmpj	Intelligent Agent Job Processor (not Java or JRE)	9.0.1
dbsnmpwd	Intelligent Agent	9.0.1
dbstart	Starts Oracle	(7.3.4)
dbua	Database Upgrade Assistant	9.2.0
dbv	Verifies datafiles	(7.3.4)
debugproxy	Oracle JVM Debugging	8.1.7
demobld	Table Build for Oracle Developer demo	(7.3.4)
demodrop	Table drop for Oracle Developer demo	(7.3.4)
deploync	JAR file deployment	8.1.7
dgmgrl	Data Manager	9.0.1
dropjava	Drops java objects	8.1.5
dumpsga	Dumps SGA contents	9.2.0
echodo	Echo command and print it	(7.3.4)
Ela	Enterprise Login Assistant	9.0.1
Emca	(Enterprise Manager?)	9.0.1
emwebsite	(Enterprise Manager?)	9.0.1
Esm	Enterprise Security Manager Command Line Utility	9.2.0
Exp	Export	(7.3.4)
extproc	External Process Agent	8.0
extractlib	Extract objects from a list of libraries	(7.3.4)
fmputl	File mapping	9.2.0
fmputlhp	File mapping	9.2.0
genagtsh	Agent shared library generation	8.1.5
genclntsh	Generate shared client library for OCI, Pro*C and XA	(7.3.4)
genksms	Generate ksms.s to relocate SGA	8.0
gennfgt	Generate list of native network libraries - nnfgt.o	8.0
gennttab	Generate list of SQL*Net protocol adapters -Output written to ntcontab.s	8.0

Binary	Description	First Available
genoccish	Generate OCCI shared object	9.2.0
gensyslib	Generate list of operating system libraries to be linked into executables. Output written to $ORACLE_HOME/lib/sysliblist	(7.3.4)
helpins	Install SQL*Plus help system	(7.3.4)
hsalloci	Heterogeneous Agent	8.1.5
hsdepxa	Heterogeneous Agent	8.1.5
hsodbc	Heterogeneous Services ODBC	8.1.6
hsots	Heterogeneous Services Oracle Transaction Service	8.1.5
imp	Import	(7.3.4)
isqlplus	Browser based SQL*Plus interface	9.2.0
jpub	Publish Java classes	8.1.5
kgmgr	Net Configuration Assistant	8.1.6
kgpmon	Unknown	8.1.5
ldapadd	LDAP management	8.1.6
ldapaddmt	LDAP management	8.1.6
ldapbind	LDAP management	8.1.6
ldapcompare	LDAP management	8.1.6
ldapdelete	LDAP management	8.1.6
ldapmoddn	LDAP management	8.1.6
ldapmodify	LDAP management	8.1.6
ldapmodifymt	LDAP management	8.1.6
ldapsearch	LDAP management	8.1.6
ldifmigrator	OID Migration Tool	9.2.0
ldifwrite	Oracle Internet Directory - write LDIF file	8.1.6
lmsgen	Binary message file generation	8.1.5
loadjava	loads java objects	8.1.5
loadpsp	loads pl/sql server pages	8.1.6
lsnrctl	Listener control	(7.3.4)
lxchknlb	Net Configuration Assistant	(7.3.4)
lxegen	NLS Calendar	(7.3.4)
lxinst	NLS Data Install	(7.3.4)
mapsga	Provides SGA map	9.2.0
maxmem	Displays RAM stats	(7.3.4)
Mig	Migrate	(7.3.4)
migprep	Migrate Prepare	8.1.5

Binary	Description	First Available
modada	Module compiler	9.2.0
names	Oracle Names	8.1.6
namesctl	Oracle Names Control	8.1.6
ncomp	Native Compiler (Java)	8.1.7
netca	Net Configuration Assistant	8.1.5
netmgr	Net Assistant	9.0.1
Nid	Set new database ID	9.2.0
Nmu7q28	Oracle Intelligent Agent	9.0.1
nmudg	Oracle Intelligent Agent	9.0.1
nmumigr8	Oracle Data Gatherer	9.0.1
ociconv	Convert OCI source from short (8.0.1) to long (8.0.2) function names	8.0
Ocm	Oracle Change Manager	9.0.1
odisrv	Oracle Internet Directory	9.0.1
odisrvreg	Oracle Internet Directory	9.0.1
oemLaunchOms	Oracle Mgmt. Server	9.0.1
oemapp	Oracle Enterprise Manager	8.1.6
oemctl	OEM Control	9.0.1
Oemevent	Oracle Intelligent Agent	8.1.5
oerr	Error Lookup	(7.3.4)
oidadmin	Oracle Internet Directory	8.1.6
oidctl	Oracle Internet Directory	8.1.7
oidldapd	Oracle Internet Directory	9.2.0
oidmon	Oracle Internet Directory	8.1.7
oidpasswd	Oracle Internet Directory	8.1.6
oidprovtool	Oracle Internet Directory	9.2.0
oidreconcile	Oracle Internet Directory	8.1.7
oidrepld	Oracle Internet Directory	9.2.0
ojspc	JSP Compiler	9.0.1
okdstry	Delete Kerberos ticket	8.1.7
okinit	New Kerberos ticket	8.1.7
oklist	Check Kerberos ticket	8.1.6
onrsd	Oracle Names	8.0
oracg	Class Generator	9.0.1
oracle	Oracle executable	(7.3.4)
oradism	Dynamic ISM	9.0.1
oraenv	Manages environment	(7.3.4)
orapwd	Manages passwords	(7.3.4)

Binary	Description	First Available
oratclsh	TCL Shell	8.0
oraxml	XML Processor	9.0.1
oraxsl	XSLT Processor	9.0.1
osh	Called from oraenv	8.0
otrccol	Oracle trace collector	(7.3.4)
otrccref	Oracle trace purge collect.dat file	(7.3.4)
otrcfmt	Oracle trace format	(7.3.4)
otrcrep	Oracle trace report	(7.3.4)
ott	Object Type Translator	8.0
ott8	Object Type Translator	9.0.1
Owm	Oracle Wallet Manager	8.1.6
passwdconvert	Unknown	9.2.0
Proc	Pro*C	(7.3.4)
procob	Pro*COBOL	(7.3.4)
procob18	Pro*COBOL	8.1.6
Profor	Pro*Fortran	8.1.6
relink	Relink executables	8.1.5
Rman	Recovery Manager	8.0
rtsora	COBOL Runtime System	(7.3.4)
runInstaller	Net Configuration Assistant	8.1.5
sbttest	Media Manager	8.1.5
schema	XML validation	9.0.1
schemasync	synchronizes schema elements; used with Oracle Directory Server	9.2.0
Sqlj	SQLJ	8.1.5
sqlldr	SQL*Loader	(7.3.4)
sqlplus	SQL*Plus	(7.3.4)
statusnc	Native Compilation Status	8.1.7
symfind	Symbolic find	(7.3.4)
sysresv	Shared Memory / Semaphores	8.1.5
tkprof	Trace output formatter	(7.3.4)
tns2nis	TNS NIS Mapping	8.1.6
tnslsnr	TNS Listener	(7.3.4)
tnsping	Listener pinger	(7.3.4)
transx	XML	9.2.0
trcasst	Trace Assistant	8.0
trcroute	Network analysis	(7.3.4)
tstshm	Shared memory	(7.3.4)

Binary	Description	First Available
Umu	LDAP	9.2.0
unzip	Unzip utility	9.2.0
Wrap	PL/SQL encrypter	(7.3.4)
Xml	XML / XSL processing	9.0.1
xmlcg	XML processing	9.2.0
Xsql	XSQL Pages	9.0.1
zip	Zip Utility	9.2.0

Table 1.3: *List of UNIX Binaries*

Windows Executables

The following table lists the Windows executables provided by Oracle. Many of the utilities provided in UNIX are also available in Windows. This list has been restricted to those utilities that are only present on the Windows platform.

Executable	Description	First Available
dbsnmp.exe	Intelligent Agent	8.1.5
dbsnmpj.exe	Intelligent Agent Job Processor (nothing to do with Java or JRE)	8.1.5
encaps.exe	SNMP encapsulation agent	Default in 9.0.1 Custom in 8i and below
encsvc.exe	SNMP encapsulation service	Default in 9.0.1 Custom in 8i and below
launch.exe	Java code launcher	8.0
launchem.exe	Enterprise Manager Launcher	8.0
ocopy.exe	File copy utility	(7.3.4)
OMSNTsrv.exe	Oracle Management Server	9.2.0
omtsreco.exe	MTS Recovery	9.0.1
OO4OCODEWIZ.EXE	Oracle Objects for OLE Code Wizard	9.2.0
OracleAdNetConnect.exe	MFC Application	8.1.7
OracleAdNetTest.exe	MFC Application	9.0.1
oradim.exe	Manages oracle instances	(7.3.4)

Executable	Description	First Available
orakill.exe	Process killer	(7.3.4)
oramts_deinst.exe	Unknown	9.2.0
Orastack.exe	Modifies stack RAM	(7.3.4)
Pagntsrv.exe	OEM Paging Server	9.0.1
tdvapp.exe	Trace Data Viewer	9.0.1
Selecthome.bat	Change oracle home	10gR2
lsqlpussvc	lsqlplus service startup	10gR2
VDOShell.exe	Oracle Expert	9.0.1
vmq.exe	SQL Analyze	9.0.1
Vtushell.exe	OEM Index Tuning Wizard	9.0.1
xpautune.exe	Oracle Expert	9.0.1
xpcoin.exe	Oracle Expert	9.0.1
xpksh.exe	Oracle Expert Command Shell	9.0.1
xpui.exe	Oracle Expert	9.0.1

Table 1.4: *Utilities Only Present on the Windows Platform*

Conclusion

This chapter defined a utility in terms relevant to an Oracle professional. The DBA now has a list of available utilities, as well as a mechanism, to discover them in the future – be it binary executables, supplied Oracle packages, new instance parameters, system events, or new v$ views.

This chapter also listed many potential Oracle utilities - those that reside in either the database itself or the $ORACLE_HOME/bin directory. The next chapter will begin the exploration and detailed analysis of the most useful Oracle utilities. The journey starts by showing those utilities that the DBA can use for general administration functions. Not every available Oracle utility will be covered, but the most useful utilities for the Oracle developer and DBA will be reviewed.

UNIX/Linux Oracle OS Utilities

Finding the OS Utilities in Linux/UNIX

Binary Discovery

Finding the new executables is slightly more difficult than finding new database objects. The standard method is to use the *dircmp* command in UNIX to compare two different directories and reports the differences, something like this:

```
dircmp -s <directory 1> <directory 2>
```

The –s option of the *dircmp* command tells UNIX to eliminate the matches from the output.

There is no similar command in Windows to compare directories and it is also more difficult to access the physical drives on separate Windows machines than UNIX machines. If nothing else, the DIR/B DOS command can be used to list the files in a directory and the output can be redirected to a file. Then the two files can then be compared using any number of tools from WinDiff to Oracle external tables.

UNIX/Linux Utilities for the Oracle Professional

UNIX provides many extra utilities to help execute UNIX command for Oracle:

- Grep - The grep command is short for Generalized Regular Expression parser.

- Awk – The awk name is short for Aho, Weinberger, and Kernighan, the folks who created the awk utility.

- Sed – The sed utility is short for String Editor. The sed utility is used to replace strings in UNIX files.

- Crontab – UNIX program scheduler

- Vi – text editor

Introduction to the UNIX Architecture

An operating system is the computer program that allows the software and the hardware to work together. The OS is the software responsible for managing all external hardware and executing all programs.

In an Oracle database, the database software works with UNIX to manage the interaction between UNIX and the Oracle data files. In addition, Oracle uses numerous UNIX structures for storing message logs, trace files and other housekeeping. The major features of UNIX and how Oracle interacts with UNIX will be covered.

Dialects of UNIX

Through the 1990s, UNIX continued to evolve and gain popularity as UNIX servers moved into mainstream data processing. Many different unique dialects of UNIX have developed, each unique to each UNIX vendor, and today's Oracle professional must be fluent in many different dialects (often called flavors) of UNIX. With the demise of DEC (Digital Equipment Corporation) and its VMS operating system, UNIX has become the dominant operating systems for the Oracle software.

One of the biggest problems for the Oracle DBA who wishes to work in the UNIX environment is that there has never been a single, unified UNIX product with total compatibility from one system to another. Most differences have arisen from different versions developed by three major early UNIX dialects - AT&T UNIX, Berkeley UNIX, and Microsoft's XENIX product. All of these UNIX flavors are similar, but no two are exactly the same.

Today, the most popular dialects of UNIX include Hewlett-Packard UNIX (HP/UX), IBM's UNIX (AIX), Sun UNIX (Solaris), and the popular Linux dialects (Red Hat Linux, SUSE Linux). This book is geared toward all versions of Oracle8i and Oracle9i, Oracle 10g, and Oracle 11g, and included are dialects of UNIX like HP/UX, IBM's AIX, Sun's Solaris, and Oracle's unbreakable Linux. Some commands in IRIX, DEC-UNIX and UNIXWARE will also be shown.

UNIX Access Control Management

In UNIX, a user named oracle is generally created to become the owner of the Oracle software on the UNIX server. In addition to the oracle user, other UNIX users may be created and granted access to certain oracle files on the server. First on the menu is how UNIX manages user IDs and groups.

UNIX group management

Groups are defined in a file called /etc/group. Each line of the /etc/group file contains group data separated by a colon ":". This file defines each group and contains the following values:

```
group name   :  group_nbr  : members of the group
root> cat /etc/group
root::0:root
bin::2:root,bin,daemon
mail::6:root
tty::7:root,tty,adm
lp::8:root,lp,adm
nuucp::9:root,nuucp
daemon::12:root,daemon
dba::102:oracle,oradev
mysql::104:
```

The next section explores how user information is stored inside UNIX.

UNIX user management

UNIX users are controlled by a special file called /etc/passwd. This file contains a series of strings separated by colons ":". The values are:

```
username : password : user_nbr : group_nbr :  default shell
root> cat /etc/passwd
oracle:x:108:102::/export/home/oracle:/bin/ksh
oradev:x:109:102::/export/home/oradev:/bin/ksh
```

From the above listing, it can be determined that the oracle user has an encrypted password in /etc/shadow, that they are user 108, and they are in group 102. The oracle user has /export/home/oracle for a home directory, and they are using the Korn shell as a default shell. For some people, the John the Ripper tool, explained later, meets the definition of a utility. But for the purposes of this book, it definitely does not.

UNIX passwords on Oracle servers

UNIX passwords are extremely vulnerable to hacking. Users can change their passwords by invoking the passwd command. Note that the listing of /etc/passwd does not contain the encrypted passwords for the user IDs, and the password column is denoted with an "x". This indicates that the system administrator is storing the passwords in another special file called /etc/shadow.

However, protecting passwords in a /etc/shadow file is not always enough to ensure security. Several tools such as John the Ripper can be used to easily crack into these UNIX files, stealing access to the Oracle server and all database data. To learn how to protect a UNIX password from hacking, see the UNIX password cracker at http://www.openwall.com/john/.

UNIX connectivity for Oracle

When the Oracle DBA creates the tnsnames.ora file to define remote databases, they often specify the host name of the foreign server that contains the remote Oracle database instead of the TCP/IP address. For example, an entry in the tnsnames.ora file for a remote database might look like this:

```
kc =
    (DESCRIPTION =
      (ADDRESS_LIST =
          (ADDRESS =
             (COMMUNITY = TCP)
             (PROTOCOL = TCP)
            (HOST = gates)
             (PORT = 1521)
            )
      )
      (CONNECT_DATA = (SID = bbq))
    )
```

This shows a TNS service name of kc, which defines a connection to a remote server named gates that contains an Oracle database named bbq. When a remote connection request is made from the UNIX server, the /etc/hosts file is accessed to get the IP address for the gates server. From the listing below, it

---

shows that the gates server is located at 192.133.13.12. In sum, the /etc/hosts file is used to isolate the IP address from the *tnsnames.ora* file. If the IP address should ever change, the UNIX systems administrator only needs to change the IP address in one place.

```
root> cat /etc/hosts
192.133.13.22  gates     gates.com
192.144.13.22  dopey  dopey.com
```

Many of the UNIX commands used to manage an Oracle database are similar, or at times, even identical to the Windows commands.

UNIX and DOS Commands

Before Windows, PCs were operated from a keyboard using a command line. PC users were required to learn these commands in order to perform any tasks using a PC. During the 1980s, Microsoft DOS dominated the PC market, while the early UNIX command systems were used on larger multi-processing servers. The main difference between UNIX and DOS is that DOS was originally designed for single-user systems, and UNIX was designed for systems with multiple users.

Although PCs have evolved into GUI interfaces such as Microsoft Windows, X-Windows, the windowed interface for UNIX systems, has never really gained general acceptance. Hence, The Oracle professional must master a bewildering number of cryptic UNIX commands in order to manage and master the Oracle database.

One of the most difficult issues for the UNIX novice is being confronted with a complex, and usually undocumented UNIX command. The cryptic nature of UNIX is such that even the most seasoned UNIX professional may have trouble deciphering the purpose of the command. In addition, there is often more than one single way to perform any number of operations within UNIX. Some UNIX professionals delight in finding the most obscure method to perform a simple operation or spend hours trying to reduce a complex operation into the absolute minimum number of commands, almost as if obscurity is one of the goals to be achieved in completing the operation.

Since UNIX and MS-DOS were developed at the same time and must accomplish similar functions, they share some common syntax. The UNIX beginner will be happy to find many common commands and concepts. Table 2.1 shows some of the commonality between UNIX and MS-DOS commands:

UNIX	MS-DOS	Command Function
--	cd -	Switch between current and last directory
cat	Type	Displays the contents of a file
cd	Cd	Moves from one directory to another
cd /u01/test	cd c:\u01\test	Change directory paths
cd ..	cd..	Go up in directory
chmod	Attrib	Sets file permissions
clear	Cls	Clear the screen
cp	copy	Copies a file (or a group of files)
diff	fc	Compare two files
cpio	xcopy	Backs up and recovers files
date	date	Display the system date
doskey	<ctl> k (3)	Display command history
export PS1='xx'	prompt	Change the command prompt text
find	grep	Find a character string in a file
gzip	dblspace	Compress a data file
ln	--	Forms a link to a file
lp	print	Queues a file for printing
lpstat	print	Displays the printing queue
ls -al	dir	Displays the contents of a directory
mem	lsdev (2)	Display RAM memory
mkdir	md	Creates a new subdirectory
move	cp (4)	Move a file to another directory
mv	rename	Renames a file
rm	del	Deletes a file (or group of files)
rmdir	rd	Deletes an existing directory
setenv (1)	set	Set an environment variable
sort	sort	Sorts lines in a file
ver	uname -a	Display OS version
Vi (emacs?)	edit	Creates and edits text

Table 2.1: *UNIX and MS-DOS Command Utilities*

As can be seen here, being productive with UNIX involves learning many commands and combinations of commands. Rather than attempting to teach every possible UNIX command, this chapter will focus on those commands most useful to perform basic Oracle database management commands.

Introduction to UNIX Utilities

Appending Data to UNIX Files

To redirect program output, UNIX provides the << and >> commands. This is very useful when the Oracle DBA wants to keep logs in the UNIX environment. A typical usage might be to write a notation to the Oracle alert log that the file has been checked for errors. The command below could be used for this purpose:

```
echo '*****Alert log checked at 2/5/2002 by Andrew Kerber ****' >> \
$DBA/$ORACLE_SID/bdump/alert_$ORACLE_SID.log
```

The >> command can also be used to append to an existing file of errors. A common application is to keep a running list of all Oracle trace file names. The following command can be used to write all new trace file names into a list. Note that the first command line uses a single ">" to recreate the *trace_file_names.lst* file, while subsequent redirects use the ">>" directive to append new entries to this file.

```
ls -al $DBA/$ORACLE_SID/bdump/*.trc  > /tmp/trace_file_names.lst
ls -al $DBA/$ORACLE_SID/udump/*.trc >> /tmp/trace_file_names.lst
ls -al $DBA/$ORACLE_SID/cdump/*.trc >> /tmp/trace_file_names.lst
```

Next, it may be necessary to suppress UNIX command output.

Redirecting Output to a NULL Device

If one does not wish to see the output of a UNIX command (typically a batch job), use the /dev/null device to suppress the output. The /dev/null device is the equivalent of the DD DUMMY syntax in the COBOL. The /dev/null device is often used in scheduled tasks (using the UNIX crontab utility) if the output from the command is not required.

The following example submits a large batch job and suppresses the output. The ampersand causes UNIX to run the job in the background (detached from the starting process), and the "2>&1" syntax tells UNIX to redirect the standard error output to standard output. All possible output from large_file.exe will be suppressed:

```
./large_job.exe & 2>&1 > /dev/null
```

The tee command can be used to redirect multiple output streams.

Common Oracle UNIX Commands

Now that the basics have been covered, next to be viewed are the common UNIX commands that are used by the Oracle DBA. Many of these commands are extremely useful to automate Oracle reporting and make Oracle management simple.

Capturing server information with UNIX

For the Oracle DBA who manages databases on multiple servers, capturing the server name is very important. This is especially true in cases where several databases with the same name exist on several servers, and the report must show the server name to properly identify the database.

One common command to gather server information is the *uname −a* command. Here is an example of the output from this command in Solaris UNIX.

```
root> uname -a
SunOS zarda 5.8 Generic_103634-03 sun4u sparc SUNW,Ultra-80
```

Here is the *uname −a* command on a HP/UX server:

```
root> uname -a
HP-UX gates B.10.20 A 9000/871 2639229148 two-user license
```

In this example, the first column is the UNIX dialect (SunOS, HP-UX), the server name (gates, zarda), the version of the OS, the serial number of the server, and miscellaneous server information. If the DBA only needs the server name for an Oracle report, extend the *uname −a* command to capture the server name by using the *awk* utility and parsing out the first column of output:

```
root> uname -a|awk '{ print $2 }'
goofy
```

Also available is the hostname command to display the server name.

```
root> hostname
zarda
```

Next to be reviewed is how the *wc* command can be used to monitor the frequency of events in the Oracle database. Contrary to its name, it has nothing at all to do with plumbing.

The UNIX wc command

The UNIX wordcount command (*wc*) is used to display the number of words or lines (or characters) in a UNIX file. The *wc* command is typically used by the Oracle DBA who is looking to monitor the contents of specific messages with the Oracle alert log. For example, count the number of words in the Oracle alert log:

```
root> cat alert_envtest.log|wc
  108313   741411 5334959
```

From the *wc* command, see that the Oracle alert log has 180,313 lines, 741,411 words and 5,334,959 characters. The *wc –l* option is used to only display the number of lines on a file.

```
root> cat alert_envtest.log|wc -l
  108313
```

A typical usage for the *wc –l* command is to count the number of specific messages in the Oracle alert log. Below the text of all ORA-600 errors in the alert .log using the *cat* and *grep* commands are displayed.

```
root> cat alert_envtest.log|grep ORA-00600
ORA-00600: internal error code, arguments: [2655], [0], [1], [], [], []
ORA-00600: internal error code, arguments: [16365], [2208470888], [1], [4]
ORA-00600: internal error code, arguments: [16365], [2209886568], [0], [4]
```

Now add the *wc –l* command to count the number of ORA-600 errors:

```
root> cat alert_envtest.log|grep ORA-00600|wc -l
    3
```

Capturing date information in UNIX

It is a common practice to capture the date from the UNIX server. As with Oracle, UNIX dates have a default date format that can be modified according to the specified needs.

The default date output for UNIX is below:

```
root> date
Tue Sep  4 10:29:40 EDT 2001
```

To change the date display format involves the use of a date format mask, very similar to using the Oracle *nls_date_format* to change Oracle dates (Table 2.2).

Format	Meaning
%d	Day of the month as a two-digit decimal number [01-31].
%e	Day of the month as a two-character decimal number
%E	Combined Emperor/Era name and year.
%H	Hour (24-hour clock) as a two-digit decimal number [00-23].
%I	Hour (12-hour clock) as a two-digit decimal number [01-12].
%j	Day of the year as a three-digit decimal number [001-366].
%m	Month as a decimal two-digit number [01-12].
%M	Minute as a decimal two-digit number [00-59].
%p	Equivalent of either AM or PM. For example, PM.
%S	Second as a two-digit decimal number
%t	Tab character.
%u	Weekday as a one-digit decimal number [1-7].
%U	Week number of the year (Sunday as the first day of the week) as a two-digit decimal number [00-53].
%V	Week number of the year (Monday as the first day of the week) as a two-digit decimal number [01-53].
%w	Weekday as a one-digit decimal number [0-6]
%W	Week number of the year (Monday as the first day of the week) as a two-digit decimal number [00-53].
%x	Current date representation. For example, 01/12/94.
%X	Current time representation. For example, 19:45:58.
%y	Year without century as a two-digit decimal number [00-99].
%Y	Year with century as a four-digit decimal number [1970-2069]. For example, 1994.

Format	Meaning
%Z	Time zone name (or no characters if time zone cannot be determined). For example, PST.

Table 2.2: *Formats for the UNIX Date Command*

This table shows that UNIX has far more date format options than Oracle.

```
root> date "+DATE: %m/%d/%y%nTIME: %H:%M:%S"
DATE: 09/04/01
TIME: 09:37:49
```

The system date from a UNIX server can be retrieved from inside a SQL*Plus script, as shown below. Spool the SQL*Plus output to a file using the UNIX date function:

```
gen.ksh
#!/bin/ksh

# First, we must set the environment . . . .
# script is called with ORACLE_SID as argument
ORACLE_SID=$1
export ORACLE_SID
ORACLE_HOME=`cat /etc/oratab|grep ^$ORACLE_SID:|cut -f2 -d':'`
export ORACLE_HOME
PATH=$ORACLE_HOME/bin:$PATH
export PATH

$ORACLE_HOME/bin/sqlplus -s /<<!

spool `hostname`_`date +%d_%m_%y`.lst
select count(*) from dba_data_files;
spool off;

exit
!
```

Once the script has run, use the UNIX *ls* command, to see that the spool file contains the UNIX hostname and the UNIX date:

```
root> ls -t|head
cheopsdb-02_04_09_01.lst
temp.ksh
get_files.ksh
```

Following is a look at how the DBA can use UNIX commands to manage connected users.

UNIX user identification

To see all users who are currently signed on to the UNIX server, the *who* command can be used. Note that the *who* command does not show Oracle users who have connected using the Oracle Database Listener. Users logged into the Oracle database using the Listener show up as Oracle processes.

```
root> who|head -20
root          ttyp1          Aug 31 19:09
tlmason       ttyp2          Sep  4 08:31
dbogstad      ttyp3          Sep  4 06:33
clarson       ttyp4          Sep  4 07:20
mgeske        ttyp5          Sep  4 06:35
vogden        ttyp6          Sep  4 06:45
crmoore       ttyp7          Sep  4 06:45
yliu          ttyp8          Sep  4 06:47
mbell         ttyp9          Sep  4 06:54
acook         ttypa          Sep  4 06:58
rwestman      ttypb          Sep  4 08:06
eboyd         ttypc          Sep  4 06:58
lhovey        ttypd          Sep  4 07:00
mepeter       ttype          Sep  4 07:10
klong         ttypf          Sep  4 07:02
ldoolitt      ttyq0          Sep  4 07:36
dwilken       ttyq1          Sep  4 08:16
```

Options can be added to the *who* command to include a count of all users on the Oracle server. In this example, there are 145 UNIX users connected to this Oracle server.

```
root> who|wc -l
145
```

Locating files in UNIX

To find the location of code that will be executed, the *which* command is used. The *which* command will search the path for the program name it is given. For example, to find the location of the SQL*Plus executable:

```
root> which sqlplus
/u01/home/oracle/product/9.1.2/bin/sqlplus
```

To find other files, the UNIX *find* command is commonly used. In chapter 8, this command will be extended to search for all files that contain specific strings:

```
root> cd /
/
root> find . -print|grep -i dbmspool.sql
./oracle/product/9.1.2/rdbms/admin/dbmspool.sql
```

In the example above, *cd* to the root directory (/) and issue a UNIX *find* command to display every file on the Oracle server. Next, *pipe* the output of the find command to *grep*, which searches for the *dbmspool.sql* file. For more details on file management commands, see Chapter 8.

Some common UNIX utility commands will be covered next.

Using grep in UNIX

The *grep* utility is the most common method used to find UNIX files that contain specific strings. Experienced users quickly learn to use the *–i* option to do a case insensitive string search.

In the example below, the goal is to find an SQL script that recompiles invalid objects.

```
root> grep -i invalid *.sql
MKSTDROL.sql:/* create role for 'invalid' users    */
RUNTHEM.sql:  4  WHERE STATUS = 'INVALID'
add_view.sql:         'IV', 'Library Cache Invalidation',
invalid.sql:Spool run_invalid.sql
invalid.sql:    status = 'INVALID'
invalid.sql:@run_invalid.sql
locks.sql:               'IV', 'Library Cache Invalidation',
```

Using awk in UNIX

The *awk* utility is used often extract a specific column of data from output or a file. For example, to create a list of UNIX process IDs for all Oracle processes on the server.

```
root> ps -ef|grep -i oracle|awk '{ print $2 }'
23308
25167
12193
25163
12155
24065
24073
```

First, issue the *ps –ef* command to get a list of all UNIX processes, and then use *grep* to filter out all processes except this that contain the string "oracle." The *awk* utility is used to extract the second column of output.

```
root> ps -ef|grep -i oracle
   oracle 23308    1  0    May 14 ?           0:06 ora_lgwr_prodb1
   oracle 25167    1  0    Apr 30 ?           0:26 ora_smon_prodc1
   oracle 25163    1  0    Apr 30 ?          41:27 ora_lgwr_prodc1
   oracle 12155    1  0 11:30:43 ?            0:01 oracleprodcars (LOCAL=NO)
   oracle 24065    1  0    Apr 30 ?           0:02 ora_pmon_rman
   oracle 24073    1  0    Apr 30 ?          10:39 ora_ckpt_rman
   oracle 24846    1  0    May 11 ?           0:48 oracleprodc1 (LOCAL=NO)

root> ps -ef|grep -i oracle|awk '{ print $2 }'
23308
25167
12193
25163
12155
24065
24073
```

File Management in UNIX

Often, an Oracle DBA is charged with the complete maintenance of all files that comprise the Oracle software. Thus, the Oracle DBA must fully understand how to manage UNIX files and directories. This management includes allocating new files, removing old trace and dump files, and managing the growth of the Oracle data files on the server.

The UNIX touch command

To create an empty file with the default owner and permissions, the touch command is used. This is the equivalent to the IEFBR14 utility on a mainframe computer, where a file is created without any contents.

```
root> touch test.exe
root> ls -al test*
-rw-r-----   1 oracle    dba               0 Aug 13 09:43 test.exe
```

Now a typical Oracle DBA example of the touch command will be shown. First, enter the UNIX *pfile* alias that has been placed in the .profile file. This leads to the location of the Oracle alert log, and the *ls –al* command shows the file:

```
cheops*testsid-/export/home/oracle
> pfile

cheops*testsid-/u01/app/oracle/admin/testsid/pfile
> ls -al
total 26140
drwxr-xr-x   2 oracle     dba             2048 Jul 18 13:36 .
drwxr-xr-x   9 oracle     dba             2048 Feb 19  2001 ..
-rw-r--r--   1 oracle     dba             2301 Aug 22 13:01 inittestsid.ora
-rw-r--r--   1 oracle     dba             1840 Mar 13 23:00 inittestsid.ora.bkup
```

Next, the *mv* command is used to move the alert log to another name. This is done so that future *grep* commands will not show old results.

```
cheops*testsid-/u01/app/oracle/admin/testsid/pfile
> mv inittestsid.ora inittestsid.ora.old
```

Finally, it is possible to recreate an empty alert log file with the touch command. This is not required since Oracle will automatically recreate the alert log the first time that it needs to write an alert message:

```
cheops*testsid-/u01/app/oracle/admin/testsid/pfile
> touch inittestsid.ora
```

Now, the *ls –al* command shows old and new alert log files.

```
cheops*testsid-/u01/app/oracle/admin/testsid/pfile
> ls -al
total 26140
drwxr-xr-x   2 oracle     dba             2048 Sep  4 16:57 .
drwxr-xr-x   9 oracle     dba             2048 Feb 19  2001 ..
-rw-r--r--   1 oracle     dba                0 Sep  4 16:57 inittestsid.ora
-rw-r--r--   1 oracle     dba             1840 Mar 13 23:00 inittestsid.ora.bkup
-rw-r--r--   1 oracle     dba             2301 Aug 22 13:01 inittestsid.ora.old
```

The UNIX chmod command

The UNIX *chmod* command (pronounced "schmod") is used to change permissions on a UNIX file. The *chmod* permissions can be assigned either by number (Table 2.3) or by a letter value.

Owner	Group	Others?	Meaning
7	7	7	Read + Write + execute
6	6	6	Write + execute
5	5	5	Read + execute
4	4	4	read only

Owner	Group	Others?	Meaning
2	2	2	write only
1	1	1	Execute only

Table 2.3: *The UNIX Numerical File Permissions*

Assume that the DBA wants to allow all UNIX users in the DBA group to write to the Oracle initialization files. First check the existing permissions.

```
root> ls -al
total 56
drwxr-sr-x   2 oracle   dba            512 Aug 31 1999  ./
drwxr-sr-x   8 oracle   dba            512 Apr 13 08:28 ../
-rw-r--r--   1 oracle   dba            819 May 23 16:11 configPUS1.ora
-rw-r--r--   1 oracle   dba           4435 May 26 15:00 initPUS1.ora
```

This shows that the *–rw-r--r-* equates to a permission of 644 because *–rw* equals 6 and *r--* equals 4. To add write permissions to the group entry, change the permissions from 644 to 664:

```
root> chmod 664 *
root> ls -al
total 56
drwxr-sr-x   2 oracle   dba            512 Aug 31 1999  ./
drwxr-sr-x   8 oracle   dba            512 Apr 13 08:28 ../
-rw-rw-r--   1 oracle   dba            819 May 23 16:11 configPUS1.ora*
-rw-rw-r--   1 oracle   dba           4435 May 26 15:00 initPUS1.ora*
```

Remember that the default UNIX file permissions are dependent upon the value of the *umask* parameter. To illustrate, begin by creating several files on the UNIX server:

```
root> umask
022
root> touch t.exe u.ora v.sql
root> ls -al
total 6
drwxr-xr-x   2 oracle   dba            512 Sep  3 15:40 .
drwxr-xr-x  22 oracle   dba           2048 Sep  3 15:40 ..
-rw-r--r--   1 oracle   dba              0 Sep  3 15:40 t.exe
-rw-r--r--   1 oracle   dba              0 Sep  3 15:40 u.ora
-rw-r--r--   1 oracle   dba              0 Sep  3 15:40 v.sql
```

Note that since *umask* is equal to 022, each of the files is created with a permission of 644. Now use *chmod* to change the permissions to all of the files to 755:

```
root> chmod 755 *
root> ls -al
total 6
drwxr-xr-x   2 oracle    dba             512 Sep  3 15:40 .
drwxr-xr-x  22 oracle    dba            2048 Sep  3 15:40 ..
-rwxr-xr-x   1 oracle    dba               0 Sep  3 15:40 t.exe
-rwxr-xr-x   1 oracle    dba               0 Sep  3 15:40 u.ora
-rwxr-xr-x   1 oracle    dba               0 Sep  3 15:40 v.sql
```

As has been already noted, the *chmod* command can be used with letter-based permission masks, as shown in Table 2.4.

Owner (u)	Group (g)	World(o)	Meaning
rwx	Rwx	rwx	Read + Write + execute
rw	Rw	rw	Read + Write
rx	Rx	rx	Read + execute
wx	Wx	wx	Write + execute
R	R	r	Read only
w	W	w	Write Only
x	X	x	Execute only

Table 2.4: *The UNIX Chmod Letter Designations*

Note how this works. In the absence of a designator (u, g, or o), the *chmod* command makes the change for owner, group and world. In the *chmod* command below, make all .ksh files executable for all users:

```
root> ls -al
-rw-r--r--   1 oracle    dba               0 Sep  3 15:40 t.exe
-rw-r--r--   1 oracle    dba               0 Sep  3 15:40 u.ora
-rw-r--r--   1 oracle    dba               0 Sep  3 15:40 v.sql

root> chmod +x *
root>ls -al
-rwxr-xr-x   1 oracle    dba               0 Sep  3 15:40 t.exe
-rwxr-xr-x   1 oracle    dba               0 Sep  3 15:40 u.ora
-rwxr-xr-x   1 oracle    dba               0 Sep  3 15:40 v.sql
```

The same operation can be done with the numeric *chmod* command. Since the execution permissions are 644, 755 is used to make all files executable:

```
root> ls -al
-rw-r--r--   1 oracle    dba               0 Sep  3 15:40 t.exe
-rw-r--r--   1 oracle    dba               0 Sep  3 15:40 u.ora
-rw-r--r--   1 oracle    dba               0 Sep  3 15:40 v.sql

root> chmod 755 *
root> ls -al
```

```
-rwxr-xr-x   1 oracle   dba          0 Sep  3 15:40 t.exe
-rwxr-xr-x   1 oracle   dba          0 Sep  3 15:40 u.ora
-rwxr-xr-x   1 oracle   dba          0 Sep  3 15:40 v.sql
```

As noted, the *chmod* command can be prefaced with a reference to the user (u), group (g) or others (o). Consider the following *chmod* command to allow others (o) to get write and execute permission:

```
root> ls -al
-rw-r--r--   1 oracle   dba          0 Sep  3 15:40 t.exe
-rw-r--r--   1 oracle   dba          0 Sep  3 15:40 u.ora
-rw-r--r--   1 oracle   dba          0 Sep  3 15:40 v.sql

root> chmod o+wx *
root>ls -al
-rw-r--rwx   1 oracle   dba          0 Sep  3 15:40 t.exe
-rw-r--rwx   1 oracle   dba          0 Sep  3 15:40 u.ora
-rw-r--rwx   1 oracle   dba          0 Sep  3 15:40 v.sql
```

Note that this is equivalent to changing the permissions from 644 to 647 as shown below:

```
root> ls -al
-rw-r--r--   1 oracle   dba          0 Sep  3 15:40 t.exe
-rw-r--r--   1 oracle   dba          0 Sep  3 15:40 u.ora
-rw-r--r--   1 oracle   dba          0 Sep  3 15:40 v.sql

root> chmod 647 *
root> ls -al
-rw-r--rwx   1 oracle   dba          0 Sep  3 15:40 t.exe
-rw-r--rwx   1 oracle   dba          0 Sep  3 15:40 u.ora
-rw-r--rwx   1 oracle   dba          0 Sep  3 15:40 v.sql
```

The *chmod* command can also be used to revoke permissions on file. As seen in the next example, revoke all permissions for read, write and execute access for everyone except the owner. In effect, the permissions are being changed from 647 to 700:

```
root> ls -al
-rw-r--rwx   1 oracle   dba          0 Sep  3 15:40 t.exe
-rw-r--rwx   1 oracle   dba          0 Sep  3 15:40 u.ora
-rw-r--rwx   1 oracle   dba          0 Sep  3 15:40 v.sql

root> chmod 700 *
root> ls -al
-rwx------   1 oracle   dba          0 Sep  3 15:40 t.exe
-rwx------   1 oracle   dba          0 Sep  3 15:40 u.ora
-rwx------   1 oracle   dba          0 Sep  3 15:40 v.sql
```

Using *chmod* to save an Oracle password in a UNIX file: There are times when there are shell scripts that access Oracle and want to store the Oracle password in a UNIX file, such that only the UNIX oracle user can read the file.

In this example, create a file with the Oracle SYSTEM password and chmod the file so that only the UNIX oracle user can view the contents:

```
root>echo manager>system_password.file
root> chmod 400 *.file
root> ls -al
-r--------   1 oracle   dba              8 Sep  3 16:17 system_password.file
```

This technique is very useful when one wants to write a shell script to access Oracle and keep the password in a single file.

In addition, the *chmod* command also has a set of plus operators (+) that can be used to add read, write, or execute permissions to a file. Some Korn shell scripts are being changed and it is best disable them for everyone until the change has been completed:

```
root> chmod -x *.ksh
root> ls -al *.ksh
-rw-r--r--   1 oracle   dba           205 May 10 09:11 a.ksh
-rw-r--r--   1 oracle   dba           303 May 10 09:11 lert.ksh
-rw-r--r--   1 oracle   dba           312 Jul 19 11:32 back.ksh
-rw-r--r--   1 oracle   dba           567 May 10 09:12 coun.ksh
```

Once the maintenance is complete, the scripts can again be made executable with the *chmod* +x command:

```
root> chmod +x *.ksh
root> ls -al *.ksh
-rwxr-xr-x   1 oracle   dba           205 May 10 09:11 a.ksh*
-rwxr-xr-x   1 oracle   dba           303 May 10 09:11 lert.ksh*
-rwxr-xr-x   1 oracle   dba           312 Jul 19 11:32 back.ksh*
-rwxr-xr-x   1 oracle   dba           567 May 10 09:12 coun.ksh*
```

> ⌂ The savvy DBA will write up a 'cheat sheet' with the basic numeric settings for the *chmod* commands, and post it in a handy location.

A very important area of Oracle UNIX administration, the management of UNIX directories, will be examined next.

Directory Management in UNIX

Detailed below are the UNIX commands that are used to create, manage and navigate between UNIX directories.

The UNIX pwd command

The *pwd* command is probably the most commonly used UNIX command. It is short for Print Working Directory, and it tells where the DBA is located in the UNIX tree structure. For example, issue the *pwd* command to see the current directory:

```
root>pwd
/export/home/oracle
```

The *pwd* command is very important, and many Oracle DBAs and UNIX system administrators place the output of the *pwd* command in their command prompt so they always know their current directory. This is done by setting the UNIX PS1 system variable:

```
PS1="
`hostname`*\${ORACLE_SID}-\${PWD}
>"
export PS1
```

With this setting, the UNIX prompt will change to always show the hostname, the $ORACLE_SID and the current working directory:

```
cheops*testsid-/u01/app/oracle/admin/testsid/pfile
>pwd
/u01/app/oracle/admin/testsid/pfile
```

The UNIX ls command

Another very frequently used UNIX command is the *ls* command. Without any arguments, the *ls* command will show a list of all files in the current directory:

```
root> ls
Mailbox                invalid.sql                 run_rpt.ksh
ad.sql                 kill_oracle_sessions.ksh    run_trunc.lst
adamf_techeops          l.ksh                       run_trunc.sql
admin                  list.lst                    schools.dmp
afiedt.buf             list2.lst                   scripts
```

```
arsd.dmp                  lockee.txt                sql
bksel.lst                 lst.lst                   sqlnet.log
```

When the −*a* and −*l* arguments are added, all of the details for each file in the current working directory are shown:

```
root> ls -al
total 928188
drwxr-xr-x  21 oracle    dba          2048 Aug 22 20:47 .
drwxr-xr-x  10 root      root          512 Jul 26 08:49 ..
-rw-------   1 oracle    qmail         437 Aug 12 20:43 .bash_history
drwxr-xr-x  11 oracle    qmail         512 Sep  3 2000 .dt
-rwxr-xr-x   1 oracle    qmail        4381 Jul 16 13:20 .profile
-rwxr-xr-x   1 oracle    qmail        3648 Sep  1 2000 .profile_old
-rw-------   1 oracle    dba          2264 Sep  3 08:06 .sh_history
drwxr-xr-x   2 oracle    dba           512 May 10 11:10 .ssh
-rw-------   1 oracle    dba          3861 May 29 06:03 Mailbox
-rw-r--r--   1 oracle    dba         12632 Apr 11 16:09 ad.sql
drwxr-xr-x   2 oracle    dba           512 Jan 26 2001 adamf_techeops
drwxr-xr-x   5 oracle    dba           512 Sep  4 2000 admin
-rwxr-xr-x   1 oracle    dba            55 Aug 22 11:56 afiedt.buf
```

Below is a listing of each of the columns in the *ls* −*al* command so their meaning is understood.

Column	Data
1	File permissions
3	file owner
4	file group
5	file size
6	last modified date
7	file name

Table 2.5: *The Columns in the ls −al UNIX Command*

The first column in *the ls −al* command shows the file permissions. The permissions are a set of letters arranged in a group of three, one for the file owner, one for the file group and another for the world.

The third and fourth columns of the *ls −al* command lists the owner and group of the file. Note that if there is super-user authority (root), change the owner and group of any file with the *chown* command. The fifth column is the file size in bytes, the sixth column lists the last modified date and the last column is the name of the file.

Displaying "Dot" files in UNIX

The *–a* option of the *ls* command is used to display the "dot" files, which are not normally seen with the *ls* command. "dot" files are those files whose name begins with a period ("."). Some "dot" files that are of special interest to the Oracle DBA:

- Command history files – These file keep a complete audit of each and every UNIX command issued by the UNIX user. These include *.sh_history*, *.bash_history* and *.ksh_history*.

- Login files – These files contain login scripts that are executed every time the user signs on to UNIX. These include *.profile*, *.cshrc*, *.kshrc* and *.bshrc*.

The UNIX cd command

The UNIX change directory (*cd*) command is used to navigate the directory structure. The *cd* command without arguments takes the DBA to the location of the UNIX home directory. The UNIX home directory is specified in the /etc/passwd file and defines where one will be immediately after logon.

```
sting*testc1-/u01/app/oracle/admin/testc1/pfile
>cd
sting*testc1-/export/home/oracle
>
```

Otherwise, the *cd* command moves one to a directory location. In this example, transfer to the $ORACLE_HOME/rdbms/admin directory:

```
sting*testc1-/export/home/oracle
>cd $ORACLE_HOME/rdbms/admin

sting*testc1-/u01/app/oracle/product/8.1.7_64/rdbms/admin
>
```

UNIX also has useful *cd* arguments for moving back and forth between two directories. In this example, use the *cd –* command to bounce back and forth from the *pfile* directory and the /etc directory:

```
sting*testc1-/u01/app/oracle/admin/testc1/pfile
>cd /etc

sting*testc1-/etc
>cd -
/u01/app/oracle/admin/testc1/pfile
```

```
sting*testc1-/u01/app/oracle/admin/testc1/pfile
>cd -
/etc

sting*testc1-/etc
>
```

The *cd* .. command is used to move up one level in the directory structure. In this example, navigate from the *pfile* directory where the *init.ora* file is located to the *bdump* directory where the Oracle alert log is located (Figure 1-4).

```
sting*testc1-/u01/app/oracle/admin/testc1/pfile
>cd ../bdump

sting*testc1-/u01/app/oracle/admin/testc1/bdump
>
```

Removing UNIX files and directories

UNIX provides the *rm* command for removing data files. The *rm* command can be very dangerous, and many Oracle DBAs make an alias for *rm*, invoking the *rm –i* option. The *rm –i* option prompts for confirmation prior to deleting a file:

```
root> alias rm='rm -i'
root> rm temp.lst
rm: remove temp.lst (yes/no)? y
```

While UNIX provides an *rmdir* command for removing directories, UNIX also provides the ability to remove entire directories by using the *rm –Rf* command. The *–R* option tells *rm* to recursively cascade through subdirectories and the *–f* option says to force deletion, even if the permissions do not allow write access. In the example below, the *rm –I* alias gives the choice to examine the files in the directory before removing them:

```
root> rm -Rf temp
rm: examine files in directory temp (yes/no)? no
```

> 💣 Warning – **Don't ever try this**: To demonstrate the horrible power of the *rm* command, the following command (when executed as root) will permanently remove all files on your entire server!
>
> root> cd /
> root> rm –Rf *

Now that the basic UNIX commands have been covered, take a closer look at how Oracle DBAs use UNIX commands in the Oracle environment.

The Oracle environment in UNIX

Upon logging onto a UNIX computer, a special login file is executed to establish the UNIX environment. Typically, these login commands perform the following functions:

- Basic UNIX environment commands
- Set the UNIX command line editor
- Set Oracle aliases
- Set a standard UNIX command prompt
- Changing the Oracle UNIX environment
- Basic UNIX environment commands

There are several settings that should be configured when logged onto UNIX. These login commands define the user environment and are critical to success in UNIX. Start with the basic environment command.

Set the shell environment

The first choice is which shell is needed as the default. The choices are c-Shell (csh), Bourne shell (sh), Korn shell (ksh), or the Bourne Again shell (bsh), more commonly known as Bash shell. In the example below, the default shell is set to the Korn shell.

```
#*************************************************************
#  Set environment to Korn shell.
#*************************************************************
ENV=.kshrc; export ENV
```

Set the umask parameter

The *umask* parameter is used to set the default file protections for a user. As shown in the following example, set the umask to 022.

```
#******************************************************************
#  Set the umask to have 755 for executables and 644 for text
#******************************************************************
umask 022
```

Set the UNIX terminal type

The following command sets the terminal type for the session.

```
#******************************************************************
#  Set the terminal to vt100
#******************************************************************
DBABRV=ora; export DBABRV
ORACLE_TERM=vt100; export ORACLE_TERM
TERM=vt100; export TERM
The UNIX command line editor
```

The next command is the setting for the command line editor. This is the set – *o* command. Observe how the command line editor makes the DBA's life in UNIX easier.

UNIX allows setting the type of command editor. Once set, a variety of shortcuts can be used to quickly redisplay previous UNIX commands. These shortcut commands will greatly reduce the amount of typing at the UNIX prompt, and a UNIX guru can always be recognized because of their use of these command shortcuts. There are two common settings for the command line editor, *emacs* and *vi*.

- set –*o emacs* – This command sets the *emacs* editor for editing online UNIX commands.

- Command completion with *emacs* – the *emacs* setting allows completing of long file names by pressing the escape key twice (<esc><esc>). For example, to *vi* the file *oracle_script_for_checking_permissions.ksh*, enter *vi* oracle <esc><esc>, and the command line will display:

  - root> *vi oracle_script_for_checking_permissions.ksh*

- Display previous commands – the *emacs* editor allow viewing of the prior command by pressing the <ctrl> p keys.

- set *–o vi* – This command sets the *vi* editor for online UNIX commands. Once a command is displayed at the UNIX prompt, use standard *vi* commands to edit the command. In addition, the set *–o vi* command allows for easy searches of the UNIX command history.

- Command completion with *vi* – the *vi* setting allows long file names to be completed by pressing the escape backslash (<esc> \). For example, to *vi* the file *oracle_script_for_checking_permissions.ksh*, enter *vi* oracle <esc> \, and the command line will display:

  - root> *vi oracle_script_for_checking_permissions.ksh*

- Display previous commands – the *vi* editor allows viewing of prior commands by pressing the <esc> k key.

- Search the command history –search for a specific command in the command history and display it on the command line by pressing the escape key and the forward slash (<esc> /). For example, to redisplay a command that contains ksh, enter <esc> /, followed by ksh. The matching command will then be displayed on the command line. To automatically set this value, place the following code in the login file *(.profile, .kshrc*

  - Backspace and Keyboard editor setting - this setting allows the following shortcuts:

    - <esc> k - to display command history

    - <esc> \ - for command completion

    - <esc> / searchstring - to find a command in the history file

    - stty erase ^? #Maps Backspace character to backspace instead of ctl-h

    - set -o vi

    - export EDITOR=vi

Once the basic UNIX environment has been set, now is the time to look at setting the UNIX environment for Oracle.

Oracle aliases for UNIX

A UNIX alias is a short command that is replaced with a larger command to save typing. A common alias used to count the number of connected users on the oracle server is *numuse*:

```
root> alias numuse='who|wc -l'
root> numuse
463
```

Here is a list of common UNIX aliases that can be added to the UNIX logon
file for the Oracle user. These perform common Oracle functions such as
checking the Oracle alert log and transferring quickly between directories.

```
#********************************
# UNIX aliases for Oracle DBAs
#********************************
   alias alert='tail -100 \
         $DBA/$ORACLE_SID/bdump/alert_$ORACLE_SID.log|more'
   alias errors='tail -100 \
         $DBA/$ORACLE_SID/bdump/alert_$ORACLE_SID.log|more'
   alias arch='cd $DBA/$ORACLE_SID/arch'
   alias bdump='cd $DBA/$ORACLE_SID/bdump'
   alias cdump='cd $DBA/$ORACLE_SID/cdump'
   alias pfile='cd $DBA/$ORACLE_SID/pfile'
   alias rm='rm -i'
   alias sid='env|grep ORACLE_SID'
   alias admin='cd $DBA/admin'
```

To illustrate the usefulness of aliases in Oracle administration, in the example
below, get to the *pfile* directory in a single command so the contents of the
init.ora file can be viewed:

```
cheops*CPRO-/home/oracle
> pfile
cheops*CPRO-/u01/app/oracle/CPRO/pfile
>ls
initCPRO.ora
```

Aliases can also be used for more sophisticated Oracle commands. For
example, the following alias can be used to display all Oracle errors in the last
400 lines of the alert log:

```
cheops*testsid-/u01/app/oracle/admin/envtest/pfile
>alias errors='tail -400 $DBA/$ORACLE_SID/bdump/alert_$ORACLE_SID.log|\
    grep ORA-'

cheops*testsid-/u01/app/oracle/admin/envtest/pfile
>errors
ORA-00604: error occurred at recursive SQL level 1
ORA-01089: immediate shutdown in progress - no operations are permitted
ORA-00604: error occurred at recursive SQL level 3
ORA-01089: immediate shutdown in progress - no operations are permitted
```

A standard UNIX prompt for Oracle users

The following code snippet in the Oracle user login file will configure a standard UNIX prompt that identifies the current server name, the value of the current $ORACLE_SID UNIX variable, and the current working directory. This standard prompt makes it very easy to know where the DBA is when navigating UNIX, and it also ensures that the DBA knows where they are located at all times.

```
#*****************************************************************
# Standard UNIX Prompt
#*****************************************************************
PS1="
`hostname`*\${ORACLE_SID}-\${PWD}
>"
```

This standardized Oracle UNIX prompt has the advantage of displaying the server name, the ORACLE_SID and the current directory. The best feature of the standard command prompt is that it also places the command prompt on the next line so that there are a full 80 characters to type UNIX commands:

```
cheops*CCPRO-/home/oracle
>pwd

/home/oracle

cheops*CCPRO-/home/oracle
>cd /u01/oradata/CPRO

cheops*CCPRO-/u01/oaradata/CPRO
>
```

Changing the Oracle environment in UNIX

A typical problem on any UNIX server is quickly setting the many environment variables necessary to change the Oracle environment to a different database.

Oracle provides a command script called *oraenv* to reset the Oracle environment, but it often does not work properly, and most experienced DBAs know that the following commands must be issued to change from one ORACLE_SID to another:

```
export ORAENV_ASK=NO;\
export ORACLE_SID='$DB';\
```

```
.TEMPHOME/bin/oraenv;\
export ORACLE_HOME;\
export ORACLE_BASE=\
   `echo ORACLE_HOME | sed -e 's:/product/.*::g'`;\
export DBA=$ORACLE_BASE/admin;\
export SCRIPT_HOME=$DBA/scripts;\
export PATH=$PATH:$SCRIPT_HOME;\
export LIB_PATH=$ORACLE_HOME/lib:$ORACLE_HOME/lib:/usr/lib '
```

Most DBAs create a UNIX alias with the same name as the ORACLE_SID. When the ORACLE_SID is entered at the command prompt, all of the required commands are executed by means of a shell script. Below is the login profile code to perform this function.

```
********************************************************************
# For every Oracle_SID in /var/opt/oracle/oratab,
# create an alias using the SID name.
# Now, entering the ORACLE_SID at the UNIX prompt will completely
# set the UNIX environment for that SID
#*******************************************************************

for DB in `cat /var/opt/oracle/oratab| \
grep -v \#|grep -v \*|cut -d":" -f1`
do
    alias $DB='export ORAENV_ASK=NO; export ORACLE_SID='$DB'; .
TEMPHOME/bin/oraenv; export ORACLE_HOME; export ORACLE_BASE=`echo
ORACLE_HOME | sed -e 's:/product/.*::g'`; export DBA=$ORACLE_BASE/admin;
xport SCRIPT_HOME=$DBA/scripts; export PATH=$PATH:$SCRIPT_HOME; export
IB_PATH=$ORACLE_HOME/lib:$ORACLE_HOME/lib:/usr/lib '
  done
```

Next, examine how this works. First there is a FOR loop in UNIX. Decompose this command and see what it is doing:

```
for DB in `cat /var/opt/oracle/oratab|\
grep -v \#|grep -v \*|cut -d":" -f1`
```

The *for DB in* command means that the script will loop once for each value of $DB. The argument to the *for DB in* command is enclosed in graves (pronounced "gra-vees"), which is the back-tick character (directly above the tab key on a PC keyboard). Arguments enclosed in graves tell UNIX to execute the command enclosed in the graves and return the result set to UNIX. In this case, the command in the graves does the following:

- cat the var/opt/oracle/oratab file (/etc/oratab in AIX). This lists all databases defined on the UNIX server:

```
root>cat /var/opt/oracle/oratab
test9i:/u01/app/oracle/product/8.1.7_64:Y
testc1:/u01/app/oracle/product/8.1.7_64:Y
```

```
#testc2:/u01/app/oracle/product/8.1.7_64:Y
testman:/u01/app/oracle/product/8.1.7_64:Y
```

- Next, notice the grep –v \# and the grep –v * commands. These ignores any lines in the oratab file that are commented-out:

```
root>cat /var/opt/oracle/oratab|grep -v \#|grep -v \*
test9i:/u01/app/oracle/product/8.1.7_64:Y
testc1:/u01/app/oracle/product/8.1.7_64:Y
testman:/u01/app/oracle/product/8.1.7_64:Y
```

- Then issue the cut -d":" -f1 command. This extracts the first column in the oratab file using the colon ":" as the column delimiter:

```
root>cat /var/opt/oracle/oratab|grep -v \#|grep -v
\*|cut -d":" -f1
test9i
testc1
testman
```

There is now a list of valid $ORACLE_SID values. Inside the FOR loop, create an alias with the value of $DB (the $ORACLE_SID name), and perform all of the required changes to reset the UNIX environment for that database.

Now to the process of dissecting complex UNIX commands. An Oracle DBA must be able to interpret complex UNIX commands.

Dissecting Complex UNIX commands

UNIX neophytes are often taken aback when they see some of the cryptic commands used in UNIX. The *pipe* command in particular lends to the difficulty of reading UNIX scripts. Once the UNIX beginner gets used to using the pipe command, much of UNIX will become more legible.

```
ps -ef|grep "ora_"|grep $ORACLE_SID|-v grep| \
awk '{ print $2 }'|-exec rm -f {} \;
```

At first glance, this command appears to be a conglomeration of cryptic letters. However, upon closer examination, this UNIX command is actually a series of commands that are joined together with the pipe operator "|". When viewed this way, the command can be viewed as a connected list of commands:

```
ps -ef
|
grep "ora_"
```

```
|
grep $ORACLE_SID
|
grep -v grep
|
awk '{ print $2 }'
|
-exec rm -f {} \;
```

By expanding the command onto separate lines using the | characters as a delimiter, one is able to examine each sub-command and see how each successive command refines the output from the prior UNIX command. Once the individual commands that comprise the whole UNIX script are revealed, one can begin to understanding each component since the result set becomes smaller and more refined with each subsequent command.

Deciphering a Complex UNIX Command

This example utilizes a one-line UNIX command that is used to kill all Oracle background processes for a specified database on the UNIX server as an example. As an Oracle DBA, there are times when it is necessary to kill all Oracle processes, or a selected sub-set of Oracle processes. This is a common UNIX script used by an Oracle DBA who wants to kill all Oracle processes when the Oracle database is "locked up" and the database cannot be stopped with the standard Oracle utilities.

The basic format of the UNIX kill command is shown below, and a single kill command can be used to kill many UNIX processes (PIDs):

```
root> kill -9 process1 process2 process3
```

Thus, the kill command can accept a list of processes, and the goal is to gather a list of processes from UNIX and use them as arguments to the kill command. The following command will kill all Oracle processes for the server because of the *–exec* syntax.

```
ps -ef|grep "ora_"|grep -v grep|awk '{print $2}'|-exec kill -9 {} \;
```

The steps within this command are as follows:

1. The *ps –ef* UNIX command displays all active processes on the server, but, the goal is to limit the command to only those processes that are running on the Oracle database.

---

2. The *grep "ora_"* command removes all but the Oracle processes:

```
root> ps -ef|grep "ora_"
  oracle 13022     1   0   Sep 30       -   0:18 ora_db02_vald
  oracle 14796 42726   0 09:00:46  pts/0  0:00 grep ora_
  oracle 17778     1   0   Sep 30       -   0:14 ora_smon_devp
  oracle 18134     1   0   Sep 30       -   0:37 ora_snp1_vald
  oracle 19516     1   0   Sep 30       -   0:24 ora_db04_prod
  oracle 21114     1   0   Sep 30       -   0:37 ora_snp0_devp
  oracle 28436     1   0   Sep 30       -   0:18 ora_arch_prod
```

3. The *grep –v grep* is used to remove the second line from the above output. The *grep –v* command is used to exclude lines with the specified string. In the output below, note that the *grep* line is now missing from the output:

```
root> ps -ef|grep "ora_"|grep -v grep
  oracle 13022     1   0   Sep 30       -   0:18 ora_db02_vald
  oracle 17778     1   0   Sep 30       -   0:14 ora_smon_devp
  oracle 18134     1   0   Sep 30       -   0:37 ora_snp1_vald
  oracle 19516     1   0   Sep 30       -   0:24 ora_db04_prod
  oracle 21114     1   0   Sep 30       -   0:37 ora_snp0_devp
  oracle 28436     1   0   Sep 30       -   0:18 ora_arch_prod
```

4. Next, use the UNIX *awk* command. The *awk* or the cut commands can be used to extract specific columns from a result set. In this case, use *awk '{ print $2 }'* to get the second column which is the Process ID (or pid) for these processes. This results in a list of process ID's to send to the kill command.

```
root> ps -ef|grep "ora_"|grep -v grep|awk '{ print $2 }'
  13022
  17778
  18134
  19516
  21114
  28436
  28956
```

5. Now there is a clean list of process IDs for the Oracle background processes. To ship the list to the next command, *pipe* the list of PIDs to the UNIX kill command by using the *–exec* UNIX command. The *–exec* command accepts a list as an argument and performs any UNIX command on the input set.

> ⌂ Note: If HP/UX or AIX is being used, also use the xargs command for this purpose.

```
ps -ef|grep "ora_"|grep -v grep|awk '{ print $2 }'|-exec kill -9 {} \;
```

6. Once the complex command is built, encapsulate the command into a single UNIX alias.

```
alias nukem = "ps -ef|grep "ora_"|grep -v grep| \
   awk '{ print $2 }'|-exec rm -f {} \;"
```

Entering the alias nukem alias at the UNIX command prompt will invoke the complex command to kill all Oracle background processes. The example is for illustration purposes only since a prudent Oracle DBA would never risk assigning such a dangerous command to an alias, or at the very least would require multiple confirmations before running the command.

Conclusion

The purpose of this chapter has been to provide an introduction to the basic UNIX commands that are used by the Oracle DBA. Some of the most common and useful UNIX commands have been covered. The main points of this chapter include:

- Listing the different dialects of UNIX

- The syntax of common UNIX commands

- Piping together multiple UNIX commands

- File and directory permissions

- Configuring the Oracle UNIX environment

- Deciphering complex UNIX commands

This book will continue with a closer look at UNIX server management. The next chapter will cover some of the internal mechanisms of the UNIX architecture, and show the most common UNIX command and utilities that are used by the Oracle DBA to monitor load on the server.

Windows Oracle OS Utilities

Oracle on Windows is probably the easiest of all Oracle versions to use. It is even easier to use if the DBA has a good understanding of Windows. On the other hand, Oracle on Windows is probably the least flexible and most frustrating version of Oracle if one is used to other Oracle platforms such as Linux.

Reasons for Using Oracle on Windows

In some ways, using Oracle on Windows is simpler than using a UNIX variant as the underlying operating system. Windows has fewer user tunable parameters than Linux and they are harder to access. Also, while many database professionals are not fond of the Windows platform for Oracle, Windows is probably the most common platform for Oracle installations. That final point alone provides enough justification to learn more about Oracle on Windows. In addition, if one is:

- Fairly new to Oracle and wants to learn more about it in an easy-to-use environment

- Experienced with Oracle and wants to experiment with more advanced features, commands, and scenarios without putting live or actual data (and one's job) at risk

- Anywhere in between new and experienced and wants to get more familiar with concepts tested on certification exams, or

- Using SQL Server and wants to see what a more powerful, flexible database looks like.

Then Oracle on Windows is a good place to start.

Oracle is the most powerful and flexible database in the world, making it also the most cost effective database in the world with a large number of pricing options. With the release of Oracle XE (Express Edition), and Oracle SQL

Developer, there are some free tools for learning about the many advantages of using Oracle in an easy-to-use Windows environment.

In addition, Oracle provides several snap-ins to monitor database activity on Windows, roughly ten categories in all, covering metrics such as physical reads per query, redo log space requests, and the frequency of recursive calls for dynamic space management.

When learning Oracle, the first step in Windows is to learn the basic Windows performance snap-ins in terms of setup, display, reporting and alerts. The second step is to install the Oracle snap-ins and start using them. Oracle's Performance Monitor snap-ins give the ability to monitor performance, generate reports and receive alerts on common Oracle database-related performance and tuning metrics.

Yet another feature in the Oracle on Windows world is the ability to configure response files so that silent, non-interactive installations of Oracle products can be performed. Response files for silent installations of Oracle are not new to either operating system. However, one's understanding about administering Windows, or at least appreciation of a Windows administrator's role, is increased by learning about the response files that Windows can use for silent/unattended installations of the Windows operating system.

Do not be surprised to learn that the template response files for Oracle are also found on the installation CDs in the /database/response directory. There are sample response files for Enterprise, Standard, and Personal editions of Oracle as well as response files for the Database Creation Assistant (DBCA) and Network Configuration Assistant (NETCA).

Windows Utilities for Monitoring Oracle

The Oracle Counters for Windows Performance Monitor package is not installed by default. In order to install it when Oracle is installed, select the custom install option. This option can also be installed later via the Oracle installer. Select both custom installation and the Oracle for Windows Performance option and that will install this package. Once Oracle Counters for Windows Performance Monitor has been installed, perform one more piece of the setup. The Oracle performance counters are set up to monitor one Oracle instance. Information about this instance must be configured in the registry. The command to configure this is:

```
operfcfg -U system -P password -D orcl
```

In this case, *orcl* is the *tnsnames* entry, not the database SID. This will update the registry to add the performance counters. Oracle can now be monitored via the window performance monitoring utility *perfmon*. Some of the things that can be monitored are:

- The Oracle Buffer Cache. This is where the cache miss ratio can be seen.

- Shared Pool Stats. This collection includes the data dictionary cache and the library cache.

- Log Buffer. Provides information on log space requests.

- Database Data Files. This object provides physical read and write per second counters.

- DBWR stats. Provides information on the DB Writer processes.

- Miscellaneous. Other statistics include dynamic space management, free lists and dynamic sorts.

By taking advantage of Oracle Counters for Windows Performance Monitor, Oracle can be easily and efficiently monitored along with the OS. As mentioned earlier, *perfmon* provides valuable performance data that is easily collected and analyzed. Some of the most important and initial counters to look at when diagnosing performance problems in an Oracle Windows environment are:

- Processor: %Processor Time. This gives a quick look at how busy the system is.

- Physical Disk: Avg. Disk sec/Read, Avg. Disk sec/Write. This provides an overview of how well the I/O subsystem is doing.

Checking Windows Services for Oracle

With Windows, in order for the Oracle database to run, it must attach itself to a running Windows process. Some DBAs think that the Windows service is the database process, but that is not true. Not only can the Windows service start and stop the database, but the service can also be started without the database starting.

One of the first things that DBAs discover when working with Windows is that most Oracle problems with the Windows service involve the service starting but the database not starting. When the Windows service is set to automatically start as the server boots, but the database does not start, the registry entry may be wrong or the service may be bad. Follow these steps:

1. Check Task Manager for the ORACLE.EXE process. If it is present, then the service started.

2. Check the Alert Log for the database. If the problem is with the database, there will probably be an entry in the alert log. If the problem is not with the database, there will not be any entry in the alert log.

3. Check the oradim.log in the $ORACLE_HOME/database directory for errors. Check the date on the log file as versions before 9i did not date/time stamp the entries.

If there are no errors in the logs, then try to start the database.

```
C:> sqlplus "/ as sysdba"
connected to an idle instance
SQL> startup
```

If the database starts, the problem is in the service.

To check the Windows service:

1. Open the registry with Regedit. Always back up the registry before making changes. Navigate to the key entry in the Windows registry:

   HKEY_LOCAL_MACHINE\SOFTWARE\ORACLE\KEY_oracle_home_name

2. There will be a key called ORA_SID_AUTOSTART. SID is the database SID. This key should be set to TRUE. If not, the server starts but not the database. There is also an ORA_SID_SHUTDOWN which should be TRUE so that if the server is shut down, the service will shutdown the database.

3. In order to set the database to manual start mode, set ORA_SID_AUTOSTART to FALSE. The service will start but not the database.

Test the Windows Oracle Service

If the ORA_SID_AUTOSTART setting was the problem, change it to TRUE and then test the service by stopping and then restarting the service to see if the database automatically starts. If it does, then reboot the Windows server to verify that the database will start automatically. Sometimes the service will work, only to fail again after a reboot. If the service fails after rebooting, recreate the service. The ORADIM utility is used to recreate the service.

- SQLPATH - If the choice is to keep all scripts in one place, SQLPATH is what needs to be used to centrally manage and store the scripts. The default location is ORACLE_HOME\dbs. Generally, this value is changed by the user as it is bad practice to store user-created SQL in a software installation directory.

- ORA_SID_AUTOSTART - In Windows, the service can run without the database instance, but the instance can not run without the service.

- Upon a reboot or startup, have the database(s) automatically start up - the service is set to start automatically, which in turn enables the instance to be started, which in turn means the database is open for business. With this parameter set, also perform shutdown and startup simply by stopping and starting the service.

- ORA_SID_SHUTDOWN - This is similar to the *autostart* parameter. If set to true, the database is shutdown when the service is stopped.

- ORA_SID_SHUTDOWNTYPE - One of three values can be set for this parameter: "a" for abort, "n" for normal, or "i" for immediate. Immediate is the default, and recommended, value. Either the entire word (abort, normal, immediate), or just the first letter may be used.

- *ORA_SID_SHUTDOWN_TIMEOUT* - To be on the safe side of things, i.e. ensure that there is a clean shutdown if not using the abort option, a time (in seconds) can be set for the service to wait before stopping.

Oracle Scripts for Windows

Every DBA will, from time to time, write his or her own utilities for managing Oracle. Thus, the basics of writing scripts against the Oracle database will be briefly covered. There are several choices for writing Oracle scripts in a Windows environment:

- .bat files - Microsoft enhanced the DOS command functions starting with Windows 2000. Even so, UNIX adherents will argue that DOS commands are not nearly as powerful as a UNIX shell script. No doubt, Windows adherents disagree with this.

- SFU - Microsoft released Windows Services for UNIX (SFU) to more closely emulate a variety of UNIX shells and UNIX utilities to ease the migration from a UNIX to a Windows environment. While SFU is certainly a more comprehensive solution than the native command prompt, it is more complicated and does not provide total compatibility for porting UNIX scripts to Windows.

- UNIX Dos - The Unix Dos Toolkit from Professional Software Solutions provides all of the UNIX-like functions. However, Unix Dos is not a free program.

What follows are some examples of writing simple Oracle scripts using windows .bat files.

Sample Invocation of Oracle from Windows

The DOS command line can be used to call Oracle. The trick is that the SQL*Plus invocation spools the output on a single command line:

```
sqlplusw -s "%DBUser%/%DBPass%@%DBTNS%" @%LOG%OraCall.sql    >
%LOG%OraCall.lst
```

Here is a Windows Oracle script with DOS commands to set the environment:

```
@ECHO off
SET DBUser=%1
SET DBPass=%2
SET DBTNS=%3
SET LOG=\temp\test\
ECHO spool %LOG%OraCall.log                              >
%LOG%OraCall.sql
ECHO set linesize 132                                    >>
%LOG%OraCall.sql
ECHO COL x_tns       NEW_VALUE v_tns      NOPRINT        >>
%LOG%OraCall.sql
ECHO COL x_dbid      NEW_VALUE v_dbid     NOPRINT        >>
%LOG%OraCall.sql
ECHO COL x_dbname    NEW_VALUE v_dbname   NOPRINT        >>
%LOG%OraCall.sql
ECHO SELECT '%DBTNS%'  x_tns     FROM dual;              >>
%LOG%OraCall.sql
ECHO SELECT dbid       x_dbid    FROM v$database;        >>
%LOG%OraCall.sql
```

```
ECHO SELECT name        x_dbname    FROM v$database;           >>
%LOG%OraCall.sql
ECHO @SQLSelect.sql                                            >>
%LOG%OraCall.sql
ECHO spool off                                                 >>
%LOG%OraCall.sql
ECHO exit                                                      >>
%LOG%OraCall.sql
sqlplusw -s "%DBUser%/%DBPass%@%DBTNS%" @%LOG%OraCall.sql   >
%LOG%OraCall.lst
```

Running a Data Pump Export from Windows

Data Pump Export was first available in Oracle 10g and is used to replace the old export/import utilities. See Chapter 6 for more information about Data Pump. Below is a very nice utility script that Jeff Hunter, Oracle Guru, wrote called *oracle_export.bat*. This is a script for exporting data from Windows.

A key learning point here is that he builds the exp parfile arguments into a DOS variable called %PARFILE% by echoing the settings to a file using the >> append command:

🖫 **oracle_export.bat**

```
c:> exp=%PARFILE%:
REM +-------------------------------------------------------------------
---+
REM | VALIDATE COMMAND-LINE
PARAMETERS                                                  |
REM +-------------------------------------------------------------------
---+

if (%1)==() goto USAGE
if (%2)==() goto USAGE
if (%3)==() goto USAGE


REM +-------------------------------------------------------------------
---+
REM | VALIDATE ENVIRONMENT
VARIABLES                                                   |
REM +-------------------------------------------------------------------
---+

REM set ORABACKUP=C:\oracle\orabackup\JEFFDB\export
REM set ORALOG=C:\oracle\custom\oracle\log
REM set ORATMP=C:\oracle\custom\oracle\temp

if (%ORALOG%)==() goto ENV_VARIABLES
if (%ORATMP%)==() goto ENV_VARIABLES
if (%ORABACKUP%)==() goto ENV_VARIABLES
```

```
REM +----------------------------------------------------------------------
---+
REM | DECLARE ALL GLOBAL
VARIABLES.                                                              |
REM +----------------------------------------------------------------------
---+

set FILENAME=export_backup_online_full_9i
set DB_USERNAME=%1%
set DB_PASSWORD=%2%
set TNS_ALIAS=%3%
set PARFILE=%ORATMP%\%FILENAME%_%TNS_ALIAS%.parfile
set LOGFILE=%ORALOG%\%FILENAME%_%TNS_ALIAS%.log
set DUMPFILE=%ORABACKUP%\exp_full_%TNS_ALIAS%.dmp


REM +----------------------------------------------------------------------
---+
REM | REMOVE OLD LOG AND PARAMETER
FILE(S).                                                                |
REM +----------------------------------------------------------------------
---+

del /q %PARFILE%
del /q %LOGFILE%


REM +----------------------------------------------------------------------
---+
REM | WRITE EXPORT PARAMETER
FILE.                                                                   |
REM +----------------------------------------------------------------------
---+

echo userid=%DB_USERNAME%/%DB_PASSWORD%@%TNS_ALIAS% > %PARFILE%
echo buffer=50000000 >> %PARFILE%
echo file=%DUMPFILE% >> %PARFILE%
echo compress=n >> %PARFILE%
echo grants=y >> %PARFILE%
echo indexes=y >> %PARFILE%
echo direct=no >> %PARFILE%
echo log=%LOGFILE% >> %PARFILE%
echo rows=y >> %PARFILE%
echo consistent=y >> %PARFILE%
echo full=y >> %PARFILE%
REM echo owner=(SCOTT) >> %PARFILE%
REM echo tables=(EMP, DEPT) >> %PARFILE%
echo triggers=y >> %PARFILE%
echo statistics=none >> %PARFILE%
echo constraints=y >> %PARFILE%


REM +----------------------------------------------------------------------
---+
REM | MOVE OLD EXPORT (DUMP)
FILE.                                                                   |
REM +----------------------------------------------------------------------
---+
```

```
del /q %DUMPFILE%.backup
move %DUMPFILE% %DUMPFILE%.backup


REM +--------------------------------------------------------------------
---+
REM | PERFORM
EXPORT.                                                                  |
REM +--------------------------------------------------------------------
---+

exp parfile=%PARFILE%


REM +--------------------------------------------------------------------
---+
REM | SCAN THE EXPORT LOGFILE FOR
ERRORS.                                    |
REM +--------------------------------------------------------------------
---+

echo ...
echo Analyzing log file for EXP- errors...
findstr /I /C:"EXP-" %LOGFILE%
if errorlevel 0 if not errorlevel 1 echo EXP- Errors:  %FILENAME%
%TNS_ALIAS% %COMPUTERNAME% %DATE% %TIME% %LOGFILE%

echo ...
echo Analyzing log file for ORA- errors...
findstr /I /C:"ORA-" %LOGFILE%
if errorlevel 0 if not errorlevel 1 echo ORA- Errors:  %FILENAME%
%TNS_ALIAS% %COMPUTERNAME% %DATE% %TIME% %LOGFILE%

echo ...
echo Analyzing log file for warnings...
findstr /I /C:"Export terminated successfully with warnings" %LOGFILE%
if errorlevel 0 if not errorlevel 1 echo WARNING: %FILENAME% %TNS_ALIAS%
%COMPUTERNAME% %DATE% %TIME% %LOGFILE%

echo ...
echo Analyzing log file for errors...
findstr /I /C:"Export terminated unsuccessfully" %LOGFILE%
if errorlevel 0 if not errorlevel 1 echo ERROR: %FILENAME% %TNS_ALIAS%
%COMPUTERNAME% %DATE% %TIME% %LOGFILE%


echo ...
echo END OF FILE REPORT
echo Filename     : %FILENAME%
echo Database     : %TNS_ALIAS%
echo Hostname     : %COMPUTERNAME%
echo Date         : %DATE%
echo Time         : %TIME%
echo EXP Log File : %LOGFILE%
```

Sending Oracle Output via Windows Email

Another handy Windows utility is the Oracle utility for sending mail. The Windows .bat file code below demonstrates how the Sendmail program is invoked from Windows. This program accepts a filename, typically the report file name, which is used as the *–attach* parameter of the Sendmail program. The recipient, sender, and subject, to, from, and subject, respectively, are accepted as arguments to the program. In the Windows .bat files, the Sendmail message text is generated dynamically using echo statements.

To make the report file appear directly within the message text, eliminate the *–attach* parameter and pass the report file to Sendmail using the *–messagefile=* parameter.

```
@ECHO OFF

REM +-----------------------------------
REM | Set up client specific variables
REM +-----------------------------------

set BC_DIR=C:\BC
set FROM=Oracle@Client.com
set TO=Client@remote-dba.net
set SUBJECT=*** Client TRACE ALERT

set FILENAME=%1

•
•
•
•
REM +-------------------------------------------------------------
REM | Build message text
REM +-------------------------------------------------------------

echo. > message.txt
echo 'Please see attached dump identified on' >> message.txt
udate >> message.txt

sendmail -messagefile=message.txt -from=%FROM% -subject="%SUBJECT%" -
attach=%FILENAME%  %TO%

:END
rm -s message.txt
rm -s %FILENAME%

exit
```

Monitoring Trace and Dump Files in Windows

As with any Oracle database, it is necessary to monitor for Oracle dump and trace files, as well as space usage. The *send alert .bat* script below is an example for a simple utility for monitoring disk space and sending the DBA a message via email when there is an alarm.

🖫 **send alert .bat**

```
@ECHO OFF

REM +---------------------------------
REM | DISK_SPACE.BAT
REM |
REM | Author:  T. Clark
REM | Written: 03/16/03
REM +---------------------------------
REM +---------------------------------
REM | Set up client specific variables
REM +---------------------------------

set BC_DIR=C:\BC

REM +-------------------------------------------------------------
REM | Define minimum space value in floating point format
REM | Example: 1E5=100,000 (100K)    1.75E5=175,000 (175K)
REM |          2E6=2,000,000 (2MB)
REM +-------------------------------------------------------------
set MINSPACE=1.75E5

ucd %BC_DIR%\script

REM +-------------------------------------------------------------
REM | Now let's go get disk space information for all disks and
REM | remove commas from the byte values
REM +-------------------------------------------------------------

df -a -t | sed -e "s/,//g" > df.txt

REM +-------------------------------------------------------------
REM | Select lines for disks that fall within the critical free
REM | space range and send them to the ALERT.TXT file
REM +-------------------------------------------------------------

getrng "-d)" -f2 -r 0,%MINSPACE% df.txt > alert.txt

REM +-------------------------------------------------------------
REM | If we found disks critically low on space, send an e-mail
REM | alert to the DBA staff
REM +-------------------------------------------------------------

test -s1 alert.txt   run: sendalrt.bat alert.txt

rm -s df.txt
rm -s alert.txt
```

```
REM +-------------------------------------
REM | Set up client specific variables
REM +-------------------------------------

set FROM=Oracle@Client.com
set TO=Client@remote-dba.net
set SUBJECT=Client Freespace Alert

REM +-------------------------------------
REM | Build the message banner
REM +-------------------------------------

echo. > message.txt
banner Disk Alert! >> message.txt
echo. >> message.txt

cat message.txt %1% >> combined.txt

REM +-------------------------------------
REM | Send the alert message
REM +-------------------------------------

sendmail -messagefile=combined.txt -subject="%SUBJECT%" -from=%FROM%   %TO%

rm message.txt
rm combined.txt
exit
```

Starting and Stopping Oracle on Windows

In Windows, the dbstart and dbshut scripts do not exist. Instead, oracle uses the oradim scripts for shutting down and starting up the database. The *nix Oracle DBA will have to become familiar with this major difference between *nix and Windows Oracle versions.

```
C:\oracle9i\bin\oradim -startup -sid ORCL92 -usrpwd manager -starttype
 SRVC,INST -pfile C:\oracle9i\admin\ORCL92\pfile\init.ora
```

Where:

- startup – Indicates that the specified instance should be started.

- sid – The SID of the database to start

- usrpwd – The password for the database user

- starttype – Specifies whether to start the instance, the service, or both (SRVC, INST)

The following command can be used to shutdown the instance with oradim:

```
C:\oracle9i\bin\oradim -shutdown -sid ORCL92 -shuttype SRVC,INST
-shutmode A
```

Notice that no password is needed to perform this task. The *shuttype* parameter specifies what is to be stopped – the service (SRVC), the instance (INST), or both (SRVC, INST). The shutmode specifies the method that should perform the shutdown – (A)bort, (I)mmediate, or (N)ormal.

Each operation, regardless of success, is logged in the oradim log file (ORACLE_HOME\database\OraDim.Log). This file should be checked for errors after each oradim command is executed.

The oradim utility provides more than just the ability to start and stop Windows databases. Oradim can create and edit databases. It also allows DBAs to configure script-based installation mechanisms, bypassing the Oracle Database Configuration Assistant's graphical user interface (GUI).

For a reference of all oradim commands, use the oradim –help command. Since oradim does not require the DBA to start up SQL*Plus and connect internally, it is a favorite utility of many DBAs. Thus, it is imperative that the Windows Oracle DBA becomes very familiar with the oradim program, especially considering its many different, and sometimes contradictory, use.

Conclusion

This chapter detailed using Oracle on the Windows platform. Several utilities are found in the Oracle Counters for Windows Performance Monitor package such as perfmon, Sendmail and Data Pump Export utilities. Also covered is how to check and test the Windows service as well as writing Oracle scripts. Other topics mentioned in this chapter were monitoring trace and dump files and starting and stopping Oracle on Windows.

The next chapter will go over Oracle utilities for server-side functions.

Oracle Utilities for Server-Side Functions

"I think we have a server issue"

Server Management

Database administrators are quite often asked to perform some database server-side tasks which seem more closely aligned to the operating system rather than the database. That is okay since it is not that unusual nor to be avoided. However, one cannot then attempt to employ the same tools that are used when performing more database-oriented tasks. The Oracle DBA will often have to utilize several database server-based command line utilities supplied by either Oracle and/or the host operating system vendor. Often the Oracle DBA's interaction with these database server command line utilities will be scripted and frequently scheduled, i.e. the script runs automatically via either the Oracle scheduler, native operating system job schedulers, and/or third party job schedulers. As such, the Oracle DBA must be aware of and comfortable with many commands executed outside of the database so as to report upon or assist with the control of it.

Within Oracle there is also a wealth of utilities to assist the DBA in the administration of server-side components, and Oracle has advanced to the point where a large part of the server-side components can be managed from within Oracle Enterprise Manager (OEM).

Some of the topics covered in this chapter include:

- External functions required to manage the Oracle database (archived redo, job scheduling, auto start, managing OS files)

- Starting and stopping instances using the auto start utilities (*oraenv, coraenv*) on Linux, Solaris, HP/UX, AIX, and Windows.

- DBA connection management (*orapwd*)

- Server monitoring (OEM, AWR external tables, *ltom, vmstat* extensions)

- File analysis (BBED, dbv, trcsess, trace analyzer)

- Process management (*orakill*)

Database Creation and the DBCA

One of the most fundamental tasks is the initial creation of a database. And although this occurs infrequently, except for possibly development and test, it is nonetheless a significantly critical task. Many of the database creation options chosen during this process will establish a fundamental performance expectation baseline. Although many of these choices can easily be modified later, some cannot. So do not rush through this task since each major Oracle release adds more options and alternatives to this universe of possibilities.

A long time ago, most DBAs had collections of scripts for creating various types of databases for differing roles across the numerous Oracle versions. Below is an historical attempt to create a single database creation shell script, *mkdb.sh.* It shows just how complex it is to write and then maintain such a script for the various Oracle versions (this script does Oracle versions 7.X to 10.X). The entire script is nearly 600 lines long so just a portion of the script is included here. The entire script can be downloaded from the Code Depot

🖫 mkdb.sh script

```
#!/bin/sh

if [ $# -ne 4 ]
then
  echo
  echo Usage: mkdb.sh SID VERS CHAR_SET NAT_CHAR_SET
  echo
  exit 1
fi

CHAR_SET=$3; export CHAR_SET
NAT_CHAR_SET=$4; export NAT_CHAR_SET

# Redirect all output to log file
LOG_FILE=$1.mkdb.log
exec 2>$LOG_FILE 1>&2

# Set default Oracle Instance database
. setdb.sh $1 $2

sqlplus "system/manager as sysdba" <<EOF
shutdown
EOF

if [ -d $ORACLE_BASE/admin/$ORACLE_SID ]; then rm -rf
$ORACLE_BASE/admin/$ORACLE_SID; fi
if [ -d $ORACLE_BASE/oradata/$ORACLE_SID ]; then rm -rf
$ORACLE_BASE/oradata/$ORACLE_SID; fi

if [ ! -d $ORACLE_BASE/admin ]; then mkdir $ORACLE_BASE/admin; fi
if [ ! -d $ORACLE_BASE/admin/$ORACLE_SID ]; then mkdir
$ORACLE_BASE/admin/$ORACLE_SID; fi
if [ ! -d $ORACLE_BASE/admin/$ORACLE_SID/bdump ]; then mkdir
$ORACLE_BASE/admin/$ORACLE_SID/bdump; fi
if [ ! -d $ORACLE_BASE/admin/$ORACLE_SID/cdump ]; then mkdir
$ORACLE_BASE/admin/$ORACLE_SID/cdump; fi
if [ ! -d $ORACLE_BASE/admin/$ORACLE_SID/udump ]; then mkdir
$ORACLE_BASE/admin/$ORACLE_SID/udump; fi
if [ ! -d $ORACLE_BASE/oradata ]; then mkdir $ORACLE_BASE/oradata; fi
if [ ! -d $ORACLE_BASE/oradata/$ORACLE_SID ]; then mkdir
$ORACLE_BASE/oradata/$ORACLE_SID; fi
if [ ! -d $ORACLE_BASE/admin/$ORACLE_SID/create ]; then mkdir
$ORACLE_BASE/admin/$ORACLE_SID/create; fi
if [ ! -d $ORACLE_BASE/admin/$ORACLE_SID/pfile ]; then mkdir
$ORACLE_BASE/admin/$ORACLE_SID/pfile; fi

cp $0 $ORACLE_BASE/admin/$ORACLE_SID/create

initora=$ORACLE_BASE/admin/$ORACLE_SID/pfile/init$ORACLE_SID.ora
```

```
dbs_initora=$ORACLE_HOME/dbs/init$ORACLE_SID.ora

### General INIT.ORA Parameters
echo # Oracle Initiailization Parameters > $initora
echo db_name = $ORACLE_SID >> $initora
echo compatible = $ORACLE_VERS >> $initora
echo control_files = \("$ORACLE_BASE/oradata/$ORACLE_SID/control_01.ctl",
"$ORACLE_BASE/oradata/$ORACLE_SID/control_02.ctl"\) >> $initora
echo background_dump_dest = $ORACLE_BASE/admin/$ORACLE_SID/bdump >> $initora
echo user_dump_dest = $ORACLE_BASE/admin/$ORACLE_SID/udump >> $initora
echo core_dump_dest = $ORACLE_BASE/admin/$ORACLE_SID/cdump >> $initora
echo db_block_size = 4096 >> $initora
echo processes = 200 >> $initora
echo open_cursors = 200 >> $initora
echo cpu_count = 4 >> $initora
echo shared_pool_size = 67108864 >> $initora
echo log_buffer = 1048576 >> $initora
echo sort_area_size = 4194304 >> $initora
echo sort_area_retained_size = 4194304 >> $initora
echo remote_login_passwordfile = EXCLUSIVE >> $initora
echo db_file_multiblock_read_count = 16 >> $initora
echo job_queue_processes = 1 >> $initora
echo log_checkpoint_timeout = 0 >> $initora
echo log_checkpoint_interval = 99999 >> $initora
echo cursor_space_for_time = true >> $initora
echo audit_trail = none >> $initora
echo timed_statistics = true >> $initora
echo sql_trace = false >> $initora
echo HASH_AREA_SIZE = 4194304 >> $initora
###
```

As comprehensive as the *mkdb*.sh script is, it does not handle OPS (Oracle Parallel Server) or RAC (Real Application Clusters) for the database versions for which it is coded, nor does it handle OMF (Oracle Managed File) or ASM (Automatic Storage Management). So Oracle solved this problem by making the Database Configuration Assistant (DBCA) both simple and comprehensive.

Starting with 10g, it has become much more efficient and effective to use DBCA for database creation. Just carefully navigate through all of its many screens and tabs so that everything is defined properly for the database's intended usage. DBCA makes single instance and RAC database creation a breeze as well as ASM configuration. The RAC portion, however, will only be active if DBCA finds the Oracle Cluster Services already installed and running. If found, then DBCA will ask whether to work with single instance or RAC, and the RAC option will offer the additional choices highlighted below.

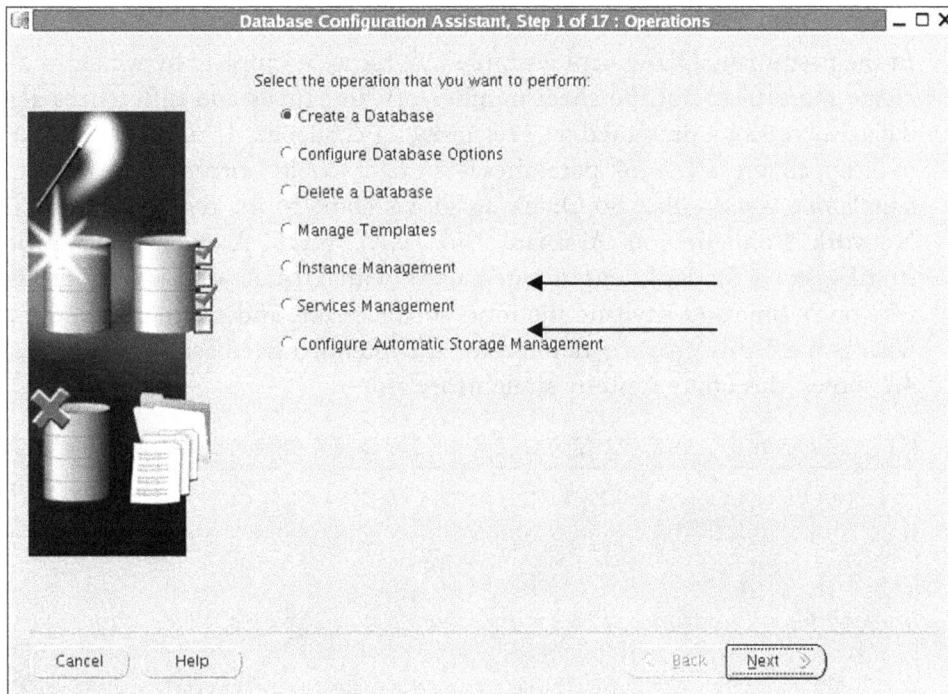

Figure 4.1: *DBCA RAC Options*

One of the more useful features of DBCA is the templates. When one is at the end of a database creation effort a named template can be created to save the current selections. Thereafter, simply choose that template to get back to those pre-defined selections. Plus, changes can be made to the selection after selecting a template as well.

SQL*NET Configuration Files: NETCA

Another fundamental task is the creation and maintenance of the SQL*Net configuration files *tnsnames.ora, listener.ora* and *sqlnet.ora* for both the database server and client machines. These files are required to provide users and their applications a network bridge by which to access their data. In theory, *tnsnames.ora* and *listener.ora* files are very simple text files with a seemingly easy syntax. In practice though, they tend to become quite large due to the dozens, if not hundreds, of databases people need access to and because of the additional challenges of properly defining load balancing, fault tolerance, and retries for RAC environments.

In the past, many DBAs kept a simple text file as a template by which to easily create these files. But the sheer number of alternatives and differences across database versions presented an ever growing challenge. If nothing else, failing to keep all the levels of parentheses straight could corrupt even seemingly simple *tnsnames.ora* files. So Oracle again has come to the rescue by having the Network Configuration Assistant (NETCA). NETCA makes this process trivial – even for RAC environments. As with DBCA, one merely needs to take one's time and navigate the tools screens, tabs, and content to verify that what is needed is properly defined for the intended database usage. As Figure 4.2 shows, this utility is pretty straightforward.

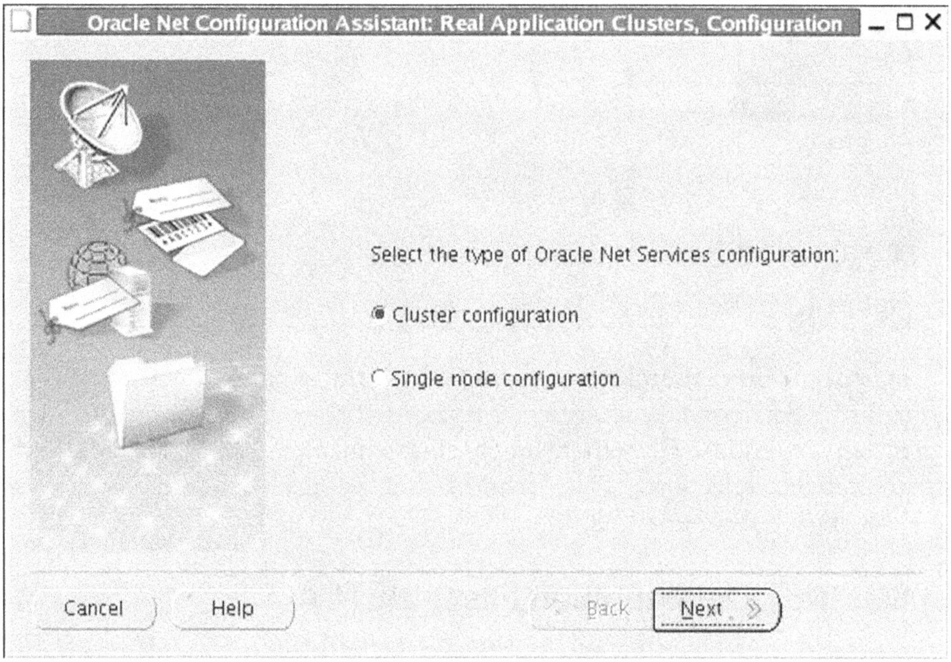

Figure 4.2: *NETCA for RAC Configuration*

External Functions

External functions are those utilities and processes that are run outside of the Oracle database and whose execution is independent of the database itself. However, the proper use of these functions is typically critical to the smooth and reliable function of the database.

Oracle Instance Management refers to the proper management of the processes that make up the Oracle instance, the most basic step of which is the instance startup and shutdown.

Auto Start and Auto Stop

Oracle comes with simple utilities to start up and shut down the database when the server starts up and shuts down. In addition, most DBAs will write scripts to shut down and start up the database on command. Often the DBA will call these scripts when bringing the database down for maintenance. If there is regularly scheduled downtime for some reason, these scripts can be called through some form of operating system scheduling software such as the UNIX *crontab* to shut down and start up the database.

Starting a Database Instance on UNIX/Linux

On UNIX and Linux, Oracle provides a very handy mechanism for easily starting and stopping database instances via the command line. These scripts read the */etc/oratab* file (*/var/opt/oratab* on some platforms). This simple text file identifies the database SID, Oracle Home directory, and whether that instance should be controlled, i.e. started or stopped, by dbstart and dbshut script executions. The */etc/oratab* example here shows that for this database server, two instances (ORLI10 and ORLI11) are controlled via these scripts, whereas the RAC instance is not.

Note: If the DBA is working with ASM based database instances, the third parameter can also accept a value of W, which simply means that the referenced database instance must wait until its associated ASM instance has been properly started by the Cluster Services (CRS).

🖫 /etc/oratab example

```
# Entries are of the form:
#   $ORACLE_SID:$ORACLE_HOME:<N|Y|W>:
#
# Multiple entries with the same $ORACLE_SID are not allowed.
#
RAC:/home/oracle/product/10.2.0/db:N
ORLI10:/home/oracle/product/10.2.0/db:Y
ORLI11:/home/oracle/product/11.1.0/db:Y
```

The command syntax for dbstart is as follows:

```
dbstart [$ORACLE_HOME]
```

This script will start all instances marked as Y or W, and produce a log file at $ORACLE_HOME/startup.log. In addition, all error and warning messages are copied to the system log. Simply set the environment variable ORACLE_TRACE=T to trace the execution.

🖫 dbstart algorithm (from script comment)

```
# Overall algorithm:
# 1) Bring up all ASM instances with 'Y' entry in status field in oratab
entry
# 2) Bring up all Database instances with 'Y' entry in status field in
#    oratab entry
# 3) If there are Database instances with 'W' entry in status field
#    then
#      iterate over all ASM instances (irrespective of 'Y' or 'N') AND
#      wait for all of them to be started
#    fi
# 4) Bring up all Database instances with 'W' entry in status field in
#    oratab entry
...
```

Below is an example of running dbstart:

```
[oracle@LINUX_10G ~]$ dbstart $ORACLE_HOME
Processing Database instance "ORLI10": log file
/home/oracle/product/10.2.0/db/startup.log
```

The dbstart command can be added to the UNIX/Linux servers' initialization or run level scripts. This enables dbstart to be executed each time the machine is booted or when it changes run levels. The method for implementing this is platform specific.

Auto Start on HP-UX, Linux, and Solaris

For HP-UX version 10 and above, Linux, and Solaris, the system initialization scripts are contained in /etc/rc<n>.d directories, where "n" is the operating system run-level. These directories contain scripts that begin with a K or S, followed by a number, and then a file name, i.e. S75cron. All scripts that begin with "S" are executed at system startup in ascending order of their number. Scripts beginning with "K" (Kill) are called at system shutdown time. Be very careful when editing those files, however. In 10gR2 and above, Oracle will properly configure the Cluster Synchronization Service (CSS) to start prior to Oracle initialization when using ASM. However, 10gR1 did not configure the CSS properly, and thus it must be manually configured. ASM requires CSS in order to run properly, so it may be necessary to edit these manually.

In general, the Oracle startup script should have a high sequence number - S99dbstart, for example - which will ensure that other system processes have been started prior to starting Oracle. Similarly, the *kill* scripts should have a low sequence number in order to shut down Oracle early in the process (K01dbshut). Also, make sure in the oratab file that the ASM instance or instances are listed before the regular database instances so that the ASM instances start prior to the corresponding database instance.

Auto Start on AIX

For AIX servers, the system initialization file is */etc/inittab* and the initialization script is */etc/rc*. A utility *(/usr/sbin/mkitab)* can be used to make an entry in the *inittab* file. The shutdown script for AIX is */usr/sbin/shutdown*.

To add the dbstart utility to the AIX initialization process, the following steps can be performed:

1. Create the script */etc/rc.oracle*. The script should contain the following:

   ```
   su oracle <<EOF
   <$ORACLE_HOME>/bin/dbstart
   EOF
   ```

2. Add the script to the inittab using the *mkitab* utility.

   ```
   $ /usr/sbin/mkitab "rcoracle:2:wait:/etc.rc.oracle >/dev/console 2>&1"
   ```

All references to <*$ORACLE_HOME*> should be replaced with the actual Oracle Home directory. Now upon system startup, the dbstart utility is normally invoked at run level 2, after networking is initialized.

Stopping Database Instance: dbshut

dbshut is an Oracle command that provides a handy mechanism for easily stopping database instances.

🖫 /etc/oratab example

```
# Entries are of the form:
#    $ORACLE_SID:$ORACLE_HOME:<N|Y|W>:
#
# Multiple entries with the same $ORACLE_SID are not allowed.
#
RAC:/home/oracle/product/10.2.0/db:N
ORLI10:/home/oracle/product/10.2.0/db:Y
ORLI11:/home/oracle/product/11.1.0/db:Y
```

The command syntax for dbshut is as follows:

```
dbshut [$ORACLE_HOME]
```

This script will stop all instances marked as Y or W, and produce a log file at $ORACLE_HOME/shutdown.log – plus all error and warning messages are copied to the system log. And if the choice is to trace the execution, simply set the environment variable ORACLE_TRACE=T.

Below is an example of running dbshut:

```
[oracle@LINUX_10G ~]$ dbshut $ORACLE_HOME
Processing Database instance "ORLI10": log file
/home/oracle/product/10.2.0/db/shutdown.log
```

Starting and Stopping on Windows

The dbstart and dbstop shell scripts do not exist on Windows platforms. The Oracle database startup and shutdown is implemented quite differently. On Windows, Oracle provides a simple utility like .exe for easily starting and stopping database services and/or instances via command line – *oradim*. Unlike UNIX, where the dbstart and dbshut scripts simply launch Oracle processes, oradim must work in the Windows paradigm of launching the Oracle processes as services.

```
C:\oracle9i\bin\oradim -startup -sid ORCL92 -usrpwd manager
-starttype SRVC,INST -pfile C:\oracle9i\admin\ORCL92\pfile\init.ora
```

- startup — Indicates that the specified instance should be started.

- sid — The SID of the database to start.

- usrpwd — The password for the database user.

- starttype — Specifies whether to start the instance, the service, or both (SRVC, INST).

Below is a screen snapshot showing a Windows machine running two database instances and a listener. Also note that unlike UNIX, on Windows the Oracle background processes are all executed within threads of just the one Oracle process.

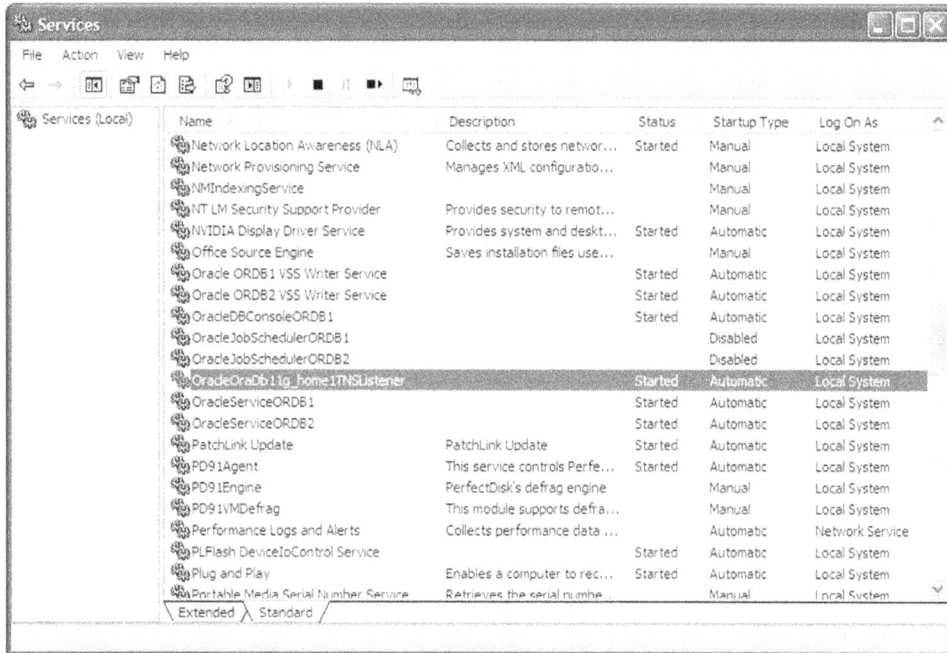

Figure 4.3: *Running Multiple Database Instances*

The oradim utility can be launched several different ways to accomplish differing tasks. Also, the parameters passed vary depending upon the purpose being invoked. It creates a log file in the directory $ORACLE_HOME\database.

To create a new instance, the syntax is as follows:

```
-NEW -SID sid | -SRVC service | -ASMSID sid | -ASMSRVC service
[-SYSPWD password] [-STARTMODE auto | manual] [-SRVCSTART system | demand]
[-PFILE file | -SPFILE] [-SHUTMODE normal | immediate | abort]
[-TIMEOUT seconds] [-RUNAS os_user/os_password]
```

To modify an existing instance, the syntax is as follows:

```
-EDIT -SID sid | -ASMSID sid
```

```
[-SYSPWD password] [-STARTMODE auto | manual] [-SRVCSTART system | demand]
[-PFILE file | -SPFILE] [-SHUTMODE normal | immediate | abort]
[-SHUTTYPE service | instance] [-RUNAS os_user/os_password]
```

To delete an existing instance, the syntax is as follows:

```
-DELETE -SID sid | -ASMSID sid | -SRVC service | -ASMSRVC service
```

To start up an existing instance, the syntax is as follows:

```
-STARTUP -SID sid | -ASMSID sid
[-SYSPWD password] [-STARTTYPE service | instance | service,instance]
[-PFILE filename | -SPFILE]
```

To shut down an existing instance, the syntax is as follows:

```
-SHUTDOWN -SID sid | -ASMSID sid
[-SYSPWD password] [-SHUTTYPE service | instance | service,instance]
[-SHUTMODE normal | immediate | abort]
```

Although no password is needed to perform this task, the Windows user must have sufficient privileges to execute this command successfully.

The *shuttype* parameter specifies what is to be stopped – the service (SRVC), the instance (INST), or both (SRVC, INST). The *shutmode* specifies the method that should perform the shutdown – (A)bort, (I)mmediate, or (N)ormal.

Each operation, regardless of success, is logged in the oradim log file (*ORACLE_HOME\database\OraDim.Log*). This file should be checked for errors after each oradim command is executed.

The oradim utility provides more than just the ability to start and stop Windows databases. Oradim can create and edit databases. It also allows DBAs to configure script-based installation mechanisms, bypassing the Oracle Database Configuration Assistant's graphical user interface (GUI).

For a reference of all oradim commands, use the oradim–help command. A good Oracle DBA will become intimately familiar with the oradim options, and DBAs that start in Linux will often create their own dbstart/dbshut scripts that call the oradim procedure.

---

lsnrctl

The listener command line utility (*lsnrctl*) provides the DBA a method for starting, stopping and checking the status of the database listener as well as several other listener management tasks. The *lsnrctl* utility can either be run as a command line invocation or as a command line interpreter, as shown in these two examples:

```
$ lsnrctl command [listener_name]

$ lsnrctl
LSNRCTL> command [listener_name]
```

The *lsnrctl* command offers the following commands:

COMMAND	DESCRIPTION
change_password	To create or change an encrypted password
exit	Exit the program
quit	Exit the program
reload	Re-read the listener.ora file without a restart
services	Lists information about services, instances, & service handlers
set	Alters parameter values for the listener until shutdown
show	Displays current parameter values for the listener
spawn	Start a program on the server where listener is running
start	Start the named listener
status	Display status of the named listener
stop	Stop the named listener
race	Start tracing for the named listener
version	Shows current version of lsnrctl utility

Table 4.1: *lsnrctl Commands and Descriptions*

emca

The Enterprise Manager Configuration Assistant (EMCA) provides the DBA a utility for configuring Oracle Enterprise Manager (OEM) for an instance. Of course, the Database Configuration Assistant offers that choice graphical when initially creating the database. However, it may happen that it is not chosen and then later needs adding. The *emca* utility is run as a command line invocation as shown here:

```
$ emca [operation] [mode] [type] [flags] [parameters]
```

Only certain combinations of emca command operations, modes and types are valid. The most common use case scenarios include:

- To configure the database control for a database, the syntax is as follows:

```
$ emca -config dbcontrol db [-repos (create | recreate)] [-cluster] [-
silent] [-backup] [parameters]
```

- To configure the central agent management for a database or an ASM instance, the syntax is as follows:

```
$ emca -config centralAgent (db | asm) [-cluster] [-silent]
[parameters]
```

- To configure both the database control and central agent management for a database, the syntax is as follows:

```
$ emca -config all db [-repos (create | recreate)] [-cluster] [-silent]
[-backup] [parameters]
```

Where the parameters are:

PARAMETER	DESCRIPTION
-respFile	Parameter input file
-SID	The database SID
-PORT	Listener port
-ORACLE_HOME	Oracle home path for database
-LISTENER_OH	Oracle home path where listener run
-HOST_USER	Host user name
-HOST_USER_PWD	Host password
-BACKUP_SCHEDULE	Daily backup schedule "HH:MM"
-EMAIL_ADDRESS	Notifications email address
-MAIL_SERVER_NAME	Notifications outgoing mail server
-ASM_OH	Oracle home for ASM
-ASM_SID	The ASM SID
-ASM_PORT	Listener port for ASM
-ASM_USER_ROLE	User role to connect to ASM instance
-ASM_USER_NAME	User name to connect to ASM instance
-ASM_USER_PWD	Password to connect to ASM instance
-DBSNMP_PWD	Password for DBSNMP user
-SYSMAN_PWD	Password for SYSMAN user
-SYS_PWD	Password for SYS user

PARAMETER	DESCRIPTION
-SRC_OH	Oracle home path for OEM database
-DBCONTROL_HTTP_PORT	Port to display OEM console
-AGENT_PORT	Port for Management Agent
-RMI_PORT	Port for RMI
-JMS_PORT	Port for JMS
-CLUSTER_NAME	Cluster name for RAC database
-DB_UNIQUE_NAME	Unique DB name for RAC database
-SERVICE_NAME	Service name for RAC database
-EM_NODE	RAC node on which db control
-EM_SID_LIST	Comma separated SID list

Table 4.2: *Enterprise Manager Configuration Assistant Parameters*

emctl

The Enterprise Manager Command Line Utility (*emctl*) provides the DBA a method to manage all aspects of the Enterprise Manager console including the OEM console, OEM agent and OMS (Oracle Management Service). The emctl utility is run as a command line invocation as shown here:

```
$ emctl [operation] [mode] [type] [flags] [parameters]
```

Only certain combinations of emctl command operations, modes and types are valid. The most common use case scenarios include:

OEM CONSOLE COMMANDS	OEM AGENT COMMANDS	OMS COMMANDS
emctl start em	emctl start agent	emctl start oms
emctl stop em	emctl stop agent	emctl stop oms
emctl status em	emctl status agent	emctl status oms

Table 4.3: *Enterprise Manager Command Line Utility Commands*

relink

On both UNIX and Linux, the DBA may occasionally find the need to relink the Oracle binaries. Sometimes a one-off patch for the OS or Oracle may require this. Not to mention that most Oracle major and minor version

---

upgrades perform the exact same relink as a final part of the installation process. The process is fairly straightforward:

1. Identify at what granularity the operation is needed

2. Shut down those database components for that level

3. Issue the relink command for the desired granularity

4. Start up those database components for that level

The relink command syntax is as follows:

```
$ relink all | oracle | network | client | client_sharedlib | interMedia |
precomp | utilities | oemagent | ldap
```

> The larger the selected granularity; for example, all the more items that must be shut down and restarted for the relink, then the longer the relink process will take.

External job scheduling

The cron daemon is the UNIX system task that runs scripted jobs on a predetermined schedule. The crontab command is used to set up the schedule for the execution of those jobs. Much of the job of crontab can now be managed by the Oracle scheduler. However, many DBAs still use crontab rather than Oracle scheduler so that scheduled jobs can be managed from a single location.

As shown in Table 4.4, the crontab command has several options with different purposes.

OPTION	PURPOSE
-e	edit the current crontab file using the text editor specified by the EDITOR environment variable or the VISUAL environment variable
-l	list the current crontab file
-r	remove the current crontab file
-u	specifies the user's crontab to be manipulated. This is usually used by root to manipulate the crontab of other users or can be used to correctly identify the crontab to be manipulated if the su command has been used to assume another identity.

Table 4.4: *Crontab Options and Purposes*

Crontab also accepts a file name and will use the specified file to create the crontab file. Many users prefer to use this option rather than the crontab -e command because it provides a master file from which the crontab is built, thus providing a backup to the crontab. The following example specifies a file called mycron.tab to be used as the input for crontab.

```
$ crontab mycron.tab
```

The crontab -l command is used to list the contents of the current crontab, as in the example below.

```
$ crontab -l
#*********************************************************
# Run the Weekly file cleanup task at 6:00AM every Monday
# and send any output to a file called cleanup.lst in the
# /tmp directory
#*********************************************************
00 06 * * 1 /home/terry/cleanup.ksh > /tmp/cleanup.lst
#*********************************************************
# Run the Weekly Management Report every Monday at 7:00 AM
# and save a copy of the report in my /home directory
#*********************************************************
00 07 * * 1 /home/terry/weekly_mgmt_rpt.ksh wprd >
/home/terry/weekly_mgmt_rpt.lst
```

Now, if deleting all the entries in the crontab is desired, use the –r option.

```
$ crontab -r
```

The format of the crontab file

The crontab file consists of a series of entries specifying what shell scripts to run and when to run it. It is also possible to document crontab entries with comments. Lines which have a pound sign (#) as the first non-blank character are considered comments. Blank lines are completely ignored. Comments cannot be specified on the same line as cron command lines; comments must be kept on their own lines within the crontab.

There are two types of command lines that can be specified in the crontab: environment variable settings and cron commands.

Environment variable settings

Each environment variable line consists of a variable name, an equal sign (=), and a value. Values that contain spaces need to be enclosed within quotes. The following are some examples of environment variable settings:

```
color = red
ORACLE_HOME = /u01/app/oracle/product/10.2.0/db_1
title = 'My Life in a Nutshell'
```

As with the operating system itself, variable names in the crontab are case-sensitive and system variables are usually defined with upper case names, while user defined variables are defined with lower case names.

Crontab command Lines

Each crontab command line is comprised of six positional fields specifying the time, date and shell script or command to be run. The format of the crontab command line is described in Table 4.5:

FIELD	VALID VALUES
Minute	0-59
Hour	0-23
Day of Month	1-31
Month	1-12
Day of Week	0-7
Command	Command path/command

Table 4.5: *Crontab Command Line Format*

In all fields which take numeric values, a single number, a range of numbers indicated with a hyphen (such as 2-4), a list of specific values separated by commas (like 2,3,4) or a combination of these designations separated by commas (such as 1,3-5) are allowed. Also allowed is an asterisk (*) indicating every possible value of this field. All conditions must be met for the entry to execute. This can all get rather confusing so make sure that one understands exactly what an entry is doing before making any changes to it.

This entry will run the script *cleanup.ksh* at 0 minutes past the hour, 6 am, every Monday. This illustrates that for a crontab to execute, all of the conditions specified must be met. So even though every day of the month has been said by making the third field a wildcard, the day also has to meet the final condition that the day is a Monday.

```
#************************************************************
# Run the Weekly Management Report every Monday at 7:00 AM
# and save a copy of the report in my /home directory
#************************************************************
00 07 * * 1 /home/bei/scripts/weekly_mgmt_rpt.ksh wprd >
/home/terry/weekly_mgmt_rpt.lst
```

This entry is similar to the previous entry, but will execute at 7:00am. Since the hour is in 24 hour format (midnight is actually represented as 00), the 07 represents 7:00 a.m. This entry again will only be run on Mondays.

```
#************************************************************
# Lunch Time Notification - run Monday-Friday at Noon -
# sends a message to all users indicating it's lunch time
#************************************************************
00 12 * * 1-5 /home/terry/lunch_time.ksh wprd > /tmp/lunch_time.lst
```

This lunch reminder is set up to run at 12:00 p.m. Monday through Friday only.

The most important thing to remember is that a crontab entry will execute every time all of its conditions are met. To take the last entry as an example, anytime it is 00 minutes past the hour of 12 on any day of the month and any month of the year and the day of the week is between Monday and Friday inclusive (1-5), this crontab will be executed.

Most crontab entries will have some wildcards, but be careful where they are used. For instance, if a * was mistakenly placed in the minute position of the last crontab example above, the script would end up running for ever minute of the 12:00 hour instead of just once at the beginning of the hour. Remember that the wildcard means all, not 'any'.

The day-of-week field accepts either zero or seven as a value for Sunday. Any of the time/date fields can also contain an asterisk (*) indicating the entire range of values. Additionally, month and day-of-week fields can contain name values, consisting of the first three letters of the month, as indicated in Table 4.6.

Field	Valid Entries (case insensitive)
Days of the week	sun, mon, tue, wed, thu, fri, sat
	SUN, MON, TUE, WED, THU, FRI, SAT
Months of year	jan, feb, mar, apr, may, jun, jul, aug, sep, oct, nov, dec
	JAN, FEB, MAR, APR, MAY, JUN, JUL, AUG, SEP, OCT, NOV, DEC

Table 4.6: *Month and Day-of-week Fields*

When numbers are used, the user can specify a range of values separated by a hyphen or a list of values separated by commas. In other words, specifying 2-5 in the hour field means 2AM, 3AM, 4AM and 5AM, while specifying 2,5 means only 2AM and 5AM.

Most people will execute shell scripts from the crontab, but any operating system command can be executed. If the command or script called in the crontab typically sends output to the screen, the move may be to redirect that output to a log file with the >> symbol so it can be checked later. The > redirection symbol will create a new file, while the >> symbol will append to an existing file, or create a new one if it does not exist. Generally, a new log file will be created with each execution, and the log file will be periodically reviewed for problems.

By default, the output from a job is emailed to the owner of the job or the user specified by the *mailto* variable. If this is unacceptable, the output can be redirected in a number of ways, including:

```
# Mail the output of the job to another user.
command | mail -s "Subject: Output of job" user

# Standard output redirected to a file.
command >> file.log

# Standard output and standard error redirected to a file.
command >> logfile 2>&1

# Throw all the output away
```

Using the OPatch Utility

The Opatch utility is used to install Oracle patches. Most Oracle DBAs are familiar with this utility. Every Oracle CPU (Critical Patch Update) is installed using this utility, as well as all other patches that Oracle produces to fix bugs and update their product. *Opatch lsinventory* detail is the command used to query opatch in order to find out what patches are installed.

OPatch creates a hidden dotted directory called *.patch_storage* in the $ORACLE_HOME. In .patch_storage are directories created by OPatch which have a name identical to the number of the patch being installed and also contain time and date of the patch installation:

```
/export/home/u04/app/oracle/product/10.1.0/db_2/.patch_storage/4193293
```

Inside each hidden Patch directory are log files describing the patch processes that have occurred. The instructions for installing each Oracle patch are included with the patch. Normally, the method is to unpack the patch, move to the directory named the same as the patch number, then type opatch napply. In versions prior to 10.2.0.4, the command is opatch apply.

Utilities for Analyzing Oracle Trace Files

There are several utilities for analyzing Oracle trace files. These include trace assist (trcasst), session tracer (trcsess), trace analyzer (trcanlzr.sql) and TKPROF. Many DBAs are very familiar with the Oracle trace facility, but just in case, here are some brief instructions for using this powerful Oracle utility. Before tracing can be enabled, the environment must first be configured by performing the following steps:

1. Enable Timed Statistics: This parameter enables the collection of certain vital statistics such as CPU execution time, wait events, and elapsed times. The resulting trace output is more meaningful with these statistics. The command to enable timed statistics is: ALTER SYSTEM SET TIMED_STATISTICS = TRUE;

2. Check the User Dump Destination Directory: The trace files generated by Oracle can be numerous and large. These files are placed by Oracle in the *user_dump_dest* directory as specified in the *init.ora*. The user dump destination can also be specified for a single session using the alter session command. Make sure that enough space exists on the device to support the number of trace files that you expect to generate.

3. Turn Tracing On: The next step in the process is to enable tracing. By default, tracing is disabled due to the burden (5-10%) it places on the database. Tracing can be defined at the session level:

```
ALTER SESSION SET SQL_TRACE = TRUE;
DBMS_SESSION.SET_SQL_TRACE(TRUE);
```

    A DBA may enable tracing for another user's session by using the following statement:

```
DBMS_SYSTEM.SET_SQL_TRACE_IN_SESSION (sid,serial#,true);
```

    The sid (Session ID) and serial# can be obtained from the *v$session* view. Once tracing with Oracle TKPROF is enabled, Oracle generates and stores the statistics in the trace file. The trace file name is version specific.

4. Enable Oracle TKPROF tracing only on those sessions that are having problems. Explain Plan is not as useful when used in conjunction with TKPROF since the trace file contains the actual execution path of the SQL statement. Use Explain Plan when anticipated execution statistics are desired without actually executing the statement.

5. When tracing a session, remember that nothing in *v$session* indicates that a session is being traced. Therefore, trace with caution and remember to disable tracing after an adequate amount of trace data has been generated.

TKPROF does not control the contents of a trace file, it simply formats them. Oracle provides multiple ways to actually generate the trace file. TKPROF is valuable for detailed trace file analysis. For those DBAs that prefer a simpler tracing mechanism with instant feedback, the autotrace utility should be used.

The trace assist (trcasst) utility is used to analyze Oracle trace files generated by most Oracle error messages. This utility will analyze the trace file and put it into a readable format.

Using the Trace Analyzer Utility

Trace Analyzer (*trcanlzr*) is an application from Oracle with much the same purpose as TKPROF. It is also designed to help analyze the trace files generated by SQL tracing. Trace Analyzer offers enhancements over TKPROF in a number of areas. Several of the key improvements are as follows:

- Trace Analyzer provides a more detailed list of wait events for every SQL statement that is part of the trace file. Only in recent versions has TKPROF provided at least limited wait information. Older versions provide no information on wait events regardless of the trace data.

- Trace Analyzer reports totals for statements that execute multiple times; whereas TKPROF would report each execution separately. This is important when tracing a process that is updating many records, but doing it one row at a time. Identifying this with TKPROF requires more manual effort.

- Trace Analyzer provides the values used by bind variables, as long as the trace file was generated at a level that includes bind variables; whereas this feature is not available with TKPROF.

Installation of Trace Analyzer is fairly straightforward as long as the instructions are followed completely. It is very similar to installing Statspack. Metalink document 224270.1 provides an adequate explanation for finding the files to accomplish the installation as well as how to install and use it. Be very careful to follow the instructions exactly.

Executing Trace Analyzer

The first step is to enable tracing at the appropriate level. For example, to provide maximum trace data, a Level 12 trace can be started for the current session:

```
SQL> ALTER SESSION SET EVENTS '10046 TRACE NAME CONTEXT FOREVER, LEVEL 12';
```

After the session executes for enough time to gain needed data, the *trcanlzr.sql* script can be executed. It requires the name of the directory object. This object points to the physical operating system directory for the *user_dump_dest*. The installation of the utility will automatically create the directory object required (named UDUMP).

```
SQL>@d:\trcanlzr.sql UDUMP asg920xr_ora_13033.trc
```

Once executed, the output will be displayed on the screen and a spool file is created in the current directory. It is possible to change the output spool file by modifying the trcanlzr.sql script.

Using the trcsess utility

When solving tuning problems, session traces are very useful and offer vital information. Traces are simple and straightforward for dedicated server sessions, but for shared server sessions, many processes are involved. The trace pertaining to the user session is scattered across different trace files belonging to different processes. This makes it difficult to get a complete picture of the life cycle of a session.

The trcsess command-line utility consolidates trace information from selected trace files based on specified criteria. The criteria include session id, client id, service name, action name and module name. This allows the compilation of multiple trace files into a single output file.

The syntax for the trcsess utility is:

```
trcsess [output=output_file_name]
[session=session_Id]
[clientid=client_Id]
[service=service_name]
[action=action_name]
```

```
[module=module_name]
[trace_files]
```

Where:

- output specifies the file where the output is generated. When this option is not specified, the standard output is used for the output.

- session consolidates the trace information for the session specified. The session ID is a combination of session index and session serial number.

- clientid consolidates the trace information given client ID.

- service consolidates the trace information for the given service name.

- action consolidates the trace information for the given action name.

- module consolidates the trace information for the given module name.

- trace_files is a list of all trace file names, separated by spaces, in which trcsess will look for trace information. The wild card character * can be used to specify the trace file names. If trace files are not specified, all the files in the current directory are checked by trcsess.

Activating trace on multiple sessions means that trace information is spread throughout many trace files. For this reason, Oracle 10g introduced the trcsess utility, allowing trace information from multiple trace files to be identified and consolidated into a single trace file. The trcsess usage is listed below.

```
trcsess [output=<output file name >]  [session=<session ID>]
[clientid=<clientid>] [service=<service name>] [action=<action name>]
[module=<module name>] <trace file names>
output=<output file name> output destination default being standard output.
session=<session Id> session to be traced.
Session id is a combination of session Index & session serial number e.g.
8.13.
clientid=<clientid> clientid to be traced.
service=<service name> service to be traced.
action=<action name> action to be traced.
module=<module name> module to be traced.
<trace_file_names> Space separated list of trace files with wild card '*'
supported.
```

Use Oracle's trcsess command-line utility to consolidate the information from all the trace files into a single output file.

```
trcsess output="hr_report.trc" service="APPS1"
module="PAYROLL" action="bulk load"
```

Then run TKPROF against the consolidated trace file to generate a report. It is recommended that one experiments some with TKPROF to become familiarized with the options available in this useful utility.

```
..\udump> tkprof hr_report.trc
output=hr_trc_report SORT=(EXEELA, PRSELA,FCHELA)
```

The oradebug utility

Oracle provides an internal and poorly documented utility called Oradebug. The *oradebug* utility provides useful functions for debugging and tracing Oracle database errors and can also be quite handy for tracing SQL statements to output to the TKPROF utility for analysis by Oracle technicians. However, there are some caveats with the use of the oradebug tool and it should be used only under the careful guidance of Oracle support to avoid potential damage to production and other critical Oracle databases.

Here are a few of the many functions available for the expert Oracle DBA with oradebug.

```
C:\oradebug>sqlplus /nolog
SQL*Plus: Release 10.2.0.1.0 - Production on Mon May 19 14:46:19 2008
Copyright (c) 1982, 2005, Oracle.  All rights reserved.
SQL> connect / as sysdba
Connected.

SQL> oradebug help
```

FUNCTION	COMMAND	DESCRIPTION
HELP	[command]	Describe one or all commands
SETMYPID		Debug current process
SETOSPID	<ospid>	Set OS pid of process to debug
SETORAPID	<orapid> ['force']	Set Oracle pid of process to debug
SHORT_STACK		Dump abridged OS stack
DUMP	<dump_name> <lvl> [addr]	Invoke named dump
DUMPSGA	[bytes]	Dump fixed SGA
DUMPLIST		Print a list of available dumps

FUNCTION	COMMAND	DESCRIPTION
EVENT	<text>	Set trace event in process
SESSION_EVENT	<text>	Set trace event in session
DUMPVAR	<p|s|uga> <name> [level]	Print/dump a fixed
PGA/SGA/UGA DUMPTY	<address> <type> <count>	Print/dump an address with type info
SETVAR	<p|s|uga> <name> <value>	Modify a fixed
PGA/SGA/UGA PEEK	<addr> <len> [level]	Print/Dump memory
POKE	<addr> <len> <value>	Modify memory
WAKEUP	<orapid>	Wake up Oracle process
SUSPEND		Suspend execution
RESUME		Resume execution
FLUSH		Flush pending writes to trace
CLOSE_TRACE		Close trace file
TRACEFILE_NAME		Get name of trace file
LKDEBUG		Invoke global enqueue service
SGATOFILE	<SGA dump dir>	Dump SGA to file
DMPCOWSGA	<SGA dump dir>	Dump & map SGA as COW
MAPCOWSGA	<SGA dump dir>	Map SGA as COW
HANGANALYZE	[level] [syslevel]	Analyze system hang
FFBEGIN		Flash Freeze the Instance
FFDEREGISTER		FF deregister instance from cluster
FFTERMINST		Call exit and terminate instance
FFRESUMEINST		Resume the flash frozen instance
FFSTATUS		Flash freeze status of instance
UNLIMIT		Unlimit the size of the trace file
PROCSTAT		Dump process statistics

Table 4.7: *List of Oradebug Functions*

As can be seen, there are quite a few options to the oradebug utility.

Using the hanganalyzer utility

Oracle provides a special hanganalyze option within oradebug and the "alter session set events" syntax to locate details about a hung session. According to Oracle documentation, hanganalyze uses kernel calls to identify blocking and waiting sessions and hanganalyze may perform automatic processstate and errorstacks trace details.

The hanganalyze can be invoked with an alter session command as follows:

```
ALTER SESSION SET EVENTS 'immediate trace name hanganalyze level 3';
```

Also, a hanganalyze trace file can be gathered to identify hung sessions with SQL*Plus when connected as SYSDBA:

```
SQL> oradebug hanganalyze 3
```

Wait at least two minutes to give time to identify process state changes.

```
SQL> oradebug hanganalyze 3
```

Open a separate SQL session and immediately generate a system state dump.

```
SQL> alter session set events 'immediate trace name SYSTEMSTATE level 10';
```

A trace dump can be done to identify hung session details in Oracle Real Application Clusters (RAC) as follows:

```
SQL> oradebug setmypid
SQL> oradebug setinst all
SQL> oradebug -g def hanganalyze 3
```

Wait at least two minutes to give time to identify process state changes.

```
SQL> oradebug -g def hanganalyze 3
```

Cautions

Oracle notes that hanganalyze run at levels higher than 3 may generate a huge number of trace files for large systems. Do not use levels higher than 3 without discussing their effects with Oracle Technical Support.

Oracle bug 1427041 for 8.1.6.2 notes that on HP/UX, the PMON process may crash the instance when the hanganalyzer syntax is invoked.

Once gathered, the trace file can be read manually or can be used as a third party tool to assist in interpreting the resulting hanganalyze trace file. The ubtools web site offers a product called iOraHangAnalyzer that claims to read the hanganalyze trace file and display details about the waiting session: "iOraHangAnalyzer is a web based tool which scans Oracle's hanganalyze trace file, and returns waiting sessions with their wait-life-cycles."

References

MetaLink Note:175006.1 - Steps to generate hanganalyze trace files

Metalink Note:215858.1 - Interpreting hanganalyze trace files to diagnose hanging and performance problems

Writing to the Oracle alert log file

While not a utility per se, the ability to write messages to the Oracle alert log is an extremely useful ability. This is being mentioned in this chapter because it is an often needed and useful, but not well documented ability.

There are many cases where the Oracle DBA may want to write custom messages directly into the standard Oracle alert log file located in $ORACLE_HOME/admin/$ORACLE_SID/bdump.

By writing custom messages to the Oracle alert log file, the default Oracle alerts can be supplemented with custom messages. Writing to the Oracle alert log is exactly the same as writing to any flat file and there are these choices:

- OS scripts and languages - Use UNIX/Linux utilities to write OS messages, e.g. RAM swapping alerts, into the alert log. Of course, all procedural languages (C++) can also write messages to the Oracle alert log.

- PL/SQL - Use the standard UTL_FILE package or call the *dbms_system*.ksdwrt procedure to write messages to the Oracle alert log file.

- SQL (read only) - Define the alert log as an external table and access the alert log messages with SQL statements.

The best method to write to the alert log is to use *sys.dbms_system.ksdwrt*. This very handy utility will write a message to the alert log; it takes two arguments, a number (1 or 2), and the text. The number indicates whether to write to alert or trace. If set to 1, it writes to a trace file. If 2, it writes to the alert log. Because it uses the *dbms_system* package, write a wrapper around the call and grant privileges to the wrapper procedure or function. Then an execute will not have to be granted on the dbms_system package. A possible function to accomplish this purpose is below:

```
create or replace function write_alert_log(log_or_trace in number,
text_message in varchar2) return number
is
begin
  SYS.DBMS_SYSTEM.KSDWRT(log_or_trace,text_message);
  return 0;
  exception
  when others then
  return 1;
end;
```

It is also possible to write to the alert log using UTL_FILE, but there are many privilege issues that arise when using this method and many more lines of programming. The easy method is to use the *dbms_system.ksdwrt* package.

Remote Connection Management

Using orapwd

The Oracle *orapwd* utility assists the DBA with granting SYSDBA and SYSOPER privileges to other users. By default, the user SYS is the only user that has these privileges. Creating a password file via *orapwd* enables remote users to connect with administrative privileges through SQL*Net.

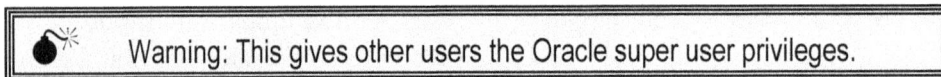

> ● Warning: This gives other users the Oracle super user privileges.

SYSOPER is a specialized database maintenance privilege that allows the granted user to perform basic operational tasks, but without the ability to look at user data. The SYSDBA privilege is the same as *connect internal* was in prior versions. It includes the following:

- Perform STARTUP and SHUTDOWN operations

- ALTER DATABASE: open, mount, back up, or change character set

- CREATE DATABASE

- DROP DATABASE

- CREATE SPFILE

- ALTER DATABASE ARCHIVELOG

- ALTER DATABASE RECOVER

- Includes the RESTRICTED SESSION privilege

The *orapwd* command syntax is:

```
$ orapwd file_name password-password [entries=users] [force=y|n]
[nosysdba=y|n]
```

Where:

- Entries specifies the maximum number of users that can be granted these special system privileges

- Force indicates whether to overwrite a previously existing password file

- NoSYSDBA indicates whether to exclude SYSDBA grants – this is for Oracle 11g Database Vault

If *orapwd* has not yet been executed, attempting to grant SYSDBA or SYSOPER privileges will result in the following error:

```
SQL> grant sysdba to scott;
ORA-01994: GRANT failed: cannot add users to public password file
```

The following steps can be performed to grant other users these privileges:

1. Create the password file. This is done by executing the following command:

   ```
   $ orapwd file=filename  password=password entries=max_users
   ```

   The filename is the name of the file that will hold the password information. The file location will default to the current directory unless the full path is specified. The contents are encrypted and are unreadable. The password required is the one for the SYS user of the database.

The *max_users* is the number of database users that can be granted SYSDBA or SYSOPER. This parameter should be set to a higher value than the number of anticipated users to prevent having to delete and recreate the password file.

2. Edit the *init.ora* parameter *remote_login_passwordfile*. This parameter must be set to either SHARED or EXCLUSIVE. When set to SHARED, the password file can be used by multiple databases, yet only the SYS user is recognized. When set to EXCLUSIVE, the file can be used by only one database, yet multiple users can exist in the file. The parameter setting can be confirmed by:

```
SQL> show parameter password

NAME                          TYPE         VALUE
----------------------------- ------------ ----------
remote_login_passwordfile     string       EXCLUSIVE
```

3. Grant SYSDBA or SYSOPER to users. When SYSDBA or SYSOPER privileges are granted to a user, that user's name and privilege information are added to the password file.

```
SQL> grant sysdba to scott;

Grant succeeded.
```

4. Confirm that the user is listed in the password file.

```
SQL> select * from v$pwfile_users;

USERNAME                          SYSDBA SYSOPER
--------------------------------- ------ -------
SYS                               TRUE   TRUE
SCOTT                             TRUE   FALSE
```

Now the user SCOTT can connect as SYSDBA. Administrative users can be connected and authenticated to a local or remote database by using the SQL*Plus *connect* command. They must connect using their username and password, and with the AS SYSDBA or AS SYSOPER clause:

```
SQL> connect scott/tiger as sysdba;
Connected.
```

The DBA utilizes the *orapwd* utility to grant SYSDBA and SYSOPER privileges to other database users. The SYS password should never be shared and should be highly classified.

Orapwd with case sensitive passwords

In the past, many people were not aware of the simple fact that Oracle passwords were not case-sensitive. In Oracle 11g, passwords became case-sensitive. The Oracle 11g password file can store passwords as case-sensitive or case-insensitive.

The password file creation utility evaluates the new parameter *ignorecase* to allow case-sensitive passwords or restrict passwords to case insensitivity. In order to create a password file with orapwd that allows case-sensitive passwords, set *ignorecase* to N.

```
[oracle@rhas4 ~]$ orapwd help=y

Usage: orapwd file=<fname> password=<password> entries=<users> force=<y/n>
ignorecase=<y/n> nosysdba=<y/n>
```

Where:

```
    file - name of password file (required),
    password - password for SYS (optional),
    entries - maximum number of distinct DBA (required),
    force - whether to overwrite existing file (optional),
    ignorecase - passwords are case-insensitive (optional),
    nosysdba - whether to shut out the SYSDBA logon (optional Database Vault
only).
```

There must be no spaces around the equal-to (=) character.

Server Monitoring Utilities

There are many utilities available for monitoring the Oracle server, both supplied by Oracle and supplied by the operating system. The Oracle DBA should become very familiar with each of these utilities and understand how to use various utilities for managing and optimizing the Oracle database.

Using vmstat

Before Oracle incorporated server-side statistics into STATSPACK, AWR and ASH, the most common way of monitoring Oracle server-side data was with the UNIX/Linux utilities such as *vmstat*, top, and glance, and sar.

In every case, the goal is to ensure that the database server has enough disk, CPU and RAM resources at all times in order to service the Oracle requests in an adequate time frame.

Server load typically changes radically over time. It is not at all unusual for an Oracle server to be CPU-bound in the morning, network-bound in the afternoon, and I/O-bound overnight.

The job of the DBA is to identify server stress over time and learn to interpret any trends in hardware consumption. For example, Oracle10g Enterprise Manager tracks server run queue waits over time and combines the CPU and paging display into a single OEM screen so that DBAs can tell when the system is experiencing server-side waits on hardware resources.

Figure 4.4 shows the CPU run queue trends over time.

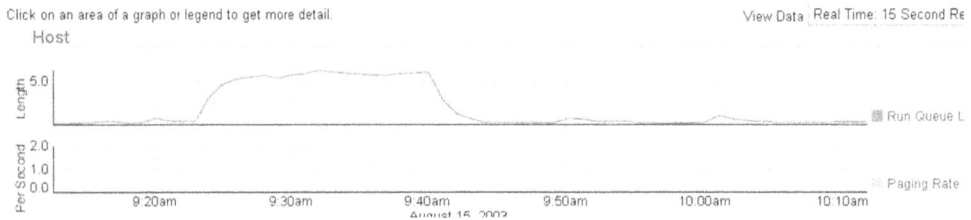

Figure 4.4: *Server CPU run queue and RAM paging values over time*

This time-based display is important because it illustrates how Oracle performance issues can be transient with short spikes of excessive hardware consumption. Due to the super-fast nature of CPU dispatching, a database might be CPU constrained for a few minutes at a time several times per day. The time series OEM display gives a quick visual clue about those times when the system is experiencing a CPU or RAM bottleneck. It is the nature of the job of a DBA to tune the system for best performance at maximum usage, even though this maximum usage may only be reached a few times in the course of a month.

Server RAM and Oracle

Traditionally, the Oracle DBA measured RAM page-in operations to judge RAM utilization on the database server as shown in Figure 4.5. All virtual memory servers (VM) anticipate RAM shortages and asynchronously page-out RAM frames in case the RAM is required for an upcoming task.

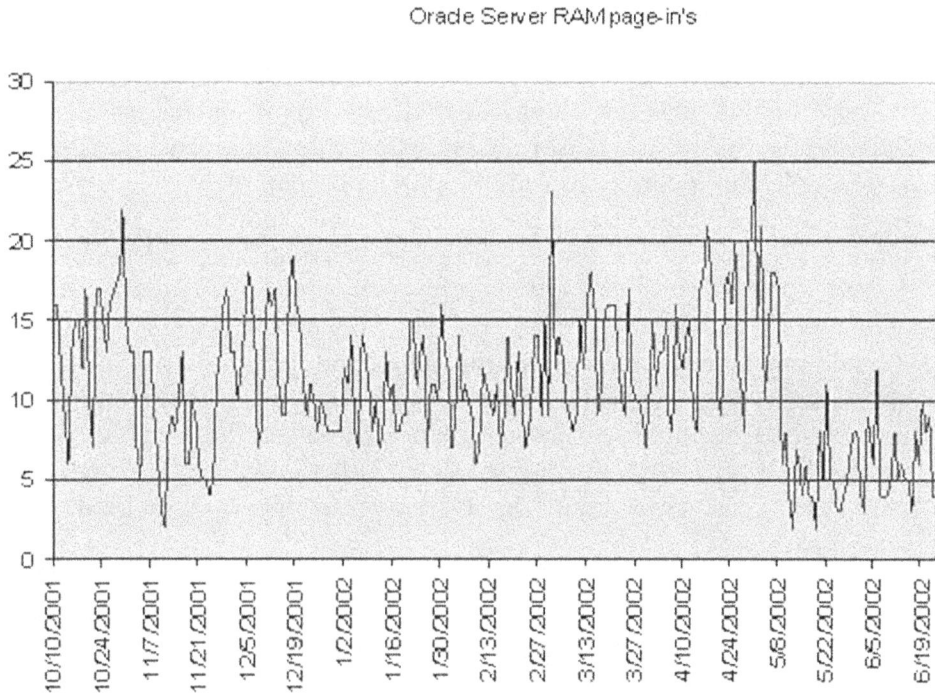

Oracle Server RAM page-in's

Figure 4.5: *Long-term Measurements of Oracle Server RAM Page-in Operations*

When the real RAM on the server is exceeded, the OS will overlay the RAM and must then page-in the saved memory frames from the swap disk on the Oracle server. However, measuring RAM usage based solely on page-ins is a mistake because the page-ins are a normal part of program startup.

To be effective as an Oracle metric, the page-in operations (from *vmstat, glance*) must be correlated with the OS scan rate. When an Oracle server begins to run low on RAM, the page-stealing daemon process awakens and UNIX begins to treat the RAM memory as a sharable resource by moving memory frames to the swap disk with paging operations.

In most UNIX and Linux implementations, the page-stealing daemon operates in two modes. When the real RAM capacity is exceeded, the page-stealing daemon will steal small chunks of the least recently used RAM memory from a program. If RAM resource demands continue to increase beyond the real capacity of the Oracle server, the daemon escalates and begins to page-out entire programs' RAM regions. Unfortunately, on Linux kernel 2.6 users have no control over it. Every parameter available for tuning kernel has been taken away from the system administrators.

Because of this, it is not always clear if the page-in operations are normal housekeeping or a serious memory shortage unless the activity of the page-stealing daemon is correlated with the page-in output. Paging occurs in kernel mode. Generally speaking, if the system exhibits more then 10% of kernel mode CPU usage, for a prolonged period of time, there is a problem with paging.

To aid in measuring real page-ins, the UNIX and Linux *vmstat* utility yields the scan rate (sr) column which designates the memory page scan rate. If the scan rate rises steadily, the page-stealing daemon's first threshold will be identified, indicating that that particular program's entire RAM memory regions are being paged-out to the swap disk. This behavior can then be correlated with the vmstat page-in (*pi*) metric.

The following is an example from a *vmstat* output. The spike in the scan rate immediately precedes an increase in page-in operations.

```
oracle > vmstat 2
      procs            memory              page
   r   b   w      avm    free   re  at    pi   po    fr   de    sr
   3   0   0   144020   12778   17   9     0   14    29    0     3
   3   0   0   144020   12737   15   0     1   34     4    0     8
   3   0   0   144020   12360    9   0     1   46     2    0    13
   1   0   0   142084   12360    5   0     3   17     0    0    21
   1   0   0   142084   12360    3   0    18    0     0    0     8
   1   0   0   140900   12360    1   0    34    0     0    0     0
   1   0   0   140900   12360    0   0    39    0     0    0     0
   1   0   0   140900   12204    0   0     3    0     0    0     0
   1   0   0   137654   12204    0   0     0    0     0    0     0
```

Fortunately, the Automatic Workload Repository (AWR) can be used to track these important external server metrics.

Tracking External Server Metrics with AWR

Oracle sets several important initialization parameters based on the number of CPUs on the Oracle server and is now more mindful of the costs of CPU cycles and I/O operations. Indeed, with each new release of Oracle, the database becomes more tuned to its external environment and more able to gather and report information from both the operating system and the database itself.

Enterprise Manager for Server & Environment

Using the new Oracle 10g Enterprise Manager (OEM) interface, the Oracle professional can now get access to external information that has never before been available in a single interface. This is important because it removes the need for the DBA to have any experience with the cumbersome OS command syntax that is required to display server-side information.

In UNIX, for example, the DBA would need to know the command-line syntax of various UNIX utilities such as sar, glance, top, lsattr, and prtconf to display server metrics. The Oracle10g OEM screens allow seamless access server-side performance metrics including:

- Oracle server-side file contents such as ALERT LOG and TRACE DUMPS

- Oracle archives redo log file performance

- Server OS kernel performance parameter values

- Server OS characteristics such as the number of CPUs, the amount of RAM, and the network

- Historical capture of CPU and RAM activity

A quick look at the Oracle 10g OEM display screens for external information reveals how the DBA is relieved of the burden of having to know and recall hundreds of server-side commands.

Oracle 10g OEM allows DBAs to quickly see the status of Oracle server-side file performance and error messages, including the alert log file, archived redo log status and file system status as shown in Figure 4.6.

Figure 4.6: *A Partial Listing of the AWR Metrics From Inside Oracle 10g Enterprise Manager*

The ability of Oracle10g OEM to monitor server-side metrics makes it a one-stop tool for monitoring both Oracle and the server. In addition, a Systems Administrator may no longer be required to buy separate, expensive tools to monitor the server and the data files. Best of all, the Oracle professional does not have to worry about a server-side problem, i.e. file-system full, causing an Oracle interruption.

The downside of using the AWR statistics is that AWR requires additional cost licensing and can be as expensive as most third party tools. The use of OEM is thoroughly covered in many other sets of documentation, so it will not be covered in this book.

Using AWR and STATSPACK for Server Monitoring

The Oracle Statspack utility can be used to capture snapshots showing the differences in system interaction over prespecified periods of time, usually each hour. Information relating to the server that is available inside Statspack includes:

- Physical disk reads

- CPUs used by specific transactions

- RAM memory used by specific transactions

One shortcoming of this Oracle statistics tool is that it does not show the aggregate demand upon the database server. The utility can be used to see resource utilization for a specific task, but the server stress cannot be seen directly. However, even if Statspack can not give all of the information needed, use some native operating system utilities to find out how many resources are consumed by the Oracle databases. In addition, write new SQL scripts to gather much of the required aggregate server-side information.

Vmstat to the Rescue

The UNIX *vmstat* utility is especially useful for monitoring the performance of Oracle databases. Vmstat can be found on almost all implementations of UNIX, including Linux. Run vmstat using the simple UNIX daemon process shown in Listing 4.1.

💾 **vmstat capture script**

```
#!/bin/ksh
#   This is the Linux version
# First, we must set the environment . . . .
ORACLE_SID=edm1
export ORACLE_SID
ORACLE_HOME=`cat /etc/oratab|grep \^$ORACLE_SID:|cut -f2 -d':'`
export ORACLE_HOME
ORACLE_HOME=/usr/app/oracle/admin/product/8/1/6
export ORACLE_HOME
PATH=$ORACLE_HOME/bin:$PATH
export PATH
MON=`echo ~oracle/mon`
export MON
SERVER_NAME=`uname -a|awk '{print $2}'`
typeset -u SERVER_NAME
export SERVER_NAME

# sample every five minutes (300 seconds) . . . .
SAMPLE_TIME=300
while true
do
   vmstat ${SAMPLE_TIME} 2 > /tmp/msg$$

# run vmstat and direct the output into the Oracle table . . .
```

```
cat /tmp/msg$$|sed 1,3d | awk  '{ printf("%s %s %s %s %s %s\n", $1, $8, $9,
$14, $15, $16) }' | while read RUNQUE PAGE_IN PAGE_OUT USER_CPU SYSTEM_CPU
IDLE_CPU
   do
     $ORACLE_HOME/bin/sqlplus -s system/manager@testb1<<EOF
     insert into sys.mon_vmstats
                         values (
                             sysdate,
                             $SAMPLE_TIME,
                             '$SERVER_NAME',
                             $RUNQUE,
                             $PAGE_IN,
                             $PAGE_OUT,
                             $USER_CPU,
                             $SYSTEM_CPU,
                             $IDLE_CPU,
                             0
                                 );
     EXIT
EOF
   done
done
rm /tmp/msg$$
```

This daemon collects server performance information every five minutes (300
seconds) and stores the server data inside Oracle tables. These Oracle *vmstat*
tables, once populated, can give interesting details about the server. For
example, one can find out usage information about how much RAM and disk
I/O is being used on the database server, as well as how many CPUs are being
used.

When analyzing vmstat output, there are several metrics to which the DBA
should pay attention. For example, keep an eye on the CPU run queue
column. The run queue should never exceed the number of CPUs on the
server. If it is noticed that the run queue starts exceeding the amount of CPUs,
it is a good indication that the server has a CPU bottleneck.

To get an idea of the RAM usage on the server, watch the page-in (pi) and
page-out (po) columns of *vmstat*'s output. By tracking common virtual memory
operations such as page-outs, this infers the times that the Oracle database is
performing a lot of work. Even though UNIX page-ins must correlate with the
vmstat's refresh rate to accurately predict RAM swapping, plotting page-ins
can tell when the server is having spikes of RAM usage.

Once captured, it is very easy to take the information about server
performance directly from the Oracle tables and plot them in a trend graph.
Rather than using an expensive statistical package such as SAS, use Microsoft

Excel. Copy and paste the data from the tables into Excel. After that, use the Chart Wizard to create a line chart that will help view server usage information and discover trends.

Using the ltom utility

Oracle introduced LTOM, the Oracle Lite Onboard Monitor (written by Carl Davis of the Oracle Center of Expertise) as an important new proactive performance monitor tool for the senior Oracle DBA. LTOM is free and can be downloaded from MetaLink.

LTOM joins the list of supplemental monitors that provide external server-side information about disk, RAM, network, and CPU influences on Oracle performance.

Oracle LTOM is unlike the reactive Oracle tuning tools that alert the DBA only after the database has already experienced a slowdown. Rather, LTOM is a proactive tool, collecting real-time data, as well as data from *vmstat*, and enabling a detailed trace mechanism. LTOM provides real-time automatic problem detection and data collection.

> 💣 WARNING - LTOM is not for beginners. The Metalink Note 352363.1 says that LTOM is an "Embedded Real-Time Data Collection and Diagnostics Platform" and explicitly notes that LTOM is only for use by experienced Oracle database administrators.

What is LTOM?

Oracle LTOM (Lite Onboard Monitor) is described as an OS independent (Java front-end) tool that works to trigger detailed trace collection whenever a LTOM user-defined threshold event (non-idle wait event and/or CPU usage) occurs. The Lite Onboard Monitor is a java program designed as a real-time diagnostic platform for deployment to a customer site.

LTOM runs on the customer's UNIX server, is tightly integrated with the host operating system and provides an integrated solution for detecting and collecting trace files for system performance issues.

The ability of LTOM to detect problems and collect data in real-time will hopefully reduce the amount of time it takes to solve problems and reduce customer downtime.

LTOM Features

The Oracle LTOM tool has the following features, centered around the concept of threshold-based data recording, i.e. trace files:

- Automatic Hang Detection
- Manual Data Recording
- Automatic Data Recording
- Automatic Session Tracing

LTOM creates no footprint on the database. All data is written to ASCII text files - either oracle session trace files located in the udump or to a specific log file associated with the respective service that is being used, i.e. manual recorder, auto recorder, hang detection or session recorder. The manual recorder writes *vmstat*, mpstat and top command info to an ascii log file.

The session recorder uses an in-memory trace buffer for the 10046 trace. Sessions are traced in-memory until they violate either a CPU or wait event rule and, at that time, the contents of the memory buffer is dumped to disk.

LTOM Wait Event Rules

LTOM implements a rule-based approach to allow the DBA to specify collection-triggering threshold rules based on the scalar values for Oracle non-idle wait events.

LTOM External Data Recording

LTOM notes the major shortcoming of Statspack and its inability to gather data about the external server environment such as disk enqueues, CPU enqueues, and RAM paging.

One of the problems with relying solely on Statspack is the inability to look at performance from a holistic point of view. Information about non-Oracle processes and the health of the operating system in terms of memory, CPU and I/O, for example, is not collected. LTOM also addresses the issue with deriving high-detail from hourly Statspack snapshots when more frequent elapsed-time metrics are needed.

Further, all static data collectors are problematic in that single sample snapshots or multiple snapshots taken at 15 or 30-minute intervals can miss problems which can occur briefly during a snapshot interval and will be averaged out over the duration of the snapshot.

The data for the LTOM in-RAM data repository includes data from both the UNIX/Linux top and *vmstat* commands. Note that many Oracle professionals have implemented external scripts to capture UNIX/Linux *vmstat* information.

LTOM Automatic Data Recording

LTOM has a rule definition component called automatic data recording that allows setting of thresholds by providing specific values for non-idle wait events. When the LTOM thresholds are triggered, data collection is enabled.

LTOM allows the definition of rules for external CPU thresholds. This is important because many 64-bit databases become CPU-bound with large RAM regions. This CPU tracing (recording amount of CPU used) is also important if the SQL optimizer (CBO) has been changed to consider CPU by setting the *_optimizer_cost_model=cpu* parameter.

LTOM Automatic Session Tracing

LTOM has a method to collect the session_id for offending SQL statements and a method to fire a 10046 SQL trace dump. LTOM uses the Oracle extended SQL*Trace utility, turning on a 10046 (super-detailed) trace on a target SQL statement.

Automatic Session Tracing uses a set of rules to determine when to turn on SQL trace for individual oracle sessions, using event 10046 level 12 trace.

In sum, LTOM is an exciting, proactive Oracle utility that overcomes many of the problems with existing reactive database monitors. In addition to system performance, the DBA must be aware of what is happening to his datafiles on the Oracle server. He needs to know how large the files are, how much space is available, and if the files have been corrupted.

File analysis

Equally important as server performance is server integrity. Not only must the DBA have a good backup and recovery strategy, which will be covered later in this book, but she must also have the ability to detect and repair file corruption when it occurs.

Using the BBED Block Editor Utility

Oracle's BBED utility (Block Browser and EDitor) is available in all releases of Oracle, from Oracle7 to Oracle11g. Designed for internal use only, BBED can be used for several functions, both legitimate and illegal. This tool means that there is effectively no privilege control between the users in the OSDBA group that can access BBED. For instance, the tool could be used to change the SYS password and status to a known value.

This would act as a safety measure if Oracle decided to be start lockout on SYS AS SYSDBA in the case of a brute force attack. BBED could also be used by an attacker, so it would be a good recommendation to remove the tool from the server.

However, it is worth keeping a copy of BBED on hand when it comes to the field of Oracle Forensics in order to recover data from the database that has been deleted by an attacker. BBED is on Windows 8i as bbed.exe or on *nix. The object files are included but need to be linked as will be shown. So, keep an unlinked copy available.

The original intent for BBED is for use by Oracle Technical support to browse, diagnose, and repair data block corruption issues. BBED is an excellent tool for browsing data blocks for those interested in examining the internal structures with data and index blocks. However, the "alter system dump" command can also dump data block contents.

💣 WARNING: NEVER use BBED in EDIT Mode unless working with Oracle technical support.

Beware, hackers might use BBED to break into an Oracle database. Tools like BBED can be used to view data directly within their data block by bypassing the Oracle layer, and because BBED writes directly to the data block, BBED could be used by hackers to update a database without logging and auditing.

Using and Linking BBED

The paper titled "Disassembling the Oracle Data Block," (http://www.orafaq.com/papers/dissassembling_the_data_block.pdf) has complete instructions for installing and using BBED. The make command tells how to linkedit BBED. What follows is a brief set of instructions for making the BBED executable and using the program:

```
make -f ins_rdbms.mk BBED=$ORACLE_HOME/bin/bbed $ORACLE_HOME/bin/bbed
```

> 🔔 BBED Safety tip: When using BBED, always stay in BROWSE mode, and only use BBED EDIT mode (with VER and REP) when completely knowledgeable.

BBED allows direct editing of the datafiles, therefore bypassing Oracle's access control. Of course, one will need to have OS access to the datafiles which should limit the use of this tool to the OS level Oracle account and the rest of OSDBA group.

On UNIX, the object files are included but need to be linked.

As the Oracle OS user:

```
cd $ORACLE_HOME/rdbms/lib
make -f ins_rdbms.mk $ORACLE_HOME/rdbms/lib/bbed.
[oracle@localhost lib]$ file bbed
bbed: ELF 32-bit LSB executable, Intel 80386, version 1 (SYSV), for
GNU/Linux 2.2.5, dynamically linked (uses shared libs), not stripped
```

Create a listfile for BBED to work from:

```
SQL> SELECT FILE#|| ' '||name||' '||bytes from v$datafile;
FILE#||''||NAME||''||BYTES
1 /u01/app/oracle/oradata/orcl/system01.dbf 513802240
2 /u01/app/oracle/oradata/orcl/undotbs01.dbf 52428800
3 /u01/app/oracle/oradata/orcl/sysaux01.dbf 293601280
```

```
4 /u01/app/oracle/oradata/orcl/users01.dbf 5242880
5 /u01/app/oracle/oradata/orcl/example01.dbf 104857600
```

And input the result into a text file called listfile.txt. Listfile.txt is then referenced in the BBED parameter file as below.

```
[oracle@localhost lib]$ vi bbed.par
blocksize=8192
listfile=/u01/app/oracle/oracle/product/10.2.0/db_4/rdbms/lib/listfile.txt
mode=edit
```

This shows the commands available:

```
BBED> HELP ALL
```

This shows the current configuration of BBED:

```
BBED> SHOW ALL
```

DBMS_ROWID is the package to use to get the necessary information to feed into BBED. BBED can be used to read individual Oracle data blocks; however, it will not find block corruption.

File Analysis

The DBV Utility (Database Verify)

The Database Verify utility (*dbv*) provides a mechanism to validate the structure of Oracle data files at the operating system level. It is a simplistic external command line utility which performs a very critical task of finding block corruption in the Oracle database – it does either an offline or online check or verification as to the validity of data files.

One common usage is to employ the utility to analyze image backups to verify their validity. The utility can only be used against datafiles and not against control files or archived redo logs. It offers two basic modes of operation: file level and segment level. The offline check is quicker when referential integrity checks are involved.

dbv Command Line Options

- File – The name of the Oracle datafile to verify. The file must be specified with full path name and file name including extension (.dbf).

- Start – The block within the file to begin the verification. If none is specified, *dbv* will begin at the first block in the file. This parameter should be used when processing large files in which the entire file does not need scanning.

- End – The last block in the data file to verify. If none is specified, *dbv* will process to the end of the file. This parameter should be used when processing large files in which the entire file does not need scanning.

- Blocksize – The database block size of the file that needs verification. This integer must be set to the *v$datafile.db_block_size* value for the data file.

If the block size is not specified, it will default to 2K. If the block size for the datafile does not equal the block size specified, *dbv* will terminate and print an error message:

```
dbv-00103: Specified BLOCKSIZE (2048) differs from actual (8192)
```

- Logfile – The name of the file to direct the *dbv* output. If none is specified, the output will be sent to the terminal. When scheduling a *dbv*-based shell script, it will be this file that needs to be checked for corruption errors.

- Feedback – A progress meter that displays a dot for *n* pages examined in the file (FEEDBACK=10000). Use this integer to provide a status indicator when *dbv* is executed against large files. This is needed to indicate that the *dbv* process is actively processing a file. This option is obviously not needed when executing *dbv* through a scheduled shell script.

- Parfile - A parameter file that can contain any of these options. The parfile should be created once and used with every *dbv* command.

- Segment_ID – A parameter that will scan a segment regardless of the number of files it spans. The format is *segment_id*=tsn.segfile.segblock.

- Userid – Used only in combination with *segment_id* to specify the username/password for the database connection.

Executing dbv and Interpreting the Output

Dbv can be executed by specifying the file name and block size of the datafile. All other parameters are optional.

```
dbv file=/usr/oracle/asg920xr/datafiles/ASG920xrsys.dbf
    blocksize=8192
```

Once executed, *dbv* provides the following output for each file it verifies:

```
Total Pages Examined         : 52480
Total Pages Processed (Data) : 36617
Total Pages Failing   (Data) : 0
Total Pages Processed (Index): 4430
Total Pages Failing   (Index): 0
Total Pages Processed (Other): 1664
Total Pages Processed (Seg)  : 0
Total Pages Failing   (Seg)  : 0
Total Pages Empty            : 9769
Total Pages Marked Corrupt   : 0
Total Pages Influx           : 0
```

The output from *dbv* is not intuitive at first glance. Following are the definitions for each data item.

- Total Pages Examined – The number of blocks inspected by *dbv*. If the entire file was scanned, this value will match the BLOCKS column for the file in *v$datafile*.

- Total Pages Processed (Data) –The number of blocks inspected by *dbv* that contained table data.

- Total Pages Failing (Data) – The number of table blocks that have corruption.

- Total Pages Processed (Index) –The number of blocks inspected by *dbv* that contained index data.

- Total Pages Failing (Index) – The number of index blocks that are corrupted.

- Total Pages Processed (Seg) – This output is new to 9i and allows the command to specify a segment that spans multiple files.

- Total Pages Failing (Seg) – The number of segment data blocks that are corrupted.

- Total Pages Empty – Number of unused blocks discovered in the file.

- Total Pages Marked Corrupt – This is the most important one. It shows the number of corrupt blocks discovered during the scan.

- Total Pages Influx – The number of pages that were reread due to the page being in use. This should only occur when executing *dbv* against hot datafiles and should never occur when running *dbv* against cold backup files.

Executing dbv against a Particular Segment

In order to execute *dbv* against a particular segment, the tablespace name, header file, and header block are needed. This command is useful when verifying particular objects that span multiple files. This is the only case, however, in which *dbv* requires a database connection.

```
SQL> select t.ts#, s.header_file, s.header_block
  2    from v$tablespace t, dba_segments s
  3    where s.owner = 'SCOTT'
  4    and s.segment_name='DEPARTMENT'
  5    and t.name = s.tablespace_name;


     TS# HEADER_FILE HEADER_BLOCK
---------- ----------- ------------
      15          12            9
```

Once these three data items are retrieved, the *dbv* command can be applied to a particular segment:

```
dbv userid=scott/tiger segment_id=15.12.9

Total Pages Examined         : 4
Total Pages Processed (Data) : 3
Total Pages Failing   (Data) : 0
Total Pages Processed (Index): 0
Total Pages Failing   (Index): 0
Total Pages Processed (Other): 0
Total Pages Processed (Seg)  : 1
Total Pages Failing   (Seg)  : 0
Total Pages Empty            : 0
Total Pages Marked Corrupt   : 0
Total Pages Influx           : 0
```

Automating dbv

DBAs should automate and execute the *dbv* utility on a regular basis. The following shell script (*dbv.ksh*) prompts for Oracle environment information,

---

File Analysis

connects to the database, and produces a command file that can be executed at the convenience of the DBA. In this script, *dbv* is executed immediately after it is generated.

🖫 dbv.ksh

```
#!/bin/ksh
# Oracle Utilities
# dbv automation script
#
#
. oraenv
    wlogfile=dbv.${ORACLE_SID}
    SQLPLUS=${ORACLE_HOME}/bin/sqlplus
    $SQLPLUS -s  system/manager >> $wlogfile <<EOF
        set echo off feedback off verify off pages 0 termout off
            linesize 150
        spool dbv.cmd
        select 'dbv file=' || name || ' blocksize=' || block_size ||
          ' feedback=' || round(blocks*.10,0) -- 10 dots per file
          from v\$datafile;
        spool off
        set feedback on verify on pages24 echo on termout on
EOF
ksh dbv.cmd
#
# End of script
```

The *dbv.ksh* script formats a *dbv* command that can be executed from the UNIX command line. The logfile for the script is *dbv. ${ORACLE_SID}*. The results of the SQL statement are placed in the *dbv.cmd* file and this file is executed at the end of the script. Notice that a feedback was specified equivalent to one dot per each 10 percent of the file processed in order to provide a status of *dbv*.

The contents of the *dbv.cmd* file are:

```
$ cat dbv.cmd

dbv file=/usr/oracle/asg920xr/datafiles/ASG920xrsys.dbf blocksize=8192 feedback=3200
dbv file=/usr/oracle/asg920xr/datafiles/undo.dbf blocksize=8192 feedback=1088
dbv file=/usr/oracle/asg920xr/datafiles/ASG920xray.dbf blocksize=8192 feedback=3200
dbv file=/usr/oracle/asg920xr/datafiles/aaa/UNDO1.dbf blocksize=8192 feedback=124
dbv file=/usr/oracle/asg920xr/datafiles/bbb/UNDO2.dbf blocksize=8192 feedback=26
dbv file=/usr/oracle/asg920xr/datafiles/ccc/UNDO3.dbf blocksize=8192 feedback=38
dbv file=/usr/oracle/asg920xr/datafiles/ddd/UNDO4.dbf blocksize=8192 feedback=51
dbv file=/usr/oracle/asg920xr/datafiles/aaa/UNDO5.dbf blocksize=8192 feedback=64
dbv file=/usr/oracle/asg920xr/datafiles/zzz/UNDO6.dbf blocksize=8192 feedback=13
dbv file=/usr/oracle/asg920xr/datafiles/aaa/undo_all1.dbf blocksize=8192 feedback=576
dbv file=/usr/oracle/asg920xr/datafiles/bbb/undo_all2.dbf blocksize=8192 feedback=26
dbv file=/usr/oracle/asg920xr/datafiles/ccc/undo_all3.dbf blocksize=8192 feedback=499
dbv file=/usr/oracle/asg920xr/datafiles/ddd/undo_all4.dbf blocksize=8192 feedback=602
dbv file=/usr/oracle/asg920xr/datafiles/aaa/undo_all5.dbf blocksize=8192 feedback=614
dbv file=/usr/oracle/asg920xr/datafiles/zzz/undo_all6.dbf blocksize=8192 feedback=13
dbv file=/data1/dbxray/datafiles/undo_all7.dbf blocksize=8192 feedback=602
dbv file=/data1/dbxray /datafiles/undo_tablespace_long2.dbf blocksize=8192 feedback=166
dbv file=/usr/oracle/asg920xr/datafiles/symbolic/UNDO8.dbf blocksize=8192 feedback=13
```

```
dbv file=/usr/oracle/asg920xr/datafiles/zzz/UNDO6a.dbf blocksize=8192feedback=1
dbv file=/usr/oracle/asg920xr/datafiles/davetest.dbf blocksize=8192 feedback=26
$
```

Notice in the *dbv.cmd* file above that the *block_size* is included for each datafile. In Oracle versions 8.1.7 and below, the following command would indicate the block size since it had to be consistent across the database.

```
SQL> show parameter db_block_size

NAME                         TYPE        VALUE
-------------------------   ----------- -------
db_block_size                integer     8192
```

In version 9, each tablespace can have its own block size and therefore, it must be included at the datafile level.

The result of the execution of the *dbv.cmd* file is:

```
dbvERIFY: Release 9.2.0.1.0 - Production on Sun Dec 29 19:15:55 2002
Copyright (c) 1982, 2002, Oracle Corporation.  All rights reserved.

dbvERIFY - Verification starting : FILE =
/usr/oracle/asg920xr/datafiles/ASG920xrsys.dbf
.........

dbvERIFY - Verification complete

Total Pages Examined         : 32000
Total Pages Processed (Data) : 16164
Total Pages Failing   (Data) : 0
Total Pages Processed (Index): 2520
Total Pages Failing   (Index): 0
Total Pages Processed (Other): 1230
Total Pages Processed (Seg)  : 0
Total Pages Failing   (Seg)  : 0
Total Pages Empty            : 12086
Total Pages Marked Corrupt   : 0
Total Pages Influx           : 0

dbvERIFY: Release 9.2.0.1.0 - Production on Sun Dec 29 19:16:06 2002

Copyright (c) 1982, 2002, Oracle Corporation.  All rights reserved.

dbvERIFY - Verification starting : FILE =
/usr/oracle/asg920xr/datafiles/undo.dbf
.........

dbvERIFY - Verification complete
```

Notice the 10 dots displayed for each datafile as it was processed. Everything looks good in this output since no pages are marked as corrupt.

Alternative Block Checking Mechanisms

There is another utility that resides completely within the database for identifying corrupt data. This command is the *analyze table* validate structure command. The *analyze* command can do things that *dbv* cannot and vice versa. The *analyze* command can validate that tables and indexes are in sync with each other. However, the *analyze* command only processes an object up to the point of its high water mark (HWM), whereas processes all blocks in a file. Block corruption can occur in blocks above the HWM.

The *analyze* command would have to be executed against an open database for each object in the database. *Dbv* can work against offline files and is much faster since it is strictly at the file level. In addition, the *analyze table* command places an exclusive lock on the object being analyzed. Alternatively, *dbv* works outside of the database in "read only" mode against the datafiles and does not lock anything. Any errors encountered by the *analyze table* command are reported in the session trace file in the user dump destination directory.

Handling Corruption

Some errors reported by *dbv* are transient in nature. Therefore, the utility should be executed on the suspect file again to confirm block corruption. If problems are again reported in the same page locations, then the file is indeed corrupt. Once one or more corrupted blocks are detected, the DBA must resolve the issue. Below are some options available to the DBA to address block corruption:

- Drop and recreate the corrupted object – If the loss of data is not an issue, this is the preferred approach. For Data Warehouses, the data can be reloaded from external sources and the loss of data is minor. For Indexes, the index can be rebuilt into another data file. However, for OLTP tables (*customer_orders*), no data can be lost without a serious negative impact on the business.

- If a few blocks are corrupt, determine which object(s) are causing the corruption. This can be done in the following query by mapping the physical file location to an object(s) contained in the file.

```
select tablespace_name, segment_type, owner,
       segment_name
  from dba_extents
 where file_id = <corrupted file id>
```

```
and <Block #>  between block_id AND block_id + blocks-1;
```

- Restore the file from a backup – The tried and true method for restoring good blocks back into the datafiles.

- Use *dbms_repair* – Dealing with block corruption is always a risky proposition, so limit the use of *dbms_repair* to extreme situations. *Dbms_repair* is a package utility supplied by Oracle that identifies and repairs block corruption (described in next section).

If the first two options are unacceptable, using *dbms_repair* can resolve some block corruption issues.

The dbms_repair Utility

Dbms_repair is a utility that can detect and repair block corruption within Oracle. It is provided by Oracle as part of the standard database installation.

Configuring the Environment

Two tables must first be created under the SYS schema before the *dbms_repair* utility can be used. Fortunately, a procedure in the package itself (*admin_tables*) creates these tables and eliminates the need to hunt for a script in *$ORACLE_HOME/rdbms/admin*.

```
dbms_repair.ADMIN_TABLES (
   table_name  IN   VARCHAR2,
   table_type  IN   BINARY_INTEGER,
   action      IN   BINARY_INTEGER,
   tablespace  IN   VARCHAR2         DEFAULT NULL);
```

- *table_name* – The name of the table to be processed, as determined by the action

- *table_type* – Either *orphan_table* or *repair_table*

- *action* – Either *create_action*, *purge_action* or *drop_action*. When *create_action* is specified, the table will be created in the SYS schema. *Purge_action* deletes all rows in the table that apply to objects that no longer exist. *Drop_action* will drop the table.

- *tablespace* – The tablespace in which the newly created table will reside. This tablespace must already exist.

The following command will be used to create the two tables needed. The command will be executed twice with different parameters, once for the *repair* table and once for the *orphan* table.

```
begin
  dbms_repair.admin_tables(
     table_name => 'REPAIR_TEST',
     table_type => dbms_repair.repair_table,
     action     => dbms_repair.create_action,
     tablespace => 'SCOTTWORK'
   );
end;

begin
  dbms_repair.admin_tables(
     table_name => 'ORPHAN_TEST',
     table_type => dbms_repair.orphan_table,
     action     => dbms_repair.create_action,
     tablespace => 'SCOTTWORK'
   );
end;
```

The two tables are now created. A describe of the two tables reveals the following:

```
SQL> desc repair_test;

 Name                                    Null?    Type
 --------------------------------------- -------- ---------------
 OBJECT_ID                               NOT NULL NUMBER
 TABLESPACE_ID                           NOT NULL NUMBER
 RELATIVE_FILE_ID                        NOT NULL NUMBER
 BLOCK_ID                                NOT NULL NUMBER
 CORRUPT_TYPE                            NOT NULL NUMBER
 SCHEMA_NAME                             NOT NULL VARCHAR2(30)
 OBJECT_NAME                             NOT NULL VARCHAR2(30)
 BASEOBJECT_NAME                                  VARCHAR2(30)
 PARTITION_NAME                                   VARCHAR2(30)
 CORRUPT_DESCRIPTION                              VARCHAR2(2000)
 REPAIR_DESCRIPTION                               VARCHAR2(200)
 MARKED_CORRUPT                          NOT NULL VARCHAR2(10)
 CHECK_TIMESTAMP                         NOT NULL DATE
 FIX_TIMESTAMP                                    DATE
 REFORMAT_TIMESTAMP                               DATE

SQL> desc orphan_test

 Name                                    Null?    Type
 --------------------------------------- -------- ---------------
 SCHEMA_NAME                             NOT NULL VARCHAR2(30)
 INDEX_NAME                              NOT NULL VARCHAR2(30)
 IPART_NAME                                       VARCHAR2(30)
 INDEX_ID                                NOT NULL NUMBER
 TABLE_NAME                              NOT NULL VARCHAR2(30)
 PART_NAME                                        VARCHAR2(30)
```

```
TABLE_ID                              NOT NULL NUMBER
KEYROWID                              NOT NULL ROWID
KEY                                   NOT NULL ROWID
DUMP_TIMESTAMP                        NOT NULL DATE
```

Repair tables will contain those objects that have corrupted blocks. Orphan tables, on the other hand, are used to contain indexes that point to corrupted data

Finding Corrupt Blocks

The *dbms_repair* utility provides a mechanism to search for corrupt database blocks. Below is the syntax for the *check_objects* procedure. Note that the only OUT parameter is the *corrupt_count*.

```
dbms_repair.CHECK_OBJECT (
    schema_name      IN  VARCHAR2,
    object_name      IN  VARCHAR2,
    partition_name   IN  VARCHAR2        DEFAULT NULL,
    object_type      IN  BINARY_INTEGER DEFAULT TABLE_OBJECT,
    repair_table_name IN VARCHAR2        DEFAULT 'REPAIR_TABLE',
    flags            IN  BINARY_INTEGER DEFAULT NULL,
    relative_fno     IN  BINARY_INTEGER DEFAULT NULL,
    block_start      IN  BINARY_INTEGER DEFAULT NULL,
    block_end        IN  BINARY_INTEGER DEFAULT NULL,
    corrupt_count       OUT BINARY_INTEGER) ;
```

- *schema_name* – Schema name of the object to be checked for corruption.

- *object_name* – Name of the table or index that will be checked for corruption.

- *partition_name* – Partition or sub-partition name to be checked.

- *object_type* – Either TABLE_OBJECT or INDEX_OBJECT as specified as an enumeration (*dbms_repair.table_object*).

- *repair_table_name* – The name of the repair table to be populated in the SYS schema.

- *flags* – Not used.

- *relative_fno* – The relative file number to be used when specifying a block range to be checked.

- *block_start* – The first block in the block range to begin checking.

- *block_end* – The last block in the block range to check.

- *corrupt_count* – The number of corrupt blocks discovered.

The code below will check the *scott.employee* table for corruption and report the number of corrupted blocks.

💾 dbms_repair.sql

```
set serveroutput on
declare corr_count binary_integer;
begin
corr_count := 0;
dbms_repair.CHECK_OBJECT (
    schema_name       => 'SCOTT',
    object_name       => 'EMPLOYEE',
    partition_name    => null,
    object_type       => dbms_repair.table_object,
    repair_table_name => 'REPAIR_TEST',
    flags             => null,
    relative_fno      => null,
    block_start       => null,
    block_end         => null,
    corrupt_count     => corr_count
    );
dbms_output.put_line(to_char(corr_count));
end;
/
# Corrupt Blocks =0

PL/SQL procedure successfully completed.
```

Once executed, the table *repair_test* can be queried in order to find more about corrupt blocks. In this case, no rows exist in the table. The repair table is only populated if the *check_object* procedure did indeed find corrupt blocks, so no rows in this table is good news!

Repairing Corrupt Blocks

The *dbms_repair* utility provides a mechanism to repair the corrupt database blocks, which is the *fix_corrupt_blocks* procedure. Corrupt blocks are not really repaired, but instead are simply marked as corrupt.

Below is the syntax for the *fix_corrupt_blocks* procedure. Note that the only OUT parameter is the *fix_count*.

```
dbms_repair.FIX_CORRUPT_BLOCKS (
    schema_name       IN  VARCHAR2,
    object_name       IN  VARCHAR2,
    partition_name    IN  VARCHAR2       DEFAULT NULL,
    object_type       IN  BINARY_INTEGER DEFAULT TABLE_OBJECT,
    repair_table_name IN  VARCHAR2       DEFAULT 'REPAIR_TABLE',
    flags             IN  BINARY_INTEGER DEFAULT NULL,
    fix_count         OUT BINARY_INTEGER);
```

- *schema_name* - The name of the schema containing the object with corrupt blocks.

- *object_name* – The name of the object needing repair.

- *partition_name* – The name of the partition or subpartition to process. If none is specified and the object is partitioned, all partitions will be processed.

- *object_type* - Either *table_object* or *index_object* as specified as an enumeration.

- *repair_table_name* – The name of the repair table.

- *flags* – Not used.

- *fix_count* – The number of blocks fixed. This should equal the same number of corrupt blocks reported.

If the object repaired is a table, then any corresponding index also needs to be fixed. The *dump_orphan_keys* procedure will indicate if any keys are broken. If they are, the index will need to be rebuilt.

Rebuilding Freelists

The *dbms_repair* utility provides a mechanism to rebuild the impacted freelists and bitmap entries after fixing block corruption. This procedure recreates the header portion of the datafile, allowing Oracle to use the newly repaired blocks.

Below is the syntax for the *rebuild_freelists* procedure:

```
dbms_repair.REBUILD_FREELISTS (
   schema_name    IN VARCHAR2,
   partition_name IN VARCHAR2      DEFAULT NULL,
   object_type    IN BINARY_INTEGER DEFAULT TABLE_OBJECT);
```

- *schema_name* – The name of the schema containing the object whose freelists need rebuilding.

- *partition_name* – The name of the partition or subpartition whose freelists are to be rebuilt.

- *object_type* – Either TABLE_OBJECT or INDEX_OBJECT as specified as an enumeration.

Dbms_repair provides a new method of addressing ORA-600 errors dealing with block corruption. The utility is very easy to use and very functional. As

---

described earlier, it is one of many potential solutions when resolving block corruption. *Dbms_repair* does basically the same thing as *analyze_table* -validate structure.

Managing files on the Oracle server have been reviewed. In the next section, the managing of user processes on the Oracle server will be detailed.

Process Management

There are times and scenarios where a user's Oracle server process on the database server may require intervention by the DBA. For example, the session may be either hung or aggressively "spinning" and thus blocking out other transactions or consuming excessive resources. When situations like this occur, the DBA needs a way to terminate the offending Oracle server process to release the operating system and database resources and thus, clear the log jam. Hopefully, this scenario should only occur occasionally.

In most cases, assuming the database itself is up and accepting new connections, the DBA can simply connect to the database, find the offending process by querying the data dictionary, and terminate it via an SQL command. The query to find the offending process and the SQL command to terminate it will look something like the following:

```
SQL> select s.username, s.osuser, s.sid, s.serial#, p.spid
  2    from v$session s,v$process p
  3   where s.paddr = p.addr
  4     and s.username is not null;

USERNAME     OSUSER            SID    SERIAL# SPID
------------ ------------ ---------- ---------- ------------
BERT         oracle           532          9 6781
BERT         BSCALZO          526         31 6889
SYSTEM       BSCALZO          535         29 7066

SQL> -- ALTER SYSTEM KILL SESSION 'sid,serial#';
SQL> alter system kill session '526,31';

System altered.
```

However, there are rare times when the database is either not up, not accepting any new connections, or the machine is just so slow that opening a new database connection is taking far too long. Likewise, this scenario should only occur very rarely and possibly not at all in an ideal world. But when it does, the DBA needs a method to terminate the session and must rely upon

---

operating system level commands. Nevertheless, far too often it is common practice to kill Oracle processes and so prevalent that even non-DBAs start to perform them on a regular basis. Make sure that the following facilities are only used under appropriate circumstance and with controlled supervision. Remember, KILL is a four-letter word and the kill utilities should be used as a last resort only.

kill

On UNIX and Linux, the Oracle process architecture follows the standard UNIX paradigm, which is that every program execution forks or spawns a process to perform that contextual task. As such, the *ps* command, even on a small system, can display hundreds to even thousands of processes and that is why a pipe to *grep* is often paired with it, as shown here:

```
[oracle@LINUX_10G ~]$ ps -ef | grep ora_
oracle    5400    1  0 10:55 ?        00:00:00 ora_pmon_ORLI10
oracle    5402    1  0 10:55 ?        00:00:00 ora_psp0_ORLI10
oracle    5404    1  0 10:55 ?        00:00:00 ora_mman_ORLI10
oracle    5406    1  0 10:55 ?        00:00:00 ora_dbw0_ORLI10
oracle    5408    1  0 10:55 ?        00:00:00 ora_lgwr_ORLI10
oracle    5410    1  0 10:55 ?        00:00:00 ora_ckpt_ORLI10
oracle    5412    1  0 10:55 ?        00:00:01 ora_smon_ORLI10
oracle    5414    1  0 10:55 ?        00:00:00 ora_reco_ORLI10
oracle    5416    1  0 10:55 ?        00:00:01 ora_cjq0_ORLI10
oracle    5418    1  0 10:55 ?        00:00:01 ora_mmon_ORLI10
oracle    5420    1  0 10:55 ?        00:00:00 ora_mmnl_ORLI10
oracle    5437    1  0 10:55 ?        00:00:00 ora_qmnc_ORLI10
oracle    5860    1  0 10:56 ?        00:00:00 ora_q000_ORLI10
oracle    6347    1  0 10:56 ?        00:00:00 ora_q001_ORLI10
oracle    6621 6552  0 10:58 pts/0    00:00:00 grep ora_
```

When there is a legitimate reason to terminate a user's SQL and the associated dedicated database server process, then the following steps are required to effect that interruption.

- Identify the correct operating system process associated with the errant SQL

- Issue the UNIX kill command for that process with the terminate flag

- Verify that the operating system process indicated terminates as planned

Following is an example where there are two users with a problem. The first user running SQL*Plus on the database server placed an exclusive lock on all the rows in a table by forgetting to place a WHERE clause in their UPDATE statement. The second user running SQL*Plus from their Windows PC is thus

---

blocked from updating the rows they need until the first user issues a commit. Further, assume that the database is not accepting any new connections, so the DBA must rely on an operating system command to kill the Oracle process. Doing a *ps* command shows both SQL*Plus sessions, where the first user's process is 6781.

```
[oracle@LINUX_10G ~]$ ps -ef | grep sqlplus
oracle    6766  6735  0 11:26 pts/1    00:00:00 sqlplus
oracle   10942  6552  0 13:52 pts/0    00:00:00 grep sqlplus
[oracle@LINUX_10G ~]$
[oracle@LINUX_10G ~]$ ps -ef | grep oracleORLI10
oracle    6781  6766  0 11:26 ?        00:00:00 oracleORLI10
(DESCRIPTION=(LOCAL=YES)(ADDRESS=(PROTOCOL=beq)))
oracle    7461     1  0 11:50 ?        00:00:00 oracleORLI10 (LOCAL=NO)
oracle   10957  6552  0 13:52 pts/0    00:00:00 grep oracleORLI10
```

So now, to kill that Oracle database dedicated server session, use the UNIX *kill* command incorporating either of the two following syntaxes:

```
kill -s SIGKILL process_id

kill -9 process_id
```

To find the names of the valid termination signal levels, simply perform a *kill –l* as shown here to see what signal level values are permissible:

```
[oracle@LINUX_10G ~]$ kill -l
 1) SIGHUP       2) SIGINT       3) SIGQUIT      4) SIGILL
 5) SIGTRAP      6) SIGABRT      7) SIGBUS       8) SIGFPE
 9) SIGKILL     10) SIGUSR1     11) SIGSEGV     12) SIGUSR2
13) SIGPIPE     14) SIGALRM     15) SIGTERM     17) SIGCHLD
18) SIGCONT     19) SIGSTOP     20) SIGTSTP     21) SIGTTIN
22) SIGTTOU     23) SIGURG      24) SIGXCPU     25) SIGXFSZ
26) SIGVTALRM   27) SIGPROF     28) SIGWINCH    29) SIGIO
30) SIGPWR      31) SIGSYS      34) SIGRTMIN    35) SIGRTMIN+1
36) SIGRTMIN+2  37) SIGRTMIN+3  38) SIGRTMIN+4  39) SIGRTMIN+5
40) SIGRTMIN+6  41) SIGRTMIN+7  42) SIGRTMIN+8  43) SIGRTMIN+9
44) SIGRTMIN+10 45) SIGRTMIN+11 46) SIGRTMIN+12 47) SIGRTMIN+13
48) SIGRTMIN+14 49) SIGRTMIN+15 50) SIGRTMAX-14 51) SIGRTMAX-13
52) SIGRTMAX-12 53) SIGRTMAX-11 54) SIGRTMAX-10 55) SIGRTMAX-9
56) SIGRTMAX-8  57) SIGRTMAX-7  58) SIGRTMAX-6  59) SIGRTMAX-5
60) SIGRTMAX-4  61) SIGRTMAX-3  62) SIGRTMAX-2  63) SIGRTMAX-1
64) SIGRTMAX
```

orakill

In Windows, there are a couple of kill utilities: the Oracle-centric *orakill* utility and the Windows *taskkill* program. If the session cannot be killed more gracefully via alter system kill session, or the instance is inaccessible via SQL, then *orakill* should be used to terminate the offending session. Access to the Windows machine containing the database must be secure to use *orakill*. Any user with access to the box could access *orakill* or the Windows Task Manager and damage database processes.

Oracle on Windows is implemented based upon threads rather than processes. So when the Windows Task Manager is viewed, all that will be seen is one ORACLE.EXE for that database instance. The individual threads for the sessions will not be visible since Task Manager only shows the process and number of threads. Look at the next screen snapshot; there are two SQL*Plus sessions connected to the database on this Windows box. Even though two sqlplus.exe processes can be seen, there is but one oracle.exe process. One would need to dig deeper than the basic Windows task management program to find the Oracle dedicated database server process' thread.

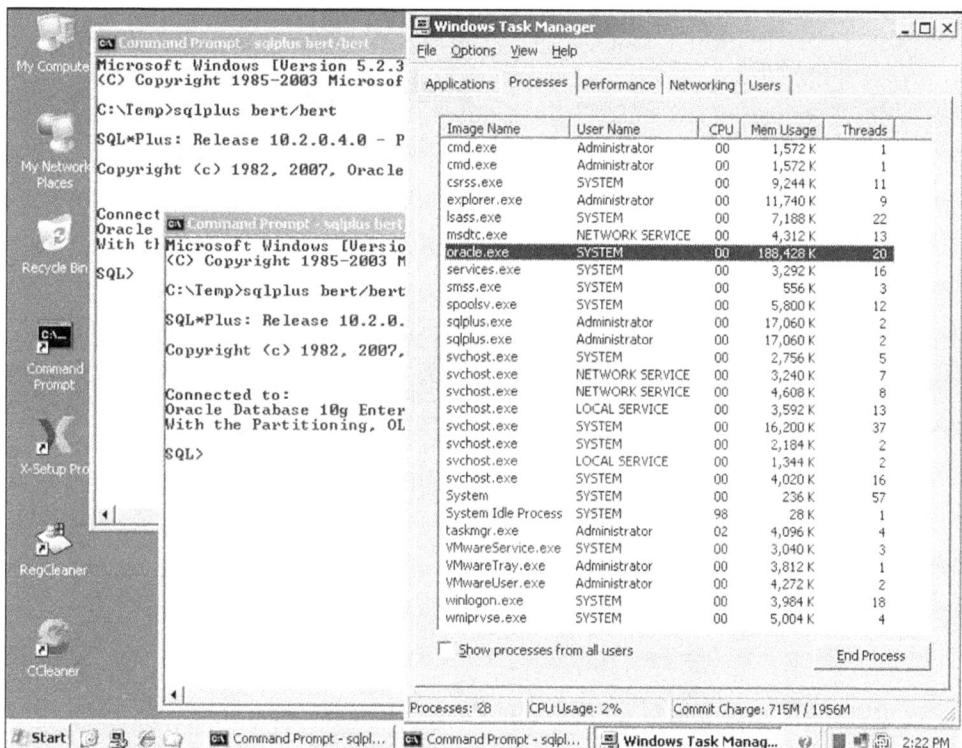

Figure 4.7: *ORACLE.EXE in Windows Task Manager*

The DBA could use a utility program, such as the free QuickSlice (qslice.exe) and PStat (pstat.exe) from the Microsoft's Resource Kit, or Process Explorer (procexp.exe), also from Microsoft. With tools like these, open the oracle.exe process and investigate into its many threads. However, if one simply selects the 1176 thread using Process Explorer and presses the KILL button, there could be a problem. These tools do not inform Oracle's PMON as to what just occurred, so they do not always make a hanging session and its locks go away. It still may be necessary to also manually run *oradebug* wakeup 1 to clear the locks, *v$session* and *v$process*. Hence, it is advisable to always use the Oracle-provided *orakill* utility instead. Just be careful, because if the wrong thread, such as a background process, is chosen, then the entire database may crash.

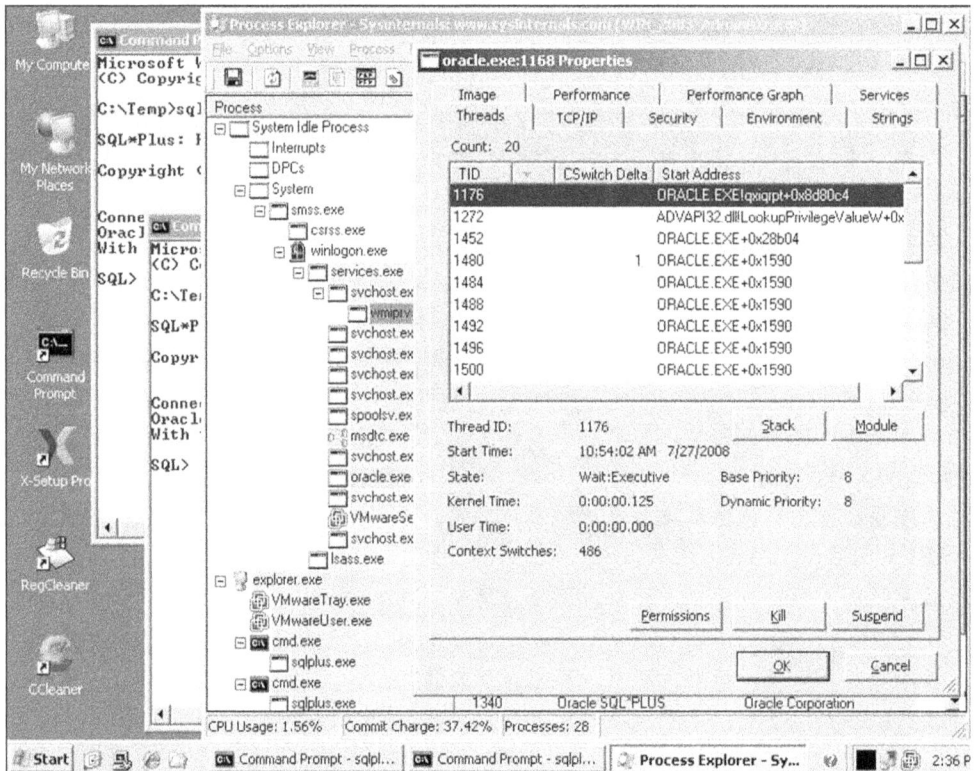

Figure 4.8: *Selecting 1176 Thread in Process Explorer*

The Windows command to kill this session would be as follows:

```
C:\oracle9i\bin>orakill ORCL92 768
```

In this example, the Windows thread corresponding to the Oracle session can be killed in the operating system without ever logging into the database. For another example, the Windows command to kill a session would be:

```
C:\oracle9i\bin>orakill ORCL92 768
```

In this example, the thread (Oracle session) was killed in the operating system without ever logging into the database. Before killing the session, the DBA may decide to view the SQL being executed by the session. This can be obtained by using the TID above (300) in the following SQL statement:

```
select
   b.username, a.sql_text
from
v$sqltext_with_newlines a, v$session b, v$process c
where
   c.spid = to_number('300', 'xxx')
and
   c.addr = b.paddr
and
   b.sql_address = a.address;
```

The *orakill* command is very simple. In fact, it is essentially the exact same syntax as the ALTER SYSTEM KILL SESSION. This means that it accepts two parameters – the SID and *v$process*.spid – which represents the thread number.

```
C:\Temp>orakill OR0310 1176

Kill of thread id 1176 in instance OR0310 successfully signaled.
```

renice

On UNIX and Linux, there may be occasions where increasing an Oracle process priority may be contemplated. While some people are dead set against this, the Oracle ADDM report can, on occasion, suggest increasing the priority of the GS processes in order to reduce global waits in a RAC environment. Remember, only the priority of a process that is owned can be changed, so login as Oracle or root to make these changes. The command syntax is as follows:

```
$ renice nice_value id [options]
```

Where the options are:

OPTION	DESCRIPTION
-g	Force who parameters to be interpreted as process group IDs
-p	Resets who interpretation to be (the default) process IDs
-u	Force who parameters to be interpreted as user names

Table 4.8: *renice Options*

The nice value can range from -20 (fastest or highest) to 19 (slowest or lowest).

trcsess

The *trcsess* command-line utility offers the DBA a way to combine or consolidate several trace files into a single trace file based upon the following criteria:

- Session Id

- Client Id

- Service name

- Action name

- Module name

This single resulting output trace file can then be fed to TKPROF or other trace file analysis tools, such as the free Hotsos plug-in for SQL Developer, to debug a particular session. When using dedicated server processes, monitoring only a single session and not doing parallel operations, there is little need for the *trcsess* utility. But when using shared server processes, monitoring several sessions concurrently, and/or doing parallel DML, the workload can span multiple trace files. In fact, it can be located on different nodes in a RAC environment if the parallel operations cross nodes. The command syntax is as follows:

```
$ trcsess [options] trace_files
```

Where the options are:

OPTION	DESCRIPTION
output=	Consolidated output trace file

OPTION	DESCRIPTION
session=	Consolidates the trace information by session id
clientid=	Consolidates the trace information by client id
service=	Consolidates the trace information by service name
action=	Consolidates the trace information by action name
module=	Consolidates the trace information by module name

Table 4.9: *trcsess Command-line Utility Options*

In the following example, all the trace files in the temporary directory are consolidated into one big trace file and are doing so just for SELECT statements:

```
C:\Temp>trcsess output=one_big.trc service=ORDB1 *.trc
```

Examining the contents of the resulting *one_big.trc* file, this shows that the *trcsess* utility has consolidated five separate trace files into one.

🖫 one_big.trc consolidated trace file

```
*** [ Windows thread id: 4860 ]
*** 2008-08-03 10:06:16.796
*** 2008-08-03 10:06:16.796
*** 2008-08-03 10:06:16.796
...
*** TRACE CONTINUED FROM FILE
c:\oracle\diag\rdbms\ordb1\ordb1\trace\ordb1_ora_4860.trc ***
...
*** TRACE CONTINUED FROM FILE
c:\oracle\diag\rdbms\ordb1\ordb1\trace\ordb1_ora_3412.trc ***
...
*** TRACE CONTINUED FROM FILE
c:\oracle\diag\rdbms\ordb1\ordb1\trace\ordb1_ora_1072.trc ***
...
*** TRACE CONTINUED FROM FILE
c:\oracle\diag\rdbms\ordb1\ordb1\trace\ordb1_ora_1716.trc ***
...
*** TRACE CONTINUED FROM FILE
c:\oracle\diag\rdbms\ordb1\ordb1\trace\ordb1_ora_2432.trc ***
...
```

TKPROF

The TKPROF command-line utility translates the plethora of performance raw data contained in trace files into a more human readable format. The trace file is a raw collection of Oracle process instrumentation data, with references and pointers that must be traversed and aggregated. While it is human readable, it's it is not human comprehendible – for it requires reformatting into a more meaningful and readable format. That's That is exactly what TKPROF does. Its command syntax is a follows:

```
$ tkprof file_name[,file_name…] [options]
```

Where the options are:

OPTION	DESCRIPTION
waits=yes|no	Record wait event summary
print=N	Lists only the first sorted SQL statement
aggregate=Y|N	Aggregate multiple users of same statement
insert=filename	Creates a file with inserts for the statistics
sys=Y|N	Include SYS and recursive SQL statements
table=schema.table	The explain table used during execution
explain=user/password	The user id and password for the explain user
record=filename	Creates a file all the non-recursive SQL statements
width=N	The output file width
sort=sort_options[,…]	Descending sort criteria for the output file

Table 4.10: *TKPROF Command-line Utility Options*

Where the sort options are:

SORT OPTION	DESCRIPTION
PRSCNT	# parses
PRSCPU	Parse CPU time
PRSELA	Parse elapsed time
PRSDSK	Parse physical reads
PRSQRY	Parse consistent mode block reads
PRSCU	Parse current mode block reads
PRSMIS	Parse library cache misses
EXECNT	# executes
EXECPU	Execute CPU time
EXEELA	Execute elapsed time
EXEDSK	Execute physical reads
EXEQRY	Execute consistent mode block reads
EXECU	Execute current mode block reads
EXEROW	Execute # rows processed
EXEMIS	Execute library cache misses
FCHCNT	# fetches

SORT OPTION	DESCRIPTION
FCHCPU	Fetch CPU time
FCHELA	Fetch elapsed time
FCHDSK	Fetch physical reads
FCHQRY	Fetch consistent mode block reads
FCHCU	Fetch current mode block reads
FCHROW	Fetch # rows processed
USERID	User ID that parsed the cursor

Table 4.11: *TKPROF Command-line Utility Sort Options*

Thus, in this example TKPROF is being asked to report on the contents of the *one_big.trc* file from the prior section to produce the *one_big.lis* report file.

```
C:\Temp>tkprof one_big.trc one_big.lis waits=yes explain=BERT/BERT
sort=FCHCPU
```

Examine a portion of each of those files to see the before and after, going from unreadable to more easily readable. Note how the *one_big.trc* file seems like nothing more than a collection of print statements at various stages of the execution with some associated counters and numerical data. This data is much easier to read in the *one_big.lis* report file.

🖫 one_big.trc consolidated trace file

```
PARSING IN CURSOR #3 len=543 dep=0 uid=42 oct=3 lid=42 tim=7241343753 hv=1890009883
ad='9ccd07d0' sqlid='fknz7njsafhsv'
select cu.firstname, cu.lastname, mr.rentaldate,
       mr.totalcharge, mt. title, mx.categoryname
from   customer cu, movierental mr, rentalitem ri,
       moviecopy mc, movietitle mt, moviecategory mx,
       (select avg(totalcharge) total from movierental) ar
where  cu.customerid = mr.customerid and
       mr.rentalid = ri.rentalid and
       ri.moviecopyid = mc.moviecopyid and
       mc.movieid = mt.movieid and
       mt.categoryid = mx.categoryid and
       mr.totalcharge <= ar.total
order by cu.lastname, cu.firstname, mr.rentaldate
END OF STMT
PARSE #3:c=0,e=75,p=0,cr=0,cu=0,mis=0,r=0,dep=0,og=1,tim=7241343744
EXEC #3:c=0,e=161,p=0,cr=0,cu=0,mis=0,r=0,dep=0,og=1,tim=7241344167
FETCH #3:c=109375,e=110611,p=0,cr=223,cu=0,mis=0,r=1,dep=0,og=1,tim=7241455269
FETCH #3:c=0,e=174,p=0,cr=0,cu=0,mis=0,r=15,dep=0,og=1,tim=7241457210
FETCH #3:c=0,e=443,p=0,cr=0,cu=0,mis=0,r=15,dep=0,og=1,tim=7241459544
FETCH #3:c=0,e=99,p=0,cr=0,cu=0,mis=0,r=15,dep=0,og=1,tim=7241461165
FETCH #3:c=0,e=214,p=0,cr=0,cu=0,mis=0,r=15,dep=0,og=1,tim=7241463715
FETCH #3:c=0,e=63,p=0,cr=0,cu=0,mis=0,r=15,dep=0,og=1,tim=7241465140
FETCH #3:c=0,e=63,p=0,cr=0,cu=0,mis=0,r=15,dep=0,og=1,tim=7241466770
FETCH #3:c=0,e=59,p=0,cr=0,cu=0,mis=0,r=15,dep=0,og=1,tim=7241468074
FETCH #3:c=0,e=63,p=0,cr=0,cu=0,mis=0,r=15,dep=0,og=1,tim=7241469784
FETCH #3:c=0,e=68,p=0,cr=0,cu=0,mis=0,r=15,dep=0,og=1,tim=7241471425
FETCH #3:c=0,e=622,p=0,cr=0,cu=0,mis=0,r=15,dep=0,og=1,tim=7241474291
```

```
FETCH #3:c=0,e=60,p=0,cr=0,cu=0,mis=0,r=15,dep=0,og=1,tim=7241475635
FETCH #3:c=0,e=679,p=0,cr=0,cu=0,mis=0,r=15,dep=0,og=1,tim=7241478094
```

💾 **one_big.lis consolidated trace file report**

```
select  cu.firstname, cu.lastname, mr.rentaldate,
        mr.totalcharge, mt. title, mx.categoryname
from    customer cu, movierental mr, rentalitem ri,
        moviecopy mc, movietitle mt, moviecategory mx,
        (select avg(totalcharge) total from movierental) ar
where   cu.customerid = mr.customerid and
        mr.rentalid = ri.rentalid and
        ri.moviecopyid = mc.moviecopyid and
        mc.movieid = mt.movieid and
        mt.categoryid = mx.categoryid and
        mr.totalcharge <= ar.total
order by cu.lastname, cu.firstname, mr.rentaldate
```

call	count	cpu	elapsed	disk	query	current	rows
Parse	4	0.00	0.00	0	0	0	0
Execute	8	0.00	0.00	0	0	0	0
Fetch	1824	0.60	0.96	0	892	0	27272
total	1836	0.60	0.96	0	892	0	27272

```
Misses in library cache during parse: 0
Parsing user id: 42  (MOVIES)
```

Using the Orastack Utility

Utilities exist for both Windows and UNIX systems that help DBAs deal with memory issues. The *orastack* utility exists on Windows systems, while the *maxmem* utility can be helpful in UNIX. The orastack utility is only available to Oracle databases on Windows platforms. It is used primarily to address the ORA-04030 error on Windows servers. The *oerr* output for the ORA-04030 error is:

```
04030, 00000, "out of process memory when trying to allocate %s bytes
(%s,%s)"
// *Cause:  Operating system process private memory has been exhausted
// *Action:
```

This error occurs when Oracle is trying to allocate memory for the session but none exists. Windows NT has a limitation of 2 GB of RAM allocated for user processes and a maximum of 2 GB for the system. The memory counter reaches the maximum addressable memory at 2 GB, and the ORA-04030 error will occur.

To conserve memory, the amount allocated for each connection process could be reduced as it is established, using the *sort area size* parameter of the instances.

The orastack utility can accomplish this. Since it functions strictly at the operating system level, there is nothing that can be done inside Oracle to limit the memory obtained upon a user connection.

The syntax of the command is the orastack keyword followed by the executable file name:

```
C:\oracle9i\bin\orastack oracle.exe

Current Reserved Memory per Thread  = 1048576
Current Committed Memory Per Thread = 4096
```

When the command is executed without specifying a new size, as shown above, the utility simply displays the memory usage and does not change anything. The reserved memory is that which is allocated and not backed up by a data store. The committed memory is that which is allocated and supported by a data store of some sort like pagefile or physical memory pages.

Notice the "Reserved Memory per Thread" of 1MB in the previous command. Each connection to the database will instantly grab a megabyte of RAM. The Oracle executable cannot be active when the command to reduce the size of the stack is executed. Once the executable is inactive, the orastack utility can be used to safely reduce the memory acquired on connection.

```
C:\oracle9i\bin\orastack oracle.exe 500000
```

After the command is executed, each session that connects to the database will consume 500K of RAM on connection. 500K should be the absolute lowest value to set this parameter.

The resetting of this value for *oracle.exe* applies only to local, non-SQL*Net connections. For connections that are initiated from the listener, the stacks on the *tnslsnr.exe* executable can be reduced by running *orastack* against *tnslsnr.exe*. This is where most connections to the database will originate.

```
C:\oracle9i\bin\orastack tnslsnr.exe 500000
```

The *orastack* utility can be used on any executable that initiates database connections.

Even though *orastack* is only available for Windows systems, other memory utilities exist on the UNIX platform. The *maxmem* utility can be used on UNIX systems to determine when the ORA-04300 error will occur. Utilizing this utility, the DBA can calculate the number of sessions that can connect to the database before the ORA-04030 error message is encountered.

The *maxmem* utility is a simple program with no command-line options:

```
$ maxmem
Memory starts at:      141728 (   229a0)
Memory ends at:     268025856 ( ff9c000)
Memory available:   267884128 ( ff79660)
```

The *maxmem* utility returns three data items, although only one is really useful to the DBA. "Memory available" indicates the number of bytes of RAM that are available. This is critical to know since ORA-04030 errors will occur when this number is less than 1,000,000 (1 MB).

If another session connects to the database, the *maxmem* utility will reflect a reduction in the memory available:

```
SQL> connect scott/tiger@ASG920;

Connected.

$ maxmem

Memory starts at:      141728 (   229a0)
Memory ends at:     267075583 ( feb3fff)
Memory available:   266933855 ( fe9165f)
```

Based on the delta in the memory available, the memory consumed by this one connection to the database is 950273 bytes, roughly 1 MB. Subsequent tests indicate that memory allocated for each connection may vary, but it is always close to 1 MB. Given that a session on this host will grab 1 MB of RAM, *awk* can be used as part of the *maxmem* command to indicate the number of sessions it will be able to support.

```
$ maxmem | awk  '$2 ~ /available/ {printf("%s%d\n","# Future Sessions:
",$3/1024/1024)}'

# Future Sessions: 251
```

This command will display the third field, divided by 1 MB, of any output line that contains "available" in the second field. This number will represent the number of additional sessions that can be handled by the database, assuming that each will take 1 MB. Based on the above output, the database can handle approximately 251 database connections before an Oracle memory error occurs. This number is an approximation based on the earlier benchmark that measured 1 MB for the connection. The DBA should include this command as part of his regular Oracle monitoring scripts on UNIX databases.

RAC Management

VIPCA

When initially creating a RAC database, the Database Configuration Assistant (DBCA) will instruct the DBA to run the *root.sh* script. Among the many other tasks it does, *root.sh* will invoke the Virtual IP Configuration Assistant (VIPCA). VIPCA is a graphical utility for defining the virtual internet protocol addresses for the RAC database in order for failover and load balancing to function properly. Even though *root.sh* calls this utility for the DBA, there are times or situations where the DBA must run it manually as well. The command is found under the CRS install and must be run as root, as shown in this example:

```
[root@LINUX_RAC]# export CRS_HOME=/home/oracle/product/10.2.0/crs
[root@LINUX_RAC]# $CRS_HOME/bin/vipca &
```

The DBA merely needs to create an entry for each node in the RAC cluster and manually assign a virtual IP address. VIPCA will then create the virtualized IP addresses necessary to support RAC failover and load balancing.

IP addresses are required for defining virtual IP resource application for each cluster node.

Node name	IP Alias Name	IP address	Subnet Mask
linux_rac	linux_rac-vip	192.168.100.105	255.255.255.0

Clear   Clear all

Cancel   Help   « Back   Next »

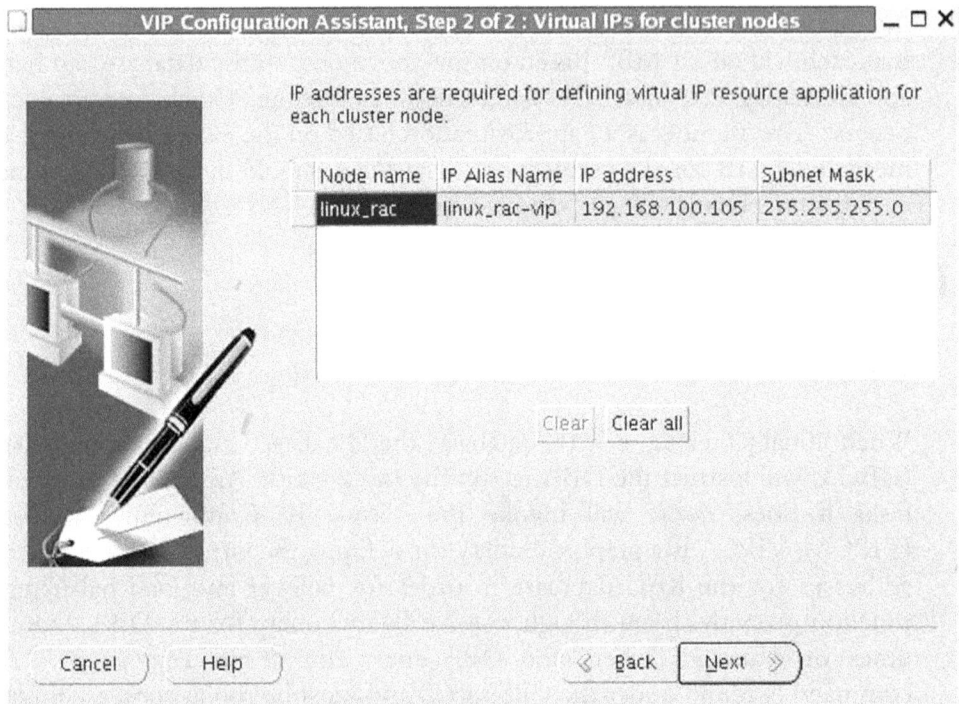

Figure 4.9: *Creating Virtualized IP Addresses in VIPCA*

For example, if the */etc/hosts* file contains the following, where *linux_rac-vip* is the alias for the virtual IP address:

```
192.168.100.104 linux_rac
192.168.100.105 linux_rac-vip
192.168.200.104 linux_rac-priv
```

Then running the *ifconfig* command will show that eth1:1 has been configured as the virtual IP address.

```
[root@LINUX_RAC]# ifconfig
eth0      Link encap:Ethernet  HWaddr 00:0C:29:4F:35:30
          inet addr:192.168.100.104  Bcast:192.168.100.255
Mask:255.255.255.0
          inet6 addr: fe80::20c:29ff:fe4f:3530/64 Scope:Link
          UP BROADCAST RUNNING MULTICAST  MTU:1500  Metric:1
          RX packets:32 errors:0 dropped:0 overruns:0 frame:0
          TX packets:20 errors:0 dropped:0 overruns:0 carrier:0
          collisions:0 txqueuelen:1000
          RX bytes:3256 (3.1 KiB)  TX bytes:1008 (1008.0 b)
          Interrupt:177 Base address:0x2024
```

```
eth1      Link encap:Ethernet  HWaddr 00:0C:29:4F:35:3A
          inet addr:192.168.200.104  Bcast:192.168.200.255
Mask:255.255.255.0
          inet6 addr: fe80::20c:29ff:fe4f:353a/64 Scope:Link
          UP BROADCAST RUNNING MULTICAST  MTU:1500  Metric:1
          RX packets:96 errors:0 dropped:0 overruns:0 frame:0
          TX packets:79 errors:0 dropped:0 overruns:0 carrier:0
          collisions:0 txqueuelen:1000
          RX bytes:8271 (8.0 KiB)  TX bytes:5502 (5.3 KiB)
          Interrupt:169 Base address:0x20a4

eth1:1    Link encap:Ethernet  HWaddr 00:0C:29:4F:35:3A
          inet addr:192.168.100.105  Bcast:192.168.100.255
Mask:255.255.255.0
          UP BROADCAST RUNNING MULTICAST  MTU:1500  Metric:1
          Interrupt:169 Base address:0x20a4
```

crsctl

The Clusterware Control command line utility (*crsctl*) provides the DBA a method to manage all aspects of the cluster services. The *crstl* utility is run as a command line invocation as shown here:

```
$ crsctl command object [options]
```

Only certain combinations of *crsctl* commands and objects are valid. The most common use case scenarios include:

```
crsctl check  crs                     - checks the viability of the CRS stack
crsctl check  cssd                    - checks the viability of CSS
crsctl check  crsd                    - checks the viability of CRS
crsctl check  evmd                    - checks the viability of EVM
crsctl set    css <parm> <value>      - sets a parameter override
crsctl get    css <parm>              - gets the value of a CSS parameter
crsctl unset  css <parm>              - sets CSS parameter to its default
crsctl query  css votedisk            - lists the voting disks used by CSS
crsctl add    css votedisk <path>     - adds a new voting disk
crsctl delete css votedisk <path>     - removes a voting disk
crsctl enable  crs                    - enables startup for all CRS daemons
crsctl disable crs                    - disables startup for all CRS daemons
crsctl start crs                      - starts all CRS daemons
crsctl stop  crs                      - stops all CRS daemons
crsctl start resources                - starts CRS resources
crsctl stop resources                 - stops  CRS resources
```

crs_start

The *crs_start* command sets the specified applications ONLINE, and attempts to start both those registered applications and their resources. The *crs_start* command supports a three basic syntax options as shown here:

```
crs_start resource_name[...] [-c cluster_node] [-q] [-f]
```

RAC Management

```
crs_start -all [-q]
crs_start [USR_attribute_name=value] [...] resource_name [-c node_name] [-q]
```

crs_stop

The *crs_stop* command sets the specified applications OFFLINE and attempts to stop both those registered applications and their resources but leaves the CRS running. The *crs_stop* command supports four basic syntax options as shown here:

```
crs_stop resource_name[...] [-f] [-q]
crs_stop -c cluster_node[...] [-q]
crs_stop -all [-q]
crs_stop [USR_attr_name=value] [...] resource_name [-q] -c cluster_node[...]
```

crs_stat

The *crs_stat* command shows the status of each registered resource in the cluster. The *crs_stat* command supports a very robust set of options as shown next:

```
[root@LINUX_RAC]# $CRS_HOME/bin/crs_stat -h
Usage:  crs_stat [resource_name [...]] [-v] [-l] [-q] [-c cluster_member]
        crs_stat [resource_name [...]] -t [-v] [-q] [-c cluster_member]
        crs_stat -p [resource_name [...]] [-q]
        crs_stat [-a] application -g
        crs_stat [-a] application -r [-c cluster_member]
        crs_stat -f [resource_name [...]] [-q] [-c cluster_member]
        crs_stat -ls [resource_name [...]] [-q]
```

Most often use, *crs_stat* with the –t option to merely display a table of the resources as shown here.

```
[root@LINUX_RAC]# $CRS_HOME/bin/crs_stat -t
Name             Type         Target    State     Host
------------------------------------------------------------
ora....C1.inst application   ONLINE    ONLINE    linux_rac
ora....C2.inst application   ONLINE    ONLINE    linux_rac
ora....AC1.srv application   ONLINE    ONLINE    linux_rac
ora....RACX.cs application   ONLINE    ONLINE    linux_rac
ora.RAC.db     application   ONLINE    ONLINE    linux_rac
ora....AC.lsnr application   ONLINE    ONLINE    linux_rac
ora....rac.gsd application   ONLINE    ONLINE    linux_rac
ora....rac.ons application   ONLINE    ONLINE    linux_rac
ora....rac.vip application   ONLINE    ONLINE    linux_rac
```

However, the *crs_stat -t* command output is neither very user friendly or readable. Thus, many people use a script such as *crsstat.sh* to improve upon that basic facility.

🖫 crsstat.sh script

```
#!/usr/bin/ksh

# Table header:echo ""
awk \
  'BEGIN {printf "%-45s %-10s %-18s\n", "HA Resource", "Target", "State";
          printf "%-45s %-10s %-18s\n", "-----------", "------", "-----";}'

$CRS_HOME/bin/crs_stat -u | awk \
 'BEGIN { FS="="; state = 0; }
 $1~/NAME/ {appname = $2; state=1};
 state == 0 {next;}
 $1~/TARGET/ && state == 1 {apptarget = $2; state=2;}
 $1~/STATE/ && state == 2 {appstate = $2; state=3;}
 state == 3 {printf "%-45s %-10s %-18s\n", appname, apptarget, appstate;
state=0;}'
```

Here is the much easier to read output of that data as formatted by *crsstat.sh*:

```
[root@LINUX_RAC ~]# ./crsstat.sh
HA Resource                              Target     State
-----------                              ------     -----
ora.RAC.RAC1.inst                        ONLINE     ONLINE on linux_rac
ora.RAC.RAC2.inst                        ONLINE     ONLINE on linux_rac
ora.RAC.RACX.RAC1.srv                     ONLINE     ONLINE on linux_rac
ora.RAC.RACX.cs                          ONLINE     ONLINE on linux_rac
ora.RAC.db                               ONLINE     ONLINE on linux_rac
ora.linux_rac.LISTENER_LINUX_RAC.lsnr    ONLINE     ONLINE on linux_rac
ora.linux_rac.gsd                        ONLINE     ONLINE on linux_rac
ora.linux_rac.ons                        ONLINE     ONLINE on linux_rac
ora.linux_rac.vip                        ONLINE     ONLINE on linux_rac
```

srvctl

The Server Control command line utility (*srvctl*) provides the DBA a method to manage all aspects of RAC and ASM database instances including their associated services. The srvctl utility is run as a command line invocation as shown here:

```
$ srvctl command object [options]
```

Only certain combinations of *srvctl* commands and objects are valid. The most common use case scenarios include:

COMMAND	OBJECT

Enable	Database
Disable	Instance
Start	Service
Stop	NodeApps
Status	ASM
Relocate	Listener

Table 4.12: *srvctl command options*

The options then depend upon the command and object type combination. For example, to start the entire RAC database (all instances on all nodes), then the command syntax is as follows:

```
$ srvctl start database -d db_name -o open_options
```

To start a specific RAC database instance or instances, the command is:

```
$ srvctl start database -d db_name -o open_options -i instance[,instance…]
```

To start the RAC node's node apps (e.g. CRS and RAC infrastructure – including ASM and listener), the command is:

```
$ srvctl start nodeapps -n node_name
```

Storage Management

ocfs2console

When using the Oracle Cluster File System version 2 (OCFS2) for the Linux RAC environments' shared storage, Oracle provides a series of command line utilities for managing OCFS. The first, *ocfs2console*, launches a simple GUI screen (Figure 4.10) to perform key fundamental OCFS administrative tasks. It must be run as root.

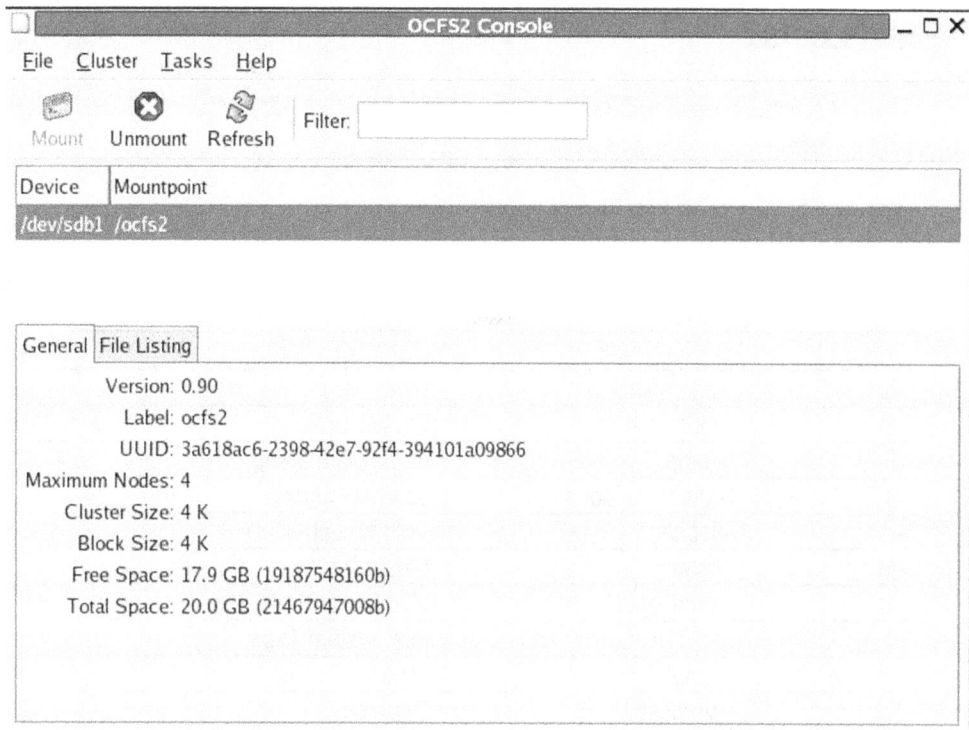

Figure 4.10: *GUI Screen in OCFS2 Console*

Besides the obvious mount and unmount available on the main menu's toolbar, *ocfs2console* supports the following five key OCFS2 administrative tasks:

Cluster → Configure Nodes: screen for defining the nodes, names, IP addresses and ports for the nodes in the cluster, which results in the population of the OCFS2 configuration file: */etc/ocfs2/cluster.conf*.

Cluster → Propagate Configuration: utility to copy the OCFS2 configuration file to all the nodes defined for that cluster.

Tools → Format: utility to format an unmounted device to contain an OCFS2 file system.

Tools → Check: utility to verify a mounted volume as containing a valid, i.e. undamaged, OCFS2 file system.

Tools → Repair: utility to attempt repairs on unmounted OCFS2 volume.

mkfs.ocfs2

The *mkfs.ocfs2* command is used to create an OCFS2 file system on a device. The command syntax is as follows:

```
mkfs.ocfs2 [options] /device blocks-count
```

Where the options are:

OPTION	LONG NAME	DESCRIPTION
-b	--block-size	Block Size
-C	--cluster-size	Cluster Size
-F	--force	Force Formatting
-J	--journal-options	Journal Options
-L	--label	Volume Label
-M	--mount	Mount Type
-N	--node-slots	Number of Node Slots
-T		File System Type
-q	--quiet	Quiet
-v	--verbose	Verbose
-V	--version	Version
	--no-backup-super	Do not backup super block

Table 4.13: *mkfs.ocfs2 Command Options*

tunefs.ocfs2

The *tunefs.ocfs2* command is used to adjust OCFS2 file system parameters on disk. The command syntax is as follows:

```
tunefs.ocfs2 [options] /device blocks-count
```

Where the options are:

OPTION	LONG NAME	DESCRIPTION
-J	--journal-options	Journal Options
-L	--label	Volume Label
-M	--mount	Mount Type
-N	--node-slots	Number of Node Slots
-S	--volume-size	Extend the size

OPTION	LONG NAME	DESCRIPTION
-Q	--query	Query B Block size in bytes T Cluster size in bytes N Number of node slots R Root directory block number Y System directory block number P First cluster group block number V Volume label U Volume uuid M Compat flags H Incompat flags O RO Compat flags
-q	--quiet	Quiet
-U	--uuid-reset	Change the volume UUID
-v	--verbose	Verbose
-V	--version	Version
	--backup-super	Backup super block

Table 4.14: *tunefs.ocfs2 Command Options*

fsck.ocfs2

The *fsck.ocfs2* command is used to check an OCFS2 file system. The command syntax is as follows:

```
fsck.ocfs2 [options] /device
```

Where the options are:

OPTION	DESCRIPTION
-b	Super Block offset to read
-B	Block Size
-f	Force
-F	Skips cluster service check
-G	Ask if mismatched inodes unused
-n	No answer to all fsck questions
-r	Recover using backup # from 1-6
-y	Yes answer to all fsck questions
-v	Verbose

OPTION	DESCRIPTION
-V	Version

Table 4.15: *fsck.ocfs2 Command Options*

mounted.ocfs2

The *mounted.ocfs2* command detects all OCFS2 volumes on a system. The command syntax is as follows:

```
mounted.ocfs2 [options] /device
```

Where the options are:

OPTION	DESCRIPTION
-d	List volumes, labels and UUID's
-f	List volumes and nodes mounted

Table 4.16: *mounted.ocfs2 Command Options*

asmtool

asmtool is a command-line utility for stamping disks, partitions and raw devices as being ASM disks, meaning it is recognized and managed by ASM. It has the following syntax:

```
$ asmtool [options] [device] [label]
```

Where the options are:

OPTION	DESCRIPTION
-add	Add or change stamp
-addprefix	Add or change stamp using prefix
-list	List available ASM disks
-delete	Remove stamps from disk
-force	Force the operation

Table 4.17: *asmtool Command Options*

asmtoolg

asmtoolg is a graphic utility for stamping disks, partitions and raw devices as being ASM disks. It performs the same operations as the prior ASMTOOL command-line utility.

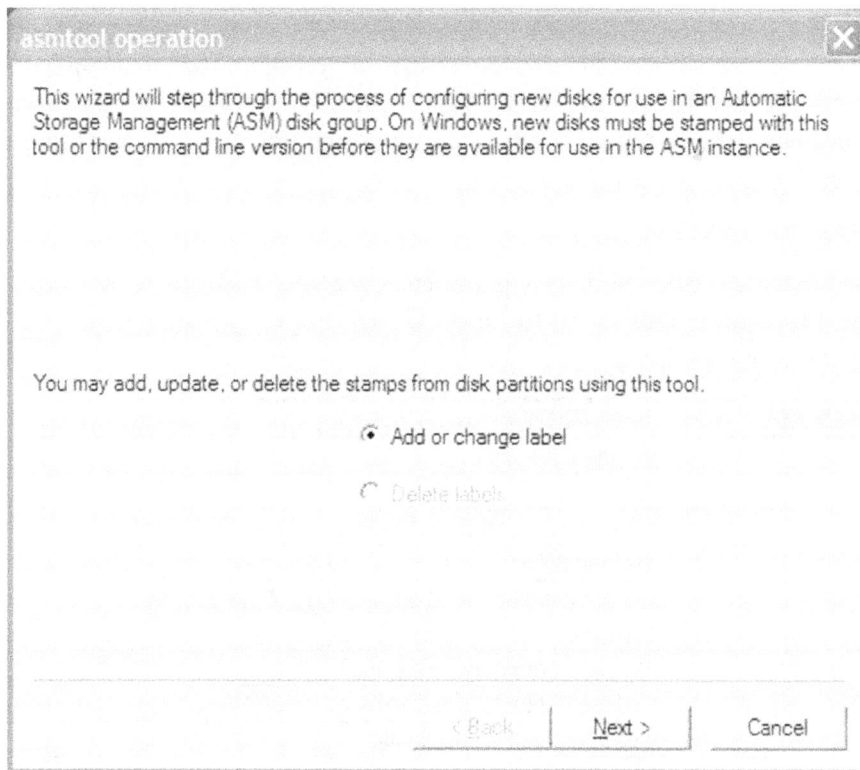

Figure 4.11: *asmtool Screen*

asmcmd

asmcmd is a command line utility for managing files and directories in ASM diskgroups. It offers UNIX-style file system commands for managing ASM directories and files. Prior to Oracle 10gR2, ASM had to be administered via OEM or SQL statements while connected to a special ASM instance.

Be aware that *asmcmd* cannot be used to create or drop disk groups, or to add or drop disks in a disk group. These ASM administrative tasks must be accomplished via SQL commands. *asmcmd* offers two modes of operation: interactive and non-interactive. Interactive mode provides a shell-like environment for executing *asmcmd* command. It resembles how SQL*Plus interactive mode works and looks like this:

```
C:\Temp>asmcmd
ASMCMD>
```

Whereas the non-interactive mode works much like the *srvctl* and *lsnctl* commands, meaning that the base *asmcmd* command is provided, its command and any command parameters are all on the operating system command line, like this:

```
C:\Temp>asmcmd ls -1
```

The *asmcmd* commands and their parameters are very UNIX-like in nature, so they will look quite familiar to those on UNIX. Here is a summary of the key commands and their purpose:

PARAMETER	DESCRIPTION
cd	Change directory
cp	Copy file
du	Disk space used by a directory and its subdirectories
exit	Exit the utility
find	Locate the path for all occurrences of the specified filename
help	Displays command assistance
ls	List the contents of a directory
lsct	List info about ASM clients
lsdg	List all disk groups and their attributes
lsdsk	List all physical disks visible to ASM
md_backup	Create a backup of the mounted diskgroups
md_restore	Restore the diskgroups from a backup
mkalias	Create an alias for a system generated filename
mkdir	Create directory
pwd	Print working directory (i.e. list current directory location)
remap	Repair a range of blocks on a disk
rm	Remove (i.e. delete) the specified files or directories
rmalias	Remove (i.e. delete) the specified alias

Table 4.18: *asmcmd Command Parameters*

Oracle 12c ASM disk scrubbing

Oracle ASM disk scrubbing is an automatic process in that it is in ASM RAID mirroring to repair rare cases of disk corruptions. When a disk corruption is detected, Oracle "breaks" the mirror for a short period of time to repair, queuing-up any updated to the mirrored disks.

Oracle ASM disk scrubbing is a new feature that checks logical data corruptions and repairs them automatically in normal and high redundancy disk groups. This feature is designed so that it does not have any impact on normal I/O in production systems. The scrubbing process repairs logical corruptions using the mirror disks. Disk scrubbing leverages the Oracle ASM rebalancing to minimize I/O overhead.

Oracle ASM disk scrubbing improves availability and reliability by proactively reading data that would otherwise not be read. Latent errors or corruption can be discovered and fixed by Oracle ASM disk scrubbing while redundant data is available.

The idea behind ASM disk scrubbing is the concept that ASM can identify those times when the database is experiencing "below average" system I/O.

Upon completion of the corruption repair, ASM applies any changes that took place during the scrubbing and then re-established the mirrored disks. ASM disk scrubbing can be done at several levels:

- **A data file**: within a disk, ASM disk scrubbing can be invoked to scrub individual disk data.

```
alter diskgroup
   data
scrub file
   '+data/orcl/datafile/example.266.806582193'
repair power high force;
```

- **A specific disk**: You can direct ASM to use the mirrored data to scrub and synchronize a mirrored disk spindle.

```
alter diskgroup
```

```
   data
scrub disk
   data_0005
repair power high force;
```

- **An ASM disk group:** Entire ASM disk groups can be done with disk scrubbing.

```
alter diskgroup
   data
scrub power low;
```

The "scrub" argument takes the following options:

- **scrub . . . repair:** This option automatically repairs disk corruptions. If the "repair" keywords is not used, Oracle will only identify corruptions and not fix them:

```
alter diskgroup
   data
scrub disk
   data_0005
repair power low; --> reports and repairs corruptions

alter diskgroup
   data
scrub disk
   data_0005
power high force;   --> reports corruptions
```

- **scrub . . . power:** If the "power" argument is specified with data scrubbing, you can have several levels of power:

```
alter diskgroup data scrub power low;

alter diskgroup data scrub power auto; --> default

alter diskgroup data scrub power high

alter diskgroup data scrub power max;
```

- **scrub . . . wait:** If the optional "wait" option is specified, the command returns after the scrubbing operation has completed. If the WAIT option is not specified, the scrubbing operation is added into the scrubbing queue and the command returns immediately.

- **scrub . . . force:** If the optional "force" option is specified, the command is processed even if the system I/O load is high or if scrubbing has been disabled internally at the system level.

It is not clear from the Oracle documentation what the meaning of the "power" argument is, other than it reflects upon the amount of system I/O load.

Conclusion

In this chapter, a wide range of server-side utilities was examined that operate ostensibly at a level one step closer to the operating system than the normal, more SQL-based administrative commands. Often these commands are once removed like this as they operate entirely outside the database itself. The most useful of these commands were covered here and are the ones that will most likely be used with any great frequency.

In the next chapter, utilities used with managing SQL will be the topic.

Oracle SQL Management Utilities

Sometime the "suits" do not understand technical issues.

Introduction

SQL is much more than just an ANSI standard language for managing and manipulating database objects and their data. It is the primary interface by which DBAs and database developers accomplish their jobs. Even in today's world of simplified graphical user interfaces (GUIs), database professionals cannot entirely avoid all tasks related to working with SQL at some level. For the application logic talks to the database via SQL, the developer writes her code as SQL. Then the DBA creates those objects using DDL, and the tuning process can involve both in refactoring the SQL to be more efficient or adding/modifying the database object definitions to indirectly improve upon the performance of that SQL.

Hence, SQL itself deserves a chapter to explain some of the key tools and techniques by which to accomplish great things via the SQL language. That starts with a basic recognition of the two most defining aspects of the language:

- SQL is a relatively simple language in terms of the basic commands.

- SQL is a set oriented language, so procedural techniques do not apply.

First, examine the simple nature of the SQL language. There are but a few commands that one must learn: CREATE, ALTER, DROP, GRANT, INSERT, UPDATE, DELETE and MERGE. However, there are many different types of database objects these commands can operate upon and whose syntaxes are different. For example, just the CREATE TABLE and CREATE INDEX commands alone possess sufficient features and options to overwhelm even senior DBAs and database application developers. So never confuse "simple by design" to mean easy to master. It is suggested that one keep the Oracle SQL Language reference manual on the desktop for it will probably be the single book which is used the most. Besides, each new version of Oracle adds a plethora of new features and options. So again, the SQL Language Reference manual is key.

Following is a very simple example that should drive this point home. If a table is going to be created within an Oracle database, there are a plethora of choices. Figure 5.1 is a partial list of the actual possibilities. However, it shows that there are many fundamental questions to answer about the nature of this table. Is it an object or a relational table? Is it clustered or not? Is it partitioned or not? Are its indexes partitioned or not? If the indexes are partitioned, then are they global or local in nature? The equation gets even more complicated if the Index Organized Tables (IOTs) are considered. The table can be organized as a heap or IOT, and then more questions will need to be asked. The point is that while the CREATE TABLE concept and syntax diagram are relatively simple in nature and thus, easy to comprehend, there are sufficient combinations of possibilities that make the overall concept and process quite daunting. Therefore, easy to read and digest does not mean easy to implement properly. Even more so, SELECT offers so many capabilities that make it the single most difficult command to claim complete mastery of.

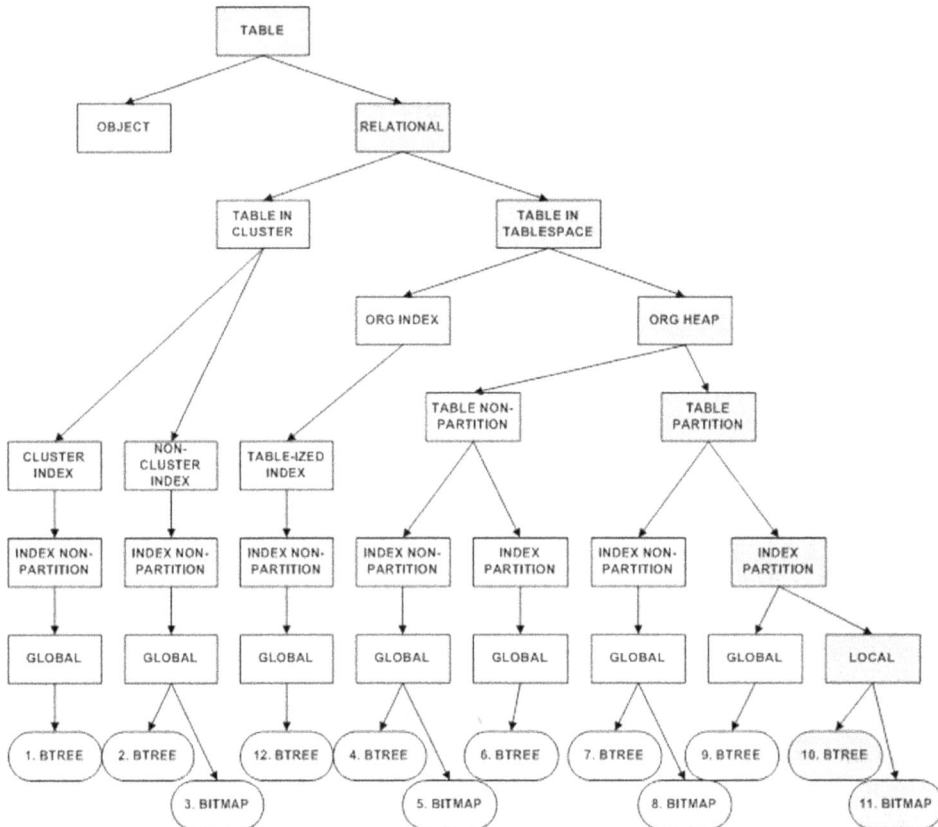

Figure 5.1: *Myriad of CREATE TABLE options*

The second key aspect of the SQL language is that it is a set oriented language and not a procedural language like traditional programming languages. This introduces two very interesting and challenging wrinkles to the equation.

When most developers are first taught programming, whether object-oriented or not, the approach to data structures and algorithms is predominantly procedural since most common instructional programming languages are procedural in nature. There are, of course, exceptions such as LISP and SQL, but they are more the exception than the norm. That essentially means that they read like a book – from top to bottom. Look at how a database JOIN operation may be coded in a procedural language:

```
FOR i := 1 TO table1.record_count
BEGIN
    record1 := table1.fetch_next
    FOR j := 1 to table2.record_count
    BEGIN
        record2 := table2.fetch_next
        result(i).record := record1.data || record2.data
    END
END
```

Most programmers can read code like that above as second nature because that is how they were taught and how they think. So for each record in table1, get the record and read all the records in table2, and for each record in table2, combine record1 and record2 data. Of course, the code above clearly does not handle any outer join scenarios. So what does the same JOIN operation in SQL look like?

```
SELECT * FROM table1 JOIN table2 USING (key_column);
```

What algorithm, if any, does this code convey? It actually expresses the desired end result versus the method by which to obtain it. So, one of the topics covered in this chapter will be querying the database to have it relate the approach that it will take to retrieve the correct data. This is known as the execution plan.

Finally, when looking at SQL language code and visualizing either the final or intermediate results, one has to think in terms of sets and therefore, set operators such as UNION, MINUS, and INTERSECT. Knowing this and actually applying it is not as easy as one would expect. Although the norm is to work with records and working with sets can sometimes feel less natural, to write truly effective and efficient SQL code, one must think and write code in terms of sets.

The reason for such an elaborate introduction on the seemingly innocent topic of SQL is to clearly show that it is critical to comprehend the language syntax, nature and results and how they interact with each other. This will make the process of examining the internal explain plans a little easier. The best place to begin is with a couple of basic utilities for working with SQL code.

SQL Utilities

SQL*Plus

SQL*Plus is a basic yet very critical command line utility. It is very reminiscent of TTY console, applications from days past. All the key interaction with SQL*Plus is via the keyboard and typed commands. While that may seem a bit quaint, most senior DBAs and senior developers prefer scripting using command line utilities like SQL*Plus. In fact, most have built up libraries or a collection of such scripts that they take with them from job to job. Figure 5.2 showcases what a basic SQL*Plus session and interaction looks like.

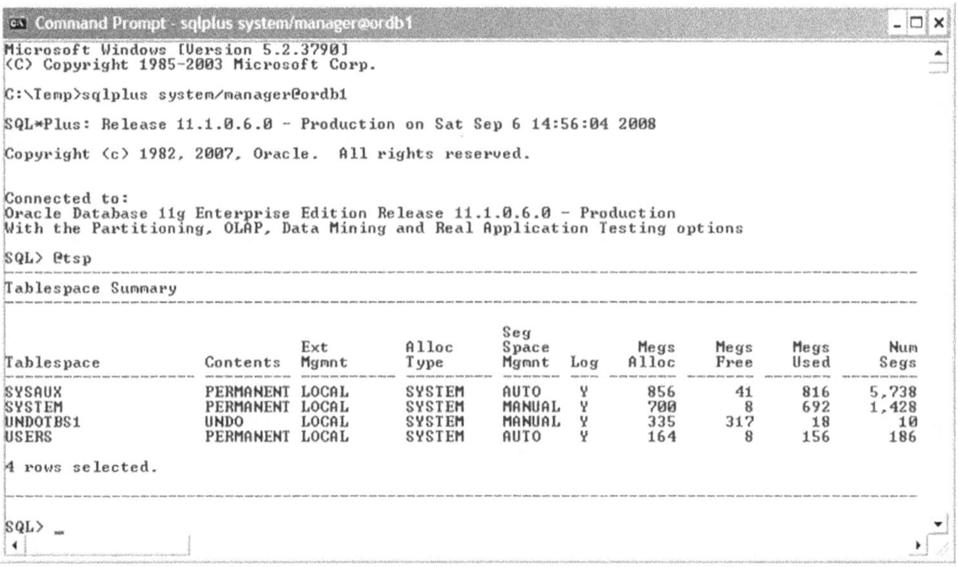

```
Command Prompt - sqlplus system/manager@ordb1
Microsoft Windows [Version 5.2.3790]
(C) Copyright 1985-2003 Microsoft Corp.

C:\Temp>sqlplus system/manager@ordb1

SQL*Plus: Release 11.1.0.6.0 - Production on Sat Sep 6 14:56:04 2008

Copyright (c) 1982, 2007, Oracle.  All rights reserved.


Connected to:
Oracle Database 11g Enterprise Edition Release 11.1.0.6.0 - Production
With the Partitioning, OLAP, Data Mining and Real Application Testing options

SQL> @tsp
------------------------------------------------------------------------------------------
Tablespace Summary
------------------------------------------------------------------------------------------

                                                     Seg
                                 Ext        Alloc    Space            Megs    Megs    Megs     Num
Tablespace              Contents  Mgmnt      Type     Mgmnt    Log    Alloc   Free    Used    Segs
----------------------- --------- ---------- -------- -------- --- ------- ------- ------- -------
SYSAUX                  PERMANENT LOCAL      SYSTEM   AUTO      Y      856      41     816   5,738
SYSTEM                  PERMANENT LOCAL      SYSTEM   MANUAL    Y      700       8     692   1,428
UNDOTBS1                UNDO      LOCAL      SYSTEM   MANUAL    Y      335     317      18      10
USERS                   PERMANENT LOCAL      SYSTEM   AUTO      Y      164       8     156     186

4 rows selected.

------------------------------------------------------------------------------------------

SQL> _
```

Figure 5.2: *SQL*Plus command line utility*

There are several key things to note about SQL*Plus. First, it supports all the basic ANSI SQL commands plus some SQL*Plus specific extensions. Some of those proprietary extensions support interaction with the command line editor, e.g. append, change, del, get, input, list and save. In fact, SQL*Plus editing works very much like the old DOS Edlin program. Other extensions support database management related tasks like connect, disconnect, shutdown, startup and password. Some extensions support scripting (accept, define, pause, prompt, undefine and variable). Finally, a large number of commands support numerous data formatting and reporting options such as break, btitle, column, compute, repfooter, repheader, set and ttile).

It is almost certain that SQL*Plus will be a valuable tool for all of the DBA's Oracle database activities. It is hard to imagine a scenario where there would not be a need for SQL*Plus on a weekly, if not daily, basis because it is simply that overwhelmingly useful.

Note: The Windows specific version of SQL*Plus (SQL*PLUSW) was a more graphical oriented application resembling SQL*Plus. However, it was discontinued. So only the simple SQL*Plus command line utility remains.

SQL Developer

For many years there was no lasting standard graphical user interface tool for working with Oracle databases. At one point, Oracle introduced Procedure Builder, a great little tool for PL/SQL developers, but it went away. Then Oracle on Windows offered Database Manager, a little lightweight OEM-like utility for managing databases, and it too disappeared. As for Oracle Enterprise Manager, it started out as a fat-Java client tool, but then became a web-based application. In addition, Application Express (APEX) is very useful for APEX work, but it is not suitable as a general-purpose Oracle database tool. Therefore, many people relied on tools like Toad® for years as a decent GUI for general purpose Oracle work.

Fortunately, Oracle finally saw the need for such a tool and built a very good freeware offering called SQL Developer. SQL Developer can be downloaded from their website as a standalone freeware offering and, starting with Oracle 11g, it is now part of the standard Oracle client install. Figure 5.3 shows what SQL Developer looks like. There are far too many features in SQL Developer to do it justice in just a brief section of one chapter of a book. Nevertheless, there are numerous blogs, discussion forums and even entire books now on the product, so search the web for information and the latest details. Note that as a Java based application, SQL Developer runs on numerous platforms and not just Microsoft Windows. So for UNIX, LINUX and even MAC-OS users, SQL Developer may well be the tool of choice. It is good to observe that

---

while SQL Developer does increasingly support SQL*Plus command syntax, it is not an entire replacement for it.

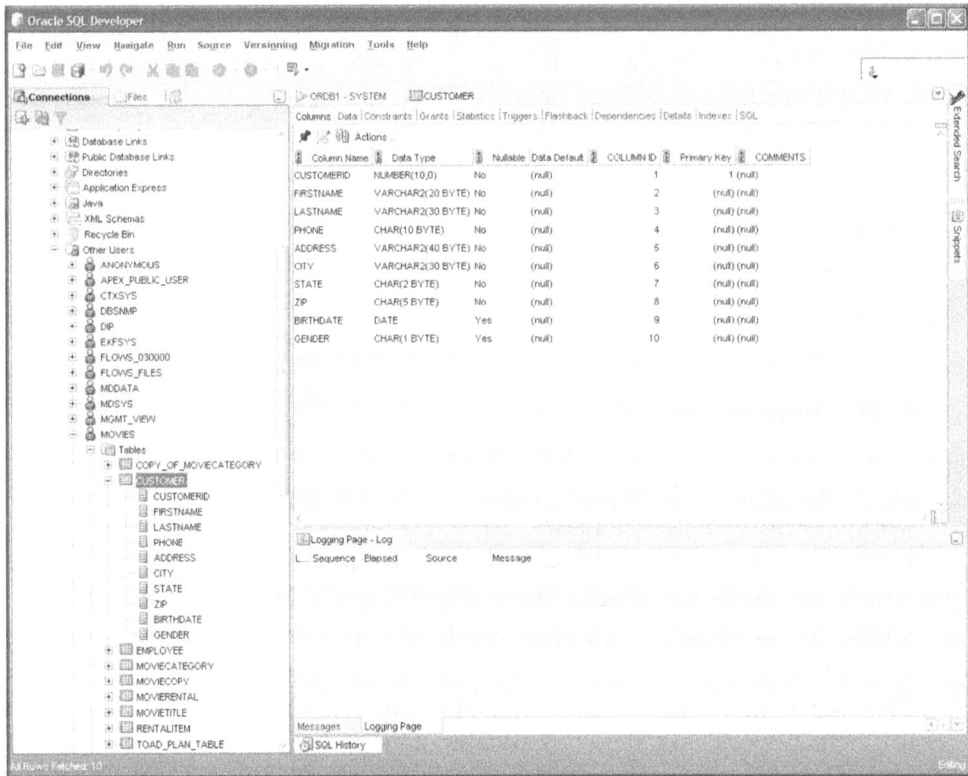

Figure 5.3: *SQL Developer*

Toad for Oracle®

It may seem odd here to list a tool from a third party vendor, but since Oracle was late to the game with SQL Developer, many people standardized on a tool from Quest Software called Toad. The letters in Toad originally stood for Tool for Oracle Application Developers. It started as a one-man effort on Compuserve, and then moved to the web at www.toadsoft.com. Later, it was acquired by Quest Software and legitimatized into a full blown, world class commercial product. However, even today, a competent and popular freeware version remains. With well over a million users worldwide, it only seemed logical to include mention of Toad here, especially since the lag time by Oracle to offer a graphical SQL tool essentially created both this market and tool.

Toad is a Microsoft Windows-only GUI for doing all things Oracle. In many respects, it was simply a precursor to Oracle's own SQL Developer, but ten years earlier. Toad has one very distinguishing trademark: the tabbed interface. While it can also display items via a tree-view or drop-down list, the early acceptance and adoption of the new-style tabbed interface was critical in its success. For many, the interface just felt right. In fact, look back again at Figure 5.3 of SQL Developer and notice how the right hand sides of the screen are similar.

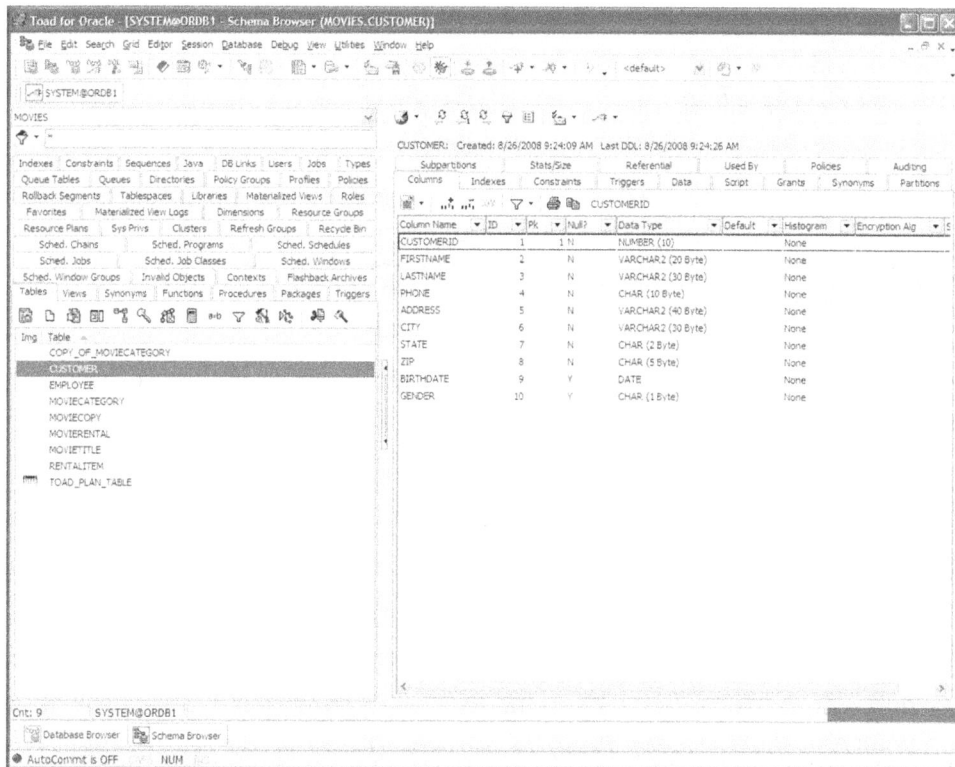

Figure 5.4: *Quest Software's Toad*

The major differences in the author's arguably biased opinion between Quest's Toad and Oracle's SQL Developer products, besides price, are highly summarized in Table 5.1 using a rating scale of 1 to 5, where 1 is the lowest and 5 is the highest. However, be aware that both tools are quite good and make most people much more productive, so in the end it often comes down to a personal choice more than anything else. Unlike products such as Microsoft Office, which seem to become the overwhelming single standard, it is quite possible to envision most companies having both products in everyday use due to both budgetary reasons and personal productivity preferences. Thus, it probably will not be one product entirely or the other for most companies.

	Toad	SQL Developer
Product Maturity	5	3
Developer Oriented Features	5	3
DBA Oriented Features	5	2 (Note 1)
Oracle Version Support	5	2 (Note 2)
Runs on Multiple Platforms	2 (Note 3)	5
Supports Multiple Databases	4 (Note 4)	5
Plug-In Extensible Architecture	1	5
Third Party Add-On Offerings	1	3 (Note 5)
Total Score	28	28

Table 5.1: *Toad vs. SQL Developer*

Oracle's Enterprise Manager is really the DBA's tool, so to keep markets and messaging clear, there is minimal overlap with most DBA features in OEM only. SQL Developer works only with more recent versions of Oracle and only offers support for versions 9.2.01 and higher, whereas Toad supports Oracle versions from 7.x on up.

Toad has been successfully run by some users via the Windows emulation package (WINE) on Linux and other platforms, but Quest does not fully support this. Quest offers a multi-database platform version of Toad as a different product that looks and feels like Toad, but works natively with numerous databases and supports working with any database that supports the ODBC 3.0 API specification.

A very promising future here, but enough companies have not yet begun to offer products and some that have offered add-on products have also been acquired by Oracle.

Advanced SQL Techniques

Login Scripts

This section will be very brief, but highlights a very useful SQL*Plus facility that can often make both SQL*Plus interactive sessions and scripting less difficult. Note too that some of the prior mentioned tools such as Toad and SQL Developer support this SQL*plus feature, although with some minor differences based upon Oracle version. For instance, prior to Oracle 11g, the *login.sql* script fired only upon startup. Whereas in 11g and Toad, it fires up each time a script is executed.

As is covered in the following sections, there will be times when SQL*Plus will be used and issue a common set of commands over and over again. Often these commands will be those that help define the environment and/or behavior for SQL*Plus during that session. For example, the six SQL*Plus commands below might well represent commands that a user wants active anytime they enter SQL*Plus or execute a SQL script.

```
SET TAB OFF
SET VERIFY OFF
SET LINESIZE 132
SET PAGESIZE 999
SET TRIMOUT ON
SET TRIMSPOOL ON
```

Obviously, typing these six commands each time SQL*Plus is entered is not an optimal solution. What about adding those six lines to the top of each of the scripts? Actually, that is also not good because if the commands are changed, then the next step will be to edit all of the scripts. The most logical idea is to simply place those six lines within their own little script *set_environment.sql*, and then simply call that script at the top of all the other scripts, such as this:

🖫 set_environment.sql script

```
SET TAB OFF
SET VERIFY OFF
SET LINESIZE 132
SET PAGESIZE 999
SET TRIMOUT ON
SET TRIMSPOOL ON
```

💾 show_init_parms.sql script

```
@SET_ENVIRONMENT

col name    format a40   heading 'Name'
col value   format a80   heading 'Value'

select NAME, VALUE
from v$parameter
where value not like '%\%'
  and value not like '%/%'
  and name not like 'log_archive_dest%'
order by name;
```

But guess what? SQL*Plus already has a built-in mechanism to do this! SQL*Plus supports the concepts of automatically executed user and site profile scripts. These are simply SQL script files containing either SQL or SQL*Plus commands that are executed automatically whenever SQL*Plus is launched. Think of these files as being like Microsoft DOS *autoexec.bat* files or a UNIX *login.sh* script. These user and site profile scripts are named *login.sql* and *glogin.sql*, respectively. When SQL*Plus first starts, it simply looks for and executes these scripts in the working directory or SQL_PATH. That is all there is to it. Here is a simple example where SQL*Plus prints "Welcome to SQL*Plus" and lists both the current database SID and connected user name. Figure 5.5 shows the *login.sql* script and its effect. Notice how the script is executed automatically upon launch. So in many cases, one can simply rely upon the *login.sql* script behavior rather than writing and then calling a new script such as *set_environment.sql*.

```
 Command Prompt - sqlplus bert/bert                                    _ □ ×
C:\Temp>
C:\Temp>
C:\Temp>
C:\Temp>
C:\Temp>
C:\Temp>type login.sql
set echo off
set heading off
set feedback off
prompt
prompt "Weclome to SQL*PLus ..."
select 'Database = '||instance_name from v$instance;
select 'UserName = '||username from user_users;
prompt
set heading on
C:\Temp>
C:\Temp>
C:\Temp>sqlplus bert/bert

SQL*Plus: Release 10.2.0.3.0 - Production on Sun Jan 27 12:18:26 2008

Copyright (c) 1982, 2006, Oracle.  All Rights Reserved.


Connected to:
Oracle Database 10g Enterprise Edition Release 10.2.0.3.0 - Production
With the Partitioning, OLAP and Data Mining options


"Weclome to SQL*PLus ..."

Database = orxp10

UserName = BERT

SQL>
SQL>
SQL>
SQL>
SQL>
```

Figure 5.5: *SQL*Plus using LOGIN.SQL script*

As to the difference between *login.sql* and *glogin.sql*: SQL*Plus provides two automatic script environmental setup options. *Login.sql* is for a particular user and is loaded from one of their local directories, whereas *glogin.sql* is more for departmental or enterprise wide standards and usually kept on shared file servers.

Dynamic SQL Scripting

Sometimes, even in today's world of super GUIs, a SQL script is still the best way to accomplish something. Also, there are always those people who steadfastly prefer command line to any GUI no matter what. So can SQL*Plus and scripting accommodate, or even facilitate, these needs? Of course, the answer is a resounding "yes". Simply embrace the advanced SQL*Plus technique known as dynamic SQL scripting or scripts that write scripts.

For example, say the DBA wants to enable or disable the already defined referential integrity within an entire schema whose list of table names can and most likely will change over time. Whether a GUI or a script is used, the mere fact that the list of table names can change adds an additional level of complexity to the challenge. So how can a one-time scripting solution be written that will handle a dynamic list of table names? The answer is with dynamic SQL scripting.

Dynamic SQL scripting is a very old and powerful trick. Just write an outer shell SQL script that will both generate and then execute the real inner shell SQL script that performs the task at hand for each of the dynamic list objects. The primary enabling technologies have always been the Oracle data dictionary and certain SQL*Plus commands – namely SPOOL and EXECUTE.

Returning to the example: view the scripts to dynamically turn on and off foreign keys for a schema. The script for the first half is to turn off the referential integrity (the reverse solution left as an exercise). Note that turning off referential integrity is intended merely as an example here and not advice of something to perform without great forethought, especially in production!

💾 ri_off.sql script

```
-- ri_off.sql
set pagesize 0
set feedback off
set term off
spool c:\temp\ri_off.tmp
select 'alter table '||owner||'.'||table_name||' disable constraint
'||constraint_name||';'
  from user_constraints
  where constraint_type = 'R'
  and status = 'ENABLED';
spool off
set term on
set feedback on
set echo on
@c:\temp\ri_off.tmp
```

Now examine just how this dynamic scripting example works. Setting page size off suppresses the SELECT command's output for the column headers and page breaks. Setting the feedback off eliminates the SELECT command's ending feedback on the number of rows processed. This is critical as commands are being created, and not the standard output useful for human reading. Setting terminal off eliminates echoing the output to the screen. Do this for two reasons: to speed up the process and because it is unknown just how much output the script could generate. The spool command then instructs SQL*Plus where to place all the output that will now be generated SQL commands. Now the SELECT command dynamically generates the desired SQL code into the spool file, and then executes that spool file since it contains the correct commands. This technique is probably one of the most powerful things one can do with SQL*Plus, so it is worth the time to review and completely understand this example.

SET TIMING ON

Sometimes when working on SQL command optimizations, all that is desired is a rough timing estimate; namely, the SQL*Plus client elapsed execution time, or simple clock time. Often that simple metric is sufficient for some very basic tuning needs. SQL*Plus has a built-in capability to do exactly this – it is the SET TIMING command. It essentially records the clock time before and after the SQL command execution, then displays the run time difference. There are two fundamental shortcomings with this technique. First, its scope is a single command, so for a script of commands, the DBA adds up those numbers himself. Second and more importantly, this timing tells nothing about the actual amount of work performed. It is like knowing that a NASCAR driver took ten seconds to circle the track without knowing the track circumference; there is no way to know how fast they were going.

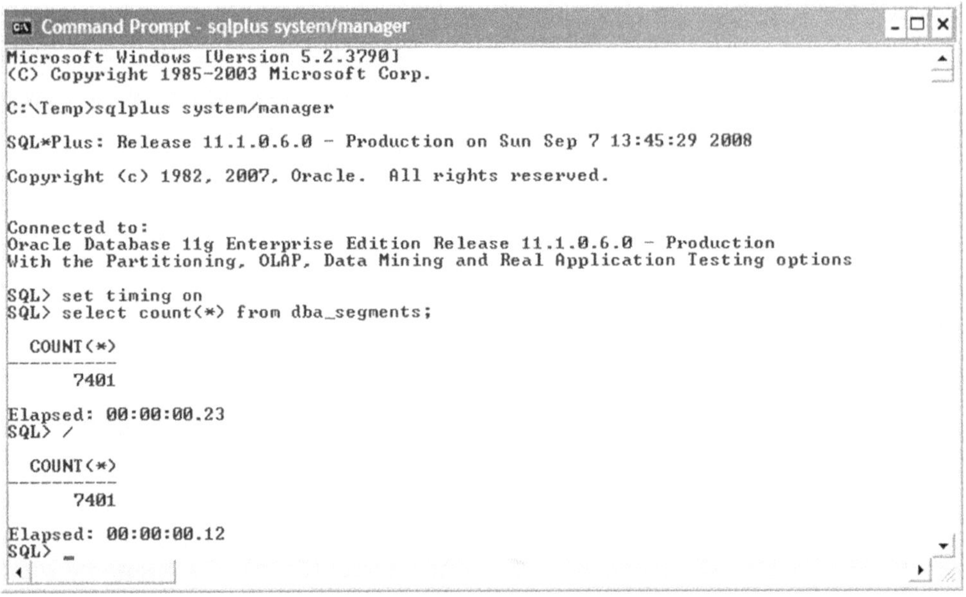
```
Command Prompt - sqlplus system/manager
Microsoft Windows [Version 5.2.3790]
(C) Copyright 1985-2003 Microsoft Corp.

C:\Temp>sqlplus system/manager

SQL*Plus: Release 11.1.0.6.0 - Production on Sun Sep 7 13:45:29 2008

Copyright (c) 1982, 2007, Oracle.  All rights reserved.


Connected to:
Oracle Database 11g Enterprise Edition Release 11.1.0.6.0 - Production
With the Partitioning, OLAP, Data Mining and Real Application Testing options

SQL> set timing on
SQL> select count(*) from dba_segments;

  COUNT(*)
----------
      7401

Elapsed: 00:00:00.23
SQL> /

  COUNT(*)
----------
      7401

Elapsed: 00:00:00.12
SQL> _
```

Figure 5.6: *SQL*Plus SET TIMING command*

TIMING START & STOP

The SQL*Plus TIMING START and STOP commands solve the script timing problem from the prior section about SET TIMING. This command permits one to define a named timer, which starts the timing process for that named context. Then later the DBA can either SHOW or STOP that timer to see the elapsed clock execution time since that timer was activated, as shown in Figure 5.7 for the *timing_demo.sql* script. Remember though, this timer and the execution time displayed are from the client machine's perspective, which means that it still suffers from the problem of not displaying the amount of actual work performed.

timing_demo.sql script

```
timing start sql_timer
select count(*) from dba_segments;
select count(*) from dba_objects where owner not in ('SYS','SYSTEM');
timing stop
```

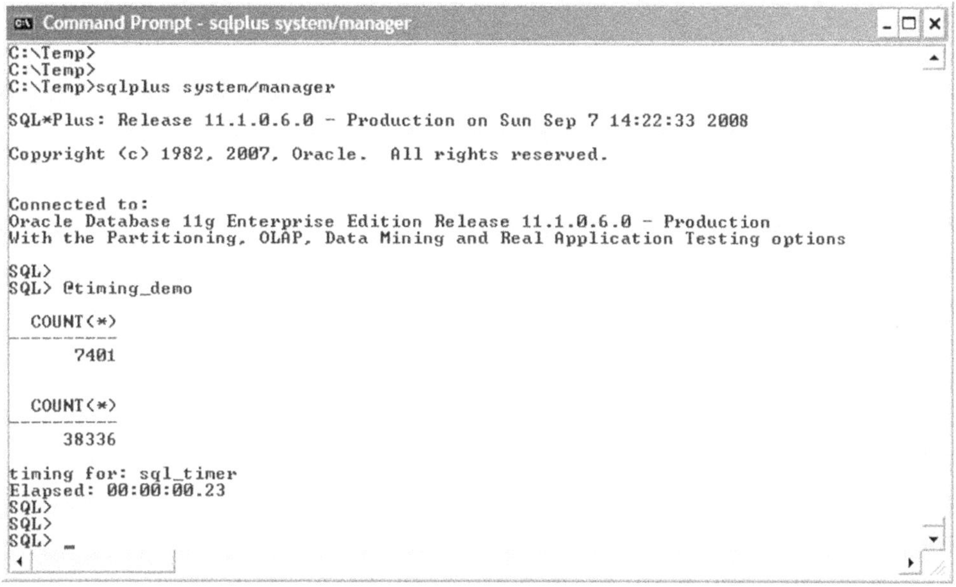

Figure 5.7: *SQL*Plus START & STOP TIMER*

Obtaining Explain Plans

At the beginning of this chapter, the different characteristics of the SQL language, namely that SQL is not a procedural language and thus less obvious to programmers on how it internally accomplishes the requested actions, was covered. This means that the SQL statement expresses itself more in terms of the end results rather than the algorithm to get there. For that purpose, Oracle provides a mechanism and utility known as Explain PlanS. In brief, this is nothing more than a query to the database to provide insight into how Oracle will most likely process the request. Note that this internal processing algorithm is based upon the optimizer's estimated cost for the operations involved and is affected by the tables' row counts, statistics and histograms. Other factors such as block size and database initialization parameters also come into play. Moreover, the database may have stored outlines, profiles or SQL Tuning Sets for some statements that will supersede what a simple stand-alone explain plan might reveal. So one must consider or factor in all these other external influences.

In order to issue SQL commands to request the explain plan information, one must have previously created an explain plan table. Oracle provides the

---

utlxplan.sql script, shown below, for this purpose. There are a few things to know about these tables that are essential. First, not all the columns are required in terms of the information returned because they may or may not have meaning based upon the SQL code and external influencing factors. However, if a column is needed, it has to be there or an error will show up. The reason for mentioning this is that often people will try to use an older version explain plan table format with a newer database which can yield such errors, thereby always making sure that the explain plan table definition is current with the database version. It is easy to forget updating these during database upgrades, so be careful.

🖫 utlxplan.sql script from Oracle 11g Release 1

```
create table PLAN_TABLE (
        statement_id       varchar2(30),
        plan_id            number,
        timestamp          date,
        remarks            varchar2(4000),
        operation          varchar2(30),
        options            varchar2(255),
        object_node        varchar2(128),
        object_owner       varchar2(30),
        object_name        varchar2(30),
        object_alias       varchar2(65),
        object_instance    numeric,
        object_type        varchar2(30),
        optimizer          varchar2(255),
        search_columns     number,
        id                 numeric,
        parent_id          numeric,
        depth              numeric,
        position           numeric,
        cost               numeric,
        cardinality        numeric,
        bytes              numeric,
        other_tag          varchar2(255),
        partition_start    varchar2(255),
        partition_stop     varchar2(255),
        partition_id       numeric,
        other              long,
        distribution       varchar2(30),
        cpu_cost           numeric,
        io_cost            numeric,
        temp_space         numeric,
        access_predicates  varchar2(4000),
        filter_predicates  varchar2(4000),
        projection         varchar2(4000),
        time               numeric,
        qblock_name        varchar2(30),
        other_xml          clob
);
```

There are three ways by which DBAs generally create explain plan tables. A single table can be created under a master schema, then a public synonym can be created for it and public access can be granted to that table. However, each user must then provide unique statement identifiers in order not to clash with each other. Also, the subject of which explain plans to retain and/or to purge is an issue since this centralized table could grow quite large over time. A second approach is to let each user create an explain plan table for their specific needs. However, this requires granting create table privilege to developers which is a practice that some DBAs prefer to avoid, even in development environments. A third, more elegant solution, is to develop a login trigger that creates a session temporary table for explain plans. Do not worry about explain tables growing over time for they purge themselves upon session termination. Also, it is far easier now to keep everyone using explain plan tables that are current because all that is needed is to modify a single trigger to get everyone updated during a patch or upgrade. The *login_plan.sql* script below creates such a trigger to automatically create the session level explain plan tables.

🖫 login_plan.sql script

```
CREATE OR REPLACE TRIGGER login_plan
AFTER LOGON
ON SCHEMA
DECLARE
  STMT VARCHAR2(4000) := 'create table PLAN_TABLE (
        statement_id          varchar2(30),
        plan_id               number,
        timestamp             date,
        remarks               varchar2(4000),
        operation             varchar2(30),
        options               varchar2(255),
        object_node           varchar2(128),
        object_owner          varchar2(30),
        object_name           varchar2(30),
        object_alias          varchar2(65),
        object_instance       numeric,
        object_type           varchar2(30),
        optimizer             varchar2(255),
        search_columns        number,
        id                    numeric,
        parent_id             numeric,
        depth                 numeric,
        position              numeric,
        cost                  numeric,
        cardinality           numeric,
        bytes                 numeric,
        other_tag             varchar2(255),
        partition_start       varchar2(255),
        partition_stop        varchar2(255),
        partition_id          numeric,
```

```
       other               long,
       distribution        varchar2(30),
       cpu_cost            numeric,
       io_cost             numeric,
       temp_space          numeric,
       access_predicates   varchar2(4000),
       filter_predicates   varchar2(4000),
       projection          varchar2(4000),
       time                numeric,
       qblock_name         varchar2(30),
       other_xml           clob
    )';
BEGIN
  EXECUTE IMMEDIATE STMT;
EXCEPTION
  WHEN OTHERS THEN
    RAISE_APPLICATION_ERROR(-20101,'login_plan trigger error');
END;
/
```

Once there is an explain plan table in place regardless of which method was chosen from those previously listed, and when Oracle informs the DBA of the internal processing algorithm for a given SQL statement, issue an EXPLAIN SQL command as shown here:

```
EXPLAIN PLAN SET STATEMENT_ID = 'BERT1' FOR SELECT * FROM MOVIES.CUSTOMER;
```

Oracle has now populated the explain plan table with the procedural logic steps it will most likely perform to return the desired results. Prior to Oracle 9i, the only way to format and display the results stored within the explain plan table was to construct a complex hierarchical (tree-walk) query such as the one shown here:

```
select lpad(' ',2*level)||operation||' '||options||' '||object_name||
       decode(partition_start,NULL,NULL,
         ' PARTS('||partition_start||'-'||partition_stop||')')||
         decode(level,1,'  [Cost = '||Cost||']',Null) QUERY_PLAN,
       Object_Node, Other_Tag
from plan_table
where statement_id = '&plan_user'
connect by prior statement_id = statement_id and
        prior id = parent_id
start with id = 1
order by statement_id;
```

In order to keep the complexities of such a query less painful, many people would encapsulate the entire explain plan information retrieval process into a single script such as the *explain_plan.sql* script shown next. Then one would simply need to cut and paste the SQL statement of concern where the script contains the text "<<< place your SQL query here >>>".

💾 explain_plan.sql script

```
set echo      off
set verify    off
set pagesize 60
set linesize 132

define plan_user='BERT'

DELETE FROM plan_table WHERE statement_id = '&plan_user';
COMMIT;

EXPLAIN PLAN SET STATEMENT_ID = '&plan_user' INTO plan_table FOR
<<< place your SQL query here >>>;

col QUERY_PLAN format a80
col Object_Node format a11
col Other_tag format a19
break on ID

select lpad(' ',2*level)||operation||' '||options||' '||object_name||
       decode(partition_start,NULL,NULL,
            ' PARTS ('||partition_start||'-'||partition_stop||')')||
            decode(level,1,'  [Cost = '||Cost||']',Null) QUERY_PLAN,
       Object_Node, Other_Tag
from plan_table
where statement_id = '&plan_user'
connect by prior statement_id = statement_id and
           prior id = parent_id
start with id = 1
order by statement_id;
```

There were scenarios where this simplistic approach was not 100% accurate nor reliable, such as some algorithms for some advanced constructs that could not be shown in a simple single level hierarchy. Thus, Oracle provided the DBMS_XPLAN PL/SQL package and the DISPLAY table function. The valid values for FORMAT are BASIC, TYPICAL, SERIAL and ALL.

ARGUMENT	TYPE	IN / OUT	DEFAULT VALUE
TABLE_NAME	VARCHAR2	IN	PLAN_TABLE
STATEMENT_ID	VARCHAR2	IN	NULL
FORMAT	VARCHAR2	IN	'TYPICAL'
FILTER_PREDS	VARCHAR2	IN	NULL

Table 5.2: *DISPLAY Table Functions*

So to fetch the explain plan steps, there is a very simple and singular SQL statement, as shown here. Plus, it is now so much simpler than before. The internal process to generate accurate explain plans has been both encapsulated and reduced to a single function that Oracle now maintains.

```
SET LINESIZE 132
SET PAGESIZE 0

SELECT * FROM table(DBMS_XPLAN.DISPLAY);
```

The DBMS_XPLAN.DISPLAY table function will yield well formatted and easily readable output like the following example explain plan for a query:

```
Plan hash value: 2174153472

---------------------------------------------------------------------------------------------
| Id  | Operation                  | Name              | Rows  | Bytes | Cost (%CPU)| Time     |
---------------------------------------------------------------------------------------------
|   0 | SELECT STATEMENT           |                   |   500 | 42000 |    43  (10)| 00:00:01 |
|   1 |  SORT ORDER BY             |                   |   500 | 42000 |    43  (10)| 00:00:01 |
|*  2 |   HASH JOIN                |                   |   500 | 42000 |    42   (8)| 00:00:01 |
|   3 |    VIEW                    | index$_join$_006  |    12 |   108 |     3   (0)| 00:00:01 |
|*  4 |     HASH JOIN              |                   |    12 |   108 |            | 00:00:01 |
|   5 |      INDEX FAST FULL SCAN  | MOVIECATEGORY_PK  |    12 |   108 |     1   (0)| 00:00:01 |
|   6 |      INDEX FAST FULL SCAN  | MOVIECATEGORY_UK  |    12 |   108 |     1   (0)| 00:00:01 |
|*  7 |    HASH JOIN               |                   |   500 | 37500 |    38   (6)| 00:00:01 |
|   8 |     TABLE ACCESS FULL      | MOVIETITLE        |   100 |  2100 |     3   (0)| 00:00:01 |
|*  9 |     HASH JOIN              |                   |   500 | 27000 |    35   (6)| 00:00:01 |
|* 10 |      TABLE ACCESS FULL     | MOVIECOPY         |   800 |  4000 |     3   (0)| 00:00:01 |
|* 11 |      HASH JOIN             |                   |   500 | 24500 |    31   (4)| 00:00:01 |
|* 12 |       HASH JOIN            |                   |   250 | 10750 |    22   (5)| 00:00:01 |
|  13 |        TABLE ACCESS FULL   | CUSTOMER          |    62 |   930 |     3   (0)| 00:00:01 |
|  14 |        NESTED LOOPS        |                   |   250 |  7000 |    18   (0)| 00:00:01 |
|  15 |         VIEW               |                   |     1 |    13 |     9   (0)| 00:00:01 |
|  16 |          SORT AGGREGATE    |                   |     1 |     3 |            |          |
|  17 |           TABLE ACCESS FULL| MOVIERENTAL       |  5000 | 15000 |     9   (0)| 00:00:01 |
|* 18 |         TABLE ACCESS FULL  | MOVIERENTAL       |   250 |  3750 |     9   (0)| 00:00:01 |
|* 19 |       TABLE ACCESS FULL    | RENTALITEM        | 10000 | 60000 |     9   (0)| 00:00:01 |
---------------------------------------------------------------------------------------------

Predicate Information (identified by operation id):
---------------------------------------------------

   2 - access("MT"."CATEGORYID"="MX"."CATEGORYID")
   4 - access(ROWID=ROWID)
   7 - access("MC"."MOVIEID"="MT"."MOVIEID")
   9 - access("RI"."MOVIECOPYID"="MC"."MOVIECOPYID")
  10 - filter("MC"."MOVIEID">0)
  11 - access("MR"."RENTALID"="RI"."RENTALID")
  12 - access("CU"."CUSTOMERID"="MR"."CUSTOMERID")
  18 - filter("MR"."TOTALCHARGE">"AR"."TOTAL")
  19 - filter("RI"."MOVIECOPYID">0)

39 rows selected.
```

Figure 5.8: *Example Explain Plan Output*

SQL*Plus AUTOTRACE

Sometimes the explain plan by itself does not provide sufficient information because although there is now an idea of the procedural logic or algorithm used to process the query, the plan itself does not provide any realistic work execution context or background by which to measure. How can one actually tell if a full table scan is really better than an indexed search if the work actual performed for each is unknown? What is needed is an extended "explain plan" capability – one where both the estimated algorithm and its net resulting workload are displayed. Fortunately, Oracle has built that exact feature into SQL*Plus, and it is one of the most useful ways to work with and/or measure explain plan effectiveness. It is called SQL*Plus AUTOTRACE.

SQL*Plus AUTOTRACE requires some initial setup before it can be used, much like explain plans, meaning that some scripts need to be run. The user must be granted a special role known as PLUSTRC in order to use AUTOTRACE, or they will see the error message shown here:

```
C:\Temp>sqlplus MOVIES/MOVIES

SQL*Plus: Release 11.1.0.6.0 - Production on Sat Sep 13 12:33:40 2008

Copyright (c) 1982, 2007, Oracle.  All rights reserved.


Connected to:
Oracle Database 11g Enterprise Edition Release 11.1.0.6.0 - Production
With the Partitioning, OLAP, Data Mining and Real Application Testing options

SQL> set autotrace on
SP2-0618: Cannot find the Session Identifier.  Check PLUSTRACE role is enabled
SP2-0611: Error enabling STATISTICS report
SQL>
```

Figure 5.9: *Error Message without PLUSTRC*

In order to setup AUTOTRACE, the DBA must perform the following two steps. First, they must run the *$ORACLE_HOME/sqlplus/admin/plustrce.sql* script shown below to create the PLUSTRACE role. Then that PLUSTRACE role simply needs to be granted as a default enabled role to any users who want to utilize this facility.

🖫 plustrce.sql script

```
set echo on

drop role plustrace;
create role plustrace;

grant select on v_$sesstat to plustrace;
grant select on v_$statname to plustrace;
grant select on v_$mystat to plustrace;
grant plustrace to dba with admin option;

set echo off
```

Once the proper setup steps have been completed, there is now a much improved explain plan output, one with both the estimated algorithm and the actual work performed to run it as shown in Figure 5.10. The SQL*Plus user merely has to include a SET AUTOTRACE ON command. Now information can be received about the actual work performs like logical reads, physical reads, sorts and such.

```
Execution Plan
----------------------------------------------------------
Plan hash value: 2174153472

---------------------------------------------------------------------------------------------
| Id  | Operation                        | Name            | Rows  | Bytes | Cost (%CPU)| Time     |
---------------------------------------------------------------------------------------------
|   0 | SELECT STATEMENT                 |                 |   500 | 42000 |    43  (10)| 00:00:01 |
|   1 |  SORT ORDER BY                   |                 |   500 | 42000 |    43  (10)| 00:00:01 |
|*  2 |   HASH JOIN                      |                 |   500 | 42000 |    42   (8)| 00:00:01 |
|   3 |    VIEW                          | index$_join$_006|    12 |   108 |     3   (0)| 00:00:01 |
|*  4 |     HASH JOIN                    |                 |    12 |   108 |            |          |
|   5 |      INDEX FAST FULL SCAN        | MOVIECATEGORY_PK|    12 |   108 |     1   (0)| 00:00:01 |
|   6 |      INDEX FAST FULL SCAN        | MOVIECATEGORY_UK|    12 |   108 |     1   (0)| 00:00:01 |
|*  7 |    HASH JOIN                     |                 |   500 | 37500 |    38   (6)| 00:00:01 |
|   8 |     TABLE ACCESS FULL            | MOVIETITLE      |   100 |  2100 |     3   (0)| 00:00:01 |
|*  9 |     HASH JOIN                    |                 |   500 | 27000 |    35   (6)| 00:00:01 |
|* 10 |      TABLE ACCESS FULL           | MOVIECOPY       |   800 |  4000 |     3   (0)| 00:00:01 |
|* 11 |      HASH JOIN                   |                 |   500 | 24500 |    31   (4)| 00:00:01 |
|* 12 |       HASH JOIN                  |                 |   250 | 10750 |    22   (5)| 00:00:01 |
|  13 |        TABLE ACCESS FULL         | CUSTOMER        |    62 |   930 |     3   (0)| 00:00:01 |
|  14 |        NESTED LOOPS              |                 |   250 |  7000 |    18   (0)| 00:00:01 |
|  15 |         VIEW                     |                 |     1 |    13 |     9   (0)| 00:00:01 |
|  16 |          SORT AGGREGATE          |                 |     1 |     3 |            |          |
|  17 |           TABLE ACCESS FULL      | MOVIERENTAL     |  5000 | 15000 |     9   (0)| 00:00:01 |
|* 18 |         TABLE ACCESS FULL        | MOVIERENTAL     |   250 |  3750 |     9   (0)| 00:00:01 |
|* 19 |       TABLE ACCESS FULL          | RENTALITEM      | 10000 | 60000 |     9   (0)| 00:00:01 |
---------------------------------------------------------------------------------------------

Predicate Information (identified by operation id):
---------------------------------------------------

   2 - access("MT"."CATEGORYID"="MX"."CATEGORYID")
   4 - access(ROWID=ROWID)
   7 - access("MC"."MOVIEID"="MT"."MOVIEID")
   9 - access("RI"."MOVIECOPYID"="MC"."MOVIECOPYID")
  10 - filter("MC"."MOVIEID">0)
  11 - access("MR"."RENTALID"="RI"."RENTALID")
  12 - access("CU"."CUSTOMERID"="MR"."CUSTOMERID")
  18 - filter("MR"."TOTALCHARGE">"AR"."TOTAL")
  19 - filter("RI"."MOVIECOPYID">0)


Statistics
----------------------------------------------------------
          0  recursive calls
          0  db block gets
        120  consistent gets
          0  physical reads
          0  redo size
     159495  bytes sent via SQL*Net to client
       2748  bytes received via SQL*Net from client
        214  SQL*Net roundtrips to/from client
          1  sorts (memory)
          0  sorts (disk)
       3182  rows processed
```

Figure 5.10: *SQL*Plus Auto-Trace Output*

Note: Although the SQl*Plus AUTOTRACE facility is easy to use and generates a lot of useful information, the DBA or developer can gather much more detailed information via the session level trace facility. This is a quick and dirty approach. When better information is needed, favor session-level trace output.

Interpreting Explain Plans

In the last two sections, all or part of the output was the explain plan or internal processing algorithm the database engine will most likely use. There are entire chapters of books written on this topic, so this book will only concentrate on the basics (reading explain plans) and show some ways to make that basic visual interpretation process much easier.

Looking back at Figure 5.6, the first step is line 17 – the table access full on the MOVIERENTAL table. Why? Because one needs to look for the rightmost uppermost plan steps, and then work downward and outward. So examine the same explain plan shown more graphically in Quest Software's Toad for Oracle® shown in Figure 5.11:

```
SELECT STATEMENT ALL_ROWS
     Cost: 43 Bytes: 42,000 Cardinality: 500
19   SORT ORDER BY
        Cost: 43 Bytes: 42,000 Cardinality: 500
18   HASH JOIN
        Cost: 42 Bytes: 42,000 Cardinality: 500
 4      VIEW VIEW MOVIES.index$_join$_006
           Cost: 3 Bytes: 108 Cardinality: 12
 3         HASH JOIN
              Cost: 1 Bytes: 108 Cardinality: 12
 1            INDEX FAST FULL SCAN INDEX (UNIQUE) MOVIES.MOVIECATEGORY_PK
                 Cost: 1 Bytes: 108 Cardinality: 12
 2            INDEX FAST FULL SCAN INDEX (UNIQUE) MOVIES.MOVIECATEGORY_UK
                 Cost: 1 Bytes: 108 Cardinality: 12
17      HASH JOIN
           Cost: 38 Bytes: 37,500 Cardinality: 500
 5         TABLE ACCESS FULL TABLE MOVIES.MOVIETITLE
              Cost: 3 Bytes: 2,100 Cardinality: 100
16         HASH JOIN
              Cost: 35 Bytes: 27,000 Cardinality: 500
 6            TABLE ACCESS FULL TABLE MOVIES.MOVIECOPY
                 Cost: 3 Bytes: 4,000 Cardinality: 800
15            HASH JOIN
                 Cost: 31 Bytes: 24,500 Cardinality: 500
13               HASH JOIN
                    Cost: 22 Bytes: 10,750 Cardinality: 250
 7                  TABLE ACCESS FULL TABLE MOVIES.CUSTOMER
                       Cost: 3 Bytes: 930 Cardinality: 62
12                  NESTED LOOPS
                       Cost: 18 Bytes: 7,000 Cardinality: 250
10                     VIEW MOVIES.
                          Cost: 9 Bytes: 13 Cardinality: 1
 9                        SORT AGGREGATE
                             Bytes: 3 Cardinality: 1
 8                           TABLE ACCESS FULL TABLE MOVIES.MOVIERENTAL
                                Cost: 9 Bytes: 15,000 Cardinality: 5,000
11                     TABLE ACCESS FULL TABLE MOVIES.MOVIERENTAL
                          Cost: 9 Bytes: 3,750 Cardinality: 250
14               TABLE ACCESS FULL TABLE MOVIES.RENTALITEM
                    Cost: 9 Bytes: 60,000 Cardinality: 10,000
```

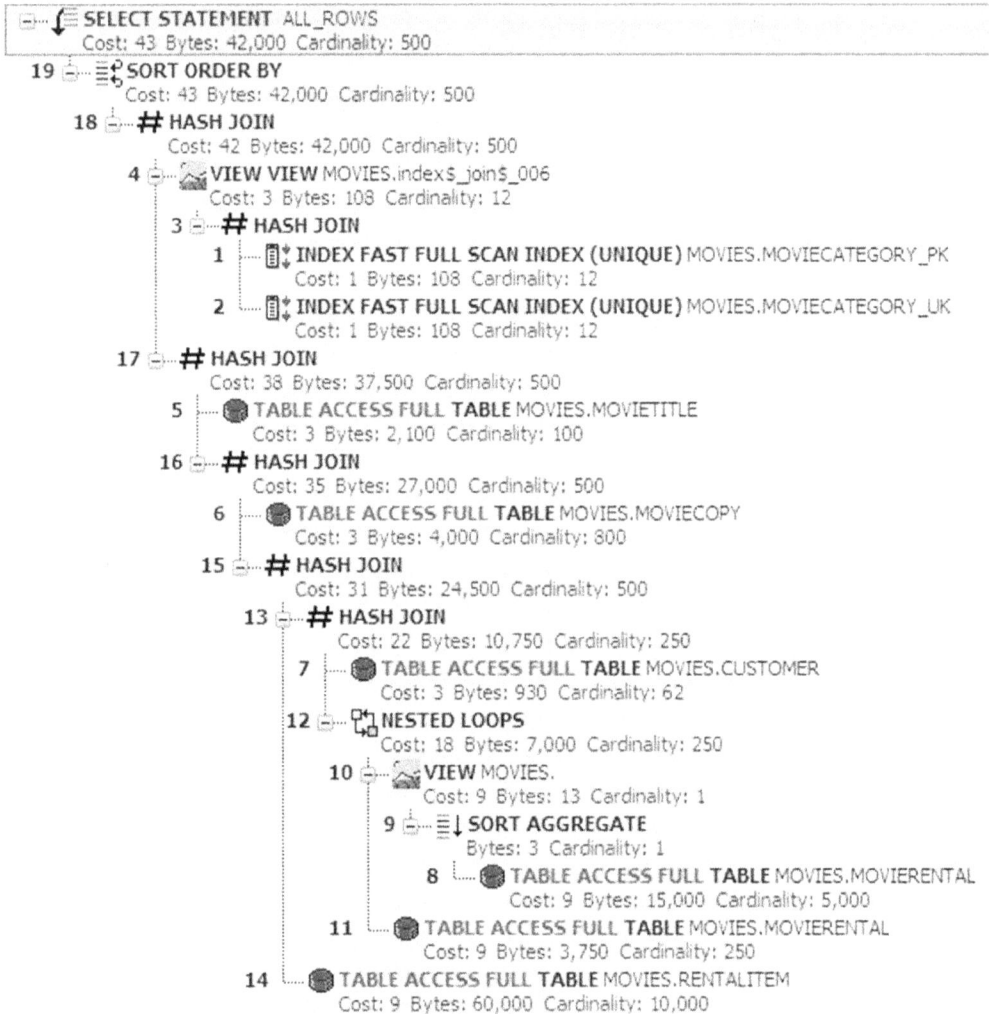

Figure 5.11: *Toad's® Tree-View Explain Plan*

The first thing to be revealed is that the plan step numbers do not match and that is okay. So look again for the rightmost uppermost. Now it is a little easier to read and interpret correctly: plan steps 8 → 9, 9 → 10, 10 → 12 and 11 → 12. Quite obviously, when viewing the actual output, play close attention to the items that appear in red. In the example above, the full table scans are red and could well be very noteworthy.

If one wants something even easier to read, here is the exact same explain plan displayed via Toad's graphic (versus tree-view) mode shown in Figure 5.12. Just start at the bottom and work upwards. Now it is far easier to see that steps 8 → 9, 9 → 10, 10 → 12 and 11 → 12.

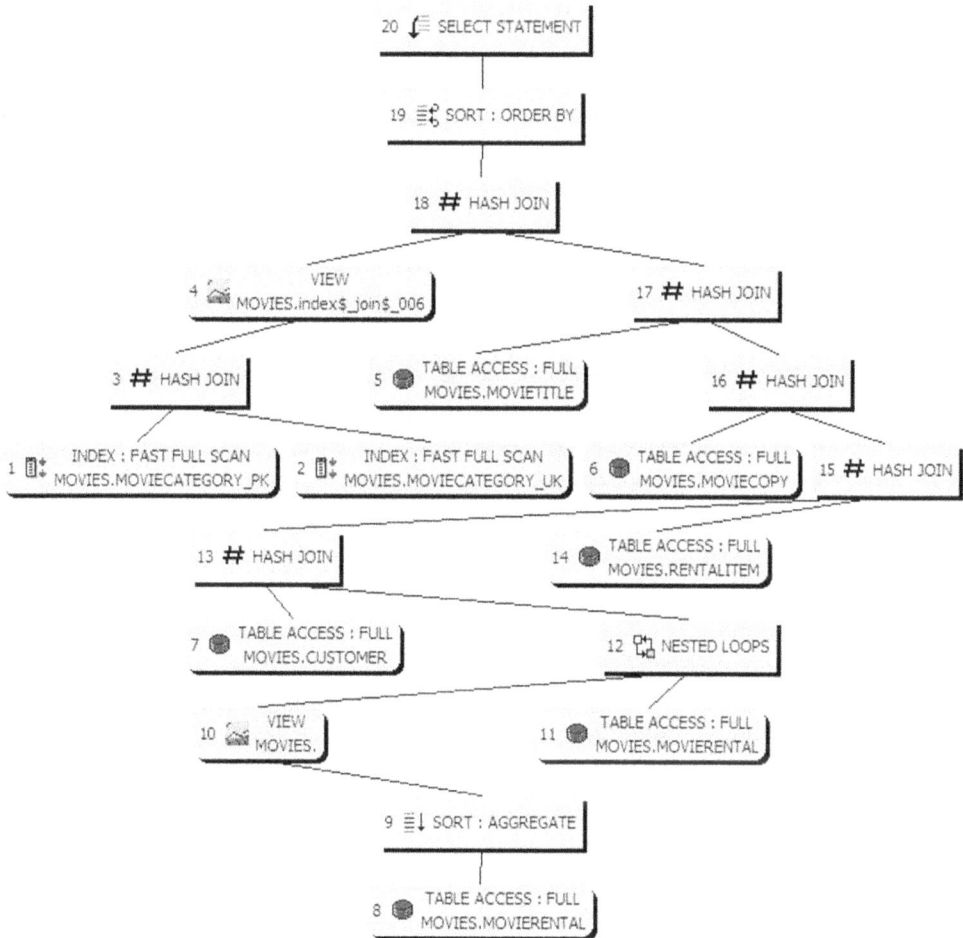

Figure 5.12: *Toad's Graphic Explain Plan*

Likewise, Oracle's SQL Developer can display a very clean and easy to read explain plan as shown in Figure 5.13. What is most noteworthy here is that SQL Developer includes the WHERE clause portion of the SQL responsible for each plan step. That can come in really handy when trying to equate what was in the code resulted as what was in the plan and why.

OPERATION	OBJECT_NAME	OPTIONS	COST
SELECT STATEMENT			43
SORT		ORDER BY	43
HASH JOIN			42
Access Predicates			
MT.CATEGORYID=MX.CATEGORYID			
VIEW	index$_join$_006		3
HASH JOIN			
Access Predicates			
ROWID=ROWID			
INDEX	MOVIECATEGORY_PK	FAST FULL SCAN	1
INDEX	MOVIECATEGORY_UK	FAST FULL SCAN	1
HASH JOIN			38
Access Predicates			
MC.MOVIEID=MT.MOVIEID			
TABLE ACCESS	MOVIETITLE	FULL	3
HASH JOIN			35
Access Predicates			
RI.MOVIECOPYID=MC.MOVIECOPYID			
TABLE ACCESS	MOVIECOPY	FULL	3
Filter Predicates			
MC.MOVIEID>0			
HASH JOIN			31
Access Predicates			
MR.RENTALID=RI.RENTALID			
HASH JOIN			22
Access Predicates			
CU.CUSTOMERID=MR.CUSTOMERID			
TABLE ACCESS	CUSTOMER	FULL	3
NESTED LOOPS			18
VIEW			9
SORT		AGGREGATE	
TABLE ACCESS	MOVIERENTAL	FULL	9
TABLE ACCESS	MOVIERENTAL	FULL	9
Filter Predicates			
MR.TOTALCHARGE>AR.TOTAL			
TABLE ACCESS	RENTALITEM	FULL	9
Filter Predicates			
RI.MOVIECOPYID>0			

Figure 5.13: *SQL Developer's Explain Plan*

So why spend all this time on showing these much easier-to-read explain plan techniques? The reason is to get a tool and concentrate on improving the plans rather than just reading them. Figure 5.12 and Figure 5.13 make the plans so transparent and so easily readable that the DBA can spend his time on trying to improve the steps. Thus, a query can be easily refactored or an optimizer hint can be added and the results show up immediately. Focusing on the information rather than reading the data will result in much more productive tuning sessions.

So how should an explain plan be improved, if this is even necessary? That is a question as loaded as religion and politics, so probably the less said the better. Too often people will focus on just one aspect of the plan – the cost. However, there have been papers written on the fallacy of this overly simplistic approach because the cost calculations depend on several *init.ora* parameter settings, object sizes and statistics. So it is possible that what shows up as a lower cost can, in fact, be wrong or maybe just not the best possible. The arguably better method is to use the cost as a rough guide, but make sure that the plan steps themselves make sense for the given context.

For example, an index range scan might seem like the more preferable choice based on just cost. But if the server is a large SMP box with lots of processors, good I/O bandwidth and few concurrently competing jobs, then a parallel full table scan might be more advisable. So it all depends because business people like the end users do not care how much CPUs, time or I/Os are consumed – they measure simply by the clock. There are times when a supposedly costlier full table scan might be preferable. One cannot simply look at the plan step costs and try to see that indexes are used throughout. The process is much more complex than that. Therefore, SQL Optimization and Tuning books such as the following are recommended reading for a more thorough explain plan analysis and explanation:

- Oracle SQL Tuning & CBO Internals, Kimberly Floss, ISBN: 0974599336
- Oracle Silver Bullets: Real-world Oracle performance Secrets, Donald K. Burleson, ISBN: 0-9759135-2-2

Conclusion

In this chapter, various SQL management concepts and the tools for accomplishing them were examined. Remember that SQL is the primary interface to the database. So SQL remains a key skill set for database professionals – even in today's world of graphical user interfaces. Because ultimately, the DBA always ends up working at the lowest level of work when tuning and that most often translates into the SQL sent to the database server from some end user, application or report.

Next to be covered is the complex world of DBA tasks with a detailed analysis of all the PL/SQL packages, command line utilities and Oracle Enterprise Manager (OEM) screens needed to perform those tasks. Even though each release of Oracle is supposedly easier to manage, with hundreds of new feature per release, the gain in simplicity is more than offset by the gain in features.

Oracle DBA Utilities

Always utilize the appropriate tools

Introduction

The typical Oracle database administrator wears many hats, often at the same time or in rapid fire succession. Because the DBA performs such a wide variety of tasks, Oracle provides numerous utilities to accommodate those needs. Furthermore, the nature of these DBA job functions spans an awesome and yet ever growing chasm of widely differing natures from reorganization, recovery and replication to the various aspects of general database management including file, space, data, task and instance management. This chapter will organize and cover that range of functionalities, all of which are generally available via command line, pre-canned PL/SQL packages, and/or exposed graphically via screens in Oracle Enterprise Manager (OEM).

Reorganization Utilities

Data Pump (EXPDP)

Data Pump Export (EXPDP) is a very modern, server based and highly scalable data unloading utility. On typical multi-processor servers with good disk-I/O subsystems, the time to unload hundreds of gigabytes to terabytes is both reliable and reasonable. And even though the dump files remain Oracle proprietary, there are also easily identifiable uses of XML within those files. Thus, uncompressed export files are semi-readable within a text editor, and as before, can be scanned with operating system commands such as string on UNIX.

As of Oracle 11g Release 2, the older client based export (i.e. exp) utility will no longer be available or supported. Data Pump Export will become the chief and only method available.

A good place to start is by identifying the most frequent data pump export command line parameters:

PARAMETER	DESCRIPTION
ATTACH	*[SCHEMA.]JOB_NAME* Name of an already existing and executing job to connect to. Need *EXP_FULL_DATABASE* privilege for other schemas
COMPRESSION	*META_DATA_ONLY | ALL | NONE | DATA_ONLY* Compress the dump file contents for the specified criteria
CONTENT	*ALL | META_DATA_ONLY | DATA_ONLY* Filter the export of dump file contents to the specified criteria
DIRECTORY	*DATA_PUMP_DIR | DIRECTORY_NAME* Name of directory object pointing to a valid server directory
DUMPFILE	*[DIRECTORY_NAME:]FILE_NAME [, ...]* The name (and optionally the directory) of the export data file

PARAMETER	DESCRIPTION
ESTIMATE	N | Y Do not export, but rather just estimate the disk space required
ESTIMATE_ONLY	BLOCKS, STATISTICS Method export uses to calculate the disk space for data only
EXCLUDE	OBJECT_TYPE[:NAME_FILTER_EXPRESSION] [, ...] Database object types as a whole or by object name filter to specifically exclude from the export
FILESIZE	INTEGER [B | K | M | G] The maximum file size permitted for any export dump file
FULL	N | Y Whether to perform a full database export or not Requires EXP_FULL_DATABASE privilege
INCLUDE	OBJECT_TYPE[:NAME_FILTER_EXPRESSION] [, ...] Database object types as a whole or by object name filter to specifically include in the export
JOB_NAME	SYS_EXPORT_<mode>_NN | JOB_NAME Name by which export job can be referenced (e.g. ATTACH)
LOGFILE	EXPORT.LOG | [DIRECTORY_NAME:]FILE_NAME The name (and optionally the directory) of the export log file
NOLOGFILE	N | Y Whether or not to suppress creation of the export log file
PARALLEL	1 | INTEGER The maximum number of concurrent threads for the export
PARFILE	[DIRECTORY_SPECIFICATION]FILE_NAME Name of the operating system specific parameter file
QUERY	[[SCHEMA.]TABLE_NAME:] FILTER_EXPRESSION Data filter condition applied to all tables or by schema and object name filters during the export
REUSE_DUMPFILES	N | Y Whether or not to overwrite pre-existing export dump files
SAMPLE	[[SCHEMA.]TABLE_NAME]N, where .000001>=N<100 Probability that a data block of rows will be included in the export's sampling of the data (i.e. subset)

PARAMETER	DESCRIPTION
SCHEMAS	SCHEMA [, ...] The schema or schemas to export Need *EXP_FULL_DATABASE* privilege for other schemas
STATUS	0	INTEGER The frequency in seconds which job displays client feedback
TABLES	*[SCHEMA.]TABLE_NAME[:PARTITION_NAME] [, ...]* List of tables for a table mode database export Restricted to a single schema
TABLESPACES	*TABLESPACE_NAME [, ...]* List of tablespaces for a tablespace mode database export
TRANSPORT_FULL_CHECK	N	Y Whether or not dependencies verified between transportable tablespace objects in the transport set to those outside the set
TRANSPORT_TABLESAPCES	*TABLESPACE_NAME [, ...]* List of tablespaces for a transportable tablespace mode database export (target database version >= source version)

Table 6.1: *Frequent EXPDP Command Line Parameters*

Moreover, to use the stop and restart data pump job capabilities, run data pump in interactive mode so as to get the data pump prompt. Then the following commands are also quite frequently useful:

PARAMETER	DESCRIPTION
CONTINUE_CLIENT	Connect client to currently executing job or restarts the job, and resumes logging mode (i.e. status output)
EXIT_CLIENT	Disconnect client connection to currently executing job and terminate the client process, but leave server job running
KILL_JOB	Detach all client processes connected to this data pump job and then terminate (i.e. kill) the currently running job
START_JOB	Start or resume the current data pump job

PARAMETER	DESCRIPTION
STOP_JOB	[IMMEDIATE] Detach all client processes connected to this data pump job and then orderly shutdown the currently running job

Table 6.2: *Additional EXPDP Parameters*

So examine some very common use cases and how data pump export would be used to extract the data.

Export Database Level

This is often referred to as a logical backup where physical backup means those performed either via RMAN, operating system commands, or via third party backup and recovery tools. One reason people used logical backup was historically for ease of recovery for when an object was accidentally dropped. However, with Oracle flashback technology, logical backups are becoming far less compelling. Another reason people performed logical backups was to avoid the perils of the Oracle database migration process when a major new version released. DBAs would simply export the entire database, perform the upgrade, and then import the database. But over the years the database migration has greatly improved, so this usage has also seen reduced importance. Probably the most prevalent reason for doing logical backups is to provide a simple backup and recovery mechanism with no additional software costs for development and test databases.

```
C:\> expdp bert/bert directory=data_pump_dir dumpfile=logical_backup.dmp
full=y
```

Remember, the user running the data pump export at the database level must have exp_full_data privilege for this option to work. Otherwise, the following Oracle errors will be returned:

```
Export: Release 11.1.0.6.0 - Production on Friday, 27 June, 2008 11:20:44
Copyright (c) 2003, 2007, Oracle.  All rights reserved.
Connected to: Oracle Database 11g Enterprise Edition Release 11.1.0.6.0 -
Production
With the Partitioning, OLAP, Data Mining and Real Application Testing
options
ORA-31631: privileges are required
ORA-39161: Full database jobs require privileges
```

Export Tablespace Level

While this may seem like a very useful, and therefore common use case, reality is that often DBAs find that tablespaces are simply containers with space for object allocation. So it is not uncommon over time to find that tablespaces have an eclectic collection of objects. But for those lucky enough and smart enough to have kept some logical rationale to tablespace object placement, here is an example of data pump entirely exporting two specific tablespaces:

```
C:\> expdp bert/bert directory=data_pump_dir dumpfile=multi_tablespace.dmp
tablespaces=users,sysaux
```

One other use for the export at the tablespace level would be if one wished to recreate the tablespace with a different block size such as a tablespace level reorganization. It would be possible to export the tablespace, drop it, recreate it with the new block size, and then import the data. Finally, the tablespace level export can be used as part of the process to merge tablespaces, but that is pretty rare.

As at the database level, the user running the data pump export at the tablespace level must have *exp_full_data* privilege for this option to work if that tablespace contains objects from schemas other than the one running the export. Otherwise, the following Oracle errors will be returned:

```
Export: Release 11.1.0.6.0 - Production on Friday, 27 June, 2008 11:20:44
Copyright (c) 2003, 2007, Oracle.  All rights reserved.
Connected to: Oracle Database 11g Enterprise Edition Release 11.1.0.6.0 -
Production
With the Partitioning, OLAP, Data Mining and Real Application Testing
options
ORA-31631: privileges are required
ORA-39161: Full database jobs require privileges
```

Export Schema Level

There are far too many good reasons to perform data pump exports at the schema level to either explain or justify them all. Suffice it to say that the export of entire schemas is probably one of the most frequently utilized modes. For example, one uses a development database where developers are writing code against a collection of related tables. Each time a developer runs some code that has yet to pass unit testing, it is possible that the data's ending state may not be entirely consistent, i.e. bug in code may invalidate the data. So

---

the developer needs a way to reset the data between runs. If the DBA makes a schema level data pump export of the base data, then it is a simple procedure to restore the data. Here is an example of exporting two specific schemas.

```
C:\> expdp bert/bert directory=data_pump_dir dumpfile=multi_schema.dmp
schemas=bert,movies
```

Note that when exporting at this level of granularity, the EXCLUDE and INCLUDE options become quite useful. For example, if one wanted to perform that exact same export without corresponding grants, indexes and statistics, here is the additional data pump export syntax required:

```
C:\> expdp bert/bert directory=data_pump_dir dumpfile=schema_exclude.dmp
schemas=bert,movies exclude=grant,index,statistics
```

And if the DBA had instead preferred to only unload those tables and views that started with the string "MOVIE", here is the data pump export command:

```
C:\> expdp bert/bert directory=data_pump_dir dumpfile=schema_include.dmp
schemas=bert,movies include=table:\"like 'MOVIES%'\"
```

Like the database and tablespace levels, the user running the data pump export at the schema level must have *exp_full_data* privilege for this option to work when requesting schemas other than the one running the export.

Export Table Level

Table level data pump export jobs are probably the second most often utilized mode. It is very easy to think in terms of tables when working with data. Table level mode just seems to be the natural granularity of choice. Return to the prior example of the developer working on code who needs the ability to refresh those tables between runs. The DBA could either export just the tables that developer needs for that programming task, or better yet, the DBA could permit and instruct the developer to export the tables being worked upon. Either way, the data pump export job would work in table mode and for the tables requested, as shown here.

```
C:\> expdp bert/bert directory=data_pump_dir dumpfile=multi_table.dmp
tables=movies.customer,movies.employee
```

Note that the table level mode data pump exports have to be sourced from but one schema, or the following error will occur:

```
C:\> expdp bert/bert directory=data_pump_dir dumpfile=multi_table.dmp
tables=movies.customer,movies.employee,bert.junk

Export: Release 11.1.0.6.0 - Production on Saturday, 28 June, 2008 6:40:21
Copyright (c) 2003, 2007, Oracle.  All rights reserved.
Connected to: Oracle Database 11g Enterprise Edition Release 11.1.0.6.0 -
Production
With the Partitioning, OLAP, Data Mining and Real Application Testing
options
UDE-00012: table mode exports only allow objects from one schema
```

Export Data Subsets

This is probably the most powerful and useful aspect of the data export process, and yet it remains highly underutilized. For instance, if one wants to extract data from a table by using a filter upon the rows being returned. That is easily accomplished via a normal SELECT command's WHERE clause placed in the query parameter passed to the export process. Then one could easily export only those customers who live in Texas as follows:

```
C:\> expdp bert/bert directory=data_pump_dir dumpfile=just_texas.dmp
schemas=movies query=movies.customer:\"where state='TX'\"
```

That seems easy enough – but there is a small catch. The QUERY clause is applied to all the tables in the export set, so all the tables better have the columns referenced by that WHERE clause. A common example would be a schema table design where each table contains a last modified date column. So if the DBA wanted to unload just records in that schema which had been modified within the past three months, here is the data pump export command for that:

```
C:\>expdp bert/bert directory=data_pump_dir dumpfile=last_mod_date.dmp
schemas=movies query=\"where last_mod_date is not null and last_mod_date >
SYSDATE-90\"
```

Yet as easy and powerful as this method is, there is another method that sometimes can be exactly what one is looking for – the subset by random sample method. If one wanted to export 10% of one's production data for use in development or test environments, then it applies the sample percentage against each object exported.

```
C:\> expdp bert/bert directory=data_pump_dir dumpfile=sample.dmp
schemas=movies sample=10
```

However, there is one major drawback to the sample method: it does not
export referentially correct subsets of data. That is because it merely applies a
simple algorithm, namely that the percentage represents the probability that a
data block of rows will be included in the export's sampling of the data. This is
plainly applied at the table level across all of its data blocks. The sample
method does not adhere to any referential integrity constraints or foreign keys
defined in the data dictionary. So if an effort to export a 10% sample of the
entire schema is made, it will generally end up with messages like those shown
below.

```
Processing object type SCHEMA_EXPORT/TABLE/CONSTRAINT/REF_CONSTRAINT
ORA-39083: Object type REF_CONSTRAINT failed to create with error:
ORA-02298: cannot validate (BERT.MOVIETITLE_FK) - parent keys not found
Failing sql is:
ALTER TABLE "BERT"."MOVIETITLE" ADD CONSTRAINT "MOVIETITLE_FK" FOREIGN KEY
("CATEGORYID") REFERENCES "BERT"."MOVIECATEGORY" ("CATE
GORYID") ENABLE
```

However, there are ways to get around this. One way could be to create a
SQL*Plus script to generate a parameter file with a series of query parameters
that would sample the data and retain the foreign key relationships. But that
would constitute a two-step process: run the script to create parameter files
and then run the data pump export with no easy way via the database to look
at the intermediate results to verify their accuracy before attempting the actual
data load. So instead, the preference is to execute the extract_data_subset.sql
SQL*Plus script, shown below, to create the subset of the data in a second
schema. Then the data can be readily examined for accuracy, and that schema
can finally be exported once it is known to be correct.

extract_data_subset.sql script

```
set linesize 200
set serveroutput on size 100000

create or replace package subsetdata
as
  procedure xgo (xsource varchar2, xtarget varchar2, xpercent integer);
end;
/
show error
create or replace package body subsetdata
as
  type tnames is table of varchar2(32);
  done_arr tnames := tnames();
  done_cnt integer := 0;
```

```
    procedure xsample (xsource varchar2, xtarget varchar2, current_table
varchar2, xpercent integer)
    is
    s1    varchar2(256) := 'create table ' || xtarget || '.' || current_table
|| '
as
select * from ' || xsource || '.' ||current_table;
    s2    varchar2(256) := 'where rownum <= (select ceil(' ||
to_char(xpercent/100) || ' * count(*))
from ' || xsource || '.' || current_table || ');';
    s3    varchar2(256) := 'create table ' || xtarget || '.' || current_table
|| ' as
select T0.* from   ' || xsource || '.' || current_table || '  T0,';
    s4    varchar2(256) := 'where';
    cnt1 integer        := 0;
    cnt2 integer        := 0;
    i    integer        := 0;
    j    integer        := 0;
    es3  varchar2(1)    := '';
    es4  varchar2(4)    := '';
    begin
    i := 0;
    es3 := ',';
    select count(*)
    into cnt1
    from dba_constraints fk,
         dba_constraints pk
    where fk.constraint_type = 'R'
      and fk.owner = xsource
      and fk.R_owner = xsource
      and fk.table_name = current_table
      and pk.constraint_type in ('P','U')
      and pk.owner = xsource
      and pk.table_name != current_table
      and fk.r_constraint_name = pk.constraint_name;
    if (cnt1 = 0) then
      dbms_output.put_line(s1);
      dbms_output.put_line(s2);
    else
      for c1 in (select pk.table_name,
                        fk.constraint_name fk_name,
                        pk.constraint_name pk_name
                 from dba_constraints fk,
                      dba_constraints pk
                 where fk.constraint_type = 'R'
                   and fk.owner = xsource
                   and fk.R_owner = xsource
                   and fk.table_name = current_table
                   and pk.constraint_type in ('P','U')
                   and pk.owner = xsource
                   and pk.table_name != current_table
                   and fk.r_constraint_name = pk.constraint_name
                ) loop
        i := i + 1;
        if (i = cnt1) then
          es3 := '';
        end if;
        s3 := s3 || '
```

```
' || xtarget || '.' || c1.table_name || '  T' || to_char(i) || es3;
       j := 0;
       es4 := ' and';
       select count(*)
       into cnt2
       from dba_cons_columns fk,
            dba_cons_columns pk
       where fk.constraint_name = c1.fk_name
         and fk.owner = xsource
         and fk.table_name = current_table
         and pk.constraint_name = c1.pk_name
         and pk.owner = xsource
         and pk.table_name != current_table
         and fk.position = pk.position;
       for c2 in (select fk.column_name fk_col,
                         pk.column_name pk_col
                  from dba_cons_columns fk,
                       dba_cons_columns pk
                  where fk.constraint_name = c1.fk_name
                    and fk.owner = xsource
                    and fk.table_name = current_table
                    and pk.constraint_name = c1.pk_name
                    and pk.owner = xsource
                    and pk.table_name != current_table
                    and fk.position = pk.position
                    order by fk.position
                 ) loop
           j := j + 1;
           if (i = cnt1) and (j = cnt2) then
             es4 := ';';
           end if;
           s4 := s4 || '
' || 'T0.' || c2.fk_col || ' = T' || to_char(i) || '.' || c2.pk_col || es4;
       end loop;
     end loop;
     dbms_output.put_line(s3);
     dbms_output.put_line(s4);
   end if;
   done_arr.extend(1);
   done_cnt := done_cnt+1;
   done_arr(done_cnt) := current_table;
 end;

 procedure xprocess (xsource varchar2, xtarget varchar2, current_table
varchar2, xpercent integer)
 is
   i    integer := 1;
   flg  integer := 1;
   cnt1 integer := 0;
   cnt2 integer := 0;
 begin
   xsample (xsource, xtarget, current_table, xpercent);
   for c1 in (select fk.table_name
             from dba_constraints fk,
                  dba_constraints pk
             where fk.constraint_type = 'R'
               and fk.owner = xsource
               and fk.R_owner = xsource
               and fk.table_name != current_table
```

```
                    and pk.constraint_type in ('P','U')
                    and pk.owner = xsource
                    and pk.table_name = current_table
                    and fk.r_constraint_name = pk.constraint_name
                ) loop
        select count(*)
        into cnt1
        from dba_constraints fk,
             dba_constraints pk
        where fk.constraint_type = 'R'
          and fk.owner = xsource
          and fk.R_owner = xsource
          and fk.table_name = c1.table_name
          and pk.constraint_type in ('P','U')
          and pk.owner = xsource
          and pk.table_name != current_table
          and fk.r_constraint_name = pk.constraint_name;
        if (cnt1 > 0) then
          cnt2 := 0;
          flg  := 0;
          for c2 in (select pk.table_name
                     from dba_constraints fk,
                          dba_constraints pk
                     where fk.constraint_type = 'R'
                       and fk.owner = xsource
                       and fk.R_owner = xsource
                       and fk.table_name = c1.table_name
                       and pk.constraint_type in ('P','U')
                       and pk.owner = xsource
                       and pk.table_name != current_table
                       and fk.r_constraint_name = pk.constraint_name
                    ) loop
            i := 1;
            while (i <= done_cnt) loop
              if (c2.table_name = done_arr(i)) then
                cnt2 := cnt2 + 1;
              end if;
              i := i + 1;
            end loop;
          end loop;
          if (cnt1 = cnt2) then
            flg := 1;
          end if;
        end if;
        if (flg = 1) then
          xprocess (xsource, xtarget, c1.table_name, xpercent);
        end if;
      end loop;
end;

procedure xgo (xsource varchar2, xtarget varchar2, xpercent integer)
is
begin
   for c1 in (select table_name
              from dba_tables tab
              where tab.owner = xsource
                and NOT EXISTS (select 1
                                from dba_constraints fk
                                where fk.constraint_type = 'R'
```

```
                                  and fk.owner = xsource
                                  and fk.R_owner = xsource
                                  and fk.table_name = tab.table_name
                         )
              ) loop
         xprocess (xsource, xtarget, c1.table_name, xpercent);
      end loop;
  end;
end;
/
show error

prompt
###
###  subsetdata.xgo(SOURCE_SCHEMA,TARGET_SCHEMA,PERCENTAGE)
###
exec subsetdata.xgo('MOVIES','BERT',10)
```

Looking at the last statement in the *extract_data_subset.sql* SQL*Plus script, simply call the *subsetdata.xgo* procedure to run, thereby specifying the source and target schemas, plus the sampling percentage. The *extract_data_subset.sql* SQL*Plus script walks the database referential integrity dependency tree and maintains it for the data sample being generated. The *extract_data_subset.sql* output, shown next, is an example of the generated script for copying 10% of the simple MOVIES demo schema copied to the BERT intermediate schema.

🖫 extract_data_subset.sql output

```
create table BERT.CUSTOMER
as
select * from MOVIES.CUSTOMER
where rownum <= (select ceil(.1 * count(*))
from MOVIES.CUSTOMER);

create table BERT.EMPLOYEE
as
select * from MOVIES.EMPLOYEE
where rownum <= (select ceil(.1 * count(*))
from MOVIES.EMPLOYEE);

create table BERT.MOVIERENTAL as
select T0.* from   MOVIES.MOVIERENTAL   T0,
 BERT.CUSTOMER   T1,
 BERT.EMPLOYEE   T2
where
 T0.CUSTOMERID = T1.CUSTOMERID and
 T0.EMPLOYEEID = T2.EMPLOYEEID;

create table BERT.MOVIECATEGORY
as
select * from MOVIES.MOVIECATEGORY
where rownum <= (select ceil(.1 * count(*))
from MOVIES.MOVIECATEGORY);
```

```
create table BERT.MOVIETITLE as
select T0.* from   MOVIES.MOVIETITLE   T0,
 BERT.MOVIECATEGORY   T1
where
 T0.CATEGORYID = T1.CATEGORYID;

create table BERT.MOVIECOPY as
select T0.* from   MOVIES.MOVIECOPY   T0,
 BERT.MOVIETITLE   T1
where
 T0.MOVIEID = T1.MOVIEID;

create table BERT.RENTALITEM as
select T0.* from   MOVIES.RENTALITEM   T0,
 BERT.MOVIERENTAL   T1,
 BERT.MOVIECOPY   T2
where
 T0.RENTALID = T1.RENTALID and
 T0.MOVIECOPYID = T2.MOVIECOPYID;
```

Now the data can be verified as correct using standard SQL SELECT commands and then export that data using the data pump export at the schema level. Although this method requires a little additional database disk space to build the subset data, disk space is so cheap and this method provides a simple method for examining intermediate results. Since it maintains referential integrity, it is obviously superior to the data pump export sample method.

Export Transportable Tablespaces

Transportable tablespaces permit the DBA to copy or move a tablespace from one Oracle database to another and are generally the fastest way to move data between Oracle databases. That is because the transportable tablespace process breaks down into two basic operations: export/import the tablespace metadata from/to the source/target database, and copy the tablespace operating system data files. Note that the DBA does need to be granted the *exp_full_database* privilege in order to unload transportable tablespaces.

Transportable tablespaces were introduced back with Oracle 8i, but over the years they have incrementally improved quite a bit. So while there are still some restrictions, e.g. source and target database must both be of the same character and national character sets, this is one area where Oracle seems to make measurable improvements with each and every release. It will be best to check with the Oracle version's documentation to verify the specific intra- and inter-version limitations. Be keenly aware of all such issues before attempting.

The complete transportable tablespace process steps are as follows:

1. Check for cross platform issues, i.e. source & target endian formats
2. Check for cross tablespace dependencies (may define export filters)
3. Alter tablespace to READ ONLY mode
4. Export the transportable tablespace set, i.e. the tablespace metadata
5. Transfer both the export file and tablespace data files to the target
6. If necessary, convert data files to correct endian format for the target
7. Import the transportable tablespace set, i.e. the tablespace metadata
8. Alter tablespace to READ WRITE mode

Now examine in detail steps one through four. The other steps are covered by the section on importing transportable tablespaces.

Step 1: Check for cross platform issues

All data at the lowest level has to have its bytes and bits formatted in some meaningful order when written to disk. This is referred to as endianness – or more simply, byte order. So while the in-memory value for 0x0A0B0C0D is always the same, how it is written to disk varies depending on hardware platform and operating system. The two alternatives are big and little endian format.

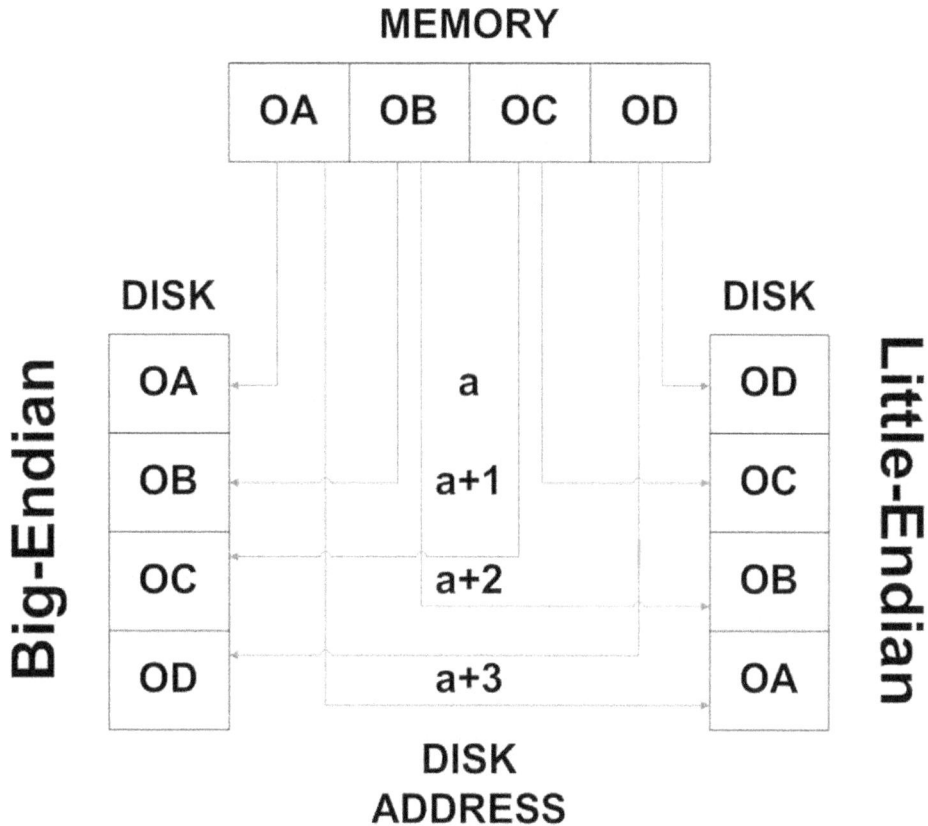

MEMORY

Figure 6.1: *Big Endian and Little Endian Format*

Fortunately, Oracle keeps a nice endian cross-reference table for DBAs to utilize, which can be queried as shown below.

```
SQL> select * from V$TRANSPORTABLE_PLATFORM ;

PLATFORM_ID PLATFORM_NAME                      ENDIAN_FORMAT
----------- ---------------------------------- --------------
          1 Solaris[tm] OE (32-bit)            Big
          2 Solaris[tm] OE (64-bit)            Big
          7 Microsoft Windows IA (32-bit)      Little
         10 Linux IA (32-bit)                  Little
          6 AIX-Based Systems (64-bit)         Big
          3 HP-UX (64-bit)                     Big
          5 HP Tru64 UNIX                      Little
          4 HP-UX IA (64-bit)                  Big
         11 Linux IA (64-bit)                  Little
         15 HP Open VMS                        Little
          8 Microsoft Windows IA (64-bit)      Little
          9 IBM zSeries Based Linux            Big
```

```
13 Linux 64-bit for AMD          Little
16 Apple Mac OS                  Big
```

So if a tablespace is going to be transported from Windows to Linux, there is no additional conversion step of the data file necessary. But if the transport is from Solaris to Linux, one would have to convert the big endian data file to little endian. For now, that conversion will be postponed until just before the import is implemented. Just record the source and target byte order natures so that one will know what, if anything, has to be done later.

Step 2: Check for cross tablespace dependencies

Transportable tablespaces must be self-contained. That means that the tablespace must stand entirely on its own with no logical or physical dependencies or references between objects in the transport set and anything outside that set. The four most common cross dependency issues include:

- A referential integrity constraint such as a foreign key between a table inside the tablespace being transported and another table outside that tablespace

- A partitioned object only partially contained within the tablespace being transported, i.e. object's partitions and/or sub-partitions span tablespaces

- A table containing LOB columns that either reference or utilize another tablespace not in the export set. Examples: LOB storage, LOB overflow, and such

- An index inside the tablespace being transported for a table in another tablespace that is outside the transport set

Fortunately, once again Oracle offers features to make this step fairly painless via the DBMS-TTS package. This package checks that a transport set is self contained.

```
DBMS_TTS.TRANSPORT_SET_CHECK (
    ts_list          IN CLOB,
    incl_constraints IN BOOLEAN DEFAULT FALSE,
    full_check       IN BOOLEAN DEFAULT FALSE);
```

Simply provide a tablespace name list separated by commas and two Boolean parameters. The first Boolean parameter is whether or not to check referential integrity constraints and this is usually set to TRUE. The second Boolean parameter indicates whether or not to perform a full check where full means anything either pointing into or out of the transport set. Once again, the recommended value is TRUE. So, of course, the defaults for both are FALSE!

This package is then executed and checked for its results via a SELECT against the transport_set_violations table as shown here. If "no rows selected" shows up, then it is good to go. Otherwise, it is best to record what the issues are and address them during the data pump export via the EXCLUDE clause.

```
SQL> exec dbms_tts.transport_set_check('ACCOUNTING',true,true)
SQL> select * from TRANSPORT_SET_VIOLATIONS;
no rows selected
```

Step 3: Alter transportable tablespace to READ ONLY mode

This is a fairly easy but quite mandatory step as the tablespace must be in READ ONLY mode for the export to succeed.

```
SQL> alter tablespace users read only;
Tablespace altered.
```

If this step is skipped, the following error messages will show up:

```
ORA-39123: Data Pump transportable tablespace job aborted
ORA-39185: The transportable tablespace failure list is
ORA-29335: tablespace 'USERS' is not read only
Job "BERT"."SYS_EXPORT_TRANSPORTABLE_01" stopped due to fatal error at
11:13:22
```

Step 4: Export the transportable tablespace set

Now comes the easiest and most obvious part of the transportable tablespace export process: the step to actually export the tablespace(s) metadata. Remember, it is just the metadata being exported, not the actual data or data files. Hence, this step is actually very quick and easy as shown here. Note that if a good job was done during Step 2's check for being self-contained, then the parameter for *transport_full_check* is probably just an extra, although generally still worthwhile, step. The data pump transportable tablespace export process has now been completed.

```
C:\> expdp bert/bert directory=data_pump_dir dumpfile=accounting.dmp
transport_tablespaces=accounting transport_full_check=y
```

IMPDP

Data pump import (IMPDP) is a very modern, server based and highly scalable data loading utility. On typical multi-processor servers with good disk-I/O subsystems, the time to load hundreds of gigabytes to terabytes is both reliable and reasonable. And even though the dump files remain Oracle proprietary, there are also easily identifiable uses of XML within those files. Therefore, uncompressed import files are semi-readable within a text editor, and as before, can be scanned with operating system commands such as string on UNIX.

Data pump import is unlikely to beat a finely tuned SQL*Loader job, nonetheless it is about as fast as one could hope for and is also very easy to use. Then all the details are kept in the data dictionary and, therefore, part of the overall database definition and backed up as such.

Start by identifying the most frequent data pump import (IMPDP) command line parameters:

PARAMETER	DESCRIPTION
ATTACH	[SCHEMA.]JOB_NAME Name of an already existing and executing job to connect to Need imp_full_database privilege for other schemas
CONTENT	ALL | META_DATA_ONLY | DATA_ONLY Filter the import of dump file contents to the specified criteria
DATA_OPTIONS	<null> | SKIP_CONSTRAINT_ERRORS Affects how non-deferred constraint violations are handled
DIRECTORY	DATA_PUMP_DIR | DIRECTORY_NAME Name of directory object pointing to a valid server directory
DUMPFILE	[DIRECTORY_NAME:]FILE_NAME [, ...] The name (and optionally directory) of the import data file
ESTIMATE	BLOCKS, STATISTICS Network import requests source to estimate data being sent

PARAMETER	DESCRIPTION
EXCLUDE	*OBJECT_TYPE[:NAME_FILTER_EXPRESSION] [, ...]* Database object types as a whole or by object name filter to specifically exclude from the import
FULL	N | Y Whether to perform a full database import or not Requires EXP_FULL_DATABASE privilege
INCLUDE	*OBJECT_TYPE[:NAME_FILTER_EXPRESSION] [, ...]* Database object types as a whole or by object name filter to specifically include in the import
JOB_NAME	*SYS_EXPORT_<mode>_NN | JOB_NAME* Name by which import job can be referenced (e.g. ATTACH)
LOGFILE	*EXPORT.LOG |* *[DIRECTORY_NAME:]FILE_NAME* The name (and optionally the directory) of the import log file
NOLOGFILE	N | Y Whether or not to suppress creation of the import log file
PARALLEL	1 | INTEGER The maximum number of concurrent threads for the import
PARFILE	*[DIRECTORY_SPECIFICATION]FILE_NAME* Name of the operating system specific parameter file
PARTITION_OPTIONS	NONE | DEPARTITION | MERGE Specifies how to implement source partitioning on the target
QUERY	*[[SCHEMA.]TABLE_NAME:]* *FILTER_EXPRESSION* Data filter condition applied to all tables or by schema and object name filters during the import
REMAP_DATA	*[schema.]tablename.column_name:[schema.]pkg.function* Function to generate new value for column during the import

PARAMETER	DESCRIPTION
REMAP_SCHEMA	*REMAP_SCHEMA=source_schema:target_schema* Permits creating objects in different schema than the export
REMAP_TABLE	*[schema.]old_tablename[.partition]:new_tablename* Naming schema for tables from created by partition options
REMAP_TABLESPACE	*source_tablespace:target_tablespace* Permits creating objects in different tablespace than the export (requires sufficient quota on the new target tablespace)
SCHEMAS	SCHEMA [, ...] The schema or schemas to import Need *IMP_FULL_DATABASE* privilege for other schemas
SKIP_UNUSABLE_INDEXES	N | Y Whether or not to skip indexes that were marked unusable during import
SQLFILE	*[directory_object:]file_name* The name (and optionally the directory) where import records all of the DDL it would have executed
STATUS	0 | INTEGER The frequency in seconds which job displays client feedback
TABLE_EXISTS_ACTION	SKIP | APPEND | TRUNCATE | REPLACE What import should do when encountering tables that already exist within the target
TABLES	*[SCHEMA.]TABLE_NAME[:PARTITION_NAME] [, ...]* List of tables for a table mode database import Restricted to a single schema
TABLESPACES	*TABLESPACE_NAME [, ...]* List of tablespaces for a tablespace mode database import

Table 6.3: *Frequent IMPDP Command Line Parameters*

Moreover, to use the stop and restart data pump job capabilities, run data pump in interactive mode by getting the data pump prompt. Then the following commands are also quite frequently useful:

PARAMETER	DESCRIPTION
CONTINUE_CLIENT	Connect client to currently executing job or restarts the job, and resumes logging mode (i.e. status output)
EXIT_CLIENT	Disconnect client connection to currently executing job and terminate the client process – but leave server job running
KILL_JOB	Detach all client processes connected to this data pump job and then terminate (i.e. kill) the currently running job
START_JOB	Start or resume the current data pump job
STOP_JOB	[IMMEDIATE] Detach all client processes connected to this data pump job and then orderly shutdown the currently running job

Table 6.4: *Additional IMPDP Parameters*

So examine some very common use cases and how data pump import is utilized to load the data.

Import Database Level

This is often referred to as a logical restore where physical restore means those performed either via RMAN, operating system commands, or via third party backup and recovery tools - or in other words, at the OS or file level. One reason people used logical restores was historically for ease of recovery for when an object was accidentally dropped. However, with Oracle flashback technology, logical restores have become far less compelling. Another reason people performed logical restores was to avoid the perils of the Oracle database migration process when a major new version released. DBAs would simply export the entire database, perform the upgrade, and then import the database. But over the years, the database migration has greatly improved, so this usage has also seen reduced importance. Probably the most prevalent reason for doing logical restores is to provide a simple backup and recovery mechanism with no additional software costs for development and test databases.

```
C:\> impdp bert/bert directory=data_pump_dir dumpfile=logical_backup.dmp
full=y
```

Remember, the user running the data pump import at the database level must have *imp_full_data* privilege for this option to work. Otherwise, the following Oracle errors will be returned:

```
Import: Release 11.1.0.6.0 - Production on Saturday, 28 June, 2008 14:04:11
Copyright (c) 2003, 2007, Oracle.  All rights reserved.
Connected to: Oracle Database 11g Enterprise Edition Release 11.1.0.6.0 -
Production
With the Partitioning, OLAP, Data Mining and Real Application Testing
options
ORA-31631: privileges are required
ORA-39161: Full database jobs require privileges
```

Import Tablespace Level

Although this may seem like a very useful and therefore common use case, the reality is that often DBAs find that tablespaces are simply containers with space for object allocation. So it is not uncommon over time to find that tablespaces have an eclectic collection of objects. But for those lucky enough and smart enough to have kept some logical rationale to tablespace object placement, here is an example of data pump entirely importing two specific tablespaces:

```
C:\> impdp bert/bert directory=data_pump_dir dumpfile=multi_tablespace.dmp
tablespaces=users,sysaux
```

One other use for the import at the tablespace level would be if one wished to recreate the tablespace with a different block size like a tablespace level reorganization. The tablespace could be exported, dropped, recreated with the new block size, and then the data could be imported. Some people have used the tablespace level import as part of the process to merge tablespaces, but that is pretty rare.

As at the database level, the user running the data pump import at the tablespace level must have *imp_full_data* privilege for this option to work if that tablespaces contains objects from schemas other than the one running the import.

Import Schema Level

Like export schema level, there are far too many good reasons to perform data pump imports at the schema level to either explain or justify them all. So use the same example of a development database where developers are writing code against a collection of related tables. Each time a developer runs some code that has yet to pass unit testing, it is possible that the data's ending state may not be entirely consistent. So the developer needs a way to reset the data between runs. If the DBA makes a schema level data pump export of the base data, then it is a simple procedure to restore the data. Here is an example of importing two specific schemas.

```
C:\> impdp bert/bert directory=data_pump_dir dumpfile=multi_schema.dmp
schemas=bert,movies
```

However, this chapter also covers a newer and arguably superior method for accomplishing this – flashback technology.

Note that when importing at this level of granularity, the EXCLUDE and INCLUDE options become quite useful. For example, if one wanted to perform that exact same import without corresponding grants, indexes and statistics, here is the additional data pump import syntax required:

```
C:\> impdp bert/bert directory=data_pump_dir dumpfile=schema_exclude.dmp
schemas=bert,movies exclude=grant,index,statistics
```

And if only those tables and views that started with the string "MOVIE" were loaded, here is the data pump import command:

```
C:\> impdp bert/bert directory=data_pump_dir dumpfile=schema_include.dmp
schemas=bert,movies include=table:\"like 'MOVIES%'\"
```

Import Table Level

Table level data pump imports jobs are probably the most often utilized mode. It is very easy to think in terms of tables when working with data. Table level mode just seems to be the natural granularity of choice. Return to the prior example of the developer working on code who needs the ability to refresh those tables between runs. The DBA could either import just the tables that developer needs for that programming task, or better yet, the DBA could permit and instruct the developer to import the tables being worked upon.

Either way, the data pump import job would work in table mode and for the tables requested, as shown here.

```
C:\> impdp bert/bert directory=data_pump_dir dumpfile=multi_table.dmp
tables=movies.customer,movies.employee
```

Note that the table level mode data pump imports have to be sourced from but one schema, or this will be the following error.

```
C:\> impdp bert/bert directory=data_pump_dir dumpfile=multi_user.dmp
tables=movies.customer,movies.employee,bert.junk

Import: Release 11.1.0.6.0 - Production on Saturday, 28 June, 2008 14:19:51
Copyright (c) 2003, 2007, Oracle.  All rights reserved.
Connected to: Oracle Database 11g Enterprise Edition Release 11.1.0.6.0 -
Production
With the Partitioning, OLAP, Data Mining and Real Application Testing
options
UDI-00012: table mode imports only allow objects from one schema
```

Import Data Subsets

This is probably the most powerful and useful aspect of the data import process, and yet it remains highly underutilized. Say that one wants to load data from a table while using a filter upon the rows being inserted. That is easily accomplished via a normal SELECT command's WHERE clause placed in the query parameter passed to the import process. So, as done before, one could easily import only those customers who live in Texas as follows:

```
C:\> impdp bert/bert directory=data_pump_dir dumpfile=all_of_movies.dmp
schemas=movies query=movies.customer:\"where state='TX'\"
```

That seems easy enough, but there is a small catch. The QUERY clause is applied to all the tables in the import set, so all the tables better have the columns referenced by that WHERE clause. A common example would be a schema table design where each table contains a last modified date column. If only records in that schema which had been modified within the past three months should be loaded, here is the data pump export command for that:

```
C:\> impdp bert/bert directory=data_pump_dir dumpfile=all_of_movies.dmp
schemas=movies query=\"where last_mod_date is not null and last_mod_date >
SYSDATE-90\"
```

But unlike the export, the data pump import does not offer a sample method, so there is really no way to externally read and filter the dump file to try to filter the input or the create more complex filtering scenarios. So plan accordingly.

Import Transportable Tablespaces

Transportable tablespaces permit the copying or moving of a tablespace from one Oracle database to another and are generally the fastest way to move data between Oracle databases. That is because the transportable tablespace process breaks down into two basic operations: export/import the tablespace metadata from/to the source/target database, and copy the tablespace operating system data files. Note that one has to be granted the *imp_full_database* privilege in order to load transportable tablespaces.

Transportable tablespaces were introduced back with Oracle 8i, but over the years they have incrementally improved quite a bit. So while there are still some restrictions like the source and target database must both be of the same character and national character sets, this is one area where Oracle seems to make measurable improvements with each and every release. So it will be best to check with the Oracle version's documentation to verify the specific intra and inter version limitations. So be keenly aware of all such issues before attempting.

Again, the complete transportable tablespace process steps are as follows:

1. Check for cross platform issues, i.e. source & target endian formats

2. Check for cross tablespace dependencies (may define export filters)

3. Alter tablespace to READ ONLY mode

4. Export the transportable tablespace set, i.e. the tablespace metadata

5. Transfer both the export file and tablespace data files to the target

6. If necessary, convert data files to correct endian format for the target

7. Import the transportable tablespace set, i.e. the tablespace metadata)

8. Alter tablespace to READ WRITE mode

Now examine in detail steps five through eight; the other steps are covered by the previous section on exporting transportable tablespaces.

Step 5: Transfer both the export file and tablespace data files to the target

This step is just as easy as it sounds. Simply copy or ftp the export tablespace set and operating system level data files for that tablespace from the source to the target. Remember to use binary mode transfer with a favorite ftp program.

Step 6: Convert data files to correct endian format for the target

Back in Step 1, the Oracle endian cross-reference table as shown below was checked so that the source database endiannes or byte order could be recorded. Now check again for the target.

```
SQL> select * from V$TRANSPORTABLE_PLATFORM ;

PLATFORM_ID PLATFORM_NAME                    ENDIAN_FORMAT
----------- -------------------------------- --------------
          1 Solaris[tm] OE (32-bit)          Big
          2 Solaris[tm] OE (64-bit)          Big
          7 Microsoft Windows IA (32-bit)    Little
         10 Linux IA (32-bit)                Little
          6 AIX-Based Systems (64-bit)       Big
          3 HP-UX (64-bit)                   Big
          5 HP Tru64 UNIX                    Little
          4 HP-UX IA (64-bit)                Big
         11 Linux IA (64-bit)                Little
         15 HP Open VMS                      Little
          8 Microsoft Windows IA (64-bit)    Little
          9 IBM zSeries Based Linux          Big
         13 Linux 64-bit for AMD             Little
         16 Apple Mac OS                     Big
```

So if a tablespace is going to be transported from Windows to Linux, there is no additional conversion step of the data file necessary. But if the transport is happening from Solaris to Linux, the big endian data file would need to be converted to little endian. The data format conversion was postponed earlier because it is better to wait until the format that is needed for the specific target de jour is apparent.

Once the target has been identified and it is discovered that a conversion is necessary, then use the Oracle RMAN utility on the target, or source, to reformat the data files with the proper byte order encoding.

```
RMAN> convert datafile 'c:\temp\accounting.dbf'
2> to platform = "Linux 64-bit for AMD"
3> from platform = "HP Tru64 UNIX"
```

```
4> db_file_name_convert =
5> "c:\oracle\oradata\ordb2\",
6> "c:\oracle\oradata\ordb3\"
7> parallelism=2;
```

There are two items above of note. First, the data file was copied into a temporary directory on the target server and not the file's final destination. This is done because it is best not to move a data file into the Oracle environment until it is ready to be absorbed, which means the byte order has already been addressed. And second, the convert was instructed about necessary file naming changes. In the example above, this tablespace is moved from database ORDB2 to ORDB3, so the data file headers need to be updated for that change.

Step 7: Import the transportable tablespace set

Now comes the easiest and most obvious part of the transportable tablespace import process: the step to actually import the tablespace(s) metadata. Also remember that it is just the metadata being imported and not the actual data or data files. Hence, this step is actually very quick and easy as shown here. If a good job was done during step 2's check for being self-contained, then the parameter for *transport_full_check* is probably just an extra, although still worthwhile, step.

```
C:\> impdp bert/bert directory=data_pump_dir dumpfile=accounting.dmp
transport_tablespaces=accounting transport_full_check=y
```

Step 8: Alter transportable tablespace to READ WRITE mode

This is a fairly easy but usually mandatory step as the tablespace to be must be placed into READ WRITE for the target database to actually be able to utilize the objects and data contained within.

```
SQL> alter tablespace users read write;
Tablespace altered.
```

If this step is skipped, the following error messages will occur:

```
ORA-00372: file 4 cannot be modified at this time
ORA-01110: data file 4: 'C:\ORACLE\ORADATA\ORDB2\USERS.DBF'
```

Import Partition Options

One of the neatest new features that data pump offers is the ability to manage partition implementation during the import process. The source table had to have been partitioned when exported. Then during the import, there are three options: NONE, DEPARTITION and MERGE. NONE means to import the structure exactly the same as it was in the source database, therefore, partitioned if it was so. DEPARTITION means to create a separate table for every partition and sub-partition. This might be useful when attempting to backwards port tables as non-partitioned for deployment in a development environment, i.e. developer sandbox. The table naming scheme is as follows: table_name_sys_pxxx or table_name_sys_subpxxx for partitions and sub-partitions, respectively. This is just table_name || parititon_name. Here is an example of a schema with fairly complex partitioning being imported with each of these three options.

```
C$\> impdp bert/bert directory=data_pump_dir dumpfile=bmf.dmp
remap_schema=BMF:BMF2 partition_options=none
C$\> impdp bert/bert directory=data_pump_dir dumpfile=bmf.dmp
remap_schema=BMF:BMF3 partition_options=departition
C$\> impdp bert/bert directory=data_pump_dir dumpfile=bmf.dmp
remap_schema=BMF:BMF4 partition_options=merge
```

Note that schema BMF2 has all the exact same counts as BMF for tables vs. partitions vs. subpartitions. So the NONE option did, in fact, import it exactly the same. Now look at BMF, which had been imported with the DEPARTITION option. It has 1387 tables! Finally, BMF4 imported with MERGE has just the eight tables and no partitions or subpartitions.

```
SQL>  select owner, count(*) from dba_tables where owner like 'BMF%' group
by owner order by 1;
BMF                            8
BMF2                           8
BMF3                        1387
BMF4                           8
SQL>  select table_owner, count(*) from dba_tab_partitions where table_owner
like 'BMF%' group by table_owner order by 1;
BMF                          194
BMF2                         194
SQL>  select table_owner, count(*) from dba_tab_subpartitions where
table_owner like 'BMF%' group by table_owner order by 1;
BMF                         1360
BMF2                        1360
```

Import Remapping Options

Often during the import process, something may need to be loaded in the target differently than it was in the source. Back in the old export days, there were the fromuser and touser parameters to load objects into a different schema. And while that was handy, it was never quite enough. Data pump has addressed this need by adding a plethora of remapping options. Look back at the prior section where there was the partition example. Was the remap_schema option being used to load into BMF2, BMF3 and BMF4 noticed? That is pretty much the same as the fromuser and touser concept. But there is more. Do another BMF schema remap where there are the objects to be created in a different tablespace as well. Here is how it is done:

```
C:\> impdp bert/bert directory=data_pump_dir dumpfile=bmf.dmp
remap_schema=BMF:BMF5 remap_tablespace=users:accounting
partition_options=none
```

If one wanted to rename tables during the import, there is the *remap_table* parameter. The most powerful remapping concept is *remap_data*. With this, a table can be loaded and the values can be changed for columns using a function that returns the same data type as that column. The function itself can be practically unlimited, except not permitted to issue either COMMIT and/or ROLLBACK commands. A strong argument could be made that this makes the Data Pump a sort of ETL (Extract, Translate and Load) toolset now because this remapping function can handle the translate portion.

DBMS_DATAPUMP

The Oracle supplied *dbms_datapump* package provides a PL/SQL API to the exact same functionality as the prior two sections about the IMPDP and EXPDP command line utilities. But the reason is not the expectation that DBAs will flock to use this programmatic interface, but rather to provide a well documented and standardized API for OEM and other third party tools to call for those users who prefer using screens. As such, this method will not be documented to the same level of detail, but rather just highlight the PL/SQL package specification reference information and a single example. Here are programmatic interfaces available from this Oracle supplied PL/SQL package followed by the simple export schema example using this API.

```
-- Add the file to the data pump import/export file set

PROCEDURE add_file (
    handle       IN   NUMBER,
    filename     IN   VARCHAR2,
    directory    IN   VARCHAR2 DEFAULT NULL,
    filesize     IN   VARCHAR2 DEFAULT NULL,
    filetype     IN   NUMBER DEFAULT KU$_FILE_TYPE_DUMP_FILE,
    reusefile    IN   NUMBER DEFAULT NULL
  );

-- Attach the current database session to a data pump job process

FUNCTION attach (
    job_name     IN   VARCHAR2 DEFAULT NULL,
    job_owner    IN   VARCHAR2 DEFAULT NULL
  )
  RETURN NUMBER;

-- Permits the specification of data pump job table data filtering

PROCEDURE data_filter (
    handle       IN   NUMBER,
    name         IN   VARCHAR2,
    value        IN   NUMBER | CLOB | VARCHAR2,
    table_name   IN   VARCHAR2 DEFAULT NULL,
    schema_name  IN   VARCHAR2 DEFAULT NULL
  );

-- Detach the current database session to a data pump job process

PROCEDURE detach (
    handle    IN   NUMBER
  );

-- Returns the extended data pump file information

PROCEDURE get_dumpfile_info (
    filename     IN     VARCHAR2,
    directory    IN     VARCHAR2,
    info_table   OUT    ku$_dumpfile_info,
    filetype     OUT    NUMBER
  );

-- Returns the status of a data pump job

FUNCTION get_status (
    handle    IN   NUMBER,
    mask      IN   INTEGER,
    timeout   IN   NUMBER DEFAULT NULL
  )
  RETURN ku$_Status;

PROCEDURE get_status (
    handle       IN   NUMBER,
    mask         IN   INTEGER,
    timeout      IN   NUMBER DEFAULT NULL,
    job_state    OUT VARCHAR2,
    status       OUT ku$_Status1010 | ku$_Status1020
```

```
    );

-- Permits the insertion of a message into the log file

PROCEDURE log_entry (
    handle          IN  NUMBER,
    message         IN  VARCHAR2,
    log_file_only   IN  NUMBER DEFAULT 0
    );

-- Permits the specification of data pump job metadata filtering

PROCEDURE metadata_filter (
    handle          IN  NUMBER,
    name            IN  VARCHAR2,
    value           IN  VARCHAR2 | CLOB,
    object_path     IN  VARCHAR2 DEFAULT NULL,
    object_type     IN  VARCHAR2 DEFAULT NULL
    );
-- Permits the specification of data pump job object re-mappings

PROCEDURE metadata_remap (
    handle          IN  NUMBER,
    name            IN  VARCHAR2,
    old_value       IN  VARCHAR2,
    value           IN  VARCHAR2,
    object_type     IN  VARCHAR2 DEFAULT NULL
    );

-- Permits the specification of data pump job metadata transformations

PROCEDURE metadata_transform (
    handle          IN  NUMBER,
    name            IN  VARCHAR2,
    value           IN  VARCHAR2 | NUMBER,
    object_type     IN  VARCHAR2 DEFAULT NULL
    );

-- Declares a new data pump job returning handle required for other API
calls

FUNCTION open (
    operation       IN  VARCHAR2,
    job_mode        IN  VARCHAR2,
    remote_link     IN  VARCHAR2 DEFAULT NULL,
    job_name        IN  VARCHAR2 DEFAULT NULL,
    version         IN  VARCHAR2 DEFAULT 'COMPATIBLE',
    compression     IN  NUMBER DEFAULT KU$_COMPRESS_METADATA
    )
    RETURN NUMBER;

-- Permits the specification of data pump job parallelization degree

PROCEDURE set_parallel (
    handle      IN  NUMBER,
    degree      IN  NUMBER
    );

-- Permits the specification of data pump job-processing options
```

```
PROCEDURE set_parameter (
    handle      IN  NUMBER,
    name        IN  VARCHAR2,
    value       IN  NUMBER | VARCHAR2
  );

-- Begin or resume the execution of a data pump job

PROCEDURE start_job (
    handle          IN  NUMBER,
    skip_current    IN  NUMBER DEFAULT 0,
    abort_step      IN  NUMBER DEFAULT 0,
    cluster_ok      IN  NUMBER DEFAULT 1,
    service_name    IN  VARCHAR2 DEFAULT NULL
  );

-- Terminate the execution of a data pump job

PROCEDURE stop_job (
    handle      IN  NUMBER,
    immediate   IN  NUMBER DEFAULT 0,
    keep_master IN  NUMBER DEFAULT NULL,
    delay       IN  NUMBER DEFAULT 60
  );

-- Runs a data pump job until it completes or aborts

PROCEDURE wait_for_job (
    handle      IN  NUMBER,
    job_state   OUT VARCHAR2
  );
```

Here is the command line version of the schema export once again that is the slightly more involved version utilizing PL/SQL API coding as the interface.

```
C:\> expdp bert/bert directory=data_pump_dir dumpfile=multi_schema.dmp
schemas=bert,movies

DECLARE
  handle NUMBER;
  status VARCHAR2(20);
BEGIN
  handle := DBMS_DATAPUMP.OPEN ('EXPORT', 'SCHEMA');
  DBMS_DATAPUMP.ADD_FILE (handle, 'multi_schema.dmp', 'DATA_PUMP_DIR');
  DBMS_DATAPUMP.METADATA_FILTER (handle, 'SCHEMA_EXPR', 'IN
(''BERT'',''MOVIES'')');
  DBMS_DATAPUMP.START_JOB (handle);
  DBMS_DATAPUMP.WAIT_FOR_JOB (handle, status);
END;
/
```

Data Pump 12c New Features

Oracle 12c offers many new features in 12c.

data pump encryption_pwd_prompt

The new 12c encryption_pwd_prompt parameter allows you to specify whether Data Pump should prompt you for the encryption password, rather than you entering it on the command line.

The default is "no" and you can specify the encryption_pwd_prompt and this parameter can be used with both expdp and impdp.

Data Pump export compression

Oracle 12c has new compression_algorithm 12c parameters for Data Pump, and 12c Oracle offers several levels of compression in Data Pump:

- **compression_algorithm=basic:** This level is not too CPU intensive and offers good compression

- **compression_algorithm=high:** This is the most CPU intensive option, but the one that many result in the smallest export dmp file.

- **compression_algorithm=medium:** This is similar to "basic" compression.

- **compression_algorithm=low:** This is for bases where the server is CPU bound and it will give the largest of the compressed files.

Here is an example invocation of expdp using the new compression_algorithm:

```
root> expdp dumpfile=mytabs.dmp tables=emp,dept compression_algorithm=high
```

impdp data pump disable_archive_logging

Oracle 12c offers disable_archive_logging in Data Pump to simply disable the writing on archived redo logs, and thereby speeding-up export operations.

You can set disable_archive_logging at several levels, globally and for specific tables and indexes:

```
transform=disable_archive_logging:Y
transform=disable_archive_logging:Y:tablename
transform=disable_archive_logging:Y:indexname
```

Here is a sample invocation of Data Pump, a schema import that disables arching logging:

```
root> impdp dumpfile=pythian.dmp table_exists_action=append schemas=scott
transform=disable_archive_logging:Y
```

In most cases you would want to run the disable archive logging parameter at the schemas level.

Data Pump 12c Logtime Parameter

The syntax for data pump logging is very straightforward. Oracle specifies four value for the logtime parameter:

- **logtime=none:** No timestamp information is displayed. (This is the default.) No timestamps on status or log file messages (same as default).
- **logtime=status:** Timestamp messages on status are displayed. Timestamps on status messages only.
- **logtime=logfile:** Same as STATUS, but only displayed for logfile messages. Timestamps on log file messages only.
- **logtime=all:** A combination of STATUS and LOGFILE. Timestamps on both status and log file messages.

Here is an example of the logtime parameter in a data pump export:

```
expdp scott/timer logtime=all directory=test
```

 As you may know, Oracle displays the progress of a data pump import or export operation to standard out. Using the logtime parameter, Oracle will add a date time stamp to each message. The Oracle docs show this simple example of the logtime parameter being used in a data pump export:

```
expdp hr DIRECTORY=dpump_dir1 \
DUMPFILE=expdat.dmp SCHEMAS=hr LOGTIME=ALL
```

The date/time information can be used to see how long it takes for specific objects to be exported, useful for planning production runtimes.

The Data Pump TRANSFORM Parameter

This 12c transform parameter instructs the Data Pump import job to modify the storage attributes of the DDL that creates the objects during the import job.

```
TRANSFORM = transform_name:value[:object_type]
transform_name: takes one of the following values:
```

- **segment_attributes:** If the value is specified as y, then segment attributes (physical attributes, storage attributes, tablespaces, and logging) are included, with appropriate DDL. The default is y.

- **storage:** If the value is specified as y, the storage clauses are included, with appropriate DDL. The default is y. This parameter is ignored if SEGMENT_ATTRIBUTES=n.

- **oid:** If the value is specified as n, the assignment of the exported OID during the creation of object tables and types is inhibited. Instead, a new OID is assigned. This can be useful for cloning schemas, but does not affect referenced objects. The default is y.

- **pctspace:** It accepts a greater-than-zero number. It represents the percentage multiplier used to alter extent allocations and the size of data files.

- **object_type:** It can take one of the following values:

```
CLUSTER,CONSTRAINT,INC_TYPE,INDEX,ROLLBACK_SEGMENT,TABLE,TABLESPACE,TYPE
impdp hr/hr TABLES=employees \
DIRECTORY=dp_dir DUMPFILE=hr_emp.dmp \
TRANSFORM=SEGMENT_ATTRIBUTES:n:table
impdp hr/hr TABLES=employees \
DIRECTORY=dp_dir DUMPFILE=hr_emp.dmp \
TRANSFORM=STORAGE:n:table
```

Oracle12c expdp view_as_tables

Prior to release 12c, Oracle expdp sometime has to go through complex gyrations when exporting view information, and Oracle has overcome this limitation by introducing the view_as_tables argument to expdp.

Invoked as "*view_as_tables=scott.empview*" the view_as_tables transforms a view at the source database into a table at the destination database, exporting all of the the columns of the view as-if they were table columns.

In a sense, the view_as_tables is an ad-hoc materialized view generator because the result set has been transformed from a view to a table.

In a case where only a small portion of a complex view is exported with *view_as_tables*, all unnecessary details that maintain the complex view are omitted.

Note: You cannot use *expdp* with the view_as_tables if you are choosing a LOB datatype column from the view.

Template tables are automatically dropped after the export operation is completed. While they exist, you can perform the following query to view their names (which all begin with KU$VAT):

```
select
    *
from
    user_tab_comments
where
    table_name like 'KU$VAT%'
```

For example, here we export a view called *scott.myview* using *views_as_tables*, naming it newtab1:

```
$ expdp xff/xifenfei views_as_tables=scott.myview:newtab1
directory=data_pump_dir dumpfile=xifenfei.dmp
Export: Release 12.1.0.0.2 - Beta on Sun Dec 16 07:56:48 2012
Copyright (c) 1982, 2012, Oracle and/or its affiliates. All rights reserved.
Connected to: Oracle Database 12c Enterprise Edition Release 12.1.0.0.2 -
64bit Beta
With the Partitioning, OLAP, Data Mining and Real Application Testing
options
Starting "XFF"."SYS_EXPORT_TABLE_01":xff/******** views_as_tables=v_xifenfei
directory=data_pump_dir
dumpfile=xifenfei.dmp
```

```
Estimate in progress using BLOCKS method...
Processing object type TABLE_EXPORT/VIEWS_AS_TABLES/TABLE_DATA
Total estimation using BLOCKS method: 16 KB
Processing object type TABLE_EXPORT/VIEWS_AS_TABLES/TABLE
. . exported "XFF"."V_XIFENFEI" 7.390 KB 3 rows
Master table "XFF"."SYS_EXPORT_TABLE_01" successfully loaded/unloaded
```

The view_as_tables allows you to specify a vie w as if it was a table and then make it into a table when using impdp:

```
$ impdp xff/xifenfei tables=v_xifenfei directory=data_pump_dir
dumpfile=xifenfei.dmp
Import: Release 12.1.0.0.2 - Beta on Sun Dec 16 07:59:05 2012
Copyright (c) 1982, 2012, Oracle and/or its affiliates. All rights reserved.
Connected to: Oracle Database 12c Enterprise Edition Release 12.1.0.0.2 -
64bit Beta
With the Partitioning, OLAP, Data Mining and Real Application Testing
options
Master table "XFF"."SYS_IMPORT_TABLE_01" successfully loaded/unloaded
Starting "XFF"."SYS_IMPORT_TABLE_01": xff/******** tables=v_xifenfei
directory=data_pump_dir
dumpfile=xifenfei.dmp
Processing object type TABLE_EXPORT/VIEWS_AS_TABLES/TABLE
ORA-39325: TABLE_EXISTS_ACTION cannot be applied to "XFF"."V_XIFENFEI".
Processing object type TABLE_EXPORT/VIEWS_AS_TABLES/TABLE_DATA
Job "XFF"."SYS_IMPORT_TABLE_01" completed with 1 error(s) at Sun Dec 16
07:59:13 2012 elapsed 0 00:00:05
```

DBMS_REDEFINITION

No database is 100% self-reliant or self-maintaining, which is a good thing for DBA job security. However, the last few major versions of Oracle have greatly increased its self-diagnostic and self-monitoring capabilities. Only database structural reorganization remains one of those tasks best left to the DBA to decide when it is appropriate to perform and when to schedule its execution. That is because data is the life blood of any modern organization, and while doing various database reorganizations, the following possibilities exist:

▪ The process could blow-up mid-stream, so data may be left offline

▪ The process is resource-intensive and takes significant time to execute

▪ Data could be momentarily inconsistent between key steps

▪ Probably advisable to consider doing a backup operation just prior to

The key point is that structural reorganizations are generally important events in any database's life cycle. Even when a reorganization activity can theoretically be performed entirely online with little or no downtime, it is often a safer bet to perform any such activities in a controlled environment. Because the one time something that can not go wrong does, the DBA will be in a better situation to resume or recover if there are not frantic customers breathing down his neck. So schedule any reorganization event with extreme caution and over- compensation.

Now with all that said, Oracle provides a robust and reliable package for performing many common online table level reorganizations – *dbms_redefinition*. Much like the *dbms_metadata* package, *dbms_redefinition* provides an almost limitless set of use cases or scenarios that it can address. Many people will probably just use the OEM graphical interface, but here is a very common example that should fulfill this key need as well as serve as a foundation for one's own modifications. The following are the key basic steps:

1. Verify that the table is a candidate for online redefinition
2. Create an interim table
3. Enable parallel DML operations
4. Start the redefinition process (and do not stop until step 9 is done)
5. Copy dependent objects
6. Check for any errors
7. Synchronize the interim table (optional)
8. Complete the redefinition
9. Drop the interim table

A common question is what is happening behind the scenes here? In other words, how and what is Oracle doing? Essentially, the redefinition package is merely an API to an intelligent materialized view with a materialized view log. So a local replication of the object shows while the reorganization occurs. Then it refreshes to get up-to-date for any transaction that occurred during reorganization.

Partition a Table

One of the most common table reorganization tasks is to partition a table that is currently not partitioned but that could benefit in manageability and/or performance by becoming partitioned. It may be that this table is a throwback from an earlier Oracle database version like those that were created long ago before partitioning was available or that it simply has grown over time to the point where partitioning makes sense. Another example might be that it is partitioned, but it is so by an older partitioning method or scheme. So if one wants to rebuild a hash partitioned table using Oracle 11g's new interval partitioning, there are many other partitioning scenarios, but the basic idea is this: the table is currently not partitioned or partitioned incorrectly, and this needs to be remedied.

Return once again to the MOVIES demo schema and partition the CUSTOMER table. And like any real world database, the rest of the database design depends on the customer, such as there are foreign keys to it. Not only that, but CUSTOMER has additional indexes and triggers. Here is the complete DDL for CUSTOMER. So as can be seen, it is much more than just a simple standalone table since there are also indexes and triggers that go with this table.

.Complete CUSTOMER table DDL

```
CREATE TABLE "MOVIES"."CUSTOMER"
(  "CUSTOMERID" NUMBER(10,0) NOT NULL ENABLE,
   "FIRSTNAME" VARCHAR2(20) NOT NULL ENABLE,
   "LASTNAME" VARCHAR2(30) NOT NULL ENABLE,
   "PHONE" CHAR(10) NOT NULL ENABLE,
   "ADDRESS" VARCHAR2(40) NOT NULL ENABLE,
   "CITY" VARCHAR2(30) NOT NULL ENABLE,
   "STATE" CHAR(2) NOT NULL ENABLE,
   "ZIP" CHAR(5) NOT NULL ENABLE,
   "BIRTHDATE" DATE,
   "GENDER" CHAR(1),
    CHECK (Gender in ('M','F')) ENABLE,
    CHECK (CustomerId > 0) ENABLE,
   `CONSTRAINT "CUSTOMER_PK" PRIMARY KEY ("CUSTOMERID")
    CONSTRAINT "CUSTOMER_UK" UNIQUE ("FIRSTNAME", "LASTNAME", "PHONE")
);

CREATE INDEX "MOVIES"."CUSTOMER_IE1" ON "MOVIES"."CUSTOMER" ("LASTNAME");
CREATE INDEX "MOVIES"."CUSTOMER_IE2" ON "MOVIES"."CUSTOMER" ("PHONE");
CREATE INDEX "MOVIES"."CUSTOMER_IE3" ON "MOVIES"."CUSTOMER" ("ZIP");
CREATE OR REPLACE TRIGGER "MOVIES"."CUSTOMER_CHECKS"
BEFORE INSERT OR UPDATE
ON customer
FOR EACH ROW
declare
-- Declare User Defined Exception
bad_length   exception;
pragma exception_init(bad_length,-20001);
bad_date     exception;
pragma exception_init(bad_date,-20002);
begin
-- Check Values for Correct Length
if (length(rtrim(:new.phone)) < 10 or
```

```
      length(rtrim(:new.state)) <  2 or
      length(rtrim(:new.zip))   <  5) then
    raise bad_length;
  end if;
  -- Check Dates for Reasonableness
  if (:new.birthdate > sysdate-18*365) then
    raise bad_date;
  end if;
  -- Force Values to All Upper Case
  :new.state  := upper(:new.state);
  :new.gender := upper(:new.gender);
exception
  when bad_length then
    raise_application_error(-20001, 'Illegal length: value shorter than
required');
  when bad_date then
    raise_application_error(-20002, 'Illegal date: value fails
reasonableness test');
end;
/
```

Step 1: Verify that the table is a candidate for online redefinition

This is a very easy step, but it is also a very critical step. If this step fails, then do not attempt to use *dbms_redefinition* to rebuild or redefine the table. Since it is known that customer has a primary key from reviewing the prior DD, then it can be verified that it can be used as the redefinition driver. Otherwise, redefinition must function utilizing the data's ROWID. Remember, *dbms_redefinition* is simply using materialized views behind the scenes.

```
BEGIN
  DBMS_REDEFINITION.CAN_REDEF_TABLE ('MOVIES', 'CUSTOMER',
DBMS_REDEFINITION.CONS_USE_PK);
END;
/
```

Step 2: Create an interim table

Assuming that the table is a valid candidate, the interim table can then be created. This will be the partitioned table for the demonstration scenario. Note that the CREATE TABLE AS SELECT (CTAS) method is being used to save time here. The rows are not actually being copied because the SELECT WHERE clause evaluates to false. This is just a relatively easy shorthand method for the copy and, of course, adding the partitioning clause.

```
create table movies.customer_interim
partition by hash(zip) partitions 8
as
select * from movies.customer
```

```
where 1=0;
```

Step 3: Enable parallel DML operations

Now for those on multi-processor database servers, parallel operations can be enabled for the session to speed up the redefinition process. This is an optional step, but generally worth considering. Just make sure not to overdo using parallelization. If there is a very fast I/O subsystem and nothing else is really running, then consider up to two or four times of the actual CPU core count. It would also be good to check the *db_writers init.ora* parameter as well because it should be more than one if the choice is to force massive parallel operations that require extensive I/O. Here are the commands for this.

```
alter session force parallel dml parallel 4;
alter session force parallel query parallel 4;
```

Step 4: Start the redefinition process

From this step forward, watch the time between steps. This means that the following steps need to happen in sequence and without major delays between them. This is pointed out because some DBAs are hesitant to put these reorganization steps in a script as they want to manually monitor each step of the process. That is fine, just do not go to lunch or home between them. If everything is ready to proceed to completion, then start the redefinition process.

```
BEGIN

DBMS_REDEFINITION.START_REDEF_TABLE('MOVIES','CUSTOMER','CUSTOMER_INTERIM');
END;
/
```

Step 5: Copy dependent objects

This step performs one of the most critical and easily forgotten steps if this process was done without *dbms_redefinition* – to automatically create any required triggers, indexes, materialized view logs, grants, and/or constraints on the table. If one refers back to the section about DDL extraction via *dbms_metadata*, it is easy to guess that Oracle is eating their own cooking internally here. Now it makes a little more sense as to why *dbms_metadata* was designed as it is. Look how easy it is to copy all dependent objects with just a single call to *dbms_redefinition*.

```
DECLARE
  num_errors PLS_INTEGER;
BEGIN
  DBMS_REDEFINITION.COPY_TABLE_DEPENDENTS ('MOVIES', 'CUSTOMER',
'CUSTOMER_INTERIM',
    DBMS_REDEFINITION.CONS_ORIG_PARAMS, TRUE, TRUE, TRUE, TRUE, num_errors);
END;
/
```

Step 6: Check for any errors

It is advisable now to check that this last operation completed successfully. This is stated because remember that it is doing quite a few things in the background here. It is quite possible for some things to need reviewing and possibly fixed manually. In most cases there should be no rows returned, so proceed.

```
select object_name, base_table_name, ddl_txt from DBA_REDEFINITION_ERRORS;
```

Step 7: Synchronize the interim table (optional)

If there has been any activity or transaction between the start of the redefinition and now, it might be advisable to resynchronize the interim table one more time. When in doubt, it is very much like chicken soup here – it may not help, but it will not hurt anything either.

```
BEGIN
  DBMS_REDEFINITION.SYNC_INTERIM_TABLE ('MOVIES', 'CUSTOMER',
'CUSTOMER_INTERIM');
END;
/
```

Step 8: Complete the redefinition

This step does two things: it severs the behind-the-scenes materialized view connection and swaps the data dictionary entries for the table and interim table. So now, what was the interim table is caught up on structural modifications and any data transactions. Thus, it is safe to make this data dictionary entry swap.

```
BEGIN
  DBMS_REDEFINITION.FINISH_REDEF_TABLE ('MOVIES', 'CUSTOMER',
'CUSTOMER_INTERIM');
END;
/
```

Step 9: Drop the interim table

The interim table is now finished which, as of the last step, is actually the original table via the dictionary entry swap done by the finish operation. So drop that table. And if there is a concern about the data, an option is to do a SELECT against the new original table to verify that nothing has been lost.

```
drop table movies.customer_interim cascade constraints purge;
```

Finally, here is the screen for doing the same thing via OEM. As was said before, most folks will probably go with this. But at least it is now evident what is going on inside.

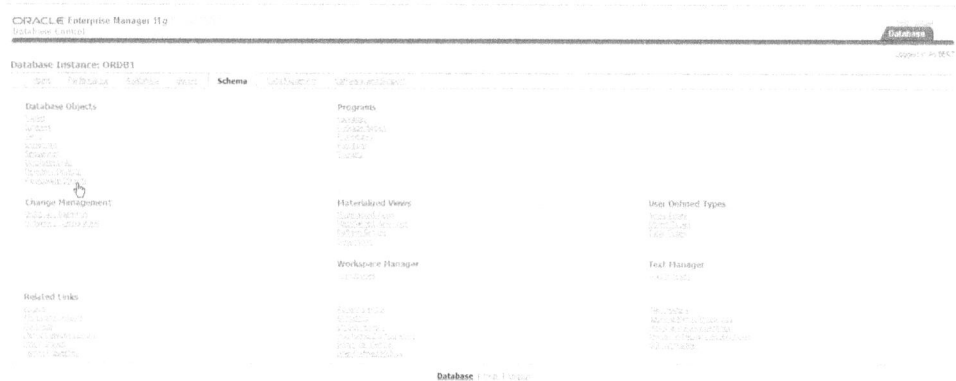

Figure 6.2: *OEM Schema Menu/Screen*

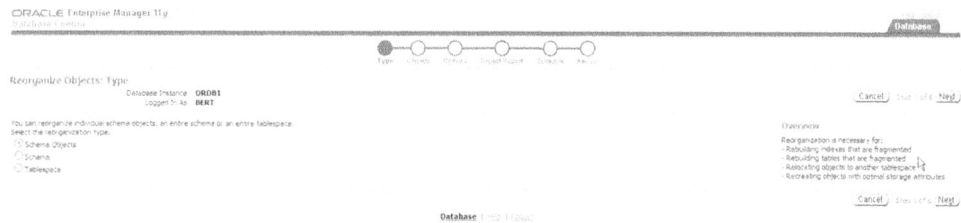

Figure 6.3: *OEM Reorganize Object Screen*

DBMS_METADATA

One of the most sacred job functions many DBAs perform is that of the "guardian of the database design", most often manifested as simply meaning the "keeper of the DDL". Even though there are many database change-management tools and data-modeling tools with model-to-database alteration/synchronization capabilities, numerous DBAs still generally rely on DDL scripts. Some DBAs might have those DDL scripts in a source-code version-control system, but even that is not the norm. So these "keepers of the DDL" have always had a staggering task in being able to produce current scripts for whatever objects the database might contain.

This challenge is only magnified by the sheer number of people, and in some cases, even applications tasked with creating database objects. In many cases, this database design sprawl is so bad that the database itself has become the central repository of the design through sheer necessity as the Oracle data dictionary may be the only guaranteed, accurate and up-to-date copy of the database design. Obviously, that is not a good place to be in, but many find themselves there nonetheless. So reverse engineering DDL from the data dictionary is quite often a necessary evil. Some people refer to reverse engineering as database, schema or object definition or DDL extraction.

In the early days when the Oracle database was much less robust and therefore much simpler, DBAs often wrote SQL scripts to generate the database objects' DDL code. These scripts simply queried that data dictionary and produced human readable SQL files of what the database design reality was at that particular time. The *old_generate_table_ddl.sql* SQL*Plus script, shown below, is a simple example of what such a script might have looked like.

🖫 old_generate_table_dll.sql script

```
set echo off
set heading off
set feedback off
set verify off
set pagesize 0
set linesize 132

define schema=&1
define CR=chr(10)
define TAB=chr(9)
col x noprint
col y noprint
select   table_name y,
```

```
        0 x,
        'CREATE TABLE ' ||
        rtrim(table_name) ||
        '('
from    dba_tables
where   owner = upper('&schema')
union
select  tc.table_name y,
        column_id x,
        decode(column_id,1,'      ',' ',    ,')||
        rtrim(column_name)|| &TAB || &TAB ||
        rtrim(data_type) ||
        rtrim(decode(data_type,'DATE',null,'LONG',null,
              'NUMBER',decode(to_char(data_precision),null,null,'('),
              '(')) ||
        rtrim(decode(data_type,
              'DATE',null,
              'CHAR',data_length,
              'VARCHAR2',data_length,
              'NUMBER',decode(to_char(data_precision),null,null,
                to_char(data_precision) || ',' || to_char(data_scale)),
              'LONG',null,
              '******ERROR')) ||
        rtrim(decode(data_type,'DATE',null,'LONG',null,
              'NUMBER',decode(to_char(data_precision),null,null,')'),
              ')')) || &TAB || &TAB ||
        rtrim(decode(nullable,'N','NOT NULL',null))
from    dba_tab_columns tc,
        dba_objects o
where   o.owner = tc.owner
and     o.object_name = tc.table_name
and     o.object_type = 'TABLE'
and     o.owner = upper('&schema')
union
select  table_name y,
        999999 x,
        ')'   || &CR
        ||'   STORAGE('                              || &CR
        ||'    INITIAL '     || initial_extent       || &CR
        ||'    NEXT '        || next_extent           || &CR
        ||'    MINEXTENTS '  || min_extents           || &CR
        ||'    MAXEXTENTS '  || max_extents           || &CR
        ||'    PCTINCREASE ' || pct_increase          || ')'  ||&CR
        ||'    INITRANS '    || ini_trans             || &CR
        ||'    MAXTRANS '    || max_trans             || &CR
        ||'    PCTFREE '     || pct_free              || &CR
        ||'    PCTUSED '     || pct_used              || &CR
        ||'    PARALLEL (DEGREE ' || rtrim(DEGREE) || ') ' || &CR
        ||'    TABLESPACE ' || rtrim(tablespace_name)      ||&CR
        ||'/'||&CR||&CR
from    dba_tables
where   owner = upper('&schema')
order by 1,2;
```

When the *old_generate_table_ddl.sql* SQL*Plus script is run against the MOVIES demo schema, here is a sample of what the generated DDL looks like for one of the tables.

🖫 old_generate_table_ddl.sql output

```
CREATE TABLE CUSTOMER(
    CUSTOMERID          NUMBER(10,0)            NOT NULL
    ,FIRSTNAME          VARCHAR2(20)            NOT NULL
    ,LASTNAME           VARCHAR2(30)            NOT NULL
    ,PHONE              CHAR(10)                NOT NULL
    ,ADDRESS            VARCHAR2(40)            NOT NULL
    ,CITY               VARCHAR2(30)            NOT NULL
    ,STATE              CHAR(2)                 NOT NULL
    ,ZIP                CHAR(5)                 NOT NULL
    ,BIRTHDATE          DATE
    ,GENDER             CHAR(1)
)
    STORAGE(
    INITIAL 1048576
    NEXT 1048576
    MINEXTENTS 1
    MAXEXTENTS 2147483645
    PCTINCREASE 0)
    INITRANS 1
    MAXTRANS 255
    PCTFREE 10
    PCTUSED
    PARALLEL (DEGREE 1)
    TABLESPACE USERS
/
```

This is not too bad. But with the plethora of table structural design options such as clustering, partitioning, index organized tables, external tables and such, it is clear that this little script would need thousands of lines of code plus more of the same for indexes and views. Also, keep in mind all the fun database objects such as materialized views, materialized view logs, queue tables, and sequences, to name a few, not to mention the entire security model for the whole enchilada such as roles and grants. It is pretty clear that DDL generation scripts such as these have met their match.

So what is a body to do? Thankfully, Oracle came to the rescue with a package to implement database object reverse engineering, namely *dbms_metadata*. Not only that, but both SQL Developer and OEM make use of it. Therefore, for those who just need a quick and easy way to peruse their databases DDL, Oracle's free SQL Developer tool is probably good enough, as shown in the following screen snapshot. But for those who want to delve even further into the mysteries of everything the dbms_metadata package can do, read on.

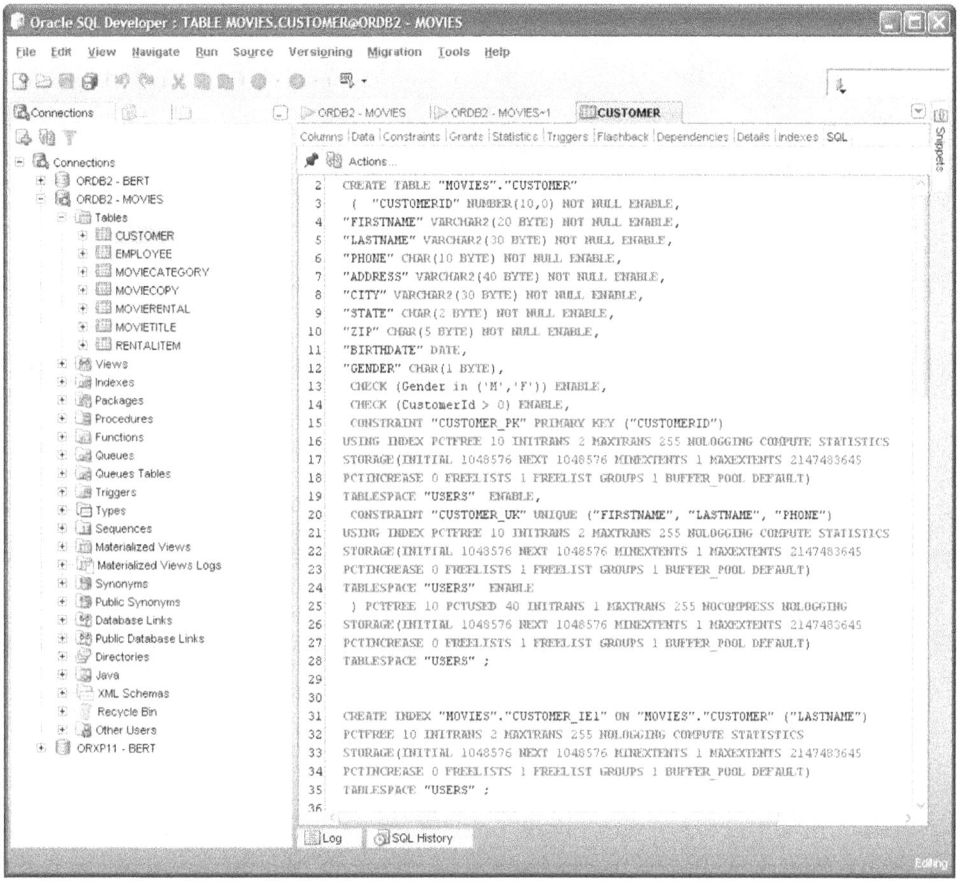

Figure 6.4: *Oracle SQL Developer*

The good news is that Oracle now provides a very robust mechanism for extracting or reverse engineering the database objects' DDL. But like anything else, there is also some bad news and here are the couple items worth note:

- Does not generate the DDL in required object dependency order for referential integrity constraints

- Is not very well documented (the Oracle Utilities manual describes the syntax and some basic cases – but not nearly enough)

- Slightly over-engineered – such references can be found on various blogs and presentations posted to the web

- IS NOT SUPPORTED FOR v7-8-9iR1 databases

- Seems to be buggy from what can be told on OTN

Please do not let the API's complexity and lack of robust documentation be a swaying factor – *dbms_metadata* is a must-have and use utility. An entire chapter could be written on just this one topic, but instead of trying to show the complete syntax reference and detailing all aspects, three very useful use case scenarios will be presented. These three examples will be used as is or serve as a good foundation upon which to add one's own modifications. And while there are just three examples, it should be noted that there are really just two ways to work with *dbms_metadata*: going for one object type at a time, or going for collections of object types simultaneously.

Extract Object

Remember the example table level DDL generation script from a few pages back? It was over 60 lines long, and yet it handled only the most basic scenarios of table DDL extraction. If that script had to be augmented for every possible permutation of table level options, that script would easily grow to a few thousand lines long. Plus, if Oracle changed either the CREATE or ALTER table syntax, then that script would have to be revisited to make sure it remained accurate for anything new. That is just too much work to tackle – especially when there is an alternative.

So examine the exact same table generation process instead using the Oracle dmbs_metadata PL/SQL package as shown in the *new_generate_table_ddl.sql* SQL*Plus script:

🖫 new_generate_table_ddl.sql script

```
set echo off
set heading off
set feedback off
set verify off
set pagesize 0
set linesize 132

define schema=&1

EXECUTE
DBMS_METADATA.SET_TRANSFORM_PARAM(DBMS_METADATA.SESSION_TRANSFORM,'PRETTY',t
rue);
EXECUTE
DBMS_METADATA.SET_TRANSFORM_PARAM(DBMS_METADATA.SESSION_TRANSFORM,'SQLTERMIN
ATOR',true);

SELECT to_char(DBMS_METADATA.GET_DDL ('TABLE', table_name, owner))
FROM   dba_tables
```

```
WHERE   owner=upper('&1');
```

In just 12 short lines, a script is created to reverse engineer all the tables for a given schema and for every possible Oracle option or feature those tables use. Furthermore, now the task of keeping such a script current is now on Oracle's shoulders. So even if Oracle adds new table options or parameters like extends or changes to the CREATE/ALTER table syntax, the script is not affected. Additionally, this DDL generation script can be extended to change or add additional objects types because it is very straightforward and easy. For example, if one wanted to switch to or add indexes, just substitute or add this command.

```
SELECT to_char(DBMS_METADATA.GET_DDL ('INDEX', index_name, table_owner))
FROM    dba_indexes
WHERE   table_owner=upper('&1');
```

Now compare the actual table CREATE TABLE DDL generated from the *new_generate_table_ddl.sql* SQL*Plus script, shown next, to the earlier output from the *old_generate_table_ddl.sql* SQL*Plus script. Note that check constraints, primary keys and unique keys have been picked up along with their storage clauses. Furthermore, even the table storage clause is more accurate with items such as NOCOMPRESS, NOLOGGING and BUFFER_POOL now covered.

new_generate_table_ddl.sql output

```
  CREATE TABLE "MOVIES"."CUSTOMER"
    (    "CUSTOMERID" NUMBER(10,0) NOT NULL ENABLE,
         "FIRSTNAME" VARCHAR2(20) NOT NULL ENABLE,
         "LASTNAME" VARCHAR2(30) NOT NULL ENABLE,
         "PHONE" CHAR(10) NOT NULL ENABLE,
         "ADDRESS" VARCHAR2(40) NOT NULL ENABLE,
         "CITY" VARCHAR2(30) NOT NULL ENABLE,
         "STATE" CHAR(2) NOT NULL ENABLE,
         "ZIP" CHAR(5) NOT NULL ENABLE,
         "BIRTHDATE" DATE,
         "GENDER" CHAR(1),
          CHECK (Gender in ('M','F')) ENABLE,
          CHECK (CustomerId > 0) ENABLE,
          CONSTRAINT "CUSTOMER_PK" PRIMARY KEY ("CUSTOMERID")
  USING INDEX PCTFREE 10 INITRANS 2 MAXTRANS 255 NOLOGGING COMPUTE
STATISTICS
  STORAGE(INITIAL 1048576 NEXT 1048576 MINEXTENTS 1 MAXEXTENTS 2147483645
  PCTINCREASE 0 FREELISTS 1 FREELIST GROUPS 1 BUFFER_POOL DEFAULT)
  TABLESPACE "USERS"  ENABLE,
          CONSTRAINT "CUSTOMER_UK" UNIQUE ("FIRSTNAME", "LASTNAME", "PHONE")
  USING INDEX PCTFREE 10 INITRANS 2 MAXTRANS 255 NOLOGGING COMPUTE
STATISTICS
  STORAGE(INITIAL 1048576 NEXT 1048576 MINEXTENTS 1 MAXEXTENTS 2147483645
```

```
PCTINCREASE 0 FREELISTS 1 FREELIST GROUPS 1 BUFFER_POOL DEFAULT)
TABLESPACE "USERS"  ENABLE
  ) PCTFREE 10 PCTUSED 40 INITRANS 1 MAXTRANS 255 NOCOMPRESS NOLOGGING
STORAGE(INITIAL 1048576 NEXT 1048576 MINEXTENTS 1 MAXEXTENTS 2147483645
PCTINCREASE 0 FREELISTS 1 FREELIST GROUPS 1 BUFFER_POOL DEFAULT)
TABLESPACE "USERS" ;
```

Extract Database

On occasion, DBAs may find the need to reverse engineer or extract an entire database. An example might be that responsibility is inherited for a pre-existing database and there are no DDL scripts that anyone knows of or is sure are accurate. Another example might be that a duplicate database needs to be created for test or development. So there are occasions where one needs to reverse engineer more than one object type or construct at a time.

Now a much more complex aspect of working with *dbms_metadata* is being introduced: extracting logical groupings of items. Start with the concept of reverse engineering or extracting the DDL for everything in the largest logical grouping of items, which is the entire database. The *generate_database_ddl.sql* SQL*Plus script generates DDL for the entire database.

🖫 generate_database_ddl.sql script

```
SET FEEDBACK OFF
SET VERIFY OFF
SET PAGESIZE 0
SET LINESIZE 1024
SET TRIMOUT ON
SET TRIMSPOOL ON
SET SERVEROUTPUT ON
SET TERMOUT OFF

COLUMN  sid NOPRINT new_value sid;
SELECT value sid from v$parameter
 where name='db_name';

SPOOL &sid._reverse_engineer.sql

DECLARE
   meta_data_handle  NUMBER;
   transform_handle  NUMBER;
   DDL               CLOB;
BEGIN
  meta_data_handle := DBMS_METADATA.OPEN ('DATABASE_EXPORT');

  DBMS_METADATA.set_filter (meta_data_handle, 'EXCLUDE_PATH_EXPR',
'=''TABLE_DATA''');

-- you can inlcude/exclude items
```

```
--  DBMS_METADATA.set_filter (meta_data_handle, 'INCLUDE_PATH_EXPR',
'=''DIRECTORY''');
--  DBMS_METADATA.set_filter (meta_data_handle, 'EXCLUDE_PATH_EXPR',
'=''DIRECTORY''');

  transform_handle:= DBMS_METADATA.add_transform (meta_data_handle, 'DDL');


  DBMS_METADATA.SET_TRANSFORM_PARAM (transform_handle, 'PRETTY',true);
  DBMS_METADATA.SET_TRANSFORM_PARAM (transform_handle,
'SQLTERMINATOR',true);

  LOOP
    DDL := DBMS_METADATA.fetch_clob (meta_data_handle);
    EXIT WHEN DDL IS NULL;
    DBMS_OUTPUT.PUT_LINE (to_char(DDL));
  END LOOP;

  DBMS_METADATA.CLOSE (meta_data_handle);
EXCEPTION
  WHEN OTHERS THEN
    DBMS_METADATA.CLOSE (meta_data_handle);
END;
/

SPOOL OFF
SET TERMOUT ON
```

The generate_database_ddl.sql SQL*Plus script demonstrates that in order to work on collections of objects with *dbms_metadata*, one must use the *dbms_metadata.open* function to define a handle. In this case, the collection is for a database export. Then simply loop through the items contained by that handle and print the DDL line one by one. Note that a filter was set to exclude the table data itself which would have generated INSERT statements for all the data. Additional filters can be added to specify an almost unlimited combination of extract scenarios.

Extract Schema

Probably the most useful reverse engineering scenario in terms of frequency of use will be the schema extraction process. Most applications and/or development projects are versioned at a very high collective level. Moreover, since applications tend to operate at the schema level where a schema may equate to one or more application functional areas, it is, therefore, also very common to want to manage or version the database at the schema level as well.

Now take the object extraction example and just add all the types of objects that may need to be reverse engineered, but that would take some work. Also like before, that script might have to change over time as new schema level objects were possible. Obviously this scenario is much like the prior database extract in that a collection of objects needs to be reversed engineered, just at the schema level this time rather than the whole database. The generate_schema_ddl.sql SQL*Plus script, as shown below, generates DDL for an entire schema.

generate_schema_ddl.sql script

```
DEFINE schema=&1

SET FEEDBACK OFF
SET VERIFY OFF
SET PAGESIZE 0
SET LINESIZE 1024
SET TRIMOUT ON
SET TRIMSPOOL ON
SET SERVEROUTPUT ON
SET TERMOUT OFF

COLUMN  sid NOPRINT new_value sid;
SELECT value sid from v$parameter
 where name='db_name';

SPOOL &sid._&schema._reverse_engineer.sql

DECLARE
   meta_data_handle   NUMBER;
   transform_handle   NUMBER;
   DDL                CLOB;
BEGIN
  meta_data_handle := DBMS_METADATA.OPEN ('SCHEMA_EXPORT');

  DBMS_METADATA.set_filter (meta_data_handle, 'SCHEMA', upper('&schema'));
  DBMS_METADATA.set_filter (meta_data_handle, 'INCLUDE_USER', true);
  DBMS_METADATA.set_filter (meta_data_handle, 'EXCLUDE_PATH_EXPR',
'=''TABLE_DATA''');

-- you can inlcude/exclude items
-- DBMS_METADATA.set_filter (meta_data_handle, 'INCLUDE_PATH_EXPR',
'=''VIEW''');
-- DBMS_METADATA.set_filter (meta_data_handle, 'EXCLUDE_PATH_EXPR',
'=''VIEW''');

  transform_handle:= DBMS_METADATA.add_transform (meta_data_handle, 'DDL');


  DBMS_METADATA.SET_TRANSFORM_PARAM (transform_handle, 'PRETTY',true);
  DBMS_METADATA.SET_TRANSFORM_PARAM (transform_handle,
'SQLTERMINATOR',true);

  LOOP
```

```
      DDL := DBMS_METADATA.fetch_clob (meta_data_handle);
      EXIT WHEN DDL IS NULL;
      DBMS_OUTPUT.PUT_LINE (to_char(DDL));
   END LOOP;

   DBMS_METADATA.CLOSE (meta_data_handle);
EXCEPTION
   WHEN OTHERS THEN
      DBMS_METADATA.CLOSE (meta_data_handle);
END;
/

SPOOL OFF
SET TERMOUT ON
```

Was it noticed that the schema and database level extract scripts are 90% the same? That is because working with groups of objects with *dbms_metadata* always works the same by simply opening and specifying some filters differently for the various granularities. So above, one opened for a *schema_export* and defined a few extra filters to handle PRETTY and SQLTERMINATOR. Shown below are tables with the various *dbms_metadata* objects types and filters. One will have to experiment on all the many possibilities.

ASSOCIATION	MATERIALIED_VIEW	ROLE_GRANT
AUDIT	MATERIALIZED_VIEW_LOG	ROLLBACK_SEGMENT
AUDIT_OBJ	OBJECT_GRANT	SEQUENCE
CLUSTER	OPERATOR	SYNONYM
COMMENT	PACKAGE	SYSTEM_GRANT
CONSTRAINT	PACKAGE_SPEC	TABLE
CONTEXT	PACKAGE_BODY	TABLE_DATA
DB_LINK	PASSWORD_HISTORY	TABLE_STATISTICS
DEFAULT_ROLE	PASSWORD_VERIFY_FUNCTION	TABLESPACE
DIMENSION	PROCEDURE	TABLESPACE_QUOTA
DIRECTORY	PROFILE	TRIGGER
FGA_POLICY	PROXY	TRUSTED_DB_LINK
FUNCTION	REF_CONSTRAINT	TYPE
INDEX_STATISTICS	REFRESH_GROUP	TYPE_SPEC
INDEX	RESOURCE_COST	TYPE_BODY
INDEXTYPE	RLS_CONTEXT	USER
JAVA_SOURCE	RLS_GROUP	VIEW
JOB	RLS_POLICY	XMLSCHEMA
LIBRARY	ROLE	

Table 6.5: *Dbms_metadata Object Types*

NAME	BASE_OBJECT_NAME_EXPR	SCHEMA
NAME_EXPR	EXCLUDE_BASE_OBJECT_NAME_EXPR	SCHEMA_EXPR
EXCLUDE_NAME_EXPR	BASE_OBJECT_SCHEMA_EXPR	INCLUDE_USER
SCHEMA	BASE_OBJECT_TYPE	SCHEMA
SCHEMA_EXPR	BASE_OBJECT_TYPE_EXPR	SCHEMA_EXPR
SPECIFICATION	BASE_OBJECT_TABLESPACE	NAME
BODY	BASE_OBJECT_TABLESPACE_EXPR	NAME_EXPR
TABLESPACE	GRANTEE	BEGIN_WITH
TABLESPACE_EXPR	PRIVNAME	BEGIN_AFTER
PRIMARY	PRIVNAME_EXPR	END_BEFORE
SECONDARY	GRANTEE_EXPR	END_WITH
BASE_OBJECT_NAME	EXCLUDE_GRANTEE_EXPR	INCLUDE_PATH_EXPR
BASE_OBJECT_SCHEMA	CUSTOM_FILTER	EXCLUDE_PATH_EXPR

Table 6.6: *DBMS_METADATA Filters*

Recovery Utilities

DBMS_FLASHBACK

At the beginning of this chapter, various use case scenarios for the data pump export and import were mentioned. One such case involved a DBA who might need the ability to restore collections of tables to some pristine state on a regular interval. In the prior section, creating restructures were illustrated where a backup or before image might be handy in case of problems during mid-restructuring. The truth is that there are many cases where the DBA would like the ability to restore a logical portion of the database back in time or to a prior SCN. But the problem is that physical backups and restores are very complex and operate more at the physical database level. Few applications are generally worthy of their own backup and recovery strategy using the physical tools to build logical or application based restore points.

However, a long time ago Oracle introduced a great concept in the SQL and PL/SQL languages called the SAVEPOINT. This was the ability to issue a database state bookmark within the application code such that one could rollback to an application based logical point in time. This was a useful technique but never really saw extensive usage. Nevertheless, it was a good concept if only it would have extended to database objects and/or even the database level itself. Well, now it does and it is Oracle's flashback technology.

Oracle flashback technology essentially lets the DBA create SAVEPOINT like bookmarks to restore to either objects or the entire database. In some respects, it is a great short term point-in-time recover technique, rather than going to a full blown backup and restore. Plus, its usage has been made so integrated, seamless and easy that it is sure to see heavy usage as time goes on. It is truly a definite must-have tool for the DBA's tool belt.

There are six flashback technologies, in chronological order of their appearance, whose topics will be examined in more detail:

- Flashback Queries (9i)

- Flashback Drop (10g)

- Flashback Tables

- Flashback Database

- Flashback Transaction (11g)

- Flashback Archives (Oracle Total Recall)

Furthermore, unlike other features covered in this chapter, it will be beneficial to learn how to utilize these various flashback technology capabilities via OEM, SQL commands and the PL/SQL API.

Note: Part of the reason for covering all the flashback technologies here, including a recap of older ones, is to hopefully lead the reader along the historical path of flashback technology development and, therefore, to perceive that each step was built on the foundations of those prior.

Flashback Queries

Oracle 9i introduced the concept of the flashback query. This can be called the "Back to the Future" or time machine type query where Oracle lets DBAs make some queries in the present as if from a database state in the not too distant past.

The black magic that makes this possible are UNDO tablespaces and automatic UNDO management and Oracle now treats those UNDO blocks as first-rate data based upon the undo_retention parameter. Using these, Oracle does its best to retain UNDO data. One can even force that availability via the UNDO tablespace RETENTION GUARANTEE option.

In its simplest form, merely add an AS OF clause to the SELECT statement to request the current execution be performed as if it were run at some prior specified time or system change number like looking backwards in time.

```
SQL> select DBMS_FLASHBACK.GET_SYSTEM_CHANGE_NUMBER from dual;

GET_SYSTEM_CHANGE_NUMBER
------------------------
                  353026

SQL> update movies.customer set zip='99999';

62 rows updated.

SQL> commit;

Commit complete.

SQL> select firstname, lastname, zip from movies.customer as of scn 353026
where rownum < 5;

FIRSTNAME           LASTNAME                        ZIP
------------------- ------------------------------- -----
Flozell             Adams                           75063
Troy                Aikman                          75063
Larry               Allen                           75063
Eric                Bjornson                        75063
```

The entire Oracle session can also be enabled to enter a "time tunnel" or "time warp" so that nothing has to be added to the SELECT command to see such historical data. In that case, simply enable and disable the flashback effect as shown here via the PL/SQL packages found in *dbms_flashback*.

```
SQL> select firstname, lastname, zip from movies.customer where rownum < 5;
```

```
FIRSTNAME            LASTNAME                        ZIP
-------------------- ------------------------------- -----
Flozell              Adams                           99999
Troy                 Aikman                          99999
Larry                Allen                           99999
Eric                 Bjornson                        99999

SQL>
SQL> execute DBMS_FLASHBACK.ENABLE_AT_SYSTEM_CHANGE_NUMBER(353026)

PL/SQL procedure successfully completed.

SQL>
SQL> select firstname, lastname, zip from movies.customer where rownum < 5;

FIRSTNAME            LASTNAME                        ZIP
-------------------- ------------------------------- -----
Flozell              Adams                           75063
Troy                 Aikman                          75063
Larry                Allen                           75063
Eric                 Bjornson                        75063

SQL> execute DBMS_FLASHBACK.DISABLE

PL/SQL procedure successfully completed.
```

Flashback Drop

Oracle 10g introduced the flashback drop concept. It is built off the new recycle bin in the database. Think of it as much like the Windows recycle bin. Now when an object is dropped, it is moved first to the recycle bin, assuming that the recycle bin has been enabled via the *recyclebin*=on *init.ora* parameter. The recycle bin simply retains the dropped objects under a new unique name.

```
SQL> drop table junk;

Table dropped.

SQL> select object_name, original_name, type from recyclebin;

OBJECT_NAME                      ORIGINAL_NAME                   TYPE
-------------------------------- ------------------------------- ------------
---
BIN$oP2i2G1STvita2AHhmFdVw==$0   JUNK                            TABLE
```

Then when a table needs to be undropped, the process is very easy by using the FLASHBACK TABLE command to restore the table as it was before the drop. When the table flashback is invoked, not only are the table and its data brought back, but so are any dependent objects and grants. It is that simple.

```
SQL> select * from junk;
```

```
        C1          C2
---------- ----------
         1           2

SQL> drop table junk;

Table dropped.

SQL> select * from junk;
select * from junk
              *
ERROR at line 1:
ORA-00942: table or view does not exist

SQL> flashback table junk to before drop;

Flashback complete.

SQL> select * from junk;

        C1          C2
---------- ----------
         1           2
```

For those who prefer a graphical interface, OEM has a rather easy screen for doing object level complete recoveries, i.e. un-drop.

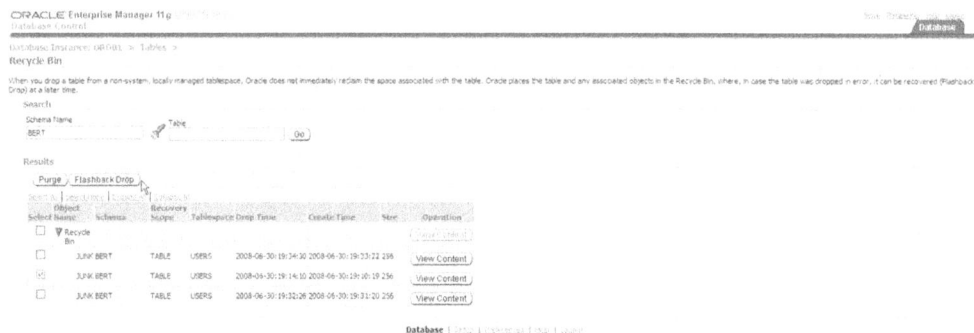

Figure 6.5: *OEM Object Level Recovery Screen*

Prior to the flashback drop capability, the best method for doing object level recoveries was the logical backup method discussed earlier in this chapter, export/import. But handling referential integrity and dependencies was a problematic manual effort requiring significant investment to get 100% right.

Flashback Tables

The next logical step in the flashback progression is to do more than simply undoing table drop, but rather to permit the table to return to its prior state as if making a flashback query permanent. Once again, there is yet another key new requirement for this latest flashback feature to work – tables must have row movement enabled. This is a feature that permits Oracle to change the ROWID of a row, otherwise they are usually immutable. Now use the prior section's flashback syntax to return a table to some prior specified time or system change number, as shown here.

```
SQL> create table junk (c1 int, c2 int) enable row movement;

Table created.

SQL> insert into junk values (1,2);

1 row created.

SQL> commit;

Commit complete.

SQL> select DBMS_FLASHBACK.GET_SYSTEM_CHANGE_NUMBER from dual;

GET_SYSTEM_CHANGE_NUMBER
------------------------
                  362096

SQL> insert into junk values (3,4);

1 row created.

SQL> commit;

Commit complete.

SQL> flashback table junk to scn 362096;

Flashback complete.

SQL> select * from junk;

        C1         C2
---------- ----------
         1          2
```

Once again, for those who prefer a graphical interface, OEM has a rather easy screen for doing object level point-in-time table recoveries or flashbacks.

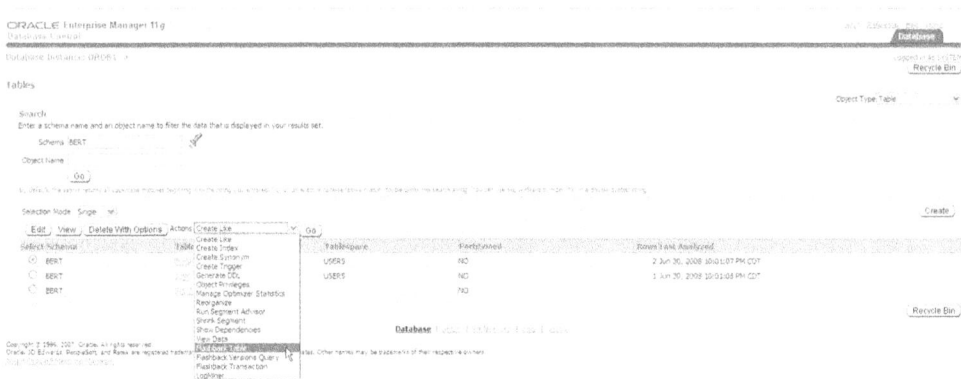

Figure 6.6: *OEM Table Screen*

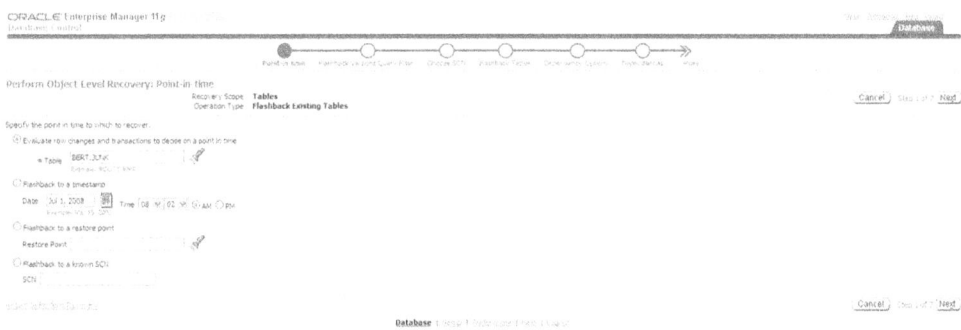

Figure 6.7: *OEM Table Flashback Screen*

Flashback Database

Continuing with the flashback technology progression, the next big step is to permit one to flashback an entire database. In essence, now is the time to perform a point-in-time recovery at the database level, all done simply and without actually doing anything in RMAN. Once again, there is yet another key new requirement for this latest flashback feature to work – the database must be running in ARCHIVELOG mode. Plus, one can only flashback to whatever online redo logs are immediately available via disk. Any further back in time requires a traditional point in time recovery via RMAN. But for many cases, even that short time span may suffice as the first-level basic point-in-time recovery strategy. The next example may look quite a bit like the last for the flashback table, so just take the database to a mounted status and issue the

FLASHBACK DATABASE command as shown. All that is changed is the scope of the operation.

```
SQL> create table junk (c1 int, c2 int) enable row movement;

Table created.

SQL> insert into junk values (1,2);

1 row created.

SQL> commit;

Commit complete.

SQL> select DBMS_FLASHBACK.GET_SYSTEM_CHANGE_NUMBER from dual;

GET_SYSTEM_CHANGE_NUMBER
-----------------------
                 365991

SQL> insert into junk values (3,4);

1 row created.

SQL> commit;

Commit complete.

SQL> connect sys/mgr as sysdba
Connected.
SQL> shutdown immediate;
Database closed.
Database dismounted.
ORACLE instance shut down.
SQL> startup mount;
ORACLE instance started.

Total System Global Area  627732480 bytes
Fixed Size                  1334996 bytes
Variable Size             398459180 bytes
Database Buffers          222298112 bytes
Redo Buffers                5640192 bytes
Database mounted.
SQL> flashback database to scn 365991;

Flashback complete.

SQL> alter database open resetlogs;

Database altered.

SQL> connect bert/bert
Connected.
SQL> select * from junk;

        C1          C2
```

```
---------- ----------
         1          2
```

The flashback technology historical progression as of Oracle 10g release 2 has now been divulged, so it is onto even bigger and better flashback capabilities with Oracle 11g. However, whereas the progression and granularities up until this point were probably fairly obvious, the next part is into less obvious but critically useful flashback techniques. Hopefully, with a decent background and understanding, one will appreciate just how one got here.

Flashback Transaction

The *dbms_flashback.transaction_backout* procedure rolls back a transaction and all its dependent transactions. As with all the other flashback technologies explained so far, the transaction back-out operation uses UNDO to create and execute the compensating or opposite transactions that return the affected data to its original state. In some respects, the granularity of this flashback operation is somewhere between the last two cases: table and database. Now go back to a subset of the database that represents some logical collection of tables and queries. It essentially implements the prior mentioned SAVEPOINT concept in the database rather than the application code. In fact, flashback transactions mostly eliminate the need for the next section on redo log file mining since it is now transparently and more easily done as shown below.

First, query the *flashback_transaction_query* view to see what transactions exist for whatever objects and/or users that may have done something that need to be undone. This view can return a lot of information in even a mildly busy database, so filtering is highly recommended. For example, see what transactions have occurred in the past day by logon user BERT and on tables owned by BERT. Note that this view offers the UNDO SQL code.

```
SQL> select xid, start_scn, operation, table_name, undo_sql from
flashback_transaction_query where start_timestamp>=sysdate-1 and
username='BERT' and table_owner='BERT';
XID               START_SCN OPERATION    TABLE_NAME
---------------- ---------- ------------ ------------
UNDO_SQL
-----------------------------------------------------------
0200030052030000    475697 DELETE       JUNK
insert into "BERT"."JUNK"("C1","C2") values ('5','6');

0200030052030000    475697 DELETE       JUNK
insert into "BERT"."JUNK"("C1","C2") values ('3','4');
```

```
0200030052030000     475697 INSERT       JUNK
delete from "BERT"."JUNK" where ROWID = 'AAAD94AAAAAAChOAAD';

0200030052030000     475697 INSERT       JUNK
delete from "BERT"."JUNK" where ROWID = 'AAAD94AAAAAAChOAAC';

0200030052030000     475697 INSERT       JUNK
delete from "BERT"."JUNK" where ROWID = 'AAAD94AAAAAAChOAAB';

0200030052030000     475697 INSERT       JUNK
delete from "BERT"."JUNK" where ROWID = 'AAAD94AAAAAAChOAAA';
```

If one wants to undo the two delete commands whose undo action was to reinsert the data that was deleted, here is the PL/SQL code for doing that.

```
SQL> select * from bert.junk;

       C1          C2
---------- ----------
        1           2
        7           8

SQL> declare
   trans_arr XID_ARRAY;
begin
   trans_arr := xid_array('0200030052030000','0200030052030000');
   dbms_flashback.transaction_backout (
       numtxns          => 1,
       xids             => trans_arr,
       options          => dbms_flashback.cascade
   );
end;
/

SQL> select * from bert.junk;

       C1          C2
---------- ----------
        1           2
        3           4
        5           6
        7           8
```

Once again, for those who prefer a graphical interface, OEM has a rather easy screen for doing object level point-in-time transaction recoveries.

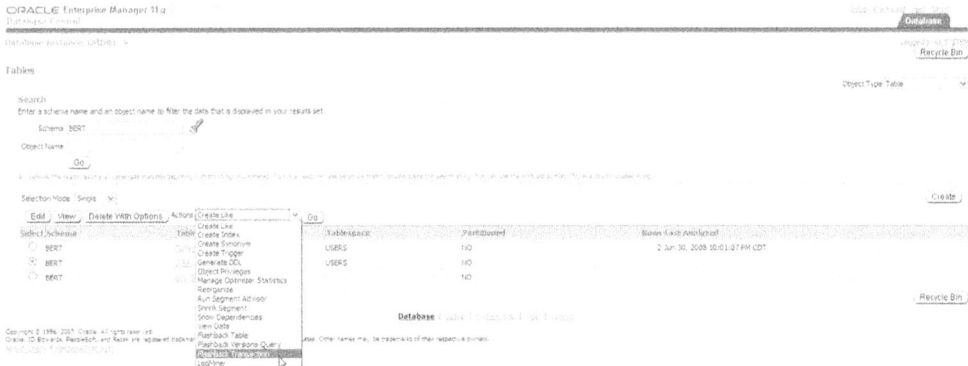

Figure 6.8: *OEM Table Screen*

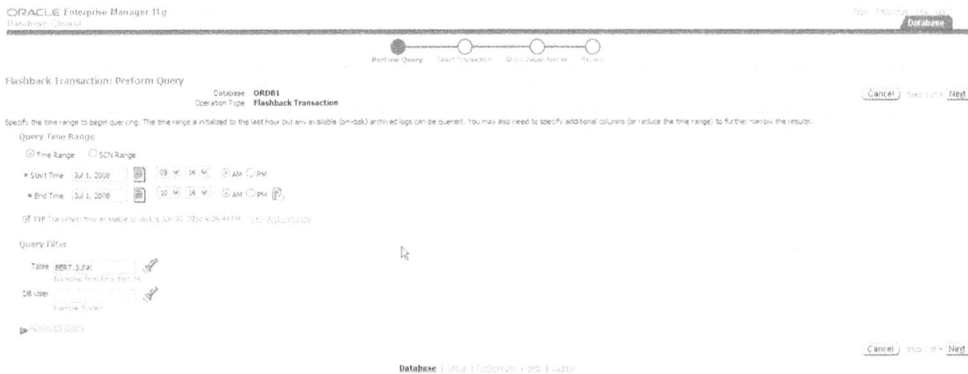

Figure 6.9: *OEM Transaction Flashback Screen*

Flashback Archives

The final piece of the puzzle in the flashback progression is the new Oracle 11g flashback archive. Define an area that provides the ability to automatically track and archive transactional data changes to specified database objects. These flashback archives become user named and managed persistence of UNDO at the specified object level. So when one needs to do a SELECT with an AS OF, rely on the object being in the chosen container for the specified duration and competing for space only with the objects one chooses. Thus, it is merely a named area to support all the prior flashback features that have just been examined.

```
SQL> create tablespace flash_archive
datafile 'c:\oracle\oradata\ordb1\flash_archive.dbf' size 50M;


Tablespace created

SQL> create flashback archive default flash_archive tablespace flash_archive
retention 30 day;

Flashback archive created.

SQL> create table bert.junk (c1 int, c2 int) flashback archive
flash_archive;

Table created.
```

DBMS_LOGMNR

With the introduction of flashback transactions, the need to perform redo log file mining is greatly diminished. It is much easier with Oracle 11g and later to use flashback transactions whenever possible. But for those on Oracle 10g or before and those who simply desire to know for knowledge sakes, now dig into the science of redo log file mining.

When an airplane crashes, the Federal Aviation Administration is quick to the disaster scene. They scour the site and the first thing they look for is the flight recorder or black box, which is actually bright orange in color and not black at all. The idea is that to research a disaster's root cause, one must look at exactly what was happening internally to see what was really occurring as opposed to what was believed or supposed to be happening. This is a critical step in all such disaster investigations because it is often the only way to be 100% sure of what happened.

The same can be said for databases, in that the best way to undo a data disaster is by examining exactly what transaction corrupted the data and then playing its opposite. That means mining the redo logs, both online and offline, to find offending SQL or DDL statements and then undoing them. This can be accomplished using the dbms_logmnr package. But first one needs to install the package as follows:

```
SQL> connect sys/mgr as sysdba
SQL> @?\/rdbms/admin/dbmslm.sql

Package created.

Grant succeeded.
```

```
Synonym created.
```

Now, for this example, assume that the data root problem or cause occurred fairly recently, as though the phone just rang with a frantic request for help, and expect to find the culprit transaction or transactions still within the online redo logs. So query the data dictionary to find the names of those files.

```
SQL> SELECT distinct member LOGFILENAME FROM V$LOGFILE;

LOGFILENAME
-------------------------------------------------------
C:\ORACLE\ORADATA\ORDB1\REDO01.LOG
C:\ORACLE\ORADATA\ORDB1\REDO02.LOG
C:\ORACLE\ORADATA\ORDB1\REDO03.LOG
C:\ORACLE\ORADATA\ORDB1\REDO04.LOG
```

Since it is fine for now to work from just those online redo log files, inform the Oracle log miner utility by registering those redo log files as the ones of interest for mining as shown here:

```
SQL> execute DBMS_LOGMNR.ADD_LOGFILE ('C:\ORACLE\ORADATA\ORDB1\REDO01.LOG');
SQL> execute DBMS_LOGMNR.ADD_LOGFILE ('C:\ORACLE\ORADATA\ORDB1\REDO02.LOG');
SQL> execute DBMS_LOGMNR.ADD_LOGFILE ('C:\ORACLE\ORADATA\ORDB1\REDO03.LOG');
SQL> execute DBMS_LOGMNR.ADD_LOGFILE ('C:\ORACLE\ORADATA\ORDB1\REDO04.LOG');
```

Log miner will require access to a data dictionary lookup reference location so that it can map object IDs to object names. The easiest and recommended source for that information is the current online data dictionary for that database. The other two options involve extracting that lookup information either into the log files or a flat file. Here is the code for using the online data dictionary.

```
execute DBMS_LOGMNR.START_LOGMNR (options =>
dbms_logmnr.dict_from_online_catalog);

PL/SQL procedure successfully completed.
```

Starting a log miner session like this results in the population of a view named *v$logmnr_contents*. Note how the query and results look pretty much the same as the new Oracle 11g flashback transaction.

```
SQL> select xid, start_scn, operation, table_name, undo_sql from
v$logmnr_contents where start_timestamp>=sysdate-1 and username='BERT' and
table_owner='BERT';
XID               START_SCN OPERATION     TABLE_NAME
---------------- ---------- ------------- ------------
```

```
UNDO_SQL
-------------------------------------------------------------
0200030052030000     475697 DELETE       JUNK
insert into "BERT"."JUNK"("C1","C2") values ('5','6');

0200030052030000     475697 DELETE       JUNK
insert into "BERT"."JUNK"("C1","C2") values ('3','4');

0200030052030000     475697 INSERT       JUNK
delete from "BERT"."JUNK" where ROWID = 'AAAD94AAAAAAChOAAD';

0200030052030000     475697 INSERT       JUNK
delete from "BERT"."JUNK" where ROWID = 'AAAD94AAAAAAChOAAC';

0200030052030000     475697 INSERT       JUNK
delete from "BERT"."JUNK" where ROWID = 'AAAD94AAAAAAChOAAB';

0200030052030000     475697 INSERT       JUNK
delete from "BERT"."JUNK" where ROWID = 'AAAD94AAAAAAChOAAA';
```

All that is left is to end the log miner session and it is done.

```
SQL> execute DBMS_LOGMNR.END_LOGMNR();;

PL/SQL procedure successfully completed.
```

Job Scheduling

DBMS_JOBS

Way back in Oracle 7, database jobs were added. Jobs were background processes run by Oracle to perform scheduled tasks. Back then, the idea was that the *dbms_jobs* processes were permitted via the *job_queue_processes init.ora* parameter and were primarily for replication purposes; namely, snapshot refreshes. Over the next few major releases, *dbms_job's* usage increased to include many additional purposes, basically to the point of serving as a generic job scheduler of sorts for many different kinds of Oracle jobs. However, there are a number of shortcomings with the *dbms_job* facility like the fact that it cannot handle job dependencies. Thus, as of Oracle 10g, the *dbms_jobs* package has been superseded by the new *dbms_scheduler* package, which is covered in the next section, and the *job_queue_processes* parameter has been deprecated. In fact, Oracle recommends disabling *dbms_job* by revoking the package execution privilege for all users. Therefore, *dbms_scheduler* is truly the clear choice now.

However, for those on older versions of Oracle or who must still maintain systems built using *dbms_jobs*, examples of *dbms_job* package usage will be examined. The two most used procedures for this package are RUN and SUBMIT. Run forces a job to begin execution immediately, and submit permits one to schedule that job to run at some time in the future, with or without a next iteration repeat specification. The most challenging part, in terms of being least obvious, is specifying the next date and interval parameters, as shown here.

```
SQL> var job number
DECLARE
  X NUMBER;
BEGIN
  SYS.DBMS_JOB.SUBMIT
    (
      job          => :job
      ,what        => 'DBMS_STATS.GATHER_SCHEMA_STATS (''BERT'');'
      ,next_date   => to_date('07/03/2008 13:49:39','mm/dd/yyyy hh24:mi:ss')
      ,interval    => 'TRUNC(LAST_DAY(SYSDATE)) + 1 + 8/24 + 30/1440'
      ,no_parse    => FALSE
    );
END;
/
SQL> print job
PL/SQL procedure successfully completed.


       JOB
----------
        21
```

The next date simply had to be a valid date, but one had to remember that any time specification that was truncated (e.g. minus minutes and seconds) meant the same as all zeroes. So '07/03/2008' without the 13:49:39 would actually mean midnight July 3rd. Likewise, the *interval* parameter was a calculation of the next date when the job would run, so it too had to be valid and was important down to the very same detailed level. Thus, next date = SYSDATE would mean run now, with an interval of SYDATE+1 meaning tomorrow at the same time as now, i.e. right now plus exactly 24 hours. If instead one wanted it run right now and then tomorrow at noon, the interval would be SYSDATE + 1 + 12/24 + 00/1440 where the 12/24 is for hours and the 00/1440 is for the minutes.

There are also three data dictionary views to check on these jobs: ALL_, DBA_ and USER_JOBS. So if the DBA wants to schedule running statistics on the BERT schema at 8:30 AM each day, here is the code to set and verify that it has been set.

```
SQL> select job, schema_user, last_date, next_date, interval, what from
dba_jobs;

JOB SCHEMA_USER  LAST_DATE NEXT_DATE INTERVAL
---- ------------ --------- --------- -----------------------
WHAT
-----------------------------------------------------------------
   1 SYSMAN       03-JUL-08 03-JUL-08 sysdate + 1 / (24 * 60)
EMD_MAINTENANCE.EXECUTE_EM_DBMS_JOB_PROCS();

  21 BERT                   03-JUL-08 TRUNC(LAST_DAY(SYSDATE))
                                      + 1 + 8/24 + 30/1440
DBMS_STATS.GATHER_SCHEMA_STATS ('BERT');
```

Finally, if one wanted to remove a job from the schedule, simply call the
REMOVE procedure like this. To see what jobs are currently running, query
the *dba_jobs_running* data dictionary view. Remember, it only shows the jobs
actually currently running, so it may not return too many rows at any given
time unless a ton of stuff has been scheduled.

```
SQL> execute dbms_job.remove(21);

PL/SQL procedure successfully completed.

SQL> select job, schema_user, last_date, next_date, interval, what from
dba_jobs;

 JOB SCHEMA_USER  LAST_DATE NEXT_DATE INTERVAL
---- ------------ --------- --------- -----------------------
WHAT
-----------------------------------------------------------------
   1 SYSMAN       03-JUL-08 03-JUL-08 sysdate + 1 / (24 * 60)
EMD_MAINTENANCE.EXECUTE_EM_DBMS_JOB_PROCS();
```

DBMS_SCHEDULER

The new *dbms_scheduler* package, available in 10g and later, is a monumental
improvement over the older *dbms_jobs* facility. In fact, not only is it more
capable in Oracle functionality and integration terms, but it also incorporates
numerous real world job scheduler concepts, such that in some cases it even
competes with actual real world job scheduling solutions outside the database
world. Not that this is necessarily an alternative, but it is believed that Oracle
took a flawed and overly simple implementation and built the best scheduler
inside the database one could hope for. Three areas where they have greatly
improved the capabilities are:

- Easier specification of start and interval values

- Ability to schedule executables as well as PL/SQL

- Tight integration with Oracle's Resource Manager

In fact, the new Oracle *dbms_scheduler* package is so robust that the following book is highly recommended where the author, Dr. Timothy Hall, does an excellent job of detailing every aspect that the new scheduler has to offer.

```
Oracle Job Scheduling: Creating Robust Task Management with dbms_job and
Oracle 10g dbms_scheduler

Author: Dr. Timothy S. Hall

Publisher: Rampant Tech Press

ISBN: 0-9744486-6-4
ISBN-13: 978-0974448664
```

And while the PL/SQL API will be investigated here in a little detail so that a fundamental understanding of its basic operation and capabilities is conveyed, another recommendation is using the OEM graphical interface shown next so that one can concentrate on the "what" needs to be done rather than the "how" it works. This is so because the employers assume the DBA generally knows how things work and they are paying to get real-world things done. Besides, as will be shown in the next few pages, Oracle has so enhanced the concept of what *dbms_scheduler* can do or be used for that the OEM GUI becomes the most efficient way to work with it.

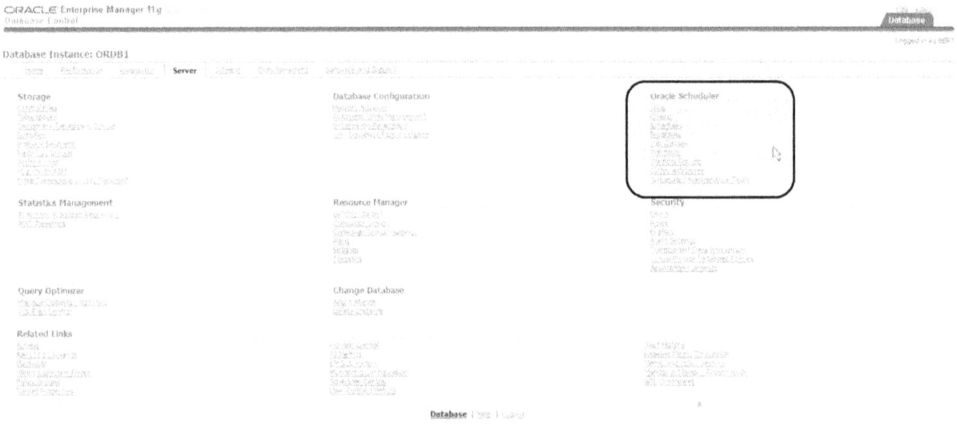

Figure 6.10: *OEM Main Menu – Scheduler Section*

The first concept needing to be done is to appreciate the hierarchy of objects that are now available to work with. The DBA should familiarize himself with the definitions below, and then examine the data model that follows in order to begin to see the nature of the things that are now possible. These concepts represent the metadata necessary to define, instantiate, and execute complex job schedules.

- Program: a program invocation command, parameter list, and definition

- Argument: parameters required to be passed in and/or out at runtime

- Schedule: a named object for when and how many times something runs

- Job: combination of what needs executed (program) and when (schedule)

- Job Instance: the occurrence of a job currently executing and/or running

- Event: message raised by the scheduler or application and passed along

- Chain: grouping of programs linked or combined for a singular objective

- Job Class: a named set of attributes assignable to or for a job description

- Window: periods of time to which resource allocations can be assigned

- Windows Groups: simple grouping of windows for ease of scheduling

That is a lot of terms to have to think about all at once, so Figure 6.11 shows a data modeling diagram of how they are generally related:

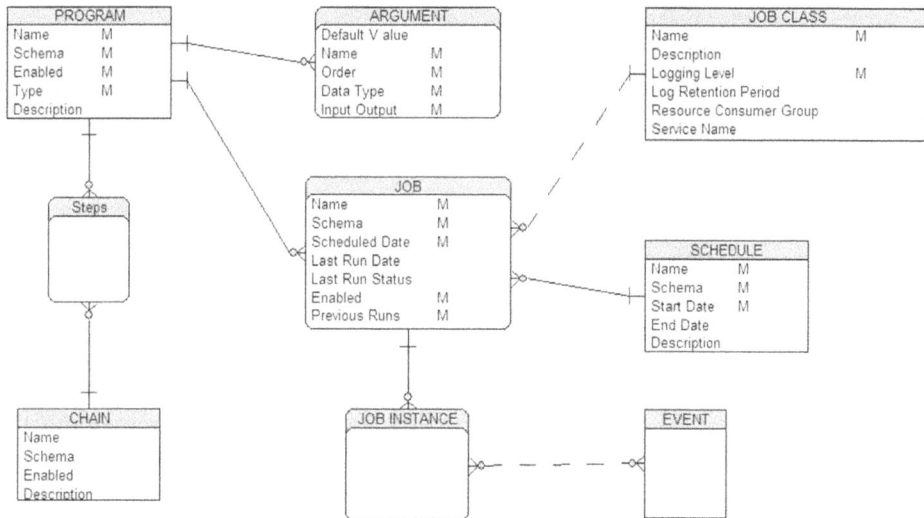

Figure 6.11: *Data Model for Scheduler Objects*

So now walk through an example of creating the semi-realistic job scheduling scenario. Start by creating two windows and windows group plus their Oracle resource manager allocations. The weeknight window should be from 3:00-4:00 AM Monday through Friday, with maintenance plan level resources. The weekend window should be from 12:00-1:00 AM Saturday and Sunday, also with maintenance plan level resources. Moreover, the two windows should be grouped together in case one wants to assign attributes to them globally. The *scheduler_windows.sql* PL/SQL code performs just these three steps:

🖫 scheduler_windows.sql code

```
BEGIN
DBMS_SCHEDULER.CREATE_WINDOW(
window_name=>'"BERT_NIGHTLY_WINDOW"',
resource_plan=>'DEFAULT_MAINTENANCE_PLAN',
start_date=>systimestamp at time zone 'America/Chicago',
duration=>numtodsinterval(60, 'minute'),
repeat_interval=>
'FREQ=WEEKLY;BYDAY=MON,TUE,WED,FRI;BYHOUR=3;BYMINUTE=0;BYSECOND=0',
end_date=>null,
window_priority=>'LOW',
comments=>'Berts nightly mainetnance window');
END;

BEGIN
DBMS_SCHEDULER.CREATE_WINDOW(
window_name=>'"BERT_WEEKEND_WINDOW"',
resource_plan=>'DEFAULT_MAINTENANCE_PLAN',
start_date=>systimestamp at time zone 'America/Chicago',
duration=>numtodsinterval(60, 'minute'),
repeat_interval=>'FREQ=WEEKLY;BYDAY=SAT,SUN;BYHOUR=0;BYMINUTE=0;BYSECOND=0',
end_date=>null,
window_priority=>'LOW',
comments=>'Berts weekend maintenance window');
END;

BEGIN
DBMS_SCHEDULER.CREATE_WINDOW_GROUP(
group_name=>'"BERT_MAINT_WINDOW"',
window_list=>'"BERT_NIGHTLY_WINDOW","BERT_WEEKEND_WINDOW"');
END;
```

Now define two simple programs that should be run during a typical maintenance activity execution: one to delete any BERT schema temporary or interim objects, and one to collect updated statistics on the remaining BERT schema objects. Moreover, the two programs should be grouped together into a chain since one always runs one then the other. The *schjeduler_programs.sql* PL/SQL code, shown below, defines those two programs and chains them together:

⊟ scheduler_programs.sql code

```
BEGIN
DBMS_SCHEDULER.CREATE_PROGRAM(
program_name=>'"BERT"."BERT_CLEAN_UP"',
program_action=>'BERT.CLEAN_UP_PACKAGE.DROP_TEMP_STUFF(''BERT'');',
program_type=>'PLSQL_BLOCK',
number_of_arguments=>0,
comments=>'Clean up temporary objects in BERT schema',
enabled=>TRUE);
END;

BEGIN
DBMS_SCHEDULER.CREATE_PROGRAM(
program_name=>'"BERT"."BERT_GET_STATS"',
program_action=>'DBMS_STATS.GATHER_SCHEMA_STATS (''BERT'');',
program_type=>'PLSQL_BLOCK',
number_of_arguments=>0,
comments=>'Gather statistics on BERT schema objects',
enabled=>TRUE);
END;

BEGIN
sys.dbms_scheduler.create_chain(
comments => 'Berts multi-step general maintenance routine',
chain_name => '"BERT"."BERT_MAINT_CHAIN"');
sys.dbms_scheduler.define_chain_step(
chain_name => '"BERT"."BERT_MAINT_CHAIN"',
step_name => '"STEP_1"',
program_name => '"BERT"."BERT_CLEAN_UP"');
sys.dbms_scheduler.alter_chain(
chain_name => '"BERT"."BERT_MAINT_CHAIN"',
step_name => '"STEP_1"',
attribute => 'pause',
value => FALSE);
sys.dbms_scheduler.alter_chain(
chain_name => '"BERT"."BERT_MAINT_CHAIN"',
step_name => '"STEP_1"',
attribute => 'skip',
value => FALSE);
sys.dbms_scheduler.define_chain_step(
chain_name => '"BERT"."BERT_MAINT_CHAIN"',
step_name => '"STEP_2"',
program_name => '"BERT"."BERT_GET_STATS"');
sys.dbms_scheduler.alter_chain(
chain_name => '"BERT"."BERT_MAINT_CHAIN"',
step_name => '"STEP_2"',
attribute => 'pause',
value => FALSE);
sys.dbms_scheduler.alter_chain(
chain_name => '"BERT"."BERT_MAINT_CHAIN"',
step_name => '"STEP_2"',
attribute => 'skip',
value => FALSE);
END;
```

Then create a job for that chain because so far the "what" one wants to do and the resources available have been defined, but it has not yet been scheduled. So create a job that can then later actually be scheduled and the *scheduler_job.sql* PL/SQL code does just that.

🖫 scheduler_job.sql code

```
BEGIN
sys.dbms_scheduler.create_job(
job_name => '"BERT"."BERT_MAINT_JOB"',
job_type => 'CHAIN',
job_action => '"BERT"."BERT_MAINT_CHAIN"',
start_date => systimestamp at time zone 'US/Central',
job_class => '"DEFAULT_JOB_CLASS"',
comments => 'Berts maintenance job',
auto_drop => FALSE,
enabled => TRUE);
END;
```

However, the job is not quite done yet because the job still needs to be scheduled to run using the *scheduler_schedule.sql* PL/SQL code, as shown below. Note how the scheduled job times here are exactly the same as the resource allocation times created in the above examples for the windows and window groups. So now a very simplistic example of the steps involved that comprise a minimal setup for a very basic real-world type schedule have been completed.

🖫 scheduler_schedule.sql code

```
BEGIN
sys.dbms_scheduler.create_schedule(
repeat_interval =>
'FREQ=WEEKLY;BYDAY=MON,TUE,WED,THU,FRI;BYHOUR=3;BYMINUTE=0;BYSECOND=0',
start_date => systimestamp at time zone 'America/Chicago',
schedule_name => '"BERT"."BERT_MAINT_NIGHLY_RUN"');
END;

BEGIN
sys.dbms_scheduler.create_schedule(
repeat_interval =>
'FREQ=WEEKLY;BYDAY=SAT,SUN;BYHOUR=0;BYMINUTE=0;BYSECOND=0',
start_date => systimestamp at time zone 'America/Chicago',
schedule_name => '"BERT"."BERT_MAINT_WEEKEND_RUN"');
END;
```

That is a tremendous amount of code. Again, it was shown mostly to give a deeper appreciation of all the work required or behind the scenes. In reality, most people are simply going to use the OEM screens for creating and managing all items related to schedules. Below is the OEM screen for very easily defining the *bert_main_weekend_run* shown above. Once the basics are

---

understood here, it advisable to use these screens exclusively and concentrate on what is being done and not how to do it.

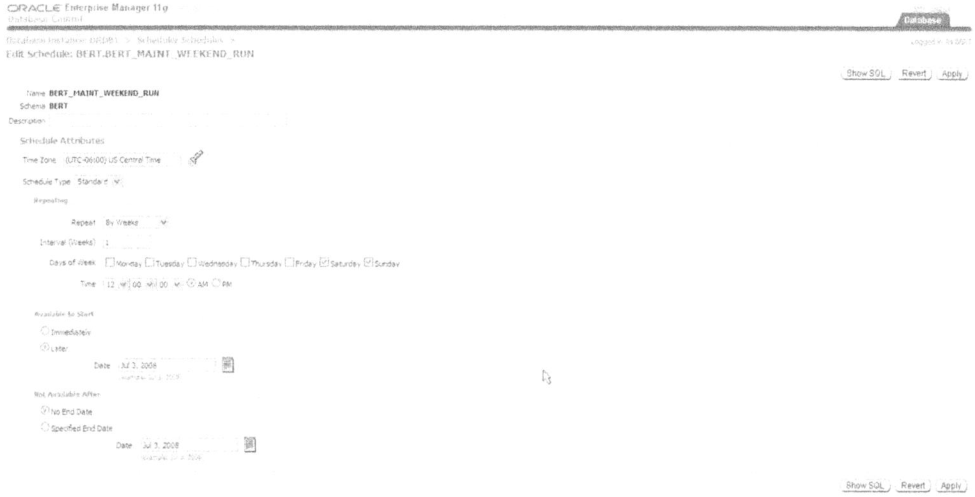

Figure 6.12: *OEM Scheduler Schedule Screen*

Access Security

DBMS_RLS

The *dbms_rls* package provides a collection of procedures for administering row level security (RLS), also commonly referred to as fine grain access control (FGAC). Essentially, RLS or FGAC appends dynamic predicates, such as WHERE clause restrictions, to DML statements at parse time. This security is completely transparent to both the end user as well as the application developer.

Note that the *dbms_rls* package itself is fairly straightforward, but the example of its usage is slightly more complex and depends heavily on application code containing proper calls to *dbms_session* for setting context. Therefore, it is advisable to review *dbms_session* later in this chapter. Plus, *dbms_rls* is available only with Oracle Enterprise Edition.

Dbms_rls is most often used to create a Virtual Private Database (VPD), which allows multiple users to access a single schema while preventing them from seeing each others' data. Think of it as schema segregation or partitioning. A single ACCOUNTING schema, tables, views and indexes can be created to hold multiple companies data, and yet still guarantee data privacy, meaning that no company can see any other companies' data. This can also be done at the application level for different classes of users. The process involves the following steps:

- Create or setup the database environment (schema, tables, views and such)

- Create one or more application contexts

- Create a login trigger for application users

- Create security policies to define dynamic predicates

- Apply, or associate, security policies with the tables

Next to be examined are the procedures that *dbms_rls* offers, followed by a fairly simple example of implementing a VPD within the pre-canned "SCOTT" schema.

There are a few enumerated constants that one must know to use this package:

```
-- Policy Types
STATIC                      CONSTANT    BINARY_INTEGER := 1;
SHARED_STATIC               CONSTANT    BINARY_INTEGER := 2;
CONTEXT_SENSITIVE           CONSTANT    BINARY_INTEGER := 3;
SHARED_CONTEXT_SENSITIVE    CONSTANT    BINARY_INTEGER := 4;
DYNAMIC                     CONSTANT    BINARY_INTEGER := 5;
XDS1                        CONSTANT    BINARY_INTEGER := 6;
XDS2                        CONSTANT    BINARY_INTEGER := 7;
XDS3                        CONSTANT    BINARY_INTEGER := 8;

-- security relevant columns options, default is null
ALL_ROWS                    CONSTANT    BINARY_INTEGER := 1;
```

add_grouped_policy is a procedure that adds a policy to the specified table, view, or synonym and associates that policy with the specified policy group. If no schema is defined, then the current session's schema is assumed. The statement type can be any combination of INDEX, SELECT, INSERT, UPDATE, or DELETE.

ARGUMENT	TYPE	IN / OUT	DEFAULT VALUE
OBJECT_SCHEMA	VARCHAR2	IN	NULL
OBJECT_NAME	VARCHAR2	IN	
POLICY_GROUP	VARCHAR2	IN	SYS_DEFAULT

POLICY_NAME	VARCHAR2	IN	
FUNCTION_SCHEMA	VARCHAR2	IN	NULL
POLICY_FUNCTION	VARCHAR2	IN	
STATEMENT_TYPES	VARCHAR2	IN	NULL
UPDATE_CHECK	BOOLEAN	IN	FALSE
ENABLED	BOOLEAN	IN	TRUE
STATIC_POLICY	BOOLEAN	IN	FALSE
POLICY_TYPE	BINARY_INTEGER	IN	NULL
LONG_PREDICATE	BOOLEAN	IN	FALSE
SEC_RELEVANT_COLS	VARCHAR2	IN	NULL
SEC_RELEVANT_COLS_OPTS	BINARY_INTEGER	IN	NULL

Table 6.7: *Add_grouped_policy Statement Types*

add_policy is a procedure that simply attaches a policy to the specified table, view, or synonym. If no schema is defined, then the current session's schema is assumed. The statement type can be any combination of INDEX, SELECT, INSERT, UPDATE, or DELETE.

ARGUMENT	TYPE	IN / OUT	DEFAULT VALUE
OBJECT_SCHEMA	VARCHAR2	IN	NULL
OBJECT_NAME	VARCHAR2	IN	
POLICY_NAME	VARCHAR2	IN	
FUNCTION_SCHEMA	VARCHAR2	IN	NULL
POLICY_FUNCTION	VARCHAR2	IN	
STATEMENT_TYPES	VARCHAR2	IN	NULL
UPDATE_CHECK	BOOLEAN	IN	FALSE
ENABLED	BOOLEAN	IN	TRUE
STATIC_POLICY	BOOLEAN	IN	FALSE
POLICY_TYPE	BINARY_INTEGER	IN	NULL
LONG_PREDICATE	BOOLEAN	IN	FALSE
SEC_RELEVANT_COLS	VARCHAR2	IN	NULL
SEC_RELEVANT_COLS_OPTS	BINARY_INTEGER	IN	NULL

Table 6.8: *Add_policy Statement Types*

add_policy_context is a procedure that defines the application context that drives the enforcement of policies such as the context that determines which application is running. If no schema is defined, then the current session's schema is assumed.

ARGUMENT	TYPE	IN / OUT	DEFAULT VALUE
OBJECT_SCHEMA	VARCHAR2	IN	NULL
OBJECT_NAME	VARCHAR2	IN	
NAMESPACE	VARCHAR2	IN	
ATTRIBUTE	VARCHAR2	IN	

Table 6.9: *Add_policy_context Statement Types*

create_policy_group is a procedure that creates a policy group. That group must be unique for each table or view.

ARGUMENT	TYPE	IN / OUT	DEFAULT VALUE
OBJECT_SCHEMA	VARCHAR2	IN	NULL
OBJECT_NAME	VARCHAR2	IN	
POLCIY_GROUP	VARCHAR2	IN	

Table 6.10: *Create_policy_group Statement Types*

delete_policy_group is a procedure that drops a policy group. Note that no policy can be in that policy group.

ARGUMENT	TYPE	IN / OUT	DEFAULT VALUE
OBJECT_SCHEMA	VARCHAR2	IN	NULL
OBJECT_NAME	VARCHAR2	IN	
POLCIY_GROUP	VARCHAR2	IN	

Table 6.11: *Delete_policy_group Statement Types*

disable_grouped_policy is a procedure that simply drops a policy associated with a policy group.

ARGUMENT	TYPE	IN / OUT	DEFAULT VALUE
OBJECT_SCHEMA	VARCHAR2	IN	NULL
OBJECT_NAME	VARCHAR2	IN	
POLCIY_GROUP	VARCHAR2	IN	
POLICY_NAME	VARCHAR2	IN	

Table 6.12: *Disable_grouped_policy Statement Types*

drop_grouped_policy is a procedure that drops, or detaches, a policy from the specified table, view, or synonym and de-associates that policy with the specified policy group. If no schema is defined, then the current session's schema is assumed.

ARGUMENT	TYPE	IN / OUT	DEFAULT VALUE
OBJECT_SCHEMA	VARCHAR2	IN	NULL
OBJECT_NAME	VARCHAR2	IN	
POLICY_GROUP	VARCHAR2	IN	SYS_DEFAULT
POLICY_NAME	VARCHAR2	IN	

Table 6.13: *Drop_grouped_policy Statement Types*

drop_policy is a procedure that simply drops a policy from the specified table, view, or synonym. If no schema is defined, then the current session's schema is assumed.

ARGUMENT	TYPE	IN / OUT	DEFAULT VALUE
OBJECT_SCHEMA	VARCHAR2	IN	NULL
OBJECT_NAME	VARCHAR2	IN	
POLICY_NAME	VARCHAR2	IN	

Table 6.14: *Drop_policy Statement Types*

drop_policy_context is a procedure that drops the application context that drives the enforcement of policies, i.e. the context that determines which application is running. If no schema is defined, then the current session's schema is assumed.

ARGUMENT	TYPE	IN / OUT	DEFAULT VALUE
OBJECT_SCHEMA	VARCHAR2	IN	NULL
OBJECT_NAME	VARCHAR2	IN	
NAMESPACE	VARCHAR2	IN	
ATTRIBUTE	VARCHAR2	IN	

Table 6.15: *Drop_policy_context Statement Types*

enable_grouped_policy is a procedure that simply enables or disables a policy associated with a policy group which causes the current transaction, if any, to commit.

ARGUMENT	TYPE	IN / OUT	DEFAULT VALUE
OBJECT_SCHEMA	VARCHAR2	IN	NULL
OBJECT_NAME	VARCHAR2	IN	
POLCIY_GROUP	VARCHAR2	IN	SYS_DEFAULT
POLICY_NAME	VARCHAR2	IN	
ENABLE	BOOLEAN	IN	TRUE

Table 6.16: *Enable_grouped_policy Statement Types*

enable_policy is a procedure that simply enables or disables a policy from the specified table, view, or synonym. If no schema is defined, then the current session's schema is assumed.

ARGUMENT	TYPE	IN / OUT	DEFAULT VALUE
OBJECT_SCHEMA	VARCHAR2	IN	NULL
OBJECT_NAME	VARCHAR2	IN	
POLICY_NAME	VARCHAR2	IN	
ENABLE	BOOLEAN	IN	TRUE

Table 6.17: *Enable_policy Statement Types*

refresh_grouped_policy is a procedure that invalidates all cursors and reparses the SQL statements associated with that policy.

ARGUMENT	TYPE	IN / OUT	DEFAULT VALUE
OBJECT_SCHEMA	VARCHAR2	IN	NULL
OBJECT_NAME	VARCHAR2	IN	NULL
POLCIY_GROUP	VARCHAR2	IN	NULL
POLICY_NAME	VARCHAR2	IN	NULL

Table 6.18: *Refresh_grouped_policy Statement Types*

refresh_policy is a procedure that invalidates all cursors and reparses the SQL statements associated with that policy.

ARGUMENT	TYPE	IN / OUT	DEFAULT VALUE
OBJECT_SCHEMA	VARCHAR2	IN	NULL
OBJECT_NAME	VARCHAR2	IN	NULL
POLICY_NAME	VARCHAR2	IN	NULL

Table 6.19: *Refresh_policy Statement Types*

The *virtual_priv_db_demo.sql* SQL*Plus script is a very simple example of creating a row-level VPD in the SCOTT schema, where user BERT can see everything and user BERT2 can only see the rows for people working in department 10.

🖫 virtual_priv_db_demo.sql script

```
connect bert/bert

set term off
drop user bert2;
drop package   emp_ctx_pkg;
drop package   boday emp_ctx_pkg;
drop context   set_emp_ctx;
drop trigger   emp_ctx_trg;
drop function set_emp_prd;
BEGIN
  DBMS_RLS.DROP_POLICY (
    object_schema    => 'scott',
    object_name      => 'emp',
    policy_name      => 'emp_policy'
  );
END;
/
set term on

grant connect to bert2 identified by bert2;
grant select on scott.emp to bert2;
```

```
CREATE OR REPLACE PACKAGE emp_ctx_pkg
IS
  PROCEDURE set_emp_ctx;
END;
/

CREATE OR REPLACE PACKAGE BODY emp_ctx_pkg
IS
  PROCEDURE set_emp_ctx
  AS
  BEGIN
    DBMS_SESSION.SET_CONTEXT('EMP_CTX', 'DNO', 10);
  END;
END;
/

CREATE OR REPLACE CONTEXT emp_ctx USING emp_ctx_pkg;

CREATE OR REPLACE TRIGGER emp_ctx_trig
AFTER LOGON ON DATABASE
BEGIN
  if (USER = 'BERT2') then
    bert.emp_ctx_pkg.set_emp_ctx;
  end if;
END;
/

CREATE OR REPLACE FUNCTION set_emp_prd(
    p_schema   IN VARCHAR2,
    p_table    IN VARCHAR2
  ) RETURN VARCHAR2
AS
  emp_pred VARCHAR2 (400);
BEGIN
  if (USER = 'BERT2') then
    emp_pred := 'deptno = SYS_CONTEXT(''emp_ctx'', ''DNO'')';
  else
    emp_pred := '1=1';
  end if;
  RETURN emp_pred;
END;
/

BEGIN
  DBMS_RLS.ADD_POLICY (
    object_schema    => 'scott',
    object_name      => 'emp',
    policy_name      => 'emp_policy',
    function_schema  => 'bert',
    policy_function  => 'set_emp_prd',
    statement_types  => 'select'
  );
END;
/

-- bert/bert
select * from scott.emp;

connect bert2/bert2;
```

```
select * from scott.emp;
```

The output from the *virtual_priv_db_demo.sql* SQL*Plus script looks like this:

🖫 virtual_priv_db_demo.sql output

```
SQL> -- bert/bert
SQL> select * from scott.emp;

    EMPNO ENAME      JOB          MGR HIREDATE      SAL  COMM DEPTNO
---------- ---------- --------- ---------- --------- ------- ----- ------
     7369 SMITH      CLERK       7902 17-DEC-80     800          20
     7499 ALLEN      SALESMAN    7698 20-FEB-81    1600   300    30
     7521 WARD       SALESMAN    7698 22-FEB-81    1250   500    30
     7566 JONES      MANAGER     7839 02-APR-81    2975          20
     7654 MARTIN     SALESMAN    7698 28-SEP-81    1250  1400    30
     7698 BLAKE      MANAGER     7839 01-MAY-81    2850          30
     7782 CLARK      MANAGER     7839 09-JUN-81    2450          10
     7788 SCOTT      ANALYST     7566 19-APR-87    3000          20
     7839 KING       PRESIDENT        17-NOV-81    5000          10
     7844 TURNER     SALESMAN    7698 08-SEP-81    1500     0    30
     7876 ADAMS      CLERK       7788 23-MAY-87    1100          20
     7900 JAMES      CLERK       7698 03-DEC-81     950          30
     7902 FORD       ANALYST     7566 03-DEC-81    3000          20
     7934 MILLER     CLERK       7782 23-JAN-82    1300          10

14 rows selected.

SQL>
SQL> connect bert2/bert2;
Connected.
SQL> select * from scott.emp;

    EMPNO ENAME      JOB          MGR HIREDATE      SAL  COMM DEPTNO
---------- ---------- --------- ---------- --------- ------- ----- ------
     7782 CLARK      MANAGER     7839 09-JUN-81    2450          10
     7839 KING       PRESIDENT        17-NOV-81    5000          10
     7934 MILLER     CLERK       7782 23-JAN-82    1300          10
```

File Security

DBMS_CRYPTO

dbms_crypto provides a modern and effectual ability to encrypt and decrypt data using any of the following cryptographic algorithms:

- Data Encryption Standard (DES)
- Triple DES (3DES, 2-key and 3-key)
- Advanced Encryption Standard (AES)
- MD5, MD4, and SHA-1 cryptographic hashes
- MD5 and SHA-1 Message Authentication Code (MAC)

Be aware that effective *dbms_crypto* usage requires a general level of security familiarity and/or expertise. Key management is entirely programmatic, thus the application, or caller of *dbms_crypto*, must supply the encryption key. Furthermore, the application is responsible for storing and retrieving keys securely. Common options for applications storing keys include within the database, on the operating system, and user self-managed. Of course, one can always rely instead upon Oracle's encrypted tables and tablespaces and their inherently automatic key management.

Dbms_obfuscation_toolkit usage should be replaced by the newer *dbms_crypto* package, available in 10g and later, which offers more modern and secure cryptographic algorithms as well as support for more database data types.

There are a few enumerated constants that one must know to use this package:

```
-- Hash Functions
HASH_MD4              CONSTANT PLS_INTEGER            :=     1;
HASH_MD5              CONSTANT PLS_INTEGER            :=     2;
HASH_SH1              CONSTANT PLS_INTEGER            :=     3;

-- MAC Functions
HMAC_MD5              CONSTANT PLS_INTEGER            :=     1;
HMAC_SH1              CONSTANT PLS_INTEGER            :=     2;

-- Block Cipher Algorithms
ENCRYPT_DES           CONSTANT PLS_INTEGER            :=     1;   -- 0x0001
ENCRYPT_3DES_2KEY     CONSTANT PLS_INTEGER            :=     2;   -- 0x0002
ENCRYPT_3DES          CONSTANT PLS_INTEGER            :=     3;   -- 0x0003
ENCRYPT_AES           CONSTANT PLS_INTEGER            :=     4;   -- 0x0004
ENCRYPT_PBE_MD5DES    CONSTANT PLS_INTEGER            :=     5;   -- 0x0005
ENCRYPT_AES128        CONSTANT PLS_INTEGER            :=     6;   -- 0x0006
ENCRYPT_AES192        CONSTANT PLS_INTEGER            :=     7;   -- 0x0007
ENCRYPT_AES256        CONSTANT PLS_INTEGER            :=     8;   -- 0x0008

-- Block Cipher Chaining Modifiers
CHAIN_CBC             CONSTANT PLS_INTEGER            :=   256;   -- 0x0100
CHAIN_CFB             CONSTANT PLS_INTEGER            :=   512;   -- 0x0200
CHAIN_ECB             CONSTANT PLS_INTEGER            :=   768;   -- 0x0300
CHAIN_OFB             CONSTANT PLS_INTEGER            :=  1024;   -- 0x0400

-- Block Cipher Padding Modifiers
PAD_PKCS5             CONSTANT PLS_INTEGER            :=  4096;   -- 0x1000
PAD_NONE              CONSTANT PLS_INTEGER            :=  8192;   -- 0x2000
PAD_ZERO              CONSTANT PLS_INTEGER            := 12288;   -- 0x3000
PAD_ORCL              CONSTANT PLS_INTEGER            := 16384;   -- 0x4000

-- Stream Cipher Algorithms
ENCRYPT_RC4           CONSTANT PLS_INTEGER            :=   129;   -- 0x0081

-- Convenience Constants for Block Ciphers
DES_CBC_PKCS5         CONSTANT PLS_INTEGER            := ENCRYPT_DES
                                                       + CHAIN_CBC
                                                       + PAD_PKCS5;
```

```
DES3_CBC_PKCS5      CONSTANT PLS_INTEGER              := ENCRYPT_3DES
                                                      + CHAIN_CBC
                                                      + PAD_PKCS5;

AES_CBC_PKCS5       CONSTANT PLS_INTEGER              := ENCRYPT_AES
                                                      + CHAIN_CBC
                                                      + PAD_PKCS5;
```

Below are the *dbms_crypto* procedures and functions but remember, security and especially this package are not for novices or security neophytes. If one loses a key or improperly implements any factors, the data will almost surely be unrecoverable.

Decrypt is an overloaded procedure for decrypting the data with the following parameters and defaults.

ARGUMENT	TYPE	IN / OUT	DEFAULT VALUE
DST	BLOB	CLOB	IN	OUT	
SRC	BLOB	IN	
TYP	PLS_INTEGER	IN	
KEY	RAW	IN	
IV	RAW	IN	NULL

Table 6.20: *Decrypt Parameters*

decrypt is also an overloaded function for decrypting the date with the following parameters and defaults, returning a RAW value.

ARGUMENT	TYPE	IN / OUT	DEFAULT VALUE
SRC	BLOB	IN	
TYP	PLS_INTEGER	IN	
KEY	RAW	IN	
IV	RAW	IN	NULL

Table 6.21: *Additional Decrypt Parameters*

Encrypt is an overloaded procedure for encrypting the data with the following parameters and defaults.

ARGUMENT	TYPE	IN / OUT	DEFAULT VALUE
DST	BLOB | CLOB	IN | OUT	
SRC	BLOB	IN	
TYP	PLS_INTEGER	IN	
KEY	RAW	IN	
IV	RAW	IN	NULL

Table 6:22: *Encrypt Parameters*

encrypt is also an overloaded function for encrypting the data with the following parameters and defaults, returning a RAW value.

ARGUMENT	TYPE	IN / OUT	DEFAULT VALUE
SRC	BLOB	IN	
TYP	PLS_INTEGER	IN	
KEY	RAW	IN	
IV	RAW	IN	NULL

Table 6.23: *Additional Encrypt Parameters*

hash is a function that accepts an input string and returns a unique identifier based upon the value as a RAW value.

ARGUMENT	TYPE	IN / OUT	DEFAULT VALUE
SRC	RAW |BLOB | CLOB	IN	
TYP	PLS_INTEGER	IN	

Table 6.24: *Hash Parameters*

MAC for message authentication code is similar to hash, but it is based off a supplied key as well as the data. It also returns the result via a RAW value.

ARGUMENT	TYPE	IN / OUT	DEFAULT VALUE
SRC	RAW |BLOB | CLOB	IN	
TYP	PLS_INTEGER	IN	
KEY	RAW	IN	

Table 6.25: *Mac Parameters*

The remaining functions provide simple random number generation, and include:

```
DBMS_CRYPTO.RANDOMBYTES (number_bytes IN POSITIVE) RETURN RAW;

DBMS_CRYPTO.RANDOMINTEGER RETURN BINARY_INTEGER;

DBMS_CRYPTO.RANDOMNUMBER RETURN NUMBER;
```

DBMS_OBFUSCATION_TOOLKIT

dbms_obfuscation_toolkit provides the capability to encrypt and decrypt data using the Data Encryption Standard (DES) or the Triple DES algorithms. The Data Encryption Standard has been an encryption standard for over 20 years. DES is a 64-bit symmetric key cipher, but the key utilizes only 56 of those bits. Triple DES (3DES) is a far stronger cipher with 128 or 192-bit keys where only 112 or 168 of those bits are used respectively, making encrypted values much harder to break. However, DES in general is being replaced by the new and more secure Advanced Encryption Standard (AES).

Des3decrypt is an overloaded procedure for decrypting the data and working with either RAW values or strings with the following parameters and defaults.

ARGUMENT	TYPE	IN / OUT	DEFAULT VALUE
INPUT | INPUT_STRING	RAW | VARCHAR2	IN	
KEY | KEY_STRING	RAW | VARCHAR2	IN	
DECRYTPED_DATA | DECRYPTED_STRING	RAW | VARCHAR2	OUT	
WHICH	PLS_INTEGER	IN	TwoKeyMode
IV | IV_STRING	RAW | VARCHAR2	IN	NULL

Table 6.26: *Des3decrypt Parameters*

Des3decrypt is also an overloaded function for decrypting the data and working with either RAW values or strings with the following parameters and defaults, returning either a RAW or VARCHAR2 value.

ARGUMENT	TYPE	IN / OUT	DEFAULT VALUE
INPUT | INPUT_STRING	RAW | VARCHAR2	IN	
KEY | KEY_STRING	RAW | VARCHAR2	IN	
WHICH	PLS_INTEGER	IN	TwoKeyMode
IV | IV_STRING	RAW | VARCHAR2	IN	NULL

Table 6.27: *Additional Des3decrypt Parameters*

Des3encrypt is an overloaded procedure for encrypting the data and working with either RAW values or strings with the following parameters and defaults.

ARGUMENT	TYPE	IN / OUT	DEFAULT VALUE
INPUT | INPUT_STRING	RAW | VARCHAR2	IN	
KEY | KEY_STRING	RAW | VARCHAR2	IN	
ENCRYTPED_DATA | ENCRYPTED_STRING	RAW | VARCHAR2	OUT	
WHICH	PLS_INTEGER	IN	TwoKeyMode
IV | IV_STRING	RAW | VARCHAR2	IN	NULL

Table 6.28: *Des3encrypt Parameters*

Des3encrypt is also an overloaded function for encrypting the data and working with either RAW values or strings with the following parameters and defaults, returning either a RAW or VARCHAR2 value.

ARGUMENT	TYPE	IN / OUT	DEFAULT VALUE
INPUT | INPUT_STRING	RAW | VARCHAR2	IN	
KEY | KEY_STRING	RAW | VARCHAR2	IN	
WHICH	PLS_INTEGER	IN	TwoKeyMode
IV | IV_STRING	RAW | VARCHAR2	IN	NULL

Table 6.29: *Additional Des3encrypt Parameters*

Des3getkey is an overloaded procedure generating an encryption key and working with either RAW values or strings with the following parameters and defaults.

ARGUMENT	TYPE	IN / OUT	DEFAULT VALUE
WHICH	PLS_INTEGER	IN	TwoKeyMode
SEED | SEED_STRING	RAW | VARCHAR2		
KEY | KEY_STRING	RAW | VARCHAR2	OUT	

Table 6.30: *Des3getkey Parameters*

Des3getkey is also an overloaded procedure generating an encryption key and working with either RAW values or strings with the following parameters and defaults, returning either a RAW or VARCHAR2 value.

ARGUMENT	TYPE	IN / OUT	DEFAULT VALUE
WHICH	PLS_INTEGER	IN	TwoKeyMode
SEED | SEED_STRING	RAW | VARCHAR2		

Table 6.31: *Additional Des3getkey Parameters*

Desdecrypt is an overloaded procedure for decrypting the data and working with either RAW values or strings with the following parameters and defaults.

ARGUMENT	TYPE	IN / OUT	DEFAULT VALUE
INPUT | INPUT_STRING	RAW | VARCHAR2	IN	
KEY | KEY_STRING	RAW | VARCHAR2	IN	
DECRYTPED_DATA | DECRYPTED_STRING	RAW | VARCHAR2	OUT	

Table 6.32: *Desdecrypt Parameters*

Desdecrypt is also an overloaded function for decrypting the data and working with either RAW values or strings with the following parameters and defaults, returning either a RAW or VARCHAR2 value.

ARGUMENT	TYPE	IN / OUT	DEFAULT VALUE
INPUT | INPUT_STRING	RAW | VARCHAR2	IN	
KEY | KEY_STRING	RAW | VARCHAR2	IN	

Table 6.33: *Additional Desdecrypt Parameters*

Desencrypt is an overloaded procedure for encrypting the data and working with either RAW values or strings with the following parameters and defaults.

ARGUMENT	TYPE	IN / OUT	DEFAULT VALUE
INPUT | INPUT_STRING	RAW | VARCHAR2	IN	
KEY | KEY_STRING	RAW | VARCHAR2	IN	
ENCRYTPED_DATA | ENCRYPTED_STRING	RAW | VARCHAR2	OUT	

Table 6.34: *Desencrypt Parameters*

Desencrypt is also an overloaded function for encrypting the data and working with either RAW values or strings with the following parameters and defaults, returning either a RAW or VARCHAR2 value.

ARGUMENT	TYPE	IN / OUT	DEFAULT VALUE
INPUT | INPUT_STRING	RAW | VARCHAR2	IN	
KEY | KEY_STRING	RAW | VARCHAR2	IN	

Table 6.35: *Additional Desencrypt Parameters*

Desgetkey is an overloaded procedure generating an encryption key and working with either RAW values or strings with the following parameters and defaults.

ARGUMENT	TYPE	IN / OUT	DEFAULT VALUE
SEED | SEED_STRING	RAW | VARCHAR2		
KEY | KEY_STRING	RAW | VARCHAR2	OUT	

Table 6.36: *Desgetkey Parameters*

Desgetkey is also an overloaded procedure generating an encryption key and working with either RAW values or strings with the following parameters and defaults, returning either a RAW or VARCHAR2 value.

ARGUMENT	TYPE	IN / OUT	DEFAULT VALUE
SEED | SEED_STRING	RAW | VARCHAR2		

Table 6.37: *Additional Desgetkey Parameters*

UTL_COMPRESS

UTL_COMPRESS provides a set of convenient yet capable data compression utilities. However, as of Oracle version 11g, features for inherent and automated compression at the table, column and/or tablespace level should be the first bet. But assuming that the need still exists to programmatically access data compression (e.g. PL/SQL code compressing UTL_FILE output stream), then UTL_COMPRESS may still be of use. If one is familiar with popular Windows compression tools such as PKZIP® and WinZip®, then this package will be very easily mastered. Finally, note that the individual files created by UTL_COMPRESS are compatible with gzip, with the –n option, and/or gunzip.

There are two basic modes of operation with UTL_COMPRESS:

- Simply compress or uncompress a source to target
- Open a context and compress or uncompress items

The first scenario is pretty much the same as when one runs zip or unzip on a file in its entirety. The second case is more like when items are added, updated or extracted to or from a zip file. That is similar to when one opens WinZip, and then drag-and-drops Windows Explorer files either into or out of that archive. So it is essentially a compression session or context, so to speak.

lz_compress is an overloaded procedure for compressing the data using the Lempel-Ziv compression algorithm with the following parameters and defaults.

ARGUMENT	TYPE	IN / OUT	DEFAULT VALUE
SRC	BLOB	BFILE	IN	
DST	BLOB	IN	OUT	
QUALITY	BINARY_INTEGER	IN	6 (values 1-9 for zip level)

Table 6.38: *Lz_compress Parameters*

lz_compress is also an overloaded function for compressing the data using the Lempel-Ziv compression algorithm, with the following parameters and defaults and returning either a RAW or BLOB value.

ARGUMENT	TYPE	IN / OUT	DEFAULT VALUE
SRC	RAW	BLOB	BFILE	IN	
QUALITY	BINARY_INTEGER	IN	6 (values 1-9 for zip level)

Table 6.39: *Additional Lz_compress Parameters*

lz_uncompress is an overloaded procedure for decompressing the data using the Lempel-Ziv compression algorithm with the following parameters and defaults.

ARGUMENT	TYPE	IN / OUT	DEFAULT VALUE
SRC	BLOB | BFILE	IN	
DST	BLOB	IN | OUT	

Table 6.40: *Lz_uncompress Parameters*

lz_uncompress is also an overloaded function for decompressing the data using the Lempel-Ziv compression algorithm with the following parameters and defaults and returning either a RAW or BLOB value.

ARGUMENT	TYPE	IN / OUT	DEFAULT VALUE
SRC	RAW | BLOB | BFILE	IN	
QUALITY	BINARY_INTEGER	IN	6 (values 1-9 for zip level)

Table 6.41: *Additional Lz_compress Parameters*

The following is a very simple example to demonstrate this first use-case scenario:

```
SQL> create table junk1 (c1 varchar2(100));

Table created.

SQL> insert into junk1 values ('This is a test');

1 row created.

SQL> commit;

Commit complete.

SQL> select * from junk1;

C1
----------------------------------------------------------------------
----
This is a test

SQL> update junk1 set c1 =
UTL_RAW.CAST_TO_VARCHAR2(UTL_COMPRESS.LZ_COMPRESS(UTL_RAW.CAST_TO_RAW(c1)));

1 row updated.

SQL> select * from junk1;

C1
----------------------------------------------------------------------
----
▼        ӧӧ╓╙,V 6Dàæ╚┌┆ 2ƒz└♫
```

The second use-case scenario is a little more involved than this very simple first example. One has to create a compressions session or context, then add and/or subtract items from that context and finally close that session or context. Again, it is very much like opening WinZip, and dragging-and-dropping Windows Explorer files into or out of that archive. The packages procedures and functions are now shown in an order that should best support such a workflow.

lz_compress_open is a function that initializes a compression session or context, returning a *binary_integer* as the handle.

ARGUMENT	TYPE	IN / OUT	DEFAULT VALUE
DST	BLOB	IN | OUT	
QUALITY	BINARY_INTEGER	IN	6 (values 1-9 for zip level)

Table 6.42: *Lz_compress_open Parameters*

lz_compress_close is a procedure that completes and otherwise finishes an existing compression session or context.

ARGUMENT	TYPE	IN / OUT	DEFAULT VALUE
HANDLE	BINARY_INTEGER	IN	
DST	BLOB	IN | OUT	

Table 6.43: *Lz_compress_close Parameters*

lz_uncompress_open is a function that initializes a decompression session or context, returning a *binary_integer* as the handle.

ARGUMENT	TYPE	IN / OUT	DEFAULT VALUE
SRC	BLOB	IN	

Table 6.44: *Lz_uncompress_open Parameters*

lz_uncompress_close is a procedure that completes and otherwise finishes an existing decompression session or context.

ARGUMENT	TYPE	IN / OUT	DEFAULT VALUE
HANDLE	BINARY_INTEGER	IN	

Table 6.45: *Lz_uncompress_close Parameters*

isopen is a function that merely lets one check the status of the compression or decompression session or context, i.e. verify the handle status. It returns a simple Boolean like True or False based upon the handle's current status.

ARGUMENT	TYPE	IN / OUT	DEFAULT VALUE
HANDLE	BINARY_INTEGER	IN	

Table 6.46: *Isopen Parameters*

Once there is an open compression or decompression session or context, then merely add or subtract items from that archive using the remaining two procedures.

lz_compress_add is a procedure that adds an item to the compression archive set. This is very much like adding a Windows file to a WinZip archive file.

File Security **283**

ARGUMENT	TYPE	IN / OUT	DEFAULT VALUE
HANDLE	BINARY_INTEGER	IN	
DST	BLOB	IN | OUT	
SRC	RAW	IN	

Table 6.47: *Lz_compress_add Parameters*

lz_uncompress_extract is a procedure that extracts a single item from the compression archive set. This is very much like extracting a Windows file from a WinZip archive file.

ARGUMENT	TYPE	IN / OUT	DEFAULT VALUE
HANDLE	BINARY_INTEGER	IN	
DST	BLOB	IN | OUT	

Table 6.48: *Lz_uncompress_extract Parameters*

UTL_ENCODE

The UTL_ENCODE package provides a collection of functions for interfacing with the UUCP (Unix to Unix CoPy) email system standards for UUENCODE (Unix-to-Unix encoding) and UUDECODE (Unix-to-Unix encoding) capabilities. Note, however, that this method of email transmission has been largely replaced by an Internet standard format known as MIME (Multipurpose Internet Mail Extensions), which is part of the SMTP (Simple Mail Transfer Protocol) de-facto standard for transmitting email. All the functions are very simple, having just one or a few inputs and returning either a RAW or VARCHAR2.

base64_decode is a function that accepts a base-64 encoded input and decodes it to its original binary value. It returns the result via a RAW value.

ARGUMENT	TYPE	IN / OUT	DEFAULT VALUE
R	RAW	IN	

Table 6.49: *Base64_decode Parameters*

base64_encode is a function that accepts a binary input and encodes it to its base-64 encoded form. It returns the result via a RAW value.

ARGUMENT	TYPE	IN / OUT	DEFAULT VALUE
R	RAW	IN	

Table 6.50: *Base64_encode Parameters*

mimeheader_decode accepts a MIME header, i.e. the internet media type whose value consists of tags and a two-part identifier for file formats on the Internet, and input for conversion and decoding and then returned as a VARCHAR2 string in the same character set as the input buffer.

ARGUMENT	TYPE	IN / OUT	DEFAULT VALUE
BUF	VARCHAR2	IN	

Table 6.51: *Mimeheader_decode Parameters*

mimeheader_encode accepts an input string for conversion and encoding to a MIME header, i.e. the internet media type whose value consists of a two-part identifier for file formats on the Internet and then returned as a VARCHAR2 string in the same character set as the input buffer.

ARGUMENT	TYPE	IN / OUT	DEFAULT VALUE
BUF	VARCHAR2	IN	
ENCODE_CHARSET	VARCHAR2	IN	NULL
ENCODING	PLS_INTEGER	IN	NULL

Table 6.52: *Mimeheader_encode Parameters*

The encoding parameter must be one of two values: UTL_ENCODE.BASE64 or UTL_ENCODE.QUOTED_PRINTAB;E.

quoted_printable_decode is a function that accepts a quoted printable format input and decodes it to its original binary value. It returns the result via a RAW value.

ARGUMENT	TYPE	IN / OUT	DEFAULT VALUE
R	RAW	IN	

Table 6.53: *Quoted_printable_decode Parameters*

---

quoted_printable_encode is a function that accepts a binary input and encodes it to its quoted printable format. It returns the result via a RAW value.

ARGUMENT	TYPE	IN / OUT	DEFAULT VALUE
R	RAW	IN	

Table 6.54: *Quoted_printable_encode Parameters*

text_decode accepts either a quoted-printable or base-64 format input for conversion and decoding and then returned as a VARCHAR2 string in the same character set as the input buffer.

ARGUMENT	TYPE	IN / OUT	DEFAULT VALUE
BUF	VARCHAR2	IN	

Table 6.55: *Text_decode Parameters*

text_encode accepts either a string input for conversion and encoding to either a quoted-printable or base-64 format and then returned as a VARCHAR2 string in the same character set as the input buffer.

ARGUMENT	TYPE	IN / OUT	DEFAULT VALUE
BUF	VARCHAR2	IN	
ENCODE_CHARSET	VARCHAR2	IN	NULL
ENCODING	PLS_INTEGER	IN	NULL

Table 6.56: *Text_encode Parameters*

UUDECODE is a function that accepts a UUENCODE format input string and decodes it to its original string value. It returns the result via a RAW value.

ARGUMENT	TYPE	IN / OUT	DEFAULT VALUE
R	RAW	IN	

Table 6.57: *UUDECODE Parameters*

UUENCODE is a function that accepts a basic data or content input string and encodes it to a UUENCODE format. It returns the result via a RAW value.

ARGUMENT	TYPE	IN / OUT	DEFAULT VALUE
R	RAW	IN	
TYPE	PLS_INTEGER	IN	
FILENAME	VARCHAR2	IN	NULL
PERMISSION	VARCHAR2	IN	NULL

Table 6.58: *UUENCODE Parameters*

Where the type must be one the following:

```
complete        CONSTANT PLS_INTEGER := 1; -- includes header and footer
header_piece    CONSTANT PLS_INTEGER := 2; -- includes header text
middle_piece    CONSTANT PLS_INTEGER := 3; -- body text only
end_piece       CONSTANT PLS_INTEGER := 4; -- includes footer text
```

Replication

DBMS_AQADM

The *dbms_aqadm* package supports configuring and managing Oracle Stream Advanced Queuing such as Queue Tables, commonly referred to as AQ. This package and some OEM screens/utilities built on top of it are the only interfaces for these types of objects. There are no native DDL commands for them, so there is no such thing as CREATE TABLE for queue tables. One must use this package. *dbms_aqadm* is a rather large and complex PL/SQL package. Thus many DBAs may simply prefer to use the OEM screens for managing queues.

There are a few enumerated constants that one must know to use this package:

```
-- retention
INFINITE                CONSTANT BINARY_INTEGER := -1;

-- message grouping
TRANSACTIONAL           CONSTANT BINARY_INTEGER := 1;
NONE                    CONSTANT BINARY_INTEGER := 0;

-- queue type
NORMAL_QUEUE            CONSTANT BINARY_INTEGER := 0;
EXCEPTION_QUEUE         CONSTANT BINARY_INTEGER := 1;
NON_PERSISTENT_QUEUE    CONSTANT BINARY_INTEGER := 2;

-- non-repudiation properties
NON_REPUDIATE_SENDER    CONSTANT BINARY_INTEGER := 1;
```

```
NON_REPUDIATE_SNDRCV         CONSTANT BINARY_INTEGER := 2;

-- protocols (note that FTP is not supported yet so it is not part of anyp).
TTC                          CONSTANT BINARY_INTEGER := 0;
HTTP                         CONSTANT BINARY_INTEGER := 1;
SMTP                         CONSTANT BINARY_INTEGER := 2;
FTP                          CONSTANT BINARY_INTEGER := 4;
ANYP                         CONSTANT BINARY_INTEGER := HTTP + SMTP;


LOGMINER_PROTOCOL            CONSTANT BINARY_INTEGER := 1;
LOGAPPLY_PROTOCOL            CONSTANT BINARY_INTEGER := 2;
TEST_PROTOCOL                CONSTANT BINARY_INTEGER := 3;

-- Constants for LDAP connection factory type
AQ_QUEUE_CONNECTION          CONSTANT BINARY_INTEGER := 1;
AQ_TOPIC_CONNECTION          CONSTANT BINARY_INTEGER := 2;

-- Constants for delivery mode
PERSISTENT                   CONSTANT BINARY_INTEGER := 1 ;
BUFFERED                     CONSTANT BINARY_INTEGER := 2 ;
PERSISTENT_OR_BUFFERED       CONSTANT BINARY_INTEGER := 3 ;

-- subscriber properties.
QUEUE_TO_QUEUE_SUBSCRIBER  CONSTANT BINARY_INTEGER := 8;

-- Constants for get/set_replay_info
LAST_ENQUEUED                CONSTANT BINARY_INTEGER := 0;
LAST_ACKNOWLEDGED            CONSTANT BINARY_INTEGER := 1;
```

add_alias_to_ldap is a procedure that creates an alias to an object like queue, agent or connection factory which is placed under the database in the LDAP hierarchy. Of course, the object must exist prior to creating an alias for it.

ARGUMENT	TYPE	IN / OUT	DEFAULT VALUE
ALIAS	VARCHAR2	IN	
OBJ_LOCATION	VARCHAR2	IN	

Table 6.59: *Add_alias_to_ldap Parameters*

add_subscriber is a procedure that adds a subscriber to queue. The rule parameter is a conditional expression string much like a WHERE clause and must be properly (double) quoted.

ARGUMENT	TYPE	IN / OUT	DEFAULT VALUE
QUEUE_NAME	VARCHAR2	IN	
SUBSCRIBER	SYS.AQ$_AGENT	IN	
RULE	VARCHAR2	IN	NULL
TRANSFORMATION	VARCHAR2	IN	NULL

ARGUMENT	TYPE	IN / OUT	DEFAULT VALUE
QUEUE_TO_QUEUE	BOOELAN	IN	FALSE
DELIVERY_MODE	PLS_INTEGER	IN	DBMS_AQADM.PERSISTENT

Table 6.60: *Add_subscriber Parameters*

alter_aq_agent is a procedure that modifies an AQ agent's registration for internet access; however, for access through HTTP, the certificate location is not required.

ARGUMENT	TYPE	IN / OUT	DEFAULT VALUE
AGENT_NAME	VARCHAR2	IN	
CERTIFICATE_LOCATION	VARCHAR2	IN	NULL
ENABLE_HTTP	BOOLEAN	IN	FALSE
ENABLE_SMTP	BOOLEAN	IN	FALSE
ENABLE_ANYP	BOOELAN	IN	FALSE

Table 6.61: *Alter_aq_agent Parameters*

alter_propagation_schedule is a procedure used to alter the parameters of a propagation schedule. If the destination parameter for the destination database link is NULL, then the destination is the local database and all messages are propagated to other local database queues.

ARGUMENT	TYPE	IN / OUT	DEFAULT VALUE
QUEUE_NAME	VARCHAR2	IN	
DESTINATION	VARCHAR2	IN	NULL
DURATION	NUMBER	IN	NULL
NEXT_TIME	VARCHAR2	IN	NULL
LATENCY	NUMBER	IN	60
DESTINATION_QUEUE	VARCHAR2	IN	NULL

Table 6:62: *Alter_propagation_schedule*

alter_queue is a procedure that modifies a queue's properties. Note that a message is automatically transferred to an exception queue if *retry_count* > *Max_retries*. Also note that the *auto_commit* parameter has been deprecated.

ARGUMENT	TYPE	IN / OUT	DEFAULT VALUE
QUEUE_NAME	VARCHAR2	IN	
MAX_RETRIES	NUMBER	IN	NULL
RETRY_DELAY	NUMBER	IN	NULL
RETENTION_TIME	NUMBER	IN	NULL
AUTO_COMMIT	BOOLEAN	IN	TRUE
COMMENT	VARCHAR2	IN	NULL

Table 6.63: *Alter_queue Parameters*

alter_queue_table is a procedure that modifies a queue table's properties. The primary instance performs the monitor scheduling and propagation for the queues in the queue table. The secondary instance is strictly for failover, i.e. when the primary instance is unavailable.

ARGUMENT	TYPE	IN / OUT	DEFAULT VALUE
QUEUE_TABLE	VARCHAR2	IN	
COMMENT	VARCHAR2	IN	NULL
PRIMARY_INSTACNE	BINARY_INTEGER	IN	NULL
SECONDARY_INSTANCE	BINARY_INTEGER	IN	NULL

Table 6.64: *Alter_queue_table Parameters*

alter_subscriber is a procedure that modifies a queue subscriber's properties. The rule parameter is a conditional expression string much like a WHERE clause, and must be properly (double) quoted. Note that this procedure permits altering both the rule and the transformation. If one wants to retain the existing value for either of them, specify the old value.

ARGUMENT	TYPE	IN / OUT	DEFAULT VALUE
QUEUE_TABLE	VARCHAR2	IN	
SUBSCRIBER	SYS.AQ$_AGENT	IN	
RULE	VARCHAR2	IN	
TRANSFORMATION	VARCHAR2	IN	

Table 6.65: *Alter_subscriber Parameters*

create_aq_agent is a procedure that creates an AQ agent's registration for internet access. However, for access through HTTP, the certificate location is not required.

ARGUMENT	TYPE	IN / OUT	DEFAULT VALUE
AGENT_NAME	VARCHAR2	IN	
CERTIFICATE_LOCATION	VARCHAR2	IN	NULL
ENABLE_HTTP	BOOLEAN	IN	FALSE
ENABLE_SMTP	BOOLEAN	IN	FALSE
ENABLE_ANYP	BOOELAN	IN	FALSE

Table 6.66: *Create_aq_agent Parameters*

create_np_queue is a procedure that creates a non-persistent RAW queue which has been deprecated as of Oracle 10gR2, so use buffered messaging instead.

ARGUMENT	TYPE	IN / OUT	DEFAULT VALUE
QUEUE	VARCHAR2	IN	
MULTIPLE_CONSUMERS	BOOLEAN	IN	FALSE
COMMENT	VARCHAR2	IN	NULL

Table 6.67: *Create_np_queue Parameters*

create_queue is a procedure that creates a message queue within the specified queue table. Note that a message is automatically transferred to an exception queue if *retry_count* >*max_retries*. Also note that the *auto_commit* parameter has been deprecated.

ARGUMENT	TYPE	IN / OUT	DEFAULT VALUE
QUEUE_NAME	VARCHAR2	IN	
QUEUE_TABLE	VARCHAR2	IN	
QUEUE_TYPE	BINARY_INTEGER	IN	NORMAL_QUEUE
MAX_RETRIES	NUMBER	IN	NULL
RETRY_DELAY	NUMBER	IN	0
RETENTION_TIME	NUMBER	IN	0
DEPENDENCY_TRACKING	BOOLEAN	IN	FALSE
COMMENT	VARCHAR2	IN	NULL
AUTO_COMMIT	BOOLEAN	IN	TRUE

Table 6.68: *Create_queue Parameters*

create_queue_table is a procedure that creates a queue table of a predefined message type. The *storage_clause* parameter takes the same text as in a standard CREATE TABLE storage clause. The primary instance performs the monitor scheduling and propagation for the queues in the queue table. The secondary instance is strictly for failover, as when the primary instance is unavailable. Also note that the *auto_commit* parameter has been deprecated.

ARGUMENT	TYPE	IN / OUT	DEFAULT VALUE
QUEUE_TABLE	VARCHAR2	IN	
QUEUE_PAYLOAD_TYPE	VARCHAR2	IN	
STORAGE_CLAUSE	VARCHAR2	IN	NULL
SORT_LIST	VARCHAR2	IN	NULL
MULTIPLE_CONSUMERS	BOOLEAN	IN	FALSE
MESSAGE_LOGGING	BINARY_INTEGER	IN	NONE
COMMENT	VARCHAR2	IN	NULL
AUTO_COMMIT	BOOLEAN	IN	TRUE
PRIMARY_INSTANCE	BINARY_INTEGER	IN	0
SECONDARY_INSTANCE	BINARY_INTEGER	IN	0
COMPATTIBLE	VARCHAR2	IN	NULL
SECURE	BOOLEAN	IN	FALSE

Table 6.69: *Create_queue_table Parameters*

del_alias_from_ldap is a procedure that drops an alias for an object, i.e. queue, agent or connection factory.

ARGUMENT	TYPE	IN / OUT	DEFAULT VALUE
ALIAS	VARCHAR2	IN	

Table 6.70: *Del_alias_from_ldap Parameters*

disable_db_access is a procedure that revokes AQ Internet agent privileges from a specified database user.

ARGUMENT	TYPE	IN / OUT	DEFAULT VALUE
AGENT_NAME	VARCHAR2	IN	
DB_USERNAME	VARCHAR2	IN	

Table 6.71: *Disable_db_access Parameters*

disable_propagation_schedule is a procedure that disables a propagation schedule. If the destination parameter for the destination database link is NULL, then the destination is the local database and all messages are propagated to other local database queues.

ARGUMENT	TYPE	IN / OUT	DEFAULT VALUE
QUEUE_NAME	VARCHAR2	IN	
DESTINATION	VARCHAR2	IN	NULL
DESTINATION_QUEUE	VARCHAR2	IN	NULL

Table 6.72: *Disable_propagation_schedule Parameters*

drop_aq_agent is a procedure that drops an AQ agent's registration for internet access.

ARGUMENT	TYPE	IN / OUT	DEFAULT VALUE
AGENT_NAME	VARCHAR2	IN	

Table 6.73: *Drop_aq_agent Parameter*

drop_queue is a procedure that drops a message queue. Note that the *auto_commit* parameter has been deprecated. Also remember to first call *stop_queue*.

ARGUMENT	TYPE	IN / OUT	DEFAULT VALUE
QUEUE_NAME	VARCHAR2	IN	
AUTO_COMMIT	BOOLEAN	IN	TRUE

Table 6.74: *Drop_queue Parameters*

drop_queue_table is a procedure that drops a queue table. The force parameter controls whether a queue table containing queues can be dropped. Note that the *auto_commit* parameter has been deprecated.

ARGUMENT	TYPE	IN / OUT	DEFAULT VALUE
QUEUE_TABLE	VARCHAR2	IN	
FORCE	BOOLEAN	IN	FALSE
AUTO_COMMIT	BOOLEAN	IN	TRUE

Table 6.75: *Drop_queue_table Parameters*

enable_db_access is a procedure that grants AQ Internet agent privileges to a specified database user.

ARGUMENT	TYPE	IN / OUT	DEFAULT VALUE
AGENT_NAME	VARCHAR2	IN	
DB_USERNAME	VARCHAR2	IN	

Table 6.76: *Enable_db_access Parameters*

enable_jms_types is a procedure that when called after *set_up_queue*, permits SYS.ANYDATA streams work for JMS types and XML types.

ARGUMENT	TYPE	IN / OUT	DEFAULT VALUE
QUEUE_TABLE	VARCHAR2	IN	

Table 6.77: *Enable_jms_types Parameter*

enable_propagation_schedule is a procedure that enables a propagation schedule. If the destination parameter for the destination database link is NULL, then the destination is the local database and all messages are propagated to other local database queues.

ARGUMENT	TYPE	IN / OUT	DEFAULT VALUE
QUEUE_NAME	VARCHAR2	IN	
DESTINATION	VARCHAR2	IN	NULL
DESTINATION_QUEUE	VARCHAR2	IN	NULL

Table 6.78: *Enable_propagation_schedule Parameters*

get_watermark is a procedure that returns the watermark value in megabytes set by *set_watermark*.

ARGUMENT	TYPE	IN / OUT	DEFAULT VALUE
WMVALUE	NUMBER	OUT	

Table 6.79: *Get_watermark Parameter*

grant_queue_privilege is a procedure for granting regular queue privileges to database users and roles. The privilege parameter access the following: ALL, ENQUEUE, and DEQUEUE.

ARGUMENT	TYPE	IN / OUT	DEFAULT VALUE
PRIVILEGE	VARCHAR2	IN	
QUEUE_NAME	VARCHAR2	IN	
GRANTEE	VARCHAR2	IN	
GRANT_OPTION	BOOLEAN	IN	FALSE

Table 6.80: *Grant_queue_privilege Parameters*

grant_system_privilege is a procedure for granting special queue privileges to database users and roles. The privilege parameter accesses the following: MANAGE_ANY, ENQUEUE_ANY, and DEQUEUE_ANY.

ARGUMENT	TYPE	IN / OUT	DEFAULT VALUE
PRIVILEGE	VARCHAR2	IN	
GRANTEE	VARCHAR2	IN	
GRANT_OPTION	BOOLEAN	IN	FALSE

Table 6.81: *Grant_system_privilege Parameters*

migrate_queue_table is a procedure for upgrading and downgrading queue tables between Oracle 8.0 and 8.1 compatible formats. Note that these are the two permissible values for the compatible parameter.

ARGUMENT	TYPE	IN / OUT	DEFAULT VALUE
QUEUE_TABLE	VARCHAR2	IN	
COMPATIBLE	VARCHAR2	IN	

Table 6.82: *Migrate_queue_table Parameters*

purge_queue_table is a procedure that purges queue table messages, plus it generates a trace file in *user_dump_dest* that details what the procedure did. The *purge_options* parameter requires using the special purge record type shown just below. When BLOCK=TRUE, then an exclusive lock is held on all queues within that queue table during the purge.

ARGUMENT	TYPE	IN / OUT	DEFAULT VALUE
QUEUE_TABLE	VARCHAR2	IN	
PURGE_CONDITION	VARCHAR2	IN	
PURGE_OPTIONS	AQ$_PURGE_OPTION_T	IN	

Table 6.83: *Purge_queue_table Parameters*

```
TYPE aq$_purge_options_t IS RECORD(
  block          boolean     DEFAULT FALSE,
  delivery_mode  PLS_INTEGER  DEFAULT dbms_aqadm.PERSISTENT
);
```

remove_subscriber is a procedure that simply drops a subscriber from a queue. It takes immediate effect, i.e. is committed.

ARGUMENT	TYPE	IN / OUT	DEFAULT VALUE
QUEUE_NAME	VARCHAR2	IN	
SUBSCRIBER	SYS.AQ$_AGENT	IN	

Table 6.84: *Remove_subscriber Parameters*

revoke_queue_privilege is a procedure for revoking regular queue privileges from database users and roles. The privilege parameter accesses the following: ALL, ENQUEUE, and DEQUEUE.

ARGUMENT	TYPE	IN / OUT	DEFAULT VALUE
PRIVILEGE	VARCHAR2	IN	
QUEUE_NAME	VARCHAR2	IN	
GRANTEE	VARCHAR2	IN	

Table 6.85: *Revoke_queue_privilege Parameters*

revoke_system_privilege is a procedure for revoking special queue privileges from database users and roles. The *privilege* parameter accesses the following: MANAGE_ANY, ENQUEUE_ANY, and DEQUEUE_ANY.

ARGUMENT	TYPE	IN / OUT	DEFAULT VALUE
PRIVILEGE	VARCHAR2	IN	
GRANTEE	VARCHAR2	IN	

Table 6.86: *Revoke_system_privilege Parameters*

schedule_propagation is a procedure that defines a propagation schedule. If the destination parameter for the destination database link is NULL, then the destination is the local database and all messages are propagated to other local database queues.

ARGUMENT	TYPE	IN / OUT	DEFAULT VALUE
QUEUE_NAME	VARCHAR2	IN	
DESTINATION	VARCHAR2	IN	NULL
START_TIME	DATE	IN	SYSDATE
DURATION	NUMBER	IN	NULL
NEXT_TIME	VARCHAR2	IN	NULL
LATENCY	NUMBER	IN	60
DESTINATION_QUEUE	VARCHAR2	IN	NULL

Table 6.87: *Schedule_propagation Parameters*

set_watermark is a procedure that defines the watermark value in megabytes, which is used to control and/or limit memory use.

ARGUMENT	TYPE	IN / OUT	DEFAULT VALUE
WMVALUE	NUMBER	OUT	

Table 6.88: *Set_watermark Parameter*

start_queue is a procedure that enables enqueuing and dequeuing for the specified queue.

ARGUMENT	TYPE	IN / OUT	DEFAULT VALUE
QUEUE_NAME	VARCHAR2	IN	
ENQUEUE	BOLLEAN	IN	TRUE
DEQUEUE	BOOLEAN	IN	TRUE

Table 6.89: *Start_queue Parameters*

stop_queue is a procedure that disables enqueuing and dequeuing for the specified queue.

ARGUMENT	TYPE	IN / OUT	DEFAULT VALUE
QUEUE_NAME	VARCHAR2	IN	
ENQUEUE	BOLLEAN	IN	TRUE
DEQUEUE	BOOLEAN	IN	TRUE

Table 6.90: *Stop_queue Parameters*

unschedule_propagation is a procedure that undefines a propagation schedule. If the destination parameter for the destination database link is NULL, then the destination is the local database and all messages are propagated to other local database queues.

ARGUMENT	TYPE	IN / OUT	DEFAULT VALUE
QUEUE_NAME	VARCHAR2	IN	
DESTINATION	VARCHAR2	IN	NULL
DESTINATION_QUEUE	VARCHAR2	IN	NULL

Table 6.91: *Unschedule_propagation Parameters*

DBMS_AQ

The *dbms_aq* package supports programmatically interfacing with Oracle Stream Advanced Queuing, such as Queue Tables, commonly referred to as AQ. Once the AQ environment has been properly configured via *dbms_sqadm*, use this package to work with the actual messages held in those queues and queue tables. So the actual work is performed via this package.

There are a few enumerated constants that one must know to use this package. Also, since this package is wrapped, one cannot see the actual constant values:

```
VISIBILITY:                  IMMEDIATE | ON_COMMIT

DEQUEUE_MODE                 BROWSE | LOCKED | REMOVE | REMOVE_NODATA

NAVIGATION:                  FIRST_MESSAGE | NEXT_MESSAGE

STATE:                       WAITING | READY | PROCESSED | EXPIRED

SEQUENCE_DEVIATION:          BEFORE | TOP

WAIT:                        FOREVER | NO_WAIT

DELAY:                       NO_DELAY

EXPIRATION:                  NONE

NAMESPACE:                   NAMESPACE_AQ | NAMESPACE_ANONYMOUS

NTFN_GROUPING_CLASS:         NTFN_GROUP_TYPE_SUMMARY | NTFN_GROUPING_TYPE_LAST

NTFN_GROUPING_REPEAT_COUNT:      NTFN_GROUPING_FOREVER
```

Bind_agent is a procedure that creates an LDAP server entry for the Oracle AQ agent. The certificate parameter is stored on the LDAP server as an attribute (usercertificate) of the Organizational Person entity. The *aq$_agent* type is shown just below.

ARGUMENT	TYPE	IN / OUT	DEFAULT VALUE
AGENT	SYS.AQ$_AGENT	IN	
CERTIFICATE	VARCHAR2	IN	NULL

Table 6.92: *Bind_agent Parameters*

```
TYPE SYS.AQ$_AGENT IS OBJECT (
  name        VARCHAR2(30),
  address     VARCHAR2(1024),
  protocol    NUMBER  DEFAULT 0
);
```

dequeue is a procedure that simply dequeues, i.e subtracts, a message from the specified queue. The *dequeue* option and message property types are shown just below.

ARGUMENT	TYPE	IN / OUT	DEFAULT VALUE
QUEUE_NAME	VARCHAR2	IN	
DEQUEUE_OPTIONS	DEQUEUE_OPTIONS_T	IN	
MESSAGE_PROPERTIES	MESSAGE_PROPERTIES_T	OUT	
PAYLOAD	STANDARD.<ADT_1>	OUT	
MSGID	RAW	OUT	

Table 6.93: *Dequeue Parameters*

```
TYPE DEQUEUE_OPTIONS_T IS RECORD (
  consumer_name    VARCHAR2(30)     DEFAULT NULL,
  dequeue_mode     BINARY_INTEGER   DEFAULT REMOVE,
  navigation       BINARY_INTEGER   DEFAULT NEXT_MESSAGE,
  visibility       BINARY_INTEGER   DEFAULT ON_COMMIT,
  wait             BINARY_INTEGER   DEFAULT FOREVER,
  msgid            RAW(16)          DEFAULT NULL,
  correlation      VARCHAR2(128)    DEFAULT NULL,
  deq_condition    VARCHAR2(4000)   DEFAULT NULL,
  signature        aq$_sig_prop     DEFAULT NULL,
  transformation   VARCHAR2(61)     DEFAULT NULL,
  delivery_mode    PLS_INTEGER      DEFAULT PERSISTENT
);

TYPE message_properties_t IS RECORD (
  priority            BINARY_INTEGER   NOT NULL DEFAULT 1,
  delay               BINARY_INTEGER   NOT NULL DEFAULT NO_DELAY,
  expiration          BINARY_INTEGER   NOT NULL DEFAULT NEVER,
  correlation         VARCHAR2(128)    DEFAULT NULL,
  attempts            BINARY_INTEGER,
  recipient_list      AQ$_RECIPIENT_LIST_T,
  exception_queue     VARCHAR2(61)     DEFAULT NULL,
  enqueue_time        DATE,
  state               BINARY_INTEGER,
  sender_id           SYS.AQ$_AGENT    DEFAULT NULL,
  original_msgid      RAW(16)          DEFAULT NULL,
  signature           aq$_sig_prop     DEFAULT NULL,
  transaction_group   VARCHAR2(30)     DEFAULT NULL,
  user_property       SYS.ANYDATA      DEFAULT NULL
  delivery_mode       PLS_INTEGER      NOT NULL DEFAULT DBMS_AQ.PERSISTENT
);
```

dequeue_array is a function that performs a bulk dequeue operation, fetching arrays of payloads, message properties and message IDs. It returns a *pls_integer* with the number of messages successfully dequeued. The *message_properties_array_t* and *msgid_array_t* types are shown below.

ARGUMENT	TYPE	IN / OUT	DEFAULT VALUE
QUEUE_NAME	VARCHAR2	IN	
DEQUEUE_OPTIONS ARRAY_SIZE	DEQUEUE_OPTIONS_T	IN	
MESSAGE_PROPERTIES_ ARRAY	MESSAGE_PROPERTIES_ T	OUT	
PAYLOAD_ARRAY	STANDARD. <COLLECTION_1>	OUT	
MSGID_ARRAY	MSGID_ARRAY_T	OUT	
ERROR_ARRAY	ERROR_ARRAY_T	OUT	

Table 6.94: *Dequeue_array Parameters*

```
TYPE MESSAGE_PROPERTIES_ARRAY_T IS VARRAY (2147483647)
  OF MESSAGE_PROPERTIES_T;

TYPE MSGID_ARRAY_T IS TABLE OF RAW(16) INDEX BY BINARY_INTEGER
```

enqueue is a procedure that simply enqueues, i.e adds, a message to the specified queue. The enqueue option and message property types are shown just below.

ARGUMENT	TYPE	IN / OUT	DEFAULT VALUE
QUEUE_NAME	VARCHAR2	IN	
ENQUEUE_OPTIONS	DEQUEUE_OPTIONS_T	IN	
MESSAGE_PROPERTIES	MESSAGE_PROPERTIES_T	OUT	
PAYLOAD	STANDARD.<ADT_1>	OUT	
MSGID	RAW	OUT	

Table 6.95: *Enqueue Parameters*

```
TYPE SYS.ENQUEUE_OPTIONS_T IS RECORD (
  visibility              BINARY_INTEGER   DEFAULT ON_COMMIT,
  relative_msgid          RAW(16)          DEFAULT NULL,
  sequence_deviation      BINARY_INTEGER   DEFAULT NULL,
  transformation          VARCHAR2(61)     DEFAULT NULL,
  delivery_mode           PLS_INTEGER      NOT NULL DEFAULT PERSISTENT
);

TYPE message_properties_t IS RECORD (
  priority                BINARY_INTEGER   NOT NULL DEFAULT 1,
  delay                   BINARY_INTEGER   NOT NULL DEFAULT NO_DELAY,
  expiration              BINARY_INTEGER   NOT NULL DEFAULT NEVER,
  correlation             VARCHAR2(128)    DEFAULT NULL,
  attempts                BINARY_INTEGER,
  recipient_list          AQ$_RECIPIENT_LIST_T,
  exception_queue         VARCHAR2(61)     DEFAULT NULL,
  enqueue_time            DATE,
  state                   BINARY_INTEGER,
  sender_id               SYS.AQ$_AGENT    DEFAULT NULL,
  original_msgid          RAW(16)          DEFAULT NULL,
  signature               aq$_sig_prop     DEFAULT NULL,
  transaction_group       VARCHAR2(30)     DEFAULT NULL,
  user_property           SYS.ANYDATA      DEFAULT NULL
  delivery_mode           PLS_INTEGER      NOT NULL DEFAULT DBMS_AQ.PERSISTENT
);
```

enqueue_array is a function that performs a bulk enqueue operation, posting arrays of payloads, message properties and message IDs. It returns a *pls_integer* with the number of messages successfully dequeued. The *message_properties_array_t* and *msgid_array_t* types are shown below.

ARGUMENT	TYPE	IN / OUT	DEFAULT VALUE
QUEUE_NAME	VARCHAR2	IN	
ENQUEUE_OPTIONS	DEQUEUE_OPTIONS_T	IN	
ARRAY_SIZE			
MESSAGE_PROPERTIES_ ARRAY	MESSAGE_PROPERTIES_ T	OUT	
PAYLOAD_ARRAY	STANDARD. <COLLECTION_1>	OUT	
MSGID_ARRAY	MSGID_ARRAY_T	OUT	
ERROR_ARRAY	ERROR_ARRAY_T		

Table 6.96: *Enqueue_array Parameters*

```
TYPE MESSAGE_PROPERTIES_ARRAY_T IS VARRAY (2147483647)
  OF MESSAGE_PROPERTIES_T;

TYPE MSGID_ARRAY_T IS TABLE OF RAW(16) INDEX BY BINARY_INTEGER
```

listen is an overloaded procedure that listens for agents on one or more queues where the address field of the agent indicates the queue to monitor. It has the two forms and uses the data types shown below. The listen delivery mode can be either persistent, buffered, or resistent_buffered.

ARGUMENT	TYPE	IN / OUT	DEFAULT VALUE
AGENT_LIST	AQ$_AGENT_LIST_T	IN	
WAIT	BINARY_INTEGER	IN	FOREVER
AGENT	SYS.AQ$_AGENT	OUT	
AGENT_LIST	AQ$_AGENT_LIST_T	IN	
WAIT	BINARY_INTEGER	IN	FOREVER
LISTEN_DELIVERY_MODE	PLS_INTEGER	IN	PERSISTENT
AGENT	SYS.AQ$_AGENT	OUT	
MESSAGE_DELIEVRY_MODE	PLS_INTEGER	OUT	

Table 6.97: *Listen Parameters*

```
TYPE SYS.AQ$_AGENT IS OBJECT (
  name       VARCHAR2(30),
  address    VARCHAR2(1024),
  protocol   NUMBER  DEFAULT 0
);

TYPE aq$_agent_list_t IS TABLE of aq$_agent INDEXED BY BINARY_INTEGER;
TYPE aq$_agent_list_t IS TABLE of aq$_agent INDEXED BY BINARY_INTEGER;
```

post is a procedure that posts anonymous subscriptions to notify any and all clients registered for notification. The *aq$_post_info* and *aq_post_infolist* types are shown next.

ARGUMENT	TYPE	IN / OUT	DEFAULT VALUE
POST_LIST	SYS.AQ$_POST_INFO_LIST	IN	
POST_COUNT	NUMBER	IN	

Table 6.98: *Post Parameters*

```
TYPE SYS.AQ$_POST_INFO IS OBJECT (
  name        VARCHAR2(128),
  namespace   NUMBER,
  payload     RAW(2000)  DEFAULT NULL
);

TYPE SYS.AQ$_POST_INFO_LIST AS VARRAY(1024) OF SYS.AQ$_POST_INFO;
```

register is a procedure that registers for notification an email address, PL/SQL procedure or HTTP UTL. The *aq$_reg_info* and *aq$_reg_infolist* types are shown next.

ARGUMENT	TYPE	IN / OUT	DEFAULT VALUE
REG_LIST	SYS.AQ$_REG_INFO_LIST	IN	
COUNT	NUMBER	IN	

Table 6.99: *Register Parameters*

```
TYPE SYS.AQ$_REG_INFO IS OBJECT (
  name                           VARCHAR2(128),
  namespace                      NUMBER,
  callback                       VARCHAR2(4000),
  context                        RAW(2000)  DEFAULT NULL,
  qosflags                       NUMBER,
  timeout                        NUMBER
  ntfn_grouping_class            NUMBER,
  ntfn_grouping_value            NUMBER     DEFAULT 600,
  ntfn_grouping_type             NUMBER,
  ntfn_grouping_start_time       TIMESTAMP WITH TIME ZONE,
  ntfn_grouping_repeat_count     NUMBER
);

TYPE SYS.AQ$_REG_INFO_LIST AS VARRAY(1024) OF SYS.AQ$_REG_INFO;
```

unbind is a procedure that simply removes form the LDAP server an AQ agent. The *aq$_agent type* is shown just below.

ARGUMENT	TYPE	IN / OUT	DEFAULT VALUE
AGENT	SYS.AQ$_AGENT	IN	

Table 6.100: *Unbind Parameter*

```
TYPE SYS.AQ$_AGENT IS OBJECT (
  name      VARCHAR2(30),
  address   VARCHAR2(1024),
  protocol  NUMBER  DEFAULT 0
);
```

unregister is a procedure that unregisters for notification an email address, PL/SQL procedure or HTTP UTL.

ARGUMENT	TYPE	IN / OUT	DEFAULT VALUE
REG_LIST	SYS.AQ$_REG_INFO_LIST	IN	
COUNT	NUMBER	IN	

Table 6.101: *Unregister Parameters*

```
TYPE SYS.AQ$_REG_INFO IS OBJECT (
  name                        VARCHAR2(128),
  namespace                   NUMBER,
  callback                    VARCHAR2(4000),
  context                     RAW(2000)  DEFAULT NULL,
  qosflags                    NUMBER,
  timeout                     NUMBER
  ntfn_grouping_class         NUMBER,
  ntfn_grouping_value         NUMBER    DEFAULT 600,
  ntfn_grouping_type          NUMBER,
  ntfn_grouping_start_time    TIMESTAMP WITH TIME ZONE,
  ntfn_grouping_repeat_count  NUMBER
);

TYPE SYS.AQ$_REG_INFO_LIST AS VARRAY(1024) OF SYS.AQ$_REG_INFO;
```

DBMS_REPUTIL

The *dbms_reputil* package provides some very basic, yet key, functions and procedures for supporting replication. Replication has many behind the scenes or shadow tables, triggers and packages that are generated to coordinate and perform the actual replication work. This package contains support subprograms called by that generated code.

Even though *dbms_reputil* may look rather simple with just seven procedures and functions, the concept of replication and what can be done is much more complex than can be elaborated here. Thus, the following book is highly recommended where the authors do an excellent job of detailing every aspect of Oracle database replication. Oracle Replication: Snapshot, Multi-master & Materialized Views Scripts. Author: Donald K. Burleson, John Garmany, Steve Karam (Publisher: Rampant Tech Press)

replication_off is a procedure that disables or suspends replication of changes. It has no parameters.

replication_on is a procedure that enables or resumes replication of changes. It has no parameters.

replication_is_on is a function that simply determines whether replication is currently active or suspended. It has no parameters and returns a Boolean.

from_remote is a function that brackets the internal replication packages so that they return TRUE when initiated, and FALSE when they complete. Think of this as a replication semaphore of types. For example, the DBA may need to code her triggers to ignore, not fire, when the update is due to replication. It has no parameters and returns a Boolean.

global_name is a function that simply returns a character sting containing the global database name. It has no parameters and returns a VARCHAR2.

make_internal_package is a procedure that synchronizes internal replication packages against the replication catalog for that table or materialized view. Do not run this procedure unless directed to do so by Oracle Support.

ARGUMENT	TYPE	IN / OUT	DEFAULT VALUE
CANON_SNAME	VARCHAR2	IN	
CANON_ONAME	VARCHAR2	IN	

Table 6.102: *Make_internal_package Parameters*

sync_up_rep is a procedure that synchronizes internal replication triggers against the replication catalog for that table or materialized view. Do not run this procedure unless directed to do so by Oracle Support.

ARGUMENT	TYPE	IN / OUT	DEFAULT VALUE
CANON_SNAME	VARCHAR2	IN	
CANON_ONAME	VARCHAR2	IN	

Table 6.103: *Sync_up_rep Parameters*

Space Management

DBMS_SPACE_ADMIN

The *dbms_space_admin* package provides a collection of procedures and functions to assist with the administration and management of locally managed tablespaces. Since locally managed tablespaces have pretty much supplanted the older data dictionary managed approach, this package has increased in significance. And since this approach lacks the data dictionary tables to query as to status, a series of packages is necessary to provide both the query and corrective measures that a DNA might need. Therefore, this package provides some very powerful capabilities, and as such, requires some common sense in its usage:

- One should have a cold database backup in case of problems

- The database must be running in RESRTICTED SESSION mode

- Should be attempted by senior DBAs comfortable with "recovery"

There are a few enumerated constants that one must know to use this package:

```
SEGMENT_VERIFY_EXTENTS            constant positive := 1;
SEGMENT_VERIFY_EXTENTS_GLOBAL     constant positive := 2;
SEGMENT_MARK_CORRUPT              constant positive := 3;
SEGMENT_MARK_VALID                constant positive := 4;
SEGMENT_DUMP_EXTENT_MAP           constant positive := 5;
TABLESPACE_VERIFY_BITMAP          constant positive := 6;
TABLESPACE_EXTENT_MAKE_FREE       constant positive := 7;
TABLESPACE_EXTENT_MAKE_USED       constant positive := 8;
SEGMENT_VERIFY_BASIC              constant positive := 9;
SEGMENT_VERIFY_DEEP               constant positive := 10;
SEGMENT_VERIFY_SPECIFIC           constant positive := 11;
HWM_CHECK                         constant positive := 12;
BMB_CHECK                         constant positive := 13;
SEG_DICT_CHECK                    constant positive := 14;
EXTENT_TS_BITMAP_CHECK            constant positive := 15;
DB_BACKPOINTER_CHECK              constant positive := 16;
EXTENT_SEGMENT_BITMAP_CHECK       constant positive := 17;
BITMAPS_CHECK                     constant positive := 18;
TS_VERIFY_BITMAPS                 constant positive := 19;
TS_VERIFY_DEEP                    constant positive := 20;
TS_VERIFY_SEGMENTS                constant positive := 21;

SEGMENT_DUMP_BITMAP_SUMMARY       constant positive := 27;

NGLOB_HBB_CHECK                   constant positive := 12;
NGLOB_FSB_CHECK                   constant positive := 13;
NGLOB_PUA_CHECK                   constant positive := 14;
NGLOB_CFS_CHECK                   constant positive := 15;
```

assm_segment_verify is a procedure that checks the consistency of the space metadata blocks, i.e. *segment_verify_basic*, as well as checks the consistency between actual data blocks and space metadata blocks like *segment_verify_deep* for the specified segment created in ASSM (Automatic Segment Space Management) tablespaces. The output is placed in a dump file named *sid_ora_process_ID.trc*.

ARGUMENT	TYPE	IN / OUT	DEFAULT VALUE
SEGMENT_OWNER	VARCHAR2	IN	
SEGMENT_NAME	VARCHAR2	IN	
SEGMENT_TYPE	VARCHAR2	IN	
PARTITION_NAME	VARCHAR2	IN	
VERIFY_OPTION	POSITIVE	IN	SEGMENT_VERIFY_BASIC
ATTRIB	POSITIVE	IN	NULL

Table 6.104: *Assm_segment_verify Parameters*

When the *verify_option* parameter is *segment_verify_basic*, then the *attrib* parameter may be one of the following:

```
HWM_CHECK                       -- high water mark check
BMB_CHECK                       -- bitmap block back pointer check
SEG_DICT_CHECK                  -- dictionary segment check
EXTENT_TS_BITMAP_CHECK          -- extent maps consistent check
DB_BACKPOINTER_CHECK            -- data block back pointer check
EXTENT_SEGMENT_BITMAP_CHECK     -- extent map match bitmap check
BITMAPS_CHECK                   -- space bitmap blocks check
```

assm_tablespace_verify is a procedure that checks the consistency of all segments created in ASSM tablespaces. It provides tablespace verification options of basic (*ts_verify_bitmaps*), deep (*ts_verify_deep*), and verify by segment (*ts_segments*). The output dump file is named *sid_ora_process_ID.trc* and in *user_dump_dest*.

ARGUMENT	TYPE	IN / OUT	DEFAULT VALUE
TABLESPACE_NAME	VARCHAR2	IN	
TS_OPTION	POSITIVE	IN	
SEGMENT_OPTION	POSITIVE	IN	NULL

Table 6.105: *Assm_tablespace_verify Parameters*

When the *ts_option* parameter is *ts_segments*, then the *segment_option* parameter may be either *segment_verify_basic* or *segment_verify_deep*.

segment_corrupt is a procedure that marks the segment as corrupt or invalid so that the correct recovery can be done. The *corrupt_option* parameter may be set to either *segment_mark_corrupt* or *segment_mark_valid*.

ARGUMENT	TYPE	IN / OUT	DEFAULT VALUE
TABLESPACE_NAME	VARCHAR2	IN	
HEADER_RELATIVE_FILE	POSITIVE	IN	
HEADER_BLOCK	POSITIVE	IN	
CORRUPT_OPTION	POSITIVE	IN	SEGMENT_MARK_CORRUPT

Table 6.106: *Segment_corrupt Parameters*

segment_drop_corrupt is a procedure that simply drops a segment marked as corrupt without reclaiming the space. For this to work, the segment should have first been marked as temporary by issuing a DROP command on it.

ARGUMENT	TYPE	IN / OUT	DEFAULT VALUE
TABLESPACE_NAME	VARCHAR2	IN	
HEADER_RELATIVE_FILE	POSITIVE	IN	
HEADER_BLOCK	POSITIVE	IN	

Table 6.107: *Segment_drop_corrupt Parameters*

segment_dump is a procedure that dumps the segment heard and bitmap blocks to *user_dump_dest*. The *dump_option* parameter may be either *segment_dump_extent_map* or *segment_dump_bitmap_summary*.

ARGUMENT	TYPE	IN / OUT	DEFAULT VALUE
TABLESPACE_NAME	VARCHAR2	IN	
HEADER_RELATIVE_FILE	POSITIVE	IN	
HEADER_BLOCK	POSITIVE	IN	
DUMP_OPTION	POSITIVE	IN	SEGMENT_DUMP_ EXTENT_MAP

Table 6.108: *Segment_dump Parameters*

segment_verify verifies the consistency of the segment extent map against the tablespace bitmaps. The *verify_option* parameter may be either *segment_verify_extents* or *segment_verify_extents_global*. The output dump file is named *sid_ora_process_ID.trc* and in *user_dump_dest*.

ARGUMENT	TYPE	IN/OUT	DEFAULT VALUE
TABLESPACE_NAME	VARCHAR2	IN	
HEADER_RELATIVE_FILE	POSITIVE	IN	
HEADER_BLOCK	POSITIVE	IN	
VERIFY_OPTION	POSITIVE	IN	SEGMENT_VERIFY_ EXTENTS

Table 6.109: *Segment_verify Parameters*

tablespace_fix_bitmaps is a procedure that marks the extent as either free or used in the tablespace bitmap.

ARGUMENT	TYPE	IN / OUT	DEFAULT VALUE
TABLESPACE_NAME	VARCHAR2	IN	
DBARRANGE_RELATIVE_FILE	POSITIVE	IN	
DBARRANGE_BEGIN_BLOCK	POSITIVE	IN	
DBARRANGE_END_BLOCK	POSITIVE	IN	
FIX_OPTION	POSITIVE	IN	

Table 6.110: *Tablespace_fix_bitmaps Parameters*

tablespace_fix_segment_states is a procedure that remedies the transient state of the segments in a tablespace in which a migration was aborted.

ARGUMENT	TYPE	IN / OUT	DEFAULT VALUE
TABLESPACE_NAME	VARCHAR2	IN	

Table 6.111: *Tablespace_fix_segment_states Parameter*

tablespace_migrate_from_local is a procedure to migrate a tablespace from locally-managed to dictionary-managed.

ARGUMENT	TYPE	IN / OUT	DEFAULT VALUE
TABLESPACE_NAME	VARCHAR2	IN	

Table 6.112: *Tablespace_migrate_from_local Parameter*

tablespace_migrate_to_local is a procedure to migrate a tablespace from dictionary-managed to locally-managed, which means user managed and not automatic segment space management. The relative file number parameter is used to place the bitmaps into a specified data file.

ARGUMENT	TYPE	IN / OUT	DEFAULT VALUE
TABLESPACE_NAME	VARCHAR2	IN	
UNIT_SIZE	POSITIVE	IN	NULL
RFNO	POSITIVE	IN	NULL

Table 6.113: *Tablespace_migrate_to_local Parameters*

tablespace_rebuild_bitmaps is a procedure that simply rebuilds the tablespace bitmaps. The relative file number parameter is used to place the bitmaps into a specified data file and the bitmap block to specify the block.

ARGUMENT	TYPE	IN / OUT	DEFAULT VALUE
TABLESPACE_NAME	VARCHAR2	IN	
BITMAP_RELATIVE_FILE	POSITIVE	IN	NULL
BITMAP_BLOCK	POSITIVE	IN	NULL

Table 6.114: *Tablespace_rebuild_bitmaps Parameters*

tablespace_rebuild_quotas is a procedure that simply rebuilds the tablespace quotas.

ARGUMENT	TYPE	IN / OUT	DEFAULT VALUE
TABLESPACE_NAME	VARCHAR2	IN	

Table 6.115: *Tablespace_rebuild_quotas Parameter*

tablespace_relocate_bitmaps is a procedure that relocates the tablespace bitmaps to the specified destination.

ARGUMENT	TYPE	IN / OUT	DEFAULT VALUE
TABLESPACE_NAME	VARCHAR2	IN	
FILNO	POSITIVE	IN	NULL
BLKNO	POSITIVE	IN	NULL

Table 6.116: *Tablespace_relocate_bitmaps Parameters*

tablespace_verify is a procedure that verifies that the bitmaps and extent maps for all the segments in the tablespace are correct.

ARGUMENT	TYPE	IN / OUT	DEFAULT VALUE
TABLESPACE_NAME	VARCHAR2	IN	
VERIFY_OPTION	POSITIVE	IN	TABLESPACE_VERIFY_BITMAP

Table 6.117: *Tablespace_verify Parameters*

DBMS_SPACE

The *dbms_space* package provides a collection of procedures and functions to assist with the analysis of segment growth and space needs. This package can greatly assist with the key DBA task commonly referred to as capacity planning. There are a few enumerated constants that one must know to use this package:

```
OBJECT_TYPE_TABLE                 constant positive := 1;
OBJECT_TYPE_NESTED_TABLE          constant positive := 2;
OBJECT_TYPE_INDEX                 constant positive := 3;
OBJECT_TYPE_CLUSTER               constant positive := 4;
OBJECT_TYPE_LOB_INDEX             constant positive := 5;
OBJECT_TYPE_LOBSEGMENT            constant positive := 6;
OBJECT_TYPE_TABLE_PARTITION       constant positive := 7;
OBJECT_TYPE_INDEX_PARTITION       constant positive := 8;
OBJECT_TYPE_TABLE_SUBPARTITION    constant positive := 9;
OBJECT_TYPE_INDEX_SUBPARTITION    constant positive := 10;
OBJECT_TYPE_LOB_PARTITION         constant positive := 11;
OBJECT_TYPE_LOB_SUBPARTITION      constant positive := 12;
OBJECT_TYPE_MV                    constant positive := 13;
OBJECT_TYPE_MVLOG                 constant positive := 14;
OBJECT_TYPE_ROLLBACK_SEGMENT      constant positive := 15;
```

Asa_recommendations is a function that returns the findings from the automatic segment advisor. However, note that this requires proper OEM licensing; namely, that the optional OEM Diagnostics Pack has been purchased. It returns that information as type *dbms_space. asa_reco_row_tb*, as shown below.

ARGUMENT	TYPE	IN / OUT	DEFAULT VALUE
ALL_RUNS	VARCHAR2	IN	TRUE
SHOW_MANUAL	VARCHAR2	IN	TRUE
SHOW_FINDINGS	VARCHAR2	IN	FALSE

Table 6.118: *Asa_recommendations Parameters*

```
type asa_reco_row is record (
  tablespace_name        varchar2(30),
  segment_owner          varchar2(30),
  segment_name           varchar2(30),
  segment_type           varchar2(18),
  partition_name         varchar2(30),
  allocated_space        number,
  used_space             number,
  reclaimable_space      number,
  chain_rowexcess        number,
  recommendations        varchar2(1000),
  c1                     varchar2(1000),
  c2                     varchar2(1000),
  c3                     varchar2(1000),
  task_id                number,
  mesg_id                number
);

type asa_reco_row_tb is table of asa_reco_row;
```

create_index_cost is a procedure that calculates or estimates the storage required to create an index on an existing table.

ARGUMENT	TYPE	IN / OUT	DEFAULT VALUE
DDL	VARCHAR2	IN	
USED_BYTES	NUMBER	OUT	
ALLOC_BYTES	NUMBER	OUT	
PLAN_TABLE	VARCHAR2	IN	NULL

Table 6.119: *Create_index_cost Parameters*

create_table_cost is an overloaded procedure that calculates or estimates the storage required to create a new table. However, remember that the answer can vary widely based upon items such as tablespace storage attributes, tablespace block size, and such. Thus, *create_table_cost* offers two versions and/or methods of operation to provide for better estimates. The first method is based on the average row size and row count, and so this method is only as good as the estimates for those values.

ARGUMENT	TYPE	IN / OUT	DEFAULT VALUE
TABLESPACE_NAME	VARCHAR2	IN	
AVG_ROW_SIZE	NUMBER	IN	
ROW_COUNT	NUMBER	IN	
PCT_FREE	NUMBER	IN	
USED_BYTES	NUMBER	OUT	
ALLOC_BYTES	NUMBER	OUT	

Table 6.120: *Create_table_cost Parameters*

The second *create_table_cost* method looks at the actual column properties like data type and size, and can often yield fairly reliable predictions. Note that the second parameter for column information requires using the *create_table_cost_columns* data type.

ARGUMENT	TYPE	IN / OUT	DEFAULT VALUE
TABLESPACE_NAME	VARCHAR2	IN	
COLINFOS	SYS. CREATE_TABLE_COST_COLUMNS	IN	
ROW_COUNT	NUMBER	IN	
PCT_FREE	NUMBER	IN	
USED_BYTES	NUMBER	OUT	
ALLOC_BYTES	NUMBER	OUT	

Table 6.121: *Create_table_cost_columns Parameters*

```
type SYS.CREATE_TABLE_COST_COLINFO is object (
  col_type varchar(200),
  col_size number
);

type SYS.CREATE_TABLE_COST_COLUMNS is varray(50000) of
create_table_cost_colinfo;
```

free_blocks is a procedure that returns information about the free blocks in an object or segment. This represents all the free space and not just the free space above the high water mark. Use the *scan_limit* parameter only if one is interested in the question, "Are there X blocks on the free list?"

ARGUMENT	TYPE	IN / OUT	DEFAULT VALUE
SEGMENT_OWNER	VARCHAR2	IN	
SEGMENT_NAME	VARCHAR2	IN	
SEGMENT_TYPE	VARCHAR2	IN	
FREELIST_GROUP_ID	NUMBER	IN	
FREE_BLKS	NUMBER	OUT	
SCAN_LIMIT	NUMBER	IN	NULL
PARTITION_NAME	VARCHAR2	IN	NULL

Table 6.122: *Free_blocks Parameters*

object_dependent_segments is a function which returns a list of all the segments that are associated with the specified object. This function is useful for walking the dependency tree of objects related to the object of interest such that one can figure an object's real overall space requirements.

ARGUMENT	TYPE	IN / OUT	DEFAULT VALUE
OBJOWNER	VARCHAR2	IN	
OBJNAME	VARCHAR2	IN	
PARTNAME	VARCHAR2	IN	
OBJTYPE	NUMBER	IN	

Table 6.123: *Object_dependent_segments Parameters*

```
type object_dependent_segment is record (
  segment_owner    varchar2(100),
  segment_name     varchar2(100),
  segment_type     varchar2(100),
  tablespace_name  varchar2(100),
  partition_name   varchar2(100),
  lob_column_name  varchar2(100)
);

type dependent_segments_table is table of object_dependent_segment;
```

object_growth_trend is a powerful function that returns the space utilization of a database object over a time period from the current time or from the Automatic Workload Repository Facilities (AWRF). However, note that this requires proper OEM licensing – namely, the Diagnostics Pack. It returns a table of *dbms_space.growth_trend_table*.

ARGUMENT	TYPE	IN / OUT	DEFAULT VALUE
OBJECT_OWNER	VARCHAR2	IN	
OBJECT_NAME	VARCHAR2	IN	
OBJECT_TYPE	VARCHAR2	IN	
PARTITION_NAME	VARCHAR2	IN	
START_TIME	TIMESTAMP	IN	
END_TIME	TIMESTAMP	IN	
INTERVAL	DSINTERVAL_UNCONSTRAINED	IN	
SKIP_INTERPOLATED	VARCHAR2	IN	
TIMEOUT_SECONDS		IN	
SINGLE_DATAPOINT_ FLAG	VARCHAR2	IN	

Table 6.124: *Dbms_space.growth_trend_table*

```
type object_growth_trend_row is record (
  timepoint       timestamp,
  space_usage     number,
  space_alloc     number,
  quality         varchar(20)
);

type object_growth_trend_table is table of object_growth_trend_row;
```

space_usage is an overloaded procedure that reveals segment space usage under the high watermark. The first form works for database objects, but only for tablespaces using auto segment space management. The FS1 through FS4 parameters stand for the ranges of blocks with free space falling in the following ranges: FS1=0-25%, FS2=25-50%, FS3=50-75% and FS4=75-100%.

ARGUMENT	TYPE	IN / OUT	DEFAULT VALUE
SEGMENT_OWNER	VARCHAR2	IN	
SEGMENT_NAME	VARCHAR2	IN	
SEGMENT_TYPE	VARCHAR2	IN	
UNFORMATTED_BLOCKS	NUMBER	OUT	
UNFORMATTED_BYTES	NUMBER	OUT	
FS1_BLOCKS	NUMBER	OUT	
FS1_BYTES	NUMBER	OUT	
FS2_BLOCKS	NUMBER	OUT	

ARGUMENT	TYPE	IN / OUT	DEFAULT VALUE
FS2_BYTES	NUMBER	OUT	
FS3_BLOcKS	NUMBER	OUT	
FS3_BYTES	NUMBER	OUT	
FS4_BLOCKS	NUMBER	OUT	
FS4_BYTES	NUMBER	OUT	
FULL_BLOCKS	NUMBER	OUT	
FULL_BYTES	NUMBER	OUT	
PARTITION_NAME	VARCHAR2	IN	NULL

Table 6.125: *Space_usage Parameters*

The second form of the *space_usage* procedure returns information about SECUREFILE LOB space usage, i.e. the Oracle 11g preferred way to store large objects basically not in the database – essentially replaces LOBs and BFILEs. The expired and unexpired values are used by the LOB to keep version data.

ARGUMENT	TYPE	IN / OUT	DEFAULT VALUE
SEGMENT_OWNER	VARCHAR2	IN	
SEGMENT_NAME	VARCHAR2	IN	
SEGMENT_TYPE	VARCHAR2	IN	
PARTITION_NAME	VARCHAR2	IN	NULL
SEGMENT_SIZE_BLOCKS	NUMBER	OUT	
SEGMENT_SIZE_BYTES	NUMBER	OUT	
USED_BLOCKS	NUMBER	OUT	
USED_BYTES	NUMBER	OUT	
EXPIRED_BLOCKS	NUMBER	OUT	
EXPIRED_BYTES	NUMBER	OUT	
UNEXPIRED_BLOCKS	NUMBER	OUT	
UNEXPIRED_BYTES	NUMBER	OUT	

Table 6.126: *Space_usage Parameters, 2nd form*

unused_space is a procedure that reveals information about unused space by a database object.

ARGUMENT	TYPE	IN / OUT	DEFAULT VALUE
SEGMENT_OWNER	VARCHAR2	IN	
SEGMENT_NAME	VARCHAR2	IN	
SEGMENT_TYPE	VARCHAR2	IN	
TOTAL_BLOCKS	NUMBER	OUT	
TOTAL_BYTES	NUMBER	OUT	
UNUSED_BLOCKS	NUMBER	OUT	
UNUSED_BYTES	NUMBER	OUT	
LAST_USED_EXTENT_FILE_ID	NUMBER	OUT	
LAST_USED_EXTENT_BLOCK_ID	NUMBER	OUT	
LAST_USED_BLOCK	NUMBER	OUT	
PARTITION_NAME	VARCHAR2	IN	NULL

Table 6.127: *Unused_space Parameters*

Data Corruption Utilities

DBVERIFY

DBVerify is a simplistic external command line utility which performs a very critical task: it does either an offline or online check or verification as to the validity of data files. The two basic modes of operation it offers are file level and segment level. The offline check is quicker when referential integrity checks are involved. Here are the table level verification mode's parameters:

PARAMETER	DESCRIPTION
USERID	Username/Password
FILE	File Name
START	Block Address
END	Block Address
BLOCKSIZE	Integer
Feedback	Integer
PARFILE	File Name

Table 6.128: *Table Level Verification Mode Parameters*

And here is a simple check of the USERS tablespace's data file.

```
C:\Temp> dbv userid=bert/bert file=C:\Oracle\oradata\ORDB1\USERS.DBF
blocksize=4096

DBVERIFY: Release 11.1.0.6.0 - Production on Tue Jul 8 15:13:42 2008

Copyright (c) 1982, 2007, Oracle.  All rights reserved.

DBVERIFY - Verification starting : FILE = C:\Oracle\oradata\ORDB1\USERS.DBF

DBVERIFY - Verification complete

Total Pages Examined         : 51200
Total Pages Processed (Data) : 610
Total Pages Failing   (Data) : 0
Total Pages Processed (Index): 815
Total Pages Failing   (Index): 0
Total Pages Processed (Other): 362
Total Pages Processed (Seg)  : 52
Total Pages Failing   (Seg)  : 0
Total Pages Empty            : 49361
Total Pages Marked Corrupt   : 0
Total Pages Influx           : 0
Total Pages Encrypted        : 0
Highest block SCN            : 1466473 (0.1466473)
```

The segment level check has fewer parameters, but the *segment_id* parameter is a little more complex, meaning it requires a three-part value to be specified which requires a data dictionary query to resolve. Here are its parameters.

PARAMETER	DESCRIPTION
USERID	Username/Password
FILE	File Name
SEGMENT_ID	Tablespace Name.Segment File.Segment Block
Feedback	Integer
PARFILE	File Name

Table 6.129: *Segment_id Parameters*

The *segment_id* requires a simple query as shown here followed by the call to invoke DBVERIFY for those values. Note that this verification mode requires SYSDBA privileges:

```
SQL> select tablespace_name, segment_name, TABLESPACE_ID, HEADER_FILE,
HEADER_BLOCK
from sys.sys_user_segs
where tablespace_name='USERS' and SEGMENT_NAME like 'JUNK%';

TABLESPACE_NAME  SEGMENT_NAME   TABLESPACE_ID HEADER_FILE HEADER_BLOCK
---------------- --------------- ------------- ----------- ------------
USERS            JUNK                       4        1024        10278
USERS            JUNK2                      4        1024        10534

C:\Temp> dbv userid=bert/bert segment_id=4.1024.10278

DBVERIFY: Release 11.1.0.6.0 - Production on Tue Jul 8 15:13:42 2008

Copyright (c) 1982, 2007, Oracle.  All rights reserved.

DBVERIFY - Verification starting : SEGMENT_ID = 4.1024.10278

DBVERIFY - Verification complete

Total Pages Examined        : 32
Total Pages Processed (Data) : 28
Total Pages Failing   (Data) : 0
Total Pages Processed (Index): 0
Total Pages Failing   (Index): 0
Total Pages Processed (Other): 0
Total Pages Processed (Seg)  : 3
Total Pages Failing   (Seg)  : 1
Total Pages Empty            : 0
Total Pages Marked Corrupt   : 0
Total Pages Influx           : 0
Total Pages Encrypted        : 0
Highest block SCN            : 1466473 (0.1466473)
```

DBMS_REPAIR

dbms_repair offers procedures that enable potential detection and repairing of corrupt blocks in tables and indexes. Nevertheless, DBAs must judge for themselves whether the database corruption is significant enough to warrant using RMAN for a recovery versus attempting to correct via *dbms_repair*. For example, a restore offers a 100% guaranteed consistent recover within a generally predictable timeframe. The DBA might spend time with *dbms_repair* to try to fix the isolated problems and still end up needing to do the recovery. So examine closely the nature and extent of the problem and what time constraints must be met. Then pick appropriately. For those who do decide to use *dbms_repair*, there a few minor but key limitations to be keenly aware of:

- Index-organized tables and LOB indexes are not supported

- LOB and out-of-line columns, i.e. nested tables and varrays, are not supported

- *check_object* does not work for clusters

- *dump_orphan_keys* does not work for bitmap or function-based indexes

- *dump_orphan_keys* does not work for indexes where length > 3950 bytes

There are a few enumerated constants that one must know to use this package:

```
--  Object Type Specification
TABLE_OBJECT constant binary_integer := 1;
INDEX_OBJECT constant binary_integer := 2;
CLUSTER_OBJECT constant binary_integer := 4;

-- Flags Specification
SKIP_FLAG     constant binary_integer := 1;
NOSKIP_FLAG   constant binary_integer := 2;

-- Admin Action Specification
CREATE_ACTION constant binary_integer := 1;
PURGE_ACTION  constant binary_integer := 2;
DROP_ACTION   constant binary_integer := 3;

-- Admin Table Type Specification
REPAIR_TABLE constant binary_integer :=1;
ORPHAN_TABLE constant binary_integer :=2;

-- Object Id Specification
ALL_INDEX_ID constant binary_integer :=0;

-- Lock Wait Specification
LOCK_NOWAIT constant binary_integer := 0;
LOCK_WAIT   constant binary_integer := 1;
```

Rather than simply listing the package procedure and functions available, a simple workflow of the common use cases will be shown because how and what is done depends upon the status of the database. So it is more important to understand the workflow required than anything else.

First, handle some mandatory prerequisite activities. Much like doing explain plans (plan_table) and table constraint checking (EXCEPTIONS INTO), the *dbms_repair* package requires the use of some highly specific tables to record its findings. So use the admin_table procedure to create them. Below are the parameters for this procedure and an example.

ARGUMENT	TYPE	IN / OUT	DEFAULT VALUE
TABLE_NAME	VARCHAR2	IN	GENERATE_DEFAULT_TABLE _NAME
TABLE_TYPE	BINARY_INTEGER	IN	
ACTION	BINARY_INTEGER	IN	
TABLESPACE	VARCHAR2	IN	NULL

Table 6.130: *Admin_table Parameters*

```
SQL> execute dbms_repair.admin_tables ('REPAIR_TABLE',
dbms_repair.repair_table, dbms_repair.create_action);

PL/SQL procedure successfully completed.

SQL> desc repair_table
 Name                                    Null?    Type
 --------------------------------------- -------- -----------------------
 ----
 OBJECT_ID                               NOT NULL NUMBER
 TABLESPACE_ID                           NOT NULL NUMBER
 RELATIVE_FILE_ID                        NOT NULL NUMBER
 BLOCK_ID                                NOT NULL NUMBER
 CORRUPT_TYPE                            NOT NULL NUMBER
 SCHEMA_NAME                             NOT NULL VARCHAR2(30)
 OBJECT_NAME                             NOT NULL VARCHAR2(30)
 BASEOBJECT_NAME                                  VARCHAR2(30)
 PARTITION_NAME                                   VARCHAR2(30)
 CORRUPT_DESCRIPTION                              VARCHAR2(2000)
 REPAIR_DESCRIPTION                               VARCHAR2(200)
 MARKED_CORRUPT                          NOT NULL VARCHAR2(10)
 CHECK_TIMESTAMP                         NOT NULL DATE
 FIX_TIMESTAMP                                    DATE
 REFORMAT_TIMESTAMP                               DATE
```

And if the problem requires orphaned index pointer-type repairs, then create a table for that need as well as shown here.

```
SQL> execute dbms_repair.admin_tables ('ORPHAN_KEY_TABLE',
dbms_repair.orphan_table, dbms_repair.create_action);

PL/SQL procedure successfully completed.

SQL> desc orphan_key_table
 Name                                    Null?    Type
 --------------------------------------- -------- -----------------------
 ----
 SCHEMA_NAME                             NOT NULL VARCHAR2(30)
 INDEX_NAME                              NOT NULL VARCHAR2(30)
 IPART_NAME                                       VARCHAR2(30)
 INDEX_ID                                NOT NULL NUMBER
```

```
TABLE_NAME                              NOT NULL VARCHAR2(30)
PART_NAME                                        VARCHAR2(30)
TABLE_ID                                NOT NULL NUMBER
KEYROWID                                NOT NULL ROWID
KEY                                     NOT NULL ROWID
DUMP_TIMESTAMP                          NOT NULL DATE
```

Second, verify if there are any problems. Even if the database has reported an error on some other operation that indicates a problem, verify that the error can be seen and fixed with *dbms_repair*. So the first step is to examine a suspect object to determine its status using the *check_object* procedure. Below are the parameters for this procedure and an example.

ARGUMENT	TYPE	IN / OUT	DEFAULT VALUE
SCHEMA_NAME	VARCHAR2	IN	
OBJECT_NAME	VARCHAR2	IN	
PARTITION_NAME	VARCHAR2	IN	NULL
OBJECT_TYPE	BINARY_INTEGER	IN	TABLE_OBJECT
REPAIR_TABLE_NAME	VARCHAR2	IN	REPAIR_TABLE
FLAGS	BINARY_INTEGER	IN	NULL
BLOCK_START	BINARY_INTEGER	IN	NULL
BLOCK_END	BINARY_INTEGER	IN	NULL
CORRUPT_COUNT	BINARY_INTEGER	OUT	

Table 6.131: *Check_object Parameters*

```
SET SERVEROUTPUT ON
DECLARE corrupt_count INT;
BEGIN
  Corrupt_count := 0;
  DBMS_REPAIR.CHECK_OBJECT (
     SCHEMA_NAME => 'BERT',
     OBJECT_NAME => 'JUNK',
     REPAIR_TABLE_NAME => 'REPAIR_TABLE',
     CORRUPT_COUNT =>  corrupt_count);
  DBMS_OUTPUT.PUT_LINE('Corrupt count = ' || TO_CHAR (corrupt_count));
END;
/
```

Then query the repair table to see what problems exist as follows:

```
SQL> SELECT OBJECT_NAME, BLOCK_ID, CORRUPT_TYPE, MARKED_CORRUPT,
CORRUPT_DESCRIPTION, REPAIR_DESCRIPTION FROM REPAIR_TABLE;
```

If the corrupt count returns a non-zero value, then one needs to fix those issues. If the problem is corrupt blocks, then use the *fix_corrupt_blocks* procedure. Below are the parameters for this procedure and an example.

ARGUMENT	TYPE	IN / OUT	DEFAULT VALUE
SCHEMA_NAME	VARCHAR2	IN	
OBJECT_NAME	VARCHAR2	IN	
PARTITION_NAME	VARCHAR2	IN	NULL
OBJECT_TYPE	BINARY_INTEGER	IN	TABLE_OBJECT
REPAIR_TABLE_NAME	VARCHAR2	IN	REPAIR_TABLE
FLAGS	BINARY_INTEGER	IN	NULL
FIX_COUNT	BINARY_INTEGER	OUT	

Table 6.132: *Fix_corrupt_blocks Parameters*

```
SET SERVEROUTPUT ON
DECLARE fix_count INT;
BEGIN
Fix_count := 0;
DBMS_REPAIR.FIX_CORRUPT_BLOCKS (
    SCHEMA_NAME => 'BERT',
    OBJECT_NAME=> 'JUNK',
    OBJECT_TYPE => dbms_repair.table_object,
    REPAIR_TABLE_NAME => 'REPAIR_TABLE',
    FIX_COUNT=> fix_count);
DBMS_OUTPUT.PUT_LINE('Fix count = ' || TO_CHAR(fix_count));
END;
/
```

If the problem is bad index entries instead like orphans, then use the *dump_orphan_keys* procedure. Below are the parameters for this procedure and an example.

ARGUMENT	TYPE	IN / OUT	DEFAULT VALUE
SCHEMA_NAME	VARCHAR2	IN	
OBJECT_NAME	VARCHAR2	IN	
PARTITION_NAME	VARCHAR2	IN	NULL
OBJECT_TYPE	BINARY_INTEGER	IN	TABLE_OBJECT
REPAIR_TABLE_NAME	VARCHAR2	IN	REPAIR_TABLE
ORPHAN_TABLE_NAME	VARCHAR2	IN	ORPHAN_KEYS_TABLE
FLAGS	BINARY_INTEGER	IN	NULL
KEY_COUNT	BINARY_INTEGER	OUT	

Table 6.133: *Dump_orphan_keys Parameters*

```
SET SERVEROUTPUT ON
DECLARE key_count INT;
BEGIN
key_count := 0;
DBMS_REPAIR.DUMP_ORPHAN_KEYS (
    SCHEMA_NAME => 'BERT',
    OBJECT_NAME => 'JUNK',
    OBJECT_TYPE => dbms_repair.index_object,
    REPAIR_TABLE_NAME => 'REPAIR_TABLE',
    ORPHAN_TABLE_NAME=> 'ORPHAN_KEY_TABLE',
    KEY_COUNT => key_count);
DBMS_OUTPUT.PUT_LINE('Orphan key count: ' || TO_CHAR(key_count));
END;
/
```

Database Session Management

DBMS_SESSION

The *dbms_session* package provides a number of useful procedures and functions related to managing and/or controlling sessions. Begin by breaking down those offerings along related lines of usefulness starting with the general purpose ones for simply getting or setting session level attributes or characteristics. They are all fairly straightforward and simple, so no examples are given for them.

```
-- Returns a unique id for a session
DBMS_SESSION.UNIQUE_SESSION_ID RETURN VARCHAR2;

-- Returns whether current session is still active
DBMS_SESSION.IS_SESSION_ALIVE (uniqueid VARCHAR2) RETURN BOOLEAN;

-- Returns whether named role is enabled for session
DBMS_SESSION.IS_ROLE_ENABLED (rolename VARCHAR2) RETURN BOOLEAN;

-- Enables and disables named role for session
-- Same as SQL command: SET ROLE
DBMS_SESSION.SET_ROLE (role_cmd VARCHAR2);

-- Permits setting session's various globalization (NLS) settings
-- Same as SQL command: ALTER SESSION SET nls_parameter = value
DBMS_SESSION.SET_NLS (param VARCHAR2, value VARCHAR2);

-- Permits setting session trace flag on or off
-- Same as SQL command: ALTER SESSION SET SQL_TRACE = boolean
DBMS_SESSION.SET_SQL_TRACE (sql_trace boolean);

-- Permits closing an open database link
-- Same as SQL command: ALTER SESSION CLOSE DATABSE LINK dblink_name
DBMS_SESSION.CLOSE_DATABASE_LINK (dblink VARCHAR2);

-- Frees up unused memory after large operations (> 100K)
DBMS_SESSION.FREE_UNUSED_USER_MEMORY;

-- Permits session to de-instantiate (i.e. unload from memory)
-- all packages and their memory, cursors, global variables, etc
DBMS_SESSION.RESET_PACKAGE;

-- Permits session to change the current resource consumer group
DBMS_SESSION.switch_current_consumer_group (
   new_consumer_group     IN  VARCHAR2,
   old_consumer_group     OUT VARCHAR2,
   initial_group_on_error IN  BOOLEAN);
```

The remaining procedures and functions primarily support row level security (RLS), also referred to as virtual private databases (VPD) and fine grained access control. Examples of using these functions are shown in the section on row level security, so identify their names, purpose, parameters and defaults.

set_identifier, *clear_set_identifier* and *clear_identifier* procedures permit setting and clearing the client ID for the session. The client ID of a session is used to map it to some corresponding global application context, which is necessary for RLS and/or VPD.

```
-- Permits setting the session application-specific identtifier
DBMS_SESSION.SET_IDENTIFIER (client_id VARCHAR2);

-- Permits clearing the session application-specific identtifier
DBMS_SESSION.CLEAR_IDENTIFIER;
```

Now move onto procedures and functions specifically for managing contexts for a session. These are a little more complicated and the following data type needs to be worked with when listing a session's active contexts:

```
TYPE AppCtxRecTyp IS RECORD (
   namespace VARCHAR2(30),
   attribute VARCHAR2(30),
   value     VARCHAR2(256));

TYPE AppCtxTabTyp IS TABLE OF AppCtxRecTyp INDEX BY BINARY_INTEGER;
```

The list_context procedure is also rather simple; it returns an array of the contexts using this data type and the count of returned entries.

```
DBMS_SESSION.LIST_CONTEXT (list OUT AppCtxTabTyp, size OUT NUMBER);
```

Here is an example of using this procedure:

🖫 .list_context_demo.sql script

```
SET SERVEROUTPUT ON
DECLARE
  array_size INT;
  array_recs DBMS_SESSION.AppCtxTabTyp;
BEGIN
  array_size := 0;
  DBMS_SESSION.LIST_CONTEXT (array_recs, array_size);
  for i in 1 .. array_size loop
    DBMS_OUTPUT.PUT_LINE('Context Name = ' || array_recs(i).namespace);
    DBMS_OUTPUT.PUT_LINE('...Atrribute = ' || array_recs(i).attribute);
    DBMS_OUTPUT.PUT_LINE('...Value     = ' || array_recs(i).value);
  end loop;
END;
/
```

The remaining three procedures are entirely for managing the corresponding global application context, which is necessary for RLS and/or VPD and whose examples are in the section on role level security.

set_context sets the specified context for a given namespace, of which there are four types: session local, globally initialized, externally initialized, and globally accessed.

ARGUMENT	TYPE	IN / OUT	DEFAULT VALUE
NAMESPACE	VARCHAR2	IN	
ATTRIBUTE	VARCHAR2	IN	
VALUE	VARCHAR2	IN	
USERNAME	VARCHAR2	IN	NULL
CLIENT_ID	VARCHAR2	IN	NULL

Table 6.134: *Set_context Parameters*

clear_context clears the named context for a given namespace.

ARGUMENT	TYPE	IN / OUT	DEFAULT VALUE
NAME_SPACE	VARCHAR2	IN	
CLIENT_IDENTIFIER	VARCHAR2	IN	
ATTRIBUTE	VARCHAR2	IN	

Table 6.135: *Clear_context Parameters*

clear_all_context clears all contexts for a given namespace.

ARGUMENT	TYPE	IN / OUT	DEFAULT VALUE
NAME_SPACE	VARCHAR2	IN	

Table 6.136: *Clear_all_context Parameters*

File Management

DBMS_FILE_TRANSFER

The *dbms_file_transfer* package, available in 10g and later, supports copying via the local file system or an ASM (Automated Storage Management) disk group as both the source and target for a binary file transfer between databases servers. An example of using this package would be to copy BFILE objects across databases. Remember, the database stores just the BFILE attributes – the data resides outside the database. So use dbms_file_transfer to copy the actual BFILE data and not just the attributes held within the database. However, there are some limitations:

- Maximum of 2 TB file size

- File size must be multiple of 512 bytes

The process is very simple. First create a database directory to read from on the source and another one on the target for the write. Then make sure that both databases have grants on the directories and the *dbms_file_transfer* package for the schemas used to perform the task. Then use one of the following three procedures.

copy_file reads a file from the local database directory and copies it to another local database directory. The DBA is able to copy any type file when working with local file systems, but ASM supports only moving database files since that is all that can be held within ASM.

ARGUMENT	TYPE	IN / OUT	DEFAULT VALUE
SOURCE_DIRECTORY_OBJECT	VARCHAR2	IN	
SOURCE_FILE_NAME	VARCHAR2	IN	
DESTINATION_ DIRECTORY_OBJECT	VARCHAR2	IN	
DESTINATION_FILE_NAME	VARCHAR2	IN	

Table 6.137: *Copy_file Parameters*

get_file reads a file from the remote database directory and copies it to the source local database directory. The DBA can copy any type file when working with local file systems, but ASM supports only moving database files since that is all that can be held within ASM.

ARGUMENT	TYPE	IN / OUT	DEFAULT VALUE
SOURCE_DIRECTORY_OBJECT	VARCHAR2	IN	
SOURCE_FILE_NAME	VARCHAR2	IN	
SOURCE_DATABASE	VARCHAR2	IN	
DESTINATION_ DIRECTORY_OBJECT	VARCHAR2	IN	
DESTINATION_FILE_NAME	VARCHAR2	IN	

Table 6.138: *Get_file Parameters*

put_file reads a file from the local database directory and copies it to the target remote database directory.

ARGUMENT	TYPE	IN / OUT	DEFAULT VALUE
SOURCE_DIRECTORY_OBJECT	VARCHAR2	IN	
SOURCE_FILE_NAME	VARCHAR2	IN	
DESTINATION_ DIRECTORY_OBJECT	VARCHAR2	IN	
DESTINATION_FILE_NAME	VARCHAR2	IN	
DESTINATION_DATABASE	VARCHAR2	IN	

Table 6.139: *Put_file Parameters*

UTL_SMTP

The UTL_SMTP package provides PL/SQL programs the capability to send emails over SMTP (Simple Mail Transfer Protocol). Note that this package requires that the Oracle XMLDB component was chosen during initial database creation or subsequent modification utilizing DBCA (Database Configuration Assistant). Otherwise, the following series of error messages will occur:

```
SQL> @send_email
DECLARE
*
ERROR at line 1:
ORA-24248: XML DB extensible security not installed
ORA-06512: at "SYS.UTL_TCP", line 17
ORA-06512: at "SYS.UTL_TCP", line 246
ORA-06512: at "SYS.UTL_SMTP", line 115
ORA-06512: at "SYS.UTL_SMTP", line 138
ORA-06512: at line 7
```

The package will be detailed shortly, but this is one occasion where an example is worth more than the reference material. The *email_myself_smtp_demo.sql* PL/SQL code, shown below, is a simple snippet of PL/SQL to email a message. Note that in this example, the author has an email server running on his PC, hence why 127.0.0.1 can be used for the mail host.

🗔 email_myself_smtp_demo.sql script

```
DECLARE
    mailhost    VARCHAR2(64) := '127.0.0.1';
    sender      VARCHAR2(64) := 'bert.scalzo@yahoo.com';
    recipient   VARCHAR2(64) := 'bert.scalzo@yahoo.com';
    mail_conn   utl_smtp.connection;
BEGIN
    mail_conn := utl_smtp.open_connection (mailhost, 25);
    utl_smtp.helo (mail_conn, mailhost);
    utl_smtp.mail (mail_conn, sender);
    utl_smtp.rcpt (mail_conn, recipient);
    utl_smtp.open_data (mail_conn);
    utl_smtp.write_data (mail_conn, 'This is a test of the emergency
broadcast system, this is only a test' || chr(13));
    utl_smtp.write_data (mail_conn, 'In the case of an actual emergency, you
would be informed where to tune' || chr(13));
    utl_smtp.close_data (mail_conn);
    utl_smtp.quit (mail_conn);
END;
/
```

That is really all there is to it. Now examine the procedures and functions provided by the UTL_SMTP package. Note that key to the process is creating an email connection and then using that on subsequent UTL_SMTP calls. One also needs to work with the following data types:

```
TYPE reply IS RECORD (
  code    PLS_INTEGER,              -- 3-digit reply code
  text    VARCHAR2(508)             -- text message
);

TYPE replies IS TABLE OF reply
    INDEX BY BINARY_INTEGER;        -- multiple reply lines
```

close_data is both a procedure and function that ends an email message by sending the proper termination sequence such as a single period at the beginning of a line. The function returns a record of type UTL_SMTP.reply.

ARGUMENT	TYPE	IN / OUT	DEFAULT VALUE
C	UTL_SMTP.CONNECTION	IN | OUT	

Table 6.140: *Close_data Parameter*

command is both a procedure and function that performs a generic SMTP command. The function returns a record of type UTL_SMTP.reply..

ARGUMENT	TYPE	IN / OUT	DEFAULT VALUE
C	UTL_SMTP.CONNECTION	IN | OUT	
CMD	VARCHAR2	IN	
ARG	VARCHAR2	IN	NULL

Table 6.141: *Command Parameters*

command_replies is a function that performs the initial handshaking with the SMTP server. It returns a data type of UTL_SMTP.replies, so there are multiple occurrences of a reply.

ARGUMENT	TYPE	IN / OUT	DEFAULT VALUE
C	UTL_SMTP.CONNECTION	IN | OUT	
CMD	VARCHAR2	IN	
ARG	VARCHAR2	IN	NULL

Table 6.142: *Command_replies Parameters*

data is both a procedure and function that specifies the email message body. The function returns a record of type UTL_SMTP.reply.

ARGUMENT	TYPE	IN / OUT	DEFAULT VALUE
C	UTL_SMTP.CONNECTION	IN | OUT	
BODY	VARCHAR2	IN	

Table 6.143: *Data Parameters*

EHLO is both a procedure and a function that performs the initial handshaking with the SMTP server with extended information returned. It returns a data type of UTL_SMTP.replies, so there are multiple occurrences of a reply.

ARGUMENT	TYPE	IN / OUT	DEFAULT VALUE
C	UTL_SMTP.CONNECTION	IN | OUT	
DOMAIN	VARCHAR2	IN	

Table 6.144: *EHLO Parameters*

HELO is both a procedure and a function that performs the initial handshaking with the SMTP server without extended information returned. It returns a record of type UTL_SMTP.reply.

ARGUMENT	TYPE	IN / OUT	DEFAULT VALUE
C	UTL_SMTP.CONNECTION	IN | OUT	
DOMAIN	VARCHAR2	IN	

Table 6.145: *HELO Parameters*

help is a function that transmits the help command. It returns a record of type UTL_SMTP.reply.

ARGUMENT	TYPE	IN / OUT	DEFAULT VALUE
C	UTL_SMTP.CONNECTION	IN | OUT	
DOMAIN	VARCHAR2	IN	NULL

Table 6.146: *Help Parameters*

mail is both a procedure and function that initiates a mail transaction. The function returns a record of type UTL_SMTP.reply.

ARGUMENT	TYPE	IN / OUT	DEFAULT VALUE
C	UTL_SMTP.CONNECTION	IN | OUT	
SENDER	VARCHAR2	IN	
PARAMETERS	VARCHAR2	IN	NULL

Table 6.147: *Mail Parameters*

NOOP is both a procedure and function that performs a NULL command. It does not actually send the mail, just prepares to send it and requires subsequent calls to RCPT and DATA to complete the transaction. The function returns a record of type UTL_SMTP.reply.

ARGUMENT	TYPE	IN / OUT	DEFAULT VALUE
C	UTL_SMTP.CONNECTION	IN | OUT	

Table 6.148: *NOOP Parameters*

open_connection is an overloaded function that takes two fairly different forms. However, each opens a connection to the SMTP server; they simply differ in their return styles. The first version returns the connection handle via and out parameter and returns UTL_SMTP.reply, shown here.

ARGUMENT	TYPE	IN / OUT	DEFAULT VALUE
HOST	VARCHAR2	IN	
PORT	PLS_INETGER	IN	25
C	UTL_SMTP.CONNECTION	OUT	
TX_TIMEOUT	PLS_INETGER	IN	NULL

Table 6.149: *Open_connection Parameters*

The second version of *open_connection* simply returns the connect handle, which is type UTL_SMTP.connection.

ARGUMENT	TYPE	IN / OUT	DEFAULT VALUE
HOST	VARCHAR2	IN	
PORT	PLS_INETGER	IN	25
TX_TIMEOUT	PLS_INETGER	IN	NULL

Table 6.150: *Open_connections Parameters, 2nd Version*

open_data is both a procedure and a function that transmits the DATA command to the SMTP server, after which one can then call *write_data* and *write_raw_data*. The function returns a record of type UTL_SMTP.reply.

ARGUMENT	TYPE	IN / OUT	DEFAULT VALUE
C	UTL_SMTP.CONNECTION	IN | OUT	

Table 6.151: *Open_data Parameter*

quit is both a procedure and function that terminates the SMTP session. The function returns a record of type UTL_SMTP.reply.

ARGUMENT	TYPE	IN / OUT	DEFAULT VALUE
C	UTL_SMTP.CONNECTION	IN | OUT	

Table 6.152: *Quit Parameter*

RCPT is both a procedure and function that specifies the recipient of the email. The function returns a record of type UTL_SMTP.reply.

ARGUMENT	TYPE	IN / OUT	DEFAULT VALUE
C	UTL_SMTP.CONNECTION	IN | OUT	
RECIPIENT	VARCHAR2	IN	
PARAMETERS	VARCHAR2	IN	NULL

Table 6.153: *RCPT Parameters*

RSET is both a procedure and function that simply terminates the current mail transaction. The function returns a record of type UTL_SMTP.reply.

ARGUMENT	TYPE	IN / OUT	DEFAULT VALUE
C	UTL_SMTP.CONNECTION	IN | OUT	

Table 6.154: *RSET Parameter*

VRFY is a function that verifies or validates the destination email address. It returns a record of type UTL_SMTP.reply.

ARGUMENT	TYPE	IN / OUT	DEFAULT VALUE
C	UTL_SMTP.CONNECTION	IN | OUT	
DOMAIN	VARCHAR2	IN	

Table 6.155: *VRFY Parameters*

write_data is a procedure that writes a portion of the email message and where repeat calls simply append data to the message.

ARGUMENT	TYPE	IN / OUT	DEFAULT VALUE
C	UTL_SMTP.CONNECTION	IN | OUT	
DATA	VARCHAR2	IN	

Table 6.156: *Write_data Parameters*

write_raw_data is also a procedure that writes a portion of the email message and where repeat calls append data to the message. The main difference is that the DATA parameter is now RAW.

ARGUMENT	TYPE	IN / OUT	DEFAULT VALUE
C	UTL_SMTP.CONNECTION	IN | OUT	
DATA	RAW	IN	

Table 6.157: *Write_raw_data parameters*

UTL_TCP

The UTL_TCP package provides PL/SQL programs the capability to communicate via TCP/IP (Transmission Control Protocol/Internet Protocol). This package requires that the Oracle XMLDB component was chosen during initial database creation or subsequent modification utilizing DBCA. Otherwise, the following series of error messages will come up:

```
SQL> @send_email
DECLARE
*
ERROR at line 1:
ORA-24248: XML DB extensible security not installed
ORA-06512: at "SYS.UTL_TCP", line 17
ORA-06512: at "SYS.UTL_TCP", line 246
ORA-06512: at "SYS.UTL_SMTP", line 115
ORA-06512: at "SYS.UTL_SMTP", line 138
ORA-06512: at line 7
```

Just like UTL_SMTP, this is one occasion where an example is worth more than the reference material. The *email_myself_tcp_demo.sql* PL/SQL code is a snippet of PL/SQL to email a message:

🖫 email_myself_tcp_demo.sql script

```
DECLARE
   sender      VARCHAR2(30)  := 'bert.scalzo@yahoo.com';
   recipient   VARCHAR2(30)  := 'bert.scalzo@yahoo.com';
   message     VARCHAR2(30)  := 'This is a test message';
   mailhost    VARCHAR2(30)  := '127.0.0.1';
   mail_conn   utl_tcp.connection;
   PROCEDURE smtp_command (command IN VARCHAR2, ok IN VARCHAR2 DEFAULT '250')
   IS
        response varchar2(3);
        len pls_integer;
   BEGIN
        len := utl_tcp.write_line (mail_conn, command);
        response := substr(utl_tcp.get_line (mail_conn), 1, 3);
   END;
BEGIN
     mail_conn := utl_tcp.open_connection (remote_host => mailhost,
remote_port => 25, charset => 'US7ASCII');
```

```
        smtp_command ('HELO ' || mailhost);
        smtp_command ('MAIL FROM: ' || sender);
        smtp_command ('RCPT TO: ' || recipient);
        smtp_command ('DATA', '354');
        smtp_command (message);
        smtp_command ('QUIT', '221');
     utl_tcp.close_connection (mail_conn);
END;
/
```

Next, examine the procedures and functions provided by the UTL_TCP package. Key to the process is creating a TCP connection and then using that on subsequent UTL_TCP calls. One also needs to work with the following data type and constants:

```
TYPE connection IS RECORD (
  remote_host    VARCHAR2(255),    -- Remote host name
  remote_port    PLS_INTEGER,      -- Remote port number
  local_host     VARCHAR2(255),    -- Local host name
  local_port     PLS_INTEGER,      -- Local port number
  charset        VARCHAR2(30),     -- Character set for on-the-wire comm.
  newline        VARCHAR2(2),      -- Newline character sequence
  tx_timeout     PLS_INTEGER,      -- Transfer time-out value (in seconds)
  private_sd     PLS_INTEGER       -- For internal use only
);

buffer_too_small                   EXCEPTION;  -- Buffer is too small for I/O
end_of_input                       EXCEPTION;  -- End of input from connection
network_error                      EXCEPTION;  -- Network error
bad_argument                       EXCEPTION;  -- Bad argument passed in API
call
partial_multibyte_char             EXCEPTION;  -- A partial multi-byte char
found
transfer_timeout                   EXCEPTION;  -- Transfer time-out occurred
network_access_denied              EXCEPTION;  -- Network access denied
buffer_too_small_errcode           CONSTANT PLS_INTEGER:= -29258;
end_of_input_errcode               CONSTANT PLS_INTEGER:= -29259;
network_error_errcode              CONSTANT PLS_INTEGER:= -29260;
bad_argument_errcode               CONSTANT PLS_INTEGER:= -29261;
partial_multibyte_char_errcode     CONSTANT PLS_INTEGER:= -29275;
transfer_timeout_errcode           CONSTANT PLS_INTEGER:= -29276;
network_access_denied_errcode      CONSTANT PLS_INTEGER:= -24247;
```

close_data is a function that determines the number of bytes available for consumption from a TCP/IP connection and returns a *pls_integer*.

ARGUMENT	TYPE	IN / OUT	DEFAULT VALUE
C	UTL_TCP.CONNECTION	IN | OUT	
TIMEOUT	PLS_INTEGER	IN	0

Table 6.158: *Close_data Parameters*

File Management

close_all_connections is a procedure that simply closes all the open TCP/IP connections. It takes no parameters.

close_connection is a procedure that closes the specified open TCP/IP connection.

ARGUMENT	TYPE	IN / OUT	DEFAULT VALUE
C	UTL_TCP.CONNECTION	IN | OUT	

Table 6.159: *Close_connection Parameter*

flush is a procedure that immediately transmits any and all data in the output buffer.

ARGUMENT	TYPE	IN / OUT	DEFAULT VALUE
C	UTL_TCP.CONNECTION	IN | OUT	

Table 6.160: *Flush Parameters*

get_line is a function that reads a line of data and returns a VARCHAR2. The *peek* parameter allows one to look ahead in the buffer without actually consuming the message.

ARGUMENT	TYPE	IN / OUT	DEFAULT VALUE
C	UTL_TCP.CONNECTION	IN | OUT	
REMOVE_CRLF	BOOLEAN	IN	FALSE
PEEK	BOOLEAN	IN	FALSE

Table 6.161: *Get_line Parameters*

get_line_nchar is a function that reads a line of data, and returns a NVARCHAR2. The peek parameter allows one to look ahead in the buffer without actually consuming the message.

ARGUMENT	TYPE	IN / OUT	DEFAULT VALUE
C	UTL_TCP.CONNECTION	IN | OUT	
REMOVE_CRLF	BOOLEAN	IN	FALSE
PEEK	BOOLEAN	IN	FALSE

Table 6.162: *Get_line_nchar Parameters*

get_raw is a function that reads data and returns it as a RAW. The *peek* parameter allows one to look ahead in the buffer without actually consuming the message. The len parameter allows specifying the number of bytes to get.

ARGUMENT	TYPE	IN / OUT	DEFAULT VALUE
C	UTL_TCP.CONNECTION	IN | OUT	
LEN	BOOLEAN	IN	1
PEEK	BOOLEAN	IN	FALSE

Table 6.163: *Get_raw Parameters*

get_text is a function that reads data, and returns it as a VARCHAR2.

ARGUMENT	TYPE	IN / OUT	DEFAULT VALUE
C	UTL_TCP.CONNECTION	IN | OUT	
LEN	BOOLEAN	IN	1
PEEK	BOOLEAN	IN	FALSE

Table 6.164: *Get_text Parameters*

get_text_nchar is a function that reads data and returns it as an NVARCHAR2.

ARGUMENT	TYPE	IN / OUT	DEFAULT VALUE
C	UTL_TCP.CONNECTION	IN | OUT	
LEN	BOOLEAN	IN	1
PEEK	BOOLEAN	IN	FALSE

Table 6.165: *Get_text_nchar Parameters*

open_connection is a function that simply opens a TCP/IP connection. It returns that connection information as type UTL_TCP.connection.

ARGUMENT	TYPE	IN / OUT	DEFAULT VALUE
REMOTE_HOST	VARCHAR2	IN	
REMOTE_PORT	PLS_INTEGER	IN	
LOCAL_HOST	VARCHAR2	IN	NULL
LOCAL_PORT	PLS_INTEGER	IN	NULL
IN_BUFFER_SIZE	PLS_INTEGER	IN	NULL
OUT_BUFFER_SIZE	PLS_INTEGER	IN	NULL
CHARSET	VARCHAR2	IN	NULL

NEWLINE	VARCHAR2	IN	CRLF
TX_TIMEOUT	PLS_INTEGER	IN	NULL

Table 6.166: *Open_connection Parameters*

read_line is a function that reads a line of data from a service and returns a *pls_integer* for the number of characters read. The *peek* parameter allows one to look ahead in the buffer without actually consuming the message.

ARGUMENT	TYPE	IN / OUT	DEFAULT VALUE
C	UTL_TCP.CONNECTION	IN	OUT	
DATA	VARCHAR2	IN	OUT	
PEEK	BOOLEAN	IN	FALSE

Table 6.167: *Read_line Parameters*

read_raw is a function that reads a line of data from a service and returns a *pls_integer* for the number of bytes read.

ARGUMENT	TYPE	IN / OUT	DEFAULT VALUE
C	UTL_TCP.CONNECTION	IN	OUT	
DATA	RAW	IN	OUT	
LEN	PLS_INTEGER	IN	1
PEEK	BOOLEAN	IN	FALSE

Table 6.168: *Read_raw parameters*

read_text is a function that reads a line of data from a service and returns a *pls_integer* for the number of characters read.

ARGUMENT	TYPE	IN / OUT	DEFAULT VALUE
C	UTL_TCP.CONNECTION	IN	OUT	
DATA	VARCHAR2	IN	OUT	
LEN	PLS_INTEGER	IN	1
PEEK	BOOLEAN	IN	FALSE

Table 6.169: *Read_text Parameters*

write_line is a function that transmits a line of data to a service and returns a *pls_integer* for the number of characters sent.

ARGUMENT	TYPE	IN / OUT	DEFAULT VALUE
C	UTL_TCP.CONNECTION	IN | OUT	
DATA	VARCHAR2	IN | OUT	

Table 6.170: *Write_line Parameters*

write_raw is a function that transmits a line of data to a service and returns a *pls_integer* for the number of bytes sent.

ARGUMENT	TYPE	IN / OUT	DEFAULT VALUE
C	UTL_TCP.CONNECTION	IN | OUT	
DATA	RAW	IN | OUT	
LEN	PLS_INTEGER	IN	1

Table 6.171: *Write_raw Parameters*

write_text is a function that transmits a line of data from a service and returns a *pls_integer* for the number of characters sent.

ARGUMENT	TYPE	IN / OUT	DEFAULT VALUE
C	UTL_TCP.CONNECTION	IN | OUT	
DATA	VARCHAR2	IN | OUT	
LEN	PLS_INTEGER	IN	1

Table 6.172: *Write_text Parameters*

ASMCMD

ASMCMD is a command line utility for managing files and directories in ASM (Automatic Storage Management) diskgroups. It offers Unix-style filesystem commands for managing ASM directories and files. Prior to Oracle 10gR2, ASM had to be administered via OEM or SQL statements while connected to a special ASM instance.

Note that ASMCMD cannot be used to create or drop diskgroups, or to add or drop disks in a disk group. These ASM administrative tasks must be accomplished via SQL commands.

ASMCMD offers two modes of operation: interactive and non-interactive. Interactive mode provides a shell-like environment for executing ASMCMD commands. It resembles how SQL*Plus interactive mode works and looks like this:

```
C:\Temp>asmcmd
ASMCMD>
```

Whereas non-interactive mode works much like the *srvctl* and *lsnctl* commands, that is that one provides the base ASMCMD command, its command and any command parameters and all on the operating system command line, like this:

```
C:\Temp>asmcmd ls -l
```

The ASMCMD commands and their parameters are very Unix-like in nature, so they will look quite familiar to those on UNIX. Here is a summary of the key commands and their purpose:

COMMAND	DESCRIPTION
cd	Change directory
cp	Copy file
du	Disk space used by a directory and its subdirectories
exit	Exit the utility
find	Locate the path for all occurrences of the specified filename
help	Displays command assistance
ls	List the contents of a directory
lsct	List info about ASM clients
lsdg	List all disk groups and their attributes
lsdsk	List all physical disks visible to ASM
md_backup	Create a backup of the mounted diskgroups
md_restore	Restore the diskgroups from a backup
mkalias	Create an alias for a system generated filename
mkdir	Create directory
pwd	Print working directory (i.e. list current directory location)
remap	Repair a range of blocks on a disk
rm	Remove (i.e. delete) the specified files or directories
rmalias	Remove (i.e. delete) the specified alias

Table 6.173: *ASMCMD Key Commands*

Instance Management

DBMS_SHARED_POOL

dbms_shared_pool provides a simple but useful programmatic access to the Oracle SGA's shared pool memory section, specifically where cursors and PL/SQL code are stored. The types of objects supported include:

- P   =   package/procedure/function
- Q   =   sequence
- R   =   trigger
- T   =   type
- JS   =   java source
- JC   =   java class
- JR   =   java resource
- JD   =   java shared data
- C   =   cursor

The PL/SQL programmatic API is as follows:

```
-- Show objects in shared pool > specified size
procedure sizes(minsize number);

-- Keep or pin the object in the shared pool (immune to aging out)
procedure keep(name varchar2, flag char DEFAULT 'P');

-- Unkeep or unpin the object in the shared pool (resume normal aging out)
procedure unkeep(name varchar2, flag char DEFAULT 'P');

-- Forces the object to immediately agre out of the shared pool
procedure purge(name varchar2, flag char DEFAULT 'P', heaps number DEFAULT
1);

-- Defines the effective size limit for a pin object request failing
procedure aborted_request_threshold(threshold_size number);
```

A very useful example of using the *dbms_shared_pool* package would be to create a database startup trigger to "pin" the most frequently used PL/SQL packages into the shared pool, assuming there is sufficient memory allocation to support it. The *pin_top4_procedures.sql* PL/SQL code shown next is an example of such a trigger for the specific database where it is known that the four packages chosen see relatively heavy use due to the nature of the database's PL/SQL code:

🖫 pin_top4_procedures.sql script

```
CREATE OR REPLACE TRIGGER SYS.PIN_HIGH_USE_PLSQL
AFTER STARTUP
ON DATABASE
BEGIN
  DBMS_SHARED_POOL.KEEP('DBMS_APPLICATION_INFO');
  DBMS_SHARED_POOL.KEEP('DBMS_SQL');
  DBMS_SHARED_POOL.KEEP('STANDARD');
  DBMS_SHARED_POOL.KEEP('DBMS_UTILITY');
END;
/
```

The following query can be run to help identify which packages might want to be included as pin candidates for the specific database.

```
SELECT owner, name, type, sharable_mem, loads, kept, executions, locks, pins
FROM v$db_object_cache outer
WHERE type in ('PROCEDURE','PACKAGE BODY', 'PACKAGE', 'FUNCTION', 'TRIGGER',
'SEQUENCE')
  AND kept = 'NO'
  and executions > ( select 2*avg(count(executions))
                     FROM v$db_object_cache inner
                     WHERE type in ('PROCEDURE','PACKAGE BODY', 'PACKAGE',
'FUNCTION', 'TRIGGER', 'SEQUENCE')
                     AND kept = 'NO'
                     group by executions)
  and loads      > ( select 2*avg(count(loads))
                     FROM v$db_object_cache inner
                     WHERE type in ('PROCEDURE','PACKAGE BODY', 'PACKAGE',
'FUNCTION', 'TRIGGER', 'SEQUENCE')
                     AND kept = 'NO'
                     group by loads)
ORDER BY executions DESC;
```

> Note: The PURGE option for doing the opposite of a PIN, can be very useful to force new explain plan considerations vs. flushing the entire shared pool.

Conclusion

In this chapter, the plethora of pre-canned PL/SQL packages, OEM facilities and command line utilities that enable DBAs to wear many hats and thereby perform a wide range of tasks was covered in detail. The scope of these tasks examined everything from reverse engineering to reorganization, from security to space management, and even replication. Therefore, it is a lot of material that was covered.

The next topic to delve into is Oracle tuning, monitoring and diagnostics which is an area that many DBAs consider paramount to being both effective and efficient.

Oracle Tuning and Monitoring Utilities

CHAPTER

7

Management judges your performance on Oracle's performance!

Introduction

One of a DBA's most challenging and yet highly rewarding activities is database monitoring, diagnostics and tuning. Therefore, expect this chapter to be like the financial or sports sections of the USA Today newspaper – the place where many people go first and often. Because as the cartoon above so truly states, management and/or customers will most often measure a DBA by the database performance even though they did not write the application code. Think of it like the racecar driver who wins or loses a race: it is the driving and not the design or mechanical condition of the racecar that day that gets the credit or the blame. It is much the same with DBAs. If the database is humming along nicely, he is the golden child at the company. But when the

---

346   Advanced Oracle Utilities

database tanks, and regardless of whether the fault lies with the database or with the application, people simply expect the DBA to make the difference. It is his problem and it must be fixed ASAP.

Fortunately, Oracle versions 10g and 11g have made the tasks of monitoring, diagnostics and tuning much easier. In many respects, the self-diagnostic and self-healing claims are warranted. When properly planned and configured, a modern Oracle database needs much less care and attention than in days past. However, that requires effective planning and efficient configuration as well as some managed best practices to maintain that happy state. This chapter will focus on the tools Oracle provides to support those efforts. Note that portions of this chapter may appear version specific, optional, or otherwise less than automatic. Failure to utilize these tools can very often be cited as the primary cause for less than optimal database performance over the long term. Moreover, several key utilities in the next chapter on advisories will depend heavily upon having correctly made appropriate choices here. Thus, this chapter should be regarded as a prerequisite for the next.

Returning to the racecar driver example, this chapter is much like the process of graduating from a road racing course. The driver requires this knowledge of the basics long before entering and participating in any actual race. The next chapter then is much like the racecar drivers' plan for a specific race on a specific date.

Tuning Utilities

DBMS_WORKLOAD_REPOSITORY

Two recent and significant additions to the Oracle database's data dictionary are more granular performance statistical data and the ability to collect that data over time. Once that performance data has been collected, it is a trivial process to perform analysis and translate that raw data into meaningful information, which often yields both problem detection as well as recommendations to solve the problems. This performance repository is known as the Automatic Workload Repository (AWR) and is managed via the PL/SQL package DBMS_WORKLOAD_REPOSITORY.

> This feature is available only in Oracle 10g and higher and specifically only for those who have purchased the optional OEM Diagnostics Pack. Furthermore, even just query access to the *dba_hist_* views where this data is collected requires a valid license.

The AWR collects and maintains this performance data when the Oracle initialization parameter *statistics_level* is set to ALL or TYPICAL (the default). Furthermore, that performance data is captured by default on the hour, called a snapshot, and kept for eight days, known as the retention period. Frequency and retention levels are fully configurable by the DBA. It is not uncommon to see snapshots taken more often and retained much longer, in some cases as much as a year. This data is kept in the SYSAUX tablespace and is the primary consumer of space within that tablespace. Obviously the more frequent the snapshots and longer the retention period, the larger the SYSAUX space needs will be. With disk space so cheap these days, just allocate a couple of gigabytes and do not worry about it. For most databases, 500 MB will be more than sufficient.

There are two key terms with AWR: snapshots and baselines. A snapshot is a numbered collection of performance data at a given time. It represents a static point-in-time of the database as expressed in all the key performance metric metadata within the data dictionary. Snapshots are the key inputs to the Automatic Database Diagnostic Monitor (ADDM) to perform relative comparisons which represent the measured workload for the delta in time. If StatsPack has been used in the past, this concept of a snapshot is pretty much the same. Baselines are simply a user named set of snapshots representing a time period, being either fixed or sliding. Baselines allow one to name and keep meaningful snapshots because baselines and their snapshots are not aged out of the AWR by the retention cleanup process, i.e. that data is not automatically deleted. Next to be examined is the interface that DBMS_WORKLOAD_REPOSITORY offers.

ash_report_html is a function that quite simply displays an Automated Session History or ASH report in HTML with multiple (pipelined) returned values of VARCHAR2(500).

ARGUMENT	TYPE	IN / OUT	DEFAULT VALUE
L_DBID	NUMBER	IN	

L_INST_NUM	NUMBER	IN	
L_BTIME	DATE	IN	
L_ETIME	DATE	IN	
L_OPTIONS	NUMBER	IN	0
L_SLOT_WIDTH	NUMBER	IN	0
L_SID	NUMBER	IN	NULL
L_SQL_ID	VARCHAR2	IN	NULL
L_WAIT_CLASS	VARCHAR2	IN	NULL
L_SERVICE_HASH	NUMBER	IN	NULL
L_MODULE	VARCHAR2	IN	NULL
L_ACTION	VARCHAR2	IN	NULL
L_CLIENT_ID	VARCHAR2	IN	NULL
L_PLSQL_ENTRY	VARCHAR2	IN	NULL

Table 7.1: *Ash_report_html Parameters*

ash_report_text is a function that displays an Automated Session History or ASH report as plain text with multiple returned values of VARCHAR2(80).

ARGUMENT	TYPE	IN / OUT	DEFAULT VALUE
L_DBID	NUMBER	IN	
L_INST_NUM	NUMBER	IN	
L_BTIME	DATE	IN	
L_ETIME	DATE	IN	
L_OPTIONS	NUMBER	IN	0
L_SLOT_WIDTH	NUMBER	IN	0
L_SID	NUMBER	IN	NULL
L_SQL_ID	VARCHAR2	IN	NULL
L_WAIT_CLASS	VARCHAR2	IN	NULL
L_SERVICE_HASH	NUMBER	IN	NULL
L_MODULE	VARCHAR2	IN	NULL
L_ACTION	VARCHAR2	IN	NULL
L_CLIENT_ID	VARCHAR2	IN	NULL
L_PLSQL_ENTRY	VARCHAR2	IN	NULL

Table 7.2: *Ash_report_text Parameters*

awr_diff_report_html is a function that displays an Automatic Workload Repository (AWR) report that compares differences between two snapshots in HTML with pipelined returned values of VARCHAR2(500).

ARGUMENT	TYPE	IN / OUT	DEFAULT VALUE
DBID1	NUMBER	IN	
INST_NUM1	NUMBER	IN	
BID1	NUMBER	IN	
EID1	NUMBER	IN	
DBID2	NUMBER	IN	
INST_NUM2	NUMBER	IN	
BID2	NUMBER	IN	
EID2	NUMBER	IN	

Table 7.3: *Awr_diff_report_html Parameters*

awr_diff_report_text is a function that displays an Automatic Workload Repository (AWR) report that compares differences between two snapshots as plain text with multiple returned values of VARCHAR2(80).

ARGUMENT	TYPE	IN / OUT	DEFAULT VALUE
DBID1	NUMBER	IN	
INST_NUM1	NUMBER	IN	
BID1	NUMBER	IN	
EID1	NUMBER	IN	
DBID2	NUMBER	IN	
INST_NUM2	NUMBER	IN	
BID2	NUMBER	IN	
EID2	NUMBER	IN	

Table 7.4: *Awr_diff_report_text Parameters*

awr_sql_report_html is a function that displays an Automatic Workload Repository (AWR) SQL report in HTML with multiple (pipelined) returned values of VARCHAR2(500).

ARGUMENT	TYPE	IN / OUT	DEFAULT VALUE
L_DBID	NUMBER	IN	
L_INST_NUM	NUMBER	IN	
L_BID	NUMBER	IN	
L_EID	NUMBER	IN	
L_SQLID	VARCHAR2	IN	

L_OPTIONS	NUMBER	IN	0

Table 7.5: *Awr_sql_report_html Parameters*

awr_sql_report_text is a function that displays an Automatic Workload Repository (AWR) SQL report as plain text with multiple returned values of VARCHAR2(120).

ARGUMENT	TYPE	IN / OUT	DEFAULT VALUE
L_DBID	NUMBER	IN	
L_INST_NUM	NUMBER	IN	
L_BID	NUMBER	IN	
L_EID	NUMBER	IN	
L_SQLID	VARCHAR2	IN	
L_OPTIONS	NUMBER	IN	0

Table 7.6: *Awr_sql_report_text Parameters*

create_baseline is both a function and a procedure that defines a baseline by either its starting snapshot ID or time and its ending snapshot ID or time. As a function, it returns the snapshot ID number.

ARGUMENT	TYPE	IN / OUT	DEFAULT VALUE
START_SNAP_ID | START_TIME	NUMBER | DATE	IN	
END_SNAP_ID | END_TIME	NUMBER | DATE	IN	
BASELINE_NAME	VARCHAR2	IN	
DBID	NUMBER	IN	NULL
EXPIRATION	NUMBER	IN	NULL

Table 7.7: *Create_baseline Parameters*

create_baseline_template is an overloaded procedure, meaning it has two forms, that defines a template for how future baselines are to be created. The first form, which creates a baseline as the period between two snapshots, is as follows:

ARGUMENT	TYPE	IN / OUT	DEFAULT VALUE
START_TIME	DATE	IN	

END_TIME	DATE	IN	
BASELINE_NAME	VARCHAR2	IN	
TEMPLATE_NAME	VARCHAR2	IN	
EXPIRATION	NUMBER	IN	
DBID	NUMBER	IN	NULL

Table 7.8: *Create_baseline_template Parameters – 1st Form*

The second form of *create_baseline_template*, which creates a baseline as the period from a user defined start time and duration, is as follows:

ARGUMENT	TYPE	IN / OUT	DEFAULT VALUE
DAY_OF_WEEK	VARCHAR2	IN	
HOUR_IN_DAY	NUMBER	IN	
DURATION	NUMBER	IN	
START_TIME	DATE	IN	
END_TIME	DATE	IN	
BASELINE_NAME_PREFIX	VARCHAR2	IN	
TEMPLATE_NAME	VARCHAR2	IN	
EXPIRATION	NUMBER	IN	
DBID	NUMBER	IN	NULL

Table 7.9: *Create_baseline_template Parameters – 2nd Form*

create_snapshot is both a function and a procedure that defines a new snapshot of performance data that is to be collected. As a function, it simply returns the snapshot ID number. The valid inputs are TYPICAL (default) and ALL. Also remember that calling this action consumes disk space in the SYSAUX tablespace.

ARGUMENT	TYPE	IN / OUT	DEFAULT VALUE
FLUSH_LEVEL	VARCHAR2	IN	'TYPICAL'

Table 7.10: *Create_snapshot Parameter*

drop_baseline is a procedure that deletes an existing baseline. When CASCADE is set to TRUE, it also deletes the pair of associated snapshots for that baseline. Otherwise, the snapshots will remain until as such time as their date and time fall outside the retention period and are then cleaned up automatically.

Advanced Oracle Utilities

ARGUMENT	TYPE	IN / OUT	DEFAULT VALUE
BASELINE_NAME	VARCHAR2	IN	
CASCADE	BOOLEAN	IN	FALSE
DBID	NUMBER	IN	NULL

Table 7.11: *Drop_baseline Parameters*

drop_baseline_template is a procedure that simply deletes an existing baseline template.

ARGUMENT	TYPE	IN / OUT	DEFAULT VALUE
TEMPLATE_NAME	VARCHAR2	IN	
DBID	NUMBER	IN	NULL

Table 7.12: *Drop_baseline_template Parameters*

drop_snapshot_range is a procedure that deletes an existing range of snapshots. The space thus freed can be utilized by future snapshots.

ARGUMENT	TYPE	IN / OUT	DEFAULT VALUE
LOW_SNAP_ID	NUMBER	IN	
HIGH_SNAP_ID	NUMBER	IN	
DBID	NUMBER	IN	NULL

Table 7.13: *Drop_snapshot_range Parameters*

modify_snapshot_settings is a procedure that permits control of three important aspects of snapshots: the frequency of the collection interval, the retention or persistence period, and the number of top SQL captured. While this call does not consume any space per se in the SYSAUX tablespace, it nonetheless defines how often snapshots are collected and for how long they are retained. Therefore, care should be taken when setting these parameters. The retention time is expressed in minutes and must be from 1 day to 100 years, where zero means keep forever. The interval is also expressed in minutes, and must be between 10 minutes and 1 year. The further apart the snapshots are spread, the harder it becomes to diagnose problems, so set accordingly.

ARGUMENT	TYPE	IN / OUT	DEFAULT VALUE
RETENTION	NUMBER	IN	NULL

INTERVAL	NUMBER	IN	NULL
TOPNSQL	NUMBER | VARCHAR2	IN	NULL |
DBID	NUMBER	IN	NULL

Table 7.14: *Modify_snapshot_setting Parameters*

The constants for these minimum and maximum values are as follows:

```
-- Minimum and Maximum values for the
-- Snapshot Interval Setting (in minutes)
MIN_INTERVAL    CONSTANT NUMBER := 10;           /* 10 minutes */
MAX_INTERVAL    CONSTANT NUMBER := 52560000;     /* 100 years */

-- Minimum and Maximum values for the
-- Snapshot Retention Setting (in minutes)
MIN_RETENTION   CONSTANT NUMBER := 1440;         /* 1 day */
MAX_RETENTION   CONSTANT NUMBER := 52560000;     /* 100 years */
```

modify_baseline_window_size is a procedure that permits one to redefine the window size of a sliding or moving window baseline. The window size is expressed in number of days and must be less than or equal to the retention period.

ARGUMENT	TYPE	IN / OUT	DEFAULT VALUE
WINDOW_SIZE	NUMBER	IN	
DBID	NUMBER	IN	NULL

Table 7.15: *Modify_baseline_window_size Parameters*

rename_baseline is a procedure that simply renames an existing baseline.

ARGUMENT	TYPE	IN / OUT	DEFAULT VALUE
OLD_BASELINE_NAME	VARCHAR2	IN	
NEW_BASELINE_NAME	VARCHAR2	IN	
DBID	NUMBER	IN	NULL

Table 7.16: *Rename_baseline Parameters*

Although PL/SQL provides this wonderful programmatic interface, most people will probably use the Oracle Enterprise Manager (OEM) screens for managing snapshots and baselines. Figure 7.1 below shows an example of deleting a snapshot range.

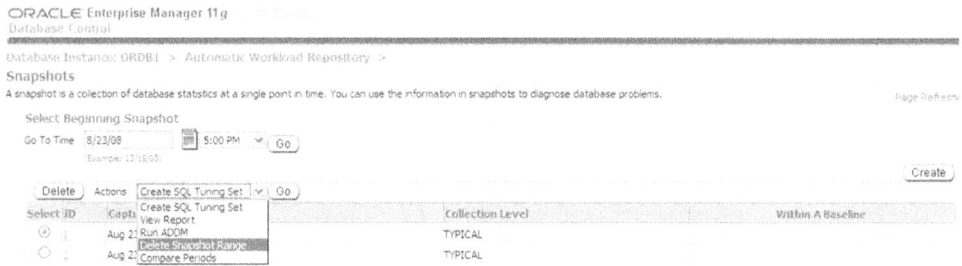

Figure 7.1 *Deleting a Snapshot Range via OEM*

DBMS_WORKLOAD_CAPTURE

Probably one of the most important new features of Oracle 10g and 11g is Real Application Testing (RAT) – the capability to easily capture the entire workload run through a database at a given time interval for replay at a later date and on another server platform or database version if desired. This permits the DBA to perform "what-if" relative comparisons for any number of scenarios. Reliable and repeatable before and after tests can now be performed for any number of database tuning or optimization efforts. For example, before and after performance results of various *init.ora* parameter changes can now be tested.

> This feature in available only in Oracle 10g and higher and specifically only for those who have purchased the Real Application Testing option. Furthermore, to fully leverage the SQL Performance Analyzer (SPA) and SQL Tuning Sets (STS), one must also license both the OEM optional Diagnostic and Tuning Packs.

RAT as a concept is actually quite easy to visualize and comprehend, as shown in Figure 7.2 of the Basic Real Application Testing Architecture.

Tuning Utilities

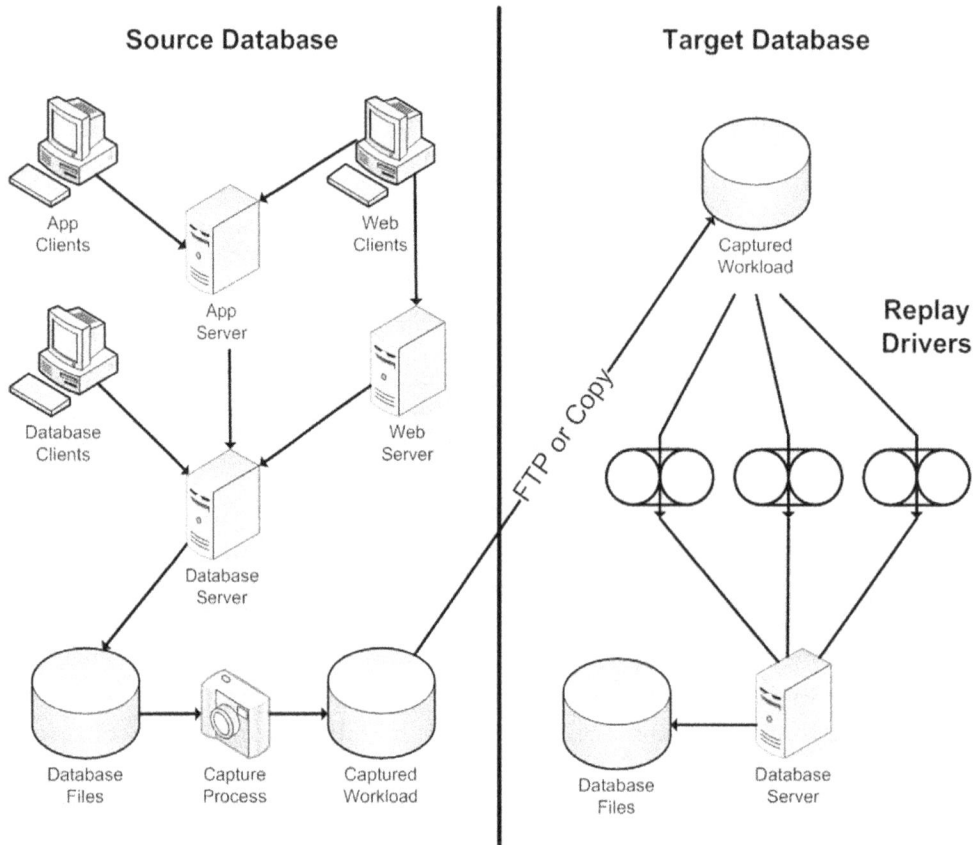

Figure 7.2 *Basic Real Application Testing Architecture*

The key information to note from Figure 7.2 of the RAT Architecture is that no matter what the source, RAT captures all database workloads sent to the database itself. The capture process, of course, strips out database internal workloads, such as extent allocations and other non-external database workloads. Furthermore, the DBA can filter further based upon user, module, program, action and such. The key point is that RAT provides a single place from which to capture any and all desired database workload. The output is files which can then be copied to another database setup and replayed by one or more replay processes.

The first step, and content of this section, is the source database workload capture process provided by the package DBMS_WORKLOAD_CAPTURE.

---

add_filter is a procedure that defines and adds a filtering condition to capture a subset of the entire workload. The attribute must be one of the following: INSTANCE_NUMBER, USER, MODULE, ACTION, PROGRAM or SERVICE. INSTANCE_NUMBER takes a numeric fvalue while the others require string value. Wildcarding is permissible for the fvalue's type string. Filters are only good for the next capture process.

ARGUMENT	TYPE	IN / OUT	DEFAULT VALUE
FNAME	VARCHAR2	IN	
FATTRIBUTE	VARCHAR2	IN	
FVALUE	NUMBER | VARCHAR2	IN	

Table 7.17: *Add_filter Parameters*

delete_capture_info is a procedure that clears the data dictionary views containing metadata for a given workload capture ID. This does not delete the captured workload files, merely the metadata definition.

ARGUMENT	TYPE	IN / OUT	DEFAULT VALUE
CAPTURE_ID	NUMBER	IN	

Table 7.18: *Delete_capture_info Parameter*

delete_filter is a procedure that deletes a pre-existing filter via its filter name. This procedure is deleting existing workload filter metadata; remember that filters expire after a workload capture run.

ARGUMENT	TYPE	IN / OUT	DEFAULT VALUE
FILTER_NAME	VARCHAR2	IN	

Table 7.19: *Delete_filter Parameter*

export_awr is a procedure that exports all the AWR snapshots for a given capture ID. Of course, the AWR snapshots must still exist at the time of this call for the procedure to function properly.

ARGUMENT	TYPE	IN / OUT	DEFAULT VALUE
CAPTURE_ID	NUMBER	IN	

Table 7.20: *Export_awr Parameter*

finish_capture is a procedure that gracefully terminates a workload capture process by signaling existing connections to stop and not permitting future connections to start. The TIMEOUT value is expressed in seconds, where zero means immediate.

ARGUMENT	TYPE	IN / OUT	DEFAULT VALUE
TIMEOUT	NUMBER	IN	30
REASON	VARCHAR2	IN	NULL

Table 7.21: *Finish_capture Parameters*

get_capture_info is a function that imports workload capture meta-data information from a directory and populates that data in the appropriate data dictionary metadata tables. It returns a NUMBER that represents either the *DBA_WORKLOAD_CAPTURE* row inserted or found already existing.

ARGUMENT	TYPE	IN / OUT	DEFAULT VALUE
DIR	VARCHAR2	IN	

Table 7.22: *Get_capture_info Parameters*

import_awr is a function that imports all the AWR snapshots for a given capture ID into a specified schema. The import will fail if the schema contains any tables with the same names as any of the AWR tables. It returns a NUMBER for the database ID.

ARGUMENT	TYPE	IN / OUT	DEFAULT VALUE
CAPTURE_ID	NUMBER	IN	
STAGING_SCHEMA	VARCHAR2	IN	

Table 7.23: *Import_awr Parameters*

report is a function that generates and returns a report for the specified workload capture. The valid report formats are 'HTML' and 'TEXT'. It returns that report as a CLOB.

ARGUMENT	TYPE	IN / OUT	DEFAULT VALUE
CAPTURE_ID	NUMBER	IN	
FORMAT	VARCHAR2	IN	

Table 7.24: *Report Parameters*

start_capture is a procedure that initiates a database wide (minus filtering) workload capture process. The DIR value must name an existing Oracle directory object with sufficient space to hold the generated workload capture files. The duration is specified in seconds, where NULL means until *finish_capture* is called. The *default_action* specifies whether filters are to be applied to INCLUDE or EXCLUDE capture information. *auto_restrict* specifies whether the database will be started in restricted session mode until the capture process begins so as to exclude any extraneous workload from being captured.

ARGUMENT	TYPE	IN / OUT	DEFAULT VALUE
NAME	VARCHAR2	IN	
DIR	VARCHAR2	IN	
DURATION	NUMBER	IN	NULL
DEFAULT_ACTION	VARCHAR2	IN	'INCLUDE'
AUTO_UNRESTIRCT	BOOLEAN	IN	TRUE

Table 7.25: *Start_capture Parameters*

Although PL/SQL provides this wonderful programmatic interface, most people will probably use the Oracle Enterprise Manager (OEM) screens for capturing and replaying of RAT workloads. Figure 7.3 below shows an example of scheduling a one-hour Real Application Testing capture process to start at 10 AM.

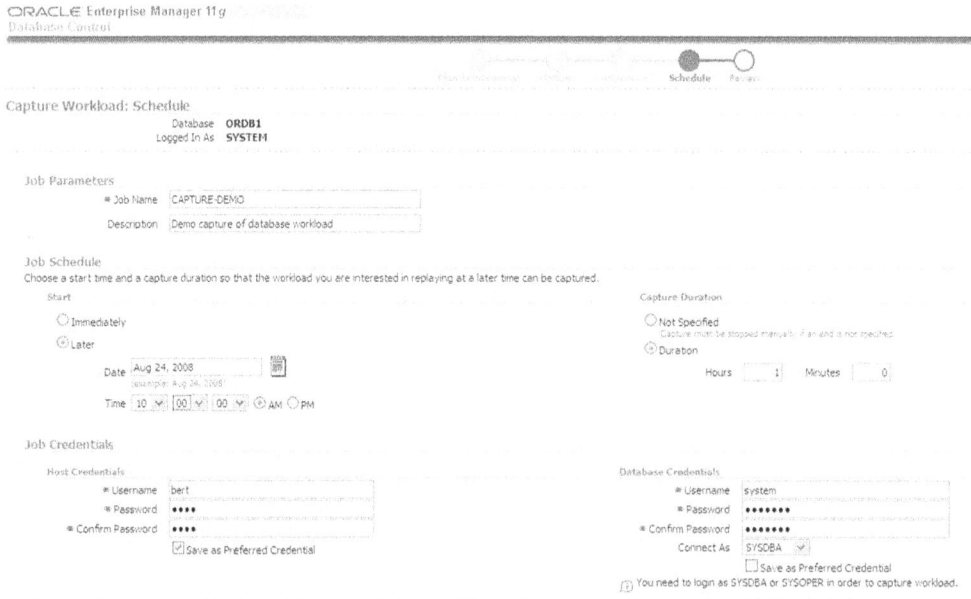

Capture Workload: Schedule

Database **ORDB1**
Logged In As **SYSTEM**

Job Parameters

* Job Name   CAPTURE-DEMO

Description   Demo capture of database workload

Job Schedule

Choose a start time and a capture duration so that the workload you are interested in replaying at a later time can be captured.

Start

○ Immediately

⊙ Later

Date   Aug 24, 2008
(example: Aug 24, 2008)

Time   10 ⌄   00 ⌄   00 ⌄   ⊙ AM ○ PM

Capture Duration

○ Not Specified
Capture must be stopped manually if an end is not specified

⊙ Duration

Hours   1   Minutes   0

Job Credentials

Host Credentials

* Username   bert
* Password   ••••
* Confirm Password   ••••

☑ Save as Preferred Credential

Database Credentials

* Username   system
* Password   •••••••
* Confirm Password   •••••••
Connect As   SYSDBA ⌄

☐ Save as Preferred Credential
ⓘ You need to login as SYSDBA or SYSOPER in order to capture workload.

Figure 7.3 *Scheduling a Real Application Testing Capture via OEM*

DBMS_WORKLOAD_REPLAY

Once the DBA has captured and copied the workload files from source to target, a method is needed for managing the replay of that workload. That is the job of the package DBMS_WORKLOAD_REPLAY. While replays are most often run against a different database, e.g. test vs. production, they can also be replayed on the source if so desired. Furthermore, the source and target can be different database platforms and/or different database versions. This permits a wide range of "what-if" testing scenarios.

> This feature in available only in Oracle 10g and higher and specifically only for those who have purchased the Real Application Testing option. Furthermore, to fully leverage the SQL Performance Analyzer (SPA) and SQL Tuning Sets (STS), one must also license both the OEM optional Diagnostic and Tuning Packs.

The next step, and content of this section, is the target database workload replay process provided by the package DBMS_WORKLOAD_REPLAY.

calibrate is a function that examines a processed workload capture directory of files and estimates/suggests the number of hosts and workload clients required to faithfully reproduce the sample workload characteristics. It returns a report for that advice as a CLOB.

ARGUMENT	TYPE	IN / OUT	DEFAULT VALUE
CAPTURE_DIRECTORY	VARCHAR2	IN	
PROCESS_PER_CPU	BINARY_INTEGER	IN	4
THREADS_PER_PROCESS	BINARY_INTEGER	IN	50

Table 7.26: *Calibrate_Parameters*

cancel_replay is a procedure that terminates a workload replay already in progress. All the workload clients are signaled to stop issuing further captured workload and to exit. A prior call to INITIALIZE_REPLAY, PREPARE_REPLAY or START_REPLAY is a prerequisite.

ARGUMENT	TYPE	IN / OUT	DEFAULT VALUE
ERROR_MESSAGE	VARCHAR2	IN	NULL

Table 7.27: *Cancel_replay Parameters*

delete_replay_info is a procedure that clears the data dictionary views containing metadata for a given workload replay ID. This does not delete the captured workload files, merely the metadata definition.

ARGUMENT	TYPE	IN / OUT	DEFAULT VALUE
REPLAY_ID	NUMBER	IN	

Table 7.28: *Delete_replay_info Parameters*

export_awr is a procedure that exports all the AWR snapshots for a given replay ID. Of course, the AWR snapshots must still exist at the time of this call for the procedure to function properly.

ARGUMENT	TYPE	IN / OUT	DEFAULT VALUE
REPLAY_ID	NUMBER	IN	

Table 7.29: *Export_awr Parameters*

get_replay_info is a function that imports workload capture meta-data information from a directory and populates that data in the appropriate data dictionary metadata tables. It returns a NUMBER that represents either the DBA_WORKLOAD_REPLAYS row inserted or found already existing.

ARGUMENT	TYPE	IN / OUT	DEFAULT VALUE
DIR	VARCHAR2	IN	

Table 7.30: *Get_replay_info Parameters*

import_awr is a function that simply imports all the AWR snapshots for a given capture ID into a specified schema. The import will fail if the schema contains any tables with the same names as any of the AWR tables. It returns a NUMBER for the database ID.

ARGUMENT	TYPE	IN / OUT	DEFAULT VALUE
REPLAY_ID	NUMBER	IN	
STAGING_SCHEMA	VARCHAR2	IN	

Table 7.31: *Import_awr Parameters*

initialize_replay is a procedure that puts the database into the proper state, i.e. INIT FOR REPLAY mode, and loads all the requisite data required for proper replay. The next logical step is *prepare_replay*.

ARGUMENT	TYPE	IN / OUT	DEFAULT VALUE
REPLAY_NAME	VARCHAR2	IN	
REPLAY_DIR	VARCHAR2	IN	

Table 7.32: *Initialize_replay Parameters*

prepare_replay is a procedure that puts the database into the proper state, i.e. PREPARE FOR REPLAY mode, after the requisite data has been loaded via *initialize_replay*. The next logical step is to instantiate one or more external replay clients. The connect time and scale time parameters specify a percentage value to potentially increase or decrease the number of concurrent users.

ARGUMENT	TYPE	IN / OUT	DEFAULT VALUE
SYNCHRONIZATION	BOOLEAN	IN	TRUE
CONNECT_TIME_SCALE	NUMBER	IN	100

ARGUMENT	TYPE	IN / OUT	DEFAULT VALUE
THINK_TIME_SCALE	NUMBER	IN	100
THINK_TIME_AUTO_CONNECT	BOOLEAN	IN	TRUE

Table 7.33: *Prepare_replay Parameters*

process_capture is a procedure that analyzes the workload capture files found in a directory and produces the metadata control files required to replay that workload capture for the current environment. A prime example of when and why this step is necessary is when the source and target databases are different versions (e.g. 10g -> 11g). It creates all new files and does not affect the original captured workload files.

ARGUMENT	TYPE	IN / OUT	DEFAULT VALUE
CAPTURE_DIR	VARCHAR2	IN	

Table 7.34: *Process_capture Parameter*

remap_connection is a procedure that reassigns captured connection information from the source to user specified connection criteria on the target. By default, NULL means to inherit that information from the replay clients' runtime environment. The REPLAY_CONNECTION string can be of any valid format for specifying database connection identifiers.

ARGUMENT	TYPE	IN / OUT	DEFAULT VALUE
CONNECTION_ID	NUMBER	IN	
REPLAY_CONNECTION	VARCHAR2	IN	NULL

Table 7.35: *Remap_connection Parameters*

report is a function that generates and returns a report for the specified workload replay. The valid report formats are 'HTML', 'TEXT' and 'XML'. It returns that report as a CLOB.

ARGUMENT	TYPE	IN / OUT	DEFAULT VALUE
CAPTURE_ID	NUMBER	IN	
FORMAT	VARCHAR2	IN	

Table 7.36: *Report Parameters*

start_replay is a procedure that initiates the workload replay. All external workload replay clients will be signaled to issue captured workload requests. This procedure has no parameters.

Although PL/SQL provides this wonderful programmatic interface, most people will probably simply use the Oracle Enterprise Manager (OEM) screens for capturing and replaying of RAT workloads. Figure 7.4 below shows an example of a verified 20% runtime performance improvement for modifying a single *init.ora* parameter where the captured workload was run with target and source the same but with just a single configuration change.

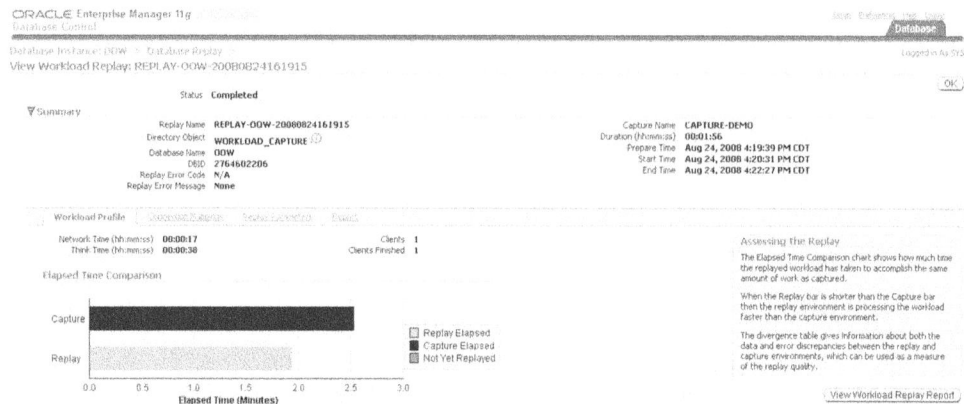

Figure 7.4 *Examining Replay Workload Results via OEM*

DBMS_ADVISOR

Now that Oracle has captured all the raw performance metrics data in the Automatic Workload Repository (AWR), the next logical step, and a great addition to the database, is to provide a comprehensive suite of advisors to offer logical suggestions for problem resolutions likely to yield the best positive results. There are so many advisors that the best way to utilize them is via the OEM screens accessible via Advisor Central as shown here in Figure 7.5. However, the PL/SQL interface will be examined for completeness.

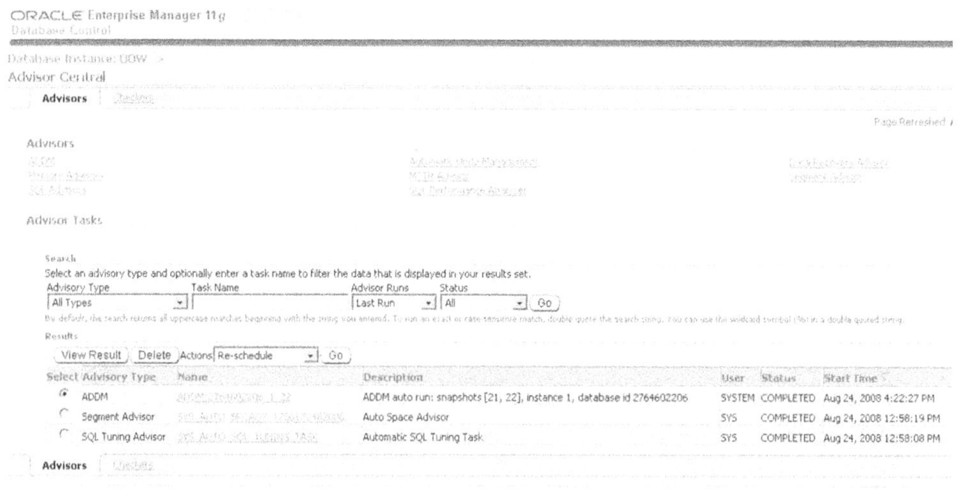

Figure 7.5 *Advisor Central in OEM*

The next chapter on Oracle Advisory & Diagnostic Utilities will examine all the various use cases and techniques for application of this package's many procedures and functions. Thus, it will represent a more task and feature oriented analysis of those capabilities. This section will limit itself to providing a simplistic yet comprehensive presentation of the package calls available, their parameters and return values, if any. Most of this content will assist in better understanding the many varied OEM screens shown in the next chapter by exposing the parameters expected. Thus even if the DBA is going to focus on the OEM screens, there is sufficient reason to skim this interface for a basic foundational understanding and appreciation.

There are some key constants one must be aware of to use this package:

```
-----------------------------------------------------------------
-- Common constants
-----------------------------------------------------------------

ADVISOR_ALL           constant number        := -995;
ADVISOR_CURRENT       constant number        := -996;
ADVISOR_DEFAULT       constant number        := -997;
ADVISOR_UNLIMITED     constant number        := -998;
ADVISOR_UNUSED        constant number        := -999;


-----------------------------------------------------------------
-- SQL Access Advisor constants
-----------------------------------------------------------------

SQLACCESS_GENERAL        constant varchar2(20) := 'SQLACCESS_GENERAL';
```

```
SQLACCESS_OLTP              constant varchar2(20) := 'SQLACCESS_OLTP';
SQLACCESS_WAREHOUSE         constant varchar2(20) := 'SQLACCESS_WAREHOUSE';

SQLACCESS_ADVISOR           constant varchar2(30) := ADV_NAME_SQLACCESS;
TUNE_MVIEW_ADVISOR          constant varchar2(30) := ADV_NAME_TUNEMV;
SQLWORKLOAD_MANAGER         constant varchar2(30) := ADV_NAME_SQLWM;
```

add_sqlwkld_ref is a procedure that creates a link between the current SQL Advisor task and a SQL Workload object. Also, much like baselines, this link or connection makes the referenced SQL Workload object persistent, which means that it is not cleaned up or removed. The IS_STS value indicates whether the workload source is an object (0) or a SQL Tuning Set (1).

ARGUMENT	TYPE	IN / OUT	DEFAULT VALUE
TASK_NAME	VARCHAR2	IN	
WORKLOAD_NAME	VARCHAR2	IN	
IS_STS	NUMBER	IN	0

Table 7.37: *Add_sqlwkld_ref Parameters*

add_sts_ref is a procedure that creates a link between the current SQL Advisor task and a SQL Tuning Set. Also, much like baselines, this link or connection makes the referenced SQL Tuning Set persistent, i.e. is not cleaned up or removed.

ARGUMENT	TYPE	IN / OUT	DEFAULT VALUE
TASK_NAME	VARCHAR2	IN	
WORKLOAD_NAME	VARCHAR2	IN	
IS_STS	VARCHAR2	IN	

Table 7.38: *Add_sts_ref Parameters*

cancel_task is a procedure that terminates the currently executing operation. This operation may take a few seconds to reply as it performs a soft interrupt which the SQL Access Advisor periodically polls for.

ARGUMENT	TYPE	IN / OUT	DEFAULT VALUE
TASK_NAME	VARCHAR2	IN	

Table 7.39: *Cancel_task Parameters*

copy_sqlwkld_tosts is a procedure that replicates the contents of a SQL Workload object to a SQL Tuning Set. The caller must create and modify SQL Tuning Set privileges. The IMPORT_MODE must be either APPEND, NEW or REPLACE.

ARGUMENT	TYPE	IN / OUT	DEFAULT VALUE
WORKLOAD_NAME	VARCHAR2	IN	
STS_NAME	VARCHAR2	IN	
IMPORT_MODE	VARCHAR2	IN	'NEW'

Table 7.40: *Copy_sqlwkld_tosts Parameters*

create_file is a procedure that creates an external file for scripts and reports from a supplied CLOB variable. All formatting must be embedded within that CLOB variable. Of course, one must have server access to the file locations desired as controlled by the *init.ora* parameter *utl_file_dir*.

ARGUMENT	TYPE	IN / OUT	DEFAULT VALUE
BUFFER	CLOB	IN	
LOCATION	VARCHAR2	IN	
FILENAME	VARCHAR2	IN	

Table 7.41: *Create_file Parameters*

create_object is an overloaded procedure where parameter *ATTR5* is optional, which is not required in one version of the call, and creates a new task object. These are generally used as input data for advisors.

ARGUMENT	TYPE	IN / OUT	DEFAULT VALUE
TASK_NAME	VARCHAR2	IN	
OBJECT_TYPE	VARCHAR2	IN	
ATTR1	VARCHAR2	IN	NULL
ATTR2	VARCHAR2	IN	NULL
ATTR3	VARCHAR2	IN	NULL
ATTR4	CLOB	IN	NULL
{ ATTR5 }	VARCHAR2	IN	NULL
OBJECT_ID	NUMBER	OUT	

Table 7.42: *Create_object Parameters*

Note that the various attribute parameters have different permissible values depending upon the object type as shown in Table 7.43 below.

OBJECT_TYPE	ATTR1	ATTR2	ATTR3	ATTR4
TABLESPACE	Tablespace Name	NULL	NULL	NULL
TABLE	Schema Name	Table Name	NULL	NULL
INDEX	Schema Name	Index Name	NULL	NULL
TABLE PARTITION	Schema Name	Table Name	Partition Name	NULL
INDEX PARTITION	Schema Name	Index Name	Subpartition Name	NULL
TABLE SUBPARTITION	Schema Name	Table Name	Partition Name	NULL
INDEX SUBPARTITION	Schema Name	Index Name	Subpartition Name	NULL
LOB	Schema Name	Segment Name	NULL	NULL
LOB PARTITION	Schema Name	Segment Name	Partition Name	NULL
LOB SUBPARTITION	Schema Name	Segment Name	Subpartition Name	NULL

Table 7.43: *Advisor Object Types Attributes*

create_task is an overloaded procedure where parameter *task_id* is optional, i.e. not required in one version of the call and creates a new advisor task. The predefined templates constants are SQLACCESS_OLTP, SQLACCESS_WAREHOUSE and SQLACCESS_GENERAL.

ARGUMENT	TYPE	IN / OUT	DEFAULT VALUE
ADVISOR_NAME	VARCHAR2	IN	
{ TASK_ID }	NUMBER	OUT	
TASK_NAME	VARCHAR2	IN	
TASK_DESC	VARCHAR2	IN	NULL
TEMPLATE	VARCHAR2	IN	NULL
IS_TEMPLATE	VARCHAR2	IN	'FALSE'
HOW_CREATED	VARCHAR2	IN	NULL

Table 7.44: *Create_task Parameters*

delete_sts_ref is a procedure that drops the link between the current SQL Advisor task and a SQL Tuning Set. The *sts_name* parameter supports wildcarding.

ARGUMENT	TYPE	IN / OUT	DEFAULT VALUE
TASK_NAME	VARCHAR2	IN	
STS_OWNER	VARCHAR2	IN	
STS_NAME	VARCHAR2	IN	

Table 7.45: *Delete_sts_ref Parameters*

delete_task is a procedure that drops an existing advisor task. The *task_name* parameter supports wildcarding.

ARGUMENT	TYPE	IN / OUT	DEFAULT VALUE
TASK_NAME	VARCHAR2	IN	

Table 7.46: *Delete_task Parameters*

execute_task is an overloaded procedure that executes the advisor analysis for the named task. Note that task execution is synchronous action, so control is not returned until it is completed. The short form of *execute_task* takes the following single parameter:

ARGUMENT	TYPE	IN / OUT	DEFAULT VALUE
TASK_NAME	VARCHAR2	IN	

Table 7.47: *Execute_task Parameter, Short Form*

Whereas the longer version of *execute_task* procedure accepts all of the following parameters:

ARGUMENT	TYPE	IN / OUT	DEFAULT VALUE
TASK_NAME	VARCHAR2	IN	
EXECUTION_TYPE	VARCHAR2	IN	NULL
EXECUTION_NAME	VARCHAR2	IN	NULL
EXECUTION_PARAMS	dbms_advisor.argList	IN	NULL
EXECUTION_DESC	VARCHAR2	IN	NULL

Table 7.48: *Execute_task Parameters, Long Form*

Where the data type for *dbms_advisor.orgList* is as follows:

```
TYPE argList IS TABLE OF sys.wri$_adv_parameters.value%TYPE;

CREATE TABLE SYS.WRI$_ADV_PARAMETERS
(
  TASK_ID       NUMBER                       NOT NULL,
  NAME          VARCHAR2(30 BYTE)            NOT NULL,
  VALUE         VARCHAR2(4000 BYTE)          NOT NULL,
  DATATYPE      NUMBER                       NOT NULL,
  FLAGS         NUMBER                       NOT NULL,
  DESCRIPTION   VARCHAR2(9 BYTE)
);
```

get_task_report is a function that generates and returns a report for the specified task. The only valid report type is TEXT, and the only valid levels are BASIC, TYPICAL and ALL. It returns that report as a CLOB.

ARGUMENT	TYPE	IN / OUT	DEFAULT VALUE
TASK_NAME	VARCHAR2	IN	
TYPE	VARCHAR2	IN	'TEXT'
LEVEL	VARCHAR2	IN	'TYPICAL'
SECTION	VARCHAR2	IN	'ALL'
OWNER_NAME	VARCHAR2	IN	NULL
EXECUTION_NAME	VARCHAR2	IN	NULL
OBJECT_ID	NUMBER	IN	NULL

Table 7.49: *Get_task_report Parameters*

get_task_script is a function that generates and returns a SQL*Plus compatible script for the specified task. The only valid script types are UNDO and IMPLEMENTATION. For the REC_ID and SCT_ID, a zero or

ADVISOR_ALL means all recommendations and actions should be generated. It returns that script as a CLOB.

ARGUMENT	TYPE	IN / OUT	DEFAULT VALUE
TASK_NAME	VARCHAR2	IN	
TYPE	VARCHAR2	IN	'IMPLEMENTATION
REC_ID	NUMBER	IN	NULL
ACT_ID	NUMBER	IN	NULL
OWNER_NAME	VARCHAR2	IN	NULL
EXECUTION_NAME	VARCHAR2	IN	NULL
OBJECT_ID	NUMBER	IN	NULL

Table 7.50: *Get_task_script Parameters*

implement_task is a procedure that simply and directly implements the recommendations for the specified task.

ARGUMENT	TYPE	IN / OUT	DEFAULT VALUE
TASK_NAME	VARCHAR2	IN	
REC_ID	NUMBER	IN	NULL
EXIT_ON_ERROR	BOOLEAN	IN	NULL

Table 7.51: *Implement_task Parameters*

interrupt_task is a procedure that performs a graceful termination, or a normal exit, of the currently executing task.

ARGUMENT	TYPE	IN / OUT	DEFAULT VALUE
TASK_NAME	VARCHAR2	IN	

Table 7.52: *Interrupt_task Parameters*

mark_recommendation is a procedure that marks a recommendation for possible implementation or import. The possible actions are ACCEPT< IGNORE and REJECT.

ARGUMENT	TYPE	IN / OUT	DEFAULT VALUE
TASK_NAME	VARCHAR2	IN	
ID	NUMBER	IN	
ACTION	VARCHAR2	IN	

Table 7.53: *Mark_recommendation Parameters*

quick_tune is a procedure that creates and executes a task that analyzes a SQL statement and generates recommendations which are saved back in the repository. Note that parameter *Attr1* must be a single SQL statement to tune and/or optimize. *Attr2* is most often the schema executing the SQL statement which is under review.

ARGUMENT	TYPE	IN / OUT	DEFAULT VALUE
ADVISOR_NAME	VARCHAR2	IN	
TASK_NAME	VARCHAR2	IN	
ATTR1	CLOB	IN	
ATTR2	VARCHAR2	IN	NULL
ATTR3	NUMBER	IN	NULL
TASK_OR_TEMPLATE	VARCHAR2	IN	NULL

Table 7.54: *Quick_tune Parameters*

reset_task is a procedure that resets a task back to its initial state. All intermediate data and recommendations are deleted.

ARGUMENT	TYPE	IN / OUT	DEFAULT VALUE
TASK_NAME	VARCHAR2	IN	

Table 7.55: *Reset_task Parameter*

set_default_task_parameter is an overloaded procedure that will modify a task's and/or template's default value for a user specified parameter. This change is not reflected in any already existing tasks, but instead only new tasks created from that point on. Refer to Table 7.58 for parameters and their values.

ARGUMENT	TYPE	IN / OUT	DEFAULT VALUE
TASK_NAME	VARCHAR2	IN	
PARAMETER	NUMBER	IN	
VALUE	VARCHAR2 | NUMBER	IN	

Table 7.56: *Set_default_task_Parameters*

set_task_parameter is an overloaded procedure that will modify a task's and/or template's default value for a user specified parameter. This change is reflected in pre-existing tasks.

ARGUMENT	TYPE	IN / OUT	DEFAULT VALUE
TASK_NAME	VARCHAR2	IN	
PARAMETER	NUMBER	IN	
VALUE	VARCHAR2 | NUMBER	IN	

Table 7.57: *Set_task_parameter Parameters*

PARAMETER	DATA TYPE	VALUES
ANALYSIS_SCOPE	STRINGLIST	ALL | EVALUATION | INDEX | MVIEW | PARTITION | TABLE
CREATION_COST	STRING	TRUE | FALSE
DAYS_TO_EXPIRE	NUMBER	30 | 0 <= integer <= 2147483647 | ADVISOR_UNLIMITED | ADVISOR_UNUSED
DEF_EM_TEMPLATE	STRING	SQLACCESS_EMTASK | task_name | template_name
DEF_INDEX_OWNER	STRING	schema name | ADVISOR_UNUSED
DEF_INDEX_TABLESPACE	STRING	tablespace name | ADVISOR_UNUSED
DEF_MVIEW_OWNER	STRING	schema name | ADVISOR_UNUSED

PARAMETER	DATA TYPE	VALUES
DEF_MVIEW_TABLESPACE	STRING	tablespace name | ADVISOR_UNUSED
DEF_MVLOG_TABLSPACE	STRING	tablespace name | ADVISOR_UNUSED
DEF_PARTITION_TABLESPACE	STRING	tablespace name | ADVISOR_UNUSED
DML_VOLATILITY	STRING	TRUE | FALSE
END_TIME	STRING	MM-DD-YYY HH24:MI:SS
EVALUATION_ONLY	STRING	TRUE | FALSE
EXECUTION_TYPE	STRINGLIST	FULL | INDEX_ONLY | MVIEW_ONLY | MVLOG_ONLY
IMPLEMENT_EXIT_ON_ERROR	STRING	TRUE | FALSE
INDEX_NAME_TEMPLATE	STRING	Literal <= 22 | TABLE | TASK_ID | SEQ
INVALID_ACTION_LIST	STRINGLIST	action list | ADVISOR_UNUSED
INVALID_MODULE_LIST	STRINGLIST	module list | ADVISOR_UNUSED
INVALID_SQLSTRING_LIST	STRINGLIST	SQL string list | ADVISOR_UNUSED
INVALID_USERNAME_LIST	STRINGLIST	username list | ADVISOR_UNUSED
JOURNALING	NUMBER	UNUSED | FATAL | ERROR | WARNING | INFORMATION | INFORMATION2 | INFORMATION3 | INFORMATION4 | INFORMATION5 | INFORMATION6
LIMITED_PARTITION_SCHEMES	NUMBER	1 <= integer <= 10 | ADVISOR_UNUSED
MAX_NUMBER_PARTITIONS	NUMBER	1 <= integer <= 4294967295 | ADVISOR_UNUSED | ADVISOR_UNLIMITED
MODE	STRING	LIMITED | COMPREHENSIVE

PARAMETER	DATA TYPE	VALUES
MVIEW_NAME_TEMPLATE	STRING	Literal <= 22 | TABLE | TASK_ID | SEQ
ORDER_LIST	STRINGLIST	BUFFER_GETS | CPU_TIME | DISK_READS | ELAPSED_TIME | EXECUTIONS | OPTIMIZER_COST | I/O | PRIORITY
PARTITION_NAME_TEMPLATE	STRING	Literal <= 22 | TABLE | TASK_ID | SEQ
PARTITIONING_GOAL	STRING	PERFROMANCE
PARTITIONING_TYPES	STRING	RANGE | HASH
RANKING_MEASURE	STRINGLIST	BUFFER_GETS | CPU_TIME | DISK_READS | ELAPSED_TIME | EXECUTIONS | OPTIMIZER_COST | I/O | PRIORITY
RECOMMEND_MV_EXACT_TEXT _MATCH	STRING	TRUE | FALSE
RECOMMENDED_TABLESPACES	STRING	TRUE | FALSE
REFRESH_MODE	STRING	ON_DEMAND | ON_COMMIT
REPORT_DATE_FORMAT	STRING	MM-DD-YYY HH24:MI:SS
SHOW_RETAINS	STRING	TRUE | FALSE
SQL_LIMIT	NUMBER	1 <= integer <= 2147483647 | ADVISOR_UNLIMITED | ADVISOR_UNUSED
START_TIME	STRING	MM-DD-YYY HH24:MI:SS
STORAGE_CHANGE	NUMBER	any integer | ADVISOR_UNLIMITED
TIME_LIMIT	NUMBER	720 | 1 <= integer <= 10000 | ADVISOR_UNLIMITED
VALID_ACTION_LIST	STRINGLIST	action name(s) | ADVISOR_UNUSED
VALID_MODULE_LIST	STRINGLIST	module name(s) | ADVISOR_UNUSED
VALID_SQLSTRING_LIST	STRINGLIST	SQL command(s) | ADVISOR_UNUSED

PARAMETER	DATA TYPE	VALUES
VALID_TABLE_LIST	STRINGLIST	schema.table Name(s) | ADVISOR_UNUSED
VALID_USERNAME_LIST	STRINGLIST	user name(s) | ADVISOR_UNUSED
WORKLOAD_SCOPE	STRING	FULL | PARTIAL

Table 7.58: *SET_*_TASK Parameters and Values*

tune_mview is an overloaded procedure that examines decomposing a single materialized view or more materialized views whose combination equals the original in content but whose performance for fast refreshes and/or queries may be superior.

ARGUMENT	TYPE	IN / OUT	DEFAULT VALUE
TASK_NAME	VARCHAR2	IN OUT	
MV_CREATE_STMT	CLOB | VARCHAR2	IN	

Table 7.59: *Tune_mview Parameters*

update_object is procedure that updates an existing task object which is generally used as input data for advisors. Refer back to Table 7.43 for the various attribute parameters' different permissible values depending upon object type.

ARGUMENT	TYPE	IN / OUT	DEFAULT VALUE
TASK_NAME	VARCHAR2	IN	
OBJECT_ID	NUMBER	IN	
ATTR1	VARCHAR2	IN	NULL
ATTR2	VARCHAR2	IN	NULL
ATTR3	VARCHAR2	IN	NULL
ATTR4	CLOB	IN	NULL
ATTR5	VARCHAR2	IN	NULL

Table 7.60: *Update_object Parameters*

update_rec_attributes is a procedure that updates and/or modifies a recommendation's owner, name and tablespace. The task must have executed at least once successfully prior to this call. The valid attribute name values are OWNER, NAME and TABLESPACE.

ARGUMENT	TYPE	IN / OUT	DEFAULT VALUE
TASK_NAME	VARCHAR2	IN	
REC_ID	NUMBER	IN	
ACTION_ID	NUMBER	IN	
ATTRIBUTE_NAME	VARCHAR2	IN	
VALUE	VARCHAR2	IN	

Table 7.61: *Update_rec_attributes Parameters*

update_task_attributes is a procedure that will modify a task's and/or template's values for a user specified attributes.

ARGUMENT	TYPE	IN / OUT	DEFAULT VALUE
TASK_NAME	VARCHAR2	IN	
NEW_NAME	VARCHAR2	IN	NULL
DESCRIPTION	VARCHAR2	IN	NULL
READ_ONLY	VARCHAR2	IN	NULL
IS_TEMPLATE	VARCHAR2	IN	NULL
HOW_CREATED	VARCHAR2	IN	NULL

Table 7.62: *Update_task_attributes Parameters*

SQL Tuning

DBMS_ADVANCED_REWRITE

One key feature for large-scale data warehousing and reporting system is the ability of the Oracle optimizer to employ query rewrites such that queries process against aggregate or summary tables and, thereby, reduce execution time and resources consumed. This process can appear externally automatic, but a great many prerequisites must first be in place, including:

- Materialized views defined and populated to contain summary or aggregate data for base tables along lines or criteria to be queried upon

- Materialized views kept fresh, or current, for base table inserts and updates

- Statistics captured

- *Init.ora* parameter *query_rewrite_enabled=true*

- Dimension database objects defined for that aggregate hierarchy

---

When all these things have been done, then it is quite possible for the Oracle optimizer to rewrite queries for generally significant orders of improvement.

Like many other advanced features within Oracle, there are Oracle Enterprise Manager (OEM) screens to support such activities. Likewise, there is a programmatic PL/SQL API as well. This section will detail that interface, even though it is highly unlikely that one will find occasion or need to call it directly.

alter_rewrite_equivalence is a procedure that modifies the equivalence declaration mode to one that is specified. Note, however, that Oracle does not recommend directly calling this procedure. The legitimate values for the rewrite mode are DISABLED, TEXT_MATCH, GENERAL and RECURSIVE.

ARGUMENT	TYPE	IN / OUT	DEFAULT VALUE
NAME	VARCHAR2	IN	
REWRITE_MODE	VARCHAR2	IN	-

Table 7.63: *alter_rewrite_equivalence Parameters*

build_safe_rewrite_equivalence is a procedure that enables the optimizer to utilize sub-materialized views to improve top-level materialized view optimization performance. It has no parameters and Oracle does not recommend directly calling this procedure either.

declare_rewrite_equivalence is an overloaded procedure that forces the optimizer to view a source and destination statement as functionally equivalent for the duration of that definition. These equivalence rewrites are honored, or implemented, by the Oracle query optimizer when the *init.ora* parameter *query_rewrite_integrity* is either TRUSTED or STALE_TOLERATED. The legitimate values for the rewrite mode are DISABLED, TEXT_MATCH, GENERAL and RECURSIVE.

ARGUMENT	TYPE	IN / OUT	DEFAULT VALUE
NAME	VARCHAR2	IN	
SOURCE_STMT	VARCHAR2	IN	
DESTINATION_STMT	VARCHAR2	IN	
VALIDATE	BOOLEAN	IN	TRUE
REWRITE_MODE	VARCHAR2	IN	'TEXT_MATCH'

Table 7.64: *Declare_rewrite_equilvalence Parameters*

drop_rewrite_equivalence is a procedure that deletes a query rewrite equivalence definition and thus renders it inactive.

ARGUMENT	TYPE	IN / OUT	DEFAULT VALUE
NAME	VARCHAR2	IN	

Table 7.65: *Drop_rewrite_equivalence Parameter*

validate_rewrite_equivalence is a procedure that simply verifies or validates the legitimacy of a query rewrite equivalence definition.

ARGUMENT	TYPE	IN / OUT	DEFAULT VALUE
NAME	VARCHAR2	IN	

Table 7.66: *Validate_rewrite_equivalence Parameter*

DBMS_STATS

With the Oracle 10g switch from the rule-based optimizer to cost based optimization, the needs and use cases for collecting statistics has increased both in terms of complexity and frequency of need. Statistics collection and management has become a first tier maintenance issue and one that the smart DBA will stay on top of at all times.

In the past, the SQL command ANALYZE was used as the primary interface to statistics and histogram collection. But once 10g switched to cost-based optimization and thus promoted statistics to a primary care issue with many varied and subtle complexities, the ANALYZE command became insufficient for general use. It did not easily support many of those advanced needs, and thus it became secondary in nature to the DBMS_STATS package. The only time the ANALYZE command is preferable is if one wants to validate or list chained rows.

Statistics has become such an important aspect that the DBMS_STATS package is one of the largest general purpose PL/SQL packages most DBAs will use on a regular basis. As such, the explanation section below is very long since it covers several dozen procedures and functions. It will be worth one's time to know the key ones and to at least be familiar with the others. As with most of the PL/SQL API calls, many are accessible via screens within Oracle Enterprise Manager (OEM), but many DBAs will find ample occasion to include such calls in their database maintenance scripts as well. So again, please look these over.

The following data types and constants are used by the DBMS_STATS package:

```
-- types for minimum/maximum values and histogram endpoints
type numarray is varray(256) of number;
type datearray is varray(256) of date;
type chararray is varray(256) of varchar2(4000);
type rawarray is varray(256) of raw(2000);
type fltarray is varray(256) of binary_float;
type dblarray is varray(256) of binary_double;

type StatRec is record (
  epc    number,
  minval raw(2000),
  maxval raw(2000),
  bkvals numarray,
  novals numarray,
  chvals chararray,
  eavs   number);

-- type for objects whose statistics may be gathered
-- make sure to maintain satisfy_obj_filter when ObjectElem type
-- is changed
type ObjectElem is record (
  ownname     varchar2(32),      -- owner
  objtype     varchar2(6),       -- 'TABLE' or 'INDEX'
  objname     varchar2(32),      -- table/index
  partname    varchar2(32),      -- partition
  subpartname varchar2(32)       -- subpartition
);
type ObjectTab is table of ObjectElem;


-- type for displaying stats difference report
type DiffRepElem is record (
  report      clob,              -- stats difference report
  maxdiffpct number);           -- max stats difference (percentage)
type DiffRepTab is table of DiffRepElem;
```

```
-- oracle decides whether to collect stats for indexes or not
AUTO_CASCADE CONSTANT BOOLEAN := null;

-- oracle decides when to invalidate depended cursors
AUTO_INVALIDATE CONSTANT BOOLEAN := null;

-- constant used to indicate auto sample size algorithms should
-- be used.
AUTO_SAMPLE_SIZE        CONSTANT NUMBER := 0;

-- constant to indicate use of the system default degree of
-- parallelism determined based on the initialization parameters.
DEFAULT_DEGREE          CONSTANT NUMBER := 32767;
-- force serial execution if the object is relatively small.
-- use the system default degree of parallelism otherwise.
AUTO_DEGREE             CONSTANT NUMBER := 32768;


--
-- Default values for key parameters passed to DBMS_STATS procedures
-- These values are specified in the DEFAULT clause when declaring the
-- corresponding parameter in any of the DBMS_STATS procedures.
--
DEFAULT_CASCADE          CONSTANT BOOLEAN  := null;
DEFAULT_DEGREE_VALUE     CONSTANT NUMBER   := 32766;
DEFAULT_ESTIMATE_PERCENT CONSTANT NUMBER   := 101;
DEFAULT_METHOD_OPT       CONSTANT VARCHAR2(1) := 'Z';
DEFAULT_NO_INVALIDATE    CONSTANT BOOLEAN  := null;
DEFAULT_GRANULARITY      CONSTANT VARCHAR2(1) := 'Z';
DEFAULT_PUBLISH          CONSTANT BOOLEAN  := true;
DEFAULT_INCREMENTAL      CONSTANT BOOLEAN  := false;
DEFAULT_STALE_PERCENT    CONSTANT NUMBER   := 10;
DEFAULT_AUTOSTATS_TARGET CONSTANT VARCHAR2(1) := 'Z';
```

alter_stats_history_retention is a procedure that modifies the retention period for statistics history. This retention period is expressed in days with valid values between 1 and 365000. In addition, there are three special values: 0 = never saved, 1 = never automatically purged, and NULL = set back to the default value.

ARGUMENT	TYPE	IN / OUT	DEFAULT VALUE
RETENTION	NUMBER	IN	

Table 7.67: *Alter_stats_history_retention Parameter*

convert_raw_value is an overloaded procedure that converts user supplied min or max values to an equivalent data-type specific value in the Oracle internal representation.

ARGUMENT	TYPE	IN / OUT	DEFAULT VALUE
RAWVAL	RAW	IN	
RESVAL	BINARY_FLOAT | BINARY_DOUBLE | DATE | NUMBER | VARCHAR2	OUT	

Table 7.68: *Convert_raw_value Parameters*

convert_raw_value_nvarchar is a procedure that converts user supplied min or max values to an equivalent data-type specific value in the Oracle internal representation.

ARGUMENT	TYPE	IN / OUT	DEFAULT VALUE
RAWVAL	RAW	IN	
RESVAL	NVARCHAR2	OUT	

Table 7.69: *Convert_raw_value_nvarchar Parameters*

convert_raw_value_rowid is a procedure that converts user supplied min or max values to an equivalent data-type specific value in the Oracle internal representation.

ARGUMENT	TYPE	IN / OUT	DEFAULT VALUE
RAWVAL	RAW	IN	
RESVAL	ROWID	OUT	

Table 7.70: *Convert_raw_value_rowid Parameters*

copy_table_stats is a procedure that copies the table, partition or subpartition statistics from source to destination and which can apply a scaling factor in the process.

ARGUMENT	TYPE	IN / OUT	DEFAULT VALUE
OWNNAME	VARCHAR2	IN	
TABNAME	VARCHAR2	IN	
SRCPARTNAME	VARCHAR2	IN	
DSTPARTNAME	VARCHAR2	IN	
SCALE_FACOTR	VARCHAR2	IN	1
FORCE	BOOLEAN	IN	FALSE

Table 7.71: *Copy_table_stats Parameters*

create_extended_stats is a function that creates a column level statistics entry for either a user specified column, column group, or an expression of columns in a table. It returns the name of this new entry as a VARCHAR2. The *extension* parameter should be either a column group list or column expression. There are some restrictions on the extensions, such as not on virtual columns, tables owned by SYS, clustered or index organized tables, a column group between 2 and 32 columns, or # extensions <= MAX (20, 10% of the total non-virtual columns). Furthermore, expressions must contain at least one column and cannot contain a subquery.

ARGUMENT	TYPE	IN / OUT	DEFAULT VALUE
OWNNAME	VARCHAR2	IN	
TABNAME	VARCHAR2	IN	
EXTENSION	VARCHAR2	IN	

Table 7.72: *Create_extended_stats Parameters*

create_stat_table is a procedure that creates in the OWNNAME's schema a table named STATTAB which can be used to hold statistics generated by procedures and functions in the DBMS_STATS package.

ARGUMENT	TYPE	IN / OUT	DEFAULT VALUE
OWNNAME	VARCHAR2	IN	
STATTAB	VARCHAR2	IN	
TBLSPACE	VARCHAR2	IN	NULL

Table 7.73: *Create_stat_table Parameters*

delete_column_stats is a procedure that drops column level statistics for the specified column, column group or column expression.

ARGUMENT	TYPE	IN / OUT	DEFAULT VALUE
OWNNAME	VARCHAR2	IN	
TABNAME	VARCHAR2	IN	
COLNAME	VARCHAR2	IN	
PARTNAME	VARCHAR2	IN	NULL
STATTAB	VARCHAR2	IN	NULL
STATID	VARCHAR2	IN	NULL
CASCADE_PARTS	BOOLEAN	IN	TRUE
STATOWN	VARCHAR2	IN	NULL
NO_INVALIDATE	BOOLEAN	IN	AUTO_INVALIDATE
FORCE	BOOLEAN	IN	FALSE
COL_STAT_TYPE	VARCHAR2	IN	'ALL'

Table 7.74: *Delete_column_stats Parameters*

delete_database_prefs is a procedure that deletes statistics preferences. The valid values for the *pname* parameter are CASCADE, DEGREE, ESTIMATE_PERCENT, METHOD_OPT, NO_INVALIDATE, GRANULARITY, PUBLISH, INCREMENTAL and STALE_PERCENT.

ARGUMENT	TYPE	IN / OUT	DEFAULT VALUE
PNAME	VARCHAR2	IN	
ADD_SYS	BOOLEAN	IN	FALSE

Table 7.75: *Delete_database_prefs Parameters*

delete_database_stats is a procedure that drops the statistics for all tables in the database.

ARGUMENT	TYPE	IN / OUT	DEFAULT VALUE
STATTAB	VARCHAR2	IN	NULL
STATID	VARCHAR2	IN	NULL
STATOWN	VARCHAR2	IN	NULL
NO_INVALIDATE	BOOLEAN	IN	AUTO_INVALIDATE
FORCE	BOOLEAN	IN	FALSE

Table 7.76: *Delete_database_stats Parameters*

delete_dictionary_stats is a procedure that drops the statistics for all data dictionary tables in the database like those owned by SYS, SYSTEM and other RDBMS component schemas.

ARGUMENT	TYPE	IN / OUT	DEFAULT VALUE
STATTAB	VARCHAR2	IN	NULL
STATID	VARCHAR2	IN	NULL
STATOWN	VARCHAR2	IN	NULL
NO_INVALIDATE	BOOLEAN	IN	AUTO_INVALIDATE
FORCE	BOOLEAN	IN	FALSE

Table 7.77: *Delete_dictionary_stats Parameters*

delete_fixed_object_stats is a procedure that drops the statistics for all SGA memory residents or fixed tables in the database, i.e. the X$ tables.

ARGUMENT	TYPE	IN / OUT	DEFAULT VALUE
STATTAB	VARCHAR2	IN	NULL
STATID	VARCHAR2	IN	NULL
STATOWN	VARCHAR2	IN	NULL
NO_INVALIDATE	BOOLEAN	IN	AUTO_INVALIDATE
FORCE	BOOLEAN	IN	FALSE

Table 7.78: *Delete_fixed_object_stats Parameters*

delete_index_stats is a procedure that drops index level statistics for the specified index.

ARGUMENT	TYPE	IN / OUT	DEFAULT VALUE
OWNNAME	VARCHAR2	IN	
INDNAME	VARCHAR2	IN	
PARTNAME	VARCHAR2	IN	NULL
STATTAB	VARCHAR2	IN	NULL
STATID	VARCHAR2	IN	NULL
CASCADE_PARTS	BOOLEAN	IN	TRUE
STATOWN	VARCHAR2	IN	NULL
NO_INVALIDATE	BOOLEAN	IN	AUTO_INVALIDATE
FORCE	BOOLEAN	IN	FALSE

Table 7.79: *Delete_index_stats Parameters*

delete_pending_stats is a procedure that deletes any pending statistics such as those that have been collected but not yet published for the specified table.

ARGUMENT	TYPE	IN / OUT	DEFAULT VALUE
OWNNAME	VARCHAR2	IN	USER
TABNAME	VARCHAR2	IN	

Table 7.80: *Delete_pending_stats Parameters*

delete_schema_prefs is a procedure that deletes statistics preferences for the schema specified. The valid values for the *pname* parameter are CASCADE, DEGREE, ESTIMATE_PERCENT, METHOD_OPT, NO_INVALIDATE, GRANULARITY, PUBLISH, INCREMENTAL and STALE_PERCENT.

ARGUMENT	TYPE	IN / OUT	DEFAULT VALUE
OWNNAME	VARCHAR2	IN	
PNAME	VARCHAR2	IN	

Table 7.81: *Delete_schema_prefs Parameters*

delete_schema_stats is a procedure that drops statistics for the specified schema.

ARGUMENT	TYPE	IN / OUT	DEFAULT VALUE
OWNNAME	VARCHAR2	IN	
STATTAB	VARCHAR2	IN	NULL
STATID	VARCHAR2	IN	NULL
STATOWN	VARCHAR2	IN	NULL
NO_INVALIDATE	BOOLEAN	IN	AUTO_INVALIDATE
FORCE	BOOLEAN	IN	FALSE

Table 7.82: *Delete_schema_stats Parameters*

delete_system_stats is a procedure that drops workload statistics. It essentially sets the state back to that of NOWORKLOAD.

ARGUMENT	TYPE	IN / OUT	DEFAULT VALUE
STATTAB	VARCHAR2	IN	NULL
STATID	VARCHAR2	IN	NULL
STATOWN	VARCHAR2	IN	NULL

Table 7.83: *Delete_system_stats Parameters*

delete_table_prefs is a procedure that deletes statistics preferences for the table specified. The valid values for the *pname* parameter are CASCADE, DEGREE, ESTIMATE_PERCENT, METHOD_OPT, NO_INVALIDATE, GRANULARITY, PUBLISH, INCREMENTAL and STALE_PERCENT.

ARGUMENT	TYPE	IN / OUT	DEFAULT VALUE
OWNNAME	VARCHAR2	IN	
TABNAME	VARCHAR2	IN	
PNAME	VARCHAR2	IN	

Table 7.84: *Delete_table_prefs Parameters*

delete_table_stats is a procedure that drops table level statistics for the specified table.

ARGUMENT	TYPE	IN / OUT	DEFAULT VALUE
OWNNAME	VARCHAR2	IN	
TABNAME	VARCHAR2	IN	
PARTNAME	VARCHAR2	IN	NULL
STATTAB	VARCHAR2	IN	NULL
STATID	VARCHAR2	IN	NULL
CASCADE_PARTS	BOOLEAN	IN	TRUE
CASCADE_COLUMNS	BOOLEAN	IN	TRUE
CASCADE_INDEXES	BOOLEAN	IN	TRUE
STATOWN	VARCHAR2	IN	NULL
NO_INVALIDATE	BOOLEAN	IN	AUTO_INVALIDATE
FORCE	BOOLEAN	IN	FALSE

Table 7.85: *Delete_table_stats Parameters*

diff_table_stats_in_history is a function that compares the collected statistics from two different historical time periods and reports on the differences. It returns those differences as multiple occurrences of type DiffRepTab (refer to data types section above).

ARGUMENT	TYPE	IN / OUT	DEFAULT VALUE
OWNNAME	VARCHAR2	IN	
TABNAME	VARCHAR2	IN	
TIME1	TIMESTAMP WITH TIME ZONE	IN	
TIME2	TIMESTAMP WITH TIME ZONE	IN	NULL
PCTTHRESHOLD	NUMBER	IN	10

Table 7.86: *Diff_table_stats_in_history Parameters*

diff_table_stats_in_pending is a function that compares the pending statistics with collected statistics from the current period and reports on the differences. It returns those differences as multiple occurrences of type DiffRepTab.

ARGUMENT	TYPE	IN / OUT	DEFAULT VALUE
OWNNAME	VARCHAR2	IN	
TABNAME	VARCHAR2	IN	
TIMESTAMP	VARCHAR2	IN	NULL
PCTTHRESHOLD	NUMBER	IN	10

Table 7.87: *Diff_table_stats_in_pending Parameters*

diff_table_stats_in_stattab is a function that compares statistics from two different sources where those sources can be two different statistics tables: a single statistics table but for different STATID references, or a statistics table and the data dictionary. It returns those differences as multiple occurrences of type DiffRepTab (refer to data types section above).

ARGUMENT	TYPE	IN / OUT	DEFAULT VALUE
OWNNAME	VARCHAR2	IN	
TABNAME	VARCHAR2	IN	
STATTAB1	VARCHAR2	IN	
STATTAB2	VARCHAR2	IN	NULL
PCTTHRESHOLD	NUMBER	IN	10
STATIS1		IN	NULL
STATID2		IN	NULL
STATTAB1OWN		IN	NULL
STATTAB2OWN		IN	NULL

Table 7.88: *Diff_table_stats_in_stattab Parameters*

drop_extended_stats is a procedure that drops a column level statistics entry for either a user specified column, column group, or an expression of columns in a table.

ARGUMENT	TYPE	IN / OUT	DEFAULT VALUE
OWNNAME	VARCHAR2	IN	
TABNAME	VARCHAR2	IN	
EXTENSION	VARCHAR2	IN	

Table 7.89: *Drop_extended_stats Parameters*

drop_stat_table is a procedure that drops user specified statistics table STATTAB which can be used to hold statistics generated by procedures and functions in the DBMS_STATS package.

ARGUMENT	TYPE	IN / OUT	DEFAULT VALUE
OWNNAME	VARCHAR2	IN	
STATTAB	VARCHAR2	IN	

Table 7.90: *Drop_stat_table Parameters*

export_column_stats is a procedure that copies column level statistics for the specified column, column group or column expression to a user defined statistics table.

ARGUMENT	TYPE	IN / OUT	DEFAULT VALUE
OWNNAME	VARCHAR2	IN	
TABNAME	VARCHAR2	IN	
COLNAME	VARCHAR2	IN	
PARTNAME	VARCHAR2	IN	NULL
STATTAB	VARCHAR2	IN	
STATID	VARCHAR2	IN	NULL
STATOWN	VARCHAR2	IN	NULL

Table 7.91: *Export_column_stats Parameters*

export_database_prefs is a procedure that exports the statistics preferences of all the tables, except those owned by Oracle such as SYS and SYSTEM.

ARGUMENT	TYPE	IN / OUT	DEFAULT VALUE
STATTAB	VARCHAR2	IN	
STATID	VARCHAR2	IN	NULL
STATOWN	VARCHAR2	IN	NULL
ADD_SYS	BOOLEAN	IN	FALSE

Table 7.92: *Export_database_prefs Parameters*

export_database_stats is a procedure that copies the statistics of all the tables, except those owned by Oracle such as SYS and SYSTEM, into the user specified statistics table.

ARGUMENT	TYPE	IN / OUT	DEFAULT VALUE
STATTAB	VARCHAR2	IN	
STATID	VARCHAR2	IN	NULL
STATOWN	VARCHAR2	IN	NULL

Table 7.93: *Export_database_stats Parameters*

export_dictionary_stats is a procedure that copies the statistics of all the data dictionary tables, except those owned by Oracle such as SYS and SYSTEM, into the user specified statistics table.

ARGUMENT	TYPE	IN / OUT	DEFAULT VALUE
STATTAB	VARCHAR2	IN	
STATID	VARCHAR2	IN	NULL
STATOWN	VARCHAR2	IN	NULL

Table 7.94: *Export_dictionary_stats Parameters*

export_fixed_object_stats is a procedure that copies the statistics of the SGA memory's fixed tables – the X$ tables – into the user specified statistics table.

ARGUMENT	TYPE	IN / OUT	DEFAULT VALUE
STATTAB	VARCHAR2	IN	
STATID	VARCHAR2	IN	NULL
STATOWN	VARCHAR2	IN	NULL

Table 7.95: *Export_fixed_object_stats Parameters*

export_index_stats is a procedure that copies the statistics of the specified index into the user specified statistics table.

ARGUMENT	TYPE	IN / OUT	DEFAULT VALUE
OWNNAME	VARCHAR2	IN	
INDNAME	VARCHAR2	IN	
PARTNAME	VARCHAR2	IN	NULL
STATTAB	VARCHAR2	IN	
STATID	VARCHAR2	IN	NULL
STATOWN	VARCHAR2	IN	NULL

Table 7.96: *Export_index_stats Parameters*

export_pending_stats is a procedure that copies the pending statistics of the specified table into the user specified statistics table.

ARGUMENT	TYPE	IN / OUT	DEFAULT VALUE
OWNNAME	VARCHAR2	IN	USER
TABNAME	VARCHAR2	IN	
STATTAB	VARCHAR2	IN	
STATID	VARCHAR2	IN	NULL
STATOWN	VARCHAR2	IN	USER

Table 7.97: *Export_pending_stats Parameters*

export_schema_prefs is a procedure that copies all the statistics preferences of the specified schema into the user specified statistics table.

ARGUMENT	TYPE	IN / OUT	DEFAULT VALUE
OWNNAME	VARCHAR2	IN	
STATTAB	VARCHAR2	IN	
STATID	VARCHAR2	IN	NULL
STATOWN	VARCHAR2	IN	NULL

Table 7.98: *Export_schema_prefs Parameters*

export_schema_stats is a procedure that copies all the statistics for all of the objects of the specified schema into the user specified statistics table.

ARGUMENT	TYPE	IN / OUT	DEFAULT VALUE
OWNNAME	VARCHAR2	IN	
STATTAB	VARCHAR2	IN	
STATID	VARCHAR2	IN	NULL
STATOWN	VARCHAR2	IN	NULL

Table 7.99: *Export_schema_stats Parameters*

export_system_stats is a procedure that copies all the system statistics into the user specified statistics table.

ARGUMENT	TYPE	IN / OUT	DEFAULT VALUE
STATTAB	VARCHAR2	IN	
STATID	VARCHAR2	IN	NULL
STATOWN	VARCHAR2	IN	NULL

Table 7.100: *Export_system_stats Parameters*

export_table_prefs is a procedure that copies all the statistics preferences of the specified table into the user specified statistics table.

ARGUMENT	TYPE	IN / OUT	DEFAULT VALUE
OWNNAME	VARCHAR2	IN	
TABNAME	VARCHAR2	IN	
STATTAB	VARCHAR2	IN	
STATID	VARCHAR2	IN	NULL
STATOWN	VARCHAR2	IN	NULL

Table 7.101: *Export_table_prefs Parameters*

export_table_stats is a procedure that copies all the statistics of the specified table into the user specified statistics table.

ARGUMENT	TYPE	IN / OUT	DEFAULT VALUE
OWNNAME	VARCHAR2	IN	
TABNAME	VARCHAR2	IN	
PARTNAME	VARCHAR2	IN	NULL
STATTAB	VARCHAR2	IN	
STATID	VARCHAR2	IN	NULL
CASCADE	VARCHAR2	IN	TRUE
STATOWN	VARCHAR2	IN	NULL

Table 7.102: *Export_table_stats Parameters*

flush_database_monitoring_info is a procedure that flushes all the in-memory monitoring information currently in the dictionary. It has no parameters.

gather_database_stats is an overloaded procedure to gather statistics for all of the database objects.

ARGUMENT	TYPE	IN / OUT	DEFAULT VALUE
ESTIMATE_PERCENT	NUMBER	IN	ESTIMATE_PERCENT
BLOCK_SAMPLE	BOOLEAN	IN	FALSE
METHOD_OPT	VARCHAR2	IN	METHOD_OPT
DEGREE	NUMBER	IN	DEGREE
GRANULARITY	VARCHAR2	IN	GRANULARITY
CASCADE	BOOLEAN	IN	CASCADE
STATTAB	VARCHAR2	IN	NULL
STATID	VARCHAR2	IN	NULL
OTPIONS	VARCHAR2	IN	GATHER
{ OBJLIST }	OBJECTTAB	OUT	
STATOWN	VARCHAR2	IN	NULL
GATHER_SYS	BOOLEAN	IN	TRUE
NO_INVALIDATE	BOOLEAN	IN	NO_INVALIDATE
OBJ_FILTER_LIST	OBJECTTAB	IN	NULL

Table 7.103: *Gather_database_stats Parameters*

gather_dictionary_stats is an overloaded procedure to gather statistics for all of the database objects for dictionary schemas such as SYS, SYSTEM and other RDBMS components.

ARGUMENT	TYPE	IN / OUT	DEFAULT VALUE
COMP_ID	VARCHAR2	IN	NULL
ESTIMATE_PERCENT	NUMBER	IN	ESTIMATE_PERCENT
BLOCK_SAMPLE	BOOLEAN	IN	FALSE
METHOD_OPT	VARCHAR2	IN	METHOD_OPT
DEGREE	NUMBER	IN	DEGREE
GRANULARITY	VARCHAR2	IN	GRANULARITY
CASCADE	BOOLEAN	IN	CASCADE
STATTAB	VARCHAR2	IN	NULL
STATID	VARCHAR2	IN	NULL
OTPIONS	VARCHAR2	IN	GATHER
{ OBJLIST }	OBJECTTAB	OUT	
STATOWN	VARCHAR2	IN	NULL
NO_INVALIDATE	BOOLEAN	IN	NO_INVALIDATE
OBJ_FILTER_LIST	OBJECTTAB	IN	NULL

Table 7.104: *Gather_dictionary_stats Parameters*

gather_fixed_object_stats is a procedure to gather statistics for all of the SGA memory tables known as fixed objects, i.e. the x$ tables.

ARGUMENT	TYPE	IN / OUT	DEFAULT VALUE
STATTAB	VARCHAR2	IN	NULL
STATID	VARCHAR2	IN	NULL
STATOWN	VARCHAR2	IN	NULL
NO_INVALIDATE	BOOLEAN	IN	NO_INVALIDATE

Table 7.105: *Gather_fixed_object_stats Parameters*

gather_index_stats is a procedure to gather all the index statistics for the user specified schema. Certain types of indexes cannot be analyzed in parallel such as cluster indexes, domain indexes and bitmap join indexes.

ARGUMENT	TYPE	IN / OUT	DEFAULT VALUE
OWNNAME	VARCHAR2	IN	
INDNAME	VARCHAR2	IN	
PARTNAME	VARCHAR2	IN	NULL
ESTIMATE_PERCENT	NUMBER	IN	ESTIMATE_PERCENT
STATTAB	VARCHAR2	IN	NULL
STATID	VARCHAR2	IN	NULL
DEGREE	NUMBER	IN	DEGREE
GRANULARITY	VARCHAR2	IN	GRANULARITY
NO_INVALIDATE	BOOLEAN	IN	NO_INVALIDATE
FORCE	BOOLEAN	IN	FALSE

Table 7.106: *Gather_index_stats Parameters*

gather_schema_stats is an overloaded procedure to gather statistics for all of the database objects for the user specified schema.

ARGUMENT	TYPE	IN / OUT	DEFAULT VALUE
OWNNAME	VARCHAR2	IN	
ESTIMATE_PERCENT	NUMBER	IN	ESTIMATE_PERCENT
BLOCK_SAMPLE	BOOLEAN	IN	FALSE
METHOD_OPT	VARCHAR2	IN	METHOD_OPT
DEGREE	NUMBER	IN	DEGREE
GRANULARITY	VARCHAR2	IN	GRANULARITY
CASCADE	BOOLEAN	IN	CASCADE

STATTAB	VARCHAR2	IN	NULL
STATID	VARCHAR2	IN	NULL
OTPIONS	VARCHAR2	IN	GATHER
{ OBJLIST }	OBJECTTAB	OUT	
STATOWN	VARCHAR2	IN	NULL
NO_INVALIDATE	BOOLEAN	IN	NO_INVALIDATE
FORCE	BOOLEAN	IN	FALSE
OBJ_FILTER_LIST	OBJECTTAB	IN	NULL

Table 7.107: *Gather_scheuma_stats Parameters*

gather_system_stats is a procedure that gathers system statistics. The interval is expressed in minutes. The gather mode must be one of the following: NOWORKLOAD, INTERVAL, START or STOP.

ARGUMENT	TYPE	IN / OUT	DEFAULT VALUE
GATHER_MODE	VARCHAR2	IN	NOWORKLOAD
INTERVAL	INTEGER	IN	NULL
STATTAB	VARCHAR2	IN	NULL
STATID	VARCHAR2	IN	NULL
STATOWN	VARCHAR2	IN	NULL

Table 7.108: *Gather_system_stats Parameters*

gather_table_stats is a procedure to gather the table and index statistics for the user specified table. Certain types of indexes cannot be analyzed in parallel such as cluster indexes, domain indexes and bitmap join indexes. However, table level statistics gathering will make heavy use of the parallel degree.

ARGUMENT	TYPE	IN / OUT	DEFAULT VALUE
OWNNAME	VARCHAR2	IN	
TABNAME	VARCHAR2	IN	
PARTNAME	VARCHAR2	IN	NULL
ESTIMATE_PERCENT	NUMBER	IN	ESTIMATE_PERCENT
BLCOK_SAMPLE	BOOELAN	IN	FALSE
METHOD_OPT	VARCHAR2	IN	METHOD_OPT
DEGREE	NUMBER	IN	DEGREE
GRANULARITY	VARCHAR2	IN	GRANULARITY
CASCADE	BOOLEAN	IN	CASCADE
STATTAB	VARCHAR2	IN	NULL

STATID	VARCHAR2	IN	NULL
STATOWN	VARCHAR2	IN	NULL
NO_INVALIDATE	BOOLEAN	IN	NO_INVALIDATE
FORCE	BOOLEAN	IN	FALSE

Table 7.109: *Gather_table_stats Parameters*

generate_stats is a procedure to create object statistics from prior statistics collections of related objects, mainly b-tree and bitmap indexes, of the specified object and schema.

ARGUMENT	TYPE	IN / OUT	DEFAULT VALUE
OWNNAME	VARCHAR2	IN	
OBJNAME	VARCHAR2	IN	
ORGANIZED	VARCHAR2	IN	7
FORCE	VARCHAR2	IN	FALSE

Table 7.110: *Generate_stats Parameters*

get_column_stats is an overloaded procedure that retrieves all the column level information for both normal and user defined statistics. The normal call to *get_column_stats* is as follows:

ARGUMENT	TYPE	IN / OUT	DEFAULT VALUE
OWNNAME	VARCHAR2	IN	
TABNAME	VARCHAR2	IN	
COLNAME	VARCHAR2	IN	
PARTNAME	VARCHAR2	IN	NULL
STATTAB	VARCHAR2	IN	NULL
STATID	VARCHAR2	IN	NULL
DISTINCT	NUMBER	OUT	
DENSITY	NUMBER	OUT	
NULLCNT	NUMBER	OUT	
SREC	StatRec	OUT	
AVGLEN	NUMBER	OUT	
STATOWN	VARCHAR2	IN	NULL

Table 7.111: *Get_column_stats Parameters, Normal Call*

The user defined statistics call to *get_column_stats* is as follows:

ARGUMENT	TYPE	IN / OUT	DEFAULT VALUE
OWNNAME	VARCHAR2	IN	
TABNAME	VARCHAR2	IN	
COLNAME	VARCHAR2	IN	
PARTNAME	VARCHAR2	IN	NULL
STATTAB	VARCHAR2	IN	NULL
STATID	VARCHAR2	IN	NULL
EXT_STATS	RAW	OUT	
STATTYPOWN	VARCHAR2	OUT	NULL
STATTYPNAME	VARCHAR2	OUT	NULL
STATOWN	VARCHAR2	IN	NULL

Table 7.112: *Get_column_stats Parameter, User Defined Statistics Call*

get_index_stats is an overloaded procedure that retrieves all the index level information for both normal and user defined statistics. The normal call to *get_index_stats* is as follows:

ARGUMENT	TYPE	IN / OUT	DEFAULT VALUE
OWNNAME	VARCHAR2	IN	
INDNAME	VARCHAR2	IN	
PARTNAME	VARCHAR2	IN	NULL
STATTAB	VARCHAR2	IN	NULL
STATID	VARCHAR2	IN	NULL
NUMROWS	NUMBER	OUT	
NUMLBLKS	NUMBER	OUT	
NUMDIST	NUMBER	OUT	
AVGLBLK	NUMBER	OUT	
AVGDBLK	NUMBER	OUT	
CLSTFCT	NUMBER	OUT	
INDLEVEL	NUMBER	OUT	
STATOWN	VARCHAR2	IN	NULL
{ GUESSQ }	NUMBER	OUT	
CACHEDBLK	NUMBER	OUT	
CACHEHIT	NUMBER	OUT	

Table 7.113: *Get_index_stats Parameters, Normal Call*

The user defined statistics call to *get_index_stats* is as follows:

ARGUMENT	TYPE	IN / OUT	DEFAULT VALUE
OWNNAME	VARCHAR2	IN	
INDNAME	VARCHAR2	IN	
PARTNAME	VARCHAR2	IN	NULL
STATTAB	VARCHAR2	IN	NULL
STATID	VARCHAR2	IN	NULL
EXT_STATS	RAW	OUT	
STATTYPOWN	VARCHAR2	OUT	NULL
STATTYPNAME	VARCHAR2	OUT	NULL
STATOWN	VARCHAR2	IN	NULL
CACHEDBLK	NUMBER	OUT	
CACHEHIT	NUMBER	OUT	

Table 7.114: *Get_index_stats Parameters, User Defined Statistics Call*

get_prefs is a function that returns the default value of the user specified preference. The valid values for the *pname* parameter are CASCADE, DEGREE, ESTIMATE_PERCENT, METHOD_OPT, NO_INVALIDATE, GRANULARITY, PUBLISH, INCREMENTAL and STALE_PERCENT.

ARGUMENT	TYPE	IN / OUT	DEFAULT VALUE
PNAME	VARCHAR2	IN	
OWNNAME	VARCHAR2	IN	NULL
TABNAME	VARCHAR2	IN	NULL

Table 7.115: *Get_prefs Parameters*

get_stats_history_availability is a function that returns the oldest timestamp for which history is available. It has no parameters and returns that value as a TIMESTAMP WITH TIMEZONE.

get_stats_history_retention is a function that returns the current retention value. It has no parameters and returns that value as a NUMBER.

get_system_stats is a procedure that retrieves the system statistics either from the user specified statistics table or the data dictionary when STABTAB is NULL. The status can be any of the following: COMPLETED, AUTOGATHERING, MANUALGATHERING and BADSTATS. The legal

---

values for *pname* include iotfrspeed, ioseektim, sreadtim, mreadtim, cpuspeed, cpuspeednw, mbrc, maxthr and slavthr.

ARGUMENT	TYPE	IN / OUT	DEFAULT VALUE
STATUS	VARCHAR2	OUT	
DSTART	DATE	OUT	
DSTOP	DATE	OUT	
PNAME	VARCHAR2	IN	
PVALUE	NUMBER	OUT	
STATTAB	VARCHAR2	IN	NULL
STATID	VARCHAR2	IN	NULL
STATDOWN	VARCHAR2	IN	NULL

Table 7.116: *Get_system_stats Parameters*

get_table_stats is a procedure that retrieves all the table level information for the user specified table.

ARGUMENT	TYPE	IN / OUT	DEFAULT VALUE
OWNNAME	VARCHAR2	IN	
TABNAME	VARCHAR2	IN	
PARTNAME	VARCHAR2	IN	NULL
STATTAB	VARCHAR2	IN	NULL
STATID	VARCHAR2	IN	NULL
NUMROWS	NUMBER	OUT	
NUMBLKS	NUMBER	OUT	
AVGRLEN	NUMBER	OUT	
STATOWN	VARCHAR2	IN	NULL
CACHEDBLK	NUMBER	OUT	
CACHEHIT	NUMBER	OUT	

Table 7.117: *Get_table_stats Parameters*

The *export_column_stats* procedure copies column level statistics for the specified column, column group or column expression from a user defined statistics table to the data dictionary.

ARGUMENT	TYPE	IN / OUT	DEFAULT VALUE
OWNNAME	VARCHAR2	IN	
TABNAME	VARCHAR2	IN	
COLNAME	VARCHAR2	IN	
PARTNAME	VARCHAR2	IN	NULL
STATTAB	VARCHAR2	IN	
STATID	VARCHAR2	IN	NULL
STATOWN	VARCHAR2	IN	NULL
NO_INVALIDATE	BOOLEAN	IN	NO_INVALIDATE
FORCE	BOOLEAN	IN	FALSE

Table 7.118: *Export_column_stats Parameters*

import_database_prefs is a procedure that imports the statistics preferences of all the tables, except those own by Oracle such as SYS and SYSTEM.

ARGUMENT	TYPE	IN / OUT	DEFAULT VALUE
STATTAB	VARCHAR2	IN	
STATID	VARCHAR2	IN	NULL
STATOWN	VARCHAR2	IN	NULL
ADD_SYS	BOOLEAN	IN	FALSE

Table 7.119: *Import_database_prefs Parameters*

import_database_stats is a procedure that copies the statistics of all the tables except those owned by Oracle, such as SYS and SYSTEM, from the user specified statistics table into the data dictionary.

ARGUMENT	TYPE	IN / OUT	DEFAULT VALUE
STATTAB	VARCHAR2	IN	
STATID	VARCHAR2	IN	NULL
STATOWN	VARCHAR2	IN	NULL
NO_INVALIDATE	BOOLEAN	IN	NO_INVALIDATE
FORCE	BOOLEAN	IN	FALSE

Table 7.120: *Import_database_stats Parameters*

import_dictionary_stats is a procedure that copies the statistics of all the data dictionary tables – those owned by Oracle, such as SYS and SYSTEM – from the user specified statistics table into the data dictionary.

ARGUMENT	TYPE	IN / OUT	DEFAULT VALUE
STATTAB	VARCHAR2	IN	
STATID	VARCHAR2	IN	NULL
STATOWN	VARCHAR2	IN	NULL
NO_INVALIDATE	BOOLEAN	IN	NO_INVALIDATE
FORCE	BOOLEAN	IN	FALSE

Table 7.121: *Import_dictionary_stats Parameters*

import_fixed_object_stats is a procedure that copies the statistics of the SGA memory's fixed tables – the x$ tables – from the user specified statistics table into the data dictionary.

ARGUMENT	TYPE	IN / OUT	DEFAULT VALUE
STATTAB	VARCHAR2	IN	
STATID	VARCHAR2	IN	NULL
STATOWN	VARCHAR2	IN	NULL
NO_INVALIDATE	BOOLEAN	IN	NO_INVALIDATE
FORCE	BOOLEAN	IN	FALSE

Table 7.122: *Import_fixed_object_stats Parameters*

import_index_stats is a procedure that copies the statistics of the specified index from the user specified statistics table into the data dictionary.

ARGUMENT	TYPE	IN / OUT	DEFAULT VALUE
OWNNAME	VARCHAR2	IN	
INDNAME	VARCHAR2	IN	
PARTNAME	VARCHAR2	IN	NULL
STATTAB	VARCHAR2	IN	
STATID	VARCHAR2	IN	NULL
STATOWN	VARCHAR2	IN	NULL
NO_INVALIDATE	BOOLEAN	IN	NO_INVALIDATE
FORCE	BOOLEAN	IN	FALSE

Table 7.123: *Import_index_stats Parameters*

import_schema_prefs is a procedure that copies all the statistics preferences from the specified schema into the user specified statistics table to the data dictionary.

ARGUMENT	TYPE	IN / OUT	DEFAULT VALUE
OWNNAME	VARCHAR2	IN	
STATTAB	VARCHAR2	IN	
STATID	VARCHAR2	IN	NULL
STATOWN	VARCHAR2	IN	NULL

Table 7.124: *Import_schema_prefs Parameters*

import_schema_stats is a procedure that copies all the statistics for all of the objects of the specified schema from the user specified statistics table to the data dictionary.

ARGUMENT	TYPE	IN / OUT	DEFAULT VALUE
OWNNAME	VARCHAR2	IN	
STATTAB	VARCHAR2	IN	
STATID	VARCHAR2	IN	NULL
STATOWN	VARCHAR2	IN	NULL
NO_INVALIDATE	BOOLEAN	IN	NO_INVALIDATE
FORCE	BOOLEAN	IN	FALSE

Table 7.125: *Import_schema_stats Parameters*

import_system_stats is a procedure that copies all the system statistics from the user specified statistics table to the data dictionary.

ARGUMENT	TYPE	IN / OUT	DEFAULT VALUE
STATTAB	VARCHAR2	IN	
STATID	VARCHAR2	IN	NULL
STATOWN	VARCHAR2	IN	NULL

Table 7.126: *Import_system_stats Parameters*

import_table_prefs is a procedure that copies all the statistics preferences of the specified table from the user specified statistics table into the data dictionary.

ARGUMENT	TYPE	IN / OUT	DEFAULT VALUE
OWNNAME	VARCHAR2	IN	
TABNAME	VARCHAR2	IN	
STATTAB	VARCHAR2	IN	
STATID	VARCHAR2	IN	NULL
STATOWN	VARCHAR2	IN	NULL

Table 7.127: *Import_table_prefs Parameters*

import_table_stats is a procedure that copies all the statistics of the specified table from the user specified statistics table to the data dictionary.

ARGUMENT	TYPE	IN / OUT	DEFAULT VALUE
OWNNAME	VARCHAR2	IN	
TABNAME	VARCHAR2	IN	
PARTNAME	VARCHAR2	IN	NULL
STATTAB	VARCHAR2	IN	
STATID	VARCHAR2	IN	NULL
CASCADE	VARCHAR2	IN	TRUE
STATOWN	VARCHAR2	IN	NULL
NO_INVALIDATE	BOOLEAN	IN	NO_INVALIDATE
FORCE	BOOLEAN	IN	FALSE

Table 7.128: *Import_table_stats Parameters*

lock_partition_stats is a procedure to lock the table statistics for the user specified partition.

ARGUMENT	TYPE	IN / OUT	DEFAULT VALUE
OWNNAME	VARCHAR2	IN	
TABNAME	VARCHAR2	IN	
PARTNAME	VARCHAR2	IN	

Table 7.129: *Lock_partition_stats Parameters*

lock_schema_stats is a procedure to lock all the table statistics for the user specified schema.

ARGUMENT	TYPE	IN / OUT	DEFAULT VALUE
OWNNAME	VARCHAR2	IN	

Table 7.130: *Lock_schema_stats Parameter*

lock_table_stats is a procedure to lock the table statistics for the user specified table.

ARGUMENT	TYPE	IN / OUT	DEFAULT VALUE
OWNNAME	VARCHAR2	IN	
TABNAME	VARCHAR2	IN	

Table 7.131: *Lock_table_stats Parameters*

prepare_column_value is an overloaded procedure that converts user supplied min, max or histogram endpoint values to an equivalent data-type specific value in the Oracle internal representation.

ARGUMENT	TYPE	IN / OUT	DEFAULT VALUE
SREC	StatRec	IN/OUT	
CHARVALS |	|CHARRAY |	IN	
DATEVALS |	DATEARRAY |		
DBLVALS |	DBLARRAY |		
FLTVALS |	FLTARRAY |		
NUMVALS |	NUMARRAY |		
RAWVALS	RAWARRAY		

Table 7.132: *Prepare_column_value Parameters*

convert_raw_value_nvarchar is a procedure that converts user supplied min, max or histogram endpoint values to an equivalent data-type specific value in the Oracle internal representation.

ARGUMENT	TYPE	IN / OUT	DEFAULT VALUE
SREC	StatRec	IN/OUT	
NVMIN	NVARCHAR2	IN	
NVMAX	NVARCHAR2	IN	

Table 7.133: *Convert_raw_value_nvarchar Parameters*

convert_raw_value_rowid is a procedure that converts user supplied min, max or histogram endpoint values to an equivalent data-type specific value in the Oracle internal representation.

ARGUMENT	TYPE	IN / OUT	DEFAULT VALUE
SREC	StatRec	IN/OUT	
RWMIN	ROWID	IN	
RWMAX	ROWID	IN	

Table 7.134: *Convert_raw_value_rowid Parameters*

publis_pending_stats is a procedure that publishes the pending statistics of the specified table.

ARGUMENT	TYPE	IN / OUT	DEFAULT VALUE
OWNNAME	VARCHAR2	IN	USER
TABNAME	VARCHAR2	IN	
NO_INVALIDATE	BOOLEAN	IN	NO_INVALIDATE
FORCE	BOOLEAN	IN	FALSE

Table 7.135: *Publis_pending_stats Parameters*

purge_stats is a procedure that purges or deletes all the statistics saved in the dictionary before the user specified date and time. If the time specified is NULL, then it purges everything older than the current time minus the statistics retention period.

ARGUMENT	TYPE	IN / OUT	DEFAULT VALUE
BEFORE_TIME	TIMESTAMP WITH TIMEZONE	IN	

Table 7.136: *Purge_stats Parameter*

reset_global_prefs_defaults is a procedure that sets all global statistics preferences to their Oracle default values. There are no parameters.

reset_param_defaults is a procedure that sets all the statistics parameters to their Oracle recommended values. There are no parameters.

---

restore_database_stats is a procedure that restores the statistics state of all tables for the entire database to that of a user specified date and time.

ARGUMENT	TYPE	IN / OUT	DEFAULT VALUE
AS_OF_TIMESTAMP	TIMESTAMP WITH TIMEZONE	IN	
FORCE	BOOLEAN	IN	FALSE
NO_INVALIDATE	BOOLEAN	IN	NO_INVALIDATE

Table 7.137: *Restore_data_stats Parameters*

restore_dictionary_stats is a procedure that restores the statistics state of all the data dictionary tables, like those owned by SYS, SYSTEM and other RDBMS components, to that of a user specified date and time.

ARGUMENT	TYPE	IN / OUT	DEFAULT VALUE
AS_OF_TIMESTAMP	TIMESTAMP WITH TIMEZONE	IN	
FORCE	BOOLEAN	IN	FALSE
NO_INVALIDATE	BOOLEAN	IN	NO_INVALIDATE

Table 7.138: *Restore_dictionary_stats Parameters*

restore_fixed_object_stats is a procedure that restores the statistics state of all the SGA memory or fixed objects, i.e. the x$ tables, to that of a user specified date and time.

ARGUMENT	TYPE	IN / OUT	DEFAULT VALUE
AS_OF_TIMESTAMP	TIMESTAMP WITH TIMEZONE	IN	
FORCE	BOOLEAN	IN	FALSE
NO_INVALIDATE	BOOLEAN	IN	NO_INVALIDATE

Table 7.139: *Restore_fixed_object_stats Parameters*

restore_schema_stats is a procedure that restores the statistics state of all tables for the user specified schema to that of a user specified date and time.

ARGUMENT	TYPE	IN / OUT	DEFAULT VALUE
OWNAME	VARCHAR2	IN	
AS_OF_TIMESTAMP	TIMESTAMP WITH TIMEZONE	IN	
FORCE	BOOLEAN	IN	FALSE
NO_INVALIDATE	BOOLEAN	IN	NO_INVALIDATE

Table 7.140: *Restore_schema_stats Parameters*

restore_system_stats is a procedure that restores the system statistics state to that of a user specified date and time.

ARGUMENT	TYPE	IN / OUT	DEFAULT VALUE
AS_OF_TIMESTAMP	TIMESTAMP WITH TIMEZONE	IN	

Table 7.141: *Restore_system_stats Parameters*

restore_table_stats is a procedure that restores the statistics state of the user specified table and its associated indexes for the user specified schema to that of a user specified date and time.

ARGUMENT	TYPE	IN / OUT	DEFAULT VALUE
OWNAME	VARCHAR2	IN	
TABNAME	VARCHAR2		
AS_OF_TIMESTAMP	TIMESTAMP WITH TIMEZONE	IN	
RESTORE_CLUSTER_INDEX	BOOLEAN	IN	FALSE
FORCE	BOOLEAN	IN	FALSE
NO_INVALIDATE	BOOLEAN	IN	NO_INVALIDATE

Table 7.142: *Restore_table_stats Parameters*

set_column_stats is an overloaded procedure that sets all the column level information for both normal and user defined statistics. The normal call to *set_column_stats* is as follows:

ARGUMENT	TYPE	IN / OUT	DEFAULT VALUE
OWNNAME	VARCHAR2	IN	
TABNAME	VARCHAR2	IN	
COLNAME	VARCHAR2	IN	
PARTNAME	VARCHAR2	IN	NULL
STATTAB	VARCHAR2	IN	NULL
STATID	VARCHAR2	IN	NULL
DISTINCT	NUMBER	IN	NULL
DENSITY	NUMBER	IN	NULL
NULLCNT	NUMBER	IN	NULL
SREC	StatRec	IN	NULL
AVGLEN	NUMBER	IN	NULL
FLAGS	NUMBER	IN	NULL
STATOWN	VARCHAR2	IN	NULL
NO_INVALIDATE	BOOLEAN	IN	NO_INVALIDATE
FORCE	BOOLEAN	IN	FALSE

Table 7.143: *Set_column_stats Parameters, Normal Call*

The user defined statistics call to *set_column_stats* is as follows:

ARGUMENT	TYPE	IN / OUT	DEFAULT VALUE
OWNNAME	VARCHAR2	IN	
TABNAME	VARCHAR2	IN	
COLNAME	VARCHAR2	IN	
PARTNAME	VARCHAR2	IN	NULL
STATTAB	VARCHAR2	IN	NULL
STATID	VARCHAR2	IN	NULL
EXT_STATS	RAW	IN	
STATTYPOWN	VARCHAR2	IN	NULL
STATTYPNAME	VARCHAR2	IN	NULL
STATOWN	VARCHAR2	IN	NULL
NO_INVALIDATE	BOOLEAN	IN	NO_INVALIDATE
FORCE	BOOLEAN	IN	FALSE

Table 7.144: *Set_column_stats Parameters, User Defined Statistics Call*

set_database_prefs is a procedure that sets statistics preferences. The valid values for the *pname* parameter are CASCADE, DEGREE, ESTIMATE_PERCENT,

METHOD_OPT, NO_INVALIDATE, GRANULARITY, PUBLISH, INCREMENTAL and STALE_PERCENT.

ARGUMENT	TYPE	IN / OUT	DEFAULT VALUE
PNAME	VARCHAR2	IN	
PVALUE	VARCHAR2	IN	
ADD_SYS	BOOLEAN	IN	FALSE

Table 7.145: *Set_database_prefs Parameters*

set_global_prefs is a procedure that sets global statistics preferences. The valid values for the *pname* parameter are CASCADE, DEGREE, ESTIMATE_PERCENT, METHOD_OPT, NO_INVALIDATE, GRANULARITY, PUBLISH, INCREMENTAL and STALE_PERCENT.

ARGUMENT	TYPE	IN / OUT	DEFAULT VALUE
PNAME	VARCHAR2	IN	

Table 7.146: *Set_global_prefs Parameter*

set_index_stats is an overloaded procedure that sets all the index level information for both normal and user defined statistics. The normal call to *set_index_stats* is as follows:

ARGUMENT	TYPE	IN / OUT	DEFAULT VALUE
OWNNAME	VARCHAR2	IN	
INDNAME	VARCHAR2	IN	
PARTNAME	VARCHAR2	IN	NULL
STATTAB	VARCHAR2	IN	NULL
STATID	VARCHAR2	IN	NULL
NUMROWS	NUMBER	IN	NULL
NUMLBLKS	NUMBER	IN	NULL
NUMDIST	NUMBER	IN	NULL
AVGLBLK	NUMBER	IN	NULL
AVGDBLK	NUMBER	IN	NULL
CLSTFCT	NUMBER	IN	NULL
INDLEVEL	NUMBER	IN	NULL
FLAGS	NUMBER	IN	NULL
STATOWN	VARCHAR2	IN	NULL
NO_INVALIDATE	BOOLEAN	IN	NO_INVALIDATE

ARGUMENT	TYPE	IN / OUT	DEFAULT VALUE
GUESSQ	NUMBER	IN	NULL
CACHEDBLK	NUMBER	IN	NULL
CACHEHIT	NUMBER	IN	NULL
FORCE	BOOLEAN	IN	FALSE

Table 7.147: *Set_index_stats Parameters, Normal Call*

The user defined statistics call to *set_index_stats* is as follows:

ARGUMENT	TYPE	IN / OUT	DEFAULT VALUE
OWNNAME	VARCHAR2	IN	
INDNAME	VARCHAR2	IN	
PARTNAME	VARCHAR2	IN	NULL
STATTAB	VARCHAR2	IN	NULL
STATID	VARCHAR2	IN	NULL
EXT_STATS	RAW	IN	
STATTYPOWN	VARCHAR2	IN	NULL
STATTYPNAME	VARCHAR2	OUT	NULL
STATOWN	VARCHAR2	IN	NULL
NO_INVALIDATE	BOOLEAN	IN	NO_INVALIDATE
CACHEDBLK	NUMBER	IN	NULL
CACHEHIT	NUMBER	IN	NULL
FORCE	BOOLEAN	IN	FALSE

Table 7.148: *Set_index_stats Parameters, User Defined Statistics Call*

set_schema_prefs is a procedure that sets all the statistics preferences for the specified schema. The valid values for the *pname* parameter are CASCADE, DEGREE, ESTIMATE_PERCENT, METHOD_OPT, NO_INVALIDATE, GRANULARITY, PUBLISH, INCREMENTAL and STALE_PERCENT.

ARGUMENT	TYPE	IN / OUT	DEFAULT VALUE
OWNNAME	VARCHAR2	IN	
PNAME	VARCHAR2	IN	
PVALUE	VARCHAR2	IN	

Table 7.149: *Set_schema_prefs Parameters*

set_system_stats is a procedure that sets all the system statistics from the user specified statistics table to the data dictionary. The legal values for *pname* include IOTFRSPEED, IOSEEKTIM, SREADTIM, MREADTIM, CPUSPEED, CPUSPEEDNW, MBRC, MAXTHR and SLAVTHR.

ARGUMENT	TYPE	IN / OUT	DEFAULT VALUE
PNAME	VARCHAR2	IN	
PVALUE	VARCHAR2	IN	
STATTAB	VARCHAR2	IN	NULL
STATID	VARCHAR2	IN	NULL
STATOWN	VARCHAR2	IN	NULL

Table 7.150: *Set_table_prefs Parameters*

set_table_prefs is a procedure that sets all the statistics preferences of the specified table from the user specified statistics table into the data dictionary. The valid values for the *pname* parameter are CASCADE, DEGREE, ESTIMATE_PERCENT, METHOD_OPT, NO_INVALIDATE, GRANULARITY, PUBLISH, INCREMENTAL and STALE_PERCENT.

ARGUMENT	TYPE	IN / OUT	DEFAULT VALUE
OWNNAME	VARCHAR2	IN	
TABNAME	VARCHAR2	IN	
PNAME	VARCHAR2	IN	
PVALUE	VARCHAR2	IN	
STATTAB	VARCHAR2	IN	
STATID	VARCHAR2	IN	NULL
STATOWN	VARCHAR2	IN	NULL

Table 7.151: *Set_table_prefs Parameters*

set_table_stats is a procedure that sets all the statistics of the specified table from the user specified statistics table to the data dictionary.

ARGUMENT	TYPE	IN / OUT	DEFAULT VALUE
OWNNAME	VARCHAR2	IN	
TABNAME	VARCHAR2	IN	
PARTNAME	VARCHAR2	IN	NULL
STATTAB	VARCHAR2	IN	NULL
STATID	VARCHAR2	IN	NULL

ARGUMENT	TYPE	IN / OUT	DEFAULT VALUE
NUMROWS	NUMBER	IN	NULL
NUMBLKS	NUMBER	IN	NULL
AVGRLEN	NUMBER	IN	NULL
FLAGS	NUMBER	IN	NULL
STATOWN	VARCHAR2	IN	NULL
NO_INVALIDATE	BOOLEAN	IN	NO_INVALIDATE
CACHEDBLK	NUMBER	IN	NULL
CACHEDHIT	NUMBER	IN	NULL
FORCE	BOOLEAN	IN	FALSE

Table 7.152: *Set_table_stats Parameters*

show_extended_stats_name is a function to display the statistics entry names for user specified extensions. It returns that name as a VARCHAR2.

ARGUMENT	TYPE	IN / OUT	DEFAULT VALUE
OWNANME	VARCHAR2	IN	
TABNAME	VARCHAR2	IN	
EXTENSION	VARCHAR2	IN	

Table 7.153: *Show_extended_stats_name Parameters*

unlock_partition_stats is a procedure to unlock the table statistics for the user specified partition.

ARGUMENT	TYPE	IN / OUT	DEFAULT VALUE
OWNNAME	VARCHAR2	IN	
TABNAME	VARCHAR2	IN	
PARTNAME	VARCHAR2	IN	

Table 7.154: *Unlock_partition_stats Parameters*

unlock_schema_stats is a procedure to unlock all the table statistics for the user specified schema.

ARGUMENT	TYPE	IN / OUT	DEFAULT VALUE
OWNNAME	VARCHAR2	IN	

Table 7.155: *Unlock_schema_stats Parameter*

unlock_table_stats is a procedure to unlock the table statistics for the user specified table.

ARGUMENT	TYPE	IN / OUT	DEFAULT VALUE
OWNNAME	VARCHAR2	IN	
TABNAME	VARCHAR2	IN	

Table 7.156: *Unlock_table_stats Parameters*

upgrade_stat_table is a procedure to upgrade an older version statistics table to the current definition.

ARGUMENT	TYPE	IN / OUT	DEFAULT VALUE
OWNNAME	VARCHAR2	IN	
STATTAB	VARCHAR2	IN	

Table 7.157: *Upgrade_stat_table Parameters*

dbms_stats 12c enhancements

Oracle 12c offers this enhancement, a new procedure named *report_stats_operations*.

dbms_stats.report_stats_operations

The new 12c *dbms_stats.report_stats_operations* now give you a window into the 12c automatic statistics collection mechanisms for creating indexes and CTAS (create table as select). Here is a sample invocation of dbms_stats.report_stats_operations:

```
SQL> variable mystatrep2 clob;

SQL> set long 1000000

SQL> begin
  2   :mystatrep2 := dbms_stats.report_stats_operations(
  3   since=>SYSTIMESTAMP-16,
  4   until=>SYSTIMESTAMP-1,
  5   detail_level=>'TYPICAL',
  6   format=>'TEXT');
  7   end;
  8   /

PL/SQL procedure successfully completed.

SQL> print mystatrep2
```

The output from *dbms_stats.report_stats_operations* report on the following data:

- Operation Id
- Operation
- Target
- Start Time
- End Time
- Status
- Total Tasks
- Successful
- Tasks
- Failed Tasks
- Active Tasks

DBMS_SQLTUNE

One of the most encouraging new areas with Oracle 10g and 11g are the many advisors, and in particular, those to assist with SQL optimization. The days of manually working solely with cryptic explain plans are essentially over. While along the way Oracle offered interim solutions such as stored outlines and profiles, the ultimate solution has now evolved resulting in the SQL Performance Analyzer (SPA), SQL Tuning Advisor and the critically important concept of SQL Tuning Sets (STS). Now one can work with small manageable SQL workload bundles called tuning sets, which include SQL Text, Bind variables, execution plans and execution statistics, and test-encapsulated scenarios for before and after relative comparisons. That, in turn, paves the way for focusing on the results rather than the explain plans resulting in those satisfactory results. Furthermore, Oracle 11g has automated candidate identification so that DBAs need only to concentrate on those flagged as being potential issues.

This feature in available only in Oracle 10g and higher and specifically only for those who have purchased the OEM optional Tuning Packs.

There are so many new database advisors, with the list seeming to grow by the minute, that the best way to utilize them is most often via the OEM screens accessible via Advisor Central as shown here in Figure 7.6. However, the PL/SQL interface in this chapter will be examined for completeness. The next chapter will focus more on the task and its processes as well as the various screens to visit.

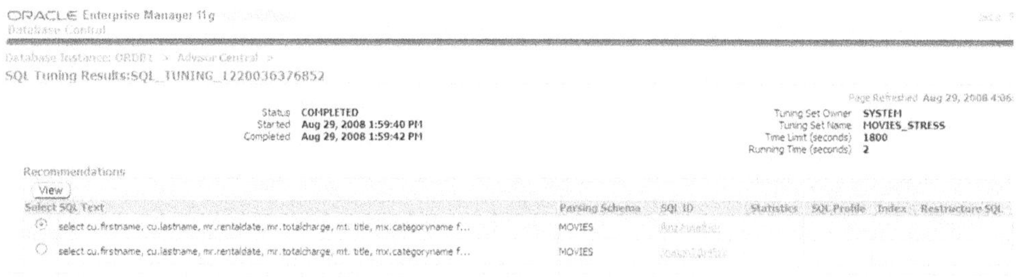

Figure 7.6: *SQL Tuning Advisor in OEM*

The following data types and constants are used by the DBMS_SQLTUNE package:

```
---------------------------------------------------------------------------
--                    global constant declarations                    --
---------------------------------------------------------------------------
--
-- sqltune advisor name
ADV_SQLTUNE_NAME  CONSTANT VARCHAR2(18) := 'SQL Tuning Advisor';


--
-- SQLTune advisor task scope parameter values
--
SCOPE_LIMITED        CONSTANT VARCHAR2(7)   := 'LIMITED';
SCOPE_COMPREHENSIVE  CONSTANT VARCHAR2(13)  := 'COMPREHENSIVE';


--
--   SQLTune advisor time_limit constants
--
TIME_LIMIT_DEFAULT  CONSTANT    NUMBER := 1800;


--
-- report type (possible values) constants
--
TYPE_TEXT           CONSTANT    VARCHAR2(4)  := 'TEXT'     ;
TYPE_XML            CONSTANT    VARCHAR2(3)  := 'XML'      ;
TYPE_HTML           CONSTANT    VARCHAR2(4)  := 'HTML'     ;


--
-- report level (possible values) constants
--
LEVEL_TYPICAL       CONSTANT    VARCHAR2(7)  := 'TYPICAL'  ;
LEVEL_BASIC         CONSTANT    VARCHAR2(5)  := 'BASIC'    ;
LEVEL_ALL           CONSTANT    VARCHAR2(3)  := 'ALL'      ;
```

```
--
-- report section (possible values) constants
--
SECTION_FINDINGS    CONSTANT   VARCHAR2(8)  := 'FINDINGS'   ;
SECTION_PLANS       CONSTANT   VARCHAR2(5)  := 'PLANS'      ;
SECTION_INFORMATION CONSTANT   VARCHAR2(11):= 'INFORMATION';
SECTION_ERRORS      CONSTANT   VARCHAR2(6)  := 'ERRORS'     ;
SECTION_ALL         CONSTANT   VARCHAR2(3)  := 'ALL'        ;
SECTION_SUMMARY     CONSTANT   VARCHAR2(7)  := 'SUMMARY'    ;

-- some common date format
DATE_FMT       constant varchar2(21)      := 'mm/dd/yyyy hh24:mi:ss';

--
-- script section constants
--
REC_TYPE_ALL             CONSTANT   VARCHAR2(3)  := 'ALL';
REC_TYPE_SQL_PROFILES    CONSTANT   VARCHAR2(8)  := 'PROFILES';
REC_TYPE_STATS           CONSTANT   VARCHAR2(10) := 'STATISTICS';
REC_TYPE_INDEXES         CONSTANT   VARCHAR2(7)  := 'INDEXES';

--
-- capture section constants
--
MODE_REPLACE_OLD_STATS CONSTANT   NUMBER := 1;
MODE_ACCUMULATE_STATS  CONSTANT   NUMBER := 2;

---- SYS.SQLSET_ROW ----


--
-- sql tuning set basic attributes
--
sql_id                    VARCHAR(13),   /* unique SQL ID */
force_matching_signature NUMBER,         /* literals, case, spaces removed */
sql_text                  CLOB,          /* unique SQL hache value */
object_list               sql_objects,   /* objects referenced by this stmt */
bind_data                 RAW(2000),     /* bind data as captured for SQL */
parsing_schema_name       VARCHAR2(30),  /* schema where the SQL is parsed */
module                    VARCHAR2(48),  /* last app. module for the SQL */
action                    VARCHAR2(32),  /* last app. action for the SQL */
elapsed_time              NUMBER,        /* elapsed time for SQL statement */
cpu_time                  NUMBER,        /* CPU time for this SQL */
buffer_gets               NUMBER,        /* number of buffer gets */
disk_reads                NUMBER,        /* number of disk reads  */
direct_writes             NUMBER,        /* number of direct writes */
rows_processed            NUMBER,        /* # of rows processed by this SQL */
fetches                   NUMBER,        /* number of fetches */
executions                NUMBER,        /* total executions of this SQL */
end_of_fetch_count        NUMBER,        /* exec. count up to end of fetch */
optimizer_cost            NUMBER,        /* Optimizer cost for this SQL */
optimizer_env             RAW(2000),     /* optimizer environment */
priority                  NUMBER,        /* user-defined priority (1,2,3) */
command_type              NUMBER,        /* statement type - INSERT, etc. */
first_load_time           VARCHAR2(19),  /* load time of parent cursor */
stat_period               NUMBER,        /* period (seconds) when the */
                                         /* stats for SQL stmt collected */
active_stat_period        NUMBER,        /* effecive time (in seconds) */
                                         /* for which SQL stmt was active */
other                     CLOB,          /* col for user defined attrs */
plan_hash_value           NUMBER,        /* plan hash value of the plan */
sql_plan                  sql_plan_table_type, /* explain plan */
bind_list                 sql_binds,     /* list of user specified binds */
```

accept_sql_profile is both a procedure and function that creates the SQL Profile recommended by the SQL Tuning Advisor. The SQL Text is supplied via a SQL Tuning Task object. The function returns the name of the SQL Profile as a VARCHAR2.

ARGUMENT	TYPE	IN / OUT	DEFAULT VALUE
TASK_NAME	VARCHAR2	IN	
OBJECT_ID	NUMBER	IN	NULL
NAME	VARCHAR2	IN	NULL
DESCRIPTION	VARCHAR2	IN	NULL
CATEGORY	VARCHAR2	IN	NULL
TASK_OWNER	VARCHAR2	IN	NULL
REPLACE	BOOLEAN	IN	FALSE
FORCE_MATCH	BOOLEAN	IN	FALSE

Table 7.158: *Accept_sql_profile Parameters*

add_sqlset_reference is a function that adds a new reference to a pre-existing SQL Tuning Set (STS). The description can be up to 256 characters. It returns the new reference's identifier as a NUMBER.

ARGUMENT	TYPE	IN / OUT	DEFAULT VALUE
SQLSET_NAME	VARCHAR2	IN	
DESCRIPTION	VARCHAR2	IN	NULL

Table 7.159: *Add_sqlset_reference Parameters*

alter_sql_profile is a procedure that modified the specified attributes of a pre-existing SQL Profile. The legal values for attributes to change are STATUS, NAME, DESCRIPTION and CATEGORY.

ARGUMENT	TYPE	IN / OUT	DEFAULT VALUE
NAME	VARCHAR2	IN	
ATTRIBUTE	VARCHAR2	IN	
VALUE	VARCHAR2	IN	

Table 7.160: *Alter_sql_profile Parameters*

cancel_tuning_task is a procedure that terminates the currently executing tuning task with a complete cleanup where all intermediate data is deleted.

ARGUMENT	TYPE	IN / OUT	DEFAULT VALUE
TASK_NAME	VARCHAR2	IN	

Table 7.161: *Cancel_tuning_task Parameter*

capture_cursor_cache_sqlset is a procedure that incrementally captures workload activity from the cursor cache into a SQL Tuning Set (STS). The capture time is expressed in seconds, the capture option can be INSERT, UPDATE or MERGE, and the capture mode can be either MODE_REPLACE_OLD_STATS or MODE_ACCUMULATE_STATS.

ARGUMENT	TYPE	IN/OUT	DEFAULT VALUE
SQLSET_NAME	VARCHAR2	IN	
TIME_LIMIT	POSITIVE	IN	1800
REPEAT_INTERVAL	POSITIVE	IN	300
CAPTURE_OPTION	VARCHAR2	IN	'MERGE'
CAPTURE_MODE	NUMBER	IN	MODE_REPLACE_OLD_STATS
BASIC_FILTER	VARCHAR2	IN	NULL
SQLSET_OWNER	VARCHAR2IN	IN	NULL

Table 7.162: *Capture_cursor_cache_sqlset Parameters*

create_sqlset is a both a procedure and function that creates a new SQL Tuning Set (STS). When used as a function, it returns the name of the new SQL Tuning Set as a VARCHAR2.

ARGUMENT	TYPE	IN / OUT	DEFAULT VALUE
SQLSET_NAME	VARCHAR2	IN	
DESCRIPTION	VARCHAR2	IN	NULL
SQLSET_OWNER	VARCHAR2	IN	NULL

Table 7.163: *Create_sqlset Parameters*

create_stgtab_sqlprof is a procedure that creates a staging table for copying SQL Profiles across systems, like those for export and import operations.

ARGUMENT	TYPE	IN / OUT	DEFAULT VALUE
TABLE_NAME	VARCHAR2	IN	

Table 7.164: *Create_stgtab_sqlprof Parameter*

create_stgtab_sqlset_sqlprof is a procedure that creates a staging table for copying SQL Tuning Sets (STS) across systems, like those for export and import operations.

ARGUMENT	TYPE	IN / OUT	DEFAULT VALUE
TABLE_NAME	VARCHAR2	IN	
SCHEMA_NAME	VARCHAR2	IN	NULL
TABLESPACE_NAME	VARCHAR2	IN	NULL

Table 7.165: *Create_stgtab_sqlset_sqlprof Parameters*

create_tuning_task is an overloaded function for creating tuning tasks via a SQL statement's text, a SQL statement's cursor cache identifier, an AWR range of snapshot identifiers, or a SQL Tuning Set. In all cases, it returns the new tuning task name as a VARCHAR2. *Create_tuning_task* based upon a SQL statement's text is as follows:

ARGUMENT	TYPE	IN / OUT	DEFAULT VALUE
SQL_TEXT	CLOB	IN	
BIND_LIST	SQLBinds	IN	NULL
USER_NAME	VARCHAR2	IN	NULL
SCOPE	VARCHAR2	IN	SCOPE_COMPREHENSIVE
TIME_LIMIT	NUMBER	IN	TIME_LIMIT_DEFAULT
TASK_NAME	VARCHAR2	IN	NULL
DESCRIPTION	VARCHAR2	IN	NULL

Table 7.166: *Create_tuning_task Parameters Based on SQL Statement's Text*

create_tuning_task based upon a SQL statement's cursor cache identifier is as follows:

ARGUMENT	TYPE	IN / OUT	DEFAULT VALUE
SQL_ID	VARCHAR2	IN	
PLAN_HASH_VALUE	NUMBER	IN	NULL

SCOPE	VARCHAR2	IN	SCOPE_COMPREHENSIVE
TIME_LIMIT	NUMBER	IN	TIME_LIMIT_DEFAULT
TASK_NAME	VARCHAR2	IN	NULL
DESCRIPTION	VARCHAR2	IN	NULL

Table 7.167: *Create_tuning_task Parameters Based on SQL Statement's Cursor Cache Identifier*

create_tuning_task based upon an AWR range of snapshot identifiers is as follows:

ARGUMENT	TYPE	IN / OUT	DEFAULT VALUE
BEGIN_SNAP	NUMBER	IN	
END_SNAP	NUMBER	IN	
SQL_ID	VARCHAR2	IN	
PLAN_HASH_VALUE	NUMBER	IN	NULL
SCOPE	VARCHAR2	IN	SCOPE_COMPREHENSIVE
TIME_LIMIT	NUMBER	IN	TIME_LIMIT_DEFAULT
TASK_NAME	VARCHAR2	IN	NULL
DESCRIPTION	VARCHAR2	IN	NULL

Table 7.168: *Create_tuning_task Parameters Based on AWR range of snapshot identifiers*

create_tuning_task based upon an SQL Tuning Set (STS) is as follows:

ARGUMENT	TYPE	IN / OUT	DEFAULT VALUE
SQLSET_NAME	VARCHAR2	IN	
BASIC_FILTER	VARCHAR2	IN	NULL
OBJECT_FILTER	VARCHAR2	IN	NULL
RANK1	VARCHAR2	IN	NULL
RANK2	VARCHAR2	IN	NULL
RANK3	VARCHAR2	IN	NULL
RESULT_PERCENT AGE	NUMBER	IN	NULL
RESULT_LIMIT	NUMBER	IN	NULL
SCOPE	VARCHAR2	IN	SCOPE_COMPREHENSIVE
TIME_LIMIT	NUMBER	IN	TIME_LIMIT_DEFAULT
TASK_NAME	VARCHAR2	IN	NULL
DESCRIPTION	VARCHAR2	IN	NULL

ARGUMENT	TYPE	IN / OUT	DEFAULT VALUE
PLAN_FILTER	VARCHAR2	IN	'MAX_ELAPSED_TIME'
SQLSET_OWNER	VARCHAR2	IN	NULL

Table 7.169: *Create_tuning_task Parameters Based on STS*

delete_sqlset is a procedure that deletes or drops the SQL statements from an STS.

ARGUMENT	TYPE	IN / OUT	DEFAULT VALUE
SQLSET_NAME	VARCHAR2	IN	
BASIC_FILTER	VARCHAR2	IN	NULL
SQLSET_OWNER	VARCHAR2	IN	NULL

Table 7.170: *Delete_sqlset Parameters*

drop_sql_profile is a procedure that drops the user specified SQL Profile.

ARGUMENT	TYPE	IN / OUT	DEFAULT VALUE
NAME	VARCHAR2	IN	
IGNORE	BOOLEAN	IN	FALSE

Table 7.171: *Drop_sql_profile Parameters*

drop_sqlset is a procedure that deletes the user specified STS and it must be inactive.

ARGUMENT	TYPE	IN / OUT	DEFAULT VALUE
SQLSET_NAME	VARCHAR2	IN	
SQLSET_OWNER	VARCHAR2	IN	NULL

Table 7.172: *Drop_sqlset Parameters*

drop_tuning_task is a procedure that deletes the user specified SQL tuning task. The task and all intermediate data are deleted.

ARGUMENT	TYPE	IN / OUT	DEFAULT VALUE
TASK_NAME	VARCHAR2	IN	

Table 7.173: *Drop_tuning_task Parameters*

execute_tuning_task is both a procedure and function that executes a pre-existing SQL tuning task. As a function, it returns the new task's name as a VARCHAR2.

ARGUMENT	TYPE	IN / OUT	DEFAULT VALUE
TASK_NAME	VARCHAR2	IN	
EXECUTION_NAME	VARCHAR2	IN	NULL
EXECUTION_PARAMS	DBMS_ADVISOR.ArgList	IN	NULL
EXECUTION_DESC	VARCHAR2	IN	NULL

Table 7.174: *Execute_tuning_task Parameters*

implement_tuning_task is a procedure that implements the SQL Profile recommendations made by the SQL Tuning Advisor.

ARGUMENT	TYPE	IN / OUT	DEFAULT VALUE
TASK_NAME	VARCHAR2	IN	
REC_TYPE	VARCHAR2	IN	REC_TYPE_SQL_PROFILES
ONWER_NAME	VARCHAR2	IN	NULL
EXECUTION_NAME	VARCHAR2	IN	NULL

Table 7.175: *Implement_tuning_task Parameters*

interrupt_tuning_task is a procedure that interrupts the currently running tuning task but does so as a normal type exit, and thus leaves intermediate results for review.

ARGUMENT	TYPE	IN / OUT	DEFAULT VALUE
TASK_NAME	VARCHAR2	IN	

Table 7.176: *Interrupt_tuning_task Parameters*

load_sqlset is a procedure that populates the user specified SQL Tuning Set (STS) with the set of selected SQL statements. It can be run multiple times and the results are simply aggregated. The valid load options are INSERT, UPDATE and MERGE. The valid update options are REPLACE and ACCUMULATE. The valid update conditions are OLD and NEW. The valid update attributes are NULL, BASIC, TYPICAL, ALL and a comma separated list of execution context attributes.

ARGUMENT	TYPE	IN / OUT	DEFAULT VALUE
SQLSET_NAME	VARCHAR2	IN	
POPULATE_CURSOR	SQLSet_Cursor	IN	
LOAD_OPTION	VARCHAR2	IN	'INSERT'
UPDATE_OPTION	VARCHAR2	IN	'REPLACE'
UPDATE_CONDITION	VARCHAR2	IN	NULL
UPDATE_ATTRIBUTES	VARCHAR2	IN	NULL
IGNORE_NULL	BOOLEAN	IN	TRUE
COMMIT_ROWS	POSITIVE	IN	NULL
SQLSET_OWNER	VARCHAR2	IN	NULL

Table 7.177: *Load_sqlset Parameters*

pack_stgtab_sqlprof is a procedure that simply copies the SQL Profile data from SYS to the user specified staging table.

ARGUMENT	TYPE	IN / OUT	DEFAULT VALUE
PROFILE_NAME	VARCHAR2	IN	'%'
PROFILE_CATEGORY	VARCHAR2	IN	'DEFAULT'
STAGING_TABLE_NAME	VARCHAR2	IN	
STAGING_SCHEMA_OWNER	VARCHAR2	IN	NULL

Table 7.178: *Pack_stgtab_sqlprof Parameters*

pack_stgtab_sqlset is a procedure that simply copies the SQL Tuning Set from SYS to the user specified staging table.

ARGUMENT	TYPE	IN / OUT	DEFAULT VALUE
SQLSET_NAME	VARCHAR2	IN	
SQLSETOWNER	VARCHAR2	IN	NULL
STAGING_TABLE_NAME	VARCHAR2	IN	
STAGING_SCHEMA_OWNER	VARCHAR2	IN	NULL

Table 7.179: *Pack_stgtab_sqlset Parameters*

remap_stgtab_sqlprof is a procedure that permits modifications to the SQL Profile data in the staging table prior to extraction.

ARGUMENT	TYPE	IN / OUT	DEFAULT VALUE

OLD_PROFILE_NAME	VARCHAR2	IN	
NEW_PROFILE_NAME	VACRHAR2	IN	NULL
PROFILE_CATEGORY	VARCHAR2	IN	'DEFAULT'
STAGING_TABLE_NAME	VARCHAR2	IN	
STAGING_SCHEMA_OWNER	VARCHAR2	IN	NULL

Table 7.180: *Remap_stgtab_sqlprof Parameters*

remap_stgtab_sqlset is a procedure that permits modifications to the STS data in the staging table prior to extraction.

ARGUMENT	TYPE	IN / OUT	DEFAULT VALUE
OLD_SQLSET_NAME	VARCHAR2	IN	
OLD_SQLSET_OWNER	VACRHAR2	IN	NULL
NEW_SQLSET_NAME	VACRHAR2	IN	NULL
NEW_SQLSET_OWNER	VACRHAR2	IN	NULL
STAGING_TABLE_NAME	VARCHAR2	IN	
STAGING_SCHEMA_OWNER	VARCHAR2	IN	NULL

Table 7.181: *Remap_stgtab_sqlset Parameters*

remove_sqlset_reference is a procedure that drops an existing reference to a pre-existing SQL Tuning Set.

ARGUMENT	TYPE	IN / OUT	DEFAULT VALUE
SQLSET_NAME	VARCHAR2	IN	
REFERENCE_ID	NUMBER	IN	

Table 7.182: *Remove_sqlset_reference Parameters*

report_auto_tuning_task is a function that displays a report based upon the automatic tuning task data. It returns that report as a CLOB.

ARGUMENT	TYPE	IN / OUT	DEFAULT VALUE
BEGIN_EXEC	VARCHAR2	IN	NULL
END_EXEC	VACRHAR2	IN	NULL
TYPE	VACRHAR2	IN	TYPE_TEXT
LEVEL	VACRHAR2	IN	LEVEL_TYPICAL
SECTION	VARCHAR2	IN	SECTION_ALL
OBJECT_ID	NUMBER	IN	NULL

RESULT_LIMIT	VARCHAR2	IN	NULL
SEGMENT_SCHEME	VARCHAR2	IN	SEGMENT_NONE

Table 7.183: *Report_auto_tuning_task Parameters*

report_sql_monitor is a function that displays a report based upon the real time SQL monitoring data being captured. It returns that report as a CLOB.

ARGUMENT	TYPE	IN / OUT	DEFAULT VALUE
SQL_ID	VARCHAR2	IN	NULL
SESSION_ID	NUMBER	IN	NULL
SESSION_SERIAL	NUMBER	IN	NULL
SQL_EXEC_START	DATE	IN	NULL
SQL_EXEC_ID	NUMBER	IN	NULL
INST_ID	NUMBER	IN	-1
START_TIME_FILTER	DATE	IN	NULL
END_TIME_FILTER	DATE	IN	NULL
INSTANCE_ID_FILTER	NUMBER	IN	NULL
PARALLEL_FILTER	VARCHAR2	IN	NULL
EVENT_DETAIL	VARCHAR2	IN	'YES'
REPORT_LEVEL	VARCHAR2	IN	'TYPICAL'
TYPE	VARCHAR2	IN	'TEXT'

Table 7.184: *Report_sql_monitor Parameters*

report_tuning_task is a function that displays a report based upon the tuning task data. It returns that report as a CLOB.

ARGUMENT	TYPE	IN / OUT	DEFAULT VALUE
TASK_NAME	VARCHAR2	IN	
TYPE	VACRHAR2	IN	TYPE_TEXT
LEVEL	VACRHAR2	IN	LEVEL_TYPICAL
SECTION	VACRHAR2	IN	SECTION_ALL
OBJECT_ID	NUMBER	IN	NULL
RESULT_LIMIT	NUMBER	IN	NULL
OWNER_NAME	VARCHAR2	IN	NULL
EXECUTION_NAME	VARCHAR2	IN	NULL

Table 7.185: *Report_tuning_task Parameters*

reset_tuning_task is a procedure that prepares a non-active SQL tuning task for re-execution, i.e. resets it to starting state.

ARGUMENT	TYPE	IN / OUT	DEFAULT VALUE
TASK_NAME	VARCHAR2	IN	

Table 7.186: *Reset_tuning_task Parameter*

resume_tuning_task is a procedure that resumes execution of a non-active SQL tuning task that was previously interrupted, meaning stopped and in a re-executable state. Note that one cannot resume a task to tune a single SQL statement. This procedure is for resuming those based on SQL Tuning Sets.

ARGUMENT	TYPE	IN / OUT	DEFAULT VALUE
TASK_NAME	VARCHAR2	IN	
BASIC_FILTER	VARCHAR2	IN	NULL

Table 7.187: *Resume_tuning_task Parameters*

script_tuning_task is a function that generates a SQL*Plus script to implement a set of tuning advisor recommendations. It returns that SQL script as a CLOB. The valid record types include ALL, PROFILES, STATISTICS and any comma separated list combining these values.

ARGUMENT	TYPE	IN / OUT	DEFAULT VALUE
TASK_NAME	VARCHAR2	IN	
REC_TYPE	VACRHAR2	IN	REC_TYPE_ALL
OBJECT_ID	NUMBER	IN	NULL
RESULT_LIMIT	NUMBER	IN	NULL
OWNER_NAME	VACRHAR2	IN	NULL
EXECUTION_NAME	VACRHAR2	IN	NULL

Table 7.188: *Script_tuning_task Parameters*

select_cursor_cache is a function that collects SQL statements live from the cursor cache and returns them one at a time, i.e. pipelined function, via a return type of SYS.SQLSET. The valid update attributes are NULL, BASIC, TYPICAL, ALL and a comma separated list of execution context attributes.

ARGUMENT	TYPE	IN / OUT	DEFAULT VALUE
BASIC_FILTER	VACRHAR2	IN	NULL
OBJECT_FILTER	VACRHAR2	IN	NULL
RANKING_MEASURE1	VACRHAR2	IN	NULL
RANKING_MEASURE2	VACRHAR2	IN	NULL
RANKING_MEASURE3	VACRHAR2	IN	NULL
RESULT_PERCENTAGE	NUMBER	IN	1
RESULT_LIMIT	NUMBER	IN	NULL
ATTRIBUTE_LIST	VACRHAR2	IN	NULL

Table 7.189: *Select_cursor_cache Parameters*

select_sqlset is a function that reads the contents of a STS and returns those values one at a time via a return type of SYS.SQLSET. The valid update attributes are NULL, BASIC, TYPICAL, ALL and a comma separated list of execution context attributes.

ARGUMENT	TYPE	IN / OUT	DEFAULT VALUE
SQLSET_NAME	VARCHAR2	IN	
BASIC_FILTER	VACRHAR2	IN	NULL
OBJECT_FILTER	VACRHAR2	IN	NULL
RANKING_MEASURE1	VACRHAR2	IN	NULL
RANKING_MEASURE2	VACRHAR2	IN	NULL
RANKING_MEASURE3	VACRHAR2	IN	NULL
RESULT_PERCENTAGE	NUMBER	IN	1
RESULT_LIMIT	NUMBER	IN	NULL
ATTRIBUTE_LIST	VACRHAR2	IN	NULL
PLAN_FILTER	VACRHAR2	IN	NULL
SQLSET_OWNER	VACRHAR2	IN	NULL

Table 7.190: *Select_sqlset Parameters*

select_workload_repository is an overloaded function that scans the contents of a range of AWR snapshots or a snapshot baseline and returns those values one at a time via a return type of SYS.SQLSET. The valid update attributes are NULL, BASIC, TYPICAL, ALL and a comma separated list of execution context attributes. The format for *select_workload_repository* when working off snapshot ranges is as follows:

ARGUMENT	TYPE	IN / OUT	DEFAULT VALUE
BEGIN_SNAP	VARCHAR2	IN	
END_SNAP	VARCHAR2	IN	
BASIC_FILTER	VACRHAR2	IN	NULL
OBJECT_FILTER	VACRHAR2	IN	NULL
RANKING_MEASURE1	VACRHAR2	IN	NULL
RANKING_MEASURE2	VACRHAR2	IN	NULL
RANKING_MEASURE3	VACRHAR2	IN	NULL
RESULT_PERCENTAGE	NUMBER	IN	1
RESULT_LIMIT	NUMBER	IN	NULL
ATTRIBUTE_LIST	VACRHAR2	IN	NULL

Table 7.191: *Select_workload_repository Parameters Working off Snapshot Ranges*

The format for *select_workload_repository* when working off a baseline representing a range of snapshots is as follows:

ARGUMENT	TYPE	IN / OUT	DEFAULT VALUE
BASELINE_NAME	VARCHAR2	IN	
BASIC_FILTER	VACRHAR2	IN	NULL
OBJECT_FILTER	VACRHAR2	IN	NULL
RANKING_MEASURE1	VACRHAR2	IN	NULL
RANKING_MEASURE2	VACRHAR2	IN	NULL
RANKING_MEASURE3	VACRHAR2	IN	NULL
RESULT_PERCENTAGE	NUMBER	IN	1
RESULT_LIMIT	NUMBER	IN	NULL
ATTRIBUTE_LIST	VACRHAR2	IN	NULL

Table 7.192: *Select_workload_repository Parameters Working off A Baseline*

set_tuning_task_parameter is an overloaded procedure that updates a SQL Tuning parameter of type VARCHAR2 or NUMBER to a user specified value. The valid values for parameter are MODE, USERNAME, DAYS_TO_EXPIRE, EXECUTION_DAYS_TO_EXPIRE, DEFAULT_EXECUTION_TYPE, TIME_LIMIT, LOCAL_TIME_LIMIT, TEST_EXECUTE, BASIC_FILTER, OBJECT_FILTER, PLAN_FILTER, RANK_MEASURE1, RANK_MEASURE2, RANK_MEASURE3, RESUME_FILTER, SQL_LIMIT, SQL_PERCENTAGE,

ACCEPT_SQL_PROFILES, MAX_AUTO_SQL_PROFILES, and MAX_SQL_PROFILES_PER_EXEC.

ARGUMENT	TYPE	IN / OUT	DEFAULT VALUE
TASK_NAME	VARCHAR2	IN	
PARAMETER	VACRHAR2	IN	
VALUE	VACRHAR2 | NUMBER	IN	

Table 7.193: *Set_tuning_task_parameter Parameters*

sqltext_to_signature is a function that simply returns the signature for user specified SQL text. The value is returned as a NUMBER.

ARGUMENT	TYPE	IN / OUT	DEFAULT VALUE
SQL_TEXT	CLOB	IN	
FORCE_MAATCH	BOOLEAN	IN	FALSE

Table 7.194: *Sqltext_to_signature Parameters*

unpack_stgtab_sqlprof is a procedure that copies the SQL Profile data from the user specified staging table to SYS, thus creating a profile.

ARGUMENT	TYPE	IN / OUT	DEFAULT VALUE
PROFILE_NAME	VARCHAR2	IN	'%'
PROFILE_CATEGORY	VARCHAR2	IN	'DEFAULT'
REPLACE	BOOLEAN	IN	
STAGING_TABLE_NAME	VARCHAR2	IN	
STAGING_SCHEMA_OWNER	VARCHAR2	IN	NULL

Table 7.195: *Unpack_stgtab_sqlprof Parameters*

unpack_stgtab_sqlset is a procedure that simply copies the SQL Tuning Set from the user specified staging table to SYS, thus creating a STS.

ARGUMENT	TYPE	IN / OUT	DEFAULT VALUE
SQLSET_NAME	VARCHAR2	IN	'%'
SQLSET_OWNER	VARCHAR2	IN	NULL
REPLACE	BOOLEAN	IN	
STAGING_TABLE_NAME	VARCHAR2	IN	
STAGING_SCHEMA_OWNER	VARCHAR2	IN	NULL

Table 7.196: *Unpack_stgtab_sqlset Parameters*

update_sqlset is an overloaded procedure that modifies the user selected fields for SQL statements within a SQL Tuning Set (STS).

ARGUMENT	TYPE	IN / OUT	DEFAULT VALUE
SQLSET_NAME	VARCHAR2	IN	
SQLSETOWNER	VARCHAR2	IN	
ATTRIBUTE_NAME	VARCHAR2	IN	
ATTRIBUTE_VALUE	VARCHAR2 | NUMBER	IN	NULL

Table 7.197: *Update_sqlset Parameters*

Monitoring

DBMS_ALERT

The DBMS_ALERT package provides a programmatic interface (API) that supports asynchronous database events or alerts which can permit an application to signal itself whenever a database value of interest is modified. This type of hand shaking is facilitated via a trigger which raises the proper signal.

register is a procedure that registers sessions' interest in alerts. A session can register interest in any number of alerts. Alert names must be 30 characters or less in length and those starting with 'ORA$' are reserved for Oracle products.

ARGUMENT	TYPE	IN / OUT	DEFAULT VALUE
NAME	VARCHAR2	IN	

Table 7.198: *Register Parameter*

remove is a procedure that deregisters sessions' interest in alerts. Removing alerts is an important performance issue since it frees up signalers.

ARGUMENT	TYPE	IN / OUT	DEFAULT VALUE
NAME	VARCHAR2	IN	

Table 7.199: *Remove Parameter*

removeall is a procedure that deregisters sessions' interest in all alerts. Removing alerts is an important performance issue since it frees up signalers. It has no parameters.

set_defaults is a procedure that sets the session's polling interval for signals of alerts. The polling interval is expressed in seconds. The default is five seconds.

ARGUMENT	TYPE	IN / OUT	DEFAULT VALUE
SENSITIVITY	NUMBER	IN	

Table 7.200: *Set_defaults Parameter*

signal is a procedure that raises the signal for a user specified alert. All sessions with a registered interest in the named alert are then notified. The message must be 1800 bytes or less in length.

ARGUMENT	TYPE	IN / OUT	DEFAULT VALUE
NAME	VARCHAR2	IN	
MESSAGE	VARCHAR2	IN	

Table 7.201: *Signal Parameters*

waitany is a procedure that waits, meaning suspends activity, until any alert is signaled that the session has a registered interest in. A return status of 0 indicates that the alert occurred, whereas a 1 means a timeout occurred instead.

ARGUMENT	TYPE	IN / OUT	DEFAULT VALUE
NAME	VARCHAR2	OUT	
MESSAGE	VARCHAR2	OUT	
STATUS	INTEGER	OUT	
TIMEOUT	NUMBER	IN	MAXWAIT

Table 7.202: *Waitany_Parameters*

DBMS_SERVER_ALERT

The DBMS_SERVER_ALERT package provides a programmatic interface (API) that supports asynchronous database events or alerts which can permit the database to signal whenever threshold values are crossed. Warning thresholds generate a severity level-5 alert, whereas critical thresholds generate a severity level-1 alert.

There are a large number of important constants one must be aware of to use this package:

```
-- operator types
OPERATOR_GT          CONSTANT BINARY_INTEGER := 0;
OPERATOR_EQ          CONSTANT BINARY_INTEGER := 1;
OPERATOR_LT          CONSTANT BINARY_INTEGER := 2;
OPERATOR_LE          CONSTANT BINARY_INTEGER := 3;
OPERATOR_GE          CONSTANT BINARY_INTEGER := 4;
OPERATOR_CONTAINS    CONSTANT BINARY_INTEGER := 5;
OPERATOR_NE          CONSTANT BINARY_INTEGER := 6;
OPERATOR_DO_NOT_CHECK CONSTANT BINARY_INTEGER := 7;

-- object types
OBJECT_TYPE_SYSTEM      CONSTANT BINARY_INTEGER := 1;
OBJECT_TYPE_FILE        CONSTANT BINARY_INTEGER := 2;
OBJECT_TYPE_SERVICE     CONSTANT BINARY_INTEGER := 3;
OBJECT_TYPE_EVENT_CLASS CONSTANT BINARY_INTEGER := 4;
OBJECT_TYPE_TABLESPACE  CONSTANT BINARY_INTEGER := 5;
OBJECT_TYPE_SESSION     CONSTANT BINARY_INTEGER := 9;

-- message levels
SUBTYPE SEVERITY_LEVEL_T IS PLS_INTEGER;
LEVEL_CRITICAL       CONSTANT PLS_INTEGER := 1;
LEVEL_WARNING        CONSTANT PLS_INTEGER := 5;
LEVEL_CLEAR          CONSTANT PLS_INTEGER := 32;

-- metrics names
AVG_USERS_WAITING      CONSTANT BINARY_INTEGER := 1000;
DB_TIME_WAITING        CONSTANT BINARY_INTEGER := 1001;
BUFFER_CACHE_HIT       CONSTANT BINARY_INTEGER := 2000;
MEMORY_SORTS_PCT       CONSTANT BINARY_INTEGER := 2001;
REDO_ALLOCATION_HIT    CONSTANT BINARY_INTEGER := 2002;
USER_TRANSACTIONS_SEC  CONSTANT BINARY_INTEGER := 2003;
PHYSICAL_READS_SEC     CONSTANT BINARY_INTEGER := 2004;
PHYSICAL_READS_TXN     CONSTANT BINARY_INTEGER := 2005;
```

```
PHYSICAL_WRITES_SEC        CONSTANT BINARY_INTEGER := 2006;
PHYSICAL_WRITES_TXN        CONSTANT BINARY_INTEGER := 2007;
PHYSICAL_READS_DIR_SEC     CONSTANT BINARY_INTEGER := 2008;
PHYSICAL_READS_DIR_TXN     CONSTANT BINARY_INTEGER := 2009;
PHYSICAL_WRITES_DIR_SEC    CONSTANT BINARY_INTEGER := 2010;
PHYSICAL_WRITES_DIR_TXN    CONSTANT BINARY_INTEGER := 2011;
PHYSICAL_READS_LOB_SEC     CONSTANT BINARY_INTEGER := 2012;
PHYSICAL_READS_LOB_TXN     CONSTANT BINARY_INTEGER := 2013;
PHYSICAL_WRITES_LOB_SEC    CONSTANT BINARY_INTEGER := 2014;
PHYSICAL_WRITES_LOB_TXN    CONSTANT BINARY_INTEGER := 2015;
REDO_GENERATED_SEC         CONSTANT BINARY_INTEGER := 2016;
REDO_GENERATED_TXN         CONSTANT BINARY_INTEGER := 2017;
LOGONS_SEC                 CONSTANT BINARY_INTEGER := 2018;
LOGONS_TXN                 CONSTANT BINARY_INTEGER := 2019;
OPEN_CURSORS_SEC           CONSTANT BINARY_INTEGER := 2020;
OPEN_CURSORS_TXN           CONSTANT BINARY_INTEGER := 2021;
USER_COMMITS_SEC           CONSTANT BINARY_INTEGER := 2022;
USER_COMMITS_TXN           CONSTANT BINARY_INTEGER := 2023;
USER_ROLLBACKS_SEC         CONSTANT BINARY_INTEGER := 2024;
USER_ROLLBACKS_TXN         CONSTANT BINARY_INTEGER := 2025;
USER_CALLS_SEC             CONSTANT BINARY_INTEGER := 2026;
USER_CALLS_TXN             CONSTANT BINARY_INTEGER := 2027;
RECURSIVE_CALLS_SEC        CONSTANT BINARY_INTEGER := 2028;
RECURSIVE_CALLS_TXN        CONSTANT BINARY_INTEGER := 2029;
SESS_LOGICAL_READS_SEC     CONSTANT BINARY_INTEGER := 2030;
SESS_LOGICAL_READS_TXN     CONSTANT BINARY_INTEGER := 2031;
DBWR_CKPT_SEC              CONSTANT BINARY_INTEGER := 2032;
BACKGROUND_CKPT_SEC        CONSTANT BINARY_INTEGER := 2033;
REDO_WRITES_SEC            CONSTANT BINARY_INTEGER := 2034;
REDO_WRITES_TXN            CONSTANT BINARY_INTEGER := 2035;
LONG_TABLE_SCANS_SEC       CONSTANT BINARY_INTEGER := 2036;
LONG_TABLE_SCANS_TXN       CONSTANT BINARY_INTEGER := 2037;
TOTAL_TABLE_SCANS_SEC      CONSTANT BINARY_INTEGER := 2038;
TOTAL_TABLE_SCANS_TXN      CONSTANT BINARY_INTEGER := 2039;
FULL_INDEX_SCANS_SEC       CONSTANT BINARY_INTEGER := 2040;
FULL_INDEX_SCANS_TXN       CONSTANT BINARY_INTEGER := 2041;
TOTAL_INDEX_SCANS_SEC      CONSTANT BINARY_INTEGER := 2042;
TOTAL_INDEX_SCANS_TXN      CONSTANT BINARY_INTEGER := 2043;
TOTAL_PARSES_SEC           CONSTANT BINARY_INTEGER := 2044;
TOTAL_PARSES_TXN           CONSTANT BINARY_INTEGER := 2045;
HARD_PARSES_SEC            CONSTANT BINARY_INTEGER := 2046;
HARD_PARSES_TXN            CONSTANT BINARY_INTEGER := 2047;
PARSE_FAILURES_SEC         CONSTANT BINARY_INTEGER := 2048;
PARSE_FAILURES_TXN         CONSTANT BINARY_INTEGER := 2049;
CURSOR_CACHE_HIT           CONSTANT BINARY_INTEGER := 2050;
DISK_SORT_SEC              CONSTANT BINARY_INTEGER := 2051;
DISK_SORT_TXN              CONSTANT BINARY_INTEGER := 2052;
ROWS_PER_SORT              CONSTANT BINARY_INTEGER := 2053;
EXECUTE_WITHOUT_PARSE      CONSTANT BINARY_INTEGER := 2054;
SOFT_PARSE_PCT             CONSTANT BINARY_INTEGER := 2055;
USER_CALLS_PCT             CONSTANT BINARY_INTEGER := 2056;
NETWORK_BYTES_SEC          CONSTANT BINARY_INTEGER := 2058;
ENQUEUE_TIMEOUTS_SEC       CONSTANT BINARY_INTEGER := 2059;
ENQUEUE_TIMEOUTS_TXN       CONSTANT BINARY_INTEGER := 2060;
ENQUEUE_WAITS_SEC          CONSTANT BINARY_INTEGER := 2061;
ENQUEUE_WAITS_TXN          CONSTANT BINARY_INTEGER := 2062;
ENQUEUE_DEADLOCKS_SEC      CONSTANT BINARY_INTEGER := 2063;
ENQUEUE_DEADLOCKS_TXN      CONSTANT BINARY_INTEGER := 2064;
ENQUEUE_REQUESTS_SEC       CONSTANT BINARY_INTEGER := 2065;
ENQUEUE_REQUESTS_TXN       CONSTANT BINARY_INTEGER := 2066;
DB_BLKGETS_SEC             CONSTANT BINARY_INTEGER := 2067;
DB_BLKGETS_TXN             CONSTANT BINARY_INTEGER := 2068;
CONSISTENT_GETS_SEC        CONSTANT BINARY_INTEGER := 2069;
CONSISTENT_GETS_TXN        CONSTANT BINARY_INTEGER := 2070;
DB_BLKCHANGES_SEC          CONSTANT BINARY_INTEGER := 2071;
DB_BLKCHANGES_TXN          CONSTANT BINARY_INTEGER := 2072;
CONSISTENT_CHANGES_SEC     CONSTANT BINARY_INTEGER := 2073;
```

```
CONSISTENT_CHANGES_TXN       CONSTANT BINARY_INTEGER := 2074;
SESSION_CPU_SEC              CONSTANT BINARY_INTEGER := 2075;
SESSION_CPU_TXN              CONSTANT BINARY_INTEGER := 2076;
CR_BLOCKS_CREATED_SEC        CONSTANT BINARY_INTEGER := 2077;
CR_BLOCKS_CREATED_TXN        CONSTANT BINARY_INTEGER := 2078;
CR_RECORDS_APPLIED_SEC       CONSTANT BINARY_INTEGER := 2079;
CR_RECORDS_APPLIED_TXN       CONSTANT BINARY_INTEGER := 2080;
RB_RECORDS_APPLIED_SEC       CONSTANT BINARY_INTEGER := 2081;
RB_RECORDS_APPLIED_TXN       CONSTANT BINARY_INTEGER := 2082;
LEAF_NODE_SPLITS_SEC         CONSTANT BINARY_INTEGER := 2083;
LEAF_NODE_SPLITS_TXN         CONSTANT BINARY_INTEGER := 2084;
BRANCH_NODE_SPLITS_SEC       CONSTANT BINARY_INTEGER := 2085;
BRANCH_NODE_SPLITS_TXN       CONSTANT BINARY_INTEGER := 2086;
PX_DOWNGRADED_25_SEC         CONSTANT BINARY_INTEGER := 2087;
PX_DOWNGRADED_50_SEC         CONSTANT BINARY_INTEGER := 2088;
PX_DOWNGRADED_75_SEC         CONSTANT BINARY_INTEGER := 2089;
PX_DOWNGRADED_SEC            CONSTANT BINARY_INTEGER := 2090;
PX_DOWNGRADED_SER_SEC        CONSTANT BINARY_INTEGER := 2091;
PX_DOWNGRADED_SEC            CONSTANT BINARY_INTEGER := 2093;
PX_DOWNGRADED_SER_SEC        CONSTANT BINARY_INTEGER := 2095;
GC_AVG_CR_GET_TIME           CONSTANT BINARY_INTEGER := 2098;
GC_AVG_CUR_GET_TIME          CONSTANT BINARY_INTEGER := 2099;
GC_BLOCKS_CORRUPT            CONSTANT BINARY_INTEGER := 2101;
GC_BLOCKS_LOST               CONSTANT BINARY_INTEGER := 2102;
LOGONS_CURRENT               CONSTANT BINARY_INTEGER := 2103;
OPEN_CURSORS_CURRENT         CONSTANT BINARY_INTEGER := 2104;
USER_LIMIT_PCT               CONSTANT BINARY_INTEGER := 2105;
SQL_SRV_RESPONSE_TIME        CONSTANT BINARY_INTEGER := 2106;
DATABASE_WAIT_TIME           CONSTANT BINARY_INTEGER := 2107;
DATABASE_CPU_TIME            CONSTANT BINARY_INTEGER := 2108;
RESPONSE_TXN                 CONSTANT BINARY_INTEGER := 2109;
ROW_CACHE_HIT                CONSTANT BINARY_INTEGER := 2110;
ROW_CACHE_MISS               CONSTANT BINARY_INTEGER := 2111;
LIBARY_CACHE_HIT             CONSTANT BINARY_INTEGER := 2112;
LIBARY_CACHE_MISS            CONSTANT BINARY_INTEGER := 2113;
SHARED_POOL_FREE_PCT         CONSTANT BINARY_INTEGER := 2114;
PGA_CACHE_HIT                CONSTANT BINARY_INTEGER := 2115;
PROCESS_LIMIT_PCT            CONSTANT BINARY_INTEGER := 2118;
SESSION_LIMIT_PCT            CONSTANT BINARY_INTEGER := 2119;
EXECUTIONS_PER_SEC           CONSTANT BINARY_INTEGER := 2121;
DB_TIME_PER_SEC              CONSTANT BINARY_INTEGER := 2123;
STREAMS_POOL_USED_PCT        CONSTANT BINARY_INTEGER := 2136;
BLOCKED_USERS                CONSTANT BINARY_INTEGER := 4000;
ELAPSED_TIME_PER_CALL        CONSTANT BINARY_INTEGER := 6000;
CPU_TIME_PER_CALL            CONSTANT BINARY_INTEGER := 6001;
AVG_FILE_READ_TIME           CONSTANT BINARY_INTEGER := 7000;
AVG_FILE_WRITE_TIME          CONSTANT BINARY_INTEGER := 7001;
TABLESPACE_PCT_FULL          CONSTANT BINARY_INTEGER := 9000;
TABLESPACE_BYT_FREE          CONSTANT BINARY_INTEGER := 9001;

-- alert reasons -- copied from kelt.h
SUBTYPE REASON_ID_T     IS PLS_INTEGER;
RSN_SLTE        CONSTANT REASON_ID_T:= 0;            -- stateless test alert
RSN_SFTE        CONSTANT REASON_ID_T:= 1;             -- stateful test alert
RSN_SYS_BFCHP   CONSTANT REASON_ID_T:= 2;          -- buffer cache hit ratio
RSN_FIL_AFRT    CONSTANT REASON_ID_T:= 3;              -- avg file read time
RSN_SVC_ELAPC   CONSTANT REASON_ID_T:= 4;           -- service elapsed time
RSN_EVC_AUWC    CONSTANT REASON_ID_T:= 5;             -- wait session count
RSN_SES_BLUSC   CONSTANT REASON_ID_T:= 6;                   -- blocked users
RSN_SYS_GBKCR   CONSTANT REASON_ID_T:= 7;      -- global cache blocks corrupt
RSN_SYS_GBKLS   CONSTANT REASON_ID_T:= 8;         -- global cache blocks lost
RSN_SFTS        CONSTANT REASON_ID_T:= 9;                 -- tablespace alert
RSN_LQWT        CONSTANT REASON_ID_T:=10;    -- long query warning on undo tbs
RSN_LQWR        CONSTANT REASON_ID_T:=11;  -- long query warn on rollback seg
RSN_OSAT        CONSTANT REASON_ID_T:=12; -- operation suspended on tablespace
RSN_OSAR        CONSTANT REASON_ID_T:=13;      -- oper suspended on rollback seg
RSN_OSAD        CONSTANT REASON_ID_T:=14;       -- operation suspended on data
```

```
RSN_OSAQ        CONSTANT REASON_ID_T:=15;       -- operation suspended on quota
RSN_SYS_MSRTP   CONSTANT REASON_ID_T:=16;            -- memory sorts ratio
RSN_SYS_RDAHP   CONSTANT REASON_ID_T:=17;        -- redo allocation hit ratio
RSN_SYS_UTXNR   CONSTANT REASON_ID_T:=18;         -- user transaction per sec
RSN_SYS_PHRDR   CONSTANT REASON_ID_T:=19;           -- physical reads per sec
RSN_SYS_PHRDX   CONSTANT REASON_ID_T:=20;           -- physical reads per txn
RSN_SYS_PHWRR   CONSTANT REASON_ID_T:=21;          -- physical writes per sec
RSN_SYS_PHWRX   CONSTANT REASON_ID_T:=22;           -- physical write per txn
RSN_SYS_PRDDR   CONSTANT REASON_ID_T:=23;    -- physical reads direct per sec
RSN_SYS_PRDDX   CONSTANT REASON_ID_T:=24;    -- physical reads direct per txn
RSN_SYS_PWRDR   CONSTANT REASON_ID_T:=25;   -- physical writes direct per sec
RSN_SYS_PWRDX   CONSTANT REASON_ID_T:=26;   -- physcial writes direct per txn
RSN_SYS_PRDLR   CONSTANT REASON_ID_T:=27;   -- phys reads direct lobs per sec
RSN_SYS_PRDLX   CONSTANT REASON_ID_T:=28;   -- phys reads direct lobs per txn
RSN_SYS_PWDLR   CONSTANT REASON_ID_T:=29;  -- phys writes direct lobs per sec
RSN_SYS_PWDLX   CONSTANT REASON_ID_T:=30;  -- phys writes direct lobs per txn
RSN_SYS_RDGNR   CONSTANT REASON_ID_T:=31;          -- redo generated per sec
RSN_SYS_LGNTR   CONSTANT REASON_ID_T:=32;                 -- logons per sec
RSN_SYS_LGNTX   CONSTANT REASON_ID_T:=33;                 -- logons per txn
RSN_SYS_OCSTR   CONSTANT REASON_ID_T:=34;           -- open cursors per sec
RSN_SYS_OCSTX   CONSTANT REASON_ID_T:=35;           -- open cursors per txn
RSN_SYS_UCMTR   CONSTANT REASON_ID_T:=36;           -- user commits per sec
RSN_SYS_UCMTP   CONSTANT REASON_ID_T:=37;        -- user commits percentage
RSN_SYS_URBKR   CONSTANT REASON_ID_T:=38;         -- user rollbacks per sec
RSN_SYS_URBKP   CONSTANT REASON_ID_T:=39;      -- user rollbacks percentage
RSN_SYS_UCALR   CONSTANT REASON_ID_T:=40;             -- user calls per sec
RSN_SYS_UCALX   CONSTANT REASON_ID_T:=41;             -- user calls per txn
RSN_SYS_RCALR   CONSTANT REASON_ID_T:=42;        -- recursive calls per sec
RSN_SYS_RCALX   CONSTANT REASON_ID_T:=43;        -- recursive calls per txn
RSN_SYS_SLRDR   CONSTANT REASON_ID_T:=44;          -- logical reads per sec
RSN_SYS_SLRDX   CONSTANT REASON_ID_T:=45;          -- logical reads per txn
RSN_SYS_DWCPR   CONSTANT REASON_ID_T:=46;        -- DBWR checkpoints per sec
RSN_SYS_BGCPR   CONSTANT REASON_ID_T:=47;  -- background checkpoints per sec
RSN_SYS_RDWRR   CONSTANT REASON_ID_T:=48;             -- redo writes per sec
RSN_SYS_RDWRX   CONSTANT REASON_ID_T:=49;             -- redo writes per txn
RSN_SYS_LTSCR   CONSTANT REASON_ID_T:=50;        -- long table scans per sec
RSN_SYS_LTSCX   CONSTANT REASON_ID_T:=51;        -- long table scans per txn
RSN_SYS_TTSCR   CONSTANT REASON_ID_T:=52;       -- total table scans per sec
RSN_SYS_TTSCX   CONSTANT REASON_ID_T:=53;       -- total table scans per txn
RSN_SYS_FISCR   CONSTANT REASON_ID_T:=54;        -- full index scans per sec
RSN_SYS_FISCX   CONSTANT REASON_ID_T:=55;        -- full index scans per txn
RSN_SYS_TISCR   CONSTANT REASON_ID_T:=56;       -- total index scans per sec
RSN_SYS_TISCX   CONSTANT REASON_ID_T:=57;       -- total index scans per txn
RSN_SYS_TPRSR   CONSTANT REASON_ID_T:=58;      -- total parse count per sec
RSN_SYS_TPRSX   CONSTANT REASON_ID_T:=59;      -- total parse count per txn
RSN_SYS_HPRSR   CONSTANT REASON_ID_T:=60;       -- hard parse count per sec
RSN_SYS_HPRSX   CONSTANT REASON_ID_T:=61;       -- hard parse count per txn
RSN_SYS_FPRSR   CONSTANT REASON_ID_T:=62;    -- parse failure count per sec
RSN_SYS_FPRSX   CONSTANT REASON_ID_T:=63;    -- parse failure count per txn
RSN_SYS_CCHTR   CONSTANT REASON_ID_T:=64;         -- cursor cache hit ratio
RSN_SYS_DSRTR   CONSTANT REASON_ID_T:=65;              -- disk sort per sec
RSN_SYS_DSRTX   CONSTANT REASON_ID_T:=66;              -- disk sort per txn
RSN_SYS_RWPST   CONSTANT REASON_ID_T:=67;                 -- rows per sort
RSN_SYS_XNPRS   CONSTANT REASON_ID_T:=68;    -- execute without parse ratio
RSN_SYS_SFPRP   CONSTANT REASON_ID_T:=69;               -- soft parse ratio
RSN_SYS_UCALP   CONSTANT REASON_ID_T:=70;               -- user calls ratio
RSN_SYS_NTWBR   CONSTANT REASON_ID_T:=71; -- network traffic volume per sec
RSN_SYS_EQTOR   CONSTANT REASON_ID_T:=72;       -- enqueue timeouts per sec
RSN_SYS_EQTOX   CONSTANT REASON_ID_T:=73;       -- enqueue timeouts per txn
RSN_SYS_EQWTR   CONSTANT REASON_ID_T:=74;          -- enqueue waits per sec
RSN_SYS_EQWTX   CONSTANT REASON_ID_T:=75;          -- enqueue waits per txn
RSN_SYS_EQDLR   CONSTANT REASON_ID_T:=76;      -- enqueue deadlocks per sec
RSN_SYS_EQDLX   CONSTANT REASON_ID_T:=77;      -- enqueue deadlocks per txn
RSN_SYS_EQRQR   CONSTANT REASON_ID_T:=78;       -- enqueue requests per sec
RSN_SYS_EQRQX   CONSTANT REASON_ID_T:=79;       -- enqueue requests per txn
RSN_SYS_DBBGR   CONSTANT REASON_ID_T:=80;          -- db block gets per sec
RSN_SYS_DBBGX   CONSTANT REASON_ID_T:=81;          -- db block gets per txn
```

```
RSN_SYS_CRGTR  CONSTANT REASON_ID_T:=82;              -- consistent read gets per sec
RSN_SYS_CRGTX  CONSTANT REASON_ID_T:=83;              -- consistent read gets per txn
RSN_SYS_DBBCR  CONSTANT REASON_ID_T:=84;                    -- db block changes per sec
RSN_SYS_DBBCX  CONSTANT REASON_ID_T:=85;                    -- db block changes per txn
RSN_SYS_CRCHR  CONSTANT REASON_ID_T:=86;          -- consistent read changes per sec
RSN_SYS_CRCHX  CONSTANT REASON_ID_T:=87;          -- consistent read changes per txn
RSN_SYS_CPUUR  CONSTANT REASON_ID_T:=88;                         -- cpu usage per sec
RSN_SYS_CPUUX  CONSTANT REASON_ID_T:=89;                         -- cpu usage per txn
RSN_SYS_CRBCR  CONSTANT REASON_ID_T:=90;               -- cr blocks created per sec
RSN_SYS_CRBCX  CONSTANT REASON_ID_T:=91;               -- cr blocks created per txn
RSN_SYS_CRRAX  CONSTANT REASON_ID_T:=92;          -- cr undo records applied per txn
RSN_SYS_RBRAR  CONSTANT REASON_ID_T:=93;      -- user rollbk undorec appl per sec
RSN_SYS_RBRAX  CONSTANT REASON_ID_T:=94;      -- user rollbk undorec appl per txn
RSN_SYS_LNSPR  CONSTANT REASON_ID_T:=95;                   -- leaf node splits per sec
RSN_SYS_LNSPX  CONSTANT REASON_ID_T:=96;                   -- leaf node splits per txn
RSN_SYS_BNSPR  CONSTANT REASON_ID_T:=97;                 -- branch node splits per sec
RSN_SYS_BNSPX  CONSTANT REASON_ID_T:=98;                 -- branch node splits per txn
RSN_SYS_PX25R  CONSTANT REASON_ID_T:=99; -- px downgraded 25% or more per sec
RSN_SYS_PX50R CONSTANT REASON_ID_T:=100; -- px downgraded 50% or more per sec
RSN_SYS_PX75R CONSTANT REASON_ID_T:=101; -- px downgraded 75% or more per sec
RSN_SYS_PXDGR CONSTANT REASON_ID_T:=102;                     -- px downgraded per sec
RSN_SYS_PXSRR CONSTANT REASON_ID_T:=103;      -- px downgraded to serial per sec
RSN_SYS_GACRT CONSTANT REASON_ID_T:=104; -- global cache average CR get time
RSN_SYS_GACUT CONSTANT REASON_ID_T:=105; -- global cache ave current get time
RSN_SYS_LGONC CONSTANT REASON_ID_T:=106;                    -- current logons count
RSN_SYS_OPCSC CONSTANT REASON_ID_T:=107;               -- current open cursors count
RSN_SYS_USLMP CONSTANT REASON_ID_T:=108;                              -- user limit %
RSN_SYS_SQSRT CONSTANT REASON_ID_T:=109;          -- sql service response time
RSN_SYS_DBWTT CONSTANT REASON_ID_T:=110;             -- database wait time ratio
RSN_SYS_DBCPT CONSTANT REASON_ID_T:=111;              -- database cpu time ratio
RSN_SYS_RSPTX CONSTANT REASON_ID_T:=112;                  -- response time per txn
RSN_SYS_RCHTR CONSTANT REASON_ID_T:=113;                   -- row cache hit ratio
RSN_SYS_LCHTR CONSTANT REASON_ID_T:=114;               -- library cache hit ratio
RSN_SYS_LCMSR CONSTANT REASON_ID_T:=115;              -- library cache miss ratio
RSN_SYS_SPFRP CONSTANT REASON_ID_T:=116;                    -- shared pool free %
RSN_SYS_PGCHR CONSTANT REASON_ID_T:=117;                       -- pga cache hit %
RSN_SYS_PRCLP CONSTANT REASON_ID_T:=118;                       -- process limit %
RSN_SYS_SESLP CONSTANT REASON_ID_T:=119;                       -- session limit %
RSN_FIL_AFWT  CONSTANT REASON_ID_T:=120;                   -- avg file write time
RSN_EVC_DTSW  CONSTANT REASON_ID_T:=121;                     -- total time waited
RSN_SYS_RCMSR CONSTANT REASON_ID_T:=122;                   -- row cache miss ratio
RSN_RADL      CONSTANT REASON_ID_T:=123;      -- recovery area disk limit alerts
RSN_SYS_RDGNX CONSTANT REASON_ID_T:=124;                    -- redo generated per txn
RSN_SYS_CRRAR CONSTANT REASON_ID_T:=125;      -- cr undo records applied per sec
RSN_SYS_THNTF CONSTANT REASON_ID_T:=126;      -- threshold notice on system type
RSN_FIL_THNTF CONSTANT REASON_ID_T:=127;       -- threshold notice on file type
RSN_EVC_THNTF CONSTANT REASON_ID_T:=128;      -- threshold notice on event class
RSN_SVC_THNTF CONSTANT REASON_ID_T:=129;         -- threshold notice on service
RSN_TBS_THNTF CONSTANT REASON_ID_T:=130;       -- threshold notice on tablespace
RSN_SVC_CPUPC CONSTANT REASON_ID_T:=131;                -- cpu time per user call
RSN_SES_THNTF CONSTANT REASON_ID_T:=132;         -- threshold notice on sessions
RSN_SFBTS     CONSTANT REASON_ID_T:=133; -- tablespace bytes based thresholds
RSN_SYS_INQPR CONSTANT REASON_ID_T:=134;            -- instance should be quiesced
RSN_FAN_INSTANCE_UP            CONSTANT REASON_ID_T:=135;        -- instance up
RSN_FAN_INSTANCE_DOWN          CONSTANT REASON_ID_T:=136;      -- instance down
RSN_FAN_SERVICE_UP             CONSTANT REASON_ID_T:=137;         -- service up
RSN_FAN_SERVICE_DOWN           CONSTANT REASON_ID_T:=138;       -- service down
RSN_FAN_SERVICE_MEMBER_UP      CONSTANT REASON_ID_T:=139;      -- svc member up
RSN_FAN_SERVICE_MEMBER_DOWN    CONSTANT REASON_ID_T:=140;    -- svc member down
RSN_FAN_SVC_PRECONNECT_UP      CONSTANT REASON_ID_T:=141;     -- preconnect up
RSN_FAN_SVC_PRECONNECT_DOWN    CONSTANT REASON_ID_T:=142;   -- preconnect down
RSN_FAN_NODE_DOWN              CONSTANT REASON_ID_T:=143;          -- node down
RSN_FAN_ASM_INSTANCE_UP        CONSTANT REASON_ID_T:=144;  -- asm instance up
RSN_FAN_ASM_INSTANCE_DOWN      CONSTANT REASON_ID_T:=145;    -- asm inst down
RSN_FAN_DATABASE_UP            CONSTANT REASON_ID_T:=146;      -- database up
RSN_FAN_DATABASE_DOWN          CONSTANT REASON_ID_T:=147;    -- database down
RSN_SYS_DBTMR CONSTANT REASON_ID_T:=148;                       -- DB Time per Sec
```

```
RSN_SYS_XCNTR CONSTANT REASON_ID_T:=149;                 -- Executions Per Sec
RSN_STR_CAPTURE_ABORTED        CONSTANT REASON_ID_T:=150;  -- capture aborted
RSN_STR_APPLY_ABORTED          CONSTANT REASON_ID_T:=151;   -- apply aborted
RSN_STR_PROPAGATION_ABORTED    CONSTANT REASON_ID_T:=152; -- propgatn aborted
RSN_STR_STREAMSPOOL_FREE_PCT   CONSTANT REASON_ID_T:=153; -- streamspool free
RSN_STR_ERROR_QUEUE            CONSTANT REASON_ID_T:=154;
                                              -- new entry in error queue
RSN_LOG_ARCHIVE_LOG_GAP        CONSTANT REASON_ID_T:=155;
                                         -- archived log gap for logminer
RSN_SYS_ACTVS CONSTANT REASON_ID_T:=156;          -- average active sessions
RSN_SYS_SRLAT CONSTANT REASON_ID_T:=157;
                               -- Avg synchronous single-blk read latency
RSN_SYS_IOMBS CONSTANT REASON_ID_T:=158;                 -- i/o megabytes
RSN_SYS_IOREQ CONSTANT REASON_ID_T:=159;                 -- i/o requests
```

expand_message is a function that expands alert messages and returns that expanded message as a VARCHAR2.

ARGUMENT	TYPE	IN / OUT	DEFAULT VALUE
USER_LANGUAGE	VARCHAR2	IN	
MESSAGE_ID	NUMBER	IN	
ARGUMENT_1	VARCHAR2	IN	
ARGUMENT_2	VARCHAR2	IN	
ARGUMENT_3	VARCHAR2	IN	
ARGUMENT_4	VARCHAR2	IN	
ARGUMENT_5	VARCHAR2	IN	

Table 7.203: *Expand_message Parameters*

get_threshold is a procedure that fetches the current threshold settings for the specified metric.

ARGUMENT	TYPE	IN / OUT	DEFAULT VALUE
METRICS_ID	BINARY_INTEGER	IN	
WARNING_OPERATOR	BINARY_INTEGER	OUT	
WARNING_VALUE	VARCHAR2	OUT	
CRITICAL_OPERATOR	BINARY_INTEGER	OUT	
CRITICAL_VALUE	VARCHAR2	OUT	
OBSERVATION_PERIOD	BINARY_INTEGER	OUT	
CONSECUTIVE_OCCURRENCES	BINARY_INTEGER	OUT	
INSTANCE_NAME	VACRHAR2	IN	
OBJECT_TYPE	BINARY_INTEGER	IN	
OBJECT_NAME	VARCHAR2	IN	

Table 7.204: *Get_threshold Parameters*

set_threshold is a procedure that defines the active threshold settings for the specified metric, both for warning and critical states.

ARGUMENT	TYPE	IN / OUT	DEFAULT VALUE
METRICS_ID	BINARY_INTEGER	IN	
WARNING_OPERATOR	BINARY_INTEGER	OUT	
WARNING_VALUE	VARCHAR2	OUT	
CRITICAL_OPERATOR	BINARY_INTEGER	OUT	
CRITICAL_VALUE	VARCHAR2	OUT	
OBSERVATION_PERIOD	BINARY_INTEGER	OUT	
CONSECUTIVE_OCCURRENCES	BINARY_INTEGER	OUT	
INSTANCE_NAME	VACRHAR2	IN	
OBJECT_TYPE	BINARY_INTEGER	IN	
OBJECT_NAME	VARCHAR2	IN	

Table 7.205: *Set_threshold Parameters*

DBMS_WARNING

The DBMS_WARNING package provides a useful method for manipulating the behavior of PL/SQL warning messages. With it, the DBA can define what warnings are treated as errors, which are displayed, and which are suppressed.

add_warning_setting_cat is a procedure that permits modification of the previously supplied warning category to a user specified value for the current session or system's warning settings. The valid categories are ALL, INFORMATIONAL, SEVERE and PERFORMANCE. The valid values are ENABLE, DISABLE and ERROR. The scope can be either SESSION or SYSTEM.

ARGUMENT	TYPE	IN / OUT	DEFAULT VALUE
WARNING_CATEGORY	VARCHAR2	IN	
WARNING_VALUE	VARCHAR2	IN	
SCOPE	VARCHAR2	IN	

Table 7.206: *Add_warning_setting_cat Parameters*

add_warning_setting_num is a procedure that permits modification of the previously supplied warning number to a user specified value for the current session or system's warning settings. The valid values are ENABLE, DISABLE and ERROR. The scope can be either SESSION or SYSTEM.

ARGUMENT	TYPE	IN / OUT	DEFAULT VALUE
WARNING_NUMBER	NUMBER	IN	
WARNING_VALUE	VARCHAR2	IN	
SCOPE	VARCHAR2	IN	

Table 7.207: *Add_warning_setting_num Parameters*

get_category is a function that, for a given message number, returns the category as a VARCHAR2.

ARGUMENT	TYPE	IN / OUT	DEFAULT VALUE
WARNING_NUMBER	PLS_INTEGER	IN	

Table 7.208: *Get_category Parameter*

get_warning_setting_cat is a function that, for the current session, returns the warning value as a VARCHAR2.

ARGUMENT	TYPE	IN / OUT	DEFAULT VALUE
WARNING_CATEGORY	VARCHAR2	IN	

Table 7.209: *Get_warning_setting_cat Parameters*

get_warning_setting_num is a function that, for the current session, returns the warning number as a VARCHAR2.

ARGUMENT	TYPE	IN / OUT	DEFAULT VALUE
WARNING_NUMBER	NUMBER	IN	

Table 7.210: *Get_warning_setting_num Parameters*

get_warning_setting_string is a function that, for the current session, returns the warning string as a VARCHAR2. There are no parameters.

set_warning_setting_string is a procedure that permits modification of the previous settings to a user specified value for the current session or system's warning settings. The valid values are ENABLE, DISABLE and ERROR. The scope can be either SESSION or SYSTEM.

ARGUMENT	TYPE	IN / OUT	DEFAULT VALUE
WARNING_VALUE	VARCHAR2	IN	
SCOPE	VARCHAR2	IN	

Table 7.211: *Set_warning_setting_string Parameters*

DBMS_MONITOR

The DBMS_MONITOR package provides a useful method for managing additional trace and statistics gathering. This can be quite useful when one wants to programmatically control tracing from within PL/SQL code where DDL commands like ALTER SESSION are supported only via dynamic SQL.

client_id_stat_disable is a procedure that disables or turns off statistics accumulation for a user specified client identifier.

ARGUMENT	TYPE	IN / OUT	DEFAULT VALUE
CLIENT_ID	VARCHAR2	IN	

Table 7.212: *Client_id_stat_disable Parameter*

client_id_stat_enable is a procedure that enables or turns on statistics accumulation for a user specified client identifier.

ARGUMENT	TYPE	IN / OUT	DEFAULT VALUE
CLIENT_ID	VARCHAR2	IN	

Table 7.213: *Client_id_stat_enable Parameter*

client_id_trace_disable is a procedure that disables tracing for a user specified client identifier.

ARGUMENT	TYPE	IN / OUT	DEFAULT VALUE
CLIENT_ID	VARCHAR2	IN	

Table 7.214: *Client_id_trace_disable Parameter*

client_id_trace_enable is a procedure that enables tracing for a user specified client identifier. The *plan_stat* parameter valid values are NEVER, FIRST_EXECUTION (same as NULL) and ALL_EXECUTIONS.

ARGUMENT	TYPE	IN / OUT	DEFAULT VALUE
CLIENT_ID	VARCHAR2	IN	
WAITS	BOOLEAN	IN	TRUE
BINDS	BOOLEAN	IN	FALSE
PLAN_STAT	VARCHAR2	IN	NULL

Table 7.215: *Client_id_trace_enable Parameters*

database_trace_disable is a procedure that disables tracing for a user specified database instance.

ARGUMENT	TYPE	IN / OUT	DEFAULT VALUE
INSTANCE_NAME	VARCHAR2	IN	

Table 7.216: *Database_trace_disable Parameter*

database_trace_enable is a procedure that enables or turns tracing for a user specified database instance. The *plan_stat* parameter valid values are NEVER, FIRST_EXECUTION (same as NULL) and ALL_EXECUTIONS.

ARGUMENT	TYPE	IN / OUT	DEFAULT VALUE
WAITS	BOOLEAN	IN	TRUE
BINDS	BOOLEAN	IN	FALSE
INSTANCE_NAME	VARCHAR2	IN	NULL
PLAN_STAT	VARCHAR2	IN	NULL

Table 7.217: *Database_trace_enable Parameters*

serv_mod_act_stat_disable is a procedure that disables statistics accumulation for user specified service, module and action. It also deletes any previously accumulated statistics.

ARGUMENT	TYPE	IN / OUT	DEFAULT VALUE
SERVICE_NAME	VARCHAR2	IN	
MODULE_NAME	VARCHAR2	IN	
ACTION_NAME	VARCHAR2	IN	ALL_ACTIONS

Table 7.218: *Serv_mod_act_stat_disable Parameters*

serv_mod_act_stat_enable is a procedure that enables statistics accumulation for all instances represented by the user specified service, module and action.

ARGUMENT	TYPE	IN / OUT	DEFAULT VALUE
SERVICE_NAME	VARCHAR2	IN	
MODULE_NAME	VARCHAR2	IN	
ACTION_NAME	VARCHAR2	IN	ALL_ACTIONS

Table 7.219: *Serv_mod_act_stat_enable Parameters*

serv_mod_act_trace_disable is a procedure that disables tracing for a user specified service, module and action.

ARGUMENT	TYPE	IN / OUT	DEFAULT VALUE
SERVICE_NAME	VARCHAR2	IN	
MODULE_NAME	VARCHAR2	IN	
ACTION_NAME	VARCHAR2	IN	ALL_ACTIONS
INSTANCE_NAME	VARCHAR2	IN	NULL

Table 7.220: *Serv_mod_act_trace_disable Parameters*

serv_mod_act_trace_enable is a procedure that enables tracing for a user specified service, module and action. The *plan_stat* parameter valid values are NEVER, FIRST_EXECUTION (same as NULL) and ALL_EXECUTIONS.

ARGUMENT	TYPE	IN / OUT	DEFAULT VALUE
SERVICE_NAME	VARCHAR2	IN	
MODULE_NAME	VARCHAR2	IN	ANY_MODULE
ACTION_NAME	VARCHAR2	IN	ANY_ACTION
WAITS	BOOLEAN	IN	TRUE
BINDS	BOOLEAN	IN	FALSE
INSTANCE_NAME	VARCHAR2	IN	NULL
PLAN_STAT	VARCHAR2	IN	NULL

Table 7.221: *Serv_mod_act_trace_enable Parameters*

session_trace_disable is a procedure that disables tracing for a user specified session. If both the session ID and serial number parameters are NULL, then that means the current session.

ARGUMENT	TYPE	IN / OUT	DEFAULT VALUE
SESSION_ID	BINARY_INTEGER	IN	NULL
SERIAL_NUM	BINARY_INTEGER	IN	NULL

Table 7.222: *Session_trace_disable Parameters*

session_trace_enable is a procedure that enables tracing for a user specified session. If both the session ID and serial number parameters are NULL, then that means the current session. The *plan_stat* parameter valid values are NEVER, FIRST_EXECUTION and ALL_EXECUTIONS.

ARGUMENT	TYPE	IN / OUT	DEFAULT VALUE
WAITS	BOOLEAN	IN	TRUE
BINDS	BOOLEAN	IN	FALSE
PLAN_STAT	VARCHAR2	IN	NULL

Table 7.223: *Session_trace_enable Parameters*

DBMS-QOPATCH

Prior to Oracle 12c, it was not easy to List Oracle patches In 12c and beyond, you can use the DBMS_QOPATCH package to list all patches.

Advanced Oracle Utilities

Rampant author Laurent Schneider, author of the book "*Advanced SQL Programming*" has these notes on DBMS_QOPATCH:

"One of a cool new feature in Oracle 12c is the ability to query Opatch. Oracle offers a set of tables and a PL/SQL package to query the Oracle Inventory. With the DBMS-QOPATCH procedure, you can query the inventory to know if a one off patch has been deployed, which components have been deployed etc. Tables related to this feature include:

- OPATCH_XML_INV
- OPATCH_XINV_TAB
- OPATCH_INST_JOB
- OPATCH_INST_PATCH

This is the base of the feature which is accessed through a PL/SQL package DBMS_QOPATCH. The DBMS_QOPATCH package has many functions, including:

- GET_OPATCH_BUGS
- GET_OPATCH_LIST
- GET_OPATCH_FILES
- IS_PATCH_INSTALLED

For example, if we execute the GET_OPATCH_BUGS (which provides bugs list in a specific patch or for all patches), the result is a XML output:

```
SQL> select dbms_qopatch.GET_OPATCH_BUGS from dual;
```

We also see these DBMS-QOPATCH package invocations:"

```
SQL> select dbms_qopatch.GET_OPATCH_FILES from dual;

SQL> select dbms_qopatch.IS_PATCH_INSTALLED from dual;

SQL> select dbms_qopatch.GET_OPATCH_LIST from dual;
```

Conclusion

In this chapter a wide range of PL/SQL programmatic APIs that provide the foundation for the challenging and rewarding activities of database monitoring, diagnostics and tuning was covered. Oracle versions 10g and 11g have made these tasks much easier, so the self-diagnostic and self-healing claims are generally true. When properly planned and configured, a modern Oracle database needs much less care and attention than in days past. However, that requires effective planning and efficient configuration as well as some managed best practices to maintain that happy state. The following chapter will detail the foundational tools Oracle provides to support such efforts.

Next to be delved into are Oracle Advisory and Diagnostic Utilities, some of whose fundamental programmatic interfaces were exposed in this chapter. The focus will extend much deeper into the task being performed which should add context to much of the reference materials from this chapter.

Oracle Advisory and Diagnostic Utilities

Introduction

When Oracle 10g was released, Oracle introduced its common manageability infrastructure, also known as the advisory framework. This framework includes server-based advisors, chief among them being the Automatic Database Diagnostic Monitor (ADDM). Embedded within ADDM, since it can call other lower-level advisors, are advisors related to SQL, memory and space management.

The named advisors include:

- SQL Tuning Advisor
- SQL Access Advisor
- PGA Advisor
- SGA Advisor
- Segment Advisor
- Undo Advisor

In release 11g, there are advisors and other tools introduced in 10g, and there are also two new utilities: the Automatic Diagnostic Repository (ADR) and the SQL Performance Advisor (SPA).

To further clarify, the following question should be addressed: Is Feature X an advisor, a utility, or both? Depending on the feature, the answer in many cases is both. Access to several advisors outside of a GUI, such as Enterprise Manager, can be accomplished by executing the underlying SQL scripts. A classic example of that is the Automatic Workload Repository. An AWR report contains several advisory-like sections. Deep inside an AWR report, there is a section on Advisory Statistics.

Advisory Statistics

- Instance Recovery Stats
- Buffer Pool Advisory
- PGA Aggr Summary
- PGA Aggr Target Stats
- PGA Aggr Target Histogram
- PGA Memory Advisory
- Shared Pool Advisory
- SGA Target Advisory
- Streams Pool Advisory
- Java Pool Advisory

Back to Top

Figure 8.1: *Advisory Statistics in AWR*

The PGA and SGA statistics captured in the report can also be obtained via canned SQL scripts.

As a caution, it is up to the DBA to determine access to use extended licensed features. If one is not licensed to use the Tuning or Diagnostics packs, for example, not only does that mean these utilities cannot be used within Enterprise Manager, or Database Control and GUI variations thereof, it also means one cannot use any script – the DBA's or Oracle's – to query the contents of any of the workload repository tables and views. If there are any doubts about what one is licensed for, contact the Oracle sales representative. The Licensing Information guide published with each release can also be reviewed.

With that caution out of the way, start by looking at two new features in 11g and then cover some historical utilities. The first two sections cover ADRCI and SQL Performance Analyzer (SPA). Both sections are somewhat lengthy because of their nature: they are quite powerful and useful. One can only hope that they will be back-ported to older versions of Oracle as that is how good they are.

ADRCI: ADR Command Interpreter

The ADR of interest here is the Automatic Diagnostic Repository, not the ADR (Automatic Data Repair) associated with LogMiner. The Automatic

Diagnostic Repository maintains diagnostic data that can be uploaded to Oracle using the Incident Packaging Service (IPS). As in the old days, part of what Oracle still asks for is a zipped or compressed set of files created by having downloaded and run the RDA tool. The remote diagnostics script(s) collected information about the system. In one sense, ADR can be thought of as a prepositioned hRDA tool within the database.

If support analysts can look at diagnostic data, then so can the DBA. From Oracle's perspective, it is easy to see where they are coming from, as in "Let's make it easier for customers to not only diagnose failure, but also to package it up and send us information in a standardized format." The side benefit of this perspective is that now the data can be seen in the same format or package. This could be done before to a large degree with RDA, but this is even better.

Changes in Oracle 11g

The architecture of how the RDBMS is installed on a computer has also undergone some significant changes. To be honest, use of Oracle 11g is going to be somewhat of a culture shock to people accustomed to older versions of Oracle. The number one shock will be saying goodbye to the Windows SQL*Plus interface for what is there now is a command prompt window. Number two is the location of dump and trace files in relation to the old admin directory. And the number three most significant shock, though there are more than just three, is how the contents of the alert log are produced. The standard alert log in 11g is an XML file. Not to worry since Oracle still provides the old version of the alert log in another directory.

Part of the new architecture includes a "diag" directory in what is analogous to ORACLE_BASE/diag/rdbms/<SID>. The arrangement of certain files is referred to as a unified directory structure and this structure can apply to more than one instance. Each instance has its own ADR Home, and just like ORACLE_HOME, there is an ADR Base.

The ADR Home turns out to be a file-based repository of diagnostic related data such as the alert log, trace files, and dumps. The idea of an ADR Home even extends to RAC and ASM. Crashes, faults, problems - whatever the errant condition is - can be viewed as incidents, and that leads back to being able to package up files relevant to an incident, hence the Incident Packaging Service. All of this is part of the fault diagnosibility infrastructure.

The command interpreter interface into the ADR is the ADRCI command-line tool (adrci.sh or adrci.exe). ADRCI enables viewing diagnostic data, viewing Health Monitor reports, and as mentioned, performing incident packaging operations.

There are two ways to access the Automatic Diagnostic Repository. One is via the Enterprise Manager Support Workbench. Since it is "known" that GUI tools are for the weak and lazy, it is best to concentrate on the command-line interface. In all seriousness, the ability to invoke the command line utility should hover around 100%, even if the database is not open or the console is not running, or host credentials are not set, or Web interface is not enabled or blocked in the environment. The idea that relying on Enterprise Manager factors in many points of failure should be coming clearer. Therefore, knowing how to use ADRCI is evidently useful.

ADRCI Command Line Interface

The commands are not too exotic and using SHOW, SET and HELP make the tool feel a lot like the listener control utility *lsnrctl*. That is another advantage of ADRCI over Enterprise Manager: the commands in ADRCI are here and now. OEM has latency issues. How many times has one seen the big red down arrow indicating the instance is down while at the same time the DBA is logged in via SQL*Plus?

By means of a quick introduction to ADRCI, here is the start of a session, some "where am I" information, and an output of help topics.

```
C:\>adrci

ADRCI: Release 11.1.0.6.0 - Beta on Sat Sep 20 15:38:12 2008

Copyright (c) 1982, 2007, Oracle.  All rights reserved.

ADR base = "c:\app\ora11g"
adrci> show home
ADR Homes:
diag\clients\user_unknown\host_411310321_11
diag\rdbms\db11\db11
diag\tnslsnr\t42\listener
adrci> help

 HELP [topic]
   Available Topics:
       CREATE REPORT
```

```
ECHO
EXIT
HELP
HOST
IPS
PURGE
RUN
SET BASE
SET BROWSER
SET CONTROL
SET ECHO
SET EDITOR
SET HOMES | HOME | HOMEPATH
SET TERMOUT
SHOW ALERT
SHOW BASE
SHOW CONTROL
SHOW HM_RUN
SHOW HOMES | HOME | HOMEPATH
SHOW INCDIR
SHOW INCIDENT
SHOW PROBLEM
SHOW REPORT
SHOW TRACEFILE
SPOOL
```

```
There are other commands intended to be used directly by Oracle, type
"HELP EXTENDED" to see the list
```

> 🔔 Notice the output is based on a Windows installation. If one wants a UNIX look-and-feel interface on a Windows PC, install Cygwin and then use UNIX commands and the vi utility to view output files.

See in the paths that "db11" is repeated. The path structure is based on diag/product_type/product_id/instance_id, where *product_id* is the database name and *instance_id* is the SID. In this example, the database name is the same as the SID, so that is why "db11" appears to repeat.

The hierarchy of directories within the repository is shown below.

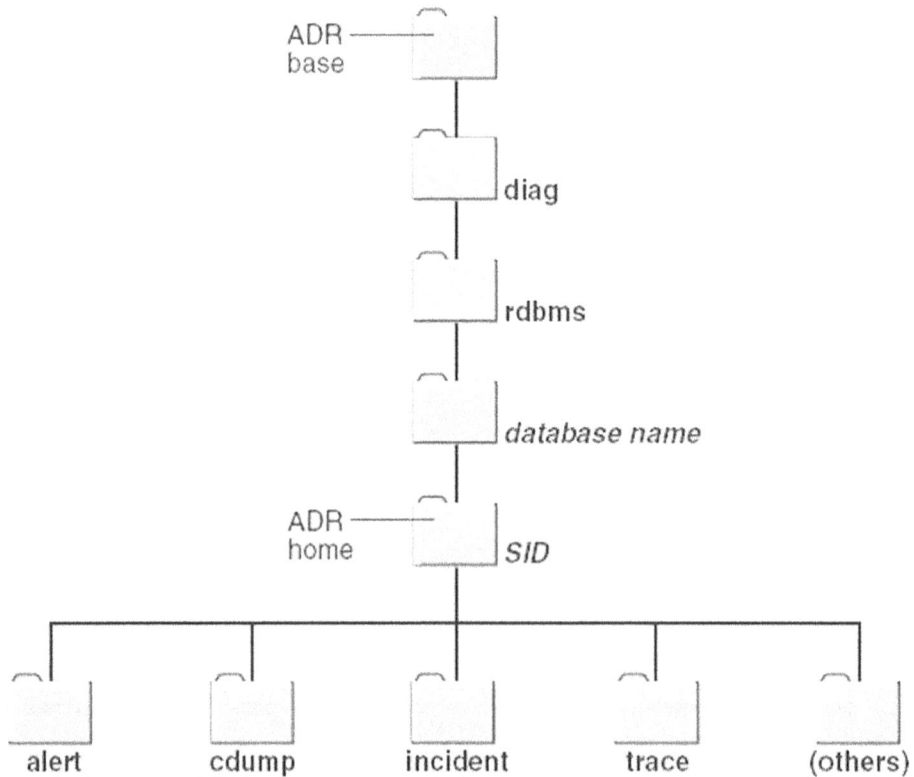

Figure 8.2: *ADR Hierarchy*

> 🔔 The *v$diag_info* data dictionary view can also be queried to determine locations of the various folders.

Being able to start the utility is obviously a good sign. Before starting, however, the platform or environment setup needs to be considered. There are a lot of things for free in a Windows environment that are not in a *NIX (all UNIX variants) one. In either case, check the *diagnostic_dest* initialization parameter value in a SQL*Plus session. On the author's PC used throughout the remainder of this chapter for examples, *diagnostic_dest* is set to C:\APP\ORA11G.

```
SQL> show parameter diag

NAME                                    TYPE        VALUE
------------------------------------    -----------  -------------
diagnostic_dest                         string      C:\APP\ORA11G
```

> 🔔 Starting in release 11g, BACKGROUND_DUMP_DEST and USER_DUMP_DEST became deprecated. Both are replaced by the new DIAGNOSTIC_DEST parameter. The location is associated with ORACLE_BASE, if set, or ORACLE_HOME/log if not.

The important information to take away here is, of course, to ensure the DBA is working in the correct environment and with the database, or instance(s), of interest. RAC nodes and ASM will have their own ADR setup, and those could be spanning a common file system.

ADR deals with problems, so create one in order to have something to work with. Is every problem reportable, that is, is any ORA error recorded in the alert log sufficient to create an incident? The answer is no. Some errors are obviously serious and others represent PEBKAC (problem exists between keyboard and chair, i.e., the user). ADRCI will report on critical problems, which are the ones that Oracle considers to be critical which may not coincide with what the DBA believes is critical.

An easy error to generate and know that it will be recorded in the alert log is to attempt to shrink a datafile to a size lower than the high-watermark. Pick a datafile at random and attempt to resize it to something obviously nonsensical.

```
SQL> select file_name from dba_data_files;

FILE_NAME
----------------------------------------------------------------
C:\APP\ORA11G\ORADATA\DB11\USERS01.DBF
C:\APP\ORA11G\ORADATA\DB11\UNDOTBS01.DBF
C:\APP\ORA11G\ORADATA\DB11\SYSAUX01.DBF
C:\APP\ORA11G\ORADATA\DB11\SYSTEM01.DBF
C:\APP\ORA11G\ORADATA\DB11\EXAMPLE01.DBF

SQL> alter database datafile 'C:\APP\ORA11G\ORADATA\DB11\SYSTEM01.DBF'
  2   resize 2M;
alter database datafile 'C:\APP\ORA11G\ORADATA\DB11\SYSTEM01.DBF'
*
ERROR at line 1:
ORA-03297: file contains used data beyond requested RESIZE value
```

The tail of the (normal) alert log has recorded the error.

```
alter database datafile 'C:\APP\ORA11G\ORADATA\DB11\SYSTEM01.DBF'
resize 2M
ORA-3297 signalled during: alter database datafile
'C:\APP\ORA11G\ORADATA\DB11\SYSTEM01.DBF'
resize 2M...
```

Keep this error in mind and generate another, more serious error. A corrupt block is pretty serious, but how does the DBA get one when he does not really want one? Use BBED, the Block Browser and Editor tool, covered elsewhere in this book. Another way to corrupt a block, and to some degree a file, is to use a Hex editor such as UltraEdit. Take a cold backup, edit the USERS01 datafile by changing a character (look for OPERATIONS and change it to PPERATIONS while in Hex edit mode), save and close, then startup the database. The following error output should show up:

```
SQL> conn / as sysdba
Connected to an idle instance.
SQL> startup
ORACLE instance started.

Total System Global Area   535662592 bytes
Fixed Size                   1334380 bytes
Variable Size              205521812 bytes
Database Buffers           322961408 bytes
Redo Buffers                 5844992 bytes
Database mounted.
ORA-01157: cannot identify/lock data file 4 - see DBWR trace file
ORA-01110: data file 4: 'C:\APP\ORA11G\ORADATA\DB11\USERS01.DBF'
```

That is a bit more serious than a user error for a wrong size while resizing a datafile. Start ADRCI and set the home to the rdbms path, but leave all homes in the SHOW HOME output.

The next step is to see what SHOW INCIDENT displays. In the output below, a CREATE_TIME column is not shown due to editing/page size limitations.

```
adrci> set homepath diag\rdbms\db11\db11
adrci> show incident

ADR Home = c:\app\ora11g\diag\rdbms\db11\db11:
*********************************************************
INCIDENT_ID          PROBLEM_KEY

-------------------- -----------------------------------
8545                 ORA 600 [kcidr_io_check_common_6]
```

```
1 rows fetched
```

Note that the database did not and does not have to be opened or have an instance running, for that matter, in order to use ADRCI.

Pretending that one is clueless about what caused this error, or realistically, had it been a true ORA-00600 or ORA-07445 error that often times mandate getting assistance from Oracle Support Services, it is now time to generate a package and finalize it before uploading into a Service Request on MetaLink.

> To recap where one is so far in the process: the tool (ADRCI) has been identified, there is a problem (an ORA-00600 error), and there is an incident (only the critical error, not the user one, but an incident can have more than one error associated with it).

The problem has an identifier or problem key, which generally speaking is the error number and the error message. One needs to start a session and choose the relevant ADR Home. So look at some other useful commands along the way to creating the package.

Use the "show home" command to see which ADR homes are available, followed by the "set homepath" as necessary. Note that more than one home can be involved in an incident. Only the rdbms home need apply in this example for viewing a specific file.

```
adrci> set homepath diag\rdbms\db11\db11
adrci> show home
ADR Homes:
diag\rdbms\db11\db11
```

With a specific home set, use ADRCI to view the tail of the XML-based alert log file. The output will have the XML stripped off. The syntax is:

```
show alert -tail [options]
```

The options are quite similar to UNIX. Using "tail –f" in an ADRCI session, one is able to view new entries into the log file as they occur. As an experiment, try using "show alert –tail –f" in an ADRCI session, and then in

---

ADRCI: ADR Command Interpreter

another session, switch the logfile via "alter system switch logfile" and the "Thread 1 advanced..." output appears in the ADRCI's session window.

> 🔔 Despite what Oracle's documentation says, using Control-C to end the live monitoring will not only end the tailing of the file, it will also terminate the ADRCI session.

Even more intuitive regarding available commands is spooling a session to a file. SPOOL ON <path/filename> and SPOOL OFF do the trick.

If it is known that there is a tracefile, or if one simply wants to view all tracefiles, the intuitive command of "show tracefile" will support that need. Yet as is well known, not all trace files are germane with respect to an incident.

Since there is an incident number, are there any trace files associated with it?

```
adrci> show tracefile -i 8545
    diag\rdbms\db11\db11\incident\incdir_8545\db11_m000_4844_i8545.trc
```

Yes, as luck has it, there is a trace file. Remember, that is luck only in the sense that one was needed for this example, but lucky in real life, no. What are the details about this incident?

ADRCI will list incident reports in a brief or detail mode, and also by a specific incident number in case there is more than one in the repository. Looking at the detailed output for this incident, the following comes up.

```
adrci> show incident -mode detail

ADR Home = c:\app\ora11g\diag\rdbms\db11\db11:
*********************************************************************

*********************************************************
INCIDENT INFO RECORD 1
*********************************************************
    INCIDENT_ID                8545
    STATUS                     ready
    CREATE_TIME                2008-09-20 18:40:36.762000 -06:00
    PROBLEM_ID                 1
    CLOSE_TIME                 <NULL>
    FLOOD_CONTROLLED           none
    ERROR_FACILITY             ORA
    ERROR_NUMBER               600
    ERROR_ARG1                 kcidr_io_check_common_6
    ERROR_ARG2                 4
```

```
ERROR_ARG3                      C:\APP\ORA11G\ORADATA\DB11\USERS01.DBF
ERROR_ARG4                      8192
ERROR_ARG5                      2
ERROR_ARG6                      4
ERROR_ARG7                      <NULL>
ERROR_ARG8                      <NULL>
SIGNALLING_COMPONENT            <NULL>
SIGNALLING_SUBCOMPONENT         <NULL>
SUSPECT_COMPONENT               <NULL>
SUSPECT_SUBCOMPONENT            <NULL>
ECID                            <NULL>
IMPACTS                         0
PROBLEM_KEY                     ORA 600 [kcidr_io_check_common_6]
FIRST_INCIDENT                  8545
FIRSTINC_TIME                   2008-09-20 18:40:36.762000 -06:00
LAST_INCIDENT                   8545
LASTINC_TIME                    2008-09-20 18:40:36.762000 -06:00
IMPACT1                         0
IMPACT2                         0
IMPACT3                         0
IMPACT4                         0
KEY_NAME                        ProcId
KEY_VALUE                       18.2
KEY_NAME                        Client ProcId
KEY_VALUE                       ORACLE.EXE.1116_4844
KEY_NAME                        SID
KEY_VALUE                       154.5
OWNER_ID                        1
INCIDENT_FILE
c:\app\ora11g\diag\rdbms\db11\db11\trace\db11_m000_4844.trc
OWNER_ID                        1
INCIDENT_FILE
c:\app\ora11g\diag\rdbms\db11\db11\incident\ ↵
incdir_8545\db11_m000_4844_i8545.trc
1 rows fetched
```

Now it is time to package the incident. Packaging an incident is a three-step process. The main part of packaging is to go from the logical to the physical. Right now, there is metadata about the incident, so create a physical set of data, i.e a set of files which contains the incident information. The steps are:

1. Create a logical package

2. Add diagnostic information to the package

3. Generate the physical package

The package can be based on one of the following attributes:

- Empty (and add items in step 2)

- Incident number

- Problem number

- Problem key
- Time interval

Different failure scenarios justify the options. The same repeated error could be grouped together by the problem key as the occurrences will have different times and incident numbers. For multiple errors, a time interval would be the most convenient grouping set. There is an error but the DBA is not sure what to hone in on yet, so an empty package is created waiting for the input. For the very specific, as in the working example, an incident number fits.

The second step is optional if anything but the empty package option was chosen. Even if something else was chosen, this is when and where additional files can be added with the restriction that they reside in the ADR base directory hierarchy. It should go without saying that if an empty package is created, then Step 2 is mandatory. ADRCI uses commands to add files to packages.

Finally, generate the physical incident package. Just like in using the old RDA tool, the DBA is required to compress the files before uploading to MetaLink. In ADRCI, create full or incremental zip files as the contents of the package. Incremental files cannot be added unless there is a complete file present. Additionally, the files can also be sequenced. How are the files associated? They are associated by the leading part of the error number and a timestamp.

Use the IPS CREATE PACKAGE [options] command to create the physical package. Given that there is an incident number, use that as follows.

```
adrci> ips create package incident 8545
Created package 1 based on incident id 8545, correlation level typical
```

What showed up? There is now a logical container identified as package 1. Assuming that no additional files are being added (Step 2), the next step is to create the zip file by generating the package.

Using C:\temp because it is easy to navigate to, the following appears:

```
adrci> ips generate package 1 in c:\temp
Generated package 1 in file c:\temp\ORA600kci_20080920194531_COM_1.zip, mode
complete
```

It is known that the incident was an ORA-00600 error with the time of package creation being September 20, 2008 around 1945 hours. It is a complete file (COM versus INC), and it is file number 1. As proof positive, the zip file exists in C:\TEMP.

Figure 8.3: *Packaged Incident File*

So what is in the zip file? Extract it and see. What will be found is a copy of the folder hierarchy, some metadata, and copies of relevant files, which includes the trace file and the alert log.

With the zipped package, the DBA is now ready to provide Oracle support with the information they need to help. Not only does the service request process change a bit with this built-in fault diagnosis and reporting capability, so does the interface to MetaLink. The changeover is phased based on the products one uses, but as of September 20, 2008, MetaLink became "My Oracle Support" for many customers.

The classic MetaLink interface can still be used for awhile, but get used to the Flash-based My Oracle Support process. It is quite sharp looking and one can tell a lot of work went into creating a more professional interface.

Do not forget to restore the cold backup. A working database is needed for the next topic.

Flood control

What happens when there are many, perhaps hundreds, of problems within a given time interval? A problem is a critical error, and an incident is an

---

occurrence of a problem. ADR, specifically the fault diagnosibility infrastructure, uses flood control to limit the number of incidents for a given problem.

The threshold levels are five incidents (same problem) within an hour, and 25 incidents (same problem) per day. After an hour or a day has passed, full recording of incidents will take place. If 50 incidents are encountered in an hour or 250 for the day, incidents beyond that, also for the same problem, are not recorded. They are still recorded to the alert log, but the ADR collection aspect of this process is suspended.

There is a complete listing of commands for ADRCI in Chapter 15 of the Oracle Database Utilities Guide. As can be imagined, there are literally hundreds of options or variations for commands. As promised in the beginning of this section, there is now a complete set of steps to not only generate an error for use within ADR, but also how to report on an incident and generate a package used by Oracle Support Services.

In summary, nothing has really changed to what takes place in a "problem detection, gather information, create service request, continue to work on problem" workflow. What has changed in Oracle 11g are some of the mechanics. Now there is a built-in repository (the ADR), a command-line (and Web interface), and how Oracle Support interacts with the DBA using Configuration Manager within My Oracle Support.

ADRCI offers the following features:

- Command-line interface with intuitive commands
- Readily accessible, does not rely on the database being open
- Automates the collection and packaging of many files
- Allows one to add one's own files
- Standardizes the content and exchange of information between you and Oracle Support

As has been seen, ADRCI is quick and easy to use. Plus, how to practice using the utility by creating one's own critical, but recoverable, error, has also been shown.

SQL Performance Analyzer

The SQL Performance Analyzer, or SPA, is another new feature introduced in release 11g. SPA, and another feature named Database Replay, fall under what is known as Real Application Testing.

The distinction between the two is that Database Replay, as its name implies, enables the replaying of events within a database. SPA, on the other hand, provides insight into how a change would play out from having run a SQL tuning set.

During a database migration or upgrade, execution plans can change. In fact, that was a problem faced by many users who upgraded to 10g. Internet Q&A forums are rife with questions and postings about how a database's performance went into the tank after upgrading to 10g even though 10g is and was much better than any prior release. So, regardless of whether the DBA is upgrading or just wanting to test the impact of adding an index, SPA will accommodate that investigation. Any activity that may impact a statement's execution plan is a candidate for using SPA to investigate the possible consequences – both good and bad.

Defining a Workflow

Using SPA is based on a five-step workflow:

1. Capture the workload

2. Gather performance metrics before the change

3. Introduce a change

4. Gather performance metrics after the change

5. Compare the before and after performance

As a testing methodology, those steps are as old as dirt. Amazingly enough, many users have a hard time adhering to this plan or any other. Oftentimes, Step 3 becomes "Introduce many changes." The interaction between changes can confound the interpretation of the results. Is the database faster because of factor X or factor Y? One just does not know.

Somewhat implied here is that the change is made elsewhere, as in not on the production instance, especially if the workload is resource intensive. Step 1 requires collecting an SQL Tuning Set (STS). Step 2 captures query statements, so inserts, updates, and deletes are not analyzed. In Step 4, SPA executes statements and generates execution plans and statistics. Finally in Step 5, review the report SPA has generated and, from there, invoke other tools such as the SQL Tuning Advisor or make changes on one's own. If needed, the cycle can be repeated.

Just like in the previous section on ADRCI, the same arguments apply for and against using Enterprise Manager and a command-line interface. The command-line interface this time around is not s separate executable, but rather, is an Oracle-supplied PL/SQL built-in named DBMS_SQLPA.

Ideally, the test system should be a clone of production. In practicality, make it as close as possible. The cost of maintaining a 3-node RAC architecture for development, and one for QA, can be prohibitive. The realization is that for whatever reason, testing is performed on a production system. SQL Performance Analyzer supports that option as well. If one can and does test on a separate server, then there is the additional task of exporting a table related to the STS and importing it into the test instance.

It should also be obvious that since SQL Performance Analyzer uses a SQL Tuning Set, the only versions from which an STS can be collected are 10g and above. If one is still using release 8i or 9i, then one must upgrade to at least 10g.

A working example

Many ad-hoc examples found on Web sites, blogs, and other books tend to use the *all_objects* data dictionary view as a source for generating test data. Therefore, for the sake of consistency, so will this example.

As mentioned, the "tool" is the DBMS_SQLPA package. Its subprograms are listed below.

- CANCEL_ANALYSIS_TASK
- CREATE_ANALYSIS_TASK
- DROP_ANALYSIS_TASK

- EXECUTE_ANALYSIS_TASK

- INTERRUPT_ANALYSIS_TASK

- REPORT_ANALYSIS_TASK

- RESET_ANALYSIS_TASK

- RESUME_ANALYSIS_TASK

- SET_ANALYSIS_TASK_PARAMETER

- SET_ANALYSIS_DEFAULT_PARAMETER

The three analysis tasks of interest here are the create, execute and report subprograms. Use the SCOTT schema, create a replica of *all_objects* and populate the new table with a dump of SELECT * from *all_objects*. A relatively easy test case or "what if" scenario concerns adding an index to the new objects table. An index on what, though?

If using 11g out of the box, the SCOTT account must be unlocked and have the password reset. To get a feel for the amount of data, there are around 53,750 objects and 24 object types. Synonyms and Java classes account for just over 90%, so in terms of selectivity, the next most populous object (views) accounts for 3% and everything else is less than that. Object type seems like a good candidate for being indexed given that most of the queries are looking names of tables, views, packages, functions, procedures and triggers.

Use CTAS (Create Table As) to create the table and then gather table statistics using DBMS_STATS.GATHER_TABLE_STATS. For the SCOTT schema, one could also use GATHER_SCHEMA_STATS because it is a relatively small schema.

The target table, in keeping with examples elsewhere, is named MY_OBJECTS.

```
create table my_objects as select * from all_objects;

exec dbms_stats.gather_table_stats ('scott','my_objects');
```

Execute a variety of SQL statements (all queries).

```
SELECT object_type, count(*) FROM my_objects
GROUP by object_type ORDER BY 2 desc;
SELECT object_name FROM my_objects
```

```
WHERE object_type = 'VIEW';
SELECT object_name FROM my_objects
WHERE object_type like 'PACKAGE%';
SELECT count(*) FROM my_objects
WHERE object_type NOT IN ('SYNONYMS','JAVA CLASS');
SELECT object_name FROM my_objects
WHERE object_type = 'EDITION';
```

Now create an SQL set using DBMS_TUNE.CREATE_SQLSET, load up a SQLSET cursor, and view what is in DBA_SQLSET_STATEMENTS.

> 🔔 The ADMINISTER SQL TUNING SET privilege will need to be
> granted to SCOTT beforehand.

```
set serveroutput on
EXEC DBMS_SQLTUNE.CREATE_SQLSET(sqlset_name => 'my_obj_sqlset');

DECLARE
  v_cursor   DBMS_SQLTUNE.SQLSET_CURSOR;
BEGIN
  OPEN v_cursor FOR
     SELECT VALUE(x)
     FROM TABLE(
       DBMS_SQLTUNE.SELECT_CURSOR_CACHE(
         basic_filter => 'sql_text LIKE ''%my_objects%''
         and parsing_schema_name = ''SCOTT''',
         attribute_list => 'ALL')) x;

  DBMS_SQLTUNE.LOAD_SQLSET
    (sqlset_name => 'my_obj_sqlset',
     populate_cursor => v_cursor);
END;
/
```

As confirmation that the tuning set is loaded, use the following query.

```
SQL> SELECT sql_text
  2  FROM dba_sqlset_statements
  3  WHERE sqlset_name = 'my_obj_sqlset';

SQL_TEXT
------------------------------------------------
SELECT object_name FROM my_objects
WHERE object_type = 'VIEW'

SELECT object_name FROM my_objects
WHERE object_type = 'EDITION'

SELECT count(*) FROM my_objects
WHERE object_type NOT IN ('SYNONYMS','JAVA CLASS')
```

```
SELECT object_type, count(*) FROM my_objects
GROUP by object_type ORDER BY 2 desc

SELECT object_name FROM my_objects
WHERE object_type like 'PACKAGE%'
```

The next steps are to get a task name for use within the call to DBMS_SQLPA.EXECUTE_ANALYSIS.

```
VARIABLE v_task VARCHAR2(64);
EXEC :v_task :=  DBMS_SQLPA.CREATE_ANALYSIS_TASK
(sqlset_name => 'my_obj_sqlset');

PRINT :v_task
```

In the working example, the task name is TASK_35. Call the before change run *before_index* and the after change run *after_index*. It is known that something is being changed, i.e. adding an index, so use something more descriptive than *before_change* and *after_change*, but that is up to the DBA. Substitute the task name or take advantage of the bind variable construct.

```
BEGIN
  DBMS_SQLPA.EXECUTE_ANALYSIS_TASK(
    task_name        => :v_task,
    execution_type   => 'test execute',
    execution_name   => 'before_index');
END;
/
```

Now at Step 3, make the change, which is to add an index to the table as well as gather table statistics.

```
CREATE INDEX idx_my_objects_type on my_objects(object_type);
exec DBMS_STATS.GATHER_TABLE_STATS
('scott','my_objects',cascade=>TRUE);
```

The after change job of *after_index* is ready to be run.

```
BEGIN
  DBMS_SQLPA.EXECUTE_ANALYSIS_TASK(
    task_name        => :v_task,
    execution_type   => 'test execute',
    execution_name   => 'after_index');
END;
/
```

Compare the runs by execution name, or if those are left out, the last two EXECUTE_ANALYSIS_TASK calls will be used.

```
BEGIN
  DBMS_SQLPA.EXECUTE_ANALYSIS_TASK(
    task_name        => :v_task,
    execution_type   => 'compare performance',
    execution_params => dbms_advisor.arglist(
      'execution_name1',
      'before_index',
      'execution_name2',
      'after_index'));
END;
/
```

Finally, the moment one has been waiting for: what is the impact of adding an index to the MY_OBJECTS table? The API to extract this information is the REPORT_ANALYSIS_TASK function of DBMS_SQLPA. There are several options, so it is worth a moment to look at some of them.

First, how does one need the report to appear? The choices are text (the default), HTML and XML. Next is the level of detail. The choices are shown below.

LEVEL	DESCRIPTION
BASIC	Same as typical
TYPICAL (default)	Information about all statements
ALL	Details of all SQL
IMPROVED	Only improved SQL
REGRESSED	Only regressed SQL
CHANGED	SQL with changed performance
UNCHANGED	Opposite of CHANGED
CHANGED_PLANS	Only SQL with plan changes
UNCHANGED_PLANS	Opposite of above
ERRORS	SQL with errors only

Table 8.1: *DBMS_SQLPA Options*

In the working example, several of the level choices would fit since it would not be unreasonable to presume there will be some improvement and change. Also, maybe there will be some degradation.

The function is shown below. Oracle's documentation shows an extra trailing right parenthesis, so delete that character if cutting and pasting from that source.

```
DBMS_SQLPA.REPORT_ANALYSIS_TASK(
  task_name       IN VARCHAR2,
  type            IN VARCHAR2 := 'text',
  level           IN VARCHAR2 := 'typical',
  section         IN VARCHAR2 := 'summary',
  object_id       IN NUMBER   := NULL,
  top_sql         IN NUMBER   := 100,
  task_owner      IN VARCHAR2 := NULL,
  execution_name  IN VARCHAR2 := NULL)
RETURN CLOB;
```

For these purposes, go with a report in HTML format. The simplest case would be to pass the task name in and default to everything else. Set up the session for spooling to include a path and file name and invoke the function by selecting from DUAL.

```
SET LONG 1000000
SET PAGESIZE 0
SET LINESIZE 200
SET LONGCHUNKSIZE 200
SET TRIMSPOOL ON
SPOOL C:\temp\spa_index_test.html
SPOOL C:\temp\spa_index_test.html
SELECT DBMS_SQLPA.REPORT_ANALYSIS_TASK
('TASK_35','HTML','ALL','ALL')
FROM   dual;
SPOOL OFF
```

Of the five statements, four of them improved, and one had no change. A section for one of the statements that improved appears as follows.

SQL Details:

Object ID   : 20
Schema Name   : SCOTT
SQL ID   : 47s9qs2y976ph
Execution Frequency : 1
SQL Text   : SELECT object_name FROM my_objects WHERE object_type like 'PACKAGE%'

Execution Statistics:

Stat Name	Impact on Workload	Value Before	Value After	Impact on SQL	% Workload Before	% Workload After
elapsed_time	6.69%	.016	0	100%	6.69%	0%
parse_time	0%	0	0	0%	0%	0%
cpu_time	9.09%	.02	0	100%	9.09%	0%
buffer_gets	18.5%	814	61	92.51%	20%	5.36%
cost	18.23%	228	14	93.86%	19.42%	3.6%
reads	0%	0	0	0%	0%	0%
writes	0%	0	0	0%	0%	0%
rows	%	422	422	%	%	%

Findings (2):

1. The performance of this SQL has improved.
2. The structure of the SQL execution plan has changed.

Figure 8.4: *Results Table*

The execution plan section shows that a full table scan was used before and the index was used after the change.

Execution Plan Before Change:

Plan Id   : 12
Plan Hash Value : 880823944

Id	Operation	Name	Rows	Bytes	Cost	Time
0	SELECT STATEMENT		2240	80640	228	00:00:03
* 1	TABLE ACCESS FULL MY_OBJECTS		2240	80640	228	00:00:03

Predicate Information (identified by operation id):

- 1 - filter("OBJECT_TYPE" LIKE 'PACKAGE%')

Execution Plan After Change:

Plan Id   : 19
Plan Hash Value : 2882451183

Id	Operation	Name	Rows	Bytes	Cost	Time
0	SELECT STATEMENT		352	12672	14	00:00:01
1	TABLE ACCESS BY INDEX ROWID	MY_OBJECTS	352	12672	14	00:00:01
* 2	INDEX RANGE SCAN	IDX_MY_OBJECTS_TYPE	352		2	00:00:01

Predicate Information (identified by operation id):

- 2 - access("OBJECT_TYPE" LIKE 'PACKAGE%')
- 2 - filter("OBJECT_TYPE" LIKE 'PACKAGE%')

Figure 8.5: *Execution Plan Comparisons*

Miscellaneous items

All in all, this was not too hard to setup and get running. There may be odd errors along the way when varying the input parameters (ORA-01478 array bind error), so try using a different format with respect to named versus positional parameters.

If there is a need to start over, use the DELETE or DROP_SQLSET procedure in DBMS_SQLTUNE. Try to make the statements as clean as possible such as avoiding extra SELECT statements and making the statement identification easy to find. For example, a table could be aliased with XXX, so that string would be unusual to find in Oracle but easy to filter on.

Enterprise Manager offers a streamlined interface into the SQL Performance Analyzer. Even though the tuning set and report were manually created, they will still be available in OEM. As an example, drilling down to TASK_35 shows a graphical comparison between sets. The two regressed SQL statements were related to internals of executing the two packages.

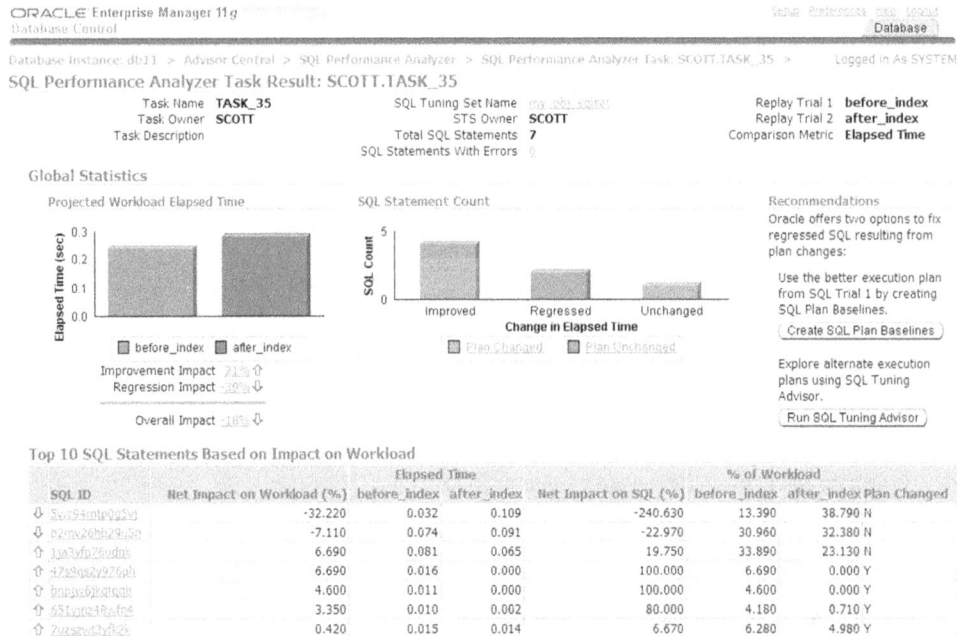

Database Instance: db11 > Advisor Central > SQL Performance Analyzer > SQL Performance Analyzer Task: SCOTT.TASK_35 >   Logged in As SYSTEM

SQL Performance Analyzer Task Result: SCOTT.TASK_35

Task Name	**TASK_35**	SQL Tuning Set Name		Replay Trial 1 **before_index**
Task Owner	**SCOTT**	STS Owner **SCOTT**		Replay Trial 2 **after_index**
Task Description		Total SQL Statements **7**		Comparison Metric **Elapsed Time**
		SQL Statements With Errors	0	

Global Statistics

Projected Workload Elapsed Time

SQL Statement Count

Recommendations
Oracle offers two options to fix regressed SQL resulting from plan changes:

Use the better execution plan from SQL Trial 1 by creating SQL Plan Baselines.

(Create SQL Plan Baselines)

Explore alternate execution plans using SQL Tuning Advisor.

(Run SQL Tuning Advisor)

☐ before_index ☐ after_index

Improvement Impact 71% ⬆
Regression Impact -18% ⬇

Overall Impact -18% ⬇

☐ Plan Changed   ☐ Plan Unchanged

Top 10 SQL Statements Based on Impact on Workload

		Elapsed Time			% of Workload		
SQL ID	Net Impact on Workload (%)	before_index	after_index	Net Impact on SQL (%)	before_index	after_index	Plan Changed
⬇ 5vr594mfp0g5v	-32.220	0.032	0.109	-240.630	13.390	38.790	N
⬇ 02mx20bb29u5n	-7.110	0.074	0.091	-22.970	30.960	32.380	N
⬆ 1ja3yfp26udnk	6.690	0.081	0.065	19.750	33.890	23.130	N
⬆ 47s9qs2y976qh	6.690	0.016	0.000	100.000	6.690	0.000	Y
⬆ bnqjv6jkgrqqp	4.600	0.011	0.000	100.000	4.600	0.000	Y
⬆ 551qpz48u4ns	3.350	0.010	0.002	80.000	4.180	0.710	Y
⬆ 7uzssw43yfk2k	0.420	0.015	0.014	6.670	6.280	4.980	Y

Figure 8.6: *SQL Performance Analyzer Graphical Results*

As mentioned in the beginning, SPA can capture differences due to most anything that affects an execution plan. Aside from DDL operations such as index creation or using hints, two other major elements can factor in to changes. One is the compatibility parameter and the other is generic parameter changes.

A change in the optimizer setting is specific enough to not be counted as a parameter change. Although it is a parameter, the setting is intrinsic to how the optimizer works as a whole. An example of a normal parameter change would be changing the *optimizer_index_cost_adj* or *db_file_multiblock_read_count* settings.

Now that the API interface is now visible, that is, the actual DBMS_SQLPA and DBMS_SQLTUNE to create the SQL tuning set, the guided workflow in Enterprise Manager will be much easier to follow along.

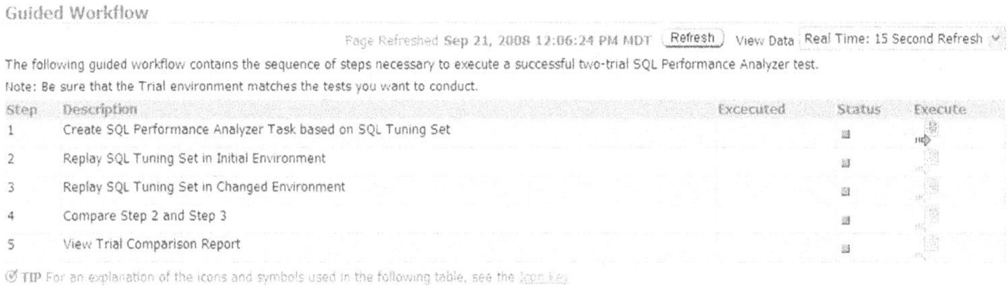

Figure 8.7: *Workflow*

To sum up so far, the SQL Performance Analyzer can be used to help validate or explore changes. It can help overcome a 100% copy of the production environment, and unlike ADRCI, SPA can be back ported to releases prior to 11g. MetaLink note 560977.1, "Real Application Testing Now Available for Earlier Releases," details the applicable versions.

After applying a patch via the opatch utility, one can capture on the older versions. However, only replay on version 11g and higher.

Finally, since SQL Performance Analyzer falls under Real Application Testing, it must be licensed. Database Replay, SQL Performance Analyzer and SQL Tuning Sets (STS) are licensable. STS can be used if the DBA licensed the Tuning Pack.

Other Utilities

The advisory framework introduced in Oracle 10g opened up quite a few portals into Oracle's internals. The RDBMS is far more instrumented than it has ever been, and hopefully that trend will continue. If one works in a split, with respect to releases, environment, how many times one wished feature X in 10g were available in 8i? That is not just limited to advisory and diagnostics, either. Flashback tabling to before some SCN is much easier to perform than a tablespace point in time recovery. It can take hours to recover from an errant commit in an older version while the time in a newer one could be a matter of seconds.

Advisor Central

Some of the named advisors are actual advisors. Some of the advisors are management interfaces to specific settings. How does one access these advisors? The advisors and Checkers can be reached via the Advisor Central link on the home page of Database Control (look near the bottom center of the home page).

At Advisor Central, links at the top of the page will send the DBA to the top-level pages for the selected topic. The advisors include:

- ADDM – analyze current or past performance
- SQL Advisors – SQL Access, SQL Tuning, and SQL Repair Advisors
- Memory Advisors – SGA and PGA advisors
- Automatic Undo Management – Undo Advisor (retention and tablespace sizing advice)
- MTTR Advisor – advice on instance recovery, media recovery and flash recovery
- SQL Performance Analyzer – Optimizer Upgrade Simulation, Parameter Change, Guided Workflow, and existing tasks
- Data Recovery Advisor – view and manage failures
- Segment Advisor – Automatic Segment Advisor information, get advice on tablespaces or schema objects

ADDM

ADDM, or the Automatic Database Diagnostic Monitor, works in conjunction with the Automatic Workload Repository, or AWR. The AWR stores performance statistics, and these statistics are then used for problem detection and self-tuning. Much like STATSPACK, it takes snapshots at regular intervals.

After the performance data has been collected, ADDM analyzes it. AWR is the hunter-gatherer, and ADDM is the thinker. The built-in functionality includes automated tasks which run in maintenance windows. One well-known maintenance window is the Oracle after-hours GATHER_STATS_JOB. The name of the job is GATHER_STATS_JOB.

Referencing the Performance Tuning Guide, this job is "created automatically at database creation time and is managed by the Scheduler. The Scheduler runs this job when the maintenance window is opened. By default, the maintenance window opens every night from 10 P.M. to 6 A.M. and all day on weekends."

The automated tasks infrastructure, known as AutoTask, schedules routine maintenance tasks. These tasks include steps needed to perform or update optimizer statistics gathering, the Automatic Segment Advisor, and the SQL Tuning Advisor. A list of common problems ADDM can detect include:

- CPU bottlenecks
- Poor connection management
- Excessive parsing
- Lock contention
- I/O capacity
- Undersizing of Oracle memory structures
- High load SQL statements
- High PL/SQL and Java time
- High checkpoint load and causes
- RAC-specific issues

Running an ADDM or AWR report (the difference in the names is analogous to how users blur the difference between database and instance at times) can be accomplished via Database Control click and point functionality or by manually running one or more SQL scripts located in $ORACLE_HOME/rdbms/admin.

The Diagnostic Pack scripts, of which ADDM falls under for licensing, can all be run as a command-line API. Many will prompt for input related to instance, dates, times, output format and snapshot coverage. The script file names and purposes are shown below. All scripts are .sql files.

NAME	PURPOSE
awrrpt	Creates the main AWR report, based on STATSPACK
awrrpti	Comparison between snapshots
addmrtp	Runs ADDM analysis on pair of AWR snapshots
addmrpti	Same as above, but used for RAC instances
ashrpt	Runs the Active Session History report, calls ashrpti
ashrpti	Worker script that supports ashrpt
awrddrpt	Runs Workload Respository Compare Periods report
awrddrpi	Worker script that supports awrddrpt
awrsqrpt	Runs Workload for a particular SQL statement
awrsqrpi	Worker script that supports awrsqrpt
awrextr	Extracts AWR info, for use with/by Oracle Support
awrload	Loads AWR data, for use with/by Oracle Support
awrinfo	Outputs general AWR info
spawrrac	Server Performance RAC report

Table 8.2: *ADDM Scripts*

The pattern on the scripts is that a script ending in -rpt typically defaults to the current DBID and instance, collects information via prompts, and passes that input to its corresponding -rpi script. The -rpi scripts can be run directly, but one will have to sort out the required/expected parameters. Some of the scripts are for overall and some are for comparison between snapshots or the repository. Many of the scripts also expect to be run as the SYS user.

SQL Tuning Advisor

Through the SQL Tuning Advisor, information ADDM has analyzed from the AWR is used to identify high load or poorly performing SQL statements. ADDM also knows about the top SQL and its impact on the system. Once a statement is identified, then ADDM can pass the statement into another analyzer, so to speak, and come up with recommendations. The SQL Tuning Advisor is the engine behind the scenes and it develops finer tuned plans along with some advice.

The recommendations fall into four categories:

- Statistics Analysis – The advisor checks the status of statistics (stale or missing) and if necessary, gathers new or updated statistics.

- SQL Profiling – What was the past execution history like? Profiling can use the history of a statement to generate a well-tuned plan. This is especially useful for applications where the DBA has no control over the code. What can be done is, via the advisor, build a better plan around the code.

- Access Path Analysis – This is a lot like what performance tuning in SQL Server does. If it is determined that an index will help a statement, the index will be automatically created. In Oracle, a recommendation will be received to build the index for it is not built for the DBA.

- SQL Structure Analysis – This component of the advisor identifies bad plans and offers suggestions as to restructuring them. Restructuring suggestions include both syntactic and semantic changes to code.

The APIs for this advisor are discussed after the next section.

SQL Access Advisor

Right behind and alongside the SQL Tuning Advisor is the SQL Access Advisor. The former helps fix or tune statements. The latter offers analysis based on recommending indexes, partitions, and materialized views. The Access Advisor works not only on single statements, but also on complete business workloads. One of the features of SQL Access Advisor is that the data that is gathered on a production system can be transferred to another system.

The SQL Tuning Advisor and SQL Access Advisor command-line APIs are accessed via the DBMS_SQLTUNE and DBMS_ADVISOR PL/SQL built-ins. The sqltrpt.sql script in the rdbms/admin directory is also part of the licensed Tuning Pack. Access to *v$sql_monitor* and *v$sql_plan_monitor* are as well.

In Oracle 11g, a new initialization parameter helps to control access to Tuning Pack and Diagnostics Pack features. The parameter *control_management_pack_access* can be set to:

- DIAGNOSTIC+TUNING – the features from both packs are enabled

- DIAGNOSTIC – only the features from the Diagnostic Pack are enabled

- NONE – features from both packs are disabled

The settings can also be controlled or accessed via Enterprise Manager (see the Setup link).

SQL Repair Advisor

The SQL Repair Advisor can be accessed via OEM or via a command-line API using the DBMS_SQLDIAG PL/SQL built-in. Two types of failures can be worked on - those related to incidents and those which are not. The distinction is that statement failure(s) related to an incident will be part of the incident package. Non-incident failures can be worked on via the SQL Worksheet and also through the Support Workbench.

The GUI approach is basically enter a query, select links related to the repair advisor, and attempt to apply a SQL patch if available. The SQL patch (not a patch as in a download from MetaLink) is a query transformation of the original statement. If the patch is accepted, then the original repairable SQL can be entered and the transformation will take care of the fix.

Finding a statement that can be repaired is the primary challenge of testing and using this feature. If the DBA finds one, the steps to repair via DBMS_SQLDIAG are shown below.

A statement is run, and an error is returned. The test table *t* is a copy of EMP in the SCOTT schema.

```
SQL> DELETE FROM scott.t1 WHERE ROWID <>
  2  (SELECT MAX(ROWID) FROM scott.t1 GROUP by empno);
(SELECT MAX(ROWID) FROM scott.t1 GROUP by empno)
 *
ERROR at line 2:
ORA-01427: single-row subquery returns more than one row
```

Create a diagnosis task using the CREATE_DIAGNOSIS_TASK subprogram. Pass in the SQL text and assign a task name for identification later.

```
DECLARE
  report_out clob;
  task_id varchar2(50);
BEGIN
  task_id := DBMS_SQLDIAG.CREATE_DIAGNOSIS_TASK(
    sql_text => 'DELETE FROM t1 WHERE ROWID <>
                (SELECT MAX(ROWID) FROM t1 GROUP by empno)',
    task_name=>'test_task1',
    problem_type=>dbms_sqldiag.problem_type_compilation_error);
END;
/
```

Optionally, view the task by querying from *dba_advisor_tasks*.

```
SELECT task_id, task_name,
to_char(created,'DD-MON HH24:MI'),
advisor_name, status
FROM dba_advisor_tasks
ORDER BY 1;
...
TASK_ID TASK_NAME  TO_CHAR(CREA ADVISOR_NAME       STATUS
------- ---------- ------------ ------------------ ---------
     54 test_task1 21-SEP 19:30 SQL Repair Advisor COMPLETED
```

Execute the diagnosis and generate a report.

```
exec dbms_sqldiag.execute_diagnosis_task('test_task1');

DECLARE
 rep_out CLOB;
BEGIN
  rep_out := dbms_sqldiag.report_diagnosis_task('test_task1',
  dbms_sqldiag.type_text);

  dbms_output.put_line('Report : ' || rep_out);
END;
/
```

The output from the report can be lengthy. Part of what the API tries is using different optimizer settings based on version. The extract below shows a path from 10.2.0.1 to 10.2.0.3 and this is just a snippet.

```
- Plan for
strategy optimizer features enabled toggle with plan directive
  (hint)
OPTIMIZER_FEATURES_ENABLE('10.2.0.1') has cost 7 with plan hash
  value 3950489424
- Plan for
strategy optimizer features enabled toggle with plan directive
  (hint)
OPTIMIZER_FEATURES_ENABLE('10.2.0.2') has cost 7 with plan hash
  value 3950489424
- Plan for
```

```
strategy optimizer features enabled toggle with plan directive
  (hint)
OPTIMIZER_FEATURES_ENABLE('10.2.0.3') has cost 7 with plan hash
  value 3950489424
```

If a patch is recommended, apply it.

```
exec DBMS_SQLDIAG.ACCEPT_SQL_PATCH ⌐⌐
 (task_name => 'test_task1', task_owner => 'SYS');
```

If needed or desired, then delete the task.

```
exec DBMS_SQLTUNE.DROP_TUNING_TASK(task_name => 'test_task1');
```

Overall, the SQL Repair Advisor is pretty easy to use, especially within OEM. The command-line API can be somewhat cryptic at times, depending on which subprogram the DBA is trying to use.

Memory Advisors (SGA and PGA)

These advisors are straightforward. There is some debate as to the validity of the findings they produce, both in a tabular format showing increase or decrease in reads as memory is increased or decreased. The tabular/graph-like data can be queried directly via canned scripts. An example of what the SGA Advisor generates in a graph is shown in Figure 8.8.

Memory Size Advice

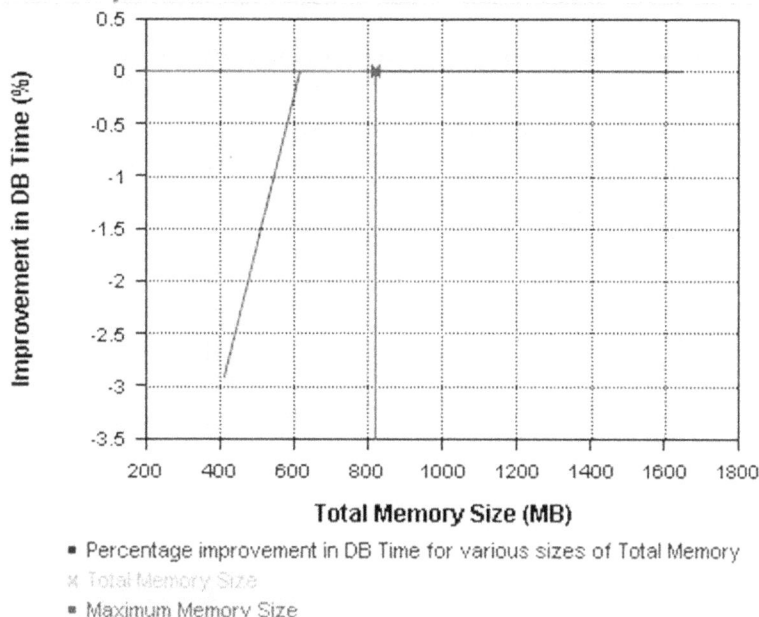

- Percentage improvement in DB Time for various sizes of Total Memory
- Total Memory Size
- Maximum Memory Size

Figure 8.8: *Memory Advice*

Sample queries for SGA target advice include those which replicate what a graph shows and what the history has been at a certain size. In this example, it can be seen that the advice has held steady at 508MB for the snapshots shown.

```
select snap_id, sga_size
from dba_hist_sga_target_advice
where sga_size_factor = 1
order by snap_id asc

  SNAP_ID    SGA_SIZE
---------- ----------
        4         508
        5         508
        6         508
        7         508
        8         508
        9         508
       10         508
       11         508
```

The relevant data dictionary views have ADVICE in them and it is a trivial matter to query those based on a snapshot ID to see what the advice was at that time.

Other Utilities

Undo Advisor

The Automated Undo Advisor is also simple to access and query. This advisor evaluates the space needed to ensure a guaranteed retention time. The retention time comes into play when considering flashback. Since flashback goes back in time, a sufficient amount of undo space, which supports the amount of time, needs to be set aside for the undo tablespace. Undo data cannot be overwritten in order for flashback to work.

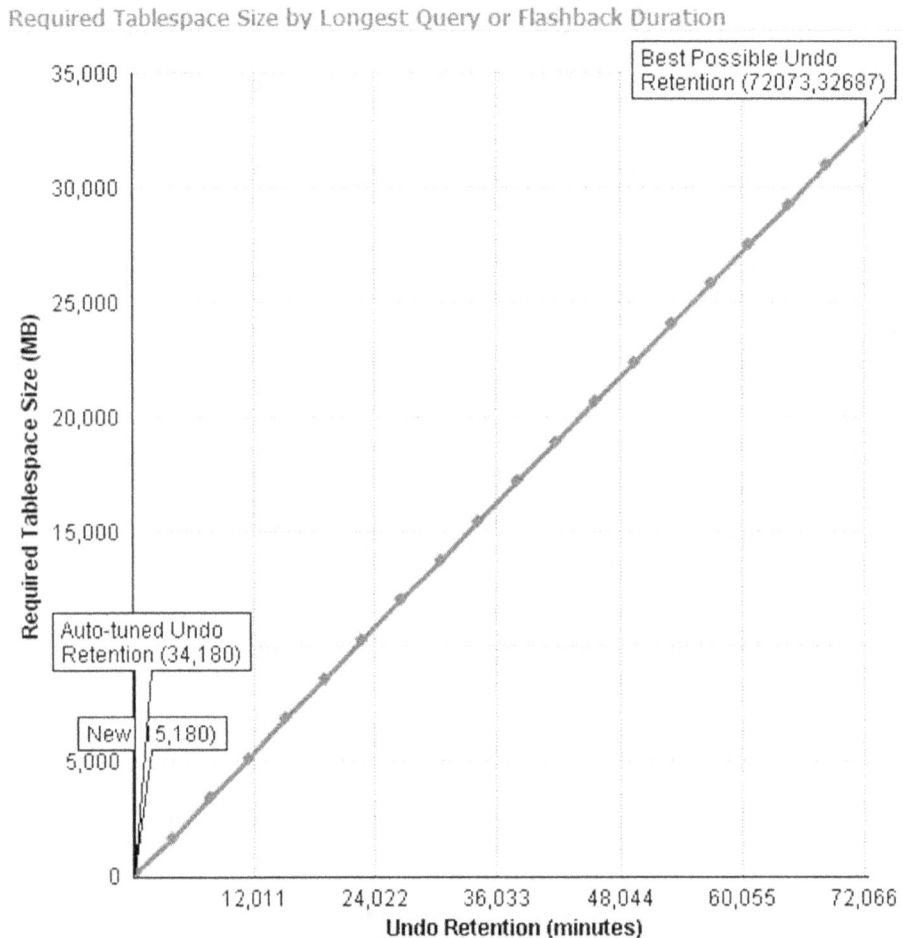

Required Tablespace Size by Longest Query or Flashback Duration

Figure 8.9: *Undo Tablespace Growth Line*

Calculating the current optimal setting can be done via a query like that below:

```
col "ACTUAL UNDO SIZE [MByte]" for 999999999
col "UNDO RETENTION [Sec]" for a20
col "OPTIMAL UNDO RETENTION [Sec]" for 999999999
SELECT d.undo_size/(1024*1024) "ACTUAL UNDO SIZE [MB]",
       SUBSTR(e.value,1,25) "UNDO RETENTION [Sec]",
       (TO_NUMBER(e.value) * TO_NUMBER(f.value) *
       g.undo_block_per_sec) / (1024*1024)
       "NEEDED UNDO SIZE [MB]"
  FROM (
       SELECT SUM(a.bytes) undo_size
         FROM v$datafile a,
              v$tablespace b,
              dba_tablespaces c
        WHERE c.contents = 'UNDO'
          AND c.status = 'ONLINE'
          AND b.name = c.tablespace_name
          AND a.ts# = b.ts#
       ) d,
       v$parameter e,
       v$parameter f,
       (
       SELECT MAX(undoblks/((end_time-begin_time)*3600*24))
         undo_block_per_sec
         FROM v$undostat
       ) g
 WHERE e.name = 'undo_retention'
   AND f.name = 'db_block_size';
```

The results for a small system running on a laptop:

```
ACTUAL UNDO SIZE [MB] UNDO RETENTION [Sec] NEEDED UNDO SIZE [MB]
-------------------- -------------------- --------------------
                 190 900                            43.5234375
```

MTTR Advisor

The MTTR Advisor (Mean Time To Recover Advisor) is enabled when two parameters are set to certain values: *statistics_level* and *fast_start_mttr_target*. The required values for *statistics_level* are TYPICAL or ALL. When the *fast_start_mttr_target* is set to a non-zero value, combined with *statistics_level* being appropriately set, the advisor is started.

Several other parameters should not be set because they will interfere with mechanisms used to meet the value or setting of *fast_start_mttr_target*. These other parameters are:

- *fast_start_io_target*
- *log_checkpoint_interval*

- *log_checkpoint_timeout*

The possible settings for *fast_start_mttr_target* range between 0 and 3600 seconds. Any setting above 3600 defaults back to 3600.

Due to what the parameter represents, the two-phase instance recovery process of roll forward and roll back, some amount of time is going to be spent on startup to apply committed transactions not yet written to datafiles and to roll back the uncommitted ones. Therefore, a setting of 0 and obviously anything less than that is not realistic. Whether the time is 10 seconds, 30 seconds, or 2 minutes, examples depend, to a degree, on how the redo logs are sized.

So, in conjunction with the redo log size and the time it takes for the database to start up regardless of what the logs have to deal with, a query from *v$instance_recovery* can be used to calibrate the optimal or practical time for the mean time to recovery. The results of the following query show the system is pretty much calibrated.

```
SELECT TARGET_MTTR, ESTIMATED_MTTR
FROM V$INSTANCE_RECOVERY;

TARGET_MTTR ESTIMATED_MTTR
----------- --------------
         37             35
```

Another ADVICE type view, *v$mttr_target_advice*, shows statistics and advisories collected by this advisor. If the advisor is not started, the following graph will not appear under the Instance Recovery section of the Recovery Settings page in OEM.

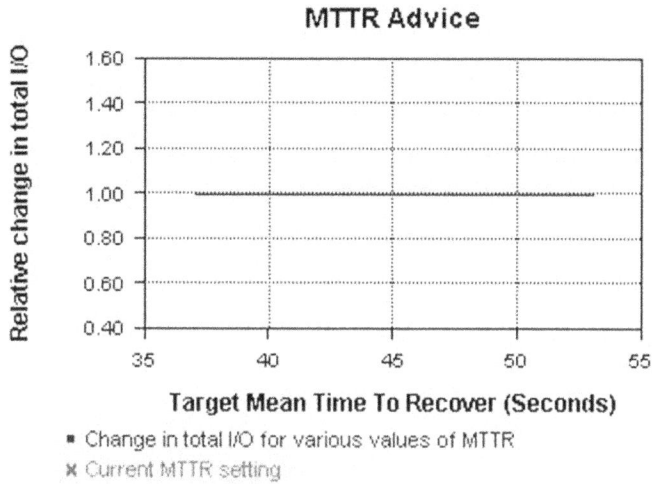

Figure 8.10: *MTTR Advice*

Data Recovery Advisor

As part of the enhanced intelligent data protection and repair present in Oracle 11g, the Data Recovery Advisor is a new feature. With this advisor, data failures can be automatically diagnosed along with reporting appropriate options for repair. The advisor can also help reduce the amount of time needed to recover.

Like many other advisors, the two interfaces used are OEM and a command-line API. The command-line API in this case is a bit different than the others because it operates inside of RMAN. Since the commands run in RMAN, this implies that the database is most likely running in archivelog mode, so that can help ensure less data loss.

The basic commands for Data Recovery Advisor are LIST FAILURE, ADVISE FAILURE, REPAIR FAILURE, and CHANGE FAILURE. Due to the nature of what this advisor is helping the DBA with, it is best to test the functionality on a test database. The database needs to experience a media failure or some type of data loss (corruption) to trigger or put this advisor into action.

Failures have two characteristics. Their status is either OPEN or CLOSED, and their priority is one of CRITICAL, HIGH, or LOW. The Data Recovery

Advisor assigns a priority of CRITICAL or HIGH to diagnosed failures. A priority of CRITICAL is significant; it implies the whole database is at risk. Loss of a control file or a SYSTEM tablespace data file would certainly qualify for this rating.

A HIGH rating means the database can continue on. An example of this would be where a non-system tablespace datafile becomes unavailable. The status in such a case could be downgraded to LOW.

The OEM interface may be slow to present failure information. As an experiment, create a 1MB datafile in its own tablespace on an attached flash drive and then pull the drive. This may terminate the instance. One's access to the database via OEM becomes quite limited. Using host credentials, connect to the database. More precisely, connect to files associated with the database, such as those in the ADR. This means, as an example, that the alert log can be viewed via OEM. The alert log records the following entry.

```
Errors in file c:\app\ora11g\diag\rdbms\db11\db11\trace\db11_ckpt_4608.trc: ORA-
01242: data file suffered media failure: database in NOARCHIVELOG mode ORA-
01110: data file 6: 'E:\FDRIVE01.DBF' ORA-01115: IO error reading block from file 6 (block # 1) ORA-
27072: File I/O error OSD-04006: ReadFile() failure, unable to read from file O/S-
Error: (OS 1006) The volume for a file has been externally altered so that the opened file is no longer valid.
```

Figure 8.11: *Alert Log Output*

In a scenario such as this, the only viable recourse is to recover the database via a command-line API such as RMAN or via traditional means such as startup mount. As this is now a backup and recovery situation, it goes beyond the scope of this chapter. After restoring the drive, starting the instance, and logging back in to OEM, the advisor now shows the critical failure, but also records it as closed for obvious reasons.

Select Failure Description	Impact	Priority	Status
▽ Data Failures			
▷ One or more non-system datafiles are corrupt	See impact for individual child failures	HIGH	CLOSED
▽ One or more non-system datafiles are missing	See impact for individual child failures	HIGH	CLOSED
Datafile 6: 'E:\FDRIVE01.DBF' is missing	Some objects in tablespace FDRIVE might be unavailable	HIGH	CLOSED

Figure 8.12: *Advisor Output in OEM*

After registering the database, or configuring it for use with RMAN, and repeating the drive failure, the instance stays open and the advisor reports the problem.

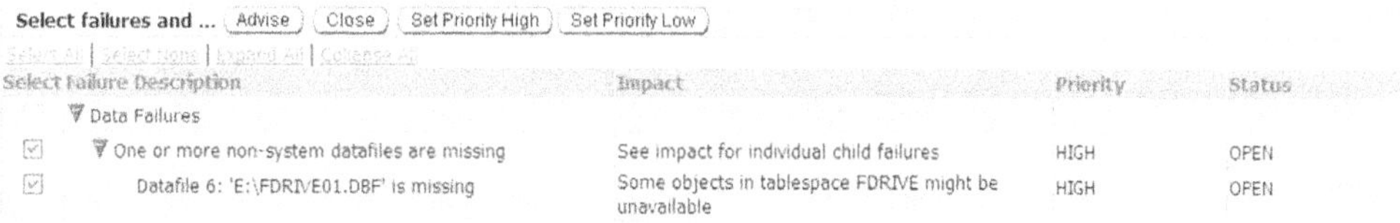

Select failures and ...   (Advise) (Close) (Set Priority High) (Set Priority Low)

Select Failure Description	Impact	Priority	Status
▼ Data Failures			
☑ ▼ One or more non-system datafiles are missing	See impact for individual child failures	HIGH	OPEN
☑ Datafile 6: 'E:\FDRIVE01.DBF' is missing	Some objects in tablespace FDRIVE might be unavailable	HIGH	OPEN

Figure 8.13: *More Advisor Output*

Click on Advise, and the advisor offers details for a manual action.

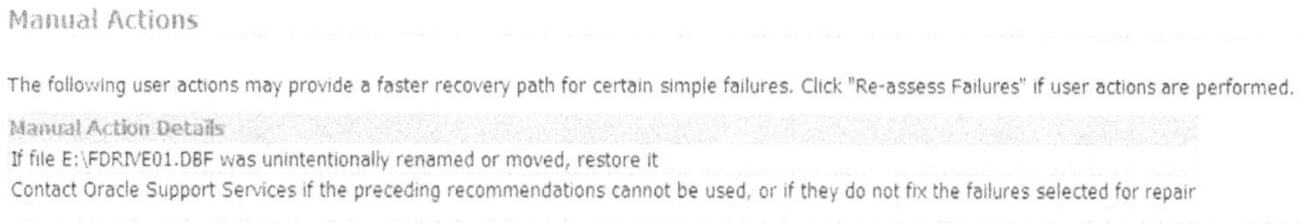

Manual Actions

The following user actions may provide a faster recovery path for certain simple failures. Click "Re-assess Failures" if user actions are performed.

Manual Action Details
If file E:\FDRIVE01.DBF was unintentionally renamed or moved, restore it
Contact Oracle Support Services if the preceding recommendations cannot be used, or if they do not fix the failures selected for repair

Figure 8.14: *Manual Actions Shown in OEM*

The RMAN version of this interface is shown below. The scenario is the same, meaning the flash drive was pulled to simulate media failure. A "startup mount" is issued. In an RMAN session, connect to the target because the rman user cannot be connected to if using the controlfile as the catalog. Once in RMAN, issue LIST FAILURE and ADVISE FAILURE commands. Note: line returns were added for formatting purposes.

```
RMAN> list failure;

using target database control file instead of recovery catalog
List of Database Failures
=========================

Failure ID Priority Status    Time Detected Summary
---------- -------- --------- ------------- -------
62         HIGH     OPEN      22-SEP-08     One or more non-system
                                            datafiles are missing

RMAN> advise failure;

List of Database Failures
=========================

Failure ID Priority Status    Time Detected Summary
---------- -------- --------- ------------- -------
62         HIGH     OPEN      22-SEP-08     One or more non-system
```

```
                                        datafiles are missing
analyzing automatic repair options; this may take some time
allocated channel: ORA_DISK_1
channel ORA_DISK_1: SID=155 device type=DISK
analyzing automatic repair options complete

Mandatory Manual Actions
========================
1. If file E:\FDRIVE01.DBF was unintentionally renamed or moved,
   restore it
2. Contact Oracle Support Services if the preceding recommendations
   cannot be used, or if they do not fix the failures selected for
   repair

Optional Manual Actions
========================
no manual actions available

Automated Repair Options
========================
no automatic repair options available
```

With this release of Oracle, the Data Recovery Advisor only operates on a single instance. In other words, it is not supported in a RAC environment. However, it can be used on a single instance, so that remains an option.

Overall, the Data Recovery Advisor can help recover a database during a time of crisis. Failure scenarios are stressing, to say the least, and having advice served up by the server, telling what needs to happen, can save time. If the database is in archivelog mode, and backups are available and once the media problem has been addressed, the advisor can preview what will take place during the repair. In an RMAN session, issue a REPAIR FAILURE PREVIEW command and view the output. If satisfactory, initiate the repair with just REPAIR FAILURE. There is also the choice of applying the repair oneself as one can have a repair script generated for oneself, which is essentially what the preview shows anyway.

> 💣 As always with recovery operations, this is something to have practiced beforehand. Learning how to perform recovery during a live event is not the most conducive learning environment and is a recipe for failure. The symbol for this warning is appropriate – the DBA does not want any bombs going off in the recovery process.

Segment Advisor

According to the Administrator's Guide, the main purpose of the Segment Advisor is to identify "segments that have space available for reclamation." For the advisor to work, it must examine the contents of the Automatic Workload Repository, and already discussed, use of the AWR requires additional licensing. Therefore, the use of the Segment Advisor is restricted if not licensed.

The advisor can run on a scheduled basis in addition to a user-directed manual one. If the advisor finds a significant amount of free space, the advice will be to perform an online segment shrink. If not eligible for shrinking, the advice may be to perform an online table redefinition. The advisor will also report on row chaining if the amount found is above a threshold value.

In the automatic mode of analyzing segment information contained in the AWR, the segments of interest are those which:

- Have the most activity

- Have the highest growth rate

- Have exceeded a critical or warning threshold (by tablespace)

The Automatic Segment Advisor job is the entity which selects the segments to be analyzed. If a segment is being analyzed when the maintenance window closes, that segment will be included at the start of the next window.

The advisor advises on three levels:

- Segment level – for a particular segment, including a partition, index or LOB column

- Object level – table or index, including partitions, and can include dependent objects

- Tablespace level – runs for all segments in the tablespace

In OEM, the DBA is taken through a guided workflow consisting of scope, objects, schedule and review.

Database **db11**   Logged In As **SYS**   (Cancel) (Back) Step 2 of 4 (Next) (Submit)

(Add)

Name	Type	Extent Management	Segment Space Management	Size (MB)	Used (MB)	Used (%)	Remove
EXAMPLE	PERMANENT	LOCAL	AUTO	100.00	77.38	77.38	
RMAN	PERMANENT	LOCAL	AUTO	9.81	8.81	89.81	
SYSAUX	PERMANENT	LOCAL	AUTO	727.56	691.12	94.99	
SYSTEM	PERMANENT	LOCAL	MANUAL	720.00	710.06	98.62	
TEMP	TEMPORARY	LOCAL	MANUAL	20.00	7.00	35.00	
UNDOTBS1	UNDO	LOCAL	MANUAL	235.00	138.75	59.04	
USERS	PERMANENT	LOCAL	AUTO	13.50	12.19	90.28	

Figure 8.15: *Tablespace List*

A history of Segment Advisor jobs can also be viewed.

Results

(View Result) (Delete) Actions Re-schedule ▾ (Go)

Select	Advisory Type	Name	Description	User	Status	Start Time
◉	Segment Advisor	SEGMENTADV_3885702	Get shrink advice based on object growth trend	SYS	RUNNING	Sep 22, 2008 4:32:50 AM
○	Segment Advisor	SYS_AUTO_SPCADV_381042292008	Auto Space Advisor	SYS	COMPLETED	Sep 21, 2008 10:10:34 PM
○	Segment Advisor	SYS_AUTO_SPCADV_529022292008	Auto Space Advisor	SYS	COMPLETED	Sep 21, 2008 6:09:54 PM
○	Segment Advisor	SYS_AUTO_SPCADV_449202192008	Auto Space Advisor	SYS	COMPLETED	Sep 21, 2008 2:09:47 PM
○	Segment Advisor	SYS_AUTO_SPCADV_478162192008	Auto Space Advisor	SYS	COMPLETED	Sep 21, 2008 10:08:48 AM
○	Segment Advisor	SYS_AUTO_SPCADV_222122192008	Auto Space Advisor	SYS	COMPLETED	Sep 21, 2008 6:02:50 AM
○	Segment Advisor	SYS_AUTO_SPCADV_526222092008	Auto Space Advisor	SYS	COMPLETED	Sep 20, 2008 4:26:19 PM
○	Segment Advisor	SYS_AUTO_SPCADV_421182092008	Auto Space Advisor	SYS	COMPLETED	Sep 20, 2008 12:21:07 PM
○	Segment Advisor	SYS_AUTO_SPCADV_510419926008	Auto Space Advisor	SYS	COMPLETED	Sep 18, 2008 10:01:40 PM

Figure 8.16: *Segment Advisor History*

The command-line API is surfaced by the DBMS_ADVISOR (and optionally, DBMS_SPACE) PL/SQL built-in. The subprograms are CREATE_TASK, CREATE_OBJECT (identify the target object), SET_TASK_PARAMETER and EXECUTE_TASK.

To view the results, use OEM, query the *dba_advisor_** dynamic views, or use the DBMS_SPACE.ASA_RECOMMENDATION procedure. The dynamic views are categorized under recommendations, findings, actions, and objects. The corresponding views are *dba_advisor_recommendations, dba_advisor_findings, dba_advisor_actions* and *dba_advisor_objects*.

Traditional Tracing Methods

The older, more traditional tracing methods are listed here with brief discussion only as a reference. More detailed information can be found in <u>Oracle Utilities Using Hidden Programs, Import/Export, SQL Loader, oradebug, Dbverify, TKPROF and More</u> (Dave Moore, Rampant TechPress, 2003).

The tracing can be viewed as either top down or bottom up, and from the specific to the general. A low-level trace would be the explain plan generated in SQL*Plus. The output there is an approximation of what the optimizer knows and is going to do. The hint syntax can be tested here as well, recalling the caution that if the hint type syntax is incorrect, the hint becomes a useless comment.

DBMS_XPLAN

The old PLAN_TABLE and explain plan format can be replaced by what DBMS_XPLAN has to offer. DBMS_XPLAN is a gateway not only to SQL statements, but also into the AWR. Armed with the SELECT_CATALOG_ROLE, a user can view several dynamic performance views. The package runs with the privileges of the calling user, so the user needs to have select privileges on *vsql_plan, vsession,* and *v$sql_plan_statistics_all*.

A simple implementation is to add EXPLAIN PLAN FOR just before a statement, and then view the plan by issuing:

```
SELECT * FROM table(DBMS_XPLAN.DISPLAY);
```

Putting it together in an example:

```
SQL> conn scott/tiger
Connected.
SQL> EXPLAIN PLAN FOR
  2  SELECT * FROM emp e, dept d
  3    WHERE e.deptno = d.deptno
  4    AND e.ename='benoit';

Explained.

SQL> set lines 110 pages 35
SQL> SELECT * FROM table(DBMS_XPLAN.DISPLAY);

PLAN_TABLE_OUTPUT
--------------------------------------------------------------------------------
Plan hash value: 3625962092
```

```
-----------------------------------------------------------------------
| Id | Operation                    | Name    | Rows | Bytes | Cost (%CPU)| Time     |
-----------------------------------------------------------------------
|  0 | SELECT STATEMENT             |         |    1 |    57 |    4   (0)| 00:00:01 |
|  1 |  NESTED LOOPS                |         |      |       |           |          |
|  2 |   NESTED LOOPS               |         |    1 |    57 |    4   (0)| 00:00:01 |
|* 3 |    TABLE ACCESS FULL         | EMP     |    1 |    37 |    3   (0)| 00:00:01 |
|* 4 |    INDEX UNIQUE SCAN         | PK_DEPT |    1 |       |    0   (0)| 00:00:01 |
|  5 |   TABLE ACCESS BY INDEX ROWID| DEPT    |    1 |    20 |    1   (0)| 00:00:01 |
-----------------------------------------------------------------------

Predicate Information (identified by operation id):
---------------------------------------------------

   3 - filter("E"."ENAME"='benoit')
   4 - access("E"."DEPTNO"="D"."DEPTNO")
```

The package has four subprograms: DISPLAY, DISPLAY_AWR, DISPLAY_CURSOR and DISPLAY_SQLSET. The DISPLAY option was just shown in the prior example. Since the SELECT statement is also a cursor, take a look at the DISPLAY_CURSOR function.

```
SQL> SELECT * FROM table(DBMS_XPLAN.DISPLAY_CURSOR);

PLAN_TABLE_OUTPUT
------------------------------------------------------------
SQL_ID  7v1g3p9b8052u, child number 0
------------------------------------
SELECT * FROM table(DBMS_XPLAN.DISPLAY)

Plan hash value: 2137789089


------------------------------------------------------------
| Id  | Operation                       | Name    | Cost  |
------------------------------------------------------------
|   0 | SELECT STATEMENT                |         |    29 |
|   1 |  COLLECTION ITERATOR PICKLER FETCH| DISPLAY |       |
------------------------------------------------------------

Note
-----
   - cpu costing is off (consider enabling it)


17 rows selected.
```

A big payoff in using DBMS_XPLAN is the quick and easy way of seeing what a statement's SQL_ID value is. Not that the DBA will be typing that odd-looking string in all that much, but it does make some more sophisticated queries easy to code since one does not have to find the ID.

The other benefit is that the ID can be used to query again from the table and be able to see past statements and their plans.

The DISPLAY function gets even more granular than being able to query on older ID. One can specify an input parameter for format. The choices are ROWS, BYTES, COST, PARTITION, and PARALLEL, to name a few.

To pull AWR information, use the DISPLAY_AWR function.

```
SELECT * FROM table(DBMS_XPLAN.DISPLAY_AWR('7v1g3p9b8052u'));
```

Going up one level would be tracing a session, either one's own or someone else's via a remote interface. Although some skilled people can read through an unformatted trace file, mere mortals can use TKPROF to format "trc" trace files. In addition to basic formatting, the actual execution plan (*explain*=y) as an input parameter will output the plans.

Becoming more sophisticated in the tracing is when wait events are also analyzed. Wait analysis is the de facto means of analyzing performance. The days of X-whatever ratios are gone, although they can be useful as trend indicators.

Tracing at the TKPROF level is good for SQL, but what about PL/SQL? That is where DBMS_PROFILER comes into play.

Above the individual session level are STATSPACK and AWR. AWR reports, or what ADDM generates from the AWR, are based on STATSPACK reports. AWR reports, however, contain much more drill down type of information. AWR reports, available since the release of Oracle 10g, also reflect the increased amount of instrumentation found within the RDBMS.

All of the data collected to obtain the big picture has to be gathered from all of the active sessions. The details, which are aggregated and summarized to create the big picture ADDM or AWR report, come from the *v$active_session_history* dynamic view. This view, and many of the related *wrh$_** views, are explained in detail in Oracle Wait Event Tuning High Performance with Wait Event Interface Analysis (Stephen Andert, Rampant TechPress, 2004).

Conclusion

There is a plethora of information Oracle collects about itself and what users are doing. With each newer release of the RDBMS engine, Oracle is becoming more self-aware and intelligent. The optimizer is becoming more sophisticated, even though at a root level, it must apply rules to the conditions it sees, and the advisory framework is then used to surface information to the database administrator. The ideal end-state would be a database that is completely self-aware and able to flawlessly diagnose and correct itself. That is a good thing, just as long as it does not become like Skynet in the Terminator series.

Oracle Developer Utilities

Introduction

What are the Oracle developer utilities? The answer to this question is, "It depends." There are utilities which clearly fall into the purview of database administrators and are not meant to be used by the general user population. On the other hand, there are many utilities meant to be used by almost every schema owner, and those utilities are not necessarily restricted to tasks a developer would be performing.

The number of utilities, referring to packaged or compiled code within the RDBMS, has witnessed a continued increase in sheer numbers as Oracle has progressed in versions. In Oracle8i, SYS-owned packages number around 140. In 9i, the count is over 300, and in 10g, over 500. This increase makes sense when one thinks about how much more powerful and capable the RDBMS has become.

The goal of this chapter is not to highlight or detail each and every package. Oracle has already done that via the "Packages and Types Reference" documentation, named "Supplied PL/SQL Packages" in older versions. The goal, however, is to highlight utility-type packages, and most of those are prefixed with UTL-.

UTL Utilities

A combined list between versions 10 and 11 shows the following:

- UTL_COLL
- UTL_COMPRESS
- UTL_DBWS (not in 11g)
- UTL_ENCODE

- UTL_FILE
- UTL_HTTP
- UTL_I18N
- UTL_INADDR
- UTL_LMS
- UTL_MAIL
- UTL_NLA
- UTL_RAW
- UTL_RECOMP
- UTL_REF
- UTL_SMTP
- UTL_SPADV (not in 10g)
- UTL_TCP
- UTL_URL

In addition to the UTL packages, this chapter will also take a look at some of the XML-related packages. In case it has not been noticed, XML within the database is becoming more and more prevalent. XML may not be seen directly, but rest assured, it is there and there in abundance. As an example, Oracle's Business Intelligence Publisher, still known as XML Publisher in versions of E-Business Suite, converts data as simple as the output from a query in SQL*Plus to an XML format that the processing engine then goes on to format.

Installation of all newer Oracle products via Oracle Universal Installer is based on an XML file. In the past, a stage.jar file was identified. Now it is a products.xml file.

Because there are so many packages, chances are pretty good that there are many the average DBA or developer has never heard of, or, if heard of, not really sure what they do. That is one of the main points of this chapter: provide some exposure to these "hidden" tools. In no particular order of importance, this chapter will start in alphabetical order with the UTL packages, and then go into the XML-related ones.

UTL_COLL

The UTL_COLL package has one subprogram named IS_LOCATOR. This is for those who work with object relational items or nested tables. In many nested tables examples, queries return the entire contents of the table. From an application developer standpoint, does one always want everything in a collection, or would it be more convenient to first perform what is essentially an existence check and then drill down to a specific element? Think of the IS_LOCATOR function as a probe of what is in a nested table.

The function specification shown in the following example is a simple test for determining if the passed-in parameter value is a locator.

```
UTL_COLL.IS_LOCATOR (
   coln IN STANDARD)
  RETURNS BOOLEAN;
```

The example shown in the Types and References Guide is not very clear as to what is taking place. The two lists shown, the first with two phone numbers in it and the second with one, are used in the example code. The key difference between the *phone_book* tables is that the second one has an additional clause associated with it: RETURN (AS) LOCATOR. The difference is not based on the fact that the nested tables have different counts.

When testing for where pno=1 is in phone_book1, that value is a locator and there is a list associated with this value. When testing in the first case (*phone_book*), it is not known if pno=1 will return anything when queried. Only what is queried shows up in the nested table.

To summarize, one can check to see if something exists, or one can get everything returned. The "everything" case is based on the default of VALUE, "which causes the entire nested table to be returned instead of just a locator to it." (Oracle Database Application Developer's Guide). When creating the object table, add RETURN AS LOCATOR and then test the location using UTL_COLL.IS_LOCATOR.

UTL_COMPRESS

Introduced in Oracle 10g, the UTL_COMPRESS package can be used to compress and uncompress large objects (raw, blob or bfile). For all practical purposes, think of UTL_COMPRESS as PL/SQL's means of compressing or zipping files. When looking at the various procedures and functions, many are prefixed with LZ. The algorithm used to perform the compression is based on the Lempel-Ziv algorithm and when used, the code is based on the LZW or Lempel-Ziv-Welch implementation.

Oracle's documentation for this package is sparse in terms of showing a full-scale example. Sparse is not even the correct word here. Nonexistent is a better descriptor. A MetaLink note (249974.1) shows two examples and various pages on the Internet can be searched.

The actual implementation of this package is pretty easy to use once an example is seen. Many of the examples shown elsewhere include a length comparison among the input, the compressed, and the uncompressed lengths. Ideally, the input and uncompressed lengths should be the same. You may find that the compressed length is longer than the input length. This occurs when the input length is small or short. The overhead of building a dictionary can make the compressed length longer than the input length.

In this simple example, create one's own input, compress it, uncompress it, and evaluate the lengths of each.

```
SET SERVEROUTPUT ON
DECLARE
l_in_blob            BLOB;
l_compressed_blob    BLOB;
l_uncompressed_blob  BLOB;
BEGIN
-- Set some values
l_in_blob       := TO_BLOB(UTL_RAW.CAST_TO_RAW
('This is a long string of words used for this example'));
l_compressed_blob    := TO_BLOB('0');
l_uncompressed_blob := TO_BLOB('0');

-- Compress the string
UTL_COMPRESS.lz_compress
(src => l_in_blob, dst => l_compressed_blob);

-- Uncompress the string
UTL_COMPRESS.lz_uncompress
(src => l_compressed_blob, dst => l_uncompressed_blob);

-- Compare the results with the input
DBMS_OUTPUT.put_line('Input length is     : ' || LENGTH(l_in_blob));
DBMS_OUTPUT.put_line('Compressed length   : ' || LENGTH(l_compressed_blob));
DBMS_OUTPUT.put_line('Uncompressed length: ' ||
LENGTH(l_uncompressed_blob));
```

```
-- Caller responsibility to free up temporary LOBs
-- See Operational Notes in the documentation
DBMS_LOB.FREETEMPORARY(l_in_blob);
DBMS_LOB.FREETEMPORARY(l_compressed_blob);
DBMS_LOB.FREETEMPORARY(l_uncompressed_blob);
END;
/

Input length is    : 52
Compressed length  : 67
Uncompressed length: 52

PL/SQL procedure successfully completed.
```

Note that the compressed length is longer than the input length. Adding a few more characters to the input string yields the following:

```
SET SERVEROUTPUT ON
DECLARE
l_in_blob            BLOB;
l_compressed_blob    BLOB;
l_uncompressed_blob  BLOB;
BEGIN
-- Set some values
l_in_blob       := TO_BLOB(UTL_RAW.CAST_TO_RAW
('This is a long string of words used for this example.
Now is the time for all good men to come to the aid of their country'));
l_compressed_blob    := TO_BLOB('0');
l_uncompressed_blob := TO_BLOB('0');

-- Compress the string
UTL_COMPRESS.lz_compress
(src => l_in_blob, dst => l_compressed_blob);

-- Uncompress the string
UTL_COMPRESS.lz_uncompress
(src => l_compressed_blob, dst => l_uncompressed_blob);

-- Compare the results with the input
DBMS_OUTPUT.put_line('Input length is    : ' || LENGTH(l_in_blob));
DBMS_OUTPUT.put_line('Compressed length  : ' || LENGTH(l_compressed_blob));
DBMS_OUTPUT.put_line('Uncompressed length: ' ||
LENGTH(l_uncompressed_blob));

-- Caller responsibility to free up temporary LOBs
-- See Operational Notes in the documentation
DBMS_LOB.FREETEMPORARY(l_in_blob);
DBMS_LOB.FREETEMPORARY(l_compressed_blob);
DBMS_LOB.FREETEMPORARY(l_uncompressed_blob);
END;
/

Input length is    : 122
Compressed length  : 113
Uncompressed length: 122

PL/SQL procedure successfully completed.
```

That little bit extra for the input string pushed it over the top in terms of having the compression take any real effect.

Note that the LZ_COMPRESS subprogram is overloaded since more than one signature method can be used to invoke it. The quality parameter is set to a default of 6. This parameter provides a trade-off between speed of compress and quality of compression. It takes quite a few more words or length of input before there is a difference in what the quality input does.

As an example, take the text about quality in the documentation and use that as the input string, and vary the quality from 1 to 9. If this block of text is used as an example, be sure to remove the single quotes around quality near the end.

"Quality is an optional compression tuning value. It allows the UTL_COMPRESS user to choose between speed and compression quality, meaning the percentage of reduction in size. A faster compression speed will result in less compression of the data. A slower compression speed will result in more compression of the data. Valid values are [1..9], with 1=fastest and 9=slowest. The default 'quality' value is 6."

At a setting of 1, the compressed length is 248, and at 9, the length becomes 245. The strength or utility of using UTL_COMPRESS comes into play when dealing with truly large objects and not just experimenting with contrived strings. For this use case, use a document, but then, a table will also be needed.

The setup steps are to create a table to hold the BLOB (Binary Large Object), create a directory with read/write for the user, put a file into the directory, initialize the record, insert a BLOB, compress it, and compare the lengths.

```
set serveroutput on
create table compress_blob (indx integer, y blob);
create directory MYDIR as 'C:\temp';
--We assume the user doing this will have read/write on MYDIR
--Copy a file into the directory, e.g., A_57KB_Word_doc.doc
--This block will take care of the insert for you, or you
--could create a separate procedure to do this
--This is simple code, does not address other PL/SQL errors
DECLARE
  ablob blob;
  abfile bfile := bfilename('MYDIR', 'A_57KB_Word_doc.doc');
  -- Gets a pointer to the file.
  a_compressed_blob blob;
```

```
  amount  integer;
  asize   integer;
  quality integer := 9;
  cursor blob_cur is select * from compress_blob;
BEGIN
--
-- compress_blob table is initialized with one record because
-- the PL/SQL BLOB locator (ablob) must point to a specific
-- EXISTING NON-NULL database BLOB.
--
-- initialize the blob locator
  insert into compress_blob values (1, empty_blob());
  select y into ablob from compress_blob where indx = 1;

  -- open the bfile and get the initial file size
  dbms_lob.fileopen(abfile);
  asize := dbms_lob.getlength(abfile);
  dbms_output.put_line('Size of input file: ' || asize);

  -- load the file and get the size
  dbms_lob.loadfromfile(ablob, abfile, asize);
  dbms_output.put_line('After loadfromfile');
  asize := dbms_lob.getlength(ablob);
  dbms_output.put_line('Size of blob: ' || asize);

  -- compress the blob
  -- you can experiment with varying the quality
  a_compressed_blob := utl_compress.lz_compress(ablob, quality);

  -- insert the compressed blob
  insert into compress_blob values (2, a_compressed_blob);

  -- compare the sizes of the blobs in the table
  dbms_output.put_line
  ('Sizes before and after insertion/compression -->');
  for c1_rec in blob_cur
    loop
    asize := dbms_lob.getlength(c1_rec.y);
    dbms_output.put_line(asize);
  end loop;
end;
/
Size of input file: 57856
After loadfromfile
Size of blob: 57856
Sizes before and after insertion/compression -->
18722
57856

PL/SQL procedure successfully completed.
```

When using a quality value of 1, the compressed size was 20868, so a value of 9 represents a 10% or so improvement. As file sizes increase, so will the amount of compression.

For production-type code, the developer will want to handle errors such as TOO_MANY_ROWS, NO_DATA_FOUND and DUP_VAL_ON_INDEX. For BLOB-related errors, a set of exception handlers, as shown in documentation like what follows, could be packaged up for reuse.

```
EXCEPTION
  when UTL_COMPRESS.INVALID_ARGUMENT then
  dbms_output.put_line('An argument was an invalid type or value.');

  when UTL_COMPRESS.BUFFER_TOO_SMALL then
  dbms_output.put_line('Compressed representation is too big.');

  when UTL_COMPRESS.DATA_ERROR then
  dbms_output.put_line('Input or output data stream has invalid format.');

  when UTL_COMPRESS.STREAM_ERROR then
  dbms_output.put_line('Error during compression/uncompression of the data
stream');

  when others then
  dbms_output.put_line('An exception occurred');
  dbms_output.put_line(sqlcode || sqlerrm);
```

Preprocessing checks such as checking if open (then closing) and vice versa could also be incorporated. Do not forget to use DBMS_LOB.FREETEMPORARY to release locked items, including the source file. For more information on UTL_COMPRESS from the DBA's perspective, please refer to this utility in Chapter 6.

UTL_DBWS

The UTL_DBWS package is for the rarefied developer; that is, someone who is very deep into Java Web services and using DII (Dynamic Invocation Interface). The DBWS in the package name represents database Web services, and what the package does is provide a wrapper on top of the Java DII. Instead of using Java-specific calls to static invocations, Oracle provides a means of using a dynamic invocation interface. Sounds pretty simple, right?

MetaLink note 428775.1, "DBWS Callout Utilities User's Guide for RDBMS 10.1 or 10.2," takes the developer through the setup steps to install DBWS Callout Utilities. In general, one will need to have Java installed and configured in the database, have JPublisher installed, and have access to an OC4J instance on the computer, which can be obtained via the OC4J version of Application Server. In essence, the database is being turned into a Web service consumer.

Installing Java and checking its status (around 20,000 SYS-owned Java objects) is documented quite well in Oracle's documentation and elsewhere on the Internet. Look for "How to Reload the JVM" on MetaLink or start with note 472937.1, "Information On Installed Database Components and Schemas" and look under the first section.

Installing JPublisher comes from installing SQLJ. If not installed, it can be obtained with the installation CD/download used to install Oracle in the first place. At the end, "jpub" should be found when entering this executable at the command line.

Get the appropriate Web services callout utility from Oracle at http://www.oracle.com/technology/sample_code/tech/java/jsp/dbwebservi ces.html.

Use J2SE 1.3.x or Oracle 9.2, and 1.4.x for releases 1 and 2 of 10g (and also works for 11g). By this point, these details probably pertain to the five or six people who use this package. There is not much in the way of documentation, so aside from OTN and MetaLink, a specialized book such as Oracle Database Programming Using Java and Web Services (Elsevier Digital Press, 2006) would be in order.

UTL_ENCODE

The UTL_ENCODE package is frequently associated with sending email. The body of an email text is encoded and the body is decoded at the receiving end. Within the package are five complementary encode and decode functions, and these are BASE64, MIMEHEADER, QUOTED_PRINTABLE, TEXT, and UUENCODE/UUDECODE. One helper package that is often used is UTL_RAW. The UTL_RAW package is used to cast a character string to a RAW datatype (more on that later). Another related package is UTL_FILE. The encoding part of UTL_ENCODE can be used to chunk files into manageable parts for UTL_FILE.

A simple example is in order. Take a short string and encode it, and then take that encoded representation of the string and decode it. The end result is that the encoded string's RAW values match going in and coming out.

```
SQL> DECLARE
  2    --note that PL/SQL variable is limited to size 32KB
  3    r RAW(32767);
  4  BEGIN
  5    r := UTL_RAW.CAST_TO_RAW('Oracle Utilites Book');
  6    dbms_output.put_line(r);
  7
  8    r := UTL_ENCODE.BASE64_ENCODE(r);
  9    dbms_output.put_line(r);
 10
 11    --now pass r into the decode function
 12    r := UTL_ENCODE.BASE64_DECODE(r);
 13    dbms_output.put_line(r);
 14  END;
 15  /
4F7261636C65205574696C6974657320426F6F6B
54334A685932786C494656306157786C6796447567A49454A766232733D
4F7261636C65205574696C6974657320426F6F6B

PL/SQL procedure successfully completed.
```

As can be seen, the before and after values match. In a similar manner, operations can be performed on human-readable text strings.

```
SQL> DECLARE
  2    v_str VARCHAR2(100);
  3  BEGIN
  4    --generate encoded value
  5    v_str := utl_encode.text_encode
  6    ('Oracle Utilities Book','WE8ISO8859P1', UTL_ENCODE.BASE64);
  7    dbms_output.put_line(v_str);
  8
  9    --take the encoded value and decode it
 10    v_str := utl_encode.text_decode
 11    (v_str,'WE8ISO8859P1', UTL_ENCODE.BASE64);
 12    dbms_output.put_line(v_str);
 13
 14  END;
 15  /
T3JhY2xlIFV0aWxpdGllcyBCb29r
Oracle Utilities Book

PL/SQL procedure successfully completed.
```

The other functions operate in the same manner. Extending this a bit more, an encoded output can be encrypted. Note the difference between encoding with this package and encryption – they are NOT the same thing.

When encoding text, pay attention to the base character set of the database. If UTF16 or EBCDIC is being used, a preliminary conversion may be necessary. If using UTF8 or ASCII, nothing else needs to be done ahead of time. UTL_ENCODE is covered in detail for the DBA in Chapter 6.

UTL_FILE

If the developer has done any file processing (reading or writing on the file system), he is certain to already be familiar with UTL_FILE. This package is similar to how C or C++ reads/writes files on a file system. The general process is to set a pointer to a file's location and name, open it, manipulate the contents, then close it.

Oracle provides an extensive set or list of exceptions which can occur when dealing with files on the operating system. If it happens that the developer is using UTL_FILE in several places, it would be worthwhile to bundle these exceptions into their own package to support code reuse.

Starting with Oracle 10g, an enhancement to UTL_FILE is the package's ability to write out the contents of a stored BLOB to the file system. Put another way, a stored JPEG file can be output. Aside from having the appropriate permissions, one may have to account for the file size and write the contents out in PL/SQL variable-sized chunks of 32KB at a time.

Another enhancement is the departure from having the location(s) specified by *utl_file_dir* in the parameter file. Previously, more than one location could be specified using this parameter as long as the locations all appeared together, meaning no other parameters in between two locations. The latest recommendation is to use a directory object. A directory location is identified to Oracle and stored within the database. Users are then granted read or write on the directory. This allows for multiple locations and more granular control of where a user can read/write. Query the *all_directories* data dictionary view for a description of all directories available to the user running the query.

As an example, take the Word document inserted as a BLOB (back in the UTL_COMPRESS section) and write back out to the file system. If the script was ran through as is, there will be a BLOB stored in the record where INDX=1 or the filename can be used. Here is an example of a procedure to write a BLOB to the MYDIR directory.

```
CREATE OR REPLACE PROCEDURE WriteBLOBToFILE
(infilename IN VARCHAR2) IS

  v_blob        BLOB;
  blob_length   INTEGER;
  out_file      UTL_FILE.FILE_TYPE;
```

```
  v_buffer      RAW(32767);
  chunk_size    BINARY_INTEGER := 32767;
  blob_position INTEGER := 1;

BEGIN

  -- Retrieve the BLOB for reading
  -- This uses a Word document
  SELECT y INTO v_blob FROM compress_blob WHERE indx = 1;

  -- Retrieve the SIZE of the BLOB
  blob_length:=DBMS_LOB.GETLENGTH(v_blob);

  -- Open a handle to the location of the BLOB file
  -- The location is the MYDIR directory
  -- wb = write in byte mode, 10g new feature
  -- The out_file picks up the name of the filename passed in
  out_file := UTL_FILE.FOPEN
    ('MYDIR', infilename, 'wb', chunk_size);

  -- Write the BLOB to file in chunks
  WHILE blob_position <= blob_length LOOP
    IF blob_position + chunk_size - 1 > blob_length THEN
      chunk_size := blob_length - blob_position + 1;
    END IF;
    DBMS_LOB.READ(v_blob, chunk_size, blob_position, v_buffer);
    UTL_FILE.PUT_RAW(out_file, v_buffer, TRUE);
    blob_position := blob_position + chunk_size;
  END LOOP;

  -- Close the file handle
  UTL_FILE.FCLOSE (out_file);
END;
/
```

Compiling the following procedure and executing it writes the "A_57KB_Word_doc.doc" file back into C:\Temp.

```
SQL> exec writeblobtofile('A_57KB_Word_doc.doc');

PL/SQL procedure successfully completed.
```

The ability to write files out like this must be safeguarded. Imagine the damage a malicious – or not – user can wreak by being able to what amounts to download from the database any document.

The UTL_FILE package contains an amazing degree of potential. The FREMOVE and FRENAME procedures do exactly what their names imply. So just as potentially dangerous as writing files out to the file system, misuse of these two procedures, inadvertent or otherwise, can be disastrous. Imagine someone playing "what if" with database files. "I wonder if I can read, write, remove, or rename a database file with UTL_FILE?" Clearly, one does not want users being able to create directory objects on database file locations.

Oracle's documentation is much more complete with respect to this package and many examples are provided therein.

UTL_HTTP

In terms of scale, the documentation behind the UTL_HTTP package is monstrous compared to many other packages. Given the huge amount of data under the covers of a Web page, it is not surprising that the number of subprograms for this package would be quite numerous.

What is a quick and dirty use of UTL_HTTP? The simplest and fastest example is one's ability to capture the source of a Web page by using PL/SQL. Coupled with spooling the output, one now has a simple means of capturing the source of virtually any Web page.

If the developer can spool to a file, she can load the file into the database. If there is a BLOB in the database, write it out to the file system. This workflow should bring to mind the idea of creating a rudimentary source control system. Not only can the developer store and generate HTML files based on a combination of UTL_FILE and UTL_HTTP, but they can be edited as well.

There are applications where the HTML for Web pages served in a framework is stored in the database. How those pages render is slightly different than creating HTML files on the file system, but the concept is the same – the database serves up the source for a page. So look at a quick example of capturing the source for a page. Use the home page of dba-oracle.com. This small body of code will generate almost 900 lines of HTML code and uses eight subprograms in the UTL_HTTP package.

```
spool get_page.html
DECLARE
 req   UTL_HTTP.REQ;
 resp  UTL_HTTP.RESP;
 value VARCHAR2(1024);
BEGIN
  req := UTL_HTTP.BEGIN_REQUEST('http://dba-oracle.com');
  UTL_HTTP.SET_HEADER(req, 'User-Agent', 'Mozilla/4.0');
  resp := UTL_HTTP.GET_RESPONSE(req);
  LOOP
    UTL_HTTP.READ_LINE(resp, value, TRUE);
```

```
      dbms_output.put_line(value);
  END LOOP;
  UTL_HTTP.END_RESPONSE(resp);
EXCEPTION
  WHEN UTL_HTTP.END_OF_BODY THEN
    UTL_HTTP.END_RESPONSE(resp);
END;
/
spool off
```

Here is the top part of the captured HTML source.

```
<!DOCTYPE HTML PUBLIC "-//IETF//DTD HTML//EN">
<html>
<head>
<META name="verify-v1"
content="03pBD3fe1Hr9cZGVzdKBKWKwK7myXtC2l7tXPLFZzbI=" />
<meta http-equiv="Content-Type" content="text/html; charset=iso-8859-1">
<meta name="GENERATOR" content="Microsoft FrontPage 6.0">
<title>Oracle Consulting, Oracle Support and Oracle Training by BC</title>
<meta name="keywords" content="Oracle Consulting, Oracle support, Oracle
Consultants,Oracle Education,Oracle
contracting,Oracle consulting,Oracle consultant,Oracle Training,Oracle dba
support,Oracle architecture,Oracle
classes,Oracle,Oracle architecture,Oracle tuning, Oracle data warehousing">
<meta name="description" content="Burleson Oracle consulting, Oracle
training and Oracle support">
</head>
```

Any Web page that can be accessed via the browser, minus those requiring authentication, can be captured. With this ability, one can sample pages and check to see if there are any differences. But what about HTTPS pages? For these pages, one needs to configure Wallet Manager. On Windows, this can be found under Start > Programs > the Oracle home > Integrated Management Tools > Wallet Manager, and in UNIX, use one found in $ORACLE_HOME/bin. Use of Wallet Manager enables the developer to capture secure Web pages, secure in the sense that this is what one is allowed to access via the wallet information.

If the returned page is large, use the REQUEST_PIECES function. This function returns a PL/SQL table of 2000 bytes. In the prior example, how many pieces were returned and what was the length? Using the example in Oracle's documentation, and correcting the error for the length output (use "len," not "i" in the last DBMS_OUTPUT), the following occurs:

```
DECLARE
   x    UTL_HTTP.HTML_PIECES;
   len PLS_INTEGER;
BEGIN
```

```
   x := UTL_HTTP.REQUEST_PIECES('http://dba-oracle.com/', 100);
   DBMS_OUTPUT.PUT_LINE(x.count || ' pieces were retrieved.');
   DBMS_OUTPUT.PUT_LINE('with total length ');
   IF x.count < 1 THEN
      DBMS_OUTPUT.PUT_LINE('0');
  ELSE
   len := 0;
   FOR i in 1..x.count LOOP
      len := len + length(x(i));
   END LOOP;
   DBMS_OUTPUT.PUT_LINE(len);
  END IF;
END;
/

23 pieces were retrieved.
with total length
44356
```

The output using this against www.oracle.com is 22 pieces with length 43086, which is quite different than what is shown in Oracle's documentation (4 pieces and length 7687).

UTL_I18N

This oddly named package is based on internationalization. Keeping the leading I and trailing N, and removing what is in-between, 18 characters are eliminated. Internationalization is then abbreviated as I18N, a small example of Oracle humor.

What is the package used for? For the most part, it is used to perform translations or lookups based on the developer's locale or input. For example, one can list out time zones.

```
DECLARE
   x   UTL_HTTP.HTML_PIECES;
   len PLS_INTEGER;
BEGIN
   x := UTL_HTTP.REQUEST_PIECES('http://www.oracle.com/', 100);
   DBMS_OUTPUT.PUT_LINE(x.count || ' pieces were retrieved.');
   DBMS_OUTPUT.PUT_LINE('with total length ');
   IF x.count < 1 THEN
      DBMS_OUTPUT.PUT_LINE('0');
  ELSE
   len := 0;
   FOR i in 1..x.count LOOP
      len := len + length(x(i));
   END LOOP;
   DBMS_OUTPUT.PUT_LINE(len);
  END IF;
END;
```

```
/
Count = 119
Pacific/Pago_Pago
Pacific/Honolulu
America/Anchorage
America/Vancouver
America/Los_Angeles
America/Tijuana
America/Edmonton
...continues...
```

How about all of the local time zones based on America?

```
DECLARE
 retval utl_i18n.string_array;
 cnt    PLS_INTEGER;
BEGIN
  retval := utl_i18n.get_local_time_zones('AMERICA');
  dbms_output.put('Count = ');
  dbms_output.put_line(retval.LAST-retval.FIRST+1);
  cnt := retval.FIRST;

  WHILE cnt IS NOT NULL LOOP
    dbms_output.put_line(retval(cnt));
    cnt := retval.NEXT(cnt);
  END LOOP;
END;
/
Count = 8
America/New_York
America/Indianapolis
America/Chicago
America/Denver
America/Phoenix
America/Los_Angeles
America/Anchorage
Pacific/Honolulu

PL/SQL procedure successfully completed.
```

Experiment with the subprograms and see what gets returned.

UTL_INADDR

This simple package can be used to get the host address and host name, both remote and local. An example of the subprograms shows the following with respect to a local host.

```
BEGIN
  DBMS_OUTPUT.PUT_LINE(UTL_INADDR.GET_HOST_NAME);
  -- get local host name
  DBMS_OUTPUT.PUT_LINE(UTL_INADDR.GET_HOST_ADDRESS);
```

```
  -- get local IP addr
END;
/
T42
10.10.10.10

PL/SQL procedure successfully completed.
```

The name of the computer running this code is T42, and the IP address, at least one of them, is 10.10.10.10, which may be recognized as a dummy address used for the Microsoft loopback adapter.

What is the host name where dba-oracle.com is hosted? The nslookup command returns an IP address of 65.109.93.192. Use this IP address and see what the host name is.

```
select
  UTL_INADDR.GET_HOST_NAME
  ('65.109.93.192')
from
  dual;

UTL_INADDR.GET_HOST_NAME('65.109.93.192')
-----------------------------------------
dba-oracle.com
```

One of Google's IP addresses is used in the following query just to show that the hostname is not the obvious name as in the previous example.

```
select
  UTL_INADDR.GET_HOST_NAME
  ('64.233.167.99')
from
  dual;

UTL_INADDR.GET_HOST_NAME('64.233.167.99')
-----------------------------------------
py-in-f99.google.com
```

UTL_LMS

The UTL_LMS package is handy when it comes to translating Oracle messages into another language. People who moderate on an Oracle-related forum have undoubtedly run across someone who posts a topic and left the error message in the poster's native tongue, which invariably is not English.

With the right adjustment of the language setting, error messages can be translated.

```
DECLARE
  s varchar2(200);
  i pls_integer;
BEGIN
  i:=utl_lms.get_message(601, 'rdbms', 'oci', 'french', s);
  dbms_output.put_line('OCI--00601 is: '||s);
END;
/

OCI—00601 is: Echec du processus de nettoyage.
```

The input parameters are *errnum, product, facility, language* and *message*.

UTL_MAIL

The UTL_MAIL package can be used to send email to recipients, including CC and BCC addresses. Because of some security issues, the package is not installed by default. As sys, two scripts in the $ORACLE_HOME/rdbms/admin directory must be run: utlmail.sql and prvtmail.plb. Once installed, then set the *smtp_out_server* parameter in the initialization parameter file. If not set, a default value of DB_DOMAIN will be used.

The package contains three procedures: SEND, SEND_ATTACH_RAW, and SEND_ATTACH_VARCHAR2. The last two procedures are overloaded. One deals with VARCHAR2 attachments and the other with RAW. The only difference between the procedures is the datatype for ATTACHMENT (RAW versus VARCHAR2).

To generate many invocations of UTL_MAIL, it is necessary to loop through addressee information. Otherwise, the developer would be executing this package one recipient at a time. Create a table with recipients, or determine a query which provides the same information, and loop through what was selected from the source table to extract addressee information.

What is different between UTL_MAIL and UTL_SMTP? The UTL_MAIL package is actually a wrapper over two other packages: UTL_TCP and UTL_SMTP. Overall, UTL_MAIL is much easier to use than UTL_SMTP. In ancient times, UTL_SMTP was Oracle's answer to sending email via PL/SQL.

Introduced in 10g, UTL_MAIL is the way to go because of its overall simplicity.

Here is a simple example of how to send email using UTL_MAIL. Replace the obvious text prompts for real data. If one does not know one's mail server, send an email to oneself and look at the header data, or ask the system administrator.

```
ALTER SYSTEM SET smtp_out_server = 'mailserver.domain.com';
DECLARE
 vSender VARCHAR2(30)  := 'sender@somewhere.com';
 vRecip  VARCHAR2(30)  := 'your.name@domain.com';
 vSubj   VARCHAR2(50)  := 'Enter the subject here';
 vMesg   VARCHAR2(4000) := 'Enter the body';
 vMType  VARCHAR2(30)  := 'text/plain; charset=us-ascii';
BEGIN
 utl_mail.send
 (vSender, vRecip, NULL, NULL, vSubj, vMesg, vMType, NULL);
END;
/
```

This example is based on sending email from a PC using Windows XP. As mentioned, once the mail package is compiled, the *smtp_out_server* parameter can be set in the SPFILE.

UTL_NLA

The UTL_NLA package represents the best area of mathematics: linear algebra! The two major areas are BLAS (Basic Linear Algebra Subprogram) and LAPACK (Linear Algebra Package). Within each area, more divisions are present. The BLAS subset has three levels (1-3) and LAPACK has two routine sets.

Use of the package presupposes a working knowledge of linear algebra. For that matter, if the developer works with linear algebra, Eigenvalues, LU decomposition, and so on, he is probably already working with other tools better suited to his needs.

For now, observe that Oracle has a highly complex and intricate math routine built-in that pertains to a very small set of users. It would be interesting to see how efficient these routines are as that is usually the limiting factor of a program's utility. Virtually all routines excel at low order systems but tend to suffer as the number of systems increases. Oracle may hold several TPC records for transaction rates, but it is doubtful it will ever hold a record for fastest LU decomposition time.

UTL_RAW

UTL_RAW has already been touched upon in earlier discussions. According to Oracle, the basic purpose of UTL_RAW is to manipulate raw datatypes. Many of the 20-plus functions are used to convert, or cast, one datatype to another. Others are related to attribute values, such as LENGTH, which was used in earlier examples.

Some of the more commonly used functions are related to VARCHAR2. The CAST_TO_RAW and CAST_TO_VARCHAR2 functions handle varchar2 to raw and vice versa conversions. For normal data or conversion operations, one would be hard pressed to describe a situation where the BIT_XOR function, as an example, came in handy.

It is usually not a good sign when all the documentation does is provide copious amounts of syntax examples and no working example whatsoever. Somewhere one missed the "Use of these subprograms is left as an exercise at the end of the chapter. Curious readers are encouraged to try the exercises."

However, the UTL_RAW is not a destination package, so to speak. It is a helper package that facilitates the functioning of other packages. The functions are all straightforward, and the three that are most likely to be used are the varchar2-related ones and length, which has already been seen in action.

UTL_RECOMP

If the developer needs to recompile invalid objects, and needs it done quickly, UTL_RECOMP may be helpful. It does not do anything that Oracle does not already do. Oracle will attempt to compile an invalid object upon first use. The main advantage to having objects in a valid status to begin with is the time savings; that is, what little bit of time it takes to compile an object while a procedure is being run will not be added to the time because the compilation time has been paid elsewhere.

What UTL_RECOMP does allow is parallel recompilation. It is like having parallel execution operations opened up for compiling objects. Oracle suggests one thread per CPU. If there are four CPUs, then the developer could use *execute utl_recomp.recomp_parallel(4)*.

There are five areas of consideration when using the package. The first is that Oracle expects to have STANDARD, DBMS_STANDARD, DBMS_JOB and DBMS_RANDOM in a valid state. The second is that the developer must be connected as SYSDBA while (third) running this via SQL*Plus. The package uses (fourth) the job queue when using the parallel option, and fifth, there should not be any DDL taking place while running this package and its procedures.

Optionally, one can recompile objects sequentially as a whole, or sequentially within a schema. If using the parallel option, one may find that writes to the SYSTEM tablespace are a bottleneck, so any gains from the multiple CPU approach are washed out by a less than optimal disk I/O situation.

Otherwise, use of this package is quite easy to implement and it does provide an alternative to running UTLRP.SQL, which, by way of interest, calls a script named UTLPRP.SQL, which is a wrapper for using UTL_RECOMP. Not surprisingly, UTLPRP.SQL can take a parameter which is the number of threads for parallel execution. Now the rest of the story is known.

If one reads in detail what the parameters are for RECOMP_SERIAL and RECOMP_PARALLEL, note that there is a *flags* parameter. It has a default of 0, and its stated purpose is that it is used for internal testing and diagnosability, suggesting hints of hidden Oracle features. Without knowing what other flag values will do, do not use anything other than what Oracle expects in the first place.

UTL_REF

The UTL_REF package is a case where the difference between definer and invoker rights matters. The security model comes into play depending on where (server versus client) the package is being called from. If on the server, it is invoker rights. If from a client, then definer rights rule. Normally, calls on the server operate with definer privileges and the owner of the package must have privileges on the underlying objects.

What is UTL_REF used for? If an object has a reference, then select that object. Somewhat like a locator, which was mentioned earlier, a row of an object table stores an object. How does one reference that object? Since the developer can use object identifiers to uniquely identify an object, a persistent pointer, or reference, can be based upon that object identifier. Coming back full circle, if there is a reference, then an object can be obtained.

The subprograms in UTL_REF include operation for deleting, locking, selecting, and updating an object. Locking an object implicitly selects it. In fact, the LOCK_OBJECT procedure is analogous to issuing a SELECT...FOR UPDATE in terms of locking a record, but in this case, an object will be locked upon.

With a reference, there is no need to know the object table name. That is the main benefit of using UTL_REF. Once the object ID is identified, i.e., the reference to it, an update can be performed or deleted on it.

Most examples use addresses or some other collection such as books, records, CDs, or animals. Here is an example using a library, or collection of books, and the use of LOCK and UPDATE.

```
DECLARE
  --both are of the same type - BOOK_t
  the_book_ref REF BOOK_t;
  the_book        BOOK_t;
BEGIN
  select REF(book)
  into the_book_ref
  from library book
  where author = 'Jones'
  and title = 'Dark Night';

  --parameters are reference and object
  --object is the same object type as the locked object
  UTL_REF.LOCK_OBJECT(the_book_ref, the_book);
  --change the title
  the_book.title := 'Stormy Night';
  --same rule applies for the lock operation
  UTL_REF.UPDATE_OBJECT(the_book_ref, the_book);
END;
/
```

Abstract data types (ADT), user-defined types (UDT) and object-oriented implementation within Oracle always seems awkward to use. This is an area where practice and repetition help to make the syntax more palatable. For the majority of database administrators and developers, use of nested tables and object types will be a rare event.

With respect to REF type items, what is more common is the use of REF cursors. REF cursors are discussed in detail in <u>Oracle PL/SQL Tuning, Expert Secrets for High Performance Programming</u> (Rampant TechPress, 2006).

UTL_SMTP

This package was introduced several versions ago. It is complex and cumbersome to use. If this package is already being used, there is probably very little new to add to what one has been using for quite a long time. If one is new to sending email from Oracle, see UTL_MAIL. It is much simpler and easier to implement. Although still supported in newer releases, it may be worthwhile to consider moving from UTL_SMTP to UTL_MAIL. Any deprecation of UTL_SMTP would have to be announced well before that takes place due to the number of legacy applications using this package. This utility is also covered in Chapter 6 from the DBA's point of view.

Here is a sample implementation of UTL_SMTP.

```
CREATE OR REPLACE PROCEDURE SEND_MAIL (
msg_to varchar2,
msg_subject varchar2,
msg_text varchar2 )
IS
c utl_smtp.connection;
rc integer;
msg_from varchar2(50) := 'Oracle9.2';
mailhost VARCHAR2(30) := '127.0.0.1'; -- local database host

BEGIN
c := utl_smtp.open_connection (mailhost, 25); -- SMTP on port 25
utl_smtp.helo(c, mailhost);
utl_smtp.mail(c, msg_from);
utl_smtp.rcpt(c, msg_to);

utl_smtp.data(c,'From: Oracle Database' || utl_tcp.crlf ||
'To: ' || msg_to || utl_tcp.crlf ||
'Subject: ' || msg_subject ||
utl_tcp.crlf || msg_text);
utl_smtp.quit(c);

EXCEPTION
WHEN UTL_SMTP.INVALID_OPERATION THEN
dbms_output.put_line(' Invalid Operation in Mail attempt
using UTL_SMTP.');
WHEN UTL_SMTP.TRANSIENT_ERROR THEN
```

```
dbms_output.put_line(' Temporary e-mail issue - try again');
WHEN UTL_SMTP.PERMANENT_ERROR THEN
dbms_output.put_line(' Permanent Error Encountered.');
END;
/
```

UTL_SPADV

This package first appeared in 11g and is used to gather and show statistics related to Oracle Streams. There are two subprograms, COLLECT_STATS and SHOW_STATS. Every parameter in COLLECT_STATS has a default value, as does every parameter in SHOW_STATS. With that in mind, there is no need to list every parameter if one wants to use something other than the default value. The way to accomplish this is to use named notation. List the parameter name followed by "=>" followed by the new value.

The SPADV part of the package takes its name from the Streams Performance Advisor. The advisor is a new feature and the best source of documentation for it (as of this writing) is in Oracle® Streams Concepts and Administration 11g Release 1 (11.1). The output from SHOW_STATS is spreadsheet ready, and one definitely needs the decoder table to interpret all of the abbreviations used in the output.

UTL_TCP

The UTL_TCP package enables PL/SQL to communicate with external servers using TCP/IP. The servers must also be using TCP/IP. The package is useful for accessing Internet protocols and email. The newer UTL_MAIL is a wrapper around this package. Examine the sample code for UTL_SMTP and one can see traces of UTL_TCP in place there as well.

The subprograms are based on GET, READ, WRITE, OPEN and CLOSE. The READ and WRITE options can handle text lines, binary data, and text data. The output from UTL_TCP requests can be captured and spooled into a file. The contents of the file will be fairly similar to what was obtained using URL_HTTP.

Here is an example set of code to GET lines from a Web site.

```
set serveroutput on
spool C:\Temp\UTL_TCP_DEMO.html
DECLARE
```

```
 conn    utl_tcp.connection;
 retval PLS_INTEGER;
BEGIN
  conn := utl_tcp.open_connection
  (remote_host => 'www.dba-oracle.com',
   remote_port => 80,
   charset => 'US7ASCII');
  retval := utl_tcp.write_line (conn, 'GET / HTTP/1.0');
  retval := utl_tcp.write_line (conn);
  BEGIN
    LOOP
      dbms_output.put_line(utl_tcp.get_line (conn, TRUE));
    END LOOP;
  EXCEPTION
    WHEN utl_tcp.end_of_input THEN
      NULL;
    WHEN OTHERS THEN
      NULL;
  END;
  BEGIN
    utl_tcp.flush(conn);
  EXCEPTION
    WHEN OTHERS THEN
      NULL;
  END;
  utl_tcp.close_connection (conn);
END;
/
spool off
```

In essence, this replicates the example shown in UTL_HTTP. The output file will have a few more artifacts from the package, but once cleaned up or commented out, the resulting HTML file will render normally in a browser. Paths to images may not resolve, so the image box may be seen on the page, but all other text and formatting will appear as seen on the actual page itself.

In comparison, using the UTL_HTTP package to scrape a Web site is easier as it requires fewer lines of code. Most of the default parameters are adequate. One that may need to be varied is the *timeout* parameter. The default of 0 means not to wait, and a null value means to wait forever. Those conditions may be extreme, so trying a small non-zero value for timeout may help connection attempts succeed more often than when set to 0. To find out more about this utility for the DBA, please refer to Chapter 6.

UTL_URL

As the last of the UTL packages, UTL_URL is useful for escaping and unescaping URLs with spaces in them. There have been URLs with "%20" in between words. That escape sequence represents a space, and a space is an

---

illegal character, so it has to be escaped. The notation is based on %hex-code format.

The following is an example of escaping spaces within a URL.

```
select
  utl_url.escape('http://www.acme.com/url with space.html')
from
  dual;

UTL_URL.ESCAPE('HTTP://WWW.ACME.COM/URLWITHSPACE.HTML')
-------------------------------------------------------------
http://www.acme.com/url%20with%20space.html
```

Likewise, the unescape function returns the URL back to its original form.

```
select
  utl_url.unescape('http://www.acme.com/url%20with%20space.html')
from
  dual;

UTL_URL.UNESCAPE('HTTP://WWW.ACME.COM/URL%20WITH%20SPACE.HTML')
-------------------------------------------------------------
http://www.acme.com/url with space.html
```

XML Utilities

DBMS_XMLGEN

How does one transform data in a table to XML format? Just as one can select and format into HTML code, and this is what takes place behind the scene in iSQL*Plus, one can select from a table and have the output be well-formed XML. Use the DBMS_XMLGEN.GETXML function to accomplish this.

The syntax is select DBMS_XMLGEN.GETXML*('your query here')* from dual and with spool and SQL*Plus settings set correctly, the output is a dump of data in XML format. Where is this useful?

Anywhere or anytime one needs to transform data into XML format, the GETXML function can be used. Of particular note, Oracle's new reporting tool Business Intelligence Publisher is intimately tied to XML. In fact, report or template development is largely driven by having an XML file representation of data to start with. Dump a portion of the data into XML format, load the XML data into an RTF document in Word, call the table wizard, and one has a report template just like that.

Of course, much more can take place with respect to manipulating the data. Oracle recommends that data selection and formatting, as much as possible, be done via the SELECT statement as opposed to forcing the RTF processing engine to manipulate the data. The RDBMS engine is obviously much more powerful than what Microsoft Word has to offer.

This select statement yields the following output:

```
SQL> select dbms_xmlgen.getxml(
  2   'select
  3   EMPNO,
  4   ENAME,
  5   JOB,
  6   MGR,
  7   HIREDATE,
  8   SAL,
  9   COMM,
 10   DEPTNO
 11   from emp
 12   where deptno=10')
 13   "XML OUTPUT"
 14   from dual;

XML OUTPUT
-------------------------------
<?xml version="1.0"?>
<ROWSET>
 <ROW>
  <EMPNO>7782</EMPNO>
  <ENAME>CLARK</ENAME>
  <JOB>MANAGER</JOB>
  <MGR>7839</MGR>
  <HIREDATE>09-JUN-81</HIREDATE>
  <SAL>2450</SAL>
  <DEPTNO>10</DEPTNO>
 </ROW>
...continued...
</ROWSET>
```

The ROWSET and ROW tags can be set via other procedures within this package. Oracle recommends that DBMS_XMLGEN be used over DBMS_XMLQUERY.

DBMS_XMLSAVE

This package can be used to upload XML data into a table. It requires a good bit of manual typing as each tag has to be quoted and concatenated. Here is an example of uploading a new record into the EMP table.

```
DECLARE
  insctx    dbms_xmlsave.ctxtype;
  n_rows    NUMBER;
  s_xml     VARCHAR2 (32767);
BEGIN
  s_xml :=
'<ROWSET>'
|| '<ROW>'
|| '<EMPNO>7783</EMPNO>'
|| '<ENAME>CLARK</ENAME>'
|| '<JOB>MANAGER</JOB>'
|| '<MGR>7839</MGR>'
|| '<SAL>2450</SAL>'
|| '<DEPTNO>10</DEPTNO>'
|| '</ROW>'
||'</ROWSET>';
insctx := dbms_xmlsave.newcontext ('EMP');
-- get the context handle
dbms_xmlsave.setrowtag (insctx, 'ROW');
n_rows := dbms_xmlsave.insertxml (insctx, s_xml);
-- this inserts the document
dbms_xmlsave.closecontext (insctx);
END;
/
```

A bit cumbersome, but it can be done. There must be an easier way.

DBMS_XMLSTORE

This package allows uploading an XML file directly and inserting the contents into a table. In this example, table EMP3 is a copy of EMP. The generated XML data file is named emp3.xml and is located in a directory object named MYDIR - C:\Temp in this example. Here is the procedure code to upload an XML file:

```
CREATE OR REPLACE PROCEDURE insertXML
(dirname IN VARCHAR2,
 filename IN VARCHAR2,
 tablename IN VARCHAR2)
IS
xmlfile BFILE;
myclob CLOB;
insCtx DBMS_XMLStore.ctxType;
rows number;
```

```
BEGIN
dbms_lob.createtemporary(myclob, TRUE, 2);

-- handle to the XML file on the OS
xmlfile := Bfilename(UPPER(dirname),filename);

-- open file
DBMS_LOB.fileOpen(xmlfile);

-- copy contents of file into empty clob
DBMS_LOB.loadFromFile
(myclob, xmlfile, dbms_lob.getLength(xmlfile));

-- context handle
insCtx := DBMS_XMLStore.newContext(UPPER(tableName));

-- this inserts the file
rows := DBMS_XMLStore.insertXML(insCtx, myclob);
dbms_output.put_line(to_char(rows) || ' rows inserted');

-- close handle
DBMS_XMLStore.closeContext(insCtx);
END insertXML;
/
```

The process to upload a file is to execute the procedure and pass in the directory object name, the file name, and the target table.

These three XML-related packages and code examples should enable one to handle basic XML file or data operations. Querying XML via XPath Query is beyond the scope of this book. However, being able to quickly generate and upload XML data is important, and as can be seen, the process is not that complicated.

Other Useful Utilities

Oerr

The oerr utility (command line executable) can be used to look up Oracle error messages. Many products within Oracle contain an msg file, or message library. It is available only on UNIX platforms and not on Windows. To receive help on how to use this tool type oerr at the command prompt.

```
%oerr
Usage: oerr facility error
```

Facility is identified by the three-letter prefix in the error string. For example, if the developer gets ORA-7300, "ora" is the facility and "7300" is the error. So type "oerr ora 7300". If one gets LCD-111, type "oerr lcd 111", and so on.

DBMS_PROFILER

This package can be used to capture time spent on PL/SQL calls. Tracing helps find wait times for SQL, but what about time spent on PL/SQL? The steps to run DBMS_PROFILER are easy to perform. Prior to running, get the latest version of the source code from MetaLink. See Note 243775.1, "Implementing and Using the PL.SQL Profiler" and download the PROF.zip file.

Once the files have been downloaded and extracted, take a look at profiler_7.html and see if this utility does not impress with what it can do. The number of times a command or instruction was executed and the execution time are readily seen in the HTML-formatted output. Best of all, this tool is free.

DBMS_DEBUG

For Forms developers, running debug in a Forms session is made easy because of the GUI interface and modal windows inside Forms Builder. In regular PL/SQL on the command line, the same is not true. Although DBMS_DEBUG can provide pretty much the same output as what is seen in Forms debugging, the overhead of running the debugger is somewhat problematic. MetaLink note 221346.1, "DBMS_DEBUG: Simple Example of Debugging An Anonymous Block" offers a fairly simple example of using the package.

The basic steps are to run two sessions. In the first, initialize debug, obtain an identifier, and call the code. A second session is then attached to the first using the identifier. So, in session one:

```
alter session set plsql_debug=true;
set serveroutput on
var x varchar2(50)
begin
  :x := dbms_debug.initialize();
  dbms_debug.debug_on();
end;
/
```

```
print x

begin
  do_whatever;
end;
/
```

In session two:

```
set serveroutput on
exec dbms_debug.attach_session('&ssid')
```

When done, turn off debugging and in session two, detach. The output is then available for viewing.

Conclusion

From release to release, the number of built-in packages within Oracle has shown a steady increase over the past ten years. It would be safe to assume this trend will continue. What defines a package as being a utility is mostly left to the interpretation of the user. The name of a package does not always belie its function. Do not think that only UTL packages are utility related. As shown in this chapter, utility-like tools can be named DBMS and even be command line executables.

In general, remember that utilities come in the following forms:

- Built-in packages
- Command line executable
- External programs, from Oracle or not

Sage advice in construction applies here as well: use the right tool for the job at hand. There are certainly plenty to choose from, so make sure the task is not being made harder when a simpler utility would have sufficed.

BBED: The Block Browser and Editor Tool

Introduction

What if one could directly read and manipulate data at the block level? Oracle provides such a tool to do exactly that, but it has to be built by the DBA. The Block Browser and Editor tool, or BBED for short, is the ticket into the contents of data blocks within an Oracle database. Here is what can be done with BBED:

- Change data
- Recover damaged or deleted data
- Alter a file header
- Corrupt and uncorrupt a block

The ability to change data is what it sounds like. Any data can be changed anywhere. What does this imply? It also means that passwords can be changed – any password. For example, the password for sys can be changed.

Deleted a row and need to recover it? What happens to data when the DBA or a user deletes it? Specifically, does the data really go away, or does something else take place? The answer is that something else takes place. Oracle marks the row(s) as deleted and makes the space available for use in the future. For example, when using files in DOS and a file was deleted, the first character of the file name was changed and the file became hidden to normal "dir" listings. Recovery tools could be used to show deleted files; the only real work was to figure out what the missing first character was. Recovering data in Oracle using BBED is roughly the same thing – one just has to find where the deleted row lives and reset some flags to make the row active again as long as the row has not been overwritten yet.

On a larger scale, the same type of recovery can be done using data files. By setting values inside the file header (the file header block), an older file can become part of the current database.

The BBED utility also gives one the power to corrupt and uncorrupt a block or reset the corrupt block marker. Use of BBED for this purpose, although interesting, is not practical in that there are better, i.e. more established and approved, ways of repairing corrupt blocks. However, if one wants to corrupt a block and test out one's RMAN skills, this would be a fairly quick way to set up that lab environment.

All of the above can be done without having access to a database in terms of being logged in or having an active instance running except for the RMAN recovery. In other words, if someone has access to BBED and access to one's datafiles, that person has access to everything in the database. Everything. If that does not convince one to safeguard the Oracle datafiles from unauthorized users, what will?

Where and how does one get BBED? In UNIX, Oracle gives the pieces needed to create the tool. The DBA does not get BBED as a live or active executable like what one gets with EXP or SQL*Plus. In older versions of Oracle on Windows, the executable was installed ready for use, but this is no longer the case. It did not even have to be the RDBMS installation to get BBED.EXE (how it is named on Windows). Using an Oracle8i client installation, BBED.EXE is installed in $ORACLE_HOME/bin by default.
In a 32-bit installation on UNIX (refers to all *NIX variants), look for two object files in $ORACLE_HOME/rdbms/lib: sbbdpt.o and ssbbded.o. In a 64-bit installation, the files will be in the lib32 directory.

```
[oracle] ls -la *bb*.o
-rw-r--r--    1 oracle    dba              1160 Nov 18  2003 sbbdpt.o
-rw-r--r--    1 oracle    dba               848 Nov 18  2003 ssbbded.o
```

To create or make the executable, use the make command as shown.

```
[oracle] make -f ins_rdbms.mk $ORACLE_HOME/rdbms/lib/bbed
```

Sample output from the make command is shown below.

```
Linking BBED utility (bbed)
rm -f /u001/app/oracle/ora904/rdbms/lib/bbed
```

Introduction   **525**

```
gcc -o /u001/app/oracle/ora904/rdbms/lib/bbed -
L/u001/app/oracle/ora904/rdbms/lib/ -L/u001/app/oracle/ora904/lib/
/u001/app/oracle/ora904/lib/s0main.o
/u001/app/oracle/ora904/rdbms/lib/ssbbded.o
/u001/app/oracle/ora904/rdbms/lib/sbbdpt.o `cat
/u001/app/oracle/ora904/lib/ldflags`    -lnsslb9 -lncrypt9 -lnsgr9 -lnzjs9 -
<some lines removed>
lcommon9 -lgeneric9  -ltrace9 -lnls9  -lcore9 -lnls9 -lcore9 -lnls9 -lxml9 -
lcore9 -lunls9 -lclient9  -lvsn9 -lwtc9 -lcommon9 -lgeneric9 -lnls9  -lcore9
-lnls9 -lcore9 -lnls9 -lxml9 -lcore9 -lunls9  `cat
/u001/app/oracle/ora904/lib/sysliblist` -Wl,-
rpath,/u001/app/oracle/ora904/lib:/lib:/usr/lib -lm    `cat
/u001/app/oracle/ora904/lib/sysliblist` -ldl -lm
```

Sample output from a 10.2.0.1 installation is shown below. The reason for showing it is to illustrate the difference between Oracle versions 9 and 10 in the flags. Put another way, there is no guarantee that one can take BBED from one version and use it on another version, but one is welcome to try.

```
[oracle@oralinux lib]$ make -f ins_rdbms.mk $ORACLE_HOME/rdbms/lib/bbed

Linking BBED utility (bbed)
rm -f /opt/oracle/product/10.2.0/db_1/rdbms/lib/bbed
gcc -o /opt/oracle/product/10.2.0/db_1/rdbms/lib/bbed -
L/opt/oracle/product/10.2.0/db_1/rdbms/lib/ -
L/opt/oracle/product/10.2.0/db_1/lib/ -
L/opt/oracle/product/10.2.0/db_1/lib/stubs/ -L/usr/lib -lirc
/opt/oracle/product/10.2.0/db_1/lib/s0main.o
/opt/oracle/product/10.2.0/db_1/rdbms/lib/ssbbded.o
/opt/oracle/product/10.2.0/db_1/rdbms/lib/sbbdpt.o `cat
/opt/oracle/product/10.2.0/db_1/lib/ldflags`    -lnsslb10 -lncrypt10 -
lnsgr10
<some lines removed>
-lclient10 -lnnetd10  -lvsn10 -lcommon10 -lgeneric10 -lsnls10 -lnls10  -
lcore10 -lsnls10 -lnls10 -lcore10 -lsnls10 -lnls10 -lxml10 -lcore10 -lunls10
-lsnls10 -lnls10 -lcore10 -lnls10  `cat
/opt/oracle/product/10.2.0/db_1/lib/sysliblist` -Wl,-
rpath,/opt/oracle/product/10.2.0/db_1/lib -lm    `cat
/opt/oracle/product/10.2.0/db_1/lib/sysliblist` -ldl -lm    -
L/opt/oracle/product/10.2.0/db_1/lib
```

To confirm the creation, see if the BBED executable was created. In this example, the make command was executed in the rdbms/lib directory. BBED can be placed anywhere the DBA likes. Also, change the permissions if needed.

```
-rwxr-xr-x    1 oracle    dba    434057 Aug 25 16:26 bbed
```

To confirm that the utility actually runs, invoke it. This example uses the 10g version, which shows release 2.0.0.0.0, and so does the 9.0.4 version. Aside from the change in the copyright, the release does not appear to have changed in quite some time.

```
[oracle@oralinux lib]$ ./bbed
Password:

BBED: Release 2.0.0.0.0 - Limited Production on Wed Aug 27 16:17:06 2008

Copyright (c) 1982, 2005, Oracle.  All rights reserved.

************* !!! For Oracle Internal Use only !!! ***************

BBED>
```

Note that one will be prompted for a password. Virtually all of the references to BBED via a search on the Internet mention that if one is motivated enough to be using BBED in the first place, then one is clever enough to determine the password on one's own. The password is blockedit. It will be seen as BLOCKEDIT in a hex dump file of BBED. Use xxd in /usr/bin to create a dump of BBED, and then look for "BBED>" in the file. A few lines up is BLOCKEDIT.

The mileage may vary, but it is possible to use BBED.EXE that shipped with Oracle 8.1.6, which was about the last time the Windows version was included in the RDBMS software installation, and use that executable against later versions of Oracle datafiles.

Before going into syntax and examples, some preliminaries are in order. First and foremost is this: BBED is an undocumented and unsupported, from a customer's perspective, utility. Unless being directed to use this tool by Oracle Support, the DBA is on his own. Do not use BBED on a production database unless one knows what one is doing. Do not use BBED on any database that one cannot afford to lose. Take a backup of any database on which this tool is going to be used.

If the DBA needs to recover data and finds herself completely stymied by every other effort made so far, this is the last resort. There may be bigger and better tools out there, but the "here and now" tool is BBED. If this tool is needed to save/rescue/recover a production database, it would be in the DBA's best interest to first take a cold backup and then take a copy of that backup as the test bed. In other words, do the work on files separate from the actual files. If the DBA is trying to restore data, transfer it from a rescue instance back into the production instance.

Oracle documentation for BBED, to include looking for it on MetaLink, or My Oracle Support as it is now known, is almost nowhere to be found in the public domain. MetaLink note 62015.1 contains (assuming it still exists within OSS) a note that "BBED is a SUPPORT ONLY tool and should NOT be discussed with customers." The contents of the note are available inside a mailing list, and support agreements prevent publishing it within this book. (See http://www.freelists.org/archives/oracle-l/04-2004/msg01068. html)

Nonetheless, information can be gleaned about this tool and others as well from the message library that accompanies Oracle software. $ORACLE_HOME/rdbms/mesg contains a file named bbedus.msg. One can cat or *vi* the file and peruse its contents to obtain an idea of how the tool works. Within the message library towards the end is a listing of valid positional parameters, one of which is HELP. Windows installations of Oracle still contain the message library even though BBED.EXE is no longer included.

Before one starts working directly with BBED, it is helpful to know one's way around data blocks in general including how to get internal block information by row within a table. That and other pieces of information commonly needed include the absolute file number, the full path and name of datafiles, datafile size in blocks, data block address, block number, block size, and the block type.

The DBA needs a reporting tool to output information about a block. There is more than one way to get this information, but the easiest is based on using the supplied PL/SQL built-in named DBMS_ROWID. This package with ten functions and one procedure has been available since at least the Oracle8i days, but use of it may be new to the DBA. Information from several functions is combined in the one procedure which makes use of OUT parameters. Create one's own wrapper procedure around DBMS_ROWID.ROWID_INFO to make it reusable. Next look at what the procedure contains (Oracle® Database PL/SQL Packages and Types Reference 10g Release 2 (10.2)).

ROWID_INFO Procedure

This procedure returns information about a ROWID, including its type, restricted or extended, and the components of the ROWID. This is a procedure and it cannot be used in a SQL statement.

```
Syntax
DBMS_ROWID.ROWID_INFO (
    rowid_in        IN   ROWID,
    ts_type_in      IN   VARCHAR2 DEFAULT 'SMALLFILE',
    rowid_type      OUT  NUMBER,
    object_number   OUT  NUMBER,
    relative_fno    OUT  NUMBER,
    block_number    OUT  NUMBER,
    row_number      OUT  NUMBER);
```

A sample *get_rowinfo* wrapper procedure is shown below.

```
create or replace procedure get_rowinfo (rid in rowid) as
  sm      varchar2(9) := 'SMALLFILE';
  rid_t   number;
  obj_n   number;
  file_n  number;
  block_n number;
  row_n   number;
begin
  DBMS_ROWID.ROWID_INFO(rid, rid_t, obj_n, file_n, block_n, row_n, sm);
  DBMS_OUTPUT.PUT_LINE('Type:             ' || to_char(rid_t));
  DBMS_OUTPUT.PUT_LINE('Data obj number: ' || to_char(obj_n));
  DBMS_OUTPUT.PUT_LINE('Relative fno:     ' || to_char(file_n));
  DBMS_OUTPUT.PUT_LINE('Block number:     ' || to_char(block_n));
  DBMS_OUTPUT.PUT_LINE('Row number:       ' || to_char(row_n));
end;
/
```

Note how placeholder variables are used for the OUT parameters and can be directly referenced. The parameter list in the code also shows the file type (SMALLFILE) being passed in last in the list. The documentation shows this as the second parameter, and that is incorrect. A describe command issued against the package shows this to be the case as well.

Start with a boiled down test database. The example throughout the rest of this chapter is based on a database named ORCL2 (use dbca to create a general purpose database). Pick a sample schema such as SCOTT to practice on. This simplifies what one has to find. The schema contains four tables (EMP, DEPT, BONUS, and SALGRADE) and two indexes, all contained in the USERS tablespace. Also, there is only one database file to contend with (users01). The DBA does not care about the other two segment names (PK_EMP and PK_DEPT) because they represent indexes, and really, why would he want to use BBED on an index? Remember, use of BBED is a last resort measure and there are so many other ways of fixing or rescuing indexes that are much safer.

As an example, get the ROWID for Scott, the analyst (EMPNO=7788) from the EMP table. If not obvious, the ROWID value that will be shown is likely to be different.

```
SQL> select rowid from emp where empno=7788;

ROWID
------------------
AAAMfMAAEAAAAgAAH
```

Plugging the ROWID into the procedure yields the following.

```
SQL> exec get_rowinfo ('AAAMfMAAEAAAAgAAH');
Type:            1
Data obj number: 51148
Relative fno:    4
Block number:    32
Row number:      7

PL/SQL procedure successfully completed.
```

Understanding the block number and row number within the block is pretty straightforward. So is the relative file number of 4 and this is easily confirmed via the following query.

```
SQL> select file#||' '||name||' '||bytes from v$datafile;

FILE#||''||NAME||''||BYTES
-------------------------------------------------------
1 /opt/app/oracle/oradata/ORCL2/system01.dbf 503316480
2 /opt/app/oracle/oradata/ORCL2/undotbs01.dbf 36700160
3 /opt/app/oracle/oradata/ORCL2/sysaux01.dbf 272629760
4 /opt/app/oracle/oradata/ORCL2/users01.dbf 5242880
5 /opt/app/oracle/oradata/ORCL2/example01.dbf 104857600
```

This means that 1 = DATA and 2 = INDEX, so seeing the "1" is confirmation one is working with the correct type. The data object number is for information and is not essential, but can also be used for confirmation. Once one knows the block and file number, one can tie them together for the

Data Block Address (dba), of which the dba value will be used quite extensively in all future BBED commands.

As an alternative to DBMS_ROWID, one could just decode the ROWID from the query based on what is known as the Extended Rowid Format Oracle uses. The base-64 decomposition of 'AAAMfMAAEAAAAAgAAH' works out to be the following.:

DATA OBJECT ID	RELATIVE FILE NO	BLOCK NUMBER	ROW SLOT(NUMBER)
AAAMfM	AAE	AAAAAg	AAH
51148	4	32	7

Oracle uses a conversion table of A-Z being 0-25 in decimal form, and a-z being 26-51. Once one has the decimal value, one can derive the binary value and then string the binary strings together to get the final value. For example, the M and f components under the data object ID are decimal values 12 and 31 whose binary values are 001100 and 011111. AAAMfM is then represented as:

000000 000000 000000 001100 011111 001100

The decimal value of this is then computed to be 51148 and matches what was shown earlier. Of course, the DBA could also just query *dba_objects* to get the DATA_OBJECT_ID value of the table.

Two other preliminary items need to be mentioned at this point. The first concerns setting up a UNIX environment. If one has the resources at work, where resources implies a totally throw-away database on a totally throw-away ORACLE_HOME installation on a server that can be down in case one has to reinstall Oracle, there is already one made. All the DBA needs to do is make the executable if not already done.

If the DBA does not have a UNIX server, how does he get access to one, i.e. the DBA is doing this on a home computer? One option is to buy a bare bones PC and install Oracle Enterprise Linux on it. Another is to install OEL on the current PC and live with booting from multiple operating systems. The boot from multiple systems on the main home PC is not the best choice, but one can make that happen with relatively little effort. If one does not like having OEL or some other brand of Linux on the PC, it can be removed later and the disk space it partitioned can be reclaimed.

The second is using a parameter file when starting BBED. Nothing new about what a parameter file is and does as it is just like parameter files used elsewhere in Oracle (exp, imp, sqlldr, etc.). What is new, however, are the parameters and their values or options. Enter *bbed help=y* to see the list. In this example, BBED is located in $ORACLE_HOME/bin after having been compiled elsewhere.

```
[oracle@oralinux ~]$ bbed help=y
PASSWORD - Required parameter
FILENAME - Database file name
BLOCKSIZE - Database block size
LISTFILE - List file name
MODE - [browse/edit]
SPOOL - Spool to logfile [no/yes]
CMDFILE - BBED command file name
LOGFILE - BBED log file name
PARFILE - Parameter file name
BIFILE - BBED before-image file name
REVERT - Rollback changes from BIFILE [no/yes]
SILENT - Hide banner [no/yes]
HELP - Show all valid parameters [no/yes]
```

Collect the file name information as shown earlier. Identify the block size of the file(s), and for the initial runs of using this tool, use the browse mode. The contents of a parameter file are shown below.

```
[oracle@oralinux bbed]$ more bbed.par
blocksize=8192
listfile=/home/oracle/bbed/orcl2files.txt
mode=browse
```

Starting a Session

To start a session using a parameter file named *bbed.par* located in a directory named BBED, use *bbed parfile=bbed.par*. Once inside a BBED session, one can invoke a help command by specifying *all* to see everything, or by a keyword, such as help set. The set command is useful and necessary for navigation between and within blocks and files. If one starts with a file based on an 8K blocksize, one could set a new filename or file number and its blocksize by using the set filename and set block commands.

Before going into an example of modifying data, check out the contents of a block. Use the one block containing all of the EMP table. If an 8K block size is used, it is highly likely all rows will be in the one block. It is known that someone in the list of employees is the president, so search for PRESIDENT after setting the data block address and also setting the offset to 0.

```
BBED> set dba 4,32
        DBA              0x01000020 (16777248 4,32)

BBED> set offset 0
        OFFSET             0

BBED> find /c PRESIDENT
 File: /opt/app/oracle/oradata/ORCL2/users01.dbf (4)
 Block: 32              Offsets: 7831 to 8191        Dba:0x01000020
 ------------------------------------------------------------------
 50524553 4944454e 54ff0777 b50b1101 010102c2 33ff02c1 0b2c0108 03c24e59
 0553434f 54540741 4e414c59 535403c2 4c430777 bb041301 010102c2 1fff02c1
 152c0108 03c24e53 05434c41 524b074d 414e4147 455203c2 4f280777 b5060901
 010103c2 1933ff02 c10b2c01 0803c24d 6305424c 414b4507 4d414e41 47455203
 c24f2807 77b50501 01010103 c21d33ff 02c11f2c 010803c2 4d37064d 41525449
 4e085341 4c45534d 414e03c2 4d630777 b5091c01 010103c2 0d3302c2 0f02c11f
 2c010803 c24c4305 4a4f4e45 53074d41 4e414745 5203c24f 280777b5 04020101
 0103c21e 4cff02c1 152c0108 03c24c16 04574152 44085341 4c45534d 414e03c2
 4d630777 b5021601 010103c2 0d3302c2 0602c11f 2c010803 c24b6405 414c4c45
 4e085341 4c45534d 414e03c2 4d630777 b5021401 010102c2 1102c204 02c11f2c
 010803c2 4a460553 4d495448 05434c45 524b03c2 50030777 b40c1101 010102c2
 09ff02c1 151006db bf

 <32 bytes per line>
```

The supported datatypes the DBA can search for are shown via *help find* at the BBED prompt. Note the absence of numeric and date datatypes.

PARAMETER	DATATYPE
x	Hexadecimal
d	Decimal
u	Unsigned decimal
o	Octal
c	Character

Table 10.1: *BBED Find Options*

If a hacker were looking for sensitive employee data, this would be a jackpot. He found a block containing PRESIDENT. To confirm his finding, he could dump the contents of the block at that offset, or position within the block, so to speak.

```
BBED> dump /v dba 4,32 offset 7831 count 32
 File: /opt/app/oracle/oradata/ORCL2/users01.dbf (4)
 Block: 32      Offsets: 7831 to 7862   Dba:0x01000020
 ------------------------------------------------------
 50524553 4944454e 54ff0777 b50b1101 l PRESIDENT..wµ...
 010102c2 33ff02c1 0b2c0108 03c24e59 l ...Â3..Á.,...ÂNY

 <16 bytes per line>
```

How many records are there in the table? Use the print command, or p for short, to print the metadata about the block. This is where knowledge of data block structure comes in handy. The struct (C-like data structure) of interest is kdbh. The following shows how many rows there are via the *kdbhnrow* value (14 in this case).

```
BBED> p kdbh
struct kdbh, 14 bytes                    @100
   ub1 kdbhflag                          @100      0x00  (NONE)
   b1 kdbhntab                           @101      1
   b2 kdbhnrow                           @102      14
   sb2 kdbhfrre                          @104      -1
   sb2 kdbhfsbo                          @106      46
   sb2 kdbhfseo                          @108      7521
   b2 kdbhavsp                           @110      7475
   b2 kdbhtosp                           @112      7475
```

Instead of examining each and every row, one could set the pointer to the last row, and then examine, or x for short, each row while spooling output. With print, numbers and dates can be displayed. As a simple example, knowing ahead of time KING is in row 9 of the EMP table, print the kdbr struct where the use of kdbr includes the row starting at 0, not 1. Row 9 in the table is kdbr[8] for these purposes.

```
BBED> print *kdbr[8]
rowdata[197]
------------
ub1 rowdata[197]                                 @7818     0x2c
```

Now that one is at offset 7818, it is a simple matter to examine the contents via the print and examine commandsand use format flags. It is known what the EMP table looks like in terms of character (c), numeric (n) and date (t) attributes. In BBED, use "x /rnccntnnn" to examine and format the output.

```
BBED> x /rnccntnnn
rowdata[197]                                     @7818
------------
flag@7818: 0x2c (KDRHFL, KDRHFF, KDRHFH)
lock@7819: 0x01
```

```
cols@7820:       8

col     0[3]  @7821:  7839
col     1[4]  @7825:  KING
col     2[9]  @7830:  PRESIDENT
col     3[0]  @7840:  *NULL*
col     4[7]  @7841:  17-NOV-81
col     5[2]  @7849:  5000
col     6[0]  @7852:  *NULL*
col     7[2]  @7853:  10
```

From a hacking or recovery standpoint, one knows the president is named King. What are the column names? Well, they are not present here, but what is to stop the DBA from deconstructing the same thing with respect to the base tables represented by the data dictionary views of *dba_tab_columns* and *dba_objects*? There is the data object ID, so finding the object name is trivial and with the object name, which becomes the table name in this case, one can get the column names from *dba_tab_columns*. The only hard part in all of this is finding the block numbers within the file, and one already knows the file is related to the SYSTEM tablespace.

As an example, the USER$ table in Oracle has a data object ID of 10. That has been the value from at least the 8i days. Who are the database users? What are their hashed passwords? That information plus much more is easily extracted. All that has been done so far is to look at data, and with just that the DBA should be able to appreciate the enormous power behind BBED. Now look at altering data.

Altering Data

The analyst named Scott in the EMP table is going to be promoted to manager. The steps to alter the table data outside of SQL*Plus are:

1. Get the ROWID if it is not already known

2. Shutdown the database and take a cold backup

3. Start BBED with a parameter file, being sure to include the relevant datafile

4. Find the data block address

5. Find the offset where the string ANALYST begins and confirm the data/location

6. Change the mode to edit unless the parfile already includes that

7. Modify the data

8. Confirm the data change

9. Apply the change

10. Restart the database and look for the change

The chosen approach is that one already knows some things about the data, e.g., the record that one wants to change and the ROWID/dba information. The dba will still be 4,32 for this example.

After shutting down the database and taking a cold backup while using the same parfile from before, a BBED session can be started. After it is started, navigate to dba 4,32 and set the offset to 0 so the DBA sees that she has a known starting position for the search/find operation to follow.

```
[oracle@oralinux bbed]$ bbed parfile=bbed.par
Password:

BBED: Release 2.0.0.0.0 - Limited Production on Sun Aug 31 17:55:58 2008

Copyright (c) 1982, 2005, Oracle.  All rights reserved.

************* !!! For Oracle Internal Use only !!! ***************

BBED> set dba 4,32
        DBA                0x01000020 (16777248 4,32)

BBED> set offset 0
        OFFSET             0
```

The find command will dump multiple lines. Since one is searching for a character string, use the c flag.

```
BBED> find /c SCOTT
 File: /opt/app/oracle/oradata/ORCL2/users01.dbf (4)
 Block: 32              Offsets: 7864 to 8191          Dba:0x01000020
------------------------------------------------------------------------
 53434f54 5407414e 414c5953 5403c24c 430777bb 04130101 0102c21f ff02c115
 2c010803 c24e5305 434c4152 4b074d41 4e414745 5203c24f 280777b5 06090101
 0103c219 33ff02c1 0b2c0108 03c24d63 05424c41 4b45074d 414e4147 455203c2
 4f280777 b5050101 010103c2 1d33ff02 c11f2c01 0803c24d 37064d41 5254494e
 0853414c 45534d41 4e03c24d 630777b5 091c0101 0103c20d 3302c20f 02c11f2c
 010803c2 4c43054a 4f4e4553 074d414e 41474552 03c24f28 0777b504 02010101
 03c21e4c ff02c115 2c010803 c24c1604 57415244 0853414c 45534d41 4e03c24d
 630777b5 02160101 0103c20d 3302c206 02c11f2c 010803c2 4b640541 4c4c454e
 0853414c 45534d41 4e03c24d 630777b5 02140101 0102c211 02c20402 c11f2c01
 0803c24a 4605534d 49544805 434c4552 4b03c250 030777b4 0c110101 0102c209
 ff02c115 1006dbbf

 <32 bytes per line>
```

Dump the current offset and confirm that SCOTT was found.

```
BBED> dump /v dba 4,32 offset 7864 count 32
 File: /opt/app/oracle/oradata/ORCL2/users01.dbf (4)
 Block: 32      Offsets: 7864 to 7895  Dba:0x01000020
-------------------------------------------------------
 53434f54 5407414e 414c5953 5403c24c l SCOTT.ANALYST.ÂL
 430777bb 04130101 0102c21f ff02c115 l C.w»......Â...Á.

 <16 bytes per line>
```

The output tells the DBA that SCOTT begins at offset 7864 within the dba. Counting over six positions is where ANALSYT should begin. To confirm this, move the offset (explicitly, although one can add or subtract positions, such as +4 or -3) to 7870 and dump the contents again.

```
BBED> set offset 7870
        OFFSET          7870

BBED> d /v
 File: /opt/app/oracle/oradata/ORCL2/users01.dbf (4)
 Block: 32      Offsets: 7870 to 7901  Dba:0x01000020
-------------------------------------------------------
 414e414c 59535403 c24c4307 77bb0413 l ANALYST.ÂLC.w»..
 01010102 c21fff02 c1152c01 0803c24e l ....Â...Á.,...ÂN

 <16 bytes per line>
```

Note the syntax used in the last dump command. If one is not sure of the location, one can always set it as done in the first dump. Now it is time to replace ANALYST with MANAGER, and that is done via the modify command. Now modify it and dump to confirm the change. Modifications can be made via one of several formats (same as find), so the easiest case for readability is finding and modifying via character strings, and that is what the /c does. Do not forget to change the EDIT mode if necessary (BBED> set mode edit).

```
BBED> modify /c MANAGER
Warning: contents of previous BIFILE will be lost. Proceed? (Y/N) Y
 File: /opt/app/oracle/oradata/ORCL2/users01.dbf (4)
 Block: 32                Offsets: 7870 to 7901        Dba:0x01000020
--------------------------------------------------------------------
 4d414e41 47455203 c24c4307 77bb0413 01010102 c21fff02 c1152c01 0803c24e

 <32 bytes per line>

BBED> d /v
 File: /opt/app/oracle/oradata/ORCL2/users01.dbf (4)
 Block: 32      Offsets: 7870 to 7901  Dba:0x01000020
-------------------------------------------------------
```

```
4d414e41 47455203 c24c4307 77bb0413 l MANAGER.ÂLC.w»..
01010102 c21fff02 c1152c01 0803c24e l ....Â...Á.,...ÂN

<16 bytes per line>
```

Now perform a sum, which is used to check or set the block's checksum value, and apply the change.

```
BBED> sum
Check value for File 4, Block 32:
current = 0x26b5, required = 0x32ae

BBED> sum apply
Check value for File 4, Block 32:
current = 0x32ae, required = 0x32ae
```

So far, so good. Assuming the change has been made in the data block, name two ways one knows of right now to check the value but not using the dump command. One is using SQL*Plus, but within BBED, one could print the row data. SCOTT's row number is still 8 (or 7 recalling that BBED starts at 0), so a combination of the following could be used:

```
BBED> p *kdbr[7]
rowdata[235]
------------
ub1 rowdata[235]                              @7856      0x2c

BBED> x /rnccntnnn
rowdata[235]                                  @7856
------------
flag@7856: 0x2c (KDRHFL, KDRHFF, KDRHFH)
lock@7857: 0x01
cols@7858:     8

col     0[3] @7859: 7788
col     1[5] @7863: SCOTT
col     2[7] @7869: MANAGER
col     3[3] @7877: 7566
col     4[7] @7881: 19-APR-87
col     5[2] @7889: 3000
col     6[0] @7892: *NULL*
col     7[2] @7893: 20
```

Recovering lost data

There are two ways to look at recovering lost data and what delineates them may be the amount of data to be recovered. The conditions may then be one row versus many rows. In the single or few rows case, editing the block directly and making the record(s) live again is the easiest way. For many rows,

---

the best bet may to be to plug in an older version of the datafile and make the datafile concurrent with the database's current state. Current state, in this case, implies making the SCN current within the file.

Undeleting a Row

Delete SCOTT's record in SQL*Plus, look at the record's information within the block, alter that information, and come back to SQL*Plus to confirm the change or resurrection, as it may be. First, what marks a row as deleted or not? Or chained, for that matter? Each row contains header information in a binary or bitmask format. The fifth position in the row flag contains the flag indicating deleted or not. There are two ways this data can be viewed. One of them, as seen within BBED, shows the values as 0x2c or 0x3c for deleted. The other way shows a D, or alter system dump datafile X block Y, and then one can view the trace file in the udump directory. Using the same file and block number, after deleting SCOTT, the trace file shows that the row is marked as deleted.

```
tab 0, row 7, @0x1e4c
tl: 2 fb: --HDFL-- lb: 0x2
```

An undeleted row shows "- - H - F L - -" plus the dumped data. What does BBED show?"

```
BBED> p *kdbr[7]
rowdata[235]
------------
ub1 rowdata[235]                          @7856      0x3c
```

On the last line, at the far right, note the 0x3c value. Undeleting the record is simply a matter of setting 0x3c back to 0x2c. So far one has searched for data and will continue to do so, and when found, the offset needs to back up a bit more to move the pointer into the row flag bitmask area. Or, having some knowledge of the data including having dumped the block into a trace file, when 0x3c and its offset value is found, that is where one needs to perform the modification.

From above, the offset of interest is 7856 to target the 3c in 0x3c. To change the flag or bit to remove the deletion, modify and update the checksum. Since the modification is being made to hexadecimal data, the "x" flag is used:

```
BBED> modify /x 2c offset 7856
Warning: contents of previous BIFILE will be lost. Proceed? (Y/N) Y
 File: /opt/app/oracle/oradata/ORCL2/users01.dbf (4)
 Block: 32            Offsets: 7856 to 8191         Dba:0x01000020
------------------------------------------------------------------------
2c020803 c24e5905 53434f54 54074d41 4e414745 5203c24c 430777bb 04130101
0102c21f ff02c115 2c000803 c24e5305 434c4152 4b074d41 4e414745 5203c24f
280777b5 06090101 0103c219 33ff02c1 0b2c0008 03c24d63 05424c41 4b45074d
414e4147 455203c2 4f280777 b5050101 010103c2 1d33ff02 c11f2c00 0803c24d
37064d41 5254494e 0853414c 45534d41 4e03c24d 630777b5 091c0101 0103c20d
3302c20f 02c11f2c 000803c2 4c43054a 4f4e4553 074d414e 41474552 03c24f28
0777b504 02010101 03c21e4c ff02c115 2c000803 c24c1604 57415244 0853414c
45534d41 4e03c24d 630777b5 02160101 0103c20d 3302c206 02c11f2c 000803c2
4b640541 4c4c454e 0853414c 45534d41 4e03c24d 630777b5 02140101 0102c211
02c20402 c11f2c00 0803c24a 4605534d 49544805 434c4552 4b03c250 030777b4
0c110101 0102c209 ff02c115 0206627f

<32 bytes per line>
```

Verify the change, and then apply it.

```
BBED> p *kdbr[7]
rowdata[235]
------------
ub1 rowdata[235]                              @7856      0x2c

BBED> sum dba 4,32 apply
Check value for File 4, Block 32:
current = 0x0e62, required = 0x0e62
```

Now the big test – is the row undeleted in the table? It appears to be.

```
SQL> select empno, ename, job from emp;

    EMPNO ENAME      JOB
---------- ---------- ---------
     7369 SMITH      CLERK
     7499 ALLEN      SALESMAN
     7521 WARD       SALESMAN
     7566 JONES      MANAGER
     7654 MARTIN     SALESMAN
     7698 BLAKE      MANAGER
     7782 CLARK      MANAGER
     7788 SCOTT      MANAGER
     7839 KING       CLERK
     7844 TURNER     SALESMAN
     7876 ADAMS      CLERK
     7900 JAMES      CLERK
     7902 FORD       ANALYST
     7934 MILLER     CLERK

14 rows selected.
```

But another query seems to say otherwise.

```
SQL> select empno, ename, job
  2  from emp where empno = 7788;

no rows selected
```

Use the verify command in BBED, along with several other outside-of-BBED utilities (analyze, DBMS_REPAIR, etc.) to validate the block structure. Is the restored structure valid?

```
BBED> verify dba 4,32
DBVERIFY - Verification starting
FILE = /opt/app/oracle/oradata/ORCL2/users01.dbf
BLOCK = 32

Block Checking: DBA = 16777248, Block Type = KTB-managed data block
data header at 0x137264
kdbchk: the amount of space used is not equal to block size
        used=613 fsc=38 avsp=7475 dtl=8088
Block 32 failed with check code 6110

DBVERIFY - Verification complete

Total Blocks Examined         : 1
Total Blocks Processed (Data) : 1
Total Blocks Failing   (Data) : 1
Total Blocks Processed (Index): 0
Total Blocks Failing   (Index): 0
Total Blocks Empty            : 0
Total Blocks Marked Corrupt   : 0
Total Blocks Influx           : 0
```

In this example, the data was restored, but the block failed to validate. Once the data is restored, take steps to check and ensure its validity. A simple way to collect the data is to perform a CTAS (Create Table As Select) using the original table as the source. The following shows there is not a difference, followed by evidence of one, and that the count is off by one.

```
SQL> select * from emp minus select * from emp2;

no rows selected

SQL> select * from emp2 minus select * from emp;

no rows selected

SQL> select empno from emp minus select empno from emp2;

no rows selected

SQL> select empno from emp2 minus select empno from emp;

     EMPNO
----------
      7788
```

```
SQL> select count(*) from emp;

  COUNT(*)
----------
        13

SQL> select count(*) from emp2;

  COUNT(*)
----------
        14
```

What can one do to remove this discrepancy? The best way – before anyone else starts trying other options – is to do what was just mentioned: make a copy of the data and put it elsewhere. Then, if one wants to start trying *dbms_repair* and other options, when one sees the following, there will not be such a desperate feeling.

```
SQL> conn / as sysdba
Connected.
SQL> declare
  2     fixed_count binary_integer;
  3  begin
  4  dbms_repair.FIX_CORRUPT_BLOCKS (
  5     schema_name        => 'SCOTT',
  6     object_name        => 'EMP',
  7     partition_name     => NULL,
  8     object_type        => dbms_repair.table_object,
  9     repair_table_name  => 'REPAIR_TABLE',
 10     flags              => NULL,
 11     fix_count          => fixed_count);
 12  dbms_output.put_line('Fixed '||to_char(fixed_count));
 13  end;
 14  /
Fixed 1

PL/SQL procedure successfully completed.

SQL> conn scott/tiger
Connected.
SQL> select * from emp;
select * from emp
            *
ERROR at line 1:
ORA-01578: ORACLE data block corrupted (file # 4, block # 32)
ORA-01110: data file 4: '/opt/app/oracle/oradata/ORCL2/users01.dbf'
```

This error leads into the next topic: corruption.

Corrupted Blocks

A value of 0xff reported in BBED and elsewhere is an indicator of the block that has been marked corrupt. Printing the block header information (kcbh) should confirm this (see the seq_kcbh line).

```
BBED> set dba 4,32
        DBA             0x01000020 (16777248 4,32)

BBED> p kcbh
struct kcbh, 20 bytes                   @0
   ub1 type_kcbh                        @0         0x06
   ub1 frmt_kcbh                        @1         0xa2
   ub1 spare1_kcbh                      @2         0x00
   ub1 spare2_kcbh                      @3         0x00
   ub4 rdba_kcbh                        @4         0x01000020
   ub4 bas_kcbh                         @8         0x000aebab
   ub2 wrp_kcbh                         @12        0x0000
   ub1 seq_kcbh                         @14        0xff
   ub1 flg_kcbh                         @15        0x04 (KCBHFCKV)
   ub2 chkval_kcbh                      @16        0x98e9
   ub2 spare3_kcbh                      @18        0x0000
```

What is the uncorrupted value for a block? This needs to be known before changing 0xff to something else. The good value is 0x01 and the offset is at 14 as indicated by the "@14" in the kcbh output. Set the dba to a known good block and confirm that 0x01 is indeed valid. In addition to the block header being set straight, one also has to fix the tail, and the BBED command tailchk can be used to check the tail. Once the tail has been modified, perform a sum with apply to effect the change.

Experimenting with trying to corrupt and uncorrupt a block, or even dealing with a block found to be corrupt after recovering data given that the data has already been rescued in a copy table is interesting but not practical. If normal tools cannot repair a corrupt block, the best option is to leave it corrupted and move on to other things. If the block becomes corrupted or fractured and one "really" needs it, try using Oracle Support. Again, if the DBA was using BBED on her own and of her own accord, she may have to plead her case to get support.

Restoring Data

This scenario of copying blocks from one file to another is based on having deleted rows in a table, and the goal is to recover the data. There is a backup of the datafile where the table data is good. The current file is not good due to a table having missing rows. Why would one use BBED to copy data, and blocks specifically, from one file to another? In other words, why would one not be using any number of other valid and more supported recovery means?

The motivation could be because it is a time issue; but remember, if using BBED on one's own, it is like playing with fire. One reason may be due to expediency and another may be related to what is on hand at the time. One only needs the relevant files: the older one and the current one. There is no need to create a clone, apply archived redo logs, wait for tapes to be mounted, and so on.

Two tricks to this recovery technique are accounting for counting and what goes in a parameter file. One has to consider from what position Oracle starts counting to identify the start point properly. It is clearly zero or one, but it makes a difference when taking information from one source and applying it to the other.

In the current instance, the 14 rows in the EMP table are deleted. So retrieve some before and after information.

```
SQL> select segment_name, header_file, header_block, blocks
  2  from dba_segments
  3  where owner = 'SCOTT' and segment_name = 'EMP';

SEGMENT_NAME HEADER_FILE HEADER_BLOCK    BLOCKS
------------ ----------- ------------ ----------
EMP                    4           27          8

SQL> conn scott/tiger
Connected.
SQL> delete from emp;

14 rows deleted.

SQL> commit;

Commit complete.

SQL> conn / as sysdba
Connected.
SQL> select segment_name, header_file, header_block, blocks
  2  from dba_segments
  3  where owner = 'SCOTT' and segment_name = 'EMP';

SEGMENT_NAME HEADER_FILE HEADER_BLOCK    BLOCKS
------------ ----------- ------------ ----------
EMP                    4           27          8
```

What this shows is that hopefully the file and block usage does not change after the deletion. Since the author knows from beforehand that the location information is going to be the same from the old file to the new one, there is no need to inspect the old file.

Start from block 27 and use 8 blocks. Or is that correct? In BBED, add one to the header_block value. The data dictionary view's start position for counting is 0, but BBED's is 1. In this example, the dba will start at 1,28 for the old file and 2,28 for the current file. The blocks to be copied are 28, 29, 30, 31, 32, 33, 34, and 35. The copy command syntax is copy dba file#,block# to dba file#,block#. It should be apparent that it is possible to copy blocks in a file to a location within the same file. Experiments with this are left for the curious reader.

Create a listfile for use inside the parameter file. The listfile will contain two files: the old one and the new one. Number them 1 and 2 (they both can not be 4, for example; the file number is their relative position BBED reads from).

```
1 /opt/app/oracle/oradata/ORCL2/backup/users01.dbf 5242880
2 /opt/app/oracle/oradata/ORCL2/users01.dbf 5242880
```

The following commands need to be applied to a closed database:

```
copy dba 1,28 to dba 2,28
copy dba 1,29 to dba 2,29
copy dba 1,30 to dba 2,30
copy dba 1,31 to dba 2,31
copy dba 1,32 to dba 2,32
copy dba 1,33 to dba 2,33
copy dba 1,34 to dba 2,34
copy dba 1,35 to dba 2,35
```

After copying the blocks, the data can be viewed in BBED.

Restoring a File

Being able to plug in an older version of a file into the current instance could be a huge save in terms of recovery. At one point in time, a file has certain values related to its state, and that state is consistent with other files in the database. When the state is off, Oracle informs the DBA about it right away via one or more error messages, especially the one about a file needing more media recovery. In a normal recovery scenario where media loss has occurred, the recovery consists of restoring a backed up copy of one or more datafiles and then applying archived redo to bring the file to a consistent state.

In the BBED recovery scenario, one will not be applying redo, but rather will be jumping the state of the file from a point in the past to a point in time consistent with the rest of the database. The specific part of the file to be edited is the file header. Information will be needed from three structs: kcvfhckp, kcvfhcpc, and kcvfhccc. Published elsewhere are decode tables for many of these items, and these are generally easy to interpret. Kernel-related codes begin with a k, fh looks like file header, and the remainder are related to checkpoints. Specifically, good values from the following are needed:

- kscnbas – last change SCN

- kcvcptim – time of the last change

- kcvfhcpc – checkpoint count

- kcvfhccc – a checkpoint checker value, which is one less than kcvfhcpc

For file headers, one is interested in the output of the kcvfh struct. The output of "p kcvfh" is long, but it is interesting to browse through the output. It is also interesting how the name of the database (ORCL2 here) appears spelled out.

```
BBED> p kcvfh
struct kcvfh, 676 bytes                    @0
   struct kcvfhbfh, 20 bytes               @0
      ub1 type_kcbh                        @0         0x0b
      ub1 frmt_kcbh                        @1         0xa2
      ub1 spare1_kcbh                      @2         0x00
      ub1 spare2_kcbh                      @3         0x00
      ub4 rdba_kcbh                        @4         0x01800001
      ub4 bas_kcbh                         @8         0x00000000
      ub2 wrp_kcbh                         @12        0x0000
      ub1 seq_kcbh                         @14        0x01
      ub1 flg_kcbh                         @15        0x04  (KCBHFCKV)
      ub2 chkval_kcbh                      @16        0x8f50
      ub2 spare3_kcbh                      @18        0x0000
   struct kcvfhhdr, 76 bytes               @20
      ub4 kccfhswv                         @20        0x00000000
      ub4 kccfhcvn                         @24        0x0a200100
      ub4 kccfhdbi                         @28        0x266ecc46
      text kccfhdbn[0]                     @32        O
      text kccfhdbn[1]                     @33        R
      text kccfhdbn[2]                     @34        C
      text kccfhdbn[3]                     @35        L
      text kccfhdbn[4]                     @36        2
```

Here is the test case. A new tablespace (BB), user (BB) and table (EMP) where the table has three rows and three columns from Scott's EMP table is created. The datafile is bb01.dbf, created with a size of 100K. A backup exists where the three rows are in place. The current instance has had a deletion of all three rows and the object is to restore the data by recovering the older datafile. Therefore, get a new list of files for use within the parameter file, and the copy of bb01.dbf will be the older version. Only two files are really needed – one with a good SCN state, and the older file, but all were listed anyway.

```
1 /opt/app/oracle/oradata/ORCL2/system01.dbf 513802240
2 /opt/app/oracle/oradata/ORCL2/undotbs01.dbf 36700160
3 /opt/app/oracle/oradata/ORCL2/sysaux01.dbf 272629760
4 /opt/app/oracle/oradata/ORCL2/users01.dbf 5242880
5 /opt/app/oracle/oradata/ORCL2/example01.dbf 104857600
6 /opt/app/oracle/oradata/ORCL2/bb01.dbf 106496
```

Replace the file and issue a startup command. One should see the error related to the "bad" file.

```
SQL> conn / as sysdba
Connected to an idle instance.
SQL> startup
ORACLE instance started.

Total System Global Area  922746880 bytes
Fixed Size                  1222624 bytes
Variable Size             281020448 bytes
Database Buffers          633339904 bytes
Redo Buffers                7163904 bytes
Database mounted.
ORA-01113: file 6 needs media recovery
ORA-01110: data file 6: '/opt/app/oracle/oradata/ORCL2/bb01.dbf'
```

The current checkpoint number is not necessarily needed, but since it can be pulled directly from the database, see what it is. It will also show up in the file itself courtesy of BBED. The current SCN is at 689110 and the bad file is at 685758.

```
SQL> select distinct checkpoint_change# from v$datafile;

CHECKPOINT_CHANGE#
------------------
            689110

SQL> select change# from v$recover_file;

   CHANGE#
----------
    685758
```

Start a BBED session and print the kcvfhckp struct. The first few lines are shown and the values of interest are the SCN and last time.

```
BBED> p kcvfhckp
struct kcvfhckp, 36 bytes              @484
   struct kcvcpscn, 8 bytes            @484
      ub4 kscnbas                      @484        0x000a83d6
      ub2 kscnwrp                      @488        0x0000
   ub4 kcvcptim                        @492        0x2799048e
```

The hexadecimal value 0x000a83d6 should convert to 689110 in base 10 (decimal). Use the scientific calculator on Windows, something on the Internet, or get the decimal value manually. The fun way is by hand. The significant part of the hex value is a83d6. Convert hex to binary where each hex character is xxxx in binary. Now there is:

a	8	3	d	6
1010	1000	0011	1101	0110

Binary 1010100001111010110 is 689110, so that is good. Now print kcvfhcpc and kcvfhccc. The SYSTEM datafile is used by setting dba 1,1.

```
BBED> p kcvfhcpc
ub4 kcvfhcpc                           @140        0x0000004a

BBED> p kcvfhccc
ub4 kcvfhccc                           @148        0x00000049
```

One other, albeit final complication in all of this is taking into account the byte ordering of data on the platform the server is running on. It is big endian versus little endian. The database is running Oracle Enterprise Linux on a PC, so that makes it little endian. The order of the first two values has to be reversed (pair by pair). To summarize the changes to be made to the older file, see the table below.

Attribute	kscnbas	kcvcptim	kcvfhcpc	kcvfhccc
Value	000a83d6 (d6830a00)	2799048e (8e049927)	4a	49
Offset	484	492	140	148

Use the modify command with /x for hexadecimal editing and a dba of file 6, block 1.

When finished with the four modify statements, perform a "sum dba x,1 apply" where "x" is your file number. If after applying the changes one receives an error upon startup, check the SCN values output from:

```
SELECT FILE#, CHANGE# FROM V$RECOVER_FILE; and
SELECT V1.GROUP#, MEMBER, SEQUENCE#, FIRST_CHANGE#
FROM V$LOG V1, V$LOGFILE V2
WHERE V1.GROUP# = V2.GROUP#;
```

If the SCN for the recovered file is wildly different from the others, the byte ordering of the hex value during the modify command might have been reversed.

```
SQL> startup
ORACLE instance started.

Total System Global Area   922746880 bytes
Fixed Size                   1222624 bytes
Variable Size              281020448 bytes
Database Buffers           633339904 bytes
Redo Buffers                 7163904 bytes
Database mounted.
ORA-01122: database file 6 failed verification check
ORA-01110: data file 6: '/opt/app/oracle/oradata/ORCL2/bb01.dbf'
ORA-01207: file is more recent than control file - old control file
```

Conclusion

The BBED utility is extremely powerful, and if used incorrectly, can cause significant damage to a database. On the other hand, as a means of being able to poke around inside data blocks and files, it can be pretty handy. The best way to learn how to use this utility is to practice on a test database. Most of the commands are self-explanatory, but several are either cryptic (only Oracle knows what they do or how) or nonfunctional altogether. Additionally, how BBED may have function in Oracle version 8 or 9 is no guarantee that the same set of steps will work in version 10 or 11.

Additional information

Map command – can be used with the v flag for more verbose output. It is used with the kcbh struct to show the block header structure. Mapping against a block header and data block produces different output. Other structs are kdbh for data header, and kdbr for row information.

Tailcheck – consists of three elements: the lower ordered two bytes of the SCN base, the block type (typically 06 for data blocks), and the SCN sequence number.

```
BBED> p tailchk
ub4 tailchk                              @8188      0x75850602
```

The hex value 0x75850602 above reflects 7585 from the base, 06 for a data block, and 02 for the sequence number.

Block header structure, found in several public sources, consists of the type, format, spare, data block address, SCN base, SCN wrap, SCN sequence, and a flag (new, delayed logging, check value saved and temporary, using values of 01, 02, 04 and 08). Dump the beginning of a block (at offset 0) and this is the first line.

Oracle Job Scheduling

Introduction to Job Scheduling

Job scheduling is an important but often overlooked part of every database environment. Even the simplest systems require scheduled jobs such as data loads, data extraction, report generation, backups and general cleanup. When scheduling these tasks, the DBA or developer has to make a choice whether to use an external scheduler provided by the operating system or an internal scheduler provided by the Oracle database.

This chapter introduces both external and internal schedulers, beginning with the external schedulers available in UNIX, Linux, and Windows systems. Then it will proceed to examine Oracle's internal scheduler and cover how to schedule jobs with the Oracle *dbms_scheduler* utility.

Fundamentals of Job Scheduling

Job scheduling is as old as data processing itself, dating back to the 1960s with the JES (job entry system) on the IBM mainframes, back in the days of punched cards. Job scheduling is not a new technology, although it is new to Oracle.

Very few Oracle systems are random in nature. Most business databases are driven by business cycles like the inline processing day, nightly batch processing and end-of-week reporting as well as monthly scheduled tasks.

Even within the realm of Oracle database administration, there is a need for regularly scheduled jobs:

- **Every 5 minutes** – check alert log for error messages, check for new dump or trace files, verify that Oracle processes are running

- **Every night** – perform hot backups, check OS disk space

- **Every Week** – clean out elderly redo log files, perform predictive analytics to seek important trends, collect table growth reports

- **Every month** – Check for database fragmentation, apply patches

It is databases with this sort of repeating cycles that are ideal for Oracle job scheduling. To understand how scheduled jobs work, start with an overview of external vs. internal job scheduling and see the differences.

UNIX Job Scheduling (cron) vs dbms_scheduler

Back before the advent of the *dbms_jobs* package (the predecessor to *dbms_scheduler*), all Oracle tasks were scheduled at the OS layer using the cron deamon with crontab files. While cron reliably executes jobs when the server is up, effective job chain management relies on sophisticated user-written shell scripts to manage internal job chain consistency.

These scripts were written in Korn shell (ksh), Bourne Again Shell (bash) or C Shell (csh) command languages, and job chaining activities like checking step status and e-mailing failures have to be coded manually. For full details on the nuances of Oracle shell scripting, see Jon Emmons' book *"Linux Shell Scripting for Oracle"* by Rampant TechPress.

In sum, using cron for Oracle job scheduling has several important drawbacks:

- It is difficult to code complex job chains – Maintaining job step status and restartability requires significant shell language coding skills.

- No centralized job location - Each UNIX/Linux user may have their own crontab file and it can be difficult to locate and manage OS scheduled tasks.

- Does not detect missed jobs – If the server is down during the time a job is executing, the OS will not inform the DBA upon server restart.

On the other hand, the *dbms_scheduler* package is not perfect either and it also has some deficiencies, foremost of which is the inability to easily communicate with the OS. For this reason, cron is still used for many OS-intensive jobs, such as scheduled jobs to clean out the archived redo log directory. Other deficiencies include:

- Difficult to shell out to the OS – Some Oracle jobs require information from the server environment (disk space, RAM usage) and these are not easy to collect within Oracle PL/SQL. Also, special techniques must be used to send signals to the OS such as when one needs to send an email or pager alert for a failed job.

- Cryptic syntax – The syntax for scheduling complex jobs requires detailed knowledge for Oracle's internal date-time formatting masks; performing error checking and restarts requires complex syntax.

While neither approach is perfect, these two approaches together allow the Oracle professional to create complex conditional job streams and automate complex nightly processing with relative ease.

Now take a closer look at the fundamentals of job scheduling for Oracle.

Job Scheduling Components

While some Oracle tasks are standalone, others require the ability to communicate with other jobs. Oracle jobs have a many-to-many relationship with other jobs, meaning that the successful completion of one job may trigger many new jobs, and the successful completion of a set of jobs may be required to trigger a single job:

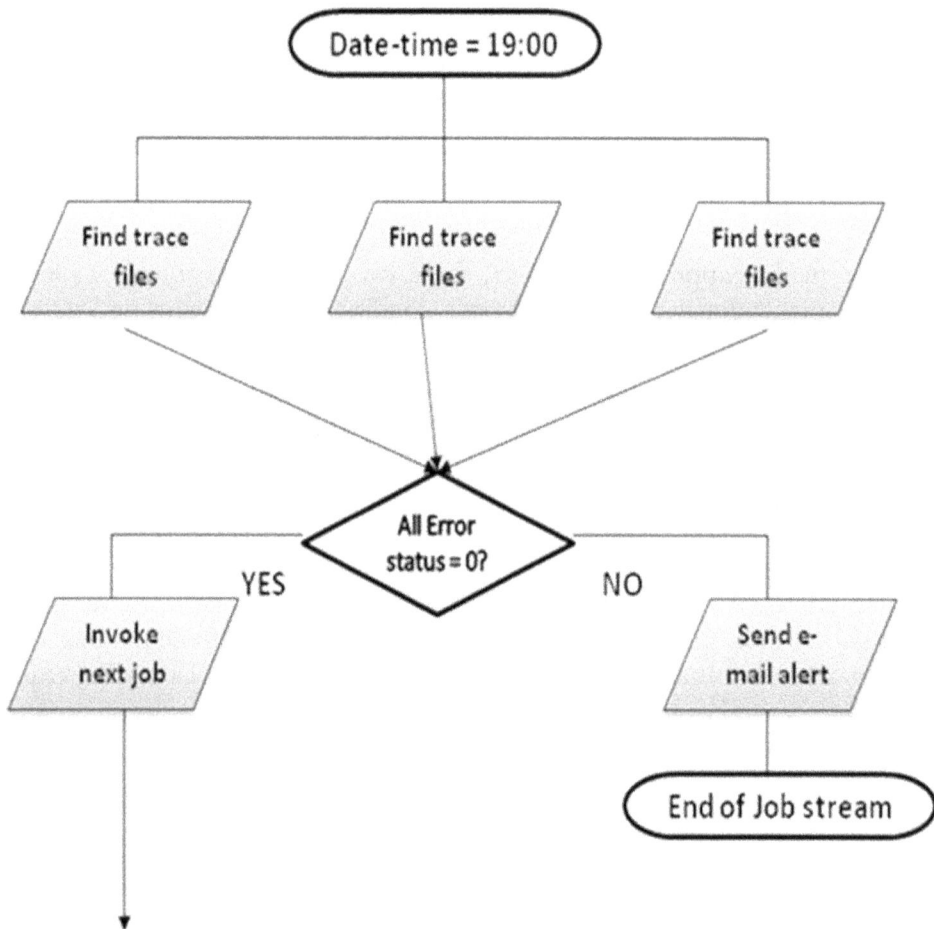

Figure 11.1: *Many-to-One Job Dependencies*

The DBA or developer also needs the ability to stop a jobstream when a task fails and invoke the appropriate error routines and notifications. Here is an example of a one-to-many conditional jobstream:

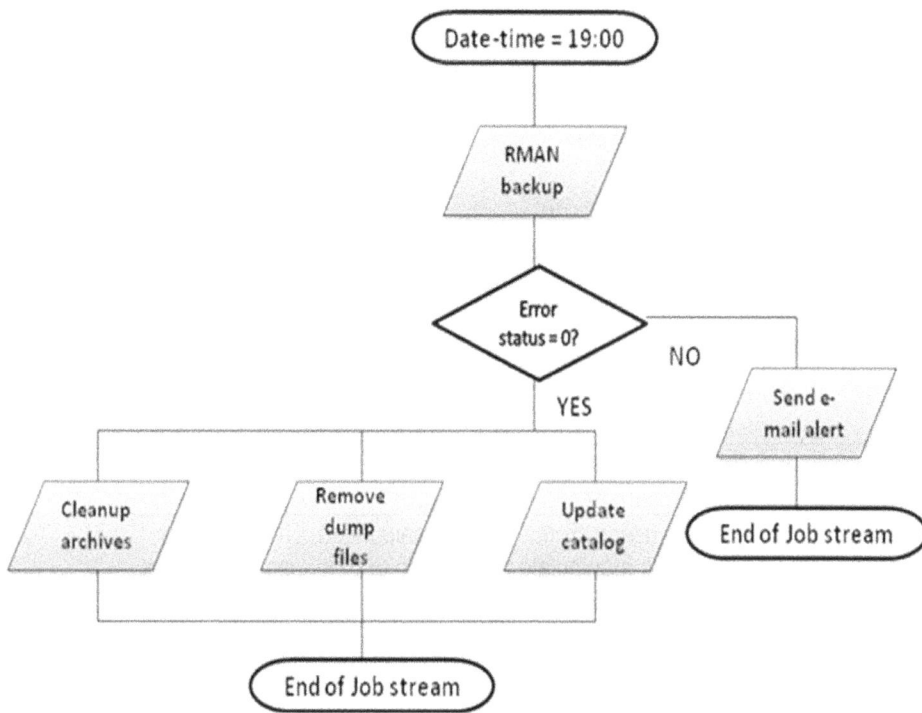

Figure 11.2: *A one-to-many conditional jobstream*

As has been noted, in UNIX and Linux environments, the most established scheduler is cron while in Windows environments, there are several schedulers available depending on the version of Windows being used. For this reason, each type of environment will be presented separately, starting with the cron scheduler. Before exploring the *dbms_scheduler* utility, take a quick look at Oracle job scheduling with cron.

Using cron and crontab to Schedule Oracle Jobs

This section will introduce the details on how to schedule Oracle shell scripts to run on a regular timetable. The cron daemon is the system task that runs scripted jobs on a predetermined schedule. The crontab command is used to tell the cron daemon what jobs the user wants to run and when to run those jobs.

Each Linux user can create his own crontab file. The administrator controls use of crontab by including users in the *cron.deny* file to disallow use of crontab.

The crontab Options

Like many Linux/UNIX utilities, the crontab command has several options, each with different purposes.

OPTION	PURPOSE
-e	edits the current crontab file using the text editor specified by the EDITOR environment variable or the VISUAL environment variable
-l	lists the current crontab file
-r	removes the current crontab file
-u	specifies the user's crontab to be manipulated. This is usually used by root to manipulate the crontab of other users or can be used to correctly identify the crontab to be manipulated if one has used the su command to assume another identity.

Table 11.1: *Crontab Options and Purposes*

The crontab –e command requires that the DBA knows the *vi* editor, which is the powerful UNIX/Linux text editor.

Here is how one would use the crontab –l (list) command to view the current cron entries for the current logged-in user:

```
$ crontab -l

#**********************************************************
# Run the Weekly file cleanup task at 6:00AM every Monday
# and send any output to a file called cleanup.lst in the
# /tmp directory
#**********************************************************
00 06 * * 1 /home/dkb/cleanup.ksh > /tmp/cleanup.lst


#**********************************************************
# Run the Weekly Management Report every Monday at 7:00 AM
# and save a copy of the report in my /home directory
#**********************************************************
00 07 * * 1 /home/dkb/weekly_mgmt_rpt.ksh wprd >
/home/terry/weekly_mgmt_rpt.lst
```

Now if one wants to delete all the entries in the crontab, use the –r option.

```
$ crontab -r
```

The Format of the crontab File

The crontab file consists of a series of entries specifying what shell scripts to run and when to run them. It is also possible to document crontab entries with comments. Lines which have a pound sign (#) as the first non-blank character are comments. Note that comments cannot be specified on the same line as cron command lines. Comments must be kept on their own lines within the crontab.

There are two types of command lines that can be specified in the crontab: environment variable settings and cron commands. The following sections will provide more detail on these two types of crontab entries.

Cron Environment Variable Settings

Each environment variable line consists of a variable name, an equal sign (=), and a value. Values that contain spaces need to be enclosed within quotes. The following are some examples of environment variable settings:

```
color = red
title = 'My Life in a Nutshell'
```

It is important to remember that variable names are case sensitive and that system variables are usually defined with upper case names, while user defined variables are defined with lower case names.

Crontab Command Line Tips

Each crontab command line is comprised of six positional fields specifying the time, date and shell script or command to be run. The format of the crontab command line is described in Table 11.2:

FIELD	MINUTE	HOUR	DAY OF MONTH	MONTH	DAY OF WEEK	COMMAND
Valid values	0-59	0-23	1-31	1-12	0-7	Command path/ command

Table 11.2: *Crontab Command Line Format*

Each of these fields can contain a single number, a range of numbers indicated with a hyphen (such as 2-4), a list of specific values separated by commas (like 2,3,4) or a combination of these designations separated by commas (such as 1,3-5). Any of these fields may also contain an asterisk (*) indicating every possible value of this field. This can all get rather confusing, so here are a few examples that are all part of the same crontab file. It has been broken up so as to explain each entry individually.

```
# Use the Korn Shell for all shell scripts
SHELL=/bin/ksh
```

This sets the default shell for these cron scripts by setting the SHELL environment variable.

```
#***********************************************************
# Run the Weekly file cleanup task at 6:00AM every Monday
# and send any output to a file called cleanup.lst in the
# /tmp directory
#***********************************************************
00 06 * * 1 /home/terry/cleanup.ksh > /tmp/cleanup.lst
```

This entry will run the script *cleanup.ksh* at 0 minutes past the hour of 6:00 am, every day of the month, every month of the year, but only on Mondays. This illustrates that for a crontab to execute, all of the conditions specified must be met. So even though it was stated that the designation is every day of the month by making the third field a wildcard, the day also has to meet the final condition that the day is a Monday.

```
#***********************************************************
# Run the Weekly Management Report every Monday at 7:00 AM
# and save a copy of the report in my /home directory
#***********************************************************
00 07 * * 1 /home/terry/weekly_mgmt_rpt.ksh wprd >
/home/terry/weekly_mgmt_rpt.lst
```

This entry is very similar but will execute at 7:00 am. Since the hour is in 24-hour format (midnight is actually represented as 00), then 07 represents 7:00 a.m. Again, this entry will only be run once a week.

```
#***********************************************************
# Weekly Full Backup - run every Sunday at 1:30AM
#***********************************************************
30 01 * * 0 /home/terry/full_backup.ksh wprd > /tmp/full_backup.lst
```

Here this script is specified to be run at 30 minutes past the hour, the first hour of the day, but only on Sundays. Remember that in the day of the week column, Sunday can be represented by either 0 or 7.

```
#***********************************************************
# Nightly Incremental Backup - run Monday-Saturday at 1:30AM
#***********************************************************
30 01 * * 1-6 /home/terry/incr_backup.ksh  > /tmp/incr_backup.lst
```

In this crontab entry, it shows the same indication for hour and minute as the last entry, but a range has been specified for the day of the week. The range 1-6 will cause the *incr_backup.ksh* to be executed at 1:30 every morning from Monday through Saturday.

```
#***********************************************************
# Low disk space alert ... run every 15 minutes, sending
# alerts to key individuals via e-mail
#***********************************************************
00,15,30,45 * * * * /home/terry/free_space.ksh > /tmp/free_space.lst
```

This entry has minutes separated by a comma indicating that it should be run at each of the indicated times. Since all the other fields are wildcards (*), the entry will be run on the hour (00), 15 minutes past the hour, 30 minutes past the hour and 45 minutes past the hour.

```
#***********************************************************
# Lunch Time Notification - run Monday-Friday at Noon -
# sends a message to all users indicating it's lunch time
#***********************************************************
00 12 * * 1-5 /home/terry/lunch_time.ksh wprd > /tmp/lunch_time.lst
```

This lunch reminder is set up to run at 12:00 p.m. Monday through Friday only.

The most important thing to remember is that a crontab entry will execute every time all of its conditions are met. To take the last entry as an example, any time it is 00 minutes past the hour of 12 on any day of the month and any month of the year and the day of the week is between Monday and Friday inclusive (1-5), this crontab will be executed.

Wildcards will be used in most crontab entries, but care must be taken in using them. For instance, if a * was mistakenly placed in the minute position of the last crontab example above, the script for every minute of the 12:00 hour would end up running instead of just once at the beginning of the hour. Someone should not need that many reminders to go to lunch!

As mentioned previously, the day-of-week field accepts either zero or seven as a value for Sunday. Any of the time/date fields can also contain an asterisk (*) indicating the entire range of values. Additionally, month and day-of-week fields can contain name values, consisting of the first three letters of the month or day, as indicated in Table 11.3 below.

FIELD	VALIE ENTRIES (case insensitive)
Days of the week	sun, mon, tue, wed, thu, fri, sat SUN, MON, TUE, WED, THU, FRI, SAT
Months of year	jan, feb, mar, apr, may, jun, jul, aug, sep, oct, nov, dec JAN, FEB, MAR, APR, MAY, JUN, JUL, AUG, SEP, OCT, NOV, DEC

Table 11.3: *Day-of-week/Month-of-year Field Values*

When numbers are used, the user can specify a range of values separated by a hyphen or a list of values separated by commas. In other words, specifying 2-5 in the hour field means 2AM, 3AM, 4AM and 5AM, while specifying 2,5 means only 2AM and 5AM.

How to specify the date and time in the crontab has been covered in detail, but what about the command? Well, most folks will write shell scripts to execute with their crontab entries but one can actually just execute a native Linux command from the crontab. Either way, make sure to put the fully qualified path to the command in the crontab. Crontab options and commands are also covered in Chapter 4 under the subject of server-side utilities.

If the command or script that is called in the crontab typically sends output to the screen, it is best to redirect that output to a log file with the >> symbol so it can be checked later. Be careful with this as the log files may get rather large over time!

Using the Windows Job Scheduler at.exe utility

The AT command can be used to schedule commands and programs on Windows NT, Windows 2000, Windows XP and Windows 2003. For the command to work, the scheduler service must be running. On Windows 2000, this can be done using the services dialog (Start → Programs → Administrative Tools → Services) or from the command line using the net command:

```
net stop "Task Scheduler"
net start "Task Scheduler"
```

The at /? command produces the following:

```
AT [\\computername] [ [id] [/DELETE] | /DELETE [/YES]]
AT [\\computername] time [/INTERACTIVE]
    [ /EVERY:date[,...] | /NEXT:date[,...]] "command"
```

A couple of simple examples of its use include:

```
C:> at 21:00 /every:m,t,th,f "c:\jobs\MyJob.bat"
Added a new job with job ID = 1

C:> at 6:00 /next:20 "c:\jobs\MyJob.bat"
Added a new job with job ID = 2
```

The first example schedules a job which runs the *c:\jobs\MyJob.bat* script at 9:00 p.m. on Mondays, Tuesdays, Thursdays and Fridays. The second example schedules a job that runs the script at 6:00 a.m. on the next 20th of the month. The current list of jobs can be displayed by issuing the AT command with no parameters:

```
C:\>at

Status ID  Day                 Time          Command Line
-------------------------------------------------------------
        1  Each M T Th F       21:00 PM      c:\jobs\MyJob.bat
        2  Next 20             06:00 AM      c:\jobs\MyJob.bat

C:\>
```

Jobs can be deleted using the /delete option:

```
C:\>at 1 /delete

C:\>at 2 /delete

C:\>at

There are no entries in the list.
```

The AT scheduler has been in Windows scheduling for many years, but recent Windows versions have introduced simpler and more flexible alternatives which will be covered in the following section.

Using the Windows Scheduled Tasks Wizard

In Windows, there is a GUI tool called the Scheduled Tasks Wizard, which is far more convenient than the AT command. It is available from the Control Panel or from the task bar (Start → Programs → Accessories → System Tools → Scheduled Tasks). The resulting dialog lists the current scheduled tasks and an Add Scheduled Task icon, as seen in Figure 11.3.

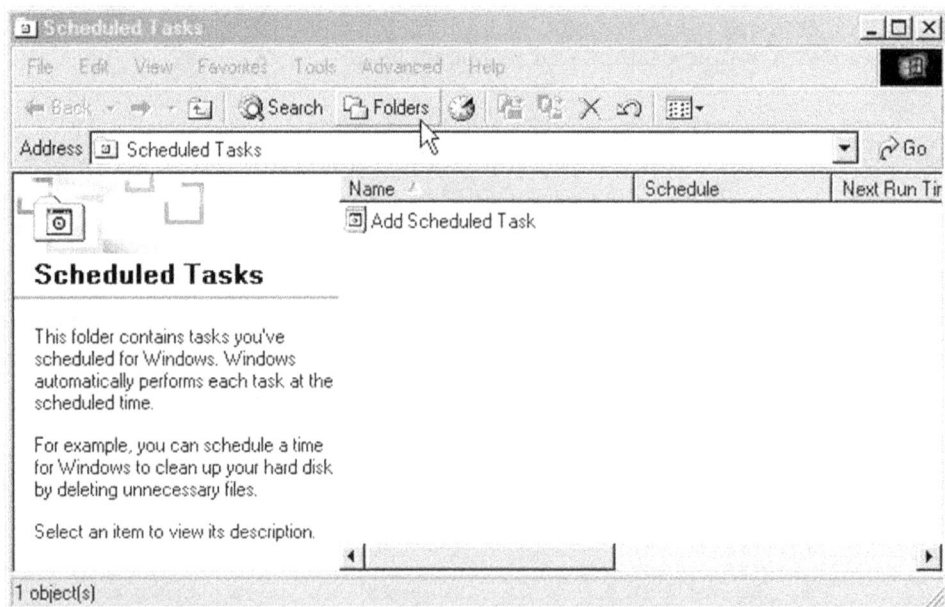

Figure 11.3: *Scheduled Tasks Dialog with no Scheduled Jobs*

To schedule a new task, simply double click on the Add Scheduled Task icon, which starts the Scheduled Tasks Wizard as shown in Figure 11.4.

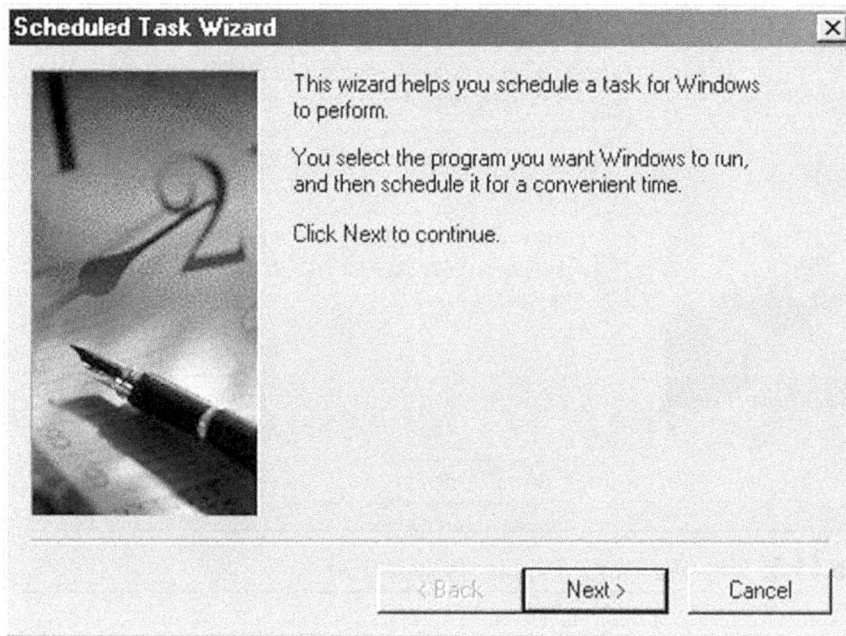

Figure 11.4: *Scheduled Tasks Wizard*

Clicking the Next button produces a list of programs that can be scheduled as shown in Figure 11.5. If the program or script that is desired is not available in the list, the Browse button allows the user to select alternatives from the file system.

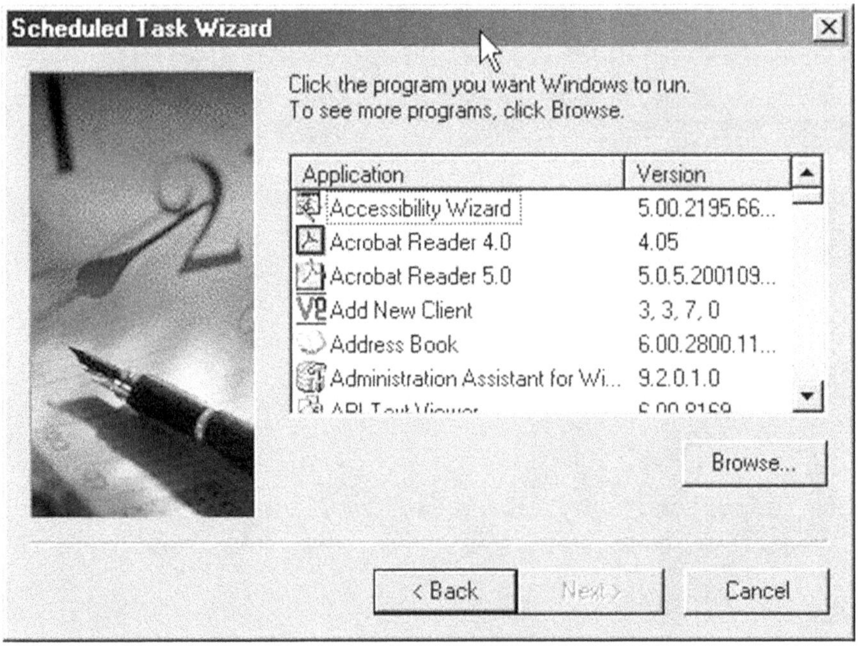

Figure 11.5: *Scheduled Tasks Wizard: Program List*

Once the relevant command or script is selected, clicking the Next button displays a screen that allows a name and basic schedule to be associated with the task as shown in Figure 11.6.

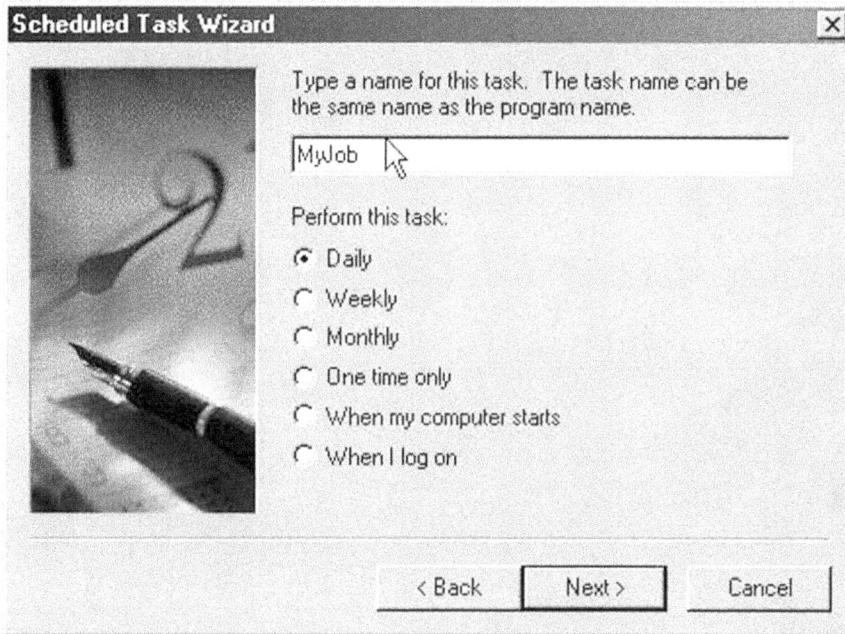

Figure 11.6: *Scheduled Tasks Wizard: Name and Basic Schedule*

The contents of the next screen vary depending on the type of basic schedule selected. Figure 11.7 shows the additional schedule information that can be defined for a daily task.

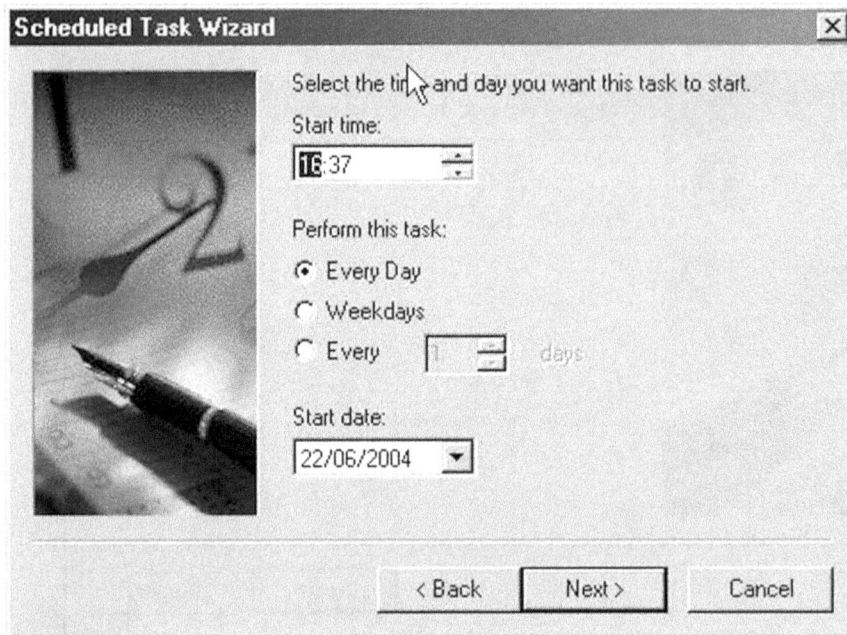

Figure 11.7: *Scheduled Tasks Wizard: Additional Scheduling Options*

The next screen permits authorization credentials for the task to be assigned, allowing the task to run as any valid operating system user. It is important that tasks run with the correct credentials as running tasks under privileged accounts can introduce potential security holes.

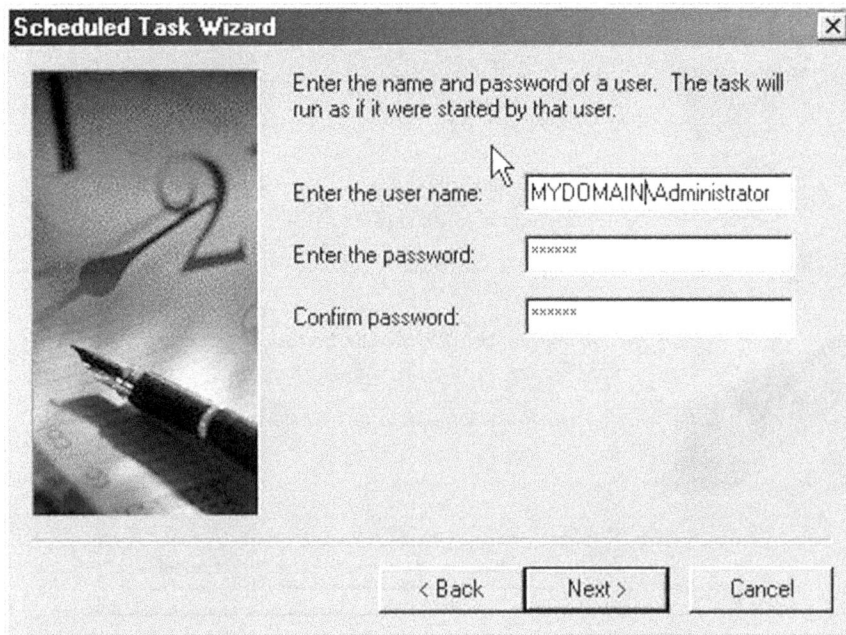

Figure 11.8: *Scheduled Tasks Wizard: Authorization Details*

Finally, a summary page is displayed which gives the option of displaying the advanced properties dialog once the job definition is complete. If this option is left unchecked, clicking the Finish button displays the original scheduled tasks list.

Figure 11.9: *Scheduled Tasks Wizard: Summary*

The newly scheduled task is now displayed in the scheduled tasks dialog:

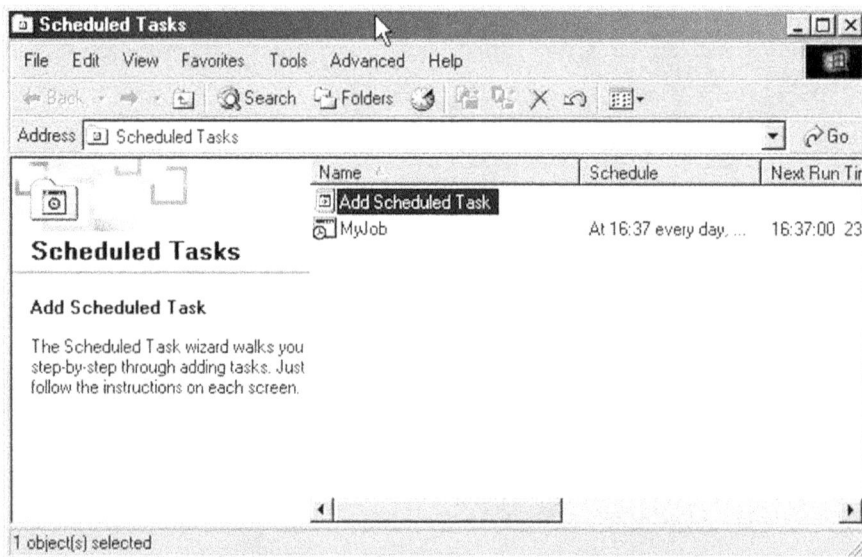

Figure 11.10: *Scheduled Tasks Dialog with Newly Scheduled Job Listed*

Right clicking on the job and selecting the Properties option from the pop-up menu, as in Figure 11.11, displays the advanced properties dialog. This dialog allows the task definition to be modified after it is created.

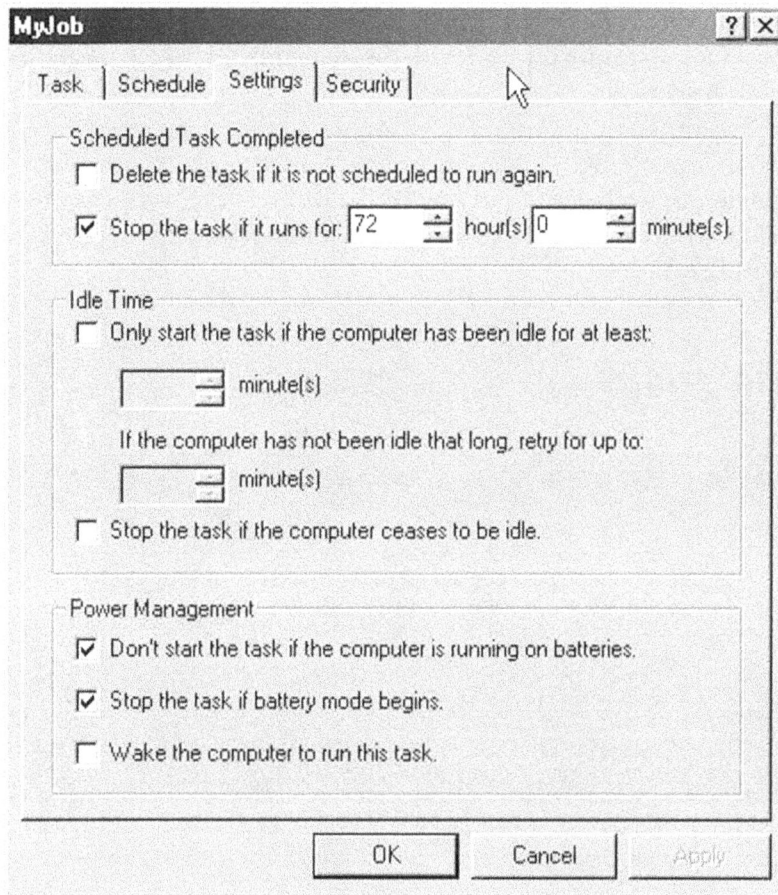

Figure 11.11: *Scheduled Job Properties Dialog*

The following section will present the SCHTASKS command which provides a more feature-rich command line alternative to the AT command.

Using the Windows Job Scheduler SCHTASKS.EXE

The SCHTASKS command was introduced in Windows XP and Windows 2003 as a more flexible and slightly more verbose replacement for the AT command. The AT command is still available for backwards compatibility, but it is no longer the preferred command line scheduling method.

As with Windows 2000, the simplest way to schedule jobs in Windows XP and Windows 2003 is via the Scheduled Tasks Wizard. However, the SCHTASKS command provides a command line API for situations in which a command line approach is preferable.

The usage notes for the SCHTASKS command are very comprehensive and include examples as well as basic syntax. The top-level usage notes are displayed below with examples indicating how more parameter specific usage notes can be obtained.

```
C:\>SCHTASKS /?

SCHTASKS /parameter [arguments]

Description:
    Enables an administrator to create, delete, query, change, run   and
    end scheduled tasks on a local or remote system. Replaces AT.exe.

Parameter List:
    /Create        Creates a new scheduled task.
    /Delete        Deletes the scheduled task(s).
    /Query         Displays all scheduled tasks.
    /Change        Changes the properties of scheduled task.
    /Run           Runs the scheduled task immediately.
    /End           Stops the currently running scheduled task.
    /?             Displays this help/usage.

Examples:
    SCHTASKS
    SCHTASKS /?
    SCHTASKS /Run /?
    SCHTASKS /End /?
    SCHTASKS /Create /?
    SCHTASKS /Delete /?
    SCHTASKS /Query  /?
    SCHTASKS /Change /?
```

To schedule a job that runs the *c:\jobs\MyJob.bat* script at 9:00 p.m. on Mondays, Tuesdays, Thursdays and Fridays, the following commands would be used:

```
SCHTASKS /Create /TN MyJob /TR C:\Jobs\MyJob.bat /ST 21:00:00 /SC weekly /D
MON,TUE,THU,FRI
The task will be created under current logged-on user name ("tim_hall").
Please enter the run as password for tim_hall: ******

SUCCESS: The scheduled task "MyJob" has successfully been created.
```

Once a task is created, it can be viewed by issuing the SCHTASKS command with no parameters:

```
C:\>SCHTASKS

TaskName                               Next Run Time            Status
==================================== =========================
MyJob                                  21:00:00, 04/06/2004
```

Tasks that are no longer needed can be deleted using the /delete option:

```
C:\>SCHTASKS /delete /TN MyJob

WARNING: Are you sure you want to remove the task "MyJob" (Y/N )? y
SUCCESS: The scheduled task "MyJob" was successfully deleted.

C:\>SCHTASKS

INFO: There are no scheduled tasks present in the system.
```

Since some of the external schedulers available on the most common operating systems have been presented, the following section will focus on the internal schedulers provided by the Oracle database.

Internal Oracle Job Scheduling

The Oracle scheduler allows jobs to be scheduled to run at a later date or on a repeating cycle. Information about the scheduling session's environment is stored along with the scheduled job, allowing jobs to run in a consistent environment each time. Scheduled jobs are placed on a job queue that is managed by a coordinator process which periodically scans the job queue looking for jobs to execute. When necessary, the coordinator process spawns job slaves to execute the jobs. The basic architecture of the Oracle scheduler is shown in Figure 11.12.

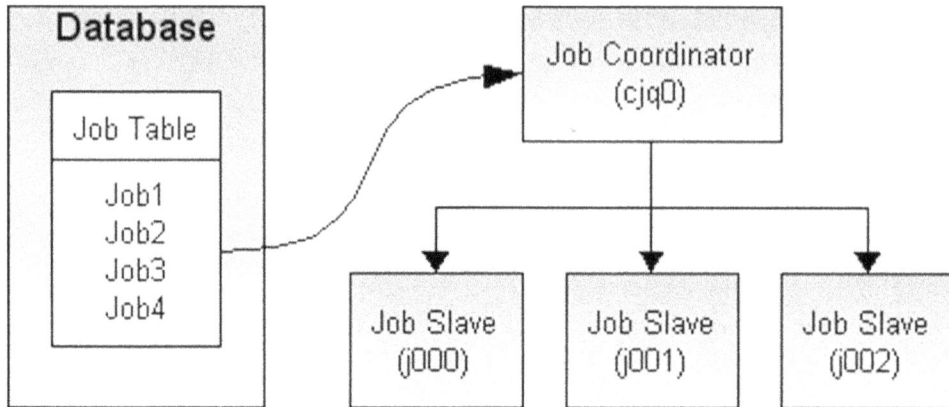

Figure 11.12: *Oracle Scheduler Architecture*

The basic architecture of *dbms_job* and *dbms_scheduler* schedulers may be similar, but the functionality and associated APIs are quite different. The Oracle 9i scheduler is extremely basic and a little clumsy, whereas the Oracle 11g scheduler is packed with features allowing job scheduling to be as simple or complicated as desired.

Oracle Scheduler Overview

By default, the Oracle 11g job coordinator process is not always running. It is started and stopped, as required. If the database detects any jobs that must be executed or windows opened in the near future, the job coordinator background process (CJQ0) is started. If there is no current job activity and no open windows, the job coordinator is stopped.

The job coordinator spawns as many job slaves (j000 to j999) as are needed to execute the outstanding jobs. A job slave gathers metadata from the scheduler tables to enable it to execute a job. Upon completion of a job, the slave process updates any relevant information in the job table, inserts data into the job run history and requests another job from the job coordinator. If a job is not available, the job slave sleeps until there is work to do. The job coordinator periodically terminates idle job slaves to reduce the slave pool.

The job table used by the scheduler is implemented using Oracle Advanced Queuing (AQ) and the supporting tables listed below:

```
select
   table_name
from
   user_tables
where
   table_name like '%SCHEDULER$_JOB%'
;

TABLE_NAME
------------------------------
SCHEDULER$_JOB_RUN_DETAILS
SCHEDULER$_JOB_STEP_STATE
AQ$_SCHEDULER$_JOBQTAB_S
SCHEDULER$_JOB
SCHEDULER$_JOBQTAB
SCHEDULER$_JOB_ARGUMENT
SCHEDULER$_JOB_CHAIN
SCHEDULER$_JOB_STEP
AQ$_SCHEDULER$_JOBQTAB_G
AQ$_SCHEDULER$_JOBQTAB_H
AQ$_SCHEDULER$_JOBQTAB_I
AQ$_SCHEDULER$_JOBQTAB_T
```

In addition to the conceptual job table, the scheduler uses several other tables to store metadata about scheduler objects.

```
select
   table_name
from
   user_tables
where
   table_name like '%SCHEDULER$%'
and
   table_name not like '%SCHEDULER$_JOB%'
;

TABLE_NAME
------------------------------
SCHEDULER$_EVENT_LOG
SCHEDULER$_WINDOW_DETAILS
SCHEDULER$_CHAIN_VARLIST
SCHEDULER$_CLASS
SCHEDULER$_GLOBAL_ATTRIBUTE
SCHEDULER$_OLDOIDS
SCHEDULER$_PROGRAM
SCHEDULER$_PROGRAM_ARGUMENT
SCHEDULER$_SCHEDULE
SCHEDULER$_WINDOW
SCHEDULER$_WINDOW_GROUP
SCHEDULER$_WINGRP_MEMBER
```

Under normal circumstances, one would not expect to interact with any of the scheduler tables directly. Information about the scheduler is displayed using the *dba_scheduler_%* views, and the *dbms_scheduler* package is used for the creation and manipulation of several scheduler objects including:

- **Schedules** - Components that define repeat intervals, allowing several jobs and windows to share a single schedule definition

- **Programs** - Components that define the work done by a job, allowing multiple jobs to share a single definition

- **Jobs** - Scheduled jobs that can be defined as individual entities or defined using existing schedules and programs

- **Job Classes** - Logical groupings of jobs that have similar resource and administration requirements. Job classes provide a link between the scheduler and the resource manager.

- **Windows** - Components that define a period of time and link it to a specific resource plan, allowing the automatic control of system resources allocated to scheduled jobs.

- **Window Groups** - Logical grouping of windows

These scheduler objects and the usage of the *dbms_scheduler* package are presented in greater detail. However, the following example demonstrates how a simple job can be scheduled in Oracle.

```
BEGIN
  DBMS_SCHEDULER.create_job (
    job_name        => 'dummy_job',
    job_type        => 'PLSQL_BLOCK',
    job_action      => 'BEGIN NULL; /* Do Nothing */ END;',
    start_date      => SYSTIMESTAMP,
    repeat_interval => 'SYSTIMESTAMP + 1 /* 1 Day */');
END;
/
```

The above example is the Oracle 11g equivalent of the job defined in the previous Oracle 9i section. From a quick look at this example, one might conclude that there is little difference between the old and the new schedulers; however, that would be an incorrect assumption.

For backwards compatibility, it is possible to schedule jobs using both the *dbms_job* and *dbms_scheduler* packages in Oracle 11g. When jobs are scheduled using the *dbms_job* package, they are still dependent on the *job_queue_processes* parameter. When this parameter is set to zero, jobs scheduled using the *dbms_job* package will not run, but those scheduled using the *dbms_scheduler* package will still run normally.

If the parameter is set to a non-zero value, the job coordinator will run permanently, but the value will only constrain the number of job slaves that can be started to run jobs scheduled using the *dbms_job* package. The value has no affect on the number of job slave processes that are allocated to jobs scheduled using the *dbms_scheduler* package.

Configuring Oracle Job Scheduling

This section will present information on how to schedule Oracle jobs using the *dbms_scheduler* package. The *dbms_scheduler* package was introduced in Oracle 10g, so the example code associated with these sections will not work on previous versions. Where appropriate, Enterprise Manager (EM) screen shots will be used to illustrate the GUI/Web alternative to using the PL/SQL API. Job Scheduling in regards to its benefit for the DBA is covered in Chapter 6 with emphasis on the *dbms_job* and *dbms_scheduler* packages.

The example code shows how objects can be created, manipulated and dropped. In a number of cases, code examples rely on previously created objects, which may have already been dropped, so they will have to be recreated before it will be possible to move on.

The following section will detail how to set up a test environment to enable the running of any example code.

Setting up a Test Environment

In order to use the examples in this chapter, it is necessary to create a user ID to work with and define a task to schedule. The following code creates a user called *job_user* and grants it the necessary privileges. Some privileges used are specific for Oracle 11g and should be ignored if a prior version is used.

```
conn sys/password as sysdba

-- Create user.
create user job_user identified by job_user default tablespace users quota
unlimited on users;
grant connect to job_user;
grant select_catalog_role to job_user;

-- Privileges for task, not for dbms_job.
grant create procedure to job_user;
grant execute on dbms_lock to job_user;
grant execute on dbms_system to job_user;
```

```
-- Oracle 10g only.
grant create job to job_user;
grant manage scheduler to job_user;

conn job_user/job_user
```

The MANAGE SCHEDULER privilege should only be granted when a user must administer job classes, windows and window groups. These objects provide a link between the scheduler and the resource manager, a feature which had traditionally required the DBA role. The roles and privileges associated with the 11g scheduler will be presented in the following text.

In the previous script, a system privilege and an object privilege were granted to *job_user* to allow the creation of a task to schedule. The following script creates a database procedure that will be used throughout this book when creating jobs. This procedure uses the *dbms_system* package to write a user defined string to the alert log at the start and end of the job.

The body of the procedure loops 100 times with a sleep of one second in each loop. It also uses the *dbms_application_info* package to write information to the *v$session* and *v$session_longops* views. The use of the *dbms_system* and *dbms_application_info* packages will be covered in more detail later in this text.

⊟ my_job_proc.sql

```
-- **************************************************
-- Parameters:
--    1) Text to identify this test job.
-- ****************************************************************

CREATE OR REPLACE PROCEDURE my_job_proc (p_text   IN   VARCHAR2) AS
  l_rindex   PLS_INTEGER;
  l_slno     PLS_INTEGER;
  l_total    NUMBER;
  l_obj      PLS_INTEGER;
BEGIN
  SYS.DBMS_SYSTEM.ksdwrt(2, 'MY_JOB_PROC Start: ' || p_text);

  DBMS_APPLICATION_INFO.set_module(
    module_name => 'my_job_proc',
    action_name => p_text || ': Start.');

  l_rindex    := Dbms_Application_Info.Set_Session_Longops_Nohint;
  l_total := 100;

  FOR i IN 1 .. l_total LOOP
    DBMS_APPLICATION_INFO.set_action(
      action_name => p_text || ': Sleep ' || i || ' of ' || l_total || '.');
```

```
    DBMS_APPLICATION_INFO.set_session_longops(
      rindex      => l_rindex,
      slno        => l_slno,
      op_name     => 'MY_JOB_PROC',
      target      => l_obj,
      context     => 0,
      sofar       => i,
      totalwork   => l_total,
      target_desc => 'MY_JOB_PROC',
      units       => 'loops');

    DBMS_LOCK.sleep(1);
  END LOOP;

  DBMS_APPLICATION_INFO.set_action(
    action_name => p_text || ': End.');

  SYS.DBMS_SYSTEM.ksdwrt(2, 'MY_JOB_PROC End: ' || p_text);
END;
/
SHOW ERRORS
```

The procedure can be tested by calling it from SQL*Plus as follows:

```
SQL> exec my_job_proc('Test It!');
```

Once the procedure has completed, the alert log should contain an entry that looks similar to the following:

```
Sat Jun 19 12:29:16 2004
MY_JOB_PROC Start: Test It!
Sat Jun 19 12:30:59 2004
MY_JOB_PROC End: Test It!
```

Obviously, these entries may be separated by other messages depending on what else has happened on the instance during the time it took for the job to run.

Now that the user named *job_user* has been created and granted privileges, it is time to schedule jobs. The first step is the examination of the *dbms_job* package.

Overview of the dbms_scheduler Functions

It quickly becomes apparent why the *dbms_scheduler* package is the recommended way to schedule jobs in Oracle. The *dbms_scheduler* package allows the user to define standard programs and schedules, which can be used

---

by many jobs. The *dbms_job* package is still present in 10g, but only for backward compatibility. The jobs created using the *dbms_job* package were very much stand-alone in nature in that they were defined with their own schedules and actions.

Support for the scheduler is built into the Oracle Enterprise Manager 11g Database Control (OEM DB Control). The majority of the scheduler objects can be managed via links from the administration page. Figure 11.13 shows the administration page with the scheduler links on the right hand side towards the bottom of the screen.

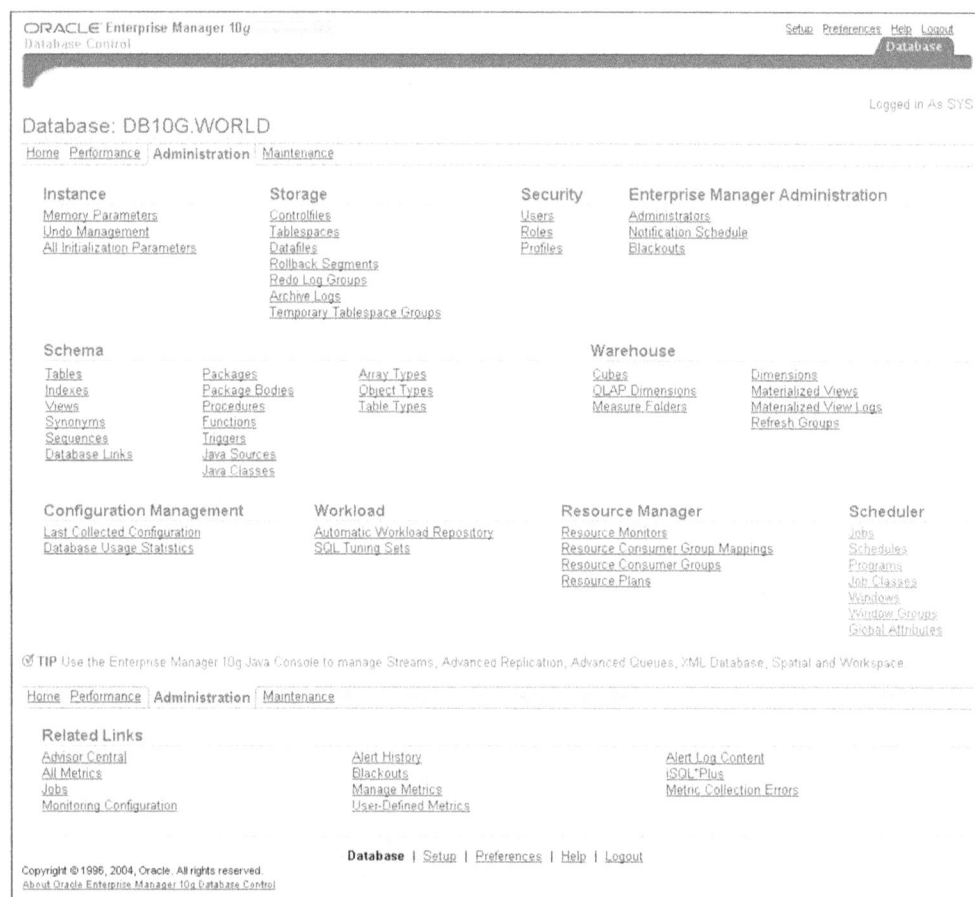

Figure 11.13: *OEM DB Control: Administration*

Job classes, windows and window groups provide a link between the scheduler and the resource manager, allowing jobs to run with a variety of resource profiles. They are considered part of the scheduler administration and require the MANAGE SCHEDULER privilege.

Specific details about the resource manager is beyond the scope of this chapter, so the sections that deal with administration objects will focus on how to create each type of object rather than how they should be used.

Programs

The *create_program* procedure is used to store metadata about a task, but it stores no schedule information.

```
PROCEDURE create_program (
  program_name             IN VARCHAR2,
  program_type             IN VARCHAR2,
  program_action           IN VARCHAR2,
  number_of_arguments      IN PLS_INTEGER DEFAULT 0,
  enabled                  IN BOOLEAN DEFAULT FALSE,
  comments                 IN VARCHAR2 DEFAULT NULL)
```

The parameters associated with this procedure and their usage are as follows:

- *program_name* - A name that uniquely identifies the program. The program name can include a schema qualifier.

- *program_type* - The type of action associated with this program (PLSQL_BLOCK, STORED_PROCEDURE or EXECUTABLE)

- *program_action* - The actual work that is done by the program

- *number_of_arguments* - The number of arguments required by this program. Programs using arguments must have their arguments defined before they can be enabled.

- *enabled* - A flag which indicates if the program is enabled or not. If the program accepts arguments, it cannot be enabled until the arguments are defined.

- *comments* - Free text, allowing the user to record additional information

The action of a program may be a PL/SQL block, a stored procedure or an OS executable file. The following examples show how each type of program is defined.

```
BEGIN
  -- PL/SQL Block.
  DBMS_SCHEDULER.create_program (
    program_name   => 'test_plsql_block_prog',
    program_type   => 'PLSQL_BLOCK',
    program_action => 'BEGIN my_job_proc(''CREATE_PROGRAM (BLOCK)''); END;',
    enabled        => TRUE,
    comments       => 'CREATE_PROGRAM test using a PL/SQL block.');
END;
/

BEGIN
  -- Stored Procedure with Arguments.
  DBMS_SCHEDULER.create_program (
    program_name       => 'test_stored_procedure_prog',
    program_type       => 'STORED_PROCEDURE',
    program_action     => 'my_job_proc',
    number_of_arguments => 1,
    enabled            => FALSE,
    comments           => 'CREATE_PROGRAM test using a procedure.');

  DBMS_SCHEDULER.define_program_argument (
    program_name     => 'test_stored_procedure_prog',
    argument_name    => 'p_text',
    argument_position => 1,
    argument_type    => 'VARCHAR2',
    default_value    => 'This is a default value.');

  DBMS_SCHEDULER.enable (name => 'test_stored_procedure_prog');
END;
/

BEGIN
  -- Shell Script (OS executable file).
  DBMS_SCHEDULER.create_program (
    program_name       => 'test_executable_prog',
    program_type       => 'EXECUTABLE',
    program_action     => '/u01/app/oracle/dba/MyJob.ksh',
    number_of_arguments => 0,
    enabled            => TRUE,
    comments           => 'CREATE_PROGRAM test using a schell script.');
END;
/
```

Programs that accept arguments must have their arguments defined before
they can be enabled. Arguments are defined, manipulated and dropped using
the *define_program_argument*, *define_metadata_argument*, and *drop_program_argument*
procedures whose call specifications are listed below.

```
PROCEDURE define_program_argument (
  program_name          IN VARCHAR2,
  argument_position     IN PLS_INTEGER,
  argument_name         IN VARCHAR2 DEFAULT NULL,
  argument_type         IN VARCHAR2,
  out_argument          IN BOOLEAN DEFAULT FALSE)
```

```
PROCEDURE define_anydata_argument(

   program_name              IN VARCHAR2,
   argument_position         IN PLS_INTEGER,
   argument_name             IN VARCHAR2 DEFAULT NULL,
   argument_type             IN VARCHAR2,
   default_value             IN SYS.ANYDATA,
   out_argument              IN BOOLEAN DEFAULT FALSE)

PROCEDURE define_metadata_argument(

   program_name              IN VARCHAR2,
   metadata_attribute        IN VARCHAR2,
   argument_position         IN PLS_INTEGER,
   argument_name             IN VARCHAR2 DEFAULT NULL)

PROCEDURE drop_program_argument (

   program_name              IN VARCHAR2,
   argument_position         IN PLS_INTEGER)

PROCEDURE drop_program_argument (

   program_name              IN VARCHAR2,
   argument_name             IN VARCHAR2)
```

The important parameters associated with these procedures and their usage are noted as follows:

- *program_name* - A name that uniquely identifies the program

- *argument_position* - The position of the argument in the call specification

- *argument_name* - The name of the argument

- *argument_type* - The datatype of the argument

- *default_value* - The argument value used if no specific value is assigned via the job

- *out_argument* - A flag that indicates the direction of the argument

Programs can be created using the Create Program screen of the OEM DB Control as shown in Figure 11.14.

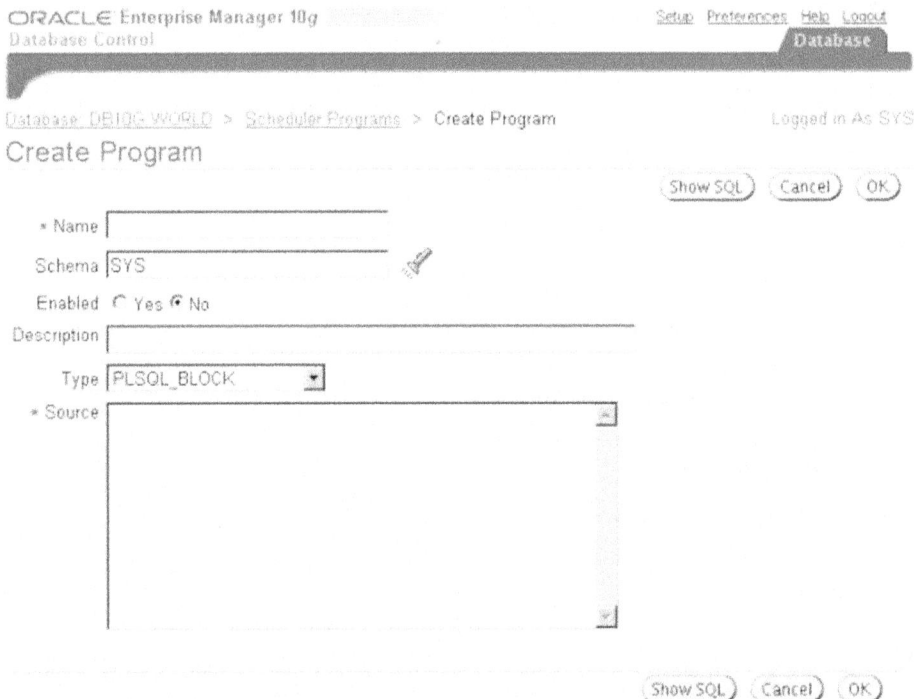

Figure 11.14: *OEM DB Control: Create Program*

Information about programs can be displayed using the *dba_scheduler_programs* view. The following script uses this view to display basic information about the currently defined programs.

🖫 programs.sql

```
set verify off

select
   owner,
   program_name,
   enabled
from
   dba_scheduler_programs
where
   owner = decode(upper('&1'), 'ALL', owner, upper('&1'));
```

The *programs.sql* script can display all programs or only those programs of a specified user.

```
SQL> @programs all

OWNER                              PROGRAM_NAME                       ENABL
---------------------------------  ---------------------------------  -----
SYS                                PURGE_LOG_PROG                     TRUE
SYS                                GATHER_STATS_PROG                  TRUE
JOB_USER                           TEST_PLSQL_BLOCK_PROG              TRUE
JOB_USER                           TEST_STORED_PROCEDURE_PROG         TRUE
JOB_USER                           TEST_EXECUTABLE_PROG               TRUE

SQL> @programs job_user

OWNER                              PROGRAM_NAME                       ENABL
---------------------------------  ---------------------------------  -----
JOB_USER                           TEST_PLSQL_BLOCK_PROG              TRUE
JOB_USER                           TEST_STORED_PROCEDURE_PROG         TRUE
JOB_USER                           TEST_EXECUTABLE_PROG               TRUE
```

Information about program arguments can be displayed using the *dba_scheduler_program_args* view. The following script uses this view to display information about the arguments of currently defined programs.

🖫 program_args.sql

```
-- ************************************************
-- Parameters:
--     1) Specific USERNAME or ALL which doesn't limit output.
--     2) Program name.
-- ******************************************************************

set verify off
column argument_name format a20
column default_value format a30

select
   argument_position,
   argument_name,
   default_value
from
   dba_scheduler_program_args
where
   owner = decode(upper('&1'), 'ALL', owner, upper('&1'))
and
   program_name = upper('&2');
```

The output from the *program_args.sql* script is displayed below.

```
SQL> @program_args job_user test_stored_procedure_prog

ARGUMENT_POSITION ARGUMENT_NAME        DEFAULT_VALUE
----------------- -------------------- ----------------------------
                1 P_TEXT               This is a default value.
```

Programs that are no longer used can be removed using the *drop_program* procedure whose call specification is listed below.

```
PROCEDURE drop_program (
  program_name            IN VARCHAR2,
  force                   IN BOOLEAN DEFAULT FALSE)
```

The parameters associated with this procedure and their usage are as follows:

- *program_name* - A name that uniquely identifies the program

- *force* - When set to TRUE, all jobs which reference the program are disabled prior to the program being dropped. If set to FALSE and jobs reference the program, an error is produced. In addition, all program arguments information is dropped.

The following examples show how the *drop_program* procedure is used.

```
BEGIN
  DBMS_SCHEDULER.drop_program (program_name => 'test_plsql_block_prog');
  DBMS_SCHEDULER.drop_program (program_name =>
'test_stored_procedure_prog');
  DBMS_SCHEDULER.drop_program (program_name => 'test_executable_prog');
END;
/
```

One can determine that the programs have been removed by checking the output of the *programs.sql* script.

```
SQL> @programs all

OWNER                           PROGRAM_NAME                    ENABL
------------------------------- ------------------------------- -----
SYS                             PURGE_LOG_PROG                  TRUE
SYS                             GATHER_STATS_PROG               TRUE
```

Program information is also available from the OEM DB Control via the Scheduler Programs screen shown in Figure 11.15.

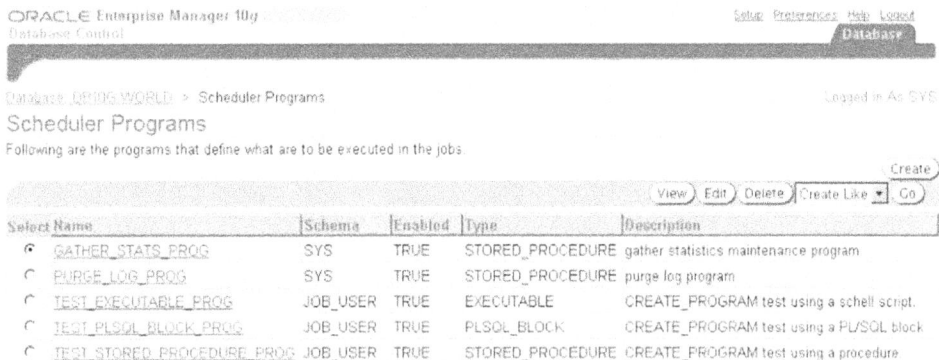

Figure 11.15: *OEM DB Control: Sheduler Programs*

Now that defining reusable programs has been explained, the next section will explain the defining of reusable schedules.

Schedules

The *create_schedule* procedure defines the start time, end time and interval that can be applied to a job.

```
PROCEDURE create_schedule (
  schedule_name           IN VARCHAR2,
  start_date              IN TIMESTAMP WITH TIME ZONE  DEFAULT NULL,
  repeat_interval         IN VARCHAR2,
  end_date                IN TIMESTAMP WITH TIME ZONE  DEFAULT NULL,
  comments                IN VARCHAR2                  DEFAULT NULL)
```

The parameters associated with this procedure and their usage are as follows:

- *schedule_name* - A name that uniquely identifies the schedule

- *start_date* - The date when this schedule will take effect. This date may be in the future if scheduled jobs are set up in advance.

- *repeat_interval* - The definition of how often the job should execute. A value of NULL indicates that the job should only run once. The repeat interval is defined using a calendaring syntax, which is new to Oracle 10g. This will be explained in more detail later.

- *end_date* - The date when this schedule will stop. This, combined with the *start_date* parameter, enables a job to be scheduled for a finite period of time.

Overview of the dbms_scheduler Functions

585

- *comments* - Free text, allowing the user to record additional information.

The following code segment defines a new schedule that runs every hour on minute "0". The lack of an *end_date* parameter value means that the job will repeat forever based on the interval.

```
BEGIN
  DBMS_SCHEDULER.create_schedule (
    schedule_name   => 'test_hourly_schedule',
    start_date      => SYSTIMESTAMP,
    repeat_interval => 'freq=hourly; byminute=0',
    end_date        => NULL,
    comments        => 'Repeats hourly, on the hour, for ever.');
END;
/
```

Schedules are created in the OEM DB Control via the Create Schedule screen shown in Figure 11.16.

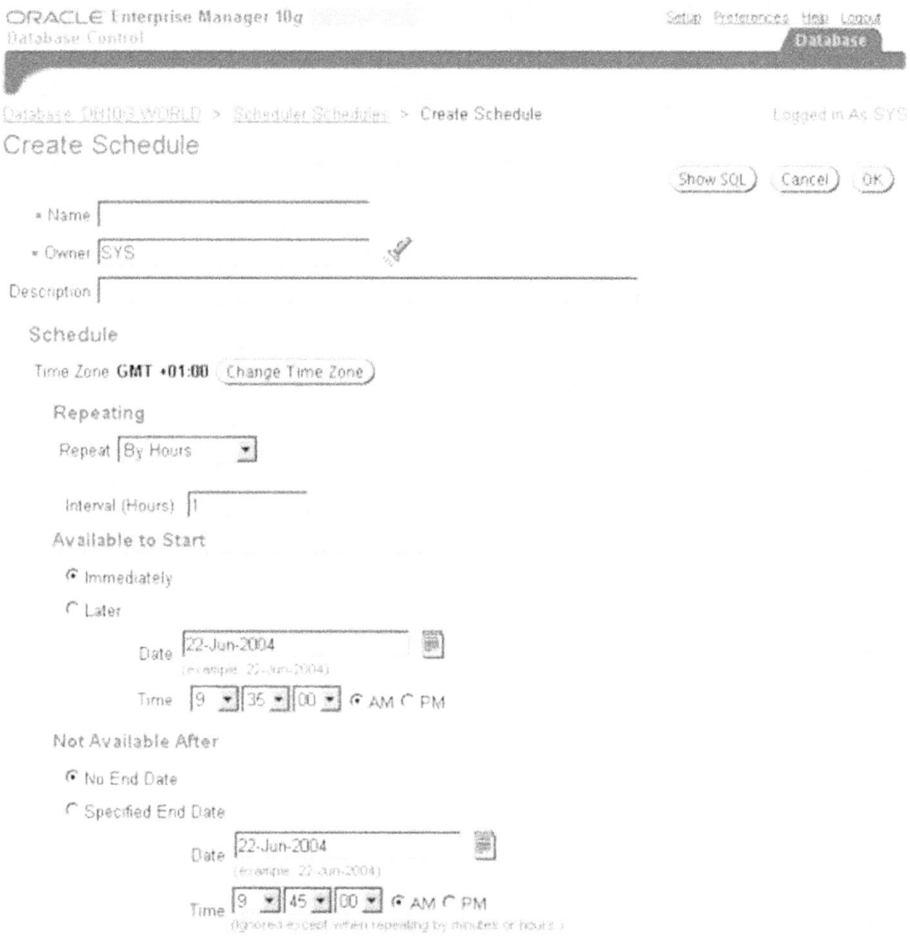

Figure 11.16: *OEM DB Control: Create Schedule*

Information about schedules can be displayed using the *dba_scheduler_schedules* view. The following script uses this view to display information about schedules for a specified user or all users.

💾 schedules.sql

```
-- **************************************************
-- Parameters:
--    1) Specific USERNAME or ALL which does not limit output.
-- ******************************************************************

set verify off

select
```

```
   owner,
   schedule_name,
   repeat_interval
from
   dba_scheduler_schedules
where
   owner = decode(upper('&1'), 'ALL', owner, upper('&1'))
;
```

The following is an example of output from the *schedules.sql* script:

```
SQL> @schedules job_user

OWNER               SCHEDULE_NAME               REPEAT_INTERVAL
-------------------------------------------------------------------
JOB_USER            TEST_HOURLY_SCHEDULE        freq=hourly; byminute=0
```

Alternately, the Scheduler Schedules screen of the OEM DB Control, shown in Figure 11.17, can be used to display schedule information.

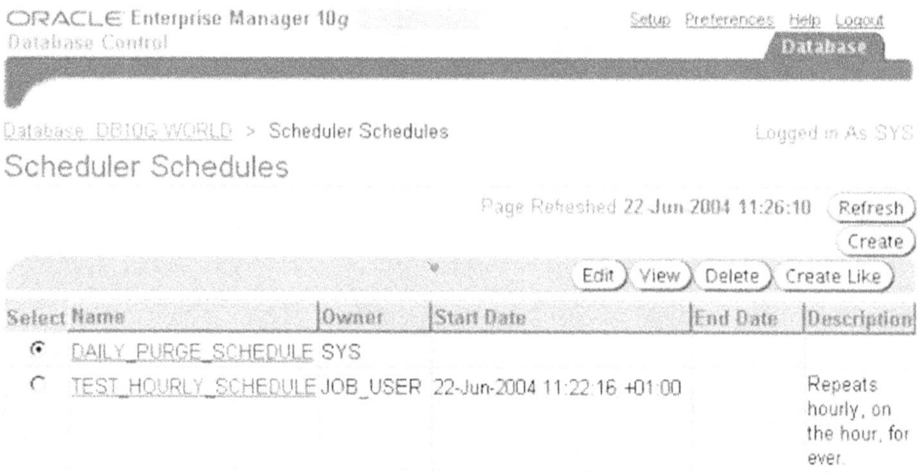

Figure 11.17: *OEM DB Control: Scheduler Schedules*

Schedules can be dropped using the *drop_schedule* procedure, whose call specification is listed below.

```
PROCEDURE drop_schedule (
   schedule_name          IN VARCHAR2,
   force                  IN BOOLEAN      DEFAULT FALSE)
```

The parameters associated with this procedure and their usage are as follows:

- *schedule_name* - A name that identifies a single schedule or a comma separated list of schedule names.

- *force* - If set to TRUE, all jobs and windows which reference this schedule are disabled prior to the schedule being dropped. If set to FALSE, the presence of dependants will produce errors.

The following examples show how the *drop_schedule* procedure is used:

```
BEGIN
  DBMS_SCHEDULER.drop_schedule (schedule_name => 'TEST_HOURLY_SCHEDULE');
END;
/
```

The output from the *schedules.sql* script shows that the schedule has been removed.

```
SQL> @schedules job_user

no rows selected
```

Now that details on how to define reusable objects such as programs and schedules have been presented, the following section will show how they are used to schedule jobs.

Creating Oracle Jobs

Jobs are what the scheduler is all about. They are created using the *create_job* procedure, which is overloaded and allows a job to be defined in one of four ways:

- Completely self-contained with the program and schedule defined inline

- Referencing both a predefined program and schedule

- Referencing a predefined program, but with an inline schedule

- Referencing a predefined schedule, but with an inline program

The following code examples rely on the previously defined programs and schedules to show how the overloads of the *create_job* procedure are used.

```
BEGIN
  -- Job defined entirely by the CREATE JOB procedure.
  DBMS_SCHEDULER.create_job (
    job_name        => 'test_full_job_definition',
    job_type        => 'PLSQL_BLOCK',
    job_action      => 'BEGIN my_job_proc(''CREATE_PROGRAM (BLOCK)'');
END;',
    start_date      => SYSTIMESTAMP,
    repeat_interval => 'freq=hourly; byminute=0',
    end_date        => NULL,
    enabled         => TRUE,
    comments        => 'Job defined entirely by the CREATE JOB procedure.');
END;
/
BEGIN
  -- Job defined by an existing program and schedule.
  DBMS_SCHEDULER.create_job (
    job_name      => 'test_prog_sched_job_definition',
    program_name  => 'test_plsql_block_prog',
    schedule_name => 'test_hourly_schedule',
    enabled       => TRUE,
    comments      => 'Job defined by an existing program and schedule.');
END;
/
BEGIN
  -- Job defined by an existing program and inline schedule.
  DBMS_SCHEDULER.create_job (
    job_name        => 'test_prog_job_definition',
    program_name    => 'test_plsql_block_prog',
    start_date      => SYSTIMESTAMP,
    repeat_interval => 'freq=hourly; byminute=0',
    end_date        => NULL,
    enabled         => TRUE,
    comments        => 'Job defined by existing program and inline
schedule.');
END;
/
BEGIN
  -- Job defined by existing schedule and inline program.
  DBMS_SCHEDULER.create_job (
    job_name      => 'test_sched_job_definition',
    schedule_name => 'test_hourly_schedule',
    job_type      => 'PLSQL_BLOCK',
    job_action    => 'BEGIN my_job_proc(''CREATE_PROGRAM (BLOCK)''); END;',
    enabled       => TRUE,
    comments      => 'Job defined by existing schedule and inline
program.');
END;
/
```

The *generate_job_name* function can be used to generate a unique name for a job.

```
FUNCTION generate_job_name (
   prefix        IN VARCHAR2 DEFAULT 'JOB$_') RETURN VARCHAR2
```

A sequence number is appended to the specified job name prefix to guarantee uniqueness. If the prefix is not specified, a standard prefix is used. The query below shows how it can be used:

```
column job_name_1 format a20
column job_name_2 format a20

select
   DBMS_SCHEDULER.generate_job_name ('test_job') as job_name_1,
   DBMS_SCHEDULER.generate_job_name as job_name_2
from
   dual;

JOB_NAME_1           JOB_NAME_2
-------------------- --------------------
TEST_JOB6            JOB$_7
```

The figures below show the Create Job (General) and Create Job (Schedule) screens, respectively. These provide a web-based alternative to the *create_job* procedure.

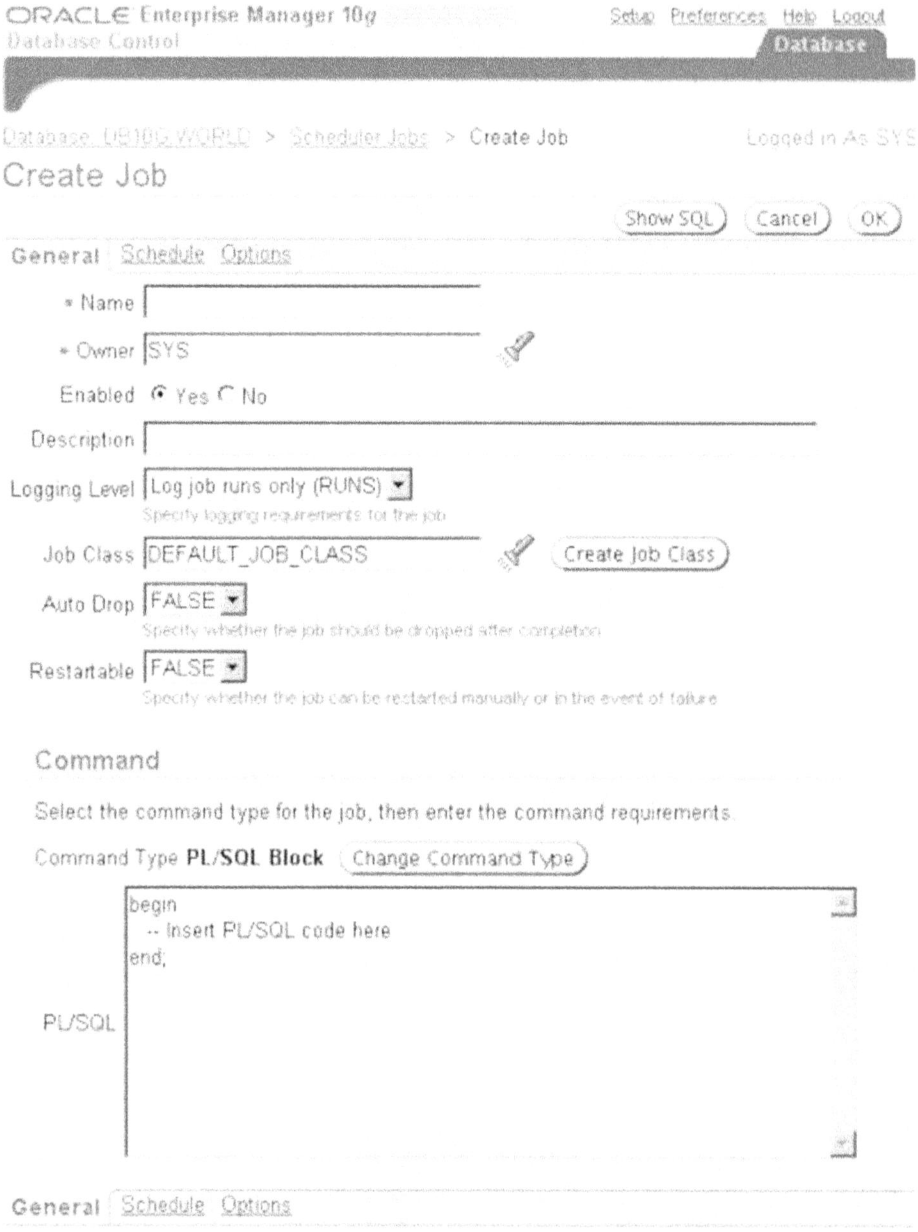

Figure 11.18: *OEM DB Control: Create Job (General)*

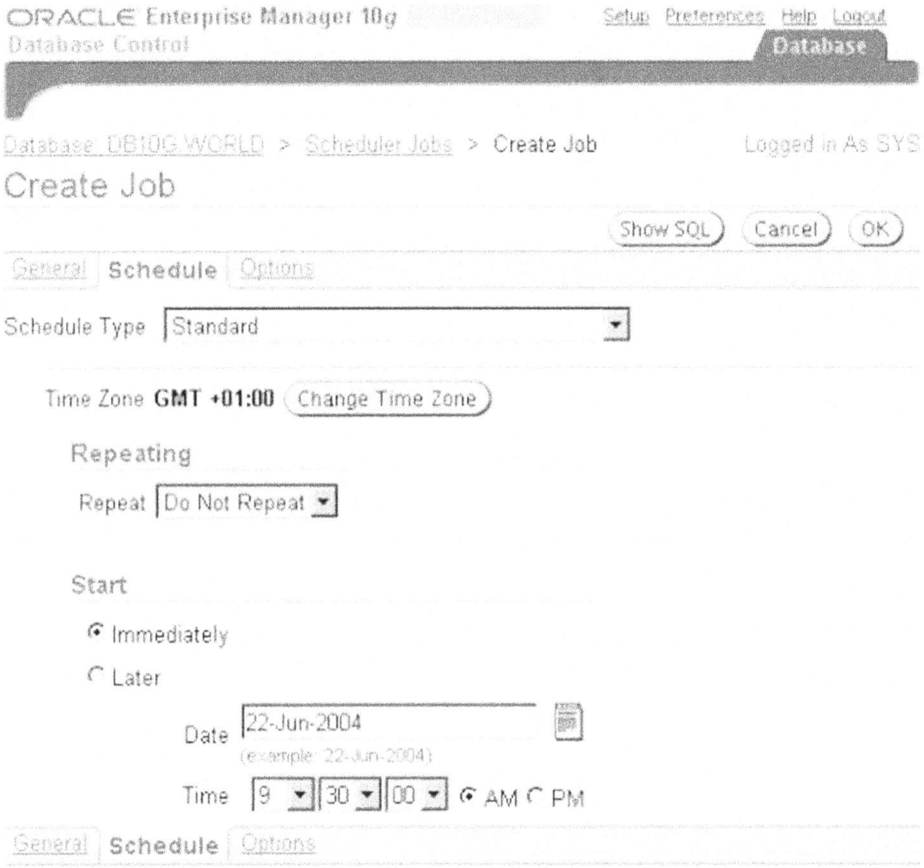

Figure 11.19: *OEM DB Control: Create Job (Schedule)*

Information about jobs can be displayed using the *dba_scheduler_jobs* view. The following script uses this view to display information about currently defined jobs.

💾 **jobs_10g.sql**

```
-- *************************************************
-- Parameters:
--    1) Specific USERNAME or ALL which doesn't limit output.
-- *****************************************************************
set verify off

select
   owner,
   job_name,
   job_class,
```

```
   enabled,
   next_run_date,
   repeat_interval
from
   dba_scheduler_jobs
where
   owner = decode(upper('&1'), 'ALL', owner, upper('&1'))
;
```

The output of the *jobs_10g.sql* script for the current user is displayed below.

```
SQL> @jobs_10g job_user

OWNER                    JOB_NAME                    JOB_CLASS                   ENABLE
------------------------ --------------------------- --------------------------- ------------------
NEXT_RUN_DATE
----------------------------------------------------------------------
REPEAT_INTERVAL
----------------------------------------------------------------

JOB_USER                 TEST_FULL_JOB_DEFINITION    DEFAULT_JOB_CLASS                   TRUE
22-JUN-04 15.00.08.900000 +01:00
freq=hourly; byminute=0

JOB_USER                 TEST_PROG_SCHED_JOB_DEFINITION DEFAULT_JOB_CLASS                TRUE
22-JUN-04 15.00.16.200000 +01:00

JOB_USER                 TEST_PROG_JOB_DEFINITION    DEFAULT_JOB_CLASS                   TRUE
22-JUN-04 15.00.09.600000 +01:00
freq=hourly; byminute=0

JOB_USER                 TEST_SCHED_JOB_DEFINITION   DEFAULT_JOB_CLASS                   TRUE
22-JUN-04 15.00.16.200000 +01:00
```

When the *test_stored_procedure_prog* program is defined, a default argument value is specified. The argument values of jobs that access predefined programs can be manipulated using the following procedures:

```
PROCEDURE set_job_argument_value (
   job_name                IN VARCHAR2,
   argument_position       IN PLS_INTEGER,
   argument_value          IN VARCHAR2)

PROCEDURE set_job_argument_value (
   job_name                IN VARCHAR2,
   argument_name           IN VARCHAR2,
   argument_value          IN VARCHAR2)

PROCEDURE set_job_anydata_value(
   job_name                IN VARCHAR2,
   argument_position       IN PLS_INTEGER,
   argument_value          IN SYS.ANYDATA)

PROCEDURE set_job_anydata_value(
   job_name                IN VARCHAR2,
   argument_name           IN VARCHAR2,
   argument_value          IN SYS.ANYDATA)

PROCEDURE reset_job_argument_value (
   job_name                IN VARCHAR2,
```

```
    argument_position        IN PLS_INTEGER)

PROCEDURE reset_job_argument_value (
  job_name                   IN VARCHAR2,
  argument_name              IN VARCHAR2)
```

The parameters associated with these procedures and their usage are as follows:

- *job_name* - A name that uniquely identifies the job

- *argument_position* - The position of the argument in the call specification

- *argument_name* - The name of the argument

- *argument_value* - The value assigned to the argument

Arguments can be referenced by name or by position and their values can be set or reset to the default value. The example below shows how the argument values for a job can be reset:

```
BEGIN
  DBMS_SCHEDULER.create_job (
    job_name        => 'argument_job_definition',
    program_name    => 'test_stored_procedure_prog',
    schedule_name   => 'test_hourly_schedule',
    enabled         => FALSE,
    comments        => 'Job defined by an existing program and schedule.');

  DBMS_SCHEDULER.set_job_argument_value (
    job_name        => 'argument_job_definition',
    argument_name   => 'p_text',
    argument_value  => 'A different argument value.');

  DBMS_SCHEDULER.enable (
    name            => 'argument_job_definition');
END;
/
```

Information about job arguments can be displayed using the *dba_scheduler_job_args* view. The following script uses this view to display argument information about a specified job.

🖫 job_arguments.sql

```
-- ************************************************
-- Parameters:
--    1) Specific USERNAME or ALL which doesn't limit output.
--    2) Job name.
-- *****************************************************************

set verify off
column argument_name format a20
```

```
column value format a30

select
   argument_position,
   argument_name,
   value
from
   dba_scheduler_job_args
where
   owner = decode(upper('&1'), 'ALL', owner, upper('&1'))
and
   job_name = upper('&2')
;
```

Using this script, one can see that the value of the job argument no longer matches the default value of the program argument.

```
SQL> @job_arguments job_user argument_job_definition

ARGUMENT_POSITION ARGUMENT_NAME       VALUE
----------------- -------------------- -----------------------------
                1 P_TEXT              A different argument value.
```

Figure 11.20 shows the information displayed on the Scheduler Jobs screen in the OEM DB Control.

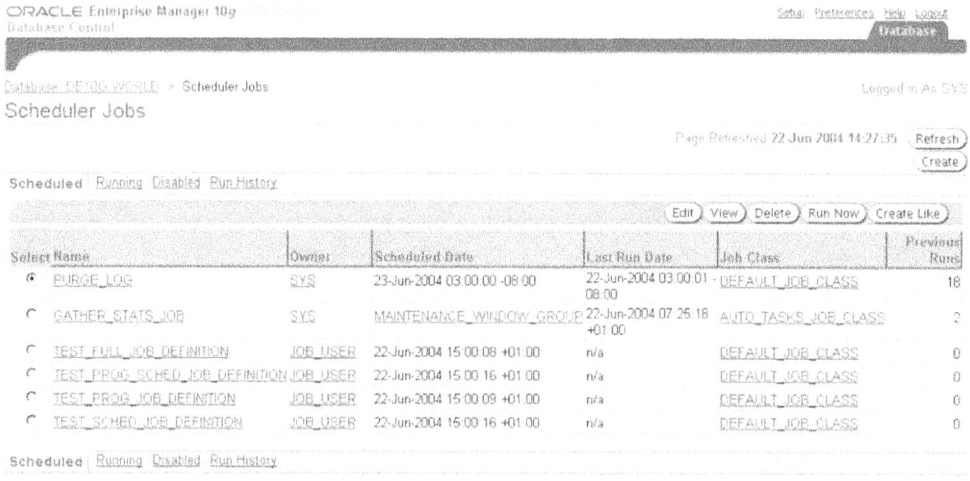

Figure 11.20: *OEM DB Control: Scheduler Jobs*

Jobs are normally run asynchronously under the control of the job coordinator, but they can also be controlled manually using the *run_job* and *stop_job* procedures.

```
PROCEDURE run_job (

  job_name                  IN VARCHAR2,
  use_current_session       IN BOOLEAN DEFAULT TRUE)

PROCEDURE stop_job (

  job_name                  IN VARCHAR2,
  force                     IN BOOLEAN DEFAULT FALSE)
```

The parameters associated with these procedures and their usage are as follows:

- *job_name* - A name that identifies a single job, a job class or a comma separated list of job names.

- *use_current_session* - When set to TRUE, the job is run in the user's current session; otherwise, a job slave runs it in the background.

- *force* - When set to FALSE, a job is stopped using the equivalent of sending a ctrl-c to the job. When TRUE, a graceful shutdown is attempted, but if this fails, the slave process is killed. Using the *force* parameter requires the user to have the MANAGE SCHEDULER system privilege.

The following code shows how the procedures can be used:

```
BEGIN
  -- Run job synchronously.
  DBMS_SCHEDULER.run_job (
    job_name            => 'test_full_job_definition',
    use_current_session => FALSE);

  -- Stop jobs.
  DBMS_SCHEDULER.stop_job (
    job_name => 'test_full_job_definition, test_prog_sched_job_definition');
END;
/
```

A new job can be created as a replica of an existing job using the *copy_job* procedure. The new job is created in the disabled state with the old job remaining unchanged.

```
PROCEDURE copy_job (

  old_job                   IN VARCHAR2,
  new_job                   IN VARCHAR2)
```

The parameters associated with this procedure and their usage are as follows:

- *old_job* - The name of the job whose attribute will be duplicated to create the new job

- *new_job* - The name of the duplicate job to be created

An example of its usage might be as follows:

```
BEGIN
  DBMS_SCHEDULER.copy_job (
    old_job => 'test_full_job_definition',
    new_job => 'new_test_full_job_definition');
END;
/
```

Jobs can be deleted using the *drop_job* procedure listed next:

```
PROCEDURE drop_job (
  job_name              IN VARCHAR2,
  force                 IN BOOLEAN      DEFAULT FALSE)
```

The parameters associated with this procedure and their usage are as follows:

- *job_name* - A name that identifies a single job, a job class name or a comma separated list

- *force* - TRUE running jobs are stopped before the job is dropped. When FALSE, dropping a job that is running will fail.

The following code shows how the *drop_job* procedure can be used:

```
BEGIN
  DBMS_SCHEDULER.drop_job (
    job_name => 'test_full_job_definition, test_prog_sched_job_definition,
                 test_prog_job_definition, test_sched_job_definition,
                 argument_job_definition',
    force    => TRUE);
END;
/
```

The output from the *jobs_10g.sql* script shows that the jobs have been removed.

```
SQL> @jobs_10g job_user

no rows selected
```

The following section will focus on job classes, which are the first of the scheduler administration objects.

Job Classes

Job classes allow the grouping of jobs with similar characteristics and resource requirements to ease administration. If the *job_class* parameter of the *create_job* procedure is undefined, the job is assigned to a job class called DEFAULT_JOB_CLASS.

Job classes are created using the *create_job_class* procedure listed below.

```
PROCEDURE create_job_class(
   job_class_name          IN VARCHAR2,
   resource_consumer_group IN VARCHAR2      DEFAULT NULL,
   service                 IN VARCHAR2      DEFAULT NULL,
   logging_level           IN PLS_INTEGER   DEFAULT
DBMS_SCHEDULER.LOGGING_RUNS,
   log_history             IN PLS_INTEGER   DEFAULT NULL,
   comments                IN VARCHAR2      DEFAULT NULL)
```

The parameters associated with this procedure and their usage are as follows:

- *job_class_name* - A name that uniquely identifies the job class

- *resource_consumer_group* - The resource consumer group associated with the job class

- *service* - The service database object the job belongs to, not the *tnsnames.ora* service

- *logging_level* - The amount of logging that should be done for this job specified by the constants *logging_off*, *logging_runs*, and *logging_full*

- *log_history* - The number of days the logging information is kept before purging

- *comments* - Free text allowing the user to record additional information

Suffice it to say that it must be decided with which resource consumer group the job class should be associated. Information about resource consumer groups can be displayed using the *dba_rsrc_consumer_groups* view.

```
select
   consumer_group
from
   dba_rsrc_consumer_groups
;

CONSUMER_GROUP
-------------------------------
```

```
OTHER_GROUPS
DEFAULT_CONSUMER_GROUP
SYS_GROUP
LOW_GROUP
AUTO_TASK_CONSUMER_GROUP
```

With this information, a new job class can be defined as follows:

```
BEGIN
  DBMS_SCHEDULER.create_job_class (
    job_class_name          => 'test_job_class',
    resource_consumer_group => 'default_consumer_group');
END;
/
```

Figure 11.21 shows the Create Job Class screen in the OEM DB Control.

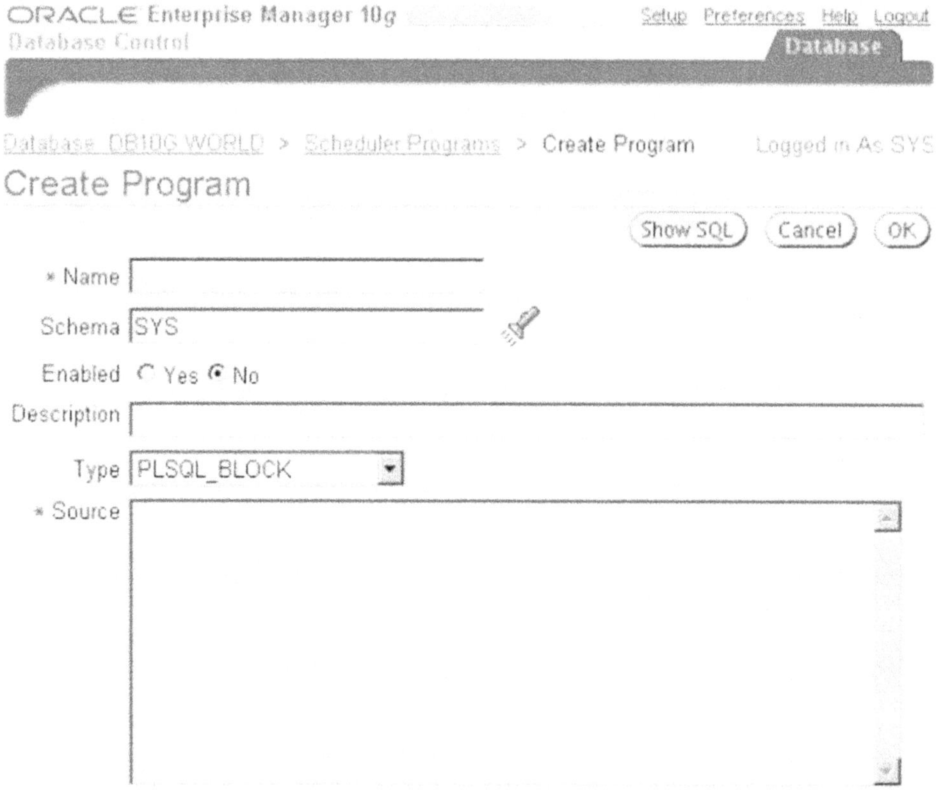

Figure 11.21: *OEM DB Control: Create Job Class*

Information about job classes can be displayed using the *dba_scheduler_job_classes* view. The following script uses this view:

🖫 job_classes.sql

```
select
   job_class_name,
   resource_consumer_group
from
   dba_scheduler_job_classes
;
```

Here is the output from the *job_classes.sql* script:

```
SQL> @job_classes


JOB_CLASS_NAME                     RESOURCE_CONSUMER_GROUP
-----------------------------      -----------------------------
DEFAULT_JOB_CLASS
AUTO_TASKS_JOB_CLASS               AUTO_TASK_CONSUMER_GROUP
TEST_JOB_CLASS                     DEFAULT_CONSUMER_GROUP

3 rows selected.
```

Figure 11.22 shows the Scheduler Job Classes screen in the OEM DB Control.

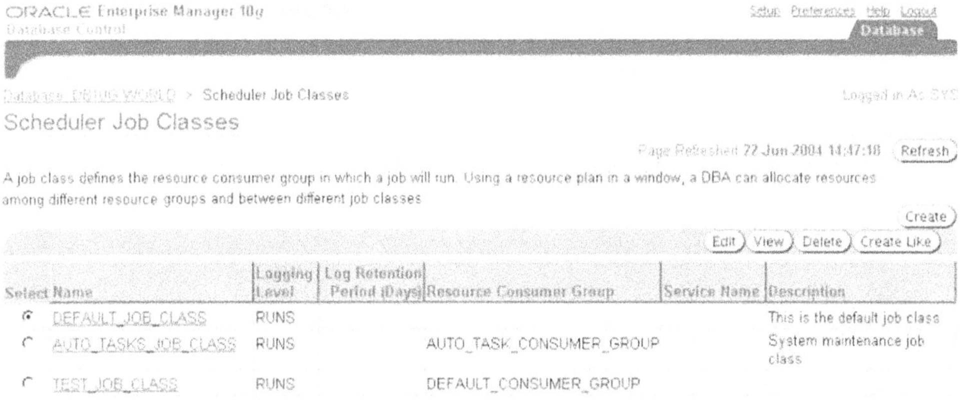

Figure 11.22: *OEM DB Control: Scheduler Job Classes*

Jobs can be assigned to a job class during creation. It is also possible to assign a job to an alternative job class after creation using one of the *set_attribute* procedure overloads.

```
BEGIN
  -- Job defined and assigned to a job class.
  DBMS_SCHEDULER.create_job (
    job_name      => 'test_prog_sched_class_job_def',
    program_name  => 'test_plsql_block_prog',
    schedule_name => 'test_hourly_schedule',
    job_class     => 'test_job_class',
    enabled       => TRUE,
    comments      => 'Job defined and assigned to a job class ');
END;
/
BEGIN
  -- Assign an existing job to a job class.
  DBMS_SCHEDULER.set_attribute (
    name      => 'test_prog_sched_job_definition',
    attribute => 'job_class',
    value     => 'test_job_class');
END;
/
```

The output from the *jobs_10g.sql* script shows that the job classes associated with these jobs have been set correctly.

```
SQL> @jobs_10g job_user

OWNER       JOB_NAME                         JOB_CLASS         ENABLE
----------  ------------------------------   ----------------  ------
NEXT_RUN_DATE
-----------------------------------------------------------------
REPEAT_INTERVAL
-----------------------------------------------------------------
JOB_USER    TEST_FULL_JOB_DEFINITION         DEFAULT_JOB_CLASS TRUE
22-JUN-04 15.00.08.900000 +01:00
freq=hourly; byminute=0

JOB_USER    TEST_PROG_SCHED_JOB_DEFINITION TEST_JOB_CLASS      TRUE
22-JUN-04 15.00.16.200000 +01:00

JOB_USER    TEST_PROG_JOB_DEFINITION         DEFAULT_JOB_CLASS TRUE
22-JUN-04 15.00.09.600000 +01:00
freq=hourly; byminute=0

JOB_USER    TEST_SCHED_JOB_DEFINITION        DEFAULT_JOB_CLASS TRUE
22-JUN-04 15.00.16.200000 +01:00

JOB_USER    ARGUMENT_JOB_DEFINITION          DEFAULT_JOB_CLASS TRUE
22-JUN-04 15.00.16.200000 +01:00

JOB_USER    TEST_PROG_SCHED_CLASS_JOB_DEF  TEST_JOB_CLASS      TRUE
22-JUN-04 15.00.16.200000 +01:00

6 rows selected.
```

Job classes can be removed using the *drop_job_class* procedure listed below:

```
PROCEDURE drop_job_class (
  job_class_name         IN VARCHAR2,
  force                  IN BOOLEAN DEFAULT FALSE)
```

The parameters associated with this procedure and their usage are as follows:

- *job_class_name* - A name that specifies a single or comma separated list of job class names

- *force* - When set to TRUE, all jobs that are assigned to the job class are disabled and have their job class set to the default. When set to FALSE, attempting to drop a job class that has dependent jobs will cause an error.

The following code example shows how a job class can be removed.

```
BEGIN
  DBMS_SCHEDULER.drop_job_class (
    job_class_name => 'test_job_class',
    force          => TRUE);
END;
/
```

The output of the *job_classes.sql* script shows that the job class has been removed successfully.

```
SQL> @job_classes

JOB_CLASS_NAME                    RESOURCE_CONSUMER_GROUP
-------------------------------   -------------------------------
DEFAULT_JOB_CLASS
AUTO_TASKS_JOB_CLASS              AUTO_TASK_CONSUMER_GROUP

2 rows selected.
```

Now that the creation of job classes has been presented, the next section will cover windows, which is another type of scheduler administration object.

Oracle Job Scheduling Windows

Windows define the times when resource plans are active. Since job classes point to resource consumer groups, and therefore resource plans, this mechanism allows control over the resources allocated to job classes and their associated jobs during specific time periods. A window can be assigned to the *schedule_name* parameter of a job instead of a schedule object.

Only one window can be active at any time with one resource plan assigned to the window. The effects of resource plan switches are instantly visible to running jobs that are assigned to job classes.

A window can be created using the *create_window* procedure with a predefined or inline schedule.

```
PROCEDURE create_window (

  window_name            IN VARCHAR2,
  resource_plan          IN VARCHAR2,
  schedule_name          IN VARCHAR2,
  duration               IN INTERVAL DAY TO SECOND,
  window_priority        IN VARCHAR2               DEFAULT 'LOW',
  comments               IN VARCHAR2               DEFAULT NULL)

PROCEDURE create_window (

  window_name            IN VARCHAR2,
  resource_plan          IN VARCHAR2,
  start_date             IN TIMESTAMP WITH TIME ZONE DEFAULT NULL,
  repeat_interval        IN VARCHAR2,
  end_date               IN TIMESTAMP WITH TIME ZONE DEFAULT NULL,
  duration               IN INTERVAL DAY TO SECOND,
  window_priority        IN VARCHAR2               DEFAULT 'LOW',
  comments               IN VARCHAR2               DEFAULT NULL)
```

The parameters associated with these procedures and their usage are as follows:

- *window_name* - A name that uniquely identifies the window

- *resource_plan* - The resource plan associated with the window. When the window opens, the system switches to use the associated resource plan. When the window closes, the system switches back to the previous resource plan.

- *schedule_name* - The name of the schedule associated with the window. If this is specified, the *start_date, repeat_interval* and *end_date* must be NULL.

- *start_date* - The date when this window will take effect. This may be in the future if the window is to be set up in advance.

- *repeat_interval* - The definition of how often the window should open. A value of NULL indicates that the window should only open once.

- *end_date* - The date when this window will stop. This, combined with the *start_date* parameter, enables a window to be scheduled for a finite period of time.

- *duration* - The length of time in minutes the window should remain open

- *window_priority* - The priority (LOW or HIGH) of the window. In the event of multiple windows opening at the same time, windows with a high priority take precedence over windows with a low priority, which is the default.

- *comments* - Free text that allows the user to record additional information

The following code shows how the *create_window* procedures can be used:

```
BEGIN
  -- Window with a predefined schedule.
  DBMS_SCHEDULER.create_window (
    window_name     => 'test_window_1',
    resource_plan   => NULL,
    schedule_name   => 'TEST_HOURLY_SCHEDULE',
    duration        => INTERVAL '30' MINUTE,
    window_priority => 'LOW',
    comments        => 'Window with a predefined schedule.');
END;
/

BEGIN
  -- Window with an inline schedule.
  DBMS_SCHEDULER.create_window (
    window_name     => 'test_window_2',
    resource_plan   => NULL,
    start_date      => SYSTIMESTAMP,
    repeat_interval => 'freq=hourly; byminute=0',
    end_date        => NULL,
    duration        => INTERVAL '30' MINUTE,
    window_priority => 'LOW',
    comments        => 'Window with an inline schedule.');
END;
/
```

The SYS user is the owner of all windows, so any schedules referenced by them must also be owned by SYS.

Figure 11.23 shows the Create Window screen in the OEM DB Control.

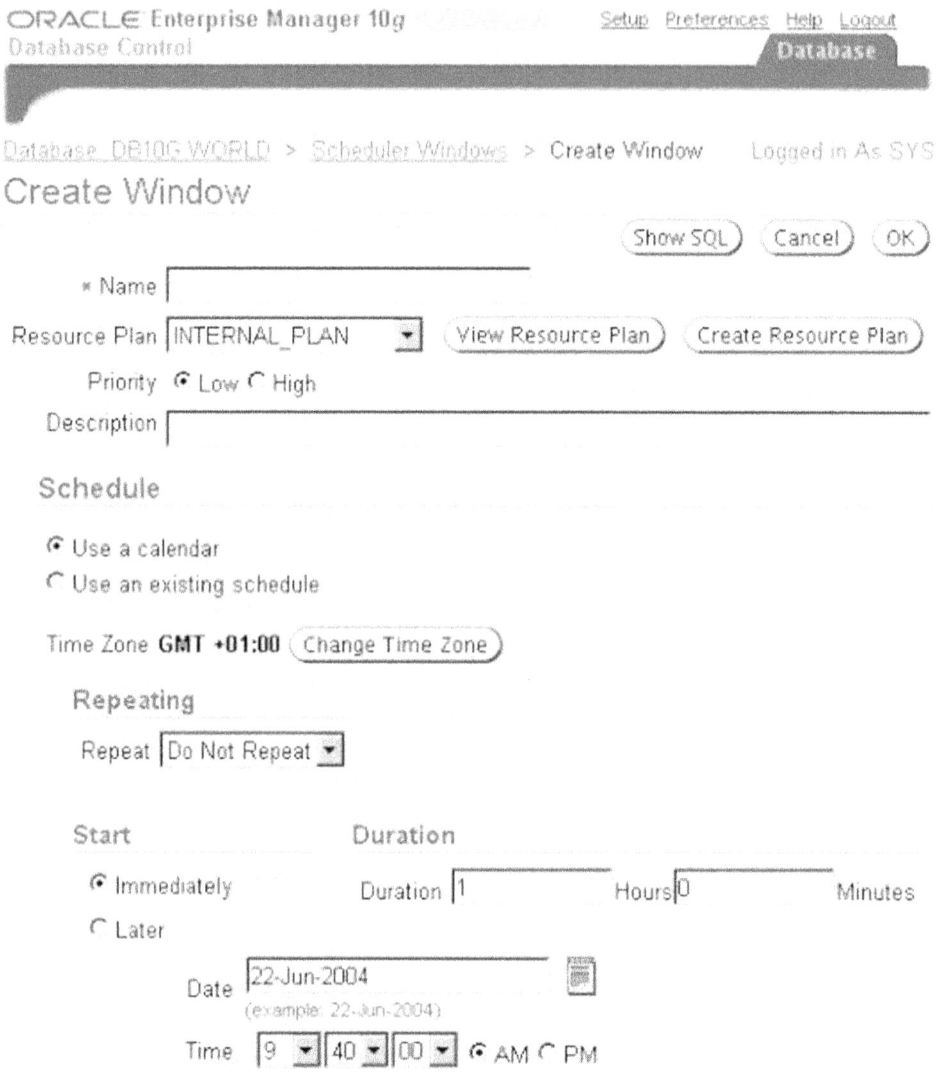

Figure 11.23: *OEM DB Control: Create Window*

Information about windows can be displayed using the *dba_scheduler_windows* view. The following script uses this view:

windows.sql

```
select
    window_name,
    resource_plan,
    enabled,
    active
from
    dba_scheduler_windows;
```

The output from the *windows.sql* script is displayed below:

```
job_user@db10g> @windows

WINDOW_NAME                        RESOURCE_PLAN            ENABL ACTIV
---------------------------------  -----------------------  ----- -----
TEST_WINDOW_1                                               TRUE  FALSE
TEST_WINDOW_2                                               TRUE  FALSE
WEEKEND_WINDOW                                              TRUE  TRUE
WEEKNIGHT_WINDOW                                            TRUE  FALSE

4 rows selected.
```

Figure 11.24 shows the Scheduler Windows screen in the OEM DB Control.

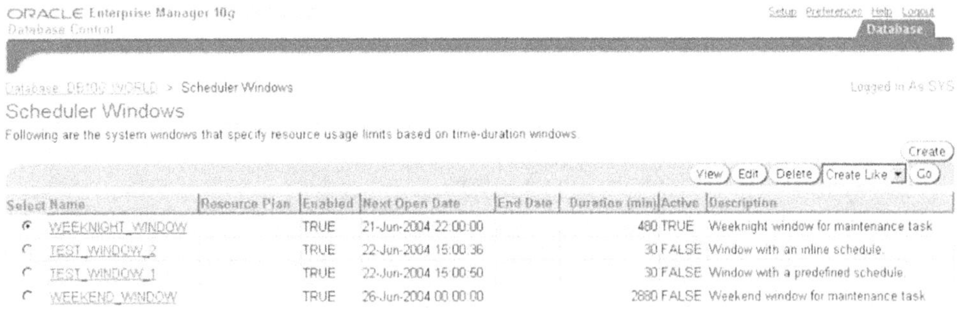

Figure 11.24: *OEM DB Control: Scheduler Windows*

The server normally controls the opening and closing of windows, but they also can be opened and closed manually using the *open_window* and *close_window* procedures.

```
PROCEDURE open_window (

  window_name            IN VARCHAR2,
  duration               IN INTERVAL DAY TO SECOND,
  force                  IN BOOLEAN DEFAULT FALSE)

PROCEDURE close_window (

  window_name            IN VARCHAR2)
```

The parameters associated with these procedures and their usage are as follows:

- *window_name* - A name that uniquely identifies the window

- *duration* - The length of time, in minutes, the window should remain open

- *force* - When set to FALSE, attempting to open a window when one is already open will result in an error unless the currently open window is the one that is attempting to open. In this case, the close time is set to the current system time plus the specified duration. Closing a window causes all jobs associated with that window to be stopped.

The following example opens, then closes, *test_window_2*. Notice how the active window switches back to *weekend_window* when *test_window_2* is closed.

```
BEGIN
  -- Open window.
  DBMS_SCHEDULER.open_window (
    window_name => 'test_window_2',
    duration    => INTERVAL '1' MINUTE,
    force       => TRUE);
END;
/

SQL> @windows

WINDOW_NAME                     RESOURCE_PLAN         ENABL ACTIV
------------------------------- --------------------- ----- -----
TEST_WINDOW_1                                         TRUE  FALSE
TEST_WINDOW_2                                         TRUE  TRUE
WEEKEND_WINDOW                                        TRUE  FALSE
WEEKNIGHT_WINDOW                                      TRUE  FALSE

4 rows selected.

BEGIN
  -- Close window.
  DBMS_SCHEDULER.close_window (
    window_name => 'test_window_2');
END;
/

SQL> @windows
```

```
WINDOW_NAME                    RESOURCE_PLAN         ENABL ACTIV
------------------------------ --------------------- ----- -----
TEST_WINDOW_1                                        TRUE  FALSE
TEST_WINDOW_2                                        TRUE  FALSE
WEEKEND_WINDOW                                       TRUE  TRUE
WEEKNIGHT_WINDOW                                     TRUE  FALSE

4 rows selected.
```

Windows can be removed using the *drop_window* procedure.

```
PROCEDURE drop_window (
  window_name             IN VARCHAR2,
  force                   IN BOOLEAN DEFAULT FALSE)
```

The parameters associated with this procedure and their usage are as follows:

- *window_name* - A single or comma separated list of window names. If a window group name is specified, all windows within that group will be dropped. In addition, all jobs that use the specified window or window group as a schedule will be disabled, although running jobs will complete normally.

- *force* - When set to FALSE, attempting to drop an open window will result in an error. When set to TRUE, the open window is closed before it is dropped.

The following example drops the two test windows that were created earlier:

```
BEGIN
  DBMS_SCHEDULER.drop_window (
    window_name => 'test_window_1,test_window_2',
    force       => TRUE);
END;
/
```

The output from the *windows.sql* script confirms that the windows have been removed successfully.

```
SQL> @windows

WINDOW_NAME              RESOURCE_PLAN         ENABL ACTIV
------------------------ ----------------- ----- -----
WEEKEND_WINDOW                                 TRUE  TRUE
WEEKNIGHT_WINDOW                               TRUE  FALSE

2 rows selected.
```

The following section will show how to group related windows together using window groups.

Job Scheduling Window Groups

A window group is a collection of related job scheduling windows which can be assigned to the *schedule_name* parameter of a job instead of a schedule object. It can be created with zero, one or many windows as group members using the *create_window_group* procedure.

```
PROCEDURE create_window_group(

  group_name              IN VARCHAR2,
  window_list             IN VARCHAR2 DEFAULT NULL,
  comments                IN VARCHAR2 DEFAULT NULL)
```

The parameters associated with this procedure and their usage are as follows:

- *group_name* - A name that uniquely identifies the window group

- *window_list* - A comma separated list of windows associated with the window group

- *comments* - Free text allowing the user to record additional information

The following code creates a window group and assigns the two test windows defined in the previous section.

```
BEGIN
  DBMS_SCHEDULER.create_window_group (
    group_name  => 'test_window_group',
    window_list => 'test_window_1, test_window_2',
    comments    => 'A test window group');
END;
/
```

Figure 11.25 shows the Create Window Group screen in the OEM DB Control.

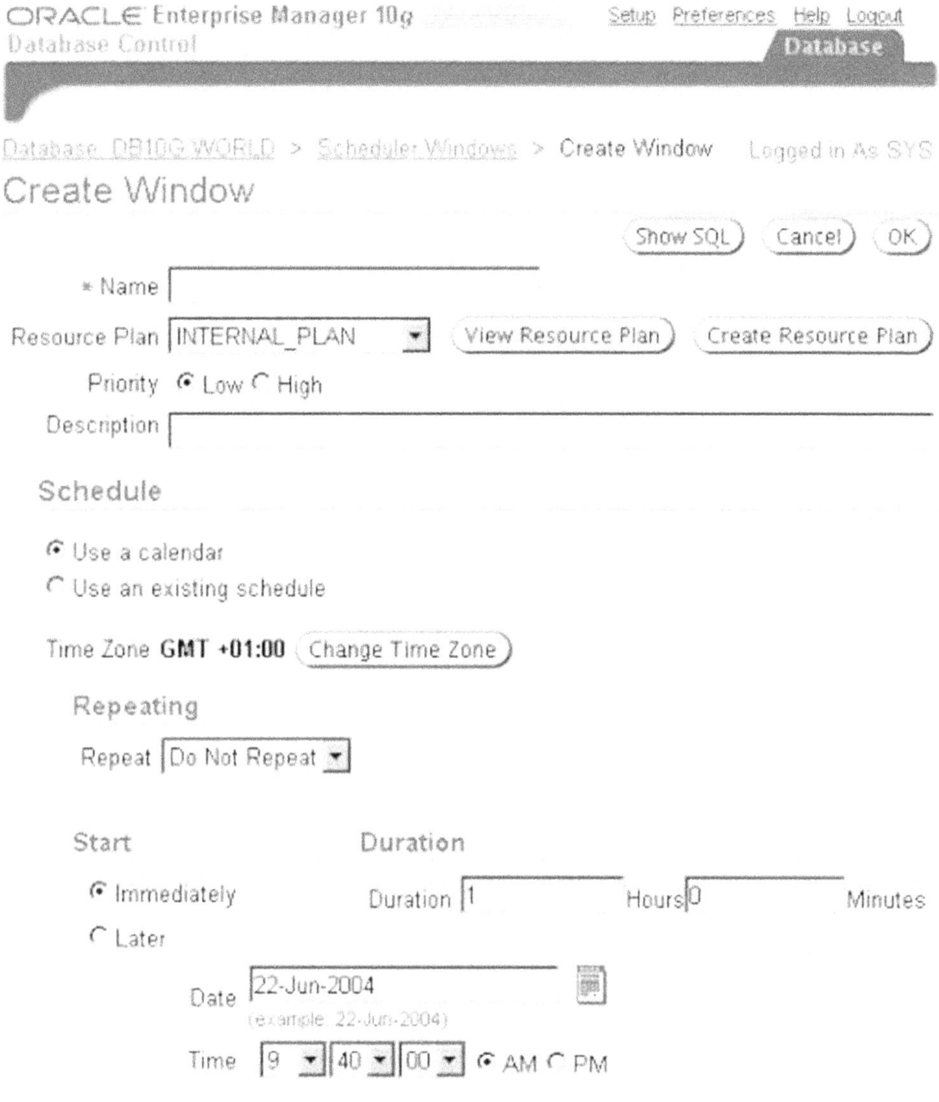

Database DB10G WORLD > Scheduler Windows > Create Window   Logged in As SYS

Create Window

(Show SQL)   (Cancel)   (OK)

* Name [   ]

Resource Plan [INTERNAL_PLAN   ▼]   (View Resource Plan)   (Create Resource Plan)

Priority ⦿ Low ○ High

Description [   ]

Schedule

⦿ Use a calendar
○ Use an existing schedule

Time Zone **GMT +01:00** (Change Time Zone)

Repeating

Repeat [Do Not Repeat ▼]

Start   Duration

⦿ Immediately   Duration [1]   Hours[0]   Minutes
○ Later

Date [22-Jun-2004   ] 🗓
     (example: 22-Jun-2004)

Time [9 ▼][40 ▼][00 ▼] ⦿ AM ○ PM

Figure 11.25: *OEM DB Control: Create Window Group*

Information about window groups can be displayed using the *dba_scheduler_window_groups* and *dba_scheduler_wingroup_members* views. The following script uses both views to display a summary of window group information.

🖫 window_groups.sql

```
prompt
prompt WINDOW GROUPS
prompt --------------

select
    window_group_name,
    enabled,
    number_of_windowS
from
    dba_scheduler_window_groups
;

prompt
prompt WINDOW GROUP MEMBERS
prompt --------------------

select
    window_group_name,
    window_name
from
    dba_scheduler_wingroup_members
;
```

The output from the *window_groups.sql* script shows that the window group was created successfully.

```
SQL> @window_groups

WINDOW GROUPS
-------------

WINDOW_GROUP_NAME                    ENABL NUMBER_OF_WINDOWS
------------------------------------ ----- -----------------
MAINTENANCE_WINDOW_GROUP             TRUE                  2
TEST_WINDOW_GROUP                    TRUE                  2

WINDOW GROUP MEMBERS
--------------------

WINDOW_GROUP_NAME                    WINDOW_NAME
------------------------------------ ----------------------------
MAINTENANCE_WINDOW_GROUP             WEEKEND_WINDOW
MAINTENANCE_WINDOW_GROUP             WEEKNIGHT_WINDOW
TEST_WINDOW_GROUP                    TEST_WINDOW_1
TEST_WINDOW_GROUP                    TEST_WINDOW_2
```

Figure 11.26 shows the Scheduler Window Groups screen in the OEM DB Control.

ORACLE Enterprise Manager 10g
Database Control

Setup Preferences Help Logout

Database

Database OR10G WORLD > Scheduler Window Groups

Logged in As SYS

Scheduler Window Groups

Create

View Edit Delete Create Like ▼ Go

Select	Name	Enabled	Number of Members
⦿	MAINTENANCE_WINDOW_GROUP	TRUE	2
○	TEST_WINDOW_GROUP	TRUE	2

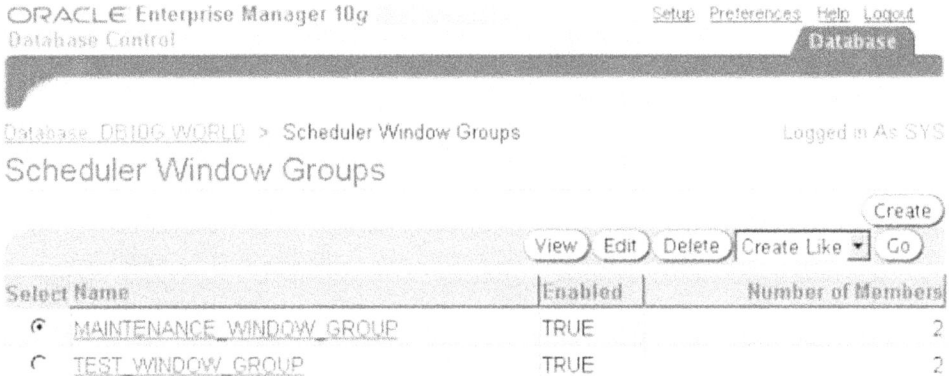

Figure 11.26: *OEM DB Control: Scheduler Window Groups*

Windows can be added and removed from a group using the *add_window_group_member* and *remove_window_group_member* procedures, respectively.

```
PROCEDURE add_window_group_member (

  group_name          IN VARCHAR2,
  window_list         IN VARCHAR2)

PROCEDURE remove_window_group_member (

  group_name          IN VARCHAR2,
  window_list         IN VARCHAR2)
```

The parameters associated with these procedures and their usage are as follows:

- *group_name* - A name that uniquely identifies the window group

- *window_list* - A comma separated list of windows to be added or removed from the window group

The following example creates a new window, adds it to a group and then removes it from the group. Figure 11.27 shows the Edit Window Group screen in the OEM DB Control. Windows can be added and removed from a window group using this screen.

Creating Oracle Jobs

613

Database: DB10G WORLD > Scheduler Window Groups > Edit Window Group: TEST_WINDOW_GROUP

Logged in As SYS

Edit Window Group: TEST_WINDOW_GROUP

Show SQL   Revert   Apply

Name **TEST_WINDOW_GROUP**

Enabled ⦿ Yes ◯ No

Members

Add/Remove Windows

Name	Resource Plan	Enabled	Next Open Date	End Date	Duration (min)	Description
TEST_WINDOW_2		TRUE	Jun 22, 2004 3:00:36 PM		30	Window with an inline schedule
TEST_WINDOW_1		TRUE	Jun 22, 2004 3:00:50 PM		30	Window with a predefined schedule

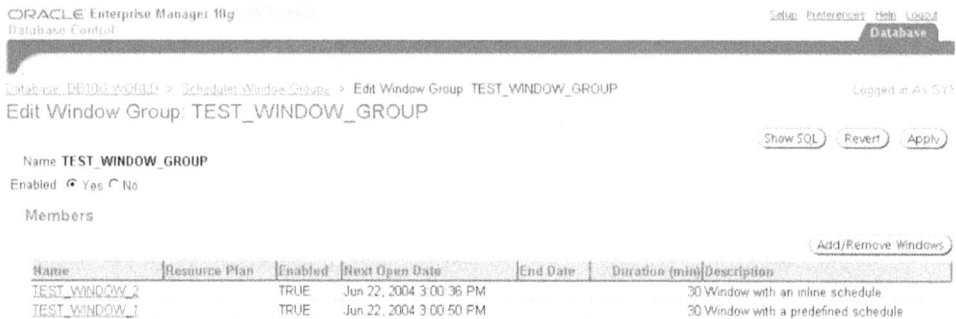

Figure 11.27: *OEM DB Control: Edit Window Group*

Windows groups are removed using the *drop_window_group* procedure.

```
PROCEDURE drop_window_group (
  group_name              IN VARCHAR2,
  force                   IN BOOLEAN DEFAULT FALSE)
```

The parameters associated with this procedure and their usage are as follows:

- *group_name* - A name that uniquely identifies the window group

- *force* - When set to FALSE, an error is produced if any jobs reference the specified window group. When set to TRUE, any dependent jobs are disabled.

The following example shows how to drop a window group:

```
BEGIN
  DBMS_SCHEDULER.drop_window_group (
    group_name => 'test_window_group',
    force       => TRUE);
END;
/
```

The output from the *window_groups.sql* script shows that the window group has been removed.

```
SQL> @window_groups

WINDOW GROUPS
-------------

WINDOW_GROUP_NAME               ENABL NUMBER_OF_WINDOWS
------------------------------- ----- -----------------
MAINTENANCE_WINDOW_GROUP        TRUE                  2


WINDOW GROUP MEMBERS
```

```
-------------------

WINDOW_GROUP_NAME                WINDOW_NAME
-------------------------------  ------------------------------
MAINTENANCE_WINDOW_GROUP         WEEKEND_WINDOW
MAINTENANCE_WINDOW_GROUP         WEEKNIGHT_WINDOW
```

The following section will explain common procedures and functions for managing the scheduler objects that have been created.

Enabling, Disabling and Setting Attributes of Scheduler Objects

All applicable scheduler objects can be enabled and disabled using the enable and disable procedures, respectively.

```
PROCEDURE disable(

  name                    IN VARCHAR2,
  force                   IN BOOLEAN DEFAULT FALSE)

PROCEDURE enable(

  name                    IN VARCHAR2)
```

The parameters associated with these procedures and their usage are as follows:

- *name* - A name that uniquely identifies the scheduler object: program, job, window, or window group

- *force* - When set to FALSE, an error is produced if the object has any dependants. When set to TRUE, the object is disabled, but any dependants remain unaltered.

The following example shows their usage:

```
BEGIN
  -- Enable programs and jobs.
  DBMS_SCHEDULER.enable (
    name  => 'test_stored_procedure_prog');

  DBMS_SCHEDULER.enable (
    name  => 'test_full_job_definition');

  -- Disable programs and jobs.
  DBMS_SCHEDULER.disable (
    name  => 'test_stored_procedure_prog',
    force => TRUE);
```

```
    DBMS_SCHEDULER.disable (
      name  => 'test_full_job_definition',
      force => TRUE);
END;
/
```

The values for individual attributes of all scheduler objects can be altered using one of the *set_attribute* overloads.

```
BEGIN
  DBMS_SCHEDULER.set_attribute (
    name      => 'test_hourly_schedule',
    attribute => 'repeat_interval',
    value     => 'freq=hourly; byminute=30');
END;
/
```

Attribute values are set to NULL using the *set_attribute_null* procedures.

```
BEGIN
  DBMS_SCHEDULER.set_attribute_null (
    name      => 'test_hourly_schedule',
    attribute => 'repeat_interval');
END;
/
```

Since the creation and maintenance of the scheduler objects has been explained in the previous section, discovering how to identify which dictionary views are available to view information about them will be presented in the following section.

Time-based Job Scheduling

In order to understand how repeat intervals of jobs are specified, a review of how Oracle handles date-time information is warranted. This section will present information on how to use dates, timestamps and intervals along with the Oracle calendar syntax to define repeat intervals for scheduled jobs.

The use of the DATE datatype used by the *dbms_job* package will be examined in the following section.

Setting Job Execution Dates

The DATE datatype is used by Oracle to store all datetime information in which a precision greater than one second is not needed. Oracle uses a seven-byte binary date format which allows Julian dates to be stored within the range of 01-Jan-4712 BC to 31-Dec-4712 AD. Table 11.4 shows how each of the seven bytes is used to store the date information:

BYTE	MEANING	NOTATION	EXAMPLE (10-JUL-2004 17:21:30)
1	Century	Divided by 100, excess-100	120
2	Year	Modulo 100, excess-100	104
3	Month	0 base	7
4	Day	0 base	10
5	Hour	excess-1	18
6	Minute	excess-1	22
7	Second	excess-1	31

Table 11.4: *Seven bytes Used to Store the Date Information*

The following example uses the *dump* function to show the contents of a stored date:

```
alter session set nls_date_format = 'DD-MON-YYYY HH24:MI:SS';

drop table date_test;

create table date_test as
select
   sysdate as now
from
   dual
;

select
   now,
   dump (now)
from
   date_test
;

NOW
------------------
DUMP(NOW)
----------------------------------------
10-JUL-2004 17:21:30
Typ=12 Len=7: 120,104,7,10,18,22,31
```

When comparing the *date* and *dump* values, subtracting 100 from the century component, then multiplying the resulting value by 100 gives a value of 2000. Subtracting the 100 from the year component gives a value of 4. The month and day components need no modification, while subtracting one from the hour, minute and second components (18, 22 and 31) give values of 17, 21 and 30.

Jobs scheduled using the *dbms_job* package use dates to define time related information, as seen in the *dbms_job.submit* procedure and the *dba_jobs* view shown below.

```
PROCEDURE submit (

   job        OUT BINARY_INTEGER,
   what       IN  VARCHAR2,
   next_date  IN  DATE DEFAULT sysdate,
   interval   IN  VARCHAR2 DEFAULT 'null',
   no_parse   IN  BOOLEAN DEFAULT FALSE,
   instance   IN  BINARY_INTEGER DEFAULT 0,
   force      IN  BOOLEAN DEFAULT FALSE)


SQL> describe dba_jobs

Name                            Null?     Type
------------------------------- --------- -------------------------
JOB                             NOT NULL  NUMBER
LOG_USER                        NOT NULL  VARCHAR2(30)
PRIV_USER                       NOT NULL  VARCHAR2(30)
SCHEMA_USER                     NOT NULL  VARCHAR2(30)
LAST_DATE                                 DATE
LAST_SEC                                  VARCHAR2(8)
THIS_DATE                                 DATE
THIS_SEC                                  VARCHAR2(8)
NEXT_DATE                       NOT NULL  DATE
NEXT_SEC                                  VARCHAR2(8)
TOTAL_TIME                                NUMBER
BROKEN                                    VARCHAR2(1)
INTERVAL                        NOT NULL  VARCHAR2(200)
FAILURES                                  NUMBER
WHAT                                      VARCHAR2(4000)
NLS_ENV                                   VARCHAR2(4000)
MISC_ENV                                  RAW(32)
INSTANCE                                  NUMBER
```

It is also the datatype that must be returned by the expression defined in the *interval* parameter of jobs scheduled using the *dbms_job* package.

Since dates are actually numbers, certain simple mathematical operations can be performed on them. Adding a whole number to a date is like adding the equivalent number of days, while adding a fraction to a date is like adding that fraction of a day to the date. The same is true in reverse for subtraction.

Table 11.5 below shows how each specific time period can be calculated. All three expressions equate to the same value, thereby allowing the DBA to pick a preferred method.

PERIOD	EXPRESSION 1	EXPRESSION 2	EXPRESSION 3	VALUE
1 Day	1	1	1	1
1 Hour	1/24	1/24	1/24	.041666667
1 Minute	1/24/60	1/(24*60)	1/1440	.000694444
1 Second	1/24/60/60	1/(24*60*60)	1/86400	.000011574

Table 11.5: *Methods of Time Period Calculation*

The following query shows how these expressions might be used to modify the value of the current operating system date:

```
alter session set nls_date_format='DD/MM/YYYY HH24:MI:SS';

select
   sysdate as current_date,
   sysdate + 1 as plus_1_day,
   sysdate + 2/24 as plus_2_hours,
   sysdate + 10/24/60 as plus_10_minutes,
   sysdate + 30/24/60/60 as plus_30_seconds
from
   dual;

alter session set nls_date_format='DD-MON-YYYY HH24:MI:SS';
```

The results of this query are listed below.

```
CURRENT_DATE         PLUS_1_DAY           PLUS_2_HOURS         PLUS_10_MINUTES
PLUS_30_SECONDS
-------------------  -------------------  -------------------  --------
10/07/2004 17:57:30 11/07/2004 17:57:30 10/07/2004 19:57:30 10/07/2004
18:07:30 10/07/2004 17:58:00
```

This introduction to the DATE datatype is a good foundation for the information presented on the TIMESTAMP datatype in the following section. The TIMESTAMP datatype is similar to the DATE datatype in many ways.

Intervals and Interval Literals

Intervals provide a way of storing a specific period of time that separates two datetime values. There is no need to store any intervals to use the Oracle scheduler, but an explanation of them will help put the information on interval literals into context.

There are currently two supported types of intervals. One specifies intervals in years and months, and the other specifies intervals in days, hours, minutes and seconds. The syntax of these datatypes is shown below.

```
INTERVAL YEAR [(year_precision)] TO MONTH
INTERVAL DAY [(day_precision)] TO SECOND [(fractional_seconds_precision)]
```

The precision elements are defined as follows:

- *year_precision* - The maximum number of digits in the year component of the interval, such that a precision of three limits the interval to a maximum of 999 years. The default value is two.

- *day_precision* - The maximum number of digits in the day component of the interval, such that a precision of four limits the interval to a maximum of 9999 days. The day precision can accept a value from zero to nine with the default value being two.

- *fraction_second_precision* - The number of digits in the fractional component of the interval. Values between zero and nine are allowed with the default value being six.

In the following example, a table is created to show how intervals can be used as column definitions:

```
create table test_interval_table (
  id             number(10),
  time_period_1  interval year to month,
  time_period_2  interval day to second,
  time_period_3  interval year (3) to month,
  time_period_4  interval day (4) to second (9)
);

SQL> describe test_interval_table

 Name                            Null?    Type
 ------------------------------- -------- ------------------------
 ID                                       NUMBER(10)
 TIME_PERIOD_1                            INTERVAL YEAR(2) TO MONTH
 TIME_PERIOD_2                            INTERVAL DAY(2) TO SECOND(6)
 TIME_PERIOD_3                            INTERVAL YEAR(3) TO MONTH
 TIME_PERIOD_4                            INTERVAL DAY(4) TO SECOND(9)
```

Interval literals are used to define intervals in an easy to understand manner. There are two separate syntax definitions, one for each type of interval. The full syntax definitions can be a little confusing, so they will be skipped in favor of examples that make their usage more clear.

The YEAR TO MONTH interval literal syntax will be presented first. The default precision for the fields is listed below along with the allowable values if specified as a trailing field.

- **YEAR** - Number of years with a default precision of two digits

- **MONTH** - Number of months with a default precision of four digits. If specified as a trailing field, it has allowable values of zero to 11.

INTERVAL LITERAL	MEANING
INTERVAL '21-2' YEAR TO MONTH	An interval of 21 years and two months
INTERVAL '100-5' YEAR(3) TO MONTH	An interval of 100 years and five months. The leading precision is specified, as it is greater than the default of two.
INTERVAL '1' YEAR	An interval of one year
INTERVAL '20' MONTH	An interval of 20 months
INTERVAL '100' YEAR(3)	An interval of 100 years. The precision must be specified as this value is beyond the default precision.
INTERVAL '10000' MONTH(5)	An interval of 10,000 months. The precision must be specified as this value is beyond the default precision.
INTERVAL '1-13' YEAR TO MONTH	Error produced. When the leading field is YEAR the allowable values for MONTH are zero to 11.

Table 11.6: *YEAR TO MONTH Intervals and Their Meanings*

These intervals from Table 11.6 can be tested by substituting them into the following query. The month syntax is converted into a years and months value.

```
select
   interval '20' month
from
   dual
;


INTERVAL'20'MONTH
-------------------------------------------------------------------
+01-08
```

A YEAR TO MONTH interval can be added to or subtracted from with the result being another YEAR TO MONTH interval.

```
select
   interval '1' year - interval '1' month
from
   dual
;
INTERVAL'1'YEAR-INTERVAL'1'MONTH
------------------------------------------------------------------
+000000000-11
```

The following examples relate to the DAY TO SECOND interval literal syntax. As with the previous example, if a trailing field is specified, it must be less significant than the previous field.

- **DAY** - Number of days with a default precision of two digits

- **HOUR** - Number of hours with a default precision of three digits. If specified as a trailing field, it has allowable values of zero to 23.

- **MINUTE** - Number of minutes with a default precision of five digits. If specified as a trailing field, it has allowable values of zero to 59.

- **SECOND** - Number of seconds with a default precision of seven digits before the decimal point and six digits after. If specified as a trailing field, it has allowable values of zero to 59.999999999.

INTERVA LITERAL	MEANING
INTERVAL '2 3:04:11.333' DAY TO SECOND(3)	2 days, 3 hours, 4 minutes, 11 seconds and 333 thousandths of a second
INTERVAL '2 3:04' DAY TO MINUTE	2 days, 3 hours, 4 minutes
INTERVAL '2 3' DAY TO HOUR	2 days, 3 hours
INTERVAL '2' DAY	2 days
INTERVAL '03:04:11.333' HOUR TO SECOND	3 hours, 4 minutes, 11 seconds and 333 thousandths of a second
INTERVAL '03:04' HOUR TO MINUTE	3 hours, 4 minutes
INTERVAL '40' HOUR	40 hours
INTERVAL '04:11.333' MINUTE TO SECOND	4 minutes, 11 seconds and 333 thousandths of a second
INTERVAL '70' MINUTE	70 minutes
INTERVAL '70' SECOND	70 seconds

INTERVA LITERAL	MEANING
INTERVAL '03:70' HOUR TO MINUTE	Error produced. When the leading field is specified, the allowable values for the trailing field must be within normal range.

Table 11.7: *DAY TO SECOND Intervals and Their Meanings*

Substituting the intervals from Table 11.7 into the following query will allow those intervals to be tested. The default precision for seconds is used because it has not been to three decimal places.

```
select
   interval '2 3:04:11.333' day to second
from
   dual
;

INTERVAL'23:04:11.333'DAYTOSECOND
-----------------------------------------------------------------
+02 03:04:11.333000
```

A DAY TO SECOND interval can be added to or subtracted from with the result being another DAY TO SECOND interval.

```
select
   interval '1' day - interval '1' second
from
   dual
;

INTERVAL'1'DAY-INTERVAL'1'SECOND
-----------------------------------------------------------------
+000000000 23:59:59.000000000
```

Intervals can also be combined with dates to manipulate date values. The following query shows how this is done:

```
select
   sysdate,
   sysdate + interval '1' month + interval '1' day - interval '3' second
from
   dual
;

SYSDATE              SYSDATE+INTERVAL'1'M
-------------------- --------------------
10-JUL-2004 19:55:53 11-AUG-2004 19:55:50
```

Now that the groundwork for using PL/SQL expressions has been covered, the calendaring syntax available in Oracle will be presented in the following section.

Calendar Syntax in Oracle Job Scheduling

Oracle introduced a calendar syntax, allowing complex job execution cycles to be defined in a simple and clear manner. The calendar syntax is listed below:

```
repeat_interval = freq=?
  [; interval=?] [; bymonth=?] [; byweekno=?]
  [; byyearday=?] [; bymonthday=?] [; byday=?]
  [; byhour=?] [; byminute=?] [; bysecond=?]
```

Before investigating what the individual clauses of this syntax mean, how the calendar strings can be tested should be explained. The *evaluate_calendar_string* procedure from the *dbms_scheduler* package returns run timestamps by evaluating a specified calendar string.

```
PROCEDURE evaluate_calendar_string (

   calendar_string    IN  VACRHAR2,
   start_date         IN  TIMESTAMP WITH TIME ZONE,
   return_date_after  IN  TIMESTAMP WITH TIME ZONE,
   next_run_date      OUT TIMESTAMP WITH TIME ZONE);
```

The parameters associated with this procedure and their usage are as follows:

- *calendar_string* - The calendar string to be evaluated

- *start_date* - The date the calendar string becomes valid. If elements of the calendar string are missing, they may be derived from elements of this date.

- *return_after_date* - Only dates after this date will be returned by the procedure. If no date is specified, the current systimestamp is used.

- *next_run_date* - The first date that matches the *calendar_string* and *start_date* and is greater than the *run_after_date*

The *test_calendar_string.sql* procedure listed below uses the *evaluate_calendar_string* procedure to display a list of run dates. For convenience, the *start_date* and *run_after_date* parameters are defaulted.

```
set serveroutput on;
alter session set nls_timestamp_format = 'DD-MON-YYYY HH24:MI:SS';

CREATE OR REPLACE PROCEDURE test_calendar_string(
  p_calendar_string  IN  VARCHAR2,
  p_iterations       IN  NUMBER DEFAULT 5)
AS
  l_start_date            TIMESTAMP := TO_TIMESTAMP('01-JAN-2004 03:04:32',
                                                    'DD-MON-YYYY HH24:MI:SS');

  l_return_date_after  TIMESTAMP := l_start_date;
  l_next_run_date      TIMESTAMP;
BEGIN
  FOR i IN 1 .. p_iterations LOOP
    DBMS_SCHEDULER.evaluate_calendar_string (
      calendar_string   => p_calendar_string,
      start_date        => l_start_date,
      return_date_after => l_return_date_after,
      next_run_date     => l_next_run_date);
    DBMS_OUTPUT.put_line('Next Run Date: ' || l_next_run_date);
    l_return_date_after := l_next_run_date;
  END LOOP;
END;
/
```

The following points contain general guidance information for the use of calendar syntax during scheduling:

- The calendar string must contain a frequency as the first clause. All other clauses are optional and can be placed in any order.

- Each clause can only be present once and must be separated by a semicolon.

- The calendar strings are not case sensitive and white spaces between clauses are allowed.

- Where a BY clause contains a list of values, the order of the list is not important.

- When there are not enough clauses to determine the precise run date, the missing clauses are derived from the *start_date*. For example, if there is no bysecond clause in the calendar string, the value of seconds from the *start_date* is used to create one.

- When a number range is not fixed, the last value of the range can be determined using a negative integer as a countback. As such, *bymonthday=-1* equates to the last day of the month. The documentation states that countbacks are not supported for fixed number ranges such as those used by the *bymonth*, *byhour*, *byminute* and *bysecond* clauses, but they do appear to work consistently.

- The first day of the week is Monday.

- A calendar string cannot specify time zones. Instead, the time zone is derived from one of the following places in this order: the *start_date*, the current session's time zone, the DEFAULT_TIMEZONE scheduler attribute, or the time zone returned by the *systimestamp* function.

Now that calendar syntax has been introduced in detail, the following section will compare the use of PL/SQL expressions and the use of calendar syntax for scheduling jobs.

Complex Date Rules for Job Execution

Prior to Oracle, the only way to define a job's repeat interval was to use a PL/SQL expression that evaluated to a date. In Oracle, the calendar syntax is the preferred way to define a job's repeat interval, although PL/SQL expression can still be used if they evaluate to a timestamp. In this section, each method will be covered and compared.

The previous section used the *test_calendar_string.sql* procedure to display the run schedule expected for a specific calendar string. Before any comparisons between the possible scheduling methods can be done, a way to test the PL/SQL expressions that are used to schedule jobs using dates and timestamps is needed. The *test_date_string* procedure listed below is similar to the *test_calendar_string* procedure, but it displays run dates defined by interval strings that might be used when scheduling jobs via the *dbms_job* package.

🔲 test_date_string.sql

```
set serveroutput on;
alter session set nls_date_format = 'DD-MON-YYYY HH24:MI:SS';

CREATE OR REPLACE PROCEDURE test_date_string(
  p_interval     IN  VARCHAR2,
  p_iterations   IN  NUMBER DEFAULT 5)
AS
  l_interval          VARCHAR2(1000) := p_interval;
  l_start_date        DATE := TO_DATE('01-JAN-2004 03:04:32',
                                      'DD-MON-YYYY HH24:MI:SS');
  l_next_run_date     DATE;
  l_start_date_str    VARCHAR2(100);
BEGIN
  FOR i IN 1 .. p_iterations LOOP
```

```
        l_start_date_str := 'TO_DATE(''' ||
                            TO_CHAR(l_start_date, 'DD-MON-YYYY HH24:MI:SS') ||
                            ''',''DD-MON-YYYY HH24:MI:SS'')';
        l_interval := REPLACE(LOWER(p_interval), 'sysdate', l_start_date_str);
        EXECUTE IMMEDIATE 'SELECT ' || l_interval || ' INTO :return FROM dual'
          INTO l_next_run_date;

        DBMS_OUTPUT.put_line('Next Run Date: ' || l_next_run_date);
        l_start_date := l_next_run_date;
    END LOOP;
END;
/
```

The *test_timestamp_string* procedure listed below is a copy of the *test_date_string*
procedure that has been adjusted to work with timestamps.

🖫 test_timestamp_string.sql

```
set serveroutput on;
alter session set nls_timestamp_format = 'DD-MON-YYYY HH24:MI:SS';

CREATE OR REPLACE PROCEDURE test_timestamp_string(
  p_interval    IN   VARCHAR2,
  p_iterations  IN   NUMBER DEFAULT 5)
AS
  l_interval        VARCHAR2(1000) := p_interval;
  l_start_ts        TIMESTAMP := TO_TIMESTAMP('01-JAN-2004 03:04:32',
                                              'DD-MON-YYYY HH24:MI:SS');

  l_next_run_ts     TIMESTAMP;
  l_start_ts_str    VARCHAR2(100);
BEGIN
  FOR i IN 1 .. p_iterations LOOP
    l_start_ts_str := 'TO_TIMESTAMP(''' ||
                      TO_CHAR(l_start_ts, 'DD-MON-YYYY HH24:MI:SS') ||
                      ''',''DD-MON-YYYY HH24:MI:SS'')';
    l_interval := REPLACE(LOWER(p_interval), 'systimestamp',
l_start_ts_str);
    EXECUTE IMMEDIATE 'SELECT ' || l_interval || ' INTO :return FROM dual'
      INTO l_next_run_ts;

    DBMS_OUTPUT.put_line('Next Run Date: ' || l_next_run_ts);
    l_start_ts := l_next_run_ts;
  END LOOP;
END;
/
```

The best way to come to grips with defining repeat intervals and comparing
the different methods available is looking at some examples. Table 11.8 lists a
range of repeat intervals along with expressions than can be used to achieve
them.

The date expressions can be used to schedule jobs using the *dbms_job* package
and the timestamp and calendar syntax expressions can be used for jobs

---

Complex Date Rules for Job Execution

scheduled using the *dbms_scheduler* package in Oracle. Where possible, a literal and interval literal example is given along with an example of the output generated by the test procedures.

INTERVAL	EXPRESSION

Every day	'sysdate + 1'
	'systimestamp + 1'
	
	'sysdate + interval "1" day'
	'systimestamp + interval "1" day'
	
	'freq=daily;'
	
	<pre>Next Run Date: 02-JAN-2004 03:04:32
	Next Run Date: 03-JAN-2004 03:04:32
	Next Run Date: 04-JAN-2004 03:04:32
	Next Run Date: 05-JAN-2004 03:04:32
	Next Run Date: 06-JAN-2004 03:04:32</pre>

Midnight every night	'trunc(sysdate) + 1'
	'trunc(systimestamp) + 1'
	
	'trunc(sysdate) + interval "1" day'
	'trunc(systimestamp) + interval "1" day'
	
	'freq=daily; byhour=0; byminute=0; bysecond=0;'
	
	<pre>Next Run Date: 02-JAN-2004 00:00:00
	Next Run Date: 03-JAN-2004 00:00:00
	Next Run Date: 04-JAN-2004 00:00:00
	Next Run Date: 05-JAN-2004 00:00:00
	Next Run Date: 06-JAN-2004 00:00:00</pre>

6:00 AM every day	'trunc(sysdate) + 1 + 6/24'
	'trunc(systimestamp) + 1 + 6/24'
	
	'trunc(sysdate) + interval "1 6" day to hour '
	'trunc(systimestamp) + interval "1 6" day to hour'
	
	'freq=daily; byhour=6; byminute=0; bysecond=0;'
	
	<pre>Next Run Date: 01-JAN-2004 06:00:00
	Next Run Date: 02-JAN-2004 06:00:00
	Next Run Date: 03-JAN-2004 06:00:00
	Next Run Date: 04-JAN-2004 06:00:00
	Next Run Date: 05-JAN-2004 06:00:00</pre>

INTERVAL	EXPRESSION
Every hour	'sysdate + 1/24' 'systimestamp + 1/24' 'sysdate + interval "1" hour' 'systimestamp + interval "1" hour' 'freq=hourly;' ``` Next Run Date: 01-JAN-2004 04:04:32 Next Run Date: 01-JAN-2004 05:04:32 Next Run Date: 01-JAN-2004 06:04:32 Next Run Date: 01-JAN-2004 07:04:32 Next Run Date: 01-JAN-2004 08:04:32 ```
Every hour, on the hour	'trunc(sysdate, "HH24") + 1/24' 'trunc(systimestamp, "HH24") + 1/24' 'trunc(sysdate, "HH24") + interval "1" hour' 'trunc(systimestamp, "HH24") + interval "1" hour' 'freq=hourly; byminute=0; bysecond=0;' ``` Next Run Date: 01-JAN-2004 04:00:00 Next Run Date: 01-JAN-2004 05:00:00 Next Run Date: 01-JAN-2004 06:00:00 Next Run Date: 01-JAN-2004 07:00:00 Next Run Date: 01-JAN-2004 08:00:00 ```
Every minute	'sysdate + 1/24/60' 'systimestamp + 1/24/60' 'sysdate + interval "1" minute' 'systimestamp + interval "1" minute' 'freq=minutely;' ``` Next Run Date: 01-JAN-2004 03:05:32 Next Run Date: 01-JAN-2004 03:06:32 Next Run Date: 01-JAN-2004 03:07:32 Next Run Date: 01-JAN-2004 03:08:32 Next Run Date: 01-JAN-2004 03:09:32 ```

INTERVAL	EXPRESSION

Every minute, on the minute	'trunc(sysdate, ''MI'') + 1/24/60'
	'trunc(systimestamp, ''MI'') + 1/24/60'
	
	'trunc(sysdate, ''MI'') + interval ''1'' minute'
	'trunc(systimestamp, ''MI'') + interval ''1'' minute'
	
	'freq=minutely; bysecond=0;'
	
	`Next Run Date: 01-JAN-2004 03:05:00`
	`Next Run Date: 01-JAN-2004 03:06:00`
	`Next Run Date: 01-JAN-2004 03:07:00`
	`Next Run Date: 01-JAN-2004 03:08:00`
	`Next Run Date: 01-JAN-2004 03:09:00`

Every hour	'sysdate + 1/24'
	'systimestamp + 1/24'
	
	'sysdate + interval ''1'' hour'
	'systimestamp + interval ''1'' hour'
	
	'freq=hourly;'
	
	`Next Run Date: 01-JAN-2004 04:04:32`
	`Next Run Date: 01-JAN-2004 05:04:32`
	`Next Run Date: 01-JAN-2004 06:04:32`
	`Next Run Date: 01-JAN-2004 07:04:32`
	`Next Run Date: 01-JAN-2004 08:04:32`

Every hour, on the hour	'trunc(sysdate, ''HH24'') + 1/24'
	'trunc(systimestamp, ''HH24'') + 1/24'
	
	'trunc(sysdate, ''HH24'') + interval ''1'' hour'
	'trunc(systimestamp, ''HH24'') + interval ''1'' hour'
	
	'freq=hourly; byminute=0; bysecond=0;'
	
	`Next Run Date: 01-JAN-2004 04:00:00`
	`Next Run Date: 01-JAN-2004 05:00:00`
	`Next Run Date: 01-JAN-2004 06:00:00`
	`Next Run Date: 01-JAN-2004 07:00:00`
	`Next Run Date: 01-JAN-2004 08:00:00`

INTERVAL	EXPRESSION

Every Monday at 9:00 AM	'trunc(next_day(sysdate, ''MONDAY'')) + 9/24'
	'trunc(next_day(systimestamp, ''MONDAY'')) + 9/24'
	
	'trunc(next_day(sysdate, ''MONDAY'')) + interval ''9'' hour'
	'trunc(next_day(systimestamp, ''MONDAY'')) + interval ''9''hour'
	
	'freq=weekly; byday=mon; byhour=9; byminute=0; bysecond=0;'
	
	`Next Run Date: 05-JAN-2004 09:00:00`
	`Next Run Date: 12-JAN-2004 09:00:00`
	`Next Run Date: 19-JAN-2004 09:00:00`
	`Next Run Date: 26-JAN-2004 09:00:00`
	`Next Run Date: 02-FEB-2004 09:00:00`

Every Monday, Wednesday and Friday at 6:00 AM	'trunc(least(next_day(sysdate, ''monday''), next_day(sysdate, ''wednesday''), next_day(sysdate, ''friday''))) + (6/24)'
	
	'trunc(least(next_day(systimestamp, ''monday''), next_day(systimestamp, ''wednesday''), next_day(systimestamp, ''friday''))) + (6/24)'
	
	'trunc(least(next_day(sysdate,''monday''), next_day(sysdate, ''wednesday''), next_day(sysdate, ''friday''))) + interval ''6'' hour'
	
	'trunc(least(next_day(systimestamp, ''monday''), next_day(systimestamp, ''wednesday''), next_day(systimestamp, ''friday''))) + interval ''6'' hour'
	
	'freq=weekly; byday=mon,wed,fri; byhour=6; byminute=0; bysecond=0;'
	
	`Next Run Date: 02-JAN-2004 06:00:00`
	`Next Run Date: 05-JAN-2004 06:00:00`
	`Next Run Date: 07-JAN-2004 06:00:00`
	`Next Run Date: 09-JAN-2004 06:00:00`
	`Next Run Date: 12-JAN-2004 06:00:00`

INTERVAL	EXPRESSION
First Monday of each quarter	'next_day(add_months(trunc(sysdate, "q"), 3), "monday")' 'next_day(add_months(trunc(systimestamp, "q"), 3), "monday")'
	'freq=monthly; bymonth=1,4,7,10; byday=1mon'

```
Next Run Date: 05-APR-2004 00:00:00
Next Run Date: 05-JUL-2004 00:00:00
Next Run Date: 04-OCT-2004 00:00:00
Next Run Date: 03-JAN-2005 00:00:00
Next Run Date: 04-APR-2005 00:00:00
```

Table 11.8: *Repeat Intervals with Their Expressions*

It would appear that all of the above expressions give exactly the same run schedule regardless of which syntax is used. In practice this not true because PL/SQL expressions can allow the run schedules of jobs to slide.

The scheduler attempts to execute all jobs on time, but in practice there is often a small delay. When a job is executed, the first thing that happens is the next run date is calculated using the specified repeat interval. Since most PL/SQL expressions use either the *sysdate* or *systimestamp* functions, the actual start date may be slightly later than the job's original next run date. Over several iterations of the job, this could add up to a noticeable difference between the times the job is expected to run and when it actually does run.

Table 11.9 gives an example of the sort of slide that might be seen if the scheduler is consistently ten seconds late in executing a job that was originally intended to run a 09:00:00 each day.

RUN	ACTUAL START DATE	NEXT RUN DATE
1	01-JAN-2004 09:00:10	02-JAN-2004 09:00:10
2	02-JAN-2004 09:00:20	03-JAN-2004 09:00:20
3	03-JAN-2004 09:00:30	04-JAN-2004 09:00:30
4	04-JAN-2004 09:00:40	05-JAN-2004 09:00:40
5	05-JAN-2004 09:00:50	06-JAN-2004 09:00:50
6	06-JAN-2004 09:01:00	07-JAN-2004 09:01:00

Table 11.9: *The Time Slide Phenomenon*

This issue becomes even more noticeable on shorter repeat intervals such as hourly runs. This behavior can be prevented by always defining PL/SQL expressions that result in a specific time rather than one relative to the current time. This is typically done using the *trunc* and *round* functions to remove the variable components. For example, 'trunc(sysdate) + 1 + 6/24' is always 06:00 tomorrow morning no matter what time it is evaluated because the time component has been truncated. The earlier examples regularly make use of the *trunc* function for the same reason.

The calendar syntax does not suffer from the problem of sliding schedules as the repeat intervals it defines are always time specific. If a component of the calendar string is not defined explicitly, it is defaulted using values from the start date specified when the job or schedule was defined. For example, a schedule with a start date of 01-JAN-2004 09:45:31 and a calendar string with no *byminute* clause would actually be assigned *byminute=45*. As a result, every *next_run_date* evaluated using this schedule would have a value of 45 minutes past the hour.

Sometimes it is either not possible or very difficult to define a repeat interval using the calendar syntax or a PL/SQL expression. In these situations, it might be easier to use a database function which returns a date or timestamp as required. The *my_schedule_function.sql* script creates a function which returns a different time interval depending on the contents of the database.

🖫 my_schedule_function.sql

```
-- Requires the following grant:
--    grant select on v_$database to job_user;
-- ************************************************************

CREATE OR REPLACE FUNCTION my_schedule_function (
  p_timestamp  IN  TIMESTAMP)
  RETURN TIMESTAMP
AS
  l_db_name     v$database.name%TYPE;
  l_timestamp   TIMESTAMP;
BEGIN
  SELECT name
  INTO   l_db_name
  FROM   v$database;

  CASE l_db_name
    WHEN 'PROD' THEN l_timestamp := p_timestamp + INTERVAL '10' MINUTE;
    WHEN 'TEST' THEN l_timestamp := p_timestamp + INTERVAL '1' HOUR;
    ELSE l_timestamp := p_timestamp + INTERVAL '1' DAY;
  END CASE;
```

```
    RETURN l_timestamp;
END;
/
```

When this script is run against the development environment with a database name of DB10G, the following run schedule is produced:

```
SQL1> exec test_timestamp_string('my_schedule_function(systimestamp)');

Next Run Date: 02-JAN-2004 03:04:32
Next Run Date: 03-JAN-2004 03:04:32
Next Run Date: 04-JAN-2004 03:04:32
Next Run Date: 05-JAN-2004 03:04:32
Next Run Date: 06-JAN-2004 03:04:32

PL/SQL procedure successfully completed.
```

The same result could be achieved by running a different schedule in each environment, but it serves to illustrate the point.

It should now be obvious that there is an almost limitless combination of possible calendar string and PL/SQL expression variations. The only way to become really confident with repeat intervals is to try as many variations as possible. The test procedures presented in this section will allow this to be done without having to actually schedule jobs and this, in turn, will save lots of time.

Creating an Oracle Job Chain

Jobs are often defined as individual tasks that are performed in isolation. Yet in some circumstances, a job consists of several tasks that must be performed as a whole in a specific sequence. Typically, this would be accomplished by combining the tasks into a single job like the one defined below.

```
DBMS_SCHEDULER.create_job (
    job_name        => 'single_job',
    job_type        => 'PLSQL_BLOCK',
    job_action      => 'BEGIN
                            task1;
                            task2;
                            task3;
                         END;',
    start_date      => SYSTIMESTAMP,
    repeat_interval => 'freq=daily; byhour=9; byminute=0; bysecond=0;',
    end_date        => NULL,
    enabled         => TRUE,
    comments        => 'Single job.');
```

The problem arises when not all tasks can be performed at the same time. For example, a batch of orders might process at midnight and produce the necessary billing paperwork at 9:00 a.m. If no dependencies are defined between these tasks, any delays in the order processing may result in the generation of the billing paperwork before the orders are complete.

In these circumstances, a job chain needs to be created such that each task in the chain is performed in sequence and the failure of a single task breaks the chain. This can be achieved in many ways, but the following methods are preferred:

- Conditional job creation

- Conditional job enabling

- Conditional job runs using Oracle Advanced Queuing

- Conditional job runs using a custom table solution

Conditional Job Creation

In this method, the first task in the chain is scheduled as a regular repeating job, but all subsequent tasks are not scheduled. Instead, as each task in the chain completes successfully, it schedules the next task as a one-off job.

In the order and billing example, the time between tasks was long and the run times were fixed, excluding delays. An example like this would not be very useful here since it would require a significant amount of time for the chain to complete successfully. Instead, assume that a process made up of three tasks must run in sequence. For the purposes of testing, the times between tasks should be relatively short and instead of fixed times, rolling times should be used.

In this example, each task will simply insert a record into a table, which can be created using the following script:

🖫 **job_chain_table.sql**

```
CREATE TABLE job_chain (
  created_timestamp   TIMESTAMP,
  task_name           VARCHAR2(20)
);
```

The *job_chain_create.sql* script creates a package specification and body that will do all the work for the example job chain.

💾 job_chain_create.sql

```
CREATE OR REPLACE PACKAGE job_chain_create AS

PROCEDURE task_1;
PROCEDURE task_2;
PROCEDURE task_3;

END job_chain_create;
/
SHOW ERRORS

CREATE OR REPLACE PACKAGE BODY job_chain_create AS

-- ------------------------------------------------------------------
PROCEDURE task_1 AS
-- ------------------------------------------------------------------
BEGIN
  DELETE FROM job_chain;
  INSERT INTO job_chain (created_timestamp, task_name)
  VALUES (systimestamp, 'TASK_1');
  COMMIT;

  -- Uncomment the following line to force a failure.
  --RAISE_APPLICATION_ERROR(-20000,
  --   'This is a fake error to prevent task_2 being executed');

  -- The work has comleted successfully so create task_2
  -- Oracle
  DBMS_SCHEDULER.create_job (
    job_name        => 'job_chain_create_task_2',
    job_type        => 'STORED_PROCEDURE',
    job_action      => 'job_chain_create.task_2',
    start_date      => SYSTIMESTAMP + INTERVAL '2' MINUTE,
    repeat_interval => NULL,
    end_date        => NULL,
    enabled         => TRUE,
    comments        => 'Second task in the create chain.');

SHOW ERRORS
```

Both task_1 and task_2 schedule a one-off job once successfully completed. Any exceptions are caught by the exception handler, which does not schedule the next job in the chain.

With the table and code in place, a job to call the first task using the *job_chain_create_job.sql* script can be scheduled.

🔲 job_chain_create_job.sql

```
-- Oracle
BEGIN
  DBMS_SCHEDULER.create_job (
    job_name        => 'job_chain_create_task_1',
    job_type        => 'STORED_PROCEDURE',
    job_action      => 'job_chain_create.task_1',
    start_date      => SYSTIMESTAMP,
    repeat_interval => NULL,
    end_date        => NULL,
    enabled         => TRUE,
    comments        => 'First task in the create chain.');
END;
/

*/
```

The *repeat_interval* (or *interval*) parameter of this job definition is set to NULL, making it a one-off job. Under normal circumstances, this job is expected to be scheduled with a repeat interval since it is the first task in the chain. However, for the purposes of this example, the less clutter on the system the better, so no unnecessary repeating jobs are scheduled.

The progress of the job can be monitored using the following query:

🔲 job_chain_query.sql

```
alter session set nls_timestamp_format = 'DD-MON-YYYY HH24:MI:SS.FF';

set linesize 100
column created_timestamp format a27
column task_name format a20

select
    *
from
    job_chain
order by
    created_timestamp
;
```

On completion of the chain, the following output from the query is expected:

```
SQL> @job_chain_query.sql

CREATED_TIMESTAMP            TASK_NAME
--------------------------   --------------------
07-AUG-2004 10:49:42.701000  TASK_1
07-AUG-2004 10:51:42.858000  TASK_2
07-AUG-2004 10:53:43.093000  TASK_3
```

The result of breaks in the chain can be tested by uncommenting the lines in the code containing the *raise_application_error* procedure calls. Uncommenting this line in task_1 would cause the chain to break during task_1, resulting in the following query output:

```
SQL> @job_chain_query.sql

CREATED_TIMESTAMP           TASK_NAME
--------------------------  --------------------
07-AUG-2004 11:03:11.827000 TASK_1
```

Commenting out the statement in task_1 and uncommenting it in task_2 would cause the chain to break in task_2, resulting in the following query output:

```
SQL> job_chain_query.sql

CREATED_TIMESTAMP           TASK_NAME
--------------------------  --------------------
07-AUG-2004 11:10:42.746000 TASK_1
07-AUG-2004 11:12:42.956000 TASK_2
```

Conditional Job Enabling

In this method, all tasks in the chain are scheduled as regular repeating jobs, but only the first job in the chain is enabled. All subsequent jobs in the chain are disabled or marked as broken prior to Oracle. As each task in the chain completes successfully, it enables the next task in the chain by enabling its associated job. Every time the first task runs, it disables the chain before starting again.

The *job_chain_enable.sql* script creates a package specification and body that will do all the work for the example job chain.

🖫 job_chain_enable.sql

```
CREATE OR REPLACE PACKAGE job_chain_enable AS

PROCEDURE task_1;
PROCEDURE task_2;
PROCEDURE task_3;

END job_chain_enable;
/
SHOW ERRORS
```

```
CREATE OR REPLACE PACKAGE BODY job_chain_enable AS

-- -------------------------------------------------------------------
PROCEDURE task_1 AS
-- -------------------------------------------------------------------
BEGIN

  -- Disable dependent jobs
  -- Oracle
  DBMS_SCHEDULER.disable ('job_chain_enable_task_2');
  DBMS_SCHEDULER.disable ('job_chain_enable_task_3');


  DELETE FROM job_chain;

  INSERT INTO job_chain (created_timestamp, task_name)
  VALUES (systimestamp, 'TASK_1');
  COMMIT;

  -- Uncomment the following line to force a failure.
  --RAISE_APPLICATION_ERROR(-20000,
  --   'This is a fake error to prevent task_2 being executed');

  -- The work has comleted successfully so enable task_2
  -- Oracle
  DBMS_SCHEDULER.enable ('job_chain_enable_task_2');

EXCEPTION
  WHEN OTHERS THEN
    -- Don't enable task_2.
    NULL;
END task_1;
-- -------------------------------------------------------------------


-- -------------------------------------------------------------------
PROCEDURE task_2 AS
-- -------------------------------------------------------------------
BEGIN

  INSERT INTO job_chain (created_timestamp, task_name)
  VALUES (systimestamp, 'TASK_2');
  COMMIT;

  -- Uncomment the following line to force a failure.
  --RAISE_APPLICATION_ERROR(-20000,
  --   'This is a fake error to prevent task_3 being executed');

  -- The work has comleted successfully so enable task_3
  -- Oracle
  DBMS_SCHEDULER.enable ('job_chain_enable_task_3');

EXCEPTION
  WHEN OTHERS THEN
    -- Don't enable task_3.
    NULL;
END task_2;
-- -------------------------------------------------------------------


-- -------------------------------------------------------------------
```

Creating an Oracle Job Chain

639

```
PROCEDURE task_3 AS
-- ----------------------------------------------------------------
BEGIN

  INSERT INTO job_chain (created_timestamp, task_name)
  VALUES (systimestamp, 'TASK_3');
  COMMIT;

END task_3;
-- ----------------------------------------------------------------

END job_chain_enable;
/
SHOW ERRORS
```

Since no jobs are created by the code, they must all be created in advance using the *job_chain_enable_jobs.sql* script. The jobs must persist, so they are generated with repeat intervals. These repeat intervals schedule them to run at 06:00, 12:00 and 18:00 respectively. Commands to remove the jobs are included and should be run once the example is completed.

💾 job_chain_enable_jobs.sql

```
-- Oracle
BEGIN
  DBMS_SCHEDULER.create_job (
    job_name        => 'job_chain_enable_task_1',
    job_type        => 'STORED_PROCEDURE',
    job_action      => 'job_chain_enable.task_1',
    start_date      => SYSTIMESTAMP,
    repeat_interval => 'freq=daily; byhour=6; byminute=0; bysecond=0;',
    end_date        => NULL,
    enabled         => TRUE,
    comments        => 'First task in the enable chain.');
END;
/

BEGIN
  DBMS_SCHEDULER.create_job (
    job_name        => 'job_chain_enable_task_2',
    job_type        => 'STORED_PROCEDURE',
    job_action      => 'job_chain_enable.task_2',
    start_date      => SYSTIMESTAMP,
    repeat_interval => 'freq=daily; byhour=12; byminute=0; bysecond=0;',
    end_date        => NULL,
    enabled         => FALSE,
    comments        => 'Second task in the enable chain.');
END;
/

BEGIN
  DBMS_SCHEDULER.create_job (
    job_name        => 'job_chain_enable_task_3',
    job_type        => 'STORED_PROCEDURE',
    job_action      => 'job_chain_enable.task_3',
```

```
    start_date       => SYSTIMESTAMP,
    repeat_interval  => 'freq=daily; byhour=18; byminute=0; bysecond=0;',
    end_date         => NULL,
    enabled          => FALSE,
    comments         => 'Third task in the enable chain.');
END;
/


-- Cleanup
/*
-- Oracle
BEGIN
  DBMS_SCHEDULER.drop_job ('job_chain_enable_task_3');
  DBMS_SCHEDULER.drop_job ('job_chain_enable_task_2');
  DBMS_SCHEDULER.drop_job ('job_chain_enable_task_1');
END;
/
```

The current job schedules for this example can be queried using the
job_queue_query.sql script listed below.

💾 job_queue_query.sql

```
set feedback off
alter session set nls_date_format = 'DD-MON-YYYY HH24:MI:SS';
alter session set nls_timestamp_format = 'DD-MON-YYYY HH24:MI:SS.FF';
alter session set nls_timestamp_tz_format = 'DD-MON-YYYY HH24:MI:SS.FF
TZH:TZM';
set feedback on

set linesize 100
column created_timestamp format a27
column next_run_date format a34
column next_date format a20

prompt
prompt USER_SCHEDULER_JOBS
select
   job_name,
   enabled,
   next_run_date
from
   user_scheduler_jobs
order by
   job_name;

prompt USER_JOBS
select
   job,
   broken,
   next_date
from
   user_jobs
order by
   job;
```

The output of this script along with the output of the *job_chain_query.sql* script is listed next:

```
SQL> @job_chain_query.sql

no rows selected

SQL> @job_queue_query.sql

USER_SCHEDULER_JOBS

JOB_NAME                    ENABL NEXT_RUN_DATE
--------------------------- ----- -----------------------------------
JOB_CHAIN_ENABLE_TASK_1     TRUE  08-AUG-2004 06:00:00.800000 +01:00
JOB_CHAIN_ENABLE_TASK_2     FALSE
JOB_CHAIN_ENABLE_TASK_3     FALSE

3 rows selected.
```

At this point, the first task is scheduled but has not been executed, hence no results in the *job_chain* table. Rather than waiting until 6:00, it can be forced to run immediately. The results below show that the first task has run and the second job has been enabled.

```
SQL> exec dbms_scheduler.run_job ('job_chain_enable_task_1');

PL/SQL procedure successfully completed.

SQL> @job_queue_query.sql

USER_SCHEDULER_JOBS

JOB_NAME                    ENABL NEXT_RUN_DATE
--------------------------- ----- -----------------------------------
JOB_CHAIN_ENABLE_TASK_1     TRUE  08-AUG-2004 06:00:00.800000 +01:00
JOB_CHAIN_ENABLE_TASK_2     TRUE  08-AUG-2004 12:00:00.200000 +01:00
JOB_CHAIN_ENABLE_TASK_3     FALSE


USER_JOBS

no rows selected

SQL> @job_chain_query.sql
```

```
CREATED_TIMESTAMP          TASK_NAME
-------------------------- --------------------
07-AUG-2004 13:52:28.227000 TASK_1
```

Next, run the second job manually. The results below show that the second task has run and the third job has been enabled.

```
SQL> exec dbms_scheduler.run_job ('job_chain_enable_task_2');

PL/SQL procedure successfully completed.

SQL> @job_chain_query.sql

CREATED_TIMESTAMP          TASK_NAME
-------------------------- --------------------
07-AUG-2004 13:52:28.227000 TASK_1
07-AUG-2004 13:59:16.666000 TASK_2


SQL> @job_queue_query.sql

USER_SCHEDULER_JOBS

JOB_NAME                   ENABL NEXT_RUN_DATE
-------------------------- ----- ----------------------------------
JOB_CHAIN_ENABLE_TASK_1    TRUE  08-AUG-2004 06:00:00.800000 +01:00
JOB_CHAIN_ENABLE_TASK_2    TRUE  08-AUG-2004 12:00:00.200000 +01:00
JOB_CHAIN_ENABLE_TASK_3    TRUE  07-AUG-2004 18:00:00.700000 +01:00


USER_JOBS

no rows selected
```

Next, run the third job manually. The results below show that the third task has run successfully.

```
SQL> exec dbms_scheduler.run_job ('job_chain_enable_task_3');

PL/SQL procedure successfully completed.

SQL> @job_chain_query.sql

CREATED_TIMESTAMP          TASK_NAME
-------------------------- --------------------
07-AUG-2004 13:52:28.227000 TASK_1
07-AUG-2004 13:59:16.666000 TASK_2
07-AUG-2004 14:02:10.948000 TASK_3


SQL> @job_queue_query.sql

USER_SCHEDULER_JOBS

JOB_NAME                   ENABL NEXT_RUN_DATE
```

```
--------------------------- ----- -----------------------------------
JOB_CHAIN_ENABLE_TASK_1      TRUE  08-AUG-2004 06:00:00.800000 +01:00
JOB_CHAIN_ENABLE_TASK_2      TRUE  08-AUG-2004 12:00:00.200000 +01:00
JOB_CHAIN_ENABLE_TASK_3      TRUE  07-AUG-2004 18:00:00.700000 +01:00


USER_JOBS

no rows selected
```

Finally, run the first job again to see that the subsequent jobs have been enabled or disabled appropriately.

```
SQL> exec dbms_scheduler.run_job ('job_chain_enable_task_1');

PL/SQL procedure successfully completed.

SQL> @job_chain_query.sql

CREATED_TIMESTAMP          TASK_NAME
-------------------------- --------------------
07-AUG-2004 14:03:55.683000 TASK_1


SQL> @job_queue_query.sql

USER_SCHEDULER_JOBS

JOB_NAME                   ENABL NEXT_RUN_DATE
-------------------------- ----- -----------------------------------
JOB_CHAIN_ENABLE_TASK_1    TRUE  08-AUG-2004 06:00:00.800000 +01:00
JOB_CHAIN_ENABLE_TASK_2    TRUE  08-AUG-2004 12:00:00.700000 +01:00
JOB_CHAIN_ENABLE_TASK_3    FALSE 07-AUG-2004 18:00:00.700000 +01:00


USER_JOBS

no rows selected
```

Care must be taken when running the pre-10g version of this code due to the way the broken procedure works. When a job has its broken flag set to FALSE, its next run date is set to the value specified by the *next_date* parameter. If this is not specified, it defaults to the current datetime. As a result, the enabled job will not run at the expected time. In this example, the *next_date* parameter has been specified as a two-minute interval for the convenience of testing, but in a real example, it must be set to an appropriate datetime value.

Conditional Job Runs Using Oracle Advanced Queuing

In this method, all tasks in the chain are scheduled as regular repeating jobs. When a task completes successfully, it places a message on a queue for the next task to read. With the exception of the first task, the first operation a task performs is read from its queue. If there is a message on the queue, the task can proceed; otherwise, it waits indefinitely for the message to arrive.

Before any code can be written, a queuing infrastructure needs to be set up using the *job_chain_aq_setup.sql* script and background information must be introduced. A full introduction to Oracle Advanced Queuing is beyond the scope of this book, so explanations will be limited to just those elements necessary to build a simple working system.

🖫 job_chain_aq_setup.sql

```
-- Grant necessary permissions
conn sys/password as sysdba

-- Create the queue payload
CREATE OR REPLACE TYPE job_user.job_chain_msg_type AS OBJECT (
  message  VARCHAR2(10)
)
/
-- Create the queue table and queues
BEGIN
  DBMS_AQADM.create_queue_table (
     queue_table            => 'job_user.job_chain_queue_tab',
     queue_payload_type     => 'job_user.job_chain_msg_type');

  DBMS_AQADM.create_queue (
     queue_name             => 'job_user.task_2_queue',
     queue_table            => 'job_user.job_chain_queue_tab');

  DBMS_AQADM.create_queue (
     queue_name             => 'job_user.task_3_queue',
     queue_table            => 'job_user.job_chain_queue_tab');

  DBMS_AQADM.start_queue (
     queue_name          => 'job_user.task_2_queue',
     enqueue             => TRUE);

  DBMS_AQADM.start_queue (
     queue_name          => 'job_user.task_3_queue',
     enqueue             => TRUE);
END;
/
grant execute on dbms_aq to job_user;

conn job_user/job_user
```

Advanced Queuing (AQ) is Oracle's implementation of a messaging system which can be used as a replacement for the *dbms_pipe* package and other Bespoke Solutions. The basic unit of any messaging system is a message with the most important element of the message being its contents, or payload.

In order to define a queue table, the payload of the messages that will be stored within it must first be defined. The *job_chain_aq_setup.sql* script contains a definition of an object type called *job_chain_msg_type* that will act as the payload. The creation of object types requires the CREATE TYPE privilege.

The payload of the message can be as simple or complicated as desired. In this case, the only concern is that the message has been sent. The particular contents are not important at this time, so the message is extremely simple.

Administration of queues is done using the *dbms_aqadm* package and requires the *aq_administrator_role* to be granted to the administrator. Alternatively, all administration can be performed by a privileged user such as SYS or SYSTEM. With the payload object defined, the queue table is created using the *create_queue_table* procedure.

Once the queue table has been created, the individual queues are created and started using the *create_queue* and *start_queue* procedures, respectively. A single queue table can hold many queues as long as each queue uses the same type for its payload.

Messages are queued and dequeued using the *dbms_aq* package. Access to this package can be granted using the *aq_user_role* role. However, access to it from a stored procedure is achieved by using the *job_chain_aq_setup.sql* script. This grants the privilege on this object directly to the test user.

The contents of the queue table can be monitored using the *job_chain_aq_query.sql* script.

🖫 job_chain_aq_query.sql

```
select
   queue,
   count(*) as messages
from
   aq$job_chain_queue_taB
group by
   queue
order by
```

```
      queue
;
```

The point has been reached where coding the specific example is desired. The
job_chain_aq.sql script creates a package specification and body that will do all
the work for the example job chain.

💾 job_chain_aq.sql

```
CREATE OR REPLACE PACKAGE job_chain_aq AS

PROCEDURE task_1;
PROCEDURE task_2;
PROCEDURE task_3;
PROCEDURE enqueue_message (p_queue_name  IN  VARCHAR2);
PROCEDURE dequeue_message (p_queue_name  IN  VARCHAR2);

END job_chain_aq;
/
SHOW ERRORS

CREATE OR REPLACE PACKAGE BODY job_chain_aq AS

-- ----------------------------------------------------------------
PROCEDURE task_1 AS
-- ----------------------------------------------------------------
BEGIN

  DELETE FROM job_chain;

  INSERT INTO job_chain (created_timestamp, task_name)
  VALUES (systimestamp, 'TASK_1');
  COMMIT;

  -- Uncomment the following line to force a failure.
  --RAISE_APPLICATION_ERROR(-20000,
  --   'This is a fake error to prevent task_2 being executed');

  -- The work has comleted successfully so signal task_2
  enqueue_message (p_queue_name => 'task_2_queue');

EXCEPTION
  WHEN OTHERS THEN
    -- Don't signal task_2.
    NULL;
END task_1;
-- ----------------------------------------------------------------


-- ----------------------------------------------------------------
PROCEDURE task_2 AS
-- ----------------------------------------------------------------
BEGIN

  dequeue_message (p_queue_name => 'task_2_queue');

  INSERT INTO job_chain (created_timestamp, task_name)
```

```
        VALUES (systimestamp, 'TASK_2');
        COMMIT;

        -- Uncomment the following line to force a failure.
        --RAISE_APPLICATION_ERROR(-20000,
        --    'This is a fake error to prevent task_3 being executed');

        -- The work has comleted successfully so signal task_3
        enqueue_message (p_queue_name => 'task_3_queue');

    EXCEPTION
      WHEN OTHERS THEN
        -- Don't signal task_3.
        NULL;
    END task_2;
    -- -------------------------------------------------------------------


    -- -------------------------------------------------------------------
    PROCEDURE task_3 AS
    -- -------------------------------------------------------------------
    BEGIN

      dequeue_message (p_queue_name => 'task_3_queue');

      INSERT INTO job_chain (created_timestamp, task_name)
      VALUES (systimestamp, 'TASK_3');
      COMMIT;

    END task_3;
    -- -------------------------------------------------------------------


    -- -------------------------------------------------------------------
    PROCEDURE enqueue_message (p_queue_name  IN  VARCHAR2) AS
    -- -------------------------------------------------------------------
      l_enqueue_options      DBMS_AQ.enqueue_options_t;
      l_message_properties   DBMS_AQ.message_properties_t;
      l_message_handle       RAW(16);
      l_job_chain_msg        job_chain_msg_type;
    BEGIN
      l_job_chain_msg := job_chain_msg_type('GO');

      DBMS_AQ.enqueue(queue_name            => 'job_user.' || p_queue_name,
                      enqueue_options       => l_enqueue_options,
                      message_properties    => l_message_properties,
                      payload               => l_job_chain_msg,
                      msgid                 => l_message_handle);
    END enqueue_message;
    -- -------------------------------------------------------------------


    -- -------------------------------------------------------------------
    PROCEDURE dequeue_message (p_queue_name  IN  VARCHAR2) AS
    -- -------------------------------------------------------------------
      l_dequeue_options      DBMS_AQ.dequeue_options_t;
      l_message_properties   DBMS_AQ.message_properties_t;
      l_message_handle       RAW(16);
      l_job_chain_msg        job_chain_msg_type;
    BEGIN
      DBMS_AQ.dequeue(queue_name            => 'job_user.' || p_queue_name,
                      dequeue_options       => l_dequeue_options,
```

```
                message_properties  => l_message_properties,
                payload             => l_job_chain_msg,
                msgid               => l_message_handle);
END dequeue_message;
-- ----------------------------------------------------------------

END job_chain_aq;
/
SHOW ERRORS
```

Next, the jobs associated with each task are scheduled. Unlike the previous
example, the job sequence is protected by the queue, so all the jobs can be
enabled.

🖫 job_chain_aq_jobs.sql

```
-- Oracle
BEGIN
  DBMS_SCHEDULER.create_job (
    job_name        => 'job_chain_aq_task_1',
    job_type        => 'STORED_PROCEDURE',
    job_action      => 'job_chain_aq.task_1',
    start_date      => SYSTIMESTAMP,
    repeat_interval => 'freq=daily; byhour=6; byminute=0; bysecond=0;',
    end_date        => NULL,
    enabled         => TRUE,
    comments        => 'First task in the AQ chain.');
END;
/
BEGIN
  DBMS_SCHEDULER.create_job (
    job_name        => 'job_chain_aq_task_2',
    job_type        => 'STORED_PROCEDURE',
    job_action      => 'job_chain_aq.task_2',
    start_date      => SYSTIMESTAMP,
    repeat_interval => 'freq=daily; byhour=12; byminute=0; bysecond=0;',
    end_date        => NULL,
    enabled         => TRUE,
    comments        => 'Second task in the AQ chain.');
END;
/
BEGIN
  DBMS_SCHEDULER.create_job (
    job_name        => 'job_chain_aq_task_3',
    job_type        => 'STORED_PROCEDURE',
    job_action      => 'job_chain_aq.task_3',
    start_date      => SYSTIMESTAMP,
    repeat_interval => 'freq=daily; byhour=18; byminute=0; bysecond=0;',
    end_date        => NULL,
    enabled         => TRUE,
    comments        => 'Third task in the AQ chain.');
END;
/

EXEC DBMS_SCHEDULER.run_job ('job_chain_aq_task_1');
-- Oracle
```

```
BEGIN
  DBMS_SCHEDULER.drop_job ('job_chain_aq_task_3');
  DBMS_SCHEDULER.drop_job ('job_chain_aq_task_2');
  DBMS_SCHEDULER.drop_job ('job_chain_aq_task_1');
END;
/
```

At this point, the tasks are scheduled but have not been executed; therefore, there are no results in the *job_chain* table or the *job_chain_queue_tab* table. Rather than waiting until 6:00, the first job is forced to run immediately. The results below show that the first task has run and there is a message waiting in the queue table on the *task_2_queue*.

```
SQL> exec dbms_scheduler.run_job ('job_chain_aq_task_1');

PL/SQL procedure successfully completed.

job_user@db10g> @job_chain_query.sql

CREATED_TIMESTAMP             TASK_NAME
---------------------------   --------------------
07-AUG-2004 18:18:36.136000   TASK_1

SQL> @job_chain_aq_query.sql

QUEUE                             MESSAGES
-----------------------------     ----------
TASK_2_QUEUE                             1
```

If the run of the second job is forced, the second task reads a message from its queue, completes its processing and places a message on the queue for the third task.

```
SQL> exec dbms_scheduler.run_job ('job_chain_aq_task_2');

PL/SQL procedure successfully completed.

SQL> @job_chain_query.sql

CREATED_TIMESTAMP             TASK_NAME
---------------------------   --------------------
07-AUG-2004 18:18:36.136000   TASK_1
07-AUG-2004 18:23:08.771000   TASK_2


SQL> @job_chain_aq_query.sql

QUEUE                             MESSAGES
-----------------------------     ----------
TASK_3_QUEUE                             1
```

If the run of the third job is forced, the third task reads a message from its queue and completes its processing.

```
SQL> exec dbms_scheduler.run_job ('job_chain_aq_task_3');

PL/SQL procedure successfully completed.

SQL> @job_chain_query.sql

CREATED_TIMESTAMP            TASK_NAME
--------------------------   --------------------
07-AUG-2004 18:18:36.136000 TASK_1
07-AUG-2004 18:23:08.771000 TASK_2
07-AUG-2004 18:26:04.972000 TASK_3


SQL> @job_chain_aq_query.sql

no rows selected
```

If manually attempting to start jobs out of sequence, the sessions hang until the appropriate message is sent.

Conditional Job Runs Using a Custom Table Solution

If none of the previous methods seem suitable, a specific solution to meet specific needs can always be built. The following example could be used as a starting point for such a solution.

The sequence of jobs is protected using the *job_chain_locks* table. The RETRIES column specifies the number of times a task should check the locks before it gives up and reschedules itself. The RETRY_DELAY column specifies the number of minutes between retries. The TASK_NAME and LOCKED columns are self-explanatory.

⊟ job_chain_locks.sql

```
CREATE TABLE job_chain_locks (
  task_name    VARCHAR2(20)                NOT NULL,
  locked       VARCHAR2(1)    DEFAULT 'Y'  NOT NULL,
  retries      NUMBER(3)      DEFAULT 0    NOT NULL,
  retry_delay  NUMBER(3)      DEFAULT 1    NOT NULL,
  CONSTRAINT job_chain_locks_pk PRIMARY KEY (task_name)
);

INSERT INTO job_chain_locks (task_name, locked, retries, retry_delay)
VALUES ('task_2', 'Y', 5, 1);

INSERT INTO job_chain_locks (task_name, locked, retries, retry_delay)
VALUES ('task_3', 'Y', 3, 1);
```

```
COMMIT;
```

The contents of the *job_chain_locks* table can be monitored using the *job_chain_locks_query.sql* script.

💾 job_chain_locks_query.sql

```
select
    *
from
    job_chain_locks
order by
    task_name;
```

The *job_chain_custom.sql* script creates a package specification and body which will do all the work for the example job chain.

💾 job_chain_custom_sql

```
CREATE OR REPLACE PACKAGE job_chain_custom AS

PROCEDURE task_1;
PROCEDURE task_2;
PROCEDURE task_3;
PROCEDURE lock_task (p_task_name  IN  job_chain_locks.task_name%TYPE,
                     p_lock       IN  BOOLEAN DEFAULT TRUE);
FUNCTION unlocked (p_task_name  IN  job_chain_locks.task_name%TYPE)
  RETURN BOOLEAN;

END job_chain_custom;
/
SHOW ERRORS


CREATE OR REPLACE PACKAGE BODY job_chain_custom AS

-- ----------------------------------------------------------------
PROCEDURE task_1 AS
-- ----------------------------------------------------------------
BEGIN

  DELETE FROM job_chain;

  INSERT INTO job_chain (created_timestamp, task_name)
  VALUES (systimestamp, 'TASK_1');
  COMMIT;

  -- Uncomment the following line to force a failure.
  --RAISE_APPLICATION_ERROR(-20000,
  --  'This is a fake error to prevent task_2 being executed');

  -- The work has comleted successfully so unlock task_2
  lock_task ('task_2', FALSE);
```

```
EXCEPTION
  WHEN OTHERS THEN
    -- Don't unlock task_2.
    NULL;
END task_1;
-- ------------------------------------------------------------------


-- ------------------------------------------------------------------
PROCEDURE task_2 AS
-- ------------------------------------------------------------------
BEGIN

  IF unlocked('task_2') THEN
    lock_task ('task_2');

    INSERT INTO job_chain (created_timestamp, task_name)
    VALUES (systimestamp, 'TASK_2');
    COMMIT;

    -- Uncomment the following line to force a failure.
    --RAISE_APPLICATION_ERROR(-20000,
    --   'This is a fake error to prevent task_3 being executed');

    -- The work has comleted successfully so unlock task_3
    lock_task ('task_3', FALSE);
  END IF;

EXCEPTION
  WHEN OTHERS THEN
    -- Don't unlock task_3.
    NULL;
END task_2;
-- ------------------------------------------------------------------


-- ------------------------------------------------------------------
PROCEDURE task_3 AS
-- ------------------------------------------------------------------
BEGIN

  IF unlocked('task_3') THEN
    lock_task ('task_3');

    INSERT INTO job_chain (created_timestamp, task_name)
    VALUES (systimestamp, 'TASK_3');
    COMMIT;
  END IF;

END task_3;
-- ------------------------------------------------------------------


-- ------------------------------------------------------------------
PROCEDURE lock_task (p_task_name  IN   job_chain_locks.task_name%TYPE,
                     p_lock       IN   BOOLEAN DEFAULT TRUE) AS
-- ------------------------------------------------------------------
  PRAGMA AUTONOMOUS_TRANSACTION;
BEGIN
  UPDATE job_chain_locks
  SET    locked = 'Y'
  WHERE  task_name = p_task_name;
```

```
    COMMIT;
END lock_task;
-- ----------------------------------------------------------------


-- ----------------------------------------------------------------
FUNCTION unlocked (p_task_name  IN  job_chain_locks.task_name%TYPE)
   RETURN BOOLEAN AS
-- ----------------------------------------------------------------
   l_jcl_row  job_chain_locks%ROWTYPE;
BEGIN
   SELECT *
   INTO   l_jcl_row
   FROM   job_chain_locks
   WHERE  task_name = p_task_name;

   IF l_jcl_row.locked != 'Y' THEN
     RETURN TRUE;
   END IF;

   FOR i IN 1 .. l_jcl_row.retries LOOP
     DBMS_LOCK.sleep(60 * l_jcl_row.retry_delay);

     SELECT locked
     INTO   l_jcl_row.locked
     FROM   job_chain_locks
     WHERE  task_name = p_task_name;

     IF l_jcl_row.locked != 'Y' THEN
        RETURN TRUE;
     END IF;
   END LOOP;

   RETURN FALSE;
EXCEPTION
  WHEN NO_DATA_FOUND THEN
     RETURN FALSE;
END unlocked;
-- ----------------------------------------------------------------

END job_chain_custom;
/
SHOW ERRORS
```

Next, the jobs associated with each task are scheduled.

💾 job_chain_custom_jobs.sql

```
-- Oracle
BEGIN
  DBMS_SCHEDULER.create_job (
    job_name        => 'job_chain_custom_task_1',
    job_type        => 'STORED_PROCEDURE',
    job_action      => 'job_chain_custom.task_1',
    start_date      => SYSTIMESTAMP,
    repeat_interval => 'freq=daily; byhour=6; byminute=0; bysecond=0;',
    end_date        => NULL,
    enabled         => TRUE,
```

```
      comments        => 'First task in the AQ chain.');
END;
/

BEGIN
  DBMS_SCHEDULER.create_job (
     job_name        => 'job_chain_custom_task_2',
     job_type        => 'STORED_PROCEDURE',
     job_action      => 'job_chain_custom.task_2',
     start_date      => SYSTIMESTAMP,
     repeat_interval => 'freq=daily; byhour=12; byminute=0; bysecond=0;',
     end_date        => NULL,
     enabled         => TRUE,
     comments        => 'Second task in the AQ chain.');
END;
/

BEGIN
  DBMS_SCHEDULER.create_job (
     job_name        => 'job_chain_custom_task_3',
     job_type        => 'STORED_PROCEDURE',
     job_action      => 'job_chain_custom.task_3',
     start_date      => SYSTIMESTAMP,
     repeat_interval => 'freq=daily; byhour=18; byminute=0; bysecond=0;',
     end_date        => NULL,
     enabled         => TRUE,
     comments        => 'Third task in the AQ chain.');
END;
/
```

At this point, the tasks are scheduled but have not been executed; hence, no results in the *job_chain* table. Rather than waiting until 6:00, the first job can be forced to run immediately. The results below show that the first task has run and second task has been unlocked.

```
SQL> exec dbms_scheduler.run_job ('job_chain_custom_task_1');

PL/SQL procedure successfully completed.

SQL> @job_chain_query.sql

CREATED_TIMESTAMP            TASK_NAME
--------------------------- --------------------
07-AUG-2004 19:54:51.010000 TASK_1

SQL> @job_chain_locks_query.sql

TASK_NAME            L   RETRIES RETRY_DELAY
-------------------- - ---------- -----------
task_2               N        5           1
task_3               Y        3           1
```

Running the second job manually results in the second task being relocked and the third task being unlocked.

```
SQL> exec dbms_scheduler.run_job ('job_chain_custom_task_2');

PL/SQL procedure successfully completed.

SQL> @job_chain_query.sql

CREATED_TIMESTAMP                TASK_NAME
-------------------------        --------------------
07-AUG-2004 19:54:51.010000 TASK_1
07-AUG-2004 19:57:29.636000 TASK_2

SQL> @job_chain_locks_query.sql

TASK_NAME               L    RETRIES RETRY_DELAY
-------------------     -    ---------- -----------
task_2                  Y          5           1
task_3                  N          3           1
```

Running the third job manually results in the second task being relocked.

```
SQL> exec dbms_scheduler.run_job ('job_chain_custom_task_3');

PL/SQL procedure successfully completed.

SQL> @job_chain_query.sql

CREATED_TIMESTAMP                TASK_NAME
-------------------------        --------------------
07-AUG-2004 19:54:51.010000 TASK_1
07-AUG-2004 19:57:29.636000 TASK_2
07-AUG-2004 19:59:11.184000 TASK_3

3 rows selected.

SQL> @job_chain_locks_query.sql

TASK_NAME               L    RETRIES RETRY_DELAY
-------------------     -    ---------- -----------
task_2                  Y          5           1
task_3                  Y          3           1

2 rows selected.
```

Attempting to run a job out of order will result in the session hanging until the task is unlocked or the appropriate number of retries has been attempted, at which point, the job is rescheduled.

```
SQL> set timing on
SQL> exec dbms_scheduler.run_job ('job_chain_custom_task_3');

PL/SQL procedure successfully completed.

Elapsed: 00:03:04.50
```

The DBA now has a variety of tools available with which to build job chains. The next section will introduce the error handling requirements associated with job scheduling.

Implementing Error Checking Routines

Proper error handling is an important part of implementing robust job scheduling. Depending on the scheduling mechanism, job failures can have differing effects.

By default, a job scheduled using the *dbms_scheduler* package does not have a limit on the maximum number of failures. If this functionality is required, it can be enforced by setting the *max_failures* attribute of the job. The *create_10g_job_failure.sql* script is the 10g equivalent of the *create_job_failure.sql* script. Notice that the *auto_drop* parameter has been set to FALSE to prevent the job from being dropped once it is disabled.

💾 create_10g_job_failure.sql

```
BEGIN
  DBMS_SCHEDULER.create_job (
    job_name        => 'force_error_job',
    job_type        => 'PLSQL_BLOCK',
    job_action      => 'BEGIN RAISE_APPLICATION_ERROR(-20000, ''Error'');
END;',
    start_date      => SYSTIMESTAMP,
    repeat_interval => 'freq=secondly;',
    end_date        => NULL,
    enabled         => TRUE,
    auto_drop       => FALSE,
    comments        => 'Job containing a forced error.');
  DBMS_SCHEDULER.set_attribute (
    name      => 'force_error_job',
    attribute => 'max_failures',
    value     => 16);
END;
/
```

The *job_run_failures_10g.sql* script queries the *dba_scheduler_jobs* view and can be used to monitor the progress of the 10g job.

🖫 job_run_failures_10g.sql

```
select
   job_name,
   enabled,
   run_count,
   max_runs,
   failure_count,
   max_failures
from
   dba_scheduler_jobs
where
   job_name = DECODE(UPPER('&1'), 'ALL', job_name, UPPER('&1'))
;
```

The output from this script is listed below:

```
SQL> @job_run_failures_10g.sql force_error_job

JOB_NAME        ENABL RUN_COUNT  MAX_RUNS  FAILURE_COUNT MAX_FAILURES
--------------- ----- ---------- --------- ------------- ------------
FORCE_ERROR_JOB TRUE         14                     14           16
```

Once the maximum number of failures has been reached, the job is disabled. If the *auto_drop* parameter had not been set, the following query would return no rows as the job would have been dropped.

```
SQL> @job_run_failures_10g.sql force_error_job

JOB_NAME        ENABL RUN_COUNT  MAX_RUNS  FAILURE_COUNT MAX_FAILURES
--------------- ----- ---------- --------- ------------- ------------
FORCE_ERROR_JOB FALSE        16                     16           16
```

Once the problem with the job is rectified, it could be restarted using the *enable* procedure.

```
SQL> exec dbms_scheduler.enable('force_error_job');

PL/SQL procedure successfully completed.
```

Alternatively, the job could be dropped using the *drop_job* procedure.

```
SQL> exec dbms_scheduler.drop_job ('force_error_job');

PL/SQL procedure successfully completed.
```

Although not directly related to errors, the maximum number of runs for a job can be limited by setting the *max_runs* parameter for a job.

🖫 create_10g_job_max_runs.sql

```
BEGIN
  DBMS_SCHEDULER.create_job (
    job_name         => 'max_runs_job',
    job_type         => 'PLSQL_BLOCK',
    job_action       => 'BEGIN NULL; END;',
    start_date       => SYSTIMESTAMP,
    repeat_interval  => 'freq=secondly;',
    end_date         => NULL,
    enabled          => TRUE,
    auto_drop        => FALSE,
    comments         => 'Job limiting maximum runs.');

  DBMS_SCHEDULER.set_attribute (
    name      => 'max_runs_job',
    attribute => 'max_runs',
    value     => 16);
END;
/
```

By monitoring the job, it can be seen that the job is disabled once it reaches its maximum number of runs.

```
SQL> @job_run_failures_10g.sql max_runs_job

JOB_NAME         ENABL RUN_COUNT MAX_RUNS FAILURE_COUNT MAX_FAILURES
---------------- ----- --------- -------- ------------- ------------
FORCE_ERROR_JOB  FALSE        16       16            16
```

The examples above show that having a job fail to complete may introduce two possible problems. The first and most obvious is that the work the job is expected to do will not complete successfully. The second, and possibly most problematic, is that the job may cease to run in the future.

The simplest way to solve this problem is to trap and handle all errors. In its simplest form, this could be done using an exception handler like the one shown in the *exception_job_proc_1.sql* procedure below.

🖫 exception_job_proc_1.sql

```
CREATE OR REPLACE PROCEDURE exception_job_proc_1 AS
BEGIN
  -- Force an error.
  RAISE_APPLICATION_ERROR(-20000, 'Forced error in exception_job_proc_1');
EXCEPTION
  WHEN OTHERS THEN
    NULL;
END exception_job_proc_1;
/
```

This exception handler will stop the job from failing if a PL/SQL exception is raised, but it will give no indication as to what caused the job to fail.

```
SQL> EXEC exception_job_proc_1;

PL/SQL procedure successfully completed.
```

Another alternative is to log an error message in the exception handler. First, the *error_logs* table to hold the error messages needs to be created.

```
CREATE TABLE error_logs (

   id                 NUMBER(10)     NOT NULL,
   prefix             VARCHAR2(100),
   data               VARCHAR2(4000)  NOT NULL,
   error_level        NUMBER(2)      NOT NULL,
   created_timestamp  TIMESTAMP      NOT NULL,
   created_by         VARCHAR2(50)   NOT NULL);

ALTER TABLE error_logs ADD (CONSTRAINT error_logs_pk PRIMARY KEY (id));

CREATE SEQUENCE error_logs_seq;
```

The usages of the table columns are listed below:

- **ID** - A system generated sequence number used as the primary key

- **PREFIX** - An optional string to identify the source of the error. This may be used to identify the job or procedure that the job is running.

- **DATA** - A string containing information about the error. This could be just the error text or some additional information like the position in the process where the error occurred and any relevant parameters.

- **ERROR_LEVEL** - A number that can be used as an indicator of the severity of the error. For example, normal errors may be level five, major errors may be level one and minor warnings may be level 10. This has a default value of five.

- **CREATED_TIMESTAMP** - A timestamp indicating the time the error was logged. This defaults to the current system time.

- **CREATED_BY** - A reference to the user who created the error. This defaults to the database user.

With the table in place, the logging code starting with the package specification in the *err.pks* script can be created. Then the package body in the *err.pkb* script can also be created.

```
-- Requirements :
/*
CREATE TABLE error_logs (
  id                 NUMBER(10)      NOT NULL,
  prefix             VARCHAR2(100),
  data               VARCHAR2(4000)  NOT NULL,
  error_level        NUMBER(2)       NOT NULL,
  created_timestamp  TIMESTAMP       NOT NULL,
  created_by         VARCHAR2(50)    NOT NULL);

ALTER TABLE error_logs ADD (CONSTRAINT error_logs_pk PRIMARY KEY (id));

CREATE SEQUENCE error_logs_seq;
*/
-- ********************************************************************

CREATE OR REPLACE PACKAGE err AS

PROCEDURE reset_defaults;

PROCEDURE logs_on;
PROCEDURE logs_off;

PROCEDURE line (p_prefix       IN  error_logs.prefix%TYPE,
                p_data         IN  error_logs.data%TYPE,
                p_error_level  IN  error_logs.error_level%TYPE DEFAULT 5,
                p_error_user   IN  error_logs.created_by%TYPE DEFAULT USER);

PROCEDURE line (p_data         IN  error_logs.data%TYPE,
                p_error_level  IN  error_logs.error_level%TYPE DEFAULT 5,
                p_error_user   IN  error_logs.created_by%TYPE DEFAULT USER);

END err;
/
SHOW ERRORS
```

```
CREATE OR REPLACE PACKAGE BODY err AS

-- Package Variables
g_logs_on  BOOLEAN := TRUE;

-- Exposed Methods

-- ----------------------------------------------------------------
PROCEDURE reset_defaults IS
-- ----------------------------------------------------------------
BEGIN
  g_logs_on := TRUE;
END;
-- ----------------------------------------------------------------


-- ----------------------------------------------------------------
PROCEDURE logs_on IS
-- ----------------------------------------------------------------
BEGIN
```

```
   g_logs_on := TRUE;
END;
-- ------------------------------------------------------------------


-- ------------------------------------------------------------------
PROCEDURE logs_off IS
-- ------------------------------------------------------------------
BEGIN
   g_logs_on := FALSE;
END;
-- ------------------------------------------------------------------


-- ------------------------------------------------------------------
PROCEDURE line (p_prefix        IN   error_logs.prefix%TYPE,
                p_data          IN   error_logs.data%TYPE,
                p_error_level   IN   error_logs.error_level%TYPE DEFAULT 5,
                p_error_user    IN   error_logs.created_by%TYPE DEFAULT USER)
IS
-- ------------------------------------------------------------------
   PRAGMA AUTONOMOUS_TRANSACTION;
BEGIN
   IF g_logs_on THEN
     INSERT INTO error_logs
     (id,
      prefix,
      data,
      error_level,
      created_timestamp,
      created_by)
     VALUES
     (error_logs_seq.NEXTVAL,
      p_prefix,
      p_data,
      p_error_level,
      SYSTIMESTAMP,
      p_error_user);

     COMMIT;
   END IF;
END;
-- ------------------------------------------------------------------


-- ------------------------------------------------------------------
PROCEDURE line (p_data          IN   error_logs.data%TYPE,
                p_error_level   IN   error_logs.error_level%TYPE DEFAULT 5,
                p_error_user    IN   error_logs.created_by%TYPE DEFAULT USER)
IS
-- ------------------------------------------------------------------
BEGIN
   line (p_prefix        => NULL,
         p_data          => p_data,
         p_error_level   => p_error_level,
         p_error_user    => p_error_user);
END;
-- ------------------------------------------------------------------


END err;
/
SHOW ERRORS
```

The *line* procedure is overloaded and this allows it to be used with or without a prefix. The main procedure is defined as an autonomous transaction, so it commits the logging data without affecting the transactions within the job. In its simplest form, error logging can be achieved by issuing the following command:

```
SQL> execute err.line('This is an error');

PL/SQL procedure successfully completed.
```

The contents of the *error_logs* table can be queried using the *list_error_logs.sql* script listed below.

list_error_logs.sql

```
-- ************************************************
-- Parameters:
--     1) Specific prefix or "all".
-- ******************************************************************

set feedback off
alter session set nls_timestamp_format='DD-MON-YYYY HH24:MI:SS';
set feedback on

set linesize 150
set verify off

column id format 99999
column prefix format a20
column data format a30
column created_timestamp format a20
column created_by format a10

select
   id,
   prefix,
   data,
   error_level,
   created_timestamp,
   created_by
from
   error_logs
where
   nvl(prefix, '~') = decode(upper('&1'), 'ALL', nvl(prefix, '~'), '&1')
order by
   id
;
```

The output from this query is displayed below.

```
SQL> @list_error_logs.sql all
```

Implementing Error Checking Routines   **663**

```
ID PREFIX   DATA              ERROR_LEVEL CREATED_TIMESTAMP     CREATED_BY
------ ------- ---------------- ----------- --------------------- ----------
   1           This is an error             5 14-AUG-2004 12:58:08  JOB_USER
```

Armed with this error logging procedure, the *exception_job_proc_1* procedure can be amended to create the *exception_job_proc_2* procedure.

exception_job_proc_2.sql

```
CREATE OR REPLACE PROCEDURE exception_job_proc_2 AS
BEGIN
  -- Force an error.
  RAISE_APPLICATION_ERROR(-20000, 'Forced error in exception_job_proc_2');
EXCEPTION
  WHEN OTHERS THEN
    ERR.line(p_prefix => 'exception_job_proc_2',
             P_data   => SQLERRM);
END exception_job_proc_2;
/
```

Running the following procedure results in the generation of the appropriate error log:

```
SQL> exec exception_job_proc_2;

PL/SQL procedure successfully completed.

SQL> @list_error_logs.sql exception_job_proc_2

ID PREFIX      DATA                          ERROR_LEVEL CREATED_TIMESTAMP     CREATED_BY
------ ------------------- ----------------------------- ----------- --------------------- --------------------
   2 exception_job_proc_2 ORA-20000: Forced error in exc    5 14-AUG-2004 13:35:02 JOB_USER
                          eption_job_proc_2
```

With this mechanism in place, PL/SQL exceptions can be monitored and their presence will not cause the jobs to fail.

This section has introduced several methods by which error checking can be implemented. Next, the following section will focus on mechanisms for sending email notifications of job failures.

Sending Email Notifications of Job Errors

Stopped here The mechanism for sending email notifications can vary depending on the version of Oracle being used. Oracle allows the use of the simpler UTL_MAIL package rather than the UTL_SMTP package available in previous versions. Note that these packages are also covered in more detail elsewhere in this book.

Using UTL_SMTP

The UTL_SMTP package was introduced in Oracle8i to give access to the SMTP protocol from PL/SQL. The package is dependent on the JServer option, which can be loaded using the Database Configuration Assistant (DBCA) or by running the following scripts as the SYS user if it is not already present.

```
CONN sys/password AS SYSDBA
@$ORACLE_HOME/javavm/install/initjvm.sql
@$ORACLE_HOME/rdbms/admin/initplsj.sql
```

Using the package to send an email requires some knowledge of the SMTP protocol, but for the purpose of this text, a simple *send_mail* procedure has been written that should be suitable for most error reporting.

💾 send_mail.sql

```
-- Parameters:
--     1) SMTP mail gateway.
--     2) From email address.
--     3) To email address.
--     4) Subject of email.
--     5) Text body of email.
-- *******************************************************************

CREATE OR REPLACE PROCEDURE send_mail (
  p_mail_host  IN   VARCHAR2,
  p_from       IN   VARCHAR2,
  p_to         IN   VARCHAR2,
  p_subject    IN   VARCHAR2,
  p_message    IN   VARCHAR2)
AS
  l_mail_conn    UTL_SMTP.connection;
BEGIN
  l_mail_conn := UTL_SMTP.open_connection (p_mail_host, 25);
  UTL_SMTP.helo(l_mail_conn, p_mail_host);
  UTL_SMTP.mail(l_mail_conn, p_from);
  UTL_SMTP.rcpt(l_mail_conn, p_to);

  UTL_SMTP.open_data (l_mail_conn);

  UTL_SMTP.write_data (l_mail_conn, 'Date: ' || TO_CHAR(SYSDATE, 'DD-MON-
YYYY HH24:MI:SS') || Chr(13));
  UTL_SMTP.write_data (l_mail_conn, 'From: ' || p_from || Chr(13));
  UTL_SMTP.write_data (l_mail_conn, 'Subject: ' || p_subject || Chr(13));
  UTL_SMTP.write_data (l_mail_conn, 'To: ' || p_to || Chr(13));
  UTL_SMTP.write_data (l_mail_conn, '' || Chr(13));
  UTL_SMTP.write_data (l_mail_conn, p_message || Chr(13));

  UTL_SMTP.close_data (l_mail_conn);
  UTL_SMTP.quit(l_mail_conn);
```

```
END send_mail;
/
SHOW ERRORS
```

The following code shows how the *send_mail* procedure can be used to send an email. Obviously, one will need to substitute the appropriate parameter values.

```
BEGIN
  send_mail(p_mail_host => 'smtp.mycompany.com',
           p_from       => 'me@mycompany.com',
           p_to         => 'you@mycompany.com',
           p_subject    => 'Test SEND_MAIL Procedure',
           p_message    => 'If you are reading this it worked!');
END;
/
```

The *p_mail_host* parameter specifies the SMTP gateway that actually sends the message.

Now that the email mechanism has been presented, how to capture errors and produce email notifications will be explained.

The simplest way to achieve this is to place all the code related to the job into a database procedure or, preferably, a packaged procedure. This allows the capture of errors using an exception handler and the generation of an appropriate email. As an example, assume there is a need for a procedure to gather database statistics for an Oracle 8i or 9i instance. A procedure like the one below might be defined.

🖫 automated_email_alert.sql

```
CREATE OR REPLACE PROCEDURE automated_email_alert AS
  l_mail_host   VARCHAR2(50) := 'smtp.mycompany.com';
  l_from        VARCHAR2(50) := 'jobs@mycompany.com';
  l_to          VARCHAR2(50) := 'tim@mycompany.com';
BEGIN
  DBMS_STATS.gather_database_stats (cascade => TRUE,
                                    options => 'GATHER AUTO');
  send_mail(p_mail_host => l_mail_host,
           p_from       => l_from,
           p_to         => l_to,
           p_subject    => 'AUTOMATED_EMAIL_ALERT (MYSID): Success',
           p_message    => 'AUTOMATED_EMAIL_ALERT (MYSID) completed
successfully!');

EXCEPTION
  WHEN OTHERS THEN
    send_mail(p_mail_host => l_mail_host,
             p_from       => l_from,
             p_to         => l_to,
```

```
                p_subject   => 'AUTOMATED_EMAIL_ALERT (MYSID): Error',
                p_message   => 'AUTOMATED_EMAIL_ALERT (MYSID) failed with the
following error:' || SQLERRM);
END automated_email_alert;
/
SHOW ERRORS
```

If this procedure were run as part of a scheduled job, an email notification would be generated whether the job completed successfully or not. In the event of an error, the associated Oracle error would be reported.

Using UTL_MAIL in Oracle

Oracle introduced the UTL_MAIL package, which provides a simpler and more intuitive email API. The package is loaded by running the following scripts as the SYS user.

```
CONN sys/password AS SYSDBA
@$ORACLE_HOME/rdbms/admin/utlmail.sql
@$ORACLE_HOME/rdbms/admin/prvtmail.plb
GRANT EXECUTE ON UTL_MAIL TO test_user;
```

Before the package can be used, the SMTP gateway must be specified by setting the *smtp_out_server* parameter. The parameter is dynamic, but the instance must be restarted before an email can be sent.

```
CONN sys/password AS SYSDBA
ALTER SYSTEM SET smtp_out_server='smtp.mycompany.com';
SHUTDOWN IMMEDIATE
STARTUP
```

With the configuration complete, it is now possible to send an email using the *send* procedure.

```
BEGIN
  UTL_MAIL.send(sender     => 'me@mycompany.com',
                recipients => 'you@mycompany.com',
                subject    => 'Test UTL_MAIL.SEND Procedure',
                message    => 'If you are reading this it worked!');
END;
/
```

As with the UTL_SMTP example, the code related to the job needs to be placed into a database procedure which captures errors using an exception handler and sends the appropriate email. The following procedure is the Oracle equivalent of the one used in the UTL_SMTP example.

---

automated_email_alert_10g.sql

```
CREATE OR REPLACE PROCEDURE automated_email_alert_10g AS
  l_mail_host   VARCHAR2(50) := 'smtp.mycompany.com';
  l_from        VARCHAR2(50) := 'jobs@mycompany.com';
  l_to          VARCHAR2(50) := 'tim@mycompany.com';
BEGIN
  DBMS_STATS.gather_database_stats (cascade => TRUE,
                                    options => 'GATHER AUTO');

  UTL_MAIL.send(sender     => l_from,
               recipients => l_to,
               subject    => 'AUTOMATED_EMAIL_ALERT_10G (MYSID): Success',
               message    => 'AUTOMATED_EMAIL_ALERT_10G (MYSID) completed
successfully!');
EXCEPTION
  WHEN OTHERS THEN
    UTL_MAIL.send(sender     => l_from,
                 recipients => l_to,
                 subject    => 'AUTOMATED_EMAIL_ALERT_10G (MYSID): Error',
                 message    => 'AUTOMATED_EMAIL_ALERT_10G (MYSID) failed
with the following error:' || SQLERRM);
END automated_email_alert_10g;
/
SHOW ERRORS
```

Next, a mechanism for running operating system commands and scripts from within PL/SQL will be introduced.

If combining these techniques with the error logging method described previously, one may wish to send additional information in the email (prefix, start and end timestamps) to help pinpoint the errors in the *error_logs* table.

Monitoring Oracle Job Execution

This section will introduce how Oracle jobs can be monitored using both database views and Oracle Enterprise Manager (OEM). The scheduler available in Oracle is radically different from the one available in previous versions of Oracle. For this reason, it will be dealt with separately. Explanations of the *dbms_application_info* and *dbms_system* packages are included as they can simplify the identification and monitoring of sessions related to scheduled jobs.

The list of currently scheduled jobs is displayed using the *dba_scheduler_jobs* view. This view provides a list of job names and the basic schedule information. The *scheduled_jobs.sql* script shows how this view is used.

🖫 scheduled_jobs.sql

```
set linesize 200

column owner format a15
column next_run_date format a25

select
   job_name,
   owner,
   nvl(to_char(next_run_date, 'DD-MON-YYYY HH24:MI:SS'), schedule_name) as
next_run_date,
   to_char(last_start_date, 'DD-MON-YYYY HH24:MI:SS') as last_run_date,
   job_class,
   run_count
from
   dba_scheduler_jobs
;
```

The output generated from the *scheduled_jobs.sql* script is shown below.

```
SQL> @scheduled_jobs

JOB_NAME                         OWNER           NEXT_RUN_DATE              LAST_RUN_DATE
JOB_CLASS                        RUN_COUNT
-------------------------------- --------------- -------------------------- -------------------- -------
------------------------- ----------
GATHER_STATS_JOB                 SYS             MAINTENANCE_WINDOW_GROUP         24-JUN-2004 08:09:39
AUTO_TASKS_JOB_CLASS          4
PURGE_LOG                        SYS             24-JUN-2004 03:00:00       23-JUN-2004 03:00:01
DEFAULT_JOB_CLASS            19
TEST_FULL_JOB_DEFINITION         JOB_USER        24-JUN-2004 08:52:00       24-JUN-2004 08:52:00
DEFAULT_JOB_CLASS           281
TEST_PROG_SCHED_CLASS_JOB_DEF    JOB_USER        24-JUN-2004 09:00:16       24-JUN-2004 08:09:39
TEST_JOB_CLASS               16
ARGUMENT_JOB_DEFINITION          JOB_USER        24-JUN-2004 09:00:16       24-JUN-2004 08:09:39
DEFAULT_JOB_CLASS            16
TEST_SCHED_JOB_DEFINITION        JOB_USER        24-JUN-2004 09:00:16       24-JUN-2004 08:09:37
DEFAULT_JOB_CLASS            16
TEST_PROG_JOB_DEFINITION         JOB_USER        24-JUN-2004 09:00:09       24-JUN-2004 08:09:38
DEFAULT_JOB_CLASS            16
TEST_PROG_SCHED_JOB_DEFINITION   JOB_USER        24-JUN-2004 09:00:16       24-JUN-2004 08:09:39
TEST_JOB_CLASS               16
```

This information is also available from OEM on the Scheduler Jobs (Scheduled) page (Administration > Jobs) shown in Figure 11.28.

Database: DB10G.WORLD > Scheduler Jobs   Logged in As SYS

Scheduler Jobs

Page Refreshed 23-Jun-2004 17:47:48   (Refresh)
(Create)

Scheduled | Running Disabled Run History

(Edit) (View) (Delete) (Run Now) (Create Like)

Select	Name	Owner	Scheduled Date	Last Run Date	Job Class	Previous Runs
⦿	GATHER_STATS_JOB	SYS	MAINTENANCE_WINDOW_GROUP	23-Jun-2004 08:19:42 +01:00	AUTO_TASKS_JOB_CLASS	3
○	PURGE_LOG	SYS	24-Jun-2004 03:00:00 -08:00	23-Jun-2004 03:00:01 -08:00	DEFAULT_JOB_CLASS	19
○	TEST_FULL_JOB_DEFINITION	JOB_USER	23-Jun-2004 17:48:00 +01:00	23-Jun-2004 17:46:00 +01:00	DEFAULT_JOB_CLASS	245
○	TEST_PROG_SCHED_CLASS_JOB_DEF	JOB_USER	23-Jun-2004 18:00:16 +01:00	23-Jun-2004 17:00:16 +01:00	TEST_JOB_CLASS	14
○	ARGUMENT_JOB_DEFINITION	JOB_USER	23-Jun-2004 18:00:16 +01:00	23-Jun-2004 17:00:16 +01:00	DEFAULT_JOB_CLASS	14
○	TEST_SCHED_JOB_DEFINITION	JOB_USER	23-Jun-2004 18:00:16 +01:00	23-Jun-2004 17:00:16 +01:00	DEFAULT_JOB_CLASS	14
○	TEST_PROG_JOB_DEFINITION	JOB_USER	23-Jun-2004 18:00:09 +01:00	23-Jun-2004 17:00:09 +01:00	DEFAULT_JOB_CLASS	14
○	TEST_PROG_SCHED_JOB_DEFINITION	JOB_USER	23-Jun-2004 18:00:16 +01:00	23-Jun-2004 17:00:16 +01:00	TEST_JOB_CLASS	14

Scheduled | Running Disabled Run History

Database | Setup | Preferences | Help | Logout

Figure 11.28: *OEM DB Control: Scheduler Jobs (Scheduled)*

The *dba_scheduler_running_jobs* view is the real starting point for job monitoring as it displays a list of the currently running jobs. Using this view, the user is able to identify the session that is actually executing the job, thereby giving the ability to monitor session level information.

The *scheduled_jobs_running.sql* script uses this view to identify the currently running jobs. The *extract* function is used to retrieve the elapsed time in seconds from the interval returned by the view.

🖫 scheduled_jobs_running.sql

```
set linesize 200
column owner format a15
column next_run_date format a20

select
  rj.job_name,
  rj.owner,
  to_char(j.next_run_date, 'DD-MON-YYYY HH24:MI:SS') as next_run_date,
  extract(second from rj.elapsed_time) as elapsed_time,
  rj.cpu_used,
  rj.session_id,
  rj.resource_consumer_group,
```

```
    j.run_count
from
    dba_scheduler_running_jobs rj,
    dba_scheduler_jobs j
where
    rj.job_name = j.job_name
order by
    rj.job_name
;
```

The output generated from the *scheduled_jobs_running.sql* script is shown below.

```
SQL> @scheduled_jobs_running

JOB_NAME                        OWNER              NEXT_RUN_DATE          ELAPSED_TIME   CPU_USED
SESSION_ID RESOURCE_CONSUMER_GROUP            RUN_COUNT
------------------------------- ---------------    --------------------   ------------   ----------
TEST_FULL_JOB_DEFINITION        JOB_USER            24-JUN-2004 09:22:00        20.69            0
272                                                 296
```

This information is also available from OEM on the Scheduler Jobs (Running) page (Administration > Jobs) shown in Figure 11.29.

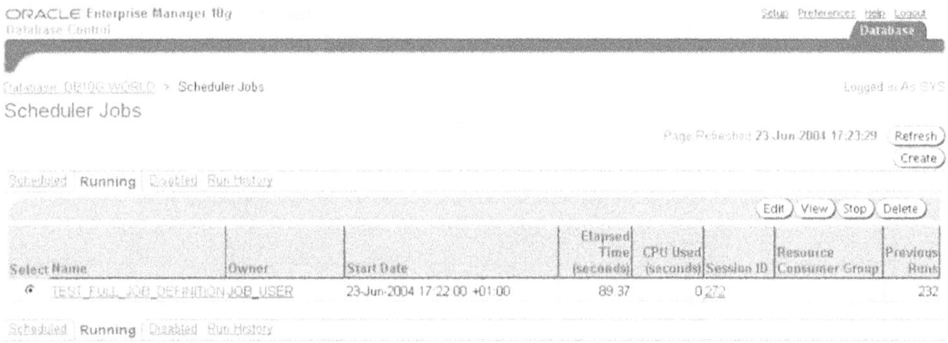

Figure 11.29: *OEM DB Control: Scheduler Jobs (Running)*

The Scheduler Jobs (Disabled) page of OEM, shown in Figure 11.30, lists all currently disabled jobs. This screen is essentially the same as the Scheduler Jobs (Scheduled) screen except the output from the *dba_scheduler_jobs* view is restricted using the ENABLED column. The *disabled_jobs.sql* script shows how the disabled jobs can be displayed.

💾 disabled_jobs.sql

```
set linesize 200

column owner format a15
column next_run_date format a25
```

```
select
    job_name,
    owner,
    nvl(to_char(next_run_date, 'DD-MON-YYYY HH24:MI:SS'), schedule_name) as
next_run_date,
    to_char(last_start_date, 'DD-MON-YYYY HH24:MI:SS') as last_run_date,
    job_class,
    run_count
from
    dba_scheduler_jobs
where
    enabled = 'FALSE'
;
```

If a job is disabled, it will be listed in the output from the *disabled_jobs.sql* script.

```
SQL> exec dbms_scheduler.disable ('test_full_job_definition', true);

PL/SQL procedure successfully completed.

SQL> @disabled_jobs

JOB_NAME                      OWNER            NEXT_RUN_DATE              LAST_RUN_DATE
JOB_CLASS                         RUN_COUNT
----------------------------- ---------------- -------------------------  -------------------- -------
------------------------- ----------
TEST_FULL_JOB_DEFINITION      JOB_USER         26-JUN-2004 13:42:00       26-JUN-2004 13:36:00
DEFAULT_JOB_CLASS                   733
```

The same information is displayed in the Scheduler Jobs (Disabled) page of OEM shown in Figure 11.30.

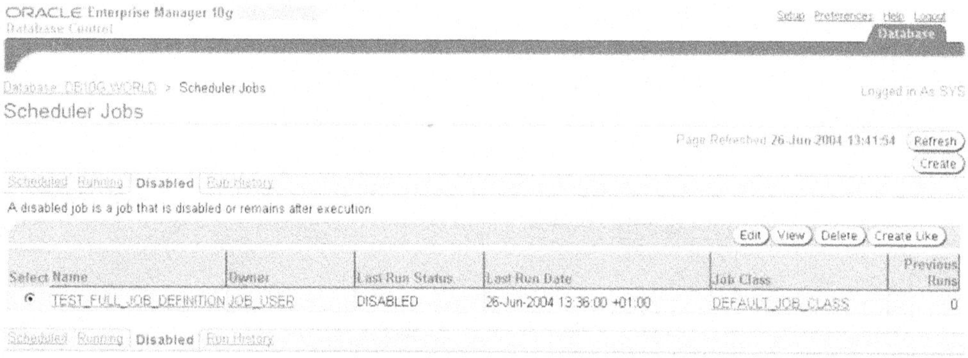

Figure 11.30: *OEM DB Control: Scheduler Jobs (Disabled)*

The *dba_scheduler_job_run_details* view provides a history of previous job runs. The *job_run_history.sql* script uses a top-n query to return a specified number of records from the history for a specified job or all jobs.

💾 job_run_history.sql

```
-- ********************************************************************
-- Parameters:
--     1) Specific job name or ALL which doesn't limit output.
--     2) Number of records to be displayed.
-- ********************************************************************

set linesize 200
set verify off

column owner format a15
column status format a10
column completion_date format a20
column run_duration format a20

select
    *
from
    (select
        job_name,
        owner,
        status,
        to_char(actual_start_date + run_duration, 'DD-MON-YYYY HH24:MI:SS')
as completion_date,
        run_duration
    from
        dba_scheduler_job_run_details
    where
        job_name = decode(upper('&1'), 'ALL', job_name, upper('&1'))
    and
        actual_start_date is not null
    order by
        (actual_start_date + run_duration) DESC) a
where
  rownum <= &2
;
```

The following output lists history information from a specific job and all jobs. The output is restricted to five rows by the second parameter.

```
SQL> @job_run_history test_sched_job_definition 5

JOB_NAME                      OWNER           STATUS     COMPLETION_DATE      RUN_DURATION
----------------------------- --------------- ---------- -------------------- ------------
TEST_SCHED_JOB_DEFINITION     JOB_USER        SUCCEEDED  24-JUN-2004 10:01:59            1
TEST_SCHED_JOB_DEFINITION     JOB_USER        SUCCEEDED  24-JUN-2004 09:01:59            1
TEST_SCHED_JOB_DEFINITION     JOB_USER        SUCCEEDED  24-JUN-2004 08:11:21            1
TEST_SCHED_JOB_DEFINITION     JOB_USER        SUCCEEDED  23-JUN-2004 18:01:59            1
TEST_SCHED_JOB_DEFINITION     JOB_USER        SUCCEEDED  23-JUN-2004 17:01:59            1

SQL> @job_run_history all 5

JOB_NAME                      OWNER           STATUS     COMPLETION_DATE      RUN_DURATION
----------------------------- --------------- ---------- -------------------- ------------
TEST_FULL_JOB_DEFINITION      JOB_USER        SUCCEEDED  24-JUN-2004 10:31:43            1
TEST_FULL_JOB_DEFINITION      JOB_USER        SUCCEEDED  24-JUN-2004 10:29:43            1
TEST_FULL_JOB_DEFINITION      JOB_USER        SUCCEEDED  24-JUN-2004 10:27:43            1
TEST_FULL_JOB_DEFINITION      JOB_USER        SUCCEEDED  24-JUN-2004 10:25:43            1
TEST_FULL_JOB_DEFINITION      JOB_USER        SUCCEEDED  24-JUN-2004 10:23:43            1
```

The Scheduler Jobs (Run History) page of OEM, shown in Figure 11.31, lists the full job run history.

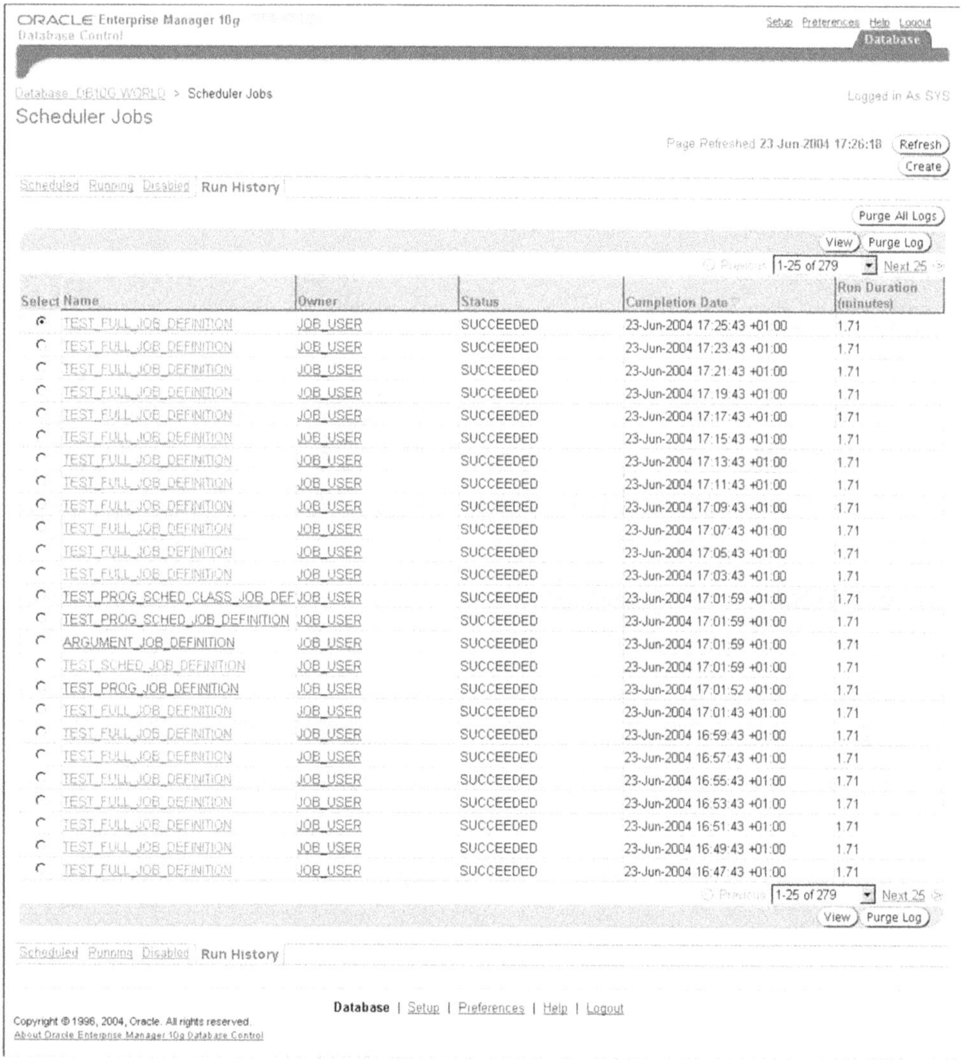

Figure 11.31: *OEM DB Control: Scheduler Jobs (Run History)*

The *scheduled_job_details.sql* script displays a summary of the information available for a specific job including a limited job history.

🖫 scheduled_job_details.sql

```
-- Parameters:
--    1) Specific job name.
--    2) Number of history records to be displayed.
-- ******************************************************************

set verify off
set feedback off
set linesize 200

column owner format a15
column comments format a50

prompt
prompt GENERAL
prompt --------

select
  job_name,
  owner,
  enabled,
  logging_level,
  job_class,
  comments
from
  dba_scheduler_jobs
where
  job_name = upper('&1');

column repeat_interval format a40
column start_date format a20
column end_date format a20
column next_run_date format a20

prompt
prompt
prompt SCHEDULE
prompt ---------

select
  repeat_interval,
  to_char(start_date, 'DD-MON-YYYY HH24:MI:SS') as start_date,
  to_char(end_date, 'DD-MON-YYYY HH24:MI:SS') as end_date,
  to_char(next_run_date, 'DD-MON-YYYY HH24:MI:SS') as next_run_date
from
  dba_scheduler_jobs
where
  job_name = upper('&1');

column job_action format a100

prompt
prompt
prompt COMMAND
prompt ---------

select
  job_action
```

```
from
  dba_scheduler_jobs
where
  job_name = upper('&1');


column status format a10
column completion_date format a20
column run_duration format a20

prompt
prompt
prompt RUN HISTORY
prompt ------------

select
   *
from
   (select
       job_name,
       owner,
       status,
       to_char(actual_start_date + run_duration, 'DD-MON-YYYY HH24:MI:SS')
as completion_date,
       run_duration
    from
       dba_scheduler_job_run_details
    where
       job_name = decode(upper('&1'), 'ALL', job_name, upper('&1'))
    and
       actual_start_date is not null
    order by
       (actual_start_date + run_duration) DESC) a
where
  rownum <= &2
;
set feedback on
```

An example of the output generated by the script is listed below:

```
SQL> @scheduled_job_details test_full_job_definition 5

GENERAL
-------

JOB_NAME                        OWNER           ENABL LOGG JOB_CLASS                     COMMENTS
------------------------------- --------------- ----- ---- ----------------------------- --
TEST_FULL_JOB_DEFINITION        JOB_USER        TRUE  RUNS DEFAULT_JOB_CLASS             Job defined
entirely by the CREATE JOB procedure.


SCHEDULE
--------

REPEAT_INTERVAL                     START_DATE           END_DATE             NEXT_RUN_DATE
----------------------------------- -------------------- -------------------- --------
FREQ=MINUTELY;INTERVAL=2     23-JUN-2004 09:22:00                              24-JUN-2004 10:42:00


COMMAND
--------

JOB_ACTION
---------------------------------------------------------------------------------------------
BEGIN my_job_proc('CREATE_PROGRAM (BLOCK)'); END;


RUN HISTORY
-----------

JOB_NAME                        OWNER           STATUS     COMPLETION_DATE      RUN_DURATION
------------------------------- --------------- ---------- -------------------- ------------
TEST_FULL_JOB_DEFINITION        JOB_USER        SUCCEEDED  24-JUN-2004 10:41:43            1
TEST_FULL_JOB_DEFINITION        JOB_USER        SUCCEEDED  24-JUN-2004 10:39:43            1
TEST_FULL_JOB_DEFINITION        JOB_USER        SUCCEEDED  24-JUN-2004 10:37:43            1
TEST_FULL_JOB_DEFINITION        JOB_USER        SUCCEEDED  24-JUN-2004 10:35:43            1
TEST_FULL_JOB_DEFINITION        JOB_USER        SUCCEEDED  24-JUN-2004 10:33:43            1
```

Clicking on a job run in the Scheduler Jobs (Run History) page produces the View Job page, shown in Figure 11.32, which contains similar information to the *scheduled_job_details.sql* script.

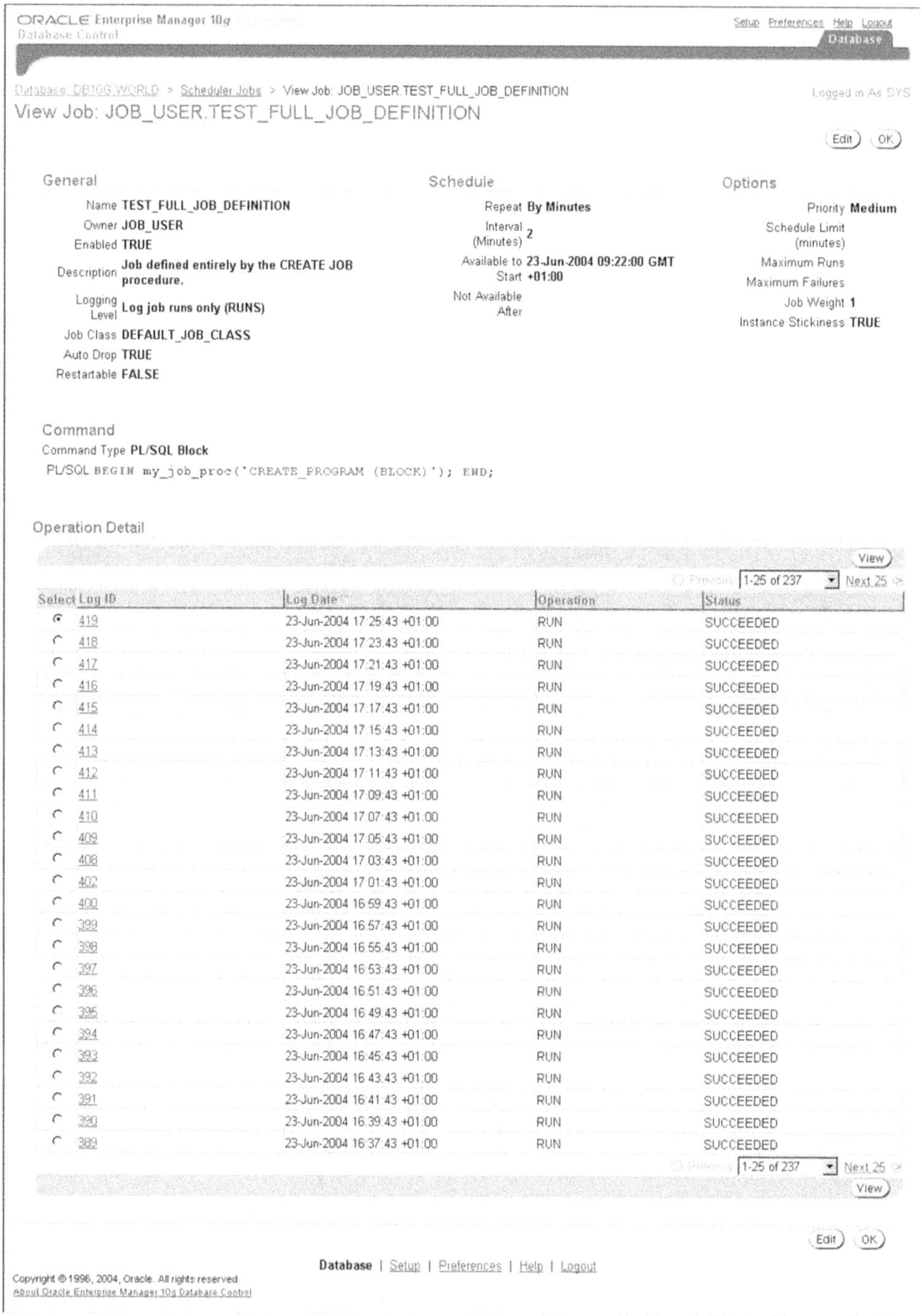

ORACLE Enterprise Manager 10g
Database Control

Setup Preferences Help Logout

Database

Database: DB10G.WORLD > Scheduler Jobs > View Job: JOB_USER.TEST_FULL_JOB_DEFINITION

Logged in As SYS

View Job: JOB_USER.TEST_FULL_JOB_DEFINITION

(Edit) (OK)

General

Name	**TEST_FULL_JOB_DEFINITION**
Owner	**JOB_USER**
Enabled	**TRUE**
Description	**Job defined entirely by the CREATE JOB procedure.**
Logging Level	**Log job runs only (RUNS)**
Job Class	**DEFAULT_JOB_CLASS**
Auto Drop	**TRUE**
Restartable	**FALSE**

Schedule

Repeat	**By Minutes**
Interval (Minutes)	**2**
Available to Start	**23-Jun-2004 09:22:00 GMT +01:00**
Not Available After	

Options

Priority	**Medium**
Schedule Limit (minutes)	
Maximum Runs	
Maximum Failures	
Job Weight	**1**
Instance Stickiness	**TRUE**

Command

Command Type **PL/SQL Block**

PL/SQL `BEGIN my_job_proc('CREATE_PROGRAM (BLOCK)'); END;`

Operation Detail

(View)

Previous 1-25 of 237 Next 25

Select	Log ID	Log Date	Operation	Status
◉	419	23-Jun-2004 17:25:43 +01:00	RUN	SUCCEEDED
○	418	23-Jun-2004 17:23:43 +01:00	RUN	SUCCEEDED
○	417	23-Jun-2004 17:21:43 +01:00	RUN	SUCCEEDED
○	416	23-Jun-2004 17:19:43 +01:00	RUN	SUCCEEDED
○	415	23-Jun-2004 17:17:43 +01:00	RUN	SUCCEEDED
○	414	23-Jun-2004 17:15:43 +01:00	RUN	SUCCEEDED
○	413	23-Jun-2004 17:13:43 +01:00	RUN	SUCCEEDED
○	412	23-Jun-2004 17:11:43 +01:00	RUN	SUCCEEDED
○	411	23-Jun-2004 17:09:43 +01:00	RUN	SUCCEEDED
○	410	23-Jun-2004 17:07:43 +01:00	RUN	SUCCEEDED
○	409	23-Jun-2004 17:05:43 +01:00	RUN	SUCCEEDED
○	408	23-Jun-2004 17:03:43 +01:00	RUN	SUCCEEDED
○	402	23-Jun-2004 17:01:43 +01:00	RUN	SUCCEEDED
○	400	23-Jun-2004 16:59:43 +01:00	RUN	SUCCEEDED
○	399	23-Jun-2004 16:57:43 +01:00	RUN	SUCCEEDED
○	398	23-Jun-2004 16:55:43 +01:00	RUN	SUCCEEDED
○	397	23-Jun-2004 16:53:43 +01:00	RUN	SUCCEEDED
○	396	23-Jun-2004 16:51:43 +01:00	RUN	SUCCEEDED
○	395	23-Jun-2004 16:49:43 +01:00	RUN	SUCCEEDED
○	394	23-Jun-2004 16:47:43 +01:00	RUN	SUCCEEDED
○	393	23-Jun-2004 16:45:43 +01:00	RUN	SUCCEEDED
○	392	23-Jun-2004 16:43:43 +01:00	RUN	SUCCEEDED
○	391	23-Jun-2004 16:41:43 +01:00	RUN	SUCCEEDED
○	390	23-Jun-2004 16:39:43 +01:00	RUN	SUCCEEDED
○	389	23-Jun-2004 16:37:43 +01:00	RUN	SUCCEEDED

Previous 1-25 of 237 Next 25

(View)

(Edit) (OK)

Database | Setup | Preferences | Help | Logout

About Oracle Enterprise Manager 10g Database Control

Figure 11.32: *OEM DB Control: View Job*

Clicking on one of the individual operations in this screen produces the Operation Detail screen, shown in Figure 11.33.

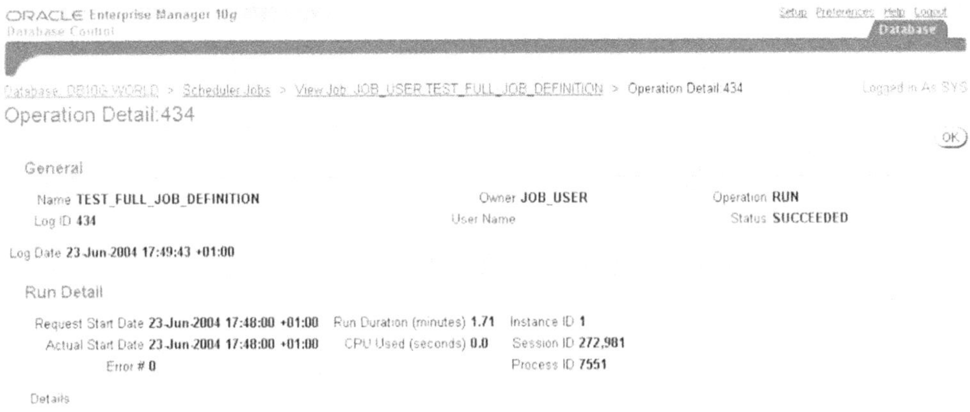

Figure 11.33: *OEM DB Control: Operation Detail*

The previous two sections showed how running jobs along with their associated sessions can be identified. The next section will focus on monitoring the individual sessions.

Killing Oracle Job Sessions

On occasion, it may be necessary to kill an Oracle session that is associated with a running job. The first step in the process is to identify the session to be killed.

Running jobs that were scheduled using the *dbms_job* package can be identified using the *dba_jobs_running* view. The *jobs_running.sql* script listed below uses this view along with the *v$session* and *v$process* views to gather all information needed about the running jobs.

🖫 running_job_processes.sql

```
set feedback off
alter session set nls_date_format='DD-MON-YYYY HH24:MI:SS';
set feedback on

select
   jr.job,
   s.username,
   s.sid,
   s.serial#,
```

```
   p.spid,
   s.lockwait,
   s.logon_time
from
   dba_jobs_running jr,
   v$session s,
   v$process p
where
   jr.sid = s.sid
and
   s.paddr = p.addr
order by
   jr.job;
```

The type of output expected from this script is listed below.

```
SQL> @running_job_processes

  JOB USERNAME      SID    SERIAL# SPID LOCKWAIT LOGON_TIME

----- ---------- ------ ---------- ---- -------- --------------------
   42 JOB_USER      265          3 3231          23-JUN-2004 08:21:25
   99 JOB_USER      272         77 3199          23-JUN-2004 08:55:35
```

Running jobs that were scheduled using the *dbms_scheduler* package can be identified using the *dba_scheduler_running_jobs* view. The following *jobs_running_10g.sql* script uses this view along with the *v$session* and *v$process* views to gather all information needed about the running jobs.

💾 running_job_processes_10g.sql

```
select
   rj.job_name,
   s.username,
   s.sid,
   s.serial#,
   p.spid,
   s.lockwait,
   s.logon_time
from
   dba_scheduler_running_jobs rj,
   v$session s,
   v$process p
where
   rj.session_id = s.sid
and
   s.paddr = p.addr
order by
   rj.job_name
;
```

The type of output expected from this script is listed below.

```
SQL> @running_job_processes_10g

JOB_NAME                  USERNAME SID SERIAL# SPID LOCK  LOGON_TIME
------------------------- -------- --- ------- ---- ----- --------------------
TEST_FULL_JOB_DEFINITION  SYS      272     125 3199       23-JUN-2004 09:22:12
```

Regardless of the job scheduling mechanism, the important thing to note is that there are *sid, serial#,* and *spid* values associated with the running jobs. The *sid* and *serial#* values are necessary in order to kill the session, while the *spid* value is necessary if the associated operating system process or thread must be killed directly.

To kill the session from within Oracle, the *sid* and *serial#* values of the relevant session can then be substituted into the following statement:

```
alter system kill session 'sid,serial#';
```

With reference to the job listed above by the *jobs_running_10g.sql* script, the statement would look like this:

```
SQL> alter system kill session '272,125';

System altered.
```

This command tells the specified session to rollback any un-committed changes and release any acquired resources before terminating cleanly. In some situations, this cleanup processing may take a considerable amount of time, in which case the session status is set to "marked for kill" until the process is complete.

Under normal circumstances, no further actions are needed, but occasionally it may be necessary to bypass this cleanup operation to speed up the release of row and object locks held by the session. Killing the operating system process or thread associated with the session releases the session's locks almost immediately, forcing the PMON process to complete the rollback operation.

> Killing the operating system processes associated with Oracle sessions should be used as a last resort. Killing the wrong process could result in an instance crash and loss of data.

In UNIX and Linux environments, the *kill* command is used to kill specific processes. In order to use this command, the operating system processes ID

Killing Oracle Job Sessions

must be specified. The *jobs_running.sql* and *jobs_running_10g.sql* scripts list the operating system process ID associated with each running job in the *spid* column. With this information, the operating system process can be killed by issuing the following command:

```
kill -9 3199
```

The *ps* command can be used to check the process list before or after killing the operating system process.

```
ps -ef | grep ora
```

In Windows environments, Oracle runs as a single multi-threaded process, so a specific process is unable to be killed. Instead, Oracle provides the *orakill.exe* command to allow a specific thread within the Oracle executable to be killed.

```
orakill.exe ORACLE_SID spid
```

The first parameter should not be confused with the *sid* value of the Oracle session. It is, in fact, the SID associated with the instance. The *spid* value in windows environments identifies the thread within the Oracle executable, rather than an operating system process ID. With reference to the job listed above by the *jobs_running_10g.sql* script, the command issued would look something like this:

```
C:> orakill.exe DB10G 3199
```

These processes can be used to kill jobs, sessions or processes as needed.

This next section will present an assortment of advanced topics related to administration of the Oracle scheduler. Topics to be covered include setting default scheduler attributes along with object specific attributes, scheduler logging, resource allocation and security.

Setting Job Scheduler Attributes

There are currently four Oracle job scheduler attributes:

- *current_open_window* (read-only)
- *default_timezone*

- *log_history*

- *max_job_slave_processes*

Management of the scheduler attributes requires the MANAGE SCHEDULER privilege. To influence the default behavior of the scheduler, three of the attributes can be altered using the *set_scheduler_attribute* procedure. These values can be displayed using the *show_scheduler_attribute.sql* script, which utilizes the *get_scheduler_attribute* procedure.

🖫 show_scheduler_attribute.sql

```
set verify off

variable v_value VARCHAR2(1000);

BEGIN
  DBMS_SCHEDULER.get_scheduler_attribute (
    attribute => '&1',
    value     => :v_value);
END;
/

print v_value
```

The following sections will present more detail regarding each of the scheduler attributes starting with the *current_open_window* attribute.

current_open_window

This is a read-only attribute which returns the name of the window that is currently open or active. The *show_scheduler_attribute.sql* script is used to display the value of the *current_open_window* attribute.

```
SQL> @show_scheduler_attribute.sql current_open_window

V_VALUE
-------------------------------------------------------------------
WEEKEND_WINDOW
```

default_timezone

As the name implies, this attribute sets the default time zone for the scheduler. When a job is scheduled using the calendar syntax to define a repeat interval, the scheduler needs to know which time zone to apply when calculating the next run date. Since a time zone cannot be specified explicitly by the calendar syntax, it must be derived from the following sources in the order noted below:

- The time zone of the job's *start_date* attribute
- The current session's time zone
- The scheduler's *default_timezone* attribute
- The time zone returned by the *systimestamp* function

The following example sets the *default_timezone* attribute to a value of 'US/Eastern' and displays the change.

```
BEGIN
  DBMS_SCHEDULER.set_scheduler_attribute (
    attribute => 'default_timezone',
    value     => 'US/Eastern');
END;
/

SQL> @show_scheduler_attribute.sql default_timezone


V_VALUE
--------------------------------------------------
US/Eastern
```

log_history

This parameter controls the length of time scheduler logs are kept. Each day the scheduler purges any logs that are older than this retention time, specified in days. Any value within the range of one to 999 can be specified with the default value being 30 days. The following example sets the *log_history* attribute to a value of 60 days and displays the change.

```
BEGIN
  DBMS_SCHEDULER.set_scheduler_attribute (
    attribute => 'log_history',
    value     => 60);
END;
/

SQL> @show_scheduler_attribute.sql log_history

V_VALUE
-------------------------------------------------
60
```

max_job_slave_processes

Unlike the scheduler in Oracle 9i, the Oracle scheduler is not constrained by the *job_queue_processes* parameter. Instead, it will start as many job slave processes as needed to cope with the current load. Although limiting the total number of job slave processes should not be necessary under normal circumstances, the *max_job_slave_processes* parameter allows the capability to do so if required. Any value within the range of one to 999 can be specified with the default value being NULL. The following example sets the *max_job_slave_processes* attribute to a value of 100 and displays the change.

```
BEGIN
  DBMS_SCHEDULER.set_scheduler_attribute (
    attribute => 'max_job_slave_processes',
    value     => 100);
END;
/

SQL> @show_scheduler_attribute.sql max_job_slave_processes

V_VALUE
---------------------------------------------
100
```

To remove this limit, simply set the value to NULL.

```
BEGIN
  DBMS_SCHEDULER.set_scheduler_attribute (
    attribute => 'max_job_slave_processes',
    value     => NULL);
END;
/

SQL> @show_scheduler_attribute.sql max_job_slave_processes

V_VALUE
---------------------------------------------
```

With that introduction to how to set scheduler attributes, the next section will present a look at how job priorities can be assigned within a job class.

Job Priorities

When several jobs within the same job class are scheduled to start at the same time, the job coordinator uses the job priority to decide which job to execute

---

first. In the following example, a job is created and its *job_priority* attribute is set to one using the *set_attribute* procedure.

```
BEGIN
  DBMS_SCHEDULER.create_job (
    job_name         => 'test_priority_job',
    job_type         => 'PLSQL_BLOCK',
    job_action       => 'BEGIN DBMS_LOCK.sleep(10); END;',
    start_date       => SYSTIMESTAMP,
    repeat_interval  => 'freq=minutely;',
    end_date         => SYSTIMESTAMP + 1/48,
    enabled          => FALSE,
    comments         => 'Job used to test priorities.');

  DBMS_SCHEDULER.set_attribute (
    name       => 'test_priority_job',
    attribute  => 'job_priority',
    value      => 1);

  DBMS_SCHEDULER.enable (name => 'test_priority_job');
END;
/
```

The attribute can be set to any value in the range from one to five, in which one is the highest priority. If a priority is not specified during the job creation, it is assigned the default value of three.

The priority of a job can be displayed using the *dba_scheduler_jobs* view, as shown by the following query:

```
select
   job_name,
   job_priority
from
   dba_scheduler_jobs
order by
   job_priority
;

JOB_NAME                        JOB_PRIORITY
------------------------------  ------------
TEST_PRIORITY_JOB                          1
GATHER_STATS_JOB                           3
PURGE_LOG                                  3
```

This introduction to priorities illustrates that assigning a priority to jobs within a job class is easy. The next section will present information on scheduler logging that is available as part of the Oracle scheduler.

Scheduler Logging

The Oracle scheduler logs a number of events including job maintenance, job run activity and window activity. It also gives some degree of control over the level of logging performed by the scheduler.

The *log_history* scheduler attribute can be used to control the volume of historical logging information. However, if a specific job or job class has a different history requirement, the *set_attribute* procedure can be used to override this value.

```
BEGIN
  -- Alter log history for a specific job.
  DBMS_SCHEDULER.set_attribute (
    name      => 'test_job',
    attribute => 'log_history',
    value     => 30);

  -- Alter log history for a specific job class.
  DBMS_SCHEDULER.set_attribute (
    name      => 'test_job_class',
    attribute => 'log_history',
    value     => 90);
END;
/
```

There are several types of scheduler logs which can be managed separately. In the following sections, information will be presented on each type of logging available, starting with job logs.

Job Logs

There are three levels of logging associated with scheduled jobs. They are noted below along with the appropriate constants defined in the *dbms_scheduler* package:

- *logging_off* - No logging
- *logging_runs* - Only run events are logged
- *logging_full* - All events that happen to a job during its lifetime are logged

The logging level of a job is typically set by associating it to a job class with the appropriate logging level. Since the default logging level for a job class is *logging_runs* and all jobs are associated with a job class, the default logging level for a job is *logging_runs*.

Alternatively, the *logging_level* parameter of a job can be set directly using the *set_attribute* procedure, as shown below.

```
BEGIN
  DBMS_SCHEDULER.set_attribute (
    name      => 'test_log_job',
    attribute => 'logging_level',
    value     => DBMS_SCHEDULER.logging_off);
END;
/
```

For security reasons, this method cannot change the logging level to a value lower than that of its associated class. For example, if the job's associated job class has a logging level of *logging_runs*, the *set_attribute* procedure could only be used to switch the job's logging level to *logging_full* and back to *logging_runs*. By doing so, administrators of the scheduler can dictate a minimum level of auditing for job execution.

The *job_log_lifecycle.sql* script creates, updates, enables and drops a job, thereby effectively producing a full lifecycle of events in the job log.

🖫 job_log_lifecycle.sql

```
BEGIN
  -- Remove all logs for this job.
  DBMS_SCHEDULER.purge_log(job_name => 'test_log_job');

  -- Create job class with full logging.
  DBMS_SCHEDULER.create_job_class (
    job_class_name          => 'test_logging_class',
    resource_consumer_group => 'default_consumer_group',
    logging_level           => DBMS_SCHEDULER.logging_full);

  -- Create job links to previous job class.
  DBMS_SCHEDULER.create_job (
    job_name    => 'test_log_job',
    job_type    => 'PLSQL_BLOCK',
    job_action  => 'BEGIN NULL; END;',
    job_class   => 'test_logging_class',
    enabled     => FALSE,
    auto_drop   => FALSE,
    comments    => 'Job used to job logs.');

  -- Update the job.
  DBMS_SCHEDULER.set_attribute (
    name      => 'test_log_job',
    attribute => 'start_date',
    value     => SYSTIMESTAMP);

  -- Enable the job.
  DBMS_SCHEDULER.enable (name => 'test_log_job');
```

```
  -- Pause to let the job run.
  DBMS_LOCK.sleep(30);

  -- Drop the job.
  DBMS_SCHEDULER.drop_job (job_name => 'test_log_job');

  -- Drop the job class.
  DBMS_SCHEDULER.drop_job_class (job_class_name => 'test_logging_class');v

END;
/
```

This script clears down any log information associated with the job it creates, allowing it to be run multiple times with the same result.

The *job_logs.sql* script uses the *dba_scheduler_job_log* view to display log information for a specific job or all jobs.

🖫 job_logs.sql

```
-- **************************************************
-- Parameters:
--      1) Specific job name or 'all' jobs.
-- ******************************************************************

set feedback off
alter session set nls_timestamp_tz_format='DD-MON-YYYY HH24:MI:SS.ff';
set feedback on

column owner format a10
column job_name format a30
column operation format a10
column status format a10
column log_date format a27

select
   owner,
   job_name,
   operation,
   status,
   log_date
from
   dba_scheduler_job_log
where
   job_name = decode(upper('&1'), 'ALL', job_name, upper('&1'))
order by
   log_date;
```

Using the previous two scripts, the sort of logging one would expect for a job with full logging enabled can be seen.

```
SQL> @ job_log_lifecycle.sql
```

```
PL/SQL procedure successfully completed.

SQL> @ job_logs.sql test_log_job

OWNER       JOB_NAME       OPERATION  STATUS     LOG_DATE
----------  -------------  ---------  ---------  --------------------------
JOB_USER    TEST_LOG_JOB   CREATE                21-AUG-2004 15:21:23.795000
JOB_USER    TEST_LOG_JOB   UPDATE                21-AUG-2004 15:21:23.811000
JOB_USER    TEST_LOG_JOB   ENABLE                21-AUG-2004 15:21:23.827000
JOB_USER    TEST_LOG_JOB   RUN        SUCCEEDED  21-AUG-2004 15:21:23.874000
JOB_USER    TEST_LOG_JOB   SUCCEEDED             21-AUG-2004 15:21:23.874000
JOB_USER    TEST_LOG_JOB   DROP                  21-AUG-2004 15:21:54.577000
```

The job logs provide only top-level information about the jobs. Further details are logged in the job run details log which is covered in the next section.

Displaying Job Run Details

Every row in the *dba_scheduler_job_log* view for a run event has an associated row in the *dba_scheduler_job_run_details* view. This view provides more details about the job run including requested start date, actual start date, duration, CPU usage and such.

The *scheduled_job_details.sql* and *job_run_history.sql* scripts use the *dba_scheduler_job_run_details* view to display the run history for a specific job.

```
SQL> @job_run_history all 5

JOB_NAME                   OWNER     STATUS     COMPLETION_DATE      RUN_DURATION
-------------------------  --------  ---------  -------------------  ------------
TEST_FULL_JOB_DEFINITION   JOB_USER  SUCCEEDED  21-AUG-2004 15:31:43            1
TEST_FULL_JOB_DEFINITION   JOB_USER  SUCCEEDED  21-AUG-2004 15:29:43            1
TEST_FULL_JOB_DEFINITION   JOB_USER  SUCCEEDED  21-AUG-2004 15:27:43            1
TEST_FULL_JOB_DEFINITION   JOB_USER  SUCCEEDED  21-AUG-2004 15:25:43            1
TEST_FULL_JOB_DEFINITION   JOB_USER  SUCCEEDED  21-AUG-2004 15:23:43            1
```

The job logs and job run detail logs allow the tracking of all job activity but do not reveal what the active resource plan was during the job runs. This information is provided by the window logs, which is covered in the next section.

Window Logs

There is no logging level associated with window logs. A window log entry is created whenever a window is created, dropped, opened, closed, overlapped, disabled or enabled. The *window_logs.sql* script uses the *dba_scheduler_window_log* view to display window log information about a specific window or all windows.

💾 window_logs.sql

```
-- ************************************************
-- Parameters:
--    1) Specific window name or 'all' windows.
-- ******************************************************************

set feedback off
alter session set nls_timestamp_tz_format='DD-MON-YYYY HH24:MI:SS';
set feedback on

column window_name format a30
column operation format a10
column status format a10
column log_date format a27

select
   window_name,
   operation,
   status,
   log_date
from
   dba_scheduler_window_log
where
   window_name = decode(upper('&1'), 'ALL', window_name, upper('&1'))
order by
   log_date;
```

An example of the output produced by this script is shown here:

```
SQL> @window_logs.sql all

WINDOW_NAME                     OPERATION  STATUS     LOG_DATE
------------------------------  ---------- ---------- --------------------
WEEKNIGHT_WINDOW                OPEN                  20-AUG-2004 07:00:01
WEEKNIGHT_WINDOW                CLOSE                 20-AUG-2004 15:00:01
WEEKNIGHT_WINDOW                OPEN                  21-AUG-2004 07:00:00
WEEKNIGHT_WINDOW                CLOSE                 21-AUG-2004 15:00:00
WEEKEND_WINDOW                  OPEN                  21-AUG-2004 15:00:02
```

Each entry in the *dba_scheduler_window_log* view for a closed operation has an associated entry in the *dba_scheduler_window_details* view. This view provides additional information including the requested start date, actual start date and window duration. The *window_details.sql* script makes use of this view.

🖫 window_details.sql

```
-- **************************************************
-- Parameters:
--    1) Specific window name or 'all' windows.
-- *********************************************************

set feedback off
alter session set nls_timestamp_tz_format='DD-MON-YYYY HH24:MI:SS';
set feedback on

set linesize 120

column window_name format a30
column log_date format a27
column actual_start_date format a27
column actual_duration format 99999

select
   window_name,
   log_date,
   actual_start_date,
   extract(minute from actual_duration) as actual_duration
from
   dba_scheduler_window_details
where
   window_name = decode(upper('&1'), 'ALL', window_name, upper('&1'))
order by
   log_date
;
```

An example of the output produced by this script is shown below.

```
SQL> @window_details.sql all

WINDOW_NAME          LOG_DATE            ACTUAL_START_DATE        ACTUAL_DURATION
-------------------- ------------------- ------------------------ ---------------
WEEKNIGHT_WINDOW     20-AUG-2004 15:00:01    19-AUG-2004 22:00:01               0
WEEKNIGHT_WINDOW     21-AUG-2004 15:00:00    20-AUG-2004 22:00:00               0
```

Now that the various types of scheduler logs have been introduced, it makes sense to examine their management. It has been shown that the contents of the scheduler logs are managed automatically, but the next section will illustrate how to manually purge the scheduler logs.

Purging Logs

On occasion, it may be necessary to manually purge the scheduler logs prior to any regularly scheduled automatic purge. This can be accomplished using the *purge_log* procedure.

```
PROCEDURE purge_log(

    log_history        IN PLS_INTEGER DEFAULT 0,
    which_log          IN VARCHAR2     DEFAULT 'JOB_AND_WINDOW_LOG',
    job_name           IN VARCHAR2     DEFAULT NULL)
```

The parameters and usages associated with this procedure are listed below:

- *log_history* - This determines the age of the logs that should be kept. Valid values range between zero and 999 with the default being zero.

- *which_log* - This indicates which log or logs should be purged. The possible parameters are *job_log*, *window_log* and *job_and_window_log*, with the latter being the default value.

- *job_name* - This limits the purge operation of a specific job, job class or comma separated list. By default, this parameter is set to NULL, which indicates logs for all jobs should be purged.

The following example shows how the procedure can be used:

```
BEGIN
  DBMS_SCHEDULER.purge_log (
    log_history => 5,
    which_log    => 'JOB_AND_WINDOW_LOG',
    job_name     => 'my_text_job');

  DBMS_SCHEDULER.purge_log (
    log_history => 15,
    which_log    => 'JOB_LOG',
    job_name     => 'my_text_job_class');

  DBMS_SCHEDULER.purge_log (
    log_history => 0,
    which_log    => 'WINDOW_LOG',
    job_name     => 'my_text_job');
END;
/
```

To purge all entries for both the job and window logs, simply call the procedure with no parameters.

```
SQL> EXECUTE DBMS_SCHEDULER.purge_log;
```

The *auto_purge* procedure uses the *log_history* values defined at the scheduler, job class and job *log_history* level to determine which logs should be purged. This procedure runs as part of the scheduled purge process, but it can also be run manually.

```
SQL> EXECUTE DBMS_SCHEDULER.auto_purge;
```

Depending on the circumstances, it is possible to manage the purging of logs manually as well as automatically. Moving on to the management of resources, it was mentioned previously that windows are involved in the link between the scheduler and the resource manager. In the following section, the link between these two functional areas will be examined.

Using the Job Resource Manager

Job classes, windows and window groups provide a link between the scheduler and the resource manager. The syntax for creating these scheduler objects was presented already, so this section will illustrate how they should be used. Since a complete investigation of the resource manager is beyond the scope of this book, this section will focus on the basic elements needed to start integrating resource management into job schedules.

The *dbms_resource_manager* package is an API which provides a means of controlling the allocation of system resources between Oracle sessions. Information about resource allocation can be displayed using the *dba_rsrc_%* views and these can be listed using the *table_comments.sql* script as shown below.

```
SQL> @table_comments.sql sys dba_rsrc

TABLE_NAME                      COMMENTS
------------------------------  ------------------------------------
DBA_RSRC_CONSUMER_GROUPS        all the resource consumer groups
DBA_RSRC_CONSUMER_GROUP_PRIVS   Switch privileges for consumer groups
DBA_RSRC_GROUP_MAPPINGS         all the consumer group mappings
DBA_RSRC_MANAGER_SYSTEM_PRIVS   system privileges for the resource
                                manager
DBA_RSRC_MAPPING_PRIORITY       the consumer group mapping attribute
                                priorities
DBA_RSRC_PLANS                  All the resource plans
DBA_RSRC_PLAN_DIRECTIVES        all the resource plan directives
```

Modifications to resource management must be complete and valid before they are applied to the system. For this reason, most operations using the *dbms_resource_manager* package are performed in a pending area where they are validated before being applied. The following code shows the procedure calls which must enclose any modifications:

```
BEGIN
```

```
  DBMS_RESOURCE_MANAGER.clear_pending_area;
  DBMS_RESOURCE_MANAGER.create_pending_area;

  -- Do something

  DBMS_RESOURCE_MANAGER.validate_pending_area;
  DBMS_RESOURCE_MANAGER.submit_pending_area;
END;
/
```

To illustrate the use of the resource manager, assume there is a system in which OLTP operations must take priority over batch operations during the day. At night, the situation is reversed so that batch operations take priority over OLTP operations.

To model this scenario, create two new consumer groups for the OLTP and batch tasks using the *create_consumer_group* procedure.

```
PROCEDURE create_consumer_group(

  consumer_group  IN  VARCHAR2,
  comment         IN  VARCHAR2,
  cpu_mth         IN  VARCHAR2 DEFAULT 'ROUND-ROBIN')
```

The *create_consumer_groups.sql* script uses this procedure to create the OLTP and batch consumer groups.

💾 create_consumer_groups.sql

```
CONN sys/password AS SYSDBA
BEGIN
  DBMS_RESOURCE_MANAGER.clear_pending_area;
  DBMS_RESOURCE_MANAGER.create_pending_area;

  -- Create the consumer groups
  DBMS_RESOURCE_MANAGER.create_consumer_group(
    consumer_group => 'oltp_consumer_group',
    comment        => 'OLTP process consumer group.');

  DBMS_RESOURCE_MANAGER.create_consumer_group(
    consumer_group => 'batch_consumer_group',
    comment        => 'Batch process consumer group.');

  DBMS_RESOURCE_MANAGER.validate_pending_area;
  DBMS_RESOURCE_MANAGER.submit_pending_area;
END;
/
```

The *consumer_groups.sql* script uses the *dba_rsrc_consumer_groups* view to display information about the consumer groups that have been created.

🖫 consumer_groups.sql

```
column comments format a60

select
   consumer_group,
   comments
from
   dba_rsrc_consumer_groups
order by
   consumer_group;
```

The output from this script is displayed below:

```
SQL> @consumer_groups.sql

CONSUMER_GROUP                 COMMENTS
-----------------------------  --------------------------------------------------
AUTO_TASK_CONSUMER_GROUP       System maintenance task consumer group
BATCH_CONSUMER_GROUP           Batch process consumer group.
DEFAULT_CONSUMER_GROUP         consumer group for users not assigned to any
                               group
LOW_GROUP                      Group of low priority sessions
OLTP_CONSUMER_GROUP            OLTP process consumer group.
OTHER_GROUPS                   consumer group for users not included in any
                               group in the active top-plan
SYS_GROUP                      Group of system sessions
```

The *delete_consumer_groups.sql* script uses the *delete_consumer_group* procedure to clean up the consumer groups created for the example. The consumer groups can only be removed if they have no dependent plan directives.

🖫 delete_consumer_groups.sql

```
BEGIN
  DBMS_RESOURCE_MANAGER.clear_pending_area();
  DBMS_RESOURCE_MANAGER.create_pending_area();

  -- Delete consumer groups.
  DBMS_RESOURCE_MANAGER.delete_consumer_group (
    consumer_group => 'oltp_consumer_group');

  DBMS_RESOURCE_MANAGER.delete_consumer_group (
    consumer_group => 'batch_consumer_group');

  DBMS_RESOURCE_MANAGER.validate_pending_area;
  DBMS_RESOURCE_MANAGER.submit_pending_area();
END;
/
```

With the consumer groups present, a resource plan can be created using the *create_plan* procedure, and it can be associated to the consumer groups using the *create_plan_directive* procedure.

```
PROCEDURE create_plan (
  plan                      IN  VARCHAR2,
  comment                   IN  VARCHAR2,
  cpu_mth                   IN  VARCHAR2 DEFAULT 'EMPHASIS',
  active_sess_pool_mth      IN  VARCHAR2 DEFAULT
'ACTIVE_SESS_POOL_ABSOLUTE',
  parallel_degree_limit_mth IN  VARCHAR2 DEFAULT
'PARALLEL_DEGREE_LIMIT_ABSOLUTE',
  queueing_mth              IN  VARCHAR2 DEFAULT 'FIFO_TIMEOUT')

PROCEDURE create_plan_directive (
  plan                      IN  VARCHAR2,
  group_or_subplan          IN  VARCHAR2,
  comment                   IN  VARCHAR2,
  cpu_p1                    IN  NUMBER DEFAULT NULL,
  cpu_p2                    IN  NUMBER DEFAULT NULL,
  cpu_p3                    IN  NUMBER DEFAULT NULL,
  cpu_p4                    IN  NUMBER DEFAULT NULL,
  cpu_p5                    IN  NUMBER DEFAULT NULL,
  cpu_p6                    IN  NUMBER DEFAULT NULL,
  cpu_p7                    IN  NUMBER DEFAULT NULL,
  cpu_p8                    IN  NUMBER DEFAULT NULL,
  active_sess_pool_p1       IN  NUMBER DEFAULT NULL,
  queueing_p1               IN  NUMBER DEFAULT NULL,
  parallel_degree_limit_p1  IN  NUMBER DEFAULT NULL,
  switch_group              IN  VARCHAR2 DEFAULT NULL,
  switch_time               IN  NUMBER DEFAULT NULL,
  switch_estimate           IN  BOOLEAN DEFAULT FALSE,
  max_est_exec_time         IN  NUMBER DEFAULT NULL,
  undo_pool                 IN  NUMBER DEFAULT NULL,
  max_idle_time             IN  NUMBER DEFAULT NULL,
  max_idle_blocker_time     IN  NUMBER DEFAULT NULL,
  switch_time_in_call       IN  NUMBER DEFAULT NULL)
```

The *day_plan.sql* script uses these procedures to create a resource plan suitable for daytime processing. The OLTP operations are associated with 80% of the CPU on level one while batch operations receive 100% of the remaining CPU at level two.

The *switch_group* and *switch_time* parameters are used in the OLTP plan directive to specify that OLTP processes lasting more than 60 seconds should be switched to the batch consumer group. The *other_groups* consumer group must be included in any valid plan as it provides resource allocation information for any processes that are not explicitly associated with the consumer groups.

🖫 day_plan.sql

```
BEGIN
  DBMS_RESOURCE_MANAGER.clear_pending_area;
  DBMS_RESOURCE_MANAGER.create_pending_area;

  -- Create a new plan
  DBMS_RESOURCE_MANAGER.create_plan(
```

```
  plan      => 'day_plan',
  comment => 'Plan suitable for daytime processing.');

-- Assign consumer groups to plan and define priorities
DBMS_RESOURCE_MANAGER.create_plan_directive (
  plan             => 'day_plan',
  group_or_subplan => 'oltp_consumer_group',
  comment          => 'Give OLTP processes higher priority - level 1',
  cpu_p1           => 80,
  switch_group     => 'batch_consumer_group',
  switch_time      => 60);

DBMS_RESOURCE_MANAGER.create_plan_directive (
  plan             => 'day_plan',
  group_or_subplan => 'batch_consumer_group',
  comment          => 'Give batch processes lower priority - level 2',
  cpu_p2           => 100);

DBMS_RESOURCE_MANAGER.create_plan_directive(
  plan             => 'day_plan',
  group_or_subplan => 'OTHER_GROUPS',
  comment          => 'all other users - level 3',
  cpu_p3           => 100);

DBMS_RESOURCE_MANAGER.validate_pending_area;
DBMS_RESOURCE_MANAGER.submit_pending_area;
END;
/
```

The *night_plan.sql* script creates a resource plan suitable for nighttime processing in which the resource allocation is the reverse of the daytime processing, such that batch processes receive 80% of the CPU at level one and OLTP operations receive 100% of the remaining CPU at level two. Once again, the *other_groups* consumer group is specified as a catch-all.

🖫 night_plan.sql

```
BEGIN
  DBMS_RESOURCE_MANAGER.clear_pending_area;
  DBMS_RESOURCE_MANAGER.create_pending_area;

  -- Create a new plan
  DBMS_RESOURCE_MANAGER.create_plan(
    plan      => 'night_plan',
    comment => 'Plan suitable for daytime processing.');

  -- Assign consumer groups to plan and define priorities
  DBMS_RESOURCE_MANAGER.create_plan_directive (
    plan             => 'night_plan',
    group_or_subplan => 'batch_consumer_group',
    comment          => 'Give batch processes lower priority - level 2',
    cpu_p1           => 80);

  DBMS_RESOURCE_MANAGER.create_plan_directive (
    plan             => 'night_plan',
```

```
      group_or_subplan => 'oltp_consumer_group',
      comment           => 'Give OLTP processes higher priority - level 1',
      cpu_p2            => 100);

   DBMS_RESOURCE_MANAGER.create_plan_directive(
      plan              => 'night_plan',
      group_or_subplan => 'OTHER_GROUPS',
      comment           => 'all other users - level 3',
      cpu_p3            => 100);

   DBMS_RESOURCE_MANAGER.validate_pending_area;
   DBMS_RESOURCE_MANAGER.submit_pending_area;
END;
/
```

The *resource_plan_directives.sql* script uses the *dba_rsrc_plan_directives* view to display information about the resource plans currently defined on the system.

🖬 resource_plan_directives.sql

```
select
   plan,
   group_or_subplan,
   status
from
   dba_rsrc_plan_directives
order by
   plan,
   group_or_subplan;
```

The output from the *resource_plan_directives.sql* script is displayed below.

```
SQL> @resource_plan_directives.sql

PLAN                          GROUP_OR_SUBPLAN              STATUS
----------------------------- ----------------------------- ------
DAY_PLAN                      BATCH_CONSUMER_GROUP          ACTIVE
DAY_PLAN                      OLTP_CONSUMER_GROUP           ACTIVE
DAY_PLAN                      OTHER_GROUPS                  ACTIVE
INTERNAL_PLAN                 OTHER_GROUPS                  ACTIVE
INTERNAL_QUIESCE              OTHER_GROUPS                  ACTIVE
INTERNAL_QUIESCE              SYS_GROUP                     ACTIVE
NIGHT_PLAN                    BATCH_CONSUMER_GROUP          ACTIVE
NIGHT_PLAN                    OLTP_CONSUMER_GROUP           ACTIVE
NIGHT_PLAN                    OTHER_GROUPS                  ACTIVE
SYSTEM_PLAN                   LOW_GROUP                     ACTIVE
SYSTEM_PLAN                   OTHER_GROUPS                  ACTIVE
SYSTEM_PLAN                   SYS_GROUP                     ACTIVE
```

The resource manager is only activated when a default resource plan is assigned. Only one resource plan can be active at any given time. Resource plan switches can be automated using scheduler windows or performed manually by setting the *resource_manager_plan* parameter using the *alter system* command as shown below.

```
alter system set resource_manager_plan = day_plan;
```

The currently active resource plan can be identified by querying the *v$rsrc_plan* view as shown in the *active_plan.sql* script:

🖫 active_plan.sql

```
select
    *
from
    v$rsrc_plan;
```

The output from the *active_plan.sql* script is displayed:

```
SQL> @active_plan.sql

NAME                            IS_TO
------------------------------- -----
DAY_PLAN                        TRUE
```

The *delete_plans.sql* script uses the *delete_plan* procedure to remove the resource plans as defined in this example. The *resource_manager_plan* parameter is unset before the plans are deleted and this deactivates the resource manager.

🖫 delete_plans.sql

```
alter system set resource_manager_plan = '';

BEGIN
  DBMS_RESOURCE_MANAGER.clear_pending_area();
  DBMS_RESOURCE_MANAGER.create_pending_area();

  -- Delete plans.
  DBMS_RESOURCE_MANAGER.delete_plan (
    plan => 'day_plan');

  DBMS_RESOURCE_MANAGER.delete_plan (
    plan => 'night_plan');

  DBMS_RESOURCE_MANAGER.validate_pending_area;
  DBMS_RESOURCE_MANAGER.submit_pending_area();
END;
/
```

With the plans present, the *create_job_classes.sql* script can be used to create job classes that are associated with the OLTP and batch consumer groups.

⊟ create_job_classes.sql

```
BEGIN
   DBMS_SCHEDULER.create_job_class(
      job_class_name          => 'oltp_job_class',
      resource_consumer_group => 'oltp_consumer_group',
      comments                => 'OLTP process job class.');

   DBMS_SCHEDULER.create_job_class(
      job_class_name          => 'batch_job_class',
      resource_consumer_group => 'batch_consumer_group',
      comments                => 'Batch process job class.');
END;
/
```

Using the *job_classes.sql* script, it can be noted that the job classes were created correctly.

```
SQL> job_classes.sql

JOB_CLASS_NAME                    RESOURCE_CONSUMER_GROUP
-------------------------------   ------------------------------
DEFAULT_JOB_CLASS
AUTO_TASKS_JOB_CLASS              AUTO_TASK_CONSUMER_GROUP
BATCH_JOB_CLASS                   BATCH_CONSUMER_GROUP
OLTP_JOB_CLASS                    OLTP_CONSUMER_GROUP
```

The *drop_job_classes.sql* script uses the *drop_job_class* procedure to remove the job classes used in this example.

⊟ drop_job_classes.sql

```
BEGIN
   DBMS_SCHEDULER.drop_job_class (
      job_class_name          => 'oltp_job_class');

   DBMS_SCHEDULER.drop_job_class (
      job_class_name          => 'batch_job_class');
END;
/
```

The consumer groups and job classes that have been created will work properly for jobs scheduled by the SYS user, but extra privileges must be granted before they can be used by other users.

First, grant the EXECUTE privilege on both job classes, and then make sure the user can switch consumer groups properly by calling the *grant_switch_consumer_group* procedure from the *dbms_resource_manager_privs* package. The *job_class_resource_privileges.sql* script performs both tasks, granting the necessary privileges to a user called *job_user*.

🖫 job_class_resource_privileges.sql

```
grant execute on oltp_job_class to job_user;
grant execute on batch_job_class to job_user;

BEGIN
  DBMS_RESOURCE_MANAGER_PRIVS.grant_switch_consumer_group (
    grantee_name   => 'JOB_USER',
    consumer_group => 'OLTP_CONSUMER_GROUP',
    grant_option   => TRUE);

  DBMS_RESOURCE_MANAGER_PRIVS.grant_switch_consumer_group (
    grantee_name   => 'JOB_USER',
    consumer_group => 'BATCH_CONSUMER_GROUP',
    grant_option   => TRUE);
END;
/
```

With the job classes and privileges in place, create a job to test the resource manager. The *test_resource_manager_job_1.sql* script connects to a user called *job_user* and creates a job associated with the *oltp_job_class* job class.

🖫 test_resource_manager_job_1.sql

```
conn job_user/job_user
BEGIN
  DBMS_SCHEDULER.create_job (
    job_name      => 'test_resource_manager_job_1',
    job_type      => 'PLSQL_BLOCK',
    job_action    => 'BEGIN DBMS_LOCK.sleep(60); END;',
    job_class     => 'oltp_job_class',
    start_date    => SYSTIMESTAMP,
    end_date      => NULL,
    enabled       => TRUE,
    comments      => 'Job to test a job classes use of the resource
manager.');
END;
/
```

The *running_job_consumer_groups.sql* script uses the *dba_scheduler_running_jobs* view to display the consumer groups associated with each running job.

🖫 running_job_consumer_groups.sql

```
select
  job_name,
  resource_consumer_group
from
  dba_scheduler_running_jobs
order by
  job_name
;
```

The output from the *running_job_consumer_groups.sql* script is displayed below:

```
SQL> @running_job_consumer_groups.sql

JOB_NAME                         RESOURCE_CONSUMER_GROUP
-------------------------------- --------------------------------
TEST_RESOURCE_MANAGER_JOB_1      OLTP_CONSUMER_GROUP
```

The *consumer_group_usage.sql* script uses the *v$rsrc_consumer_group* view to monitor the relative usage of each consumer group.

🖫 consumer_group_usage.sql

```
select
   name,
   consumed_cpu_time
from
   v$rsrc_consumer_group
;
```

The output from this script is:

```
SQL> @consumer_group_usage.sql

NAME                             CONSUMED_CPU_TIME
-------------------------------- -----------------
BATCH_CONSUMER_GROUP                             0
OTHER_GROUPS                                  2502
OLTP_CONSUMER_GROUP                             49
```

With the resource allocations and job classes defined, all that is left to do is to define windows to automatically switch between the day and night processing plans. The *create_windows.sql* script creates a 10-hour window associated with daytime processing and a 14-hour window associated with nighttime processing with both windows added to a newly created window group.

🖫 create_windows.sql

```
BEGIN
  DBMS_SCHEDULER.create_window (
    window_name     => 'day_window',
    resource_plan   => 'day_plan',
    start_date      => SYSTIMESTAMP,
    repeat_interval => 'freq=daily; byhour=8; byminute=0; bysecond=0;',
    end_date        => NULL,
    duration        => INTERVAL '10' HOUR,
    window_priority => 'HIGH',
    comments        => 'Day time processing window.');

  DBMS_SCHEDULER.create_window (
    window_name     => 'night_window',
```

```
    resource_plan    => 'night_plan',
    start_date       => SYSTIMESTAMP,
    repeat_interval => 'freq=daily; byhour=18; byminute=0; bysecond=0;',
    end_date         => NULL,
    duration         => INTERVAL '14' HOUR,
    window_priority => 'HIGH',
    comments         => 'Night time processing window.');

  DBMS_SCHEDULER.create_window_group (
    group_name  => 'processing_window_group',
    window_list => 'day_window, night_window',
    comments    => '24 hour processing window group');
END;
/
```

Using the *windows.sql* script, it can be seen that the windows were created successfully.

```
SQL> @windows.sql

WINDOW_NAME               RESOURCE_PLAN                  ENABL ACTIV
-----------------------   ------------------------------ ----- -----
DAY_WINDOW                DAY_PLAN                       TRUE  FALSE
NIGHT_WINDOW              NIGHT_PLAN                     TRUE  FALSE
WEEKEND_WINDOW                                           TRUE  TRUE
WEEKNIGHT_WINDOW                                         TRUE  FALSE
```

Rather than waiting for the windows to open automatically, they can be forced to open and the effects on the active resource plan can be monitored. To do this, open the nighttime window using the *open_window* procedure, and then use the *active_plan.sql* script to display the resource plan currently active on the system.

```
BEGIN
  DBMS_SCHEDULER.open_window (
    window_name => 'night_window',
    duration    => INTERVAL '30' MINUTE,
    force       => TRUE);
END;
/

SQL> @active_plan.sql

NAME                            IS_TO
------------------------------- -----
NIGHT_PLAN                      TRUE
```

The output from the *active_plan.sql* script shows that opening the nighttime window has activated the nighttime resource plan as expected. Now open the daytime window.

```
BEGIN
  DBMS_SCHEDULER.open_window (
    window_name => 'day_window',
    duration    => INTERVAL '30' MINUTE,
    force       => TRUE);
END;
/

SQL> @active_plan.sql

NAME                             IS_TO
------------------------------   -----
DAY_PLAN                         TRUE
```

As expected, opening the daytime window has activated the daytime resource plan.

Windows can overlap, but it is not recommended since only one window can be open at any given time. When windows overlap, Oracle decides which one should open by using the following rules:

- If overlapping windows have the same priority, the currently open window will remain open.

- If overlapping windows have different priorities, the window with the highest priority will open and the lower priority window will be closed.

- When a window closes, the overlapping window with the highest percentage time remaining will open.

- When an open window is dropped, it is automatically closed.

The *drop_windows.sql* script uses the *drop_window* and *drop_window_group* procedures to remove the windows and window group defined in this example.

🖫 drop_windows.sql
```
BEGIN
  DBMS_SCHEDULER.drop_window (
    window_name     => 'day_window',
    force           => TRUE);

  DBMS_SCHEDULER.drop_window (
    window_name     => 'night_window',
    force           => TRUE);

  DBMS_SCHEDULER.drop_window_group (
    group_name  => 'processing_window_group',
    force           => TRUE);
END;
/
```

This section has shown how resource plans are created, linked to job classes and switched by Windows. Armed with this information, it should be quite simple to create resource allocation schemes to suit various scheduling needs.

Now that information on how to manage the allocation of resources between jobs has been presented, the next section will detail how scheduler objects can be transferred between databases.

Export/Import and the Scheduler

Jobs defined using the *dbms_jobs* package can be exported and imported using the *exp* and *imp* utilities at both the schema and full database level.

The import and export of scheduler objects defined using the *dbms_scheduler* package is only supported via the new *datapump* utilities (*expdp* and *impdp*). These utilities are also capable of transferring legacy job definitions. The export process generates Data Definition Language (DDL) which is used to recreate the scheduler objects as they were originally defined including time zone information. The following simple example shows how these utilities work. First, a directory object for the *expdp* and *impdp* utilities to work with must be created.

```
conn system/password
create or replace directory export_dir AS '/tmp/';
grant read, write on directory export_dir to job_user;
```

Then, a basic job to be exported by the *expdp* utility is created.

```
conn job_user/job_user
BEGIN
  DBMS_SCHEDULER.create_job (
    job_name        => 'test_expdp_job_1',
    job_type        => 'PLSQL_BLOCK',
    job_action      => 'BEGIN DBMS_LOCK.sleep(10); END;',
    start_date      => SYSTIMESTAMP,
    repeat_interval => 'freq=hourly;',
    end_date        => SYSTIMESTAMP + 1,
    enabled         => TRUE,
    comments        => 'Job to test expdp.');
END;
/
```

From the operating system prompt, run the *expdp* utility to export the *job_user* schema. The following listing shows both the export command and the export log output:

```
expdp system/password schemas=JOB_USER directory=EXPORT_DIR
dumpfile=JOB_USER.dmp
 logfile=expdpJOB_USER.log

Export: Release 10.1.0.2.0 - Production on Saturday, 11 September, 2004
17:47

Copyright (c) 2003, Oracle.  All rights reserved.

Connected to: Oracle Database 10g Enterprise Edition Release 10.1.0.2.0 -
Production
With the Partitioning, OLAP and Data Mining options
FLASHBACK automatically enabled to preserve database integrity.
Starting "SYSTEM"."SYS_EXPORT_SCHEMA_01":  system/******** schemas=JOB_USER
dire
ctory=EXPORT_DIR dumpfile=JOB_USER.dmp logfile=expdpJOB_USER.log
Estimate in progress using BLOCKS method...
Total estimation using BLOCKS method: 0 KB
Processing object type SCHEMA_EXPORT/USER
Processing object type SCHEMA_EXPORT/SYSTEM_GRANT
Processing object type SCHEMA_EXPORT/ROLE_GRANT
Processing object type SCHEMA_EXPORT/DEFAULT_ROLE
Processing object type SCHEMA_EXPORT/TABLESPACE_QUOTA
Processing object type SCHEMA_EXPORT/SE_PRE_SCHEMA_PROCOBJACT/PROCACT_SCHEMA
Processing object type SCHEMA_EXPORT/PROCEDURE/PROCEDURE
Processing object type SCHEMA_EXPORT/PROCEDURE/ALTER_PROCEDURE
Processing object type SCHEMA_EXPORT/SE_POST_SCHEMA_PROCOBJACT/PROCOBJ
Master table "SYSTEM"."SYS_EXPORT_SCHEMA_01" successfully loaded/unloaded
******************************************************************
Dump file set for SYSTEM.SYS_EXPORT_SCHEMA_01 is:
  /tmp/JOB_USER.DMP
Job "SYSTEM"."SYS_EXPORT_SCHEMA_01" successfully completed at 17:48
```

On completion of the export, the *impdp* utility can be run with the *sqlfile* parameter set to create a DDL script containing all the object creation code. The following listing shows both the import command and the import log output:

```
impdp system/password sqlfile=JOBS.sql directory=EXPORT_DIR
dumpfile=JOB_USER.dmp
 logfile=impdpJOB_USER.log

Import: Release 10.1.0.2.0 - Production on Saturday, 11 September, 2004
17:48

Copyright (c) 2003, Oracle.  All rights reserved.

Connected to: Oracle Database 10g Enterprise Edition Release 10.1.0.2.0 -
Produc
tion
```

```
With the Partitioning, OLAP and Data Mining options
Master table "SYSTEM"."SYS_SQL_FILE_FULL_01" successfully loaded/unloaded
Starting "SYSTEM"."SYS_SQL_FILE_FULL_01":  system/******** sqlfile=JOBS.sql
dire
ctory=EXPORT_DIR dumpfile=JOB_USER.dmp logfile=impdpJOB_USER.log
Processing object type SCHEMA_EXPORT/USER
Processing object type SCHEMA_EXPORT/SYSTEM_GRANT
Processing object type SCHEMA_EXPORT/ROLE_GRANT
Processing object type SCHEMA_EXPORT/DEFAULT_ROLE
Processing object type SCHEMA_EXPORT/TABLESPACE_QUOTA
Processing object type SCHEMA_EXPORT/SE_PRE_SCHEMA_PROCOBJACT/PROCACT_SCHEMA
Processing object type SCHEMA_EXPORT/PROCEDURE/PROCEDURE
Processing object type SCHEMA_EXPORT/PROCEDURE/ALTER_PROCEDURE
Processing object type SCHEMA_EXPORT/SE_POST_SCHEMA_PROCOBJACT/PROCOBJ
Job "SYSTEM"."SYS_SQL_FILE_FULL_01" successfully completed at 17:48
```

The resulting *sqlfile* (JOBS.sql) contains creation DDL for all the *job_user* schema objects including the following job creation script code.

```
BEGIN
dbms_scheduler.create_job ('"TEST_EXPDP_JOB_1"',
job_type=>'PLSQL_BLOCK', job_action=>
'BEGIN DBMS_LOCK.sleep(10); END;'
, number_of_arguments=>0,
start_date=>'11-SEP-04 17.43.18.552000 +01:00', repeat_interval=>
'freq=hourly;'
, end_date=>'12-SEP-04 17.43.18.000000 +01:00',
job_class=>'"DEFAULT_JOB_CLASS"', enabled=>FALSE, auto_drop=>TRUE,comments=>
'Job to test expdp.'
);
dbms_scheduler.enable('"TEST_EXPDP_JOB_1"');
COMMIT;
END;
/
```

> It can be helpful to keep scheduler object definitions as text files in a source control system. As a result, the object definitions would be loaded using the original text files rather than transferring them between databases.

The new *datapump* utilities that were just introduced, *expdp* and *impdp*, are covered in more detail in the beginning of Chapter 6, Oracle DBA Utilities.

Now that methods for importing and exporting jobs to and from the scheduler have been established, the focus of the following section will shift to information on the use of services and instance stickiness in Real Application Clusters (RAC) environments.

Job Services and Instance Stickiness

Services allow the classification or grouping of applications within a database. This permits application priorities and resource allocation to be managed more effectively. Services can be defined and utilized in both single-node and Real Application Clusters (RAC) environments. The RAC is where they are most useful as they facilitate the coordination of grid computing.

A job class can be assigned to a service which affects how jobs associated with the job class are executed. When using RAC, jobs belonging to a job class will only run in a RAC instance that is assigned to the specific service. The following rules apply to job classes in relation to services:

- All job classes are assigned to a service. If a service is not explicitly specified, the job class is assigned to the default service, meaning it can run on any RAC instance in the cluster.

- Dropping a service will cause any dependent job classes to be reassigned to the default service.

- Specifying a nonexistent service will cause the job class creation to fail.

Services can be configured using the Database Configuration Assistant (DBCA), *srvctl* utility or the *dbms_service* package. More information concerning DBCA and its various components in regards to server-side functions can be found in Chapter 4. The *dbms_service* package is limited to service administration on a single node while the *dbca* and *srvctl* utilities can perform cluster-wide configuration and administration. Examples of administering services with the *dbms_service* package are shown below.

```
BEGIN
  -- Create a new service associated with the specified TSN service name.
  DBMS_SERVICE.create_service (
    service_name => 'test_service',
    network_name => 'DB10G.MYDOMAIN.COM');

  -- Start the specified service.
  DBMS_SERVICE.start_service (
    service_name => ' test_service');

  -- Disconnects all sessions associated with the specified service.
  DBMS_SERVICE.disconnect_session (
    service_name => 'test_service');

  -- Stop the specified service.
  DBMS_SERVICE.stop_service (
    service_name => 'test_service');

  -- Delete the specified service.
  DBMS_SERVICE.delete_service (
    service_name => 'test_service');
END;
/
```

Some examples of using the *srvctl* utility to do similar actions are listed below.

```
# Create the service on two nodes.
srvctl add service -d DB10G -s TEST_SERVICE -r DB10G1,DB10G2

# Stop and start the service on a single or multiple nodes.
srvctl stop service -d DB10G -s TEST_SERVICE -i DB10G1,DB10G2
srvctl start service -d DB10G -s TEST_SERVICE -i DB10G1

# Disable and enable the service on a single or multiple nodes.
srvctl disable service -d DB10G -s TEST_SERVICE -i DB10G1,DB10G2
srvctl enable service -d DB10G -s TEST_SERVICE -i DB10G1

# Display the current status of the service.
srvctl status service -d DB10G -s TEST_SERVICE -v

# Remove the service from both nodes.
srvctl remove service -d DB10G -s TEST_SERVICE -i DB10G1,DB10G2
```

Once a service is present, it can be assigned to a job class during creation or subsequently using the *set_attribute* procedure, as shown below.

```
BEGIN
  DBMS_SCHEDULER.create_job_class (
    job_class_name => 'test_job_class',
    service        => 'test_service');

  DBMS_SCHEDULER.set_attribute (
    name      => 'test_job_class',
    attribute => 'service',
    value     => 'admin_service');
END;
/
```

The following scenario will explain more specifically how services can be used to partition applications in a three-node RAC environment.

For services to function correctly, the Global Services Daemon (GSD) must be running on each node in the cluster. The GSDs are started using the *gsdctl* utility, which is part of the Cluster Ready Services (CRS) installation, so they must be started from that environment.

```
# Set environment.
export ORACLE_HOME=/u01/app/oracle/product/10.1.0/crs
export PATH=$ORACLE_HOME/bin:$PATH

# Start GSD daemon.
gsdctl start
```

Once the GSDs are running, the user must check that the cluster configuration is correct. The following command and output show the expected configuration for a three-node database called ORCL.

```
srvctl config database -d ORCL
server01 ORCL1 /u01/app/oracle/product/10.1.0/db_1
server02 ORCL2 /u01/app/oracle/product/10.1.0/db_1
server03 ORCL3 /u01/app/oracle/product/10.1.0/db_1
```

This configuration is typically performed during the cluster database creation, but it can be performed subsequently using the following commands.

```
srvctl add database -d ORCL -o /u01/app/oracle/product/10.1.0/db_1
srvctl add instance -d ORCL -i ORCL1 -n server01
srvctl add instance -d ORCL -i ORCL2 -n server02
srvctl add instance -d ORCL -i ORCL3 -n server03
```

Assume that two applications should run in the following way:

- OLTP - Should run on nodes one and two of the RAC, but is able to run on node three if nodes one and two are not available.

- BATCH - Should run on node three, but is able to run on nodes one and two if node three is not available.

To meet this requirement, the following services can be created:

```
# Set environment.
export ORACLE_HOME=/u01/app/oracle/product/10.1.0/db_1
export PATH=$ORACLE_HOME/bin:$PATH

# Create services.
srvctl add service -d ORCL -s OLTP_SERVICE -r ORCL1,ORCL2 -a
ORCL1,ORCL2,ORCL3
srvctl add service -d ORCL -s BATCH_SERVICE -r ORCL3 -a ORCL1,ORCL2,ORCL3
```

The OLTP_SERVICE is able to run on all RAC nodes, indicated by the -a option, but will run in preference on nodes one and two, indicated by the -r option. The BATCH_SERVICE is able to run on all RAC nodes, indicated by the -a option, but will run in preference on node three, indicated by the -r option.

The services can be started and stopped using the following commands:

```
srvctl start service -d ORCL -s OLTP_SERVICE
srvctl start service -d ORCL -s BATCH_SERVICE

srvctl stop service -d ORCL -s OLTP_SERVICE
srvctl stop service -d ORCL -s BATCH_SERVICE
```

The Oracle scheduler allows jobs to be linked with job classes, which in turn can be linked to services to allow jobs to run on specific nodes in a RAC environment. To support the requirements for the job, two job classes might have to be created as follows:

```
-- Create OLTP and BATCH job classes.
BEGIN
  DBMS_SCHEDULER.create_job_class(
    job_class_name => 'OLTP_JOB_CLASS',
    service        => 'OLTP_SERVICE');

  DBMS_SCHEDULER.create_job_class(
    job_class_name => 'BATCH_JOB_CLASS',
    service        => 'BATCH_SERVICE');
END;
/

-- Make sure the relevant users have access to the job classes.
GRANT EXECUTE ON sys.oltp_job_class TO job_user;
GRANT EXECUTE ON sys.batch_job_class TO job_user;
```

These job classes can then be assigned to existing jobs or during job creation.

```
-- Create a job associated with a job class.
BEGIN
  DBMS_SCHEDULER.create_job (
    job_name        => 'my_user.oltp_job_test',
    job_type        => 'PLSQL_BLOCK',
    job_action      => 'BEGIN NULL; END;',
    start_date      => SYSTIMESTAMP,
    repeat_interval => 'FREQ=DAILY;',
    job_class       => 'SYS.OLTP_JOB_CLASS',
    end_date        => NULL,
    enabled         => TRUE,
    comments        => 'Job linked to the OLTP_JOB_CLASS.');
END;
/

-- Assign a job class to an existing job.
EXEC DBMS_SCHEDULER.set_attribute ('MY_BATCH_JOB', 'JOB_CLASS',
'BATCH_JOB_CLASS');
```

The use of services is not restricted to scheduled jobs. These services can be used in the *tnsnames.ora* file to influence which nodes are used for each application. An example of the *tnsnames.ora* file entries are displayed below.

```
OLTP =
  (DESCRIPTION =
    (LOAD_BALANCE = ON)
    (FAILOVER = ON)
    (ADDRESS = (PROTOCOL = TCP)(HOST = server01)(PORT = 1521))
    (ADDRESS = (PROTOCOL = TCP)(HOST = server02)(PORT = 1521))
    (ADDRESS = (PROTOCOL = TCP)(HOST = server03)(PORT = 1521))
    (CONNECT_DATA =
      (SERVICE_NAME = OLTP_SERVICE)
      (FAILOVER_MODE =
        (TYPE = SELECT)
        (METHOD = BASIC)
        (RETRIES = 20)
        (DELAY = 1)
      )
    )
  )

BATCH =
  (DESCRIPTION =
    (LOAD_BALANCE = ON)
    (FAILOVER = ON)
    (ADDRESS = (PROTOCOL = TCP)(HOST = server01)(PORT = 1521))
    (ADDRESS = (PROTOCOL = TCP)(HOST = server02)(PORT = 1521))
    (ADDRESS = (PROTOCOL = TCP)(HOST = server03)(PORT = 1521))
    (CONNECT_DATA =
      (SERVICE_NAME = BATCH_SERVICE)
      (FAILOVER_MODE =
        (TYPE = SELECT)
        (METHOD = BASIC)
        (RETRIES = 20)
        (DELAY = 1)
      )
    )
  )
```

As long as applications use the appropriate connection identifier, they should only connect to the nodes associated to the service.

Although not directly related to services, it is sensible to discuss the concept of instance stickiness at this point. It has been shown that services can be used to associate jobs to one or more RAC instances in the cluster, but having a job run on a different instance each time can result in performance issues. For example, a job on the first node of the cluster may be executed, during which time all the data necessary to perform the job is read from the disk into the buffer cache. On the second execution, the job runs on the second node.

As most of the data necessary to perform the job is already in the cache of the first node, the data must be passed across the clusters interconnect before the second job can proceed. If the job had executed on the first node again, this network transfer would not have been necessary. This is the reason for instance stickiness.

The *instance_stickiness* parameter for an individual job defaults to TRUE, meaning that the job will run repeatedly on the same node, assuming it is available and not severely overloaded. The default value can be modified using the *set_attribute* procedure:

```
BEGIN
  DBMS_SCHEDULER.set_attribute (    name       => 'test_stickiness_job',
attribute => 'instance_stickiness',    value    => FALSE);
END;
/
```

With the *instance_stickiness* parameter set to FALSE, the job can run on any available node in the cluster.

Conclusion

This chapter covered the fundamentals of job scheduling including both external schedulers like ones available in Unix, Linux and Windows as well as Oracle's internal scheduler. Various tools such as the crontab command, *dbms_scheduler* and *dbms_jobs* packages, and Scheduled Tasks Wizard in Windows were introduced with more emphasis put on the preferred scheduling method for scheduling jobs in Oracle, *dbms_scheduler*.

Another area of job scheduling that was covered concerned time-based scheduling. Such components as intervals, which is a way of storing a specific period of time that separates two datetime values, calendar syntax and Oracle job chains were explained in detail. This chapter also showed how to identify and correct errors, how to email notifications of errors and how jobs can be monitored via using both database views and Oracle Enterprise Manager (OEM).

The chapter concluded with information regarding scheduler attributes, job priorities, scheduler logging, and details about the Job Resource Manager.

Index

Index

About Bert Scalzo

Bert Scalzo is a Database Architect for Quest Software and a member of the TOAD team. He has worked with Oracle databases for well over two decades, starting with version 4. His work history includes time at Oracle Education and Oracle Consulting, plus he holds several Oracle Masters certifications. Mr. Scalzo also has an extensive academic background - including a BS, MS and PhD in Computer Science, an MBA and several insurance industry designations.

Mr. Scalzo is an accomplished speaker and has presented at numerous Oracle conferences and user groups - including OOW, ODTUG, IOUGA, OAUG, RMOUG, et al. His key areas of DBA interest are Data Modeling, Database Benchmarking, Database Tuning & Optimization, Star Schema Data Warehouses and Linux. Mr. Scalzo has written articles for Oracle's Technology Network (OTN), Oracle Magazine, Oracle Informant, PC Week (eWeek), Dell PowerEdge Magazine, The Linux Journal, www.linux.com, and www.orafaq.com.

He also has written six books: *Oracle DBA Guide to Data Warehousing and Star Schemas*, *TOAD Handbook*, *TOAD Pocket Reference* (2nd Edition), *Database Benchmarking: Practical Methods for Oracle 10g & SQL Server 2005*, *Oracle on VMware: Expert Tips for Database Virtualization*, and *Advanced Oracle Utilities: The Definitive Reference*. Mr. Scalzo can be reached via email at bert.scalzo@quest.com or bert.scalzo@yahoo.com.

About Andy Kerber

Andrew Kerber is an experienced Oracle RAC DBA consultant and a graduate of West Point with a Bachelor of Science in Computer Science and a more than a decade of progressive DBA experience working with mission-critical systems. Andy is also an Oracle Certified Professional (OCP) and Oracle Ace.

Beyond the realm of Oracle database administration, Andy has broad technical skills ranging from PL/SQL administration and tuning to the installation and troubleshooting of complex multi-instance cluster databases. As a veteran of numerous Oracle RAC implementations, Andy is well versed in the hands-on management of RAC maintenance, upgrades and migration. Andrew has dedicated his life to Oracle technology and spends a great deal of his time exploring new Oracle features and improving his expert skills.

Andrew is happily married with two children and enjoys spending his Friday nights watching his son's high school football games.

About Donald K. Burleson

Donald K. Burleson is one of the world's top Oracle Database experts with more than 20 years of full-time DBA experience. He specializes in creating database architectures for very large online databases and he has worked with some of the world's most powerful and complex systems.

A former Adjunct Professor, Don Burleson has written 30 books, published more than 100 articles in National Magazines, and serves as Editor-in-Chief of Rampant TechPress. Don is a popular lecturer and teacher and is a frequent speaker at Oracle Openworld and other international database conferences.

About Steve Callan

Steve Callan is an Oracle Certified Professional (OCP) with over 20 years of progressive hands-on technical experience and nearly a decade managing mission-critical Oracle databases. He is also a Microsoft Certified Professional (MCP), and is proficient in SQL Server 2005.

Mr. Callan is a multi-faceted expert with significant experience using Oracle Application Server technology, performing all of the duties of an Oracle Application Server DBA and leveraging his technical skills with application server extension technologies, including HTML, JSP, JavaScript, CSS, Apache and Tomcat. He also has experience as a developer using Apex (HTML-DB), SQL*Forms and SQL*Reports.

Steve is also an experienced UNIX Systems Administrator, performing critical UNIX system admin duties, knowledgeable in all areas of UNIX administration including installation and configuration, security and multi-tiered UNIX architectures.

A former senior U.S. Military officer, Steve is a graduate of the prestigious United States Military Academy at West Point, earning his wings as an attack helicopter pilot. Steve has a Masters Degree in Software and Information Systems from Regis University, and a Masters Degree in Industrial Engineering from New Mexico State University. He has also completed all Ph.D. coursework for his pending doctorate in Mathematical & Computer Sciences at the Colorado School of Mines. Steve has contributed to the Oracle community by writing over 100 articles for DatabaseJournal.com and has volunteer over 900 answers on the Oracle Technical Network forums.

About Mike Reed

When he first started drawing, Mike Reed drew just to amuse himself. It wasn't long, though, before he knew he wanted to be an artist. Today he does illustrations for children's books, magazines, catalogs, and ads.

He also teaches illustration at the College of Visual Art in St. Paul, Minnesota. Mike Reed says, "Making pictures is like acting — you can paint yourself into the action." He often paints on the computer, but he also draws in pen and ink and paints in acrylics. He feels that learning to draw well is the key to being a successful artist.

Mike is regarded as one of the nation's premier illustrators and is the creator of the popular "Flame Warriors" illustrations at www.flamewarriors.com, a website devoted to Internet insults. "To enter his Flame Warriors site is sort of like entering a hellish Sesame Street populated by Oscar the Grouch and 83 of his relatives." – Los Angeles Times.
(http://redwing.hutman.net/%7Emreed/warriorshtm/lat.htm)

Mike Reed has always enjoyed reading. As a young child, he liked the Dr. Seuss books. Later, he started reading biographies and war stories. One reason why he feels lucky to be an illustrator is because he can listen to books on tape while he works. Mike is available to provide custom illustrations for all manner of publications at reasonable prices. Mike can be reached at www.mikereedillustration.com.

About Jeff Smith

Jeff Smith is a solution architect at Quest Software. Jeff has seven years of IT experience and is a certified Toad expert. Jeff is the primary author of the Toad Handbook, 2nd Edition, published by O'Reilly.

Jeff holds a bachelor's degree in Computer Science from West Virginia University and is a frequent contributor to the popular Toad Soft and a recent member of ODTUG. Jeff is a regular speaker at Toad User Groups and Oracle User Groups worldwide.

www.ingramcontent.com/pod-product-compliance
Lightning Source LLC
Chambersburg PA
CBHW080339220326
41598CB00030B/4548